An Introduction to Programming Using

Visual Basic® 2005

Sixth Edition

AN INTRODUCTION TO PROGRAMMING USING
VISUAL BASIC® 2005
SIXTH EDITION

David I. Schneider

University of Maryland

PEARSON

Prentice
Hall

Upper Saddle River, NJ 07458

Library of Congress Cataloging-in-Publication Data on File

Vice President and Editorial Director, ECS: *Marcia J. Horton*
Executive Editor: *Tracy Dunkelberger*
Editorial Assistant: *Christianna Lee*
Executive Managing Editor: *Vince O'Brien*
Managing Editor: *Camille Trentacoste*
Production Editor: *Rose Kernan*
Director of Creative Services: *Paul Belfanti*
Cover Designer: *Jonathan Boylan*
Managing Editor, AV Management and Production: *Patricia Burns*
Art Editor: *Xioahong Zhu*
Manufacturing Manager: *Alexis Heydt-Long*
Manufacturing Buyer: *Lisa McDowell*
Marketing Manager: *Robin O'Brien*

© 2006, 2003, 1999, 1998, 1997, 1995 Pearson Education, Inc.
Pearson Prentice Hall
Pearson Education, Inc.
Upper Saddle River, NJ 07458

Pearson Prentice Hall™ is a trademark of Pearson Education, Inc.

The author and publisher of this book have used their best efforts in preparing this book. These efforts include the development, research, and testing of the theories and programs to determine their effectiveness. The author and publisher make no warranty of any kind, expressed or implied, with regard to these programs or the documentation contained in this book. The author and publisher shall not be liable in any event for incidental or consequential damages in connection with, or arising out of, the furnishing, performance, or use of these programs.

Printed in the United States of America
10 9 8 7 6 5 4 3 2

ISBN 0-13-030654-1

Pearson Education Ltd., *London*
Pearson Education Australia Pty. Ltd., *Sydney*
Pearson Education Singapore, Pte. Ltd.
Pearson Education North Asia Ltd., *Hong Kong*
Pearson Education Canada, Inc., *Toronto*
Pearson Educacíon de Mexico, S.A. de C.V.
Pearson Education—Japan, *Tokyo*
Pearson Education Malaysia, Pte. Ltd.
Pearson Education Inc., Upper Saddle River, New Jersey

CONTENTS

Preface xi

Acknowledgments xiii

The Companion Website for Students and Instructors xv

Using this Book for a Short or Condensed Course xvi

1 An Introduction to Computers and Visual Basic 2005   1

1.1 An Introduction to Computers 2

1.2 Using Windows 4

1.3 Files and Folders 12

1.4 An Introduction to Visual Basic 2005 18

1.5 Biographical History of Computing 21

2 Problem Solving   29

2.1 Program-Development Cycle 30

2.2 Programming Tools 32

3 Fundamentals of Programming in Visual Basic 41

3.1 Visual Basic Controls 42

3.2 Visual Basic Events 60

3.3 Numbers 73

v

3.4   Strings 88

3.5   Input and Output 105

Summary 127

Programming Projects 128

4   General Procedures   131

4.1   Sub Procedures, Part I 132

4.2   Sub Procedures, Part II 154

4.3   Function Procedures. 169

4.4   Modular Design 183

Summary 188

Programming Projects 188

5   Decisions   193

5.1   Relational and Logical Operators 194

5.2   If Blocks 201

5.3   Select Case Blocks 218

5.4   A Case Study: Weekly Payroll 235

Summary 243

Programming Projects 243

6 Repetition 247

6.1 Do Loops 248

6.2 Processing Lists of Data with Do Loops 261

6.3 For . . . Next Loops 277

6.4 A Case Study: Analyze a Loan 291

Summary 301

Programming Projects 301

7 Arrays 307

7.1 Creating and Accessing Arrays 308

7.2 Using Arrays 326

7.3 Some Additional Types of Arrays 341

7.4 Sorting and Searching 356

7.5 Two-Dimensional Arrays 377

7.6 A Case Study: A Sophisticated Cash Register 392

Summary 401

Programming Projects 402

8 Sequential Files 411

8.1 Sequential Files 412

8.2 Using Sequential Files 430

8.3 A Case Study: Recording Checks and Deposits 442

Summary 454

Programming Projects 454

9 Additional Controls and Objects 461

9.1 List Boxes, Combo Boxes, and the File-Opening Control 462

9.2 Seven Elementary Controls 472

9.3 Four Additional Objects 484

9.4 Graphics 496

Summary 509

Programming Projects 510

10 Database Management 517

10.1 An Introduction to Databases 518

10.2 Relational Databases and SQL 531

Summary 548

Programming Projects 549

11 Object-Oriented Programming 551

11.1 Classes and Objects 552

11.2 Arrays of Objects; Events; Containment 569

11.3 Inheritance 582

Summary 601

Programming Projects 602

Appendices 605

Appendix A ANSI Values 605

Appendix B How To 607

Appendix C Converting from Visual Basic 6.0 to Visual Basic 2005 621

Appendix D Visual Basic Debugging Tools 627

Answers to Selected Odd-Numbered Exercises 637

Index 725

PREFACE

Since its introduction in 1991, Visual Basic has been the most widely used programming language in the world. The latest incarnation of Visual Basic is called Visual Basic 2005. Visual Basic programmers are enthusiastically embracing the new features of the language. Likewise, students learning their first programming language will find Visual Basic 2005 the ideal tool to understand the development of computer programs.

My objectives when writing this text were as follows:

1. *To develop focused chapters.* Rather than covering many topics superficially, I concentrate on important subjects and cover them thoroughly.

2. *To use examples and exercises that students can appreciate and with which they can relate, and feel comfortable.* I frequently use real data. Examples do not have so many embellishments that students are distracted from the programming techniques illustrated.

3. *To produce compactly written text that students will find both readable and informative.* The main points of each topic are discussed first, and then the peripheral details are presented as comments.

4. *To teach good programming practices that are in step with modern programming methodology.* Problem-solving techniques and structured programming are discussed early and used throughout the book. The style follows object-oriented programming principles.

5. *To provide insights into the major applications of computers.*

Unique and Distinguishing Features

Exercises for Most Sections. Each section that teaches programming has an exercise set. The exercises both reinforce the understanding of the key ideas of the section and challenge the student to explore applications. Most of the exercise sets require the student to trace programs, find errors, and write programs. The answers to all the odd-numbered exercises in Chapters 1 through 8 and selected odd-numbered exercises from Chapters 9, 10, and 11 are given at the end of the text.

Practice Problems. Practice Problems are carefully selected exercises located at the end of a section, just before the exercise set. Complete solutions are given following the exercise set. The practice problems often focus on points that are potentially confusing or are best appreciated after the student has worked on them. The reader should seriously attempt the practice problems and study their solutions before moving on to the exercises.

Programming Projects. Beginning with Chapter 3, chapters contain programming projects. The programming projects not only reflect the variety of ways that computers are used in the business community, but also present some games and general-interest topics. The large number and range of difficulty of the programming projects provide the flexibility to adapt the course to the interests and abilities of the students. Some programming projects in later chapters can be assigned as end-of-the-semester projects.

Comments. Extensions and fine points of new topics are deferred to the "Comments" portion at the end of each section so that they will not interfere with the flow of the presentation.

Case Studies. Each of the four case studies focuses on an important programming application. The problems are analyzed and the programs are developed with top-down charts and pseudocode. The programs can be found on the companion website at *www.prenhall.com/schneider*.

Chapter Summaries. In Chapters 3 through 11, the key results are stated and the important terms are summarized at the end of the chapter.

Procedures. The early introduction of procedures in Chapter 4 allows structured programming to be used in simple situations before being applied to complex problems. However, the text is written so that the presentation of procedures easily can be postponed until decision and repetition structures have been presented. In Chapters 5 and 6 (and Sections 7.1 and 7.2), all programs using procedures appear at the ends of sections and can be deferred or omitted.

Arrays. Arrays are introduced gently in two sections. The first section presents the basic definitions and avoids procedures. The second section presents the techniques for manipulating arrays and shows how to pass arrays to procedures.

How To Appendix. Appendix B provides a compact, step-by-step reference on how to carry out standard tasks in the Visual Basic environment.

Appendix on Debugging. Placing of the discussion of Visual Basic's sophisticated debugger in Appendix D allows the instructor flexibility in deciding when to cover this topic.

Companion Website. The companion website contains all the examples, case studies, and data files referenced in the book as well as additional NetSearch terms, Destination Links, online study guide with additional exercises and learning resources for students.

Instructor Resource Center. The Instructor Resource Center contains solutions to every exercise and programming project, a test item file for each chapter, PowerPoint lecture slides, and data files for all the examples and programs featured in the book. Contact your local Prentice Hall Sales Representative for information on how to download these resources.

What's New in the Sixth Edition

1. Suggestions from students and reviewers have been incorporated as much as possible.

2. The real-life data in the examples and exercises have been updated and revised.

3. The version of Visual Basic has been upgraded from VB.NET to Visual Basic 2005 and the relevant new features of Visual Basic 2005 have been explained.

4. A section on graphics has been added

5. Nine programming projects have been added.

ACKNOWLEDGMENTS

Many talented instructors, students, and programmers provided helpful comments and constructive suggestions during the preparation of this text. For their contributions to the quality of the first four editions of the book I extend my gratitude to A. Abonomah, University of Akron; Timothy Babbitt, Rochester Institute of Technology; William Barnett, Northwestern State University; Sherry Barriclow, Grand Valley State University; Robert Berman, Wayne State University; William Burrows, University of Washington; David Chao, San Francisco State University; Christopher Chisolm, University of Nebraska, Omaha; Robert Coil, Cincinnati State Technical and Community College; Gary Cornell, University of Connecticut; Ronit Dancis; John DaPonte, Southern Connecticut State University; Ward Deutschman, Briarcliff; Ralph Duffy, North Seattle Community College; Charles Fairchild; Pat Fenton, West Valley College; David Fichbohm, Golden Gate University; Robert Fritz, American River College; Matthew Goddard, New Hampshire Technical College; Mickie Goodro, Casper College; Wade T. Graves, Grayson Community College; Christine Griffin; Gary Haw, MIPS Software Development Inc.; Shelly Hawkins, Microsoft; Tom Janicki, Kent State University; Dana Johnson, North Dakota State University; Dan Joseph, Rochester Institute of Technology; Del Kimber, Clemson University; Wanda Kunkle, Rowan College; Paul Lecoq, San Francisco Community College; David Leitch, Devry Institute; David Letcher, The College of New Jersey; Kieran Mathieson, Oakland University; Charlie Miri, Delaware Tech; George Nezlek, DePaul University; Ron Notes, Hebrew Academy of Greater Washington; Mike Paul, Berry University; T. S. Pennington, Maple Woods Community College; Arland Richmond, Computer Learning Center; David Rosser, Essex County College; Arturo Salazar, San Francisco State; Susanne Peterson, Microsoft; Janie Schwark, Microsoft; Mike Talber, Portland Community College; Steve Turek, Devry Institute of Technology, Kansas City; Jac Van Deventer, Washington State University; Randy Weinberg, St. Cloud State University; Laurie Werner, Miami University; Melinda, White, Santa Fe Community College; Ronald Williams, Central Piedmont Community College; Amit Kalani, CIStems Solutions LLC; Priti Kalani, MobiEcast Corporation; Chris Panell, Heald College; Kevin Parker, Idaho State University; TJ Racoosin, rSolutions; and Bill Tinker, Aries Software.

The current edition benefited greatly from the valuable comments of the following knowledgeable reviewers:

Joe Mast, Eastern Mennonite University
Joe Brady, University of Delaware
Jim McKeown, Dakota State University
Syd Shewchuk, Heald College
Sara Rushinek, University of Miami
Chakib Chraibi, Barry University

Many people are involved in the successful publication of a book. I wish to thank the dedicated team at Prentice Hall whose support and diligence made this textbook possible, especially Marcia Horton, editor-in-chief, and Camille Trentacoste, managing editor.

I also express my thanks to Marc Leager, a talented programmer, who helped with the development of the book, and provided valuable insights and careful proofreading. I am grateful to Shaun Szot for his valuable proofreading. Production editor, Rose Kernan, and compositor Rebecca Evans did a fantastic job producing the book and keeping it on schedule.

I extend special thanks to my editor Tracy Dunkelberger. Her ideas and enthusiasm helped immensely with the preparation of the book.

THE COMPANION WEBSITE FOR STUDENTS AND INSTRUCTORS

How to Access the Companion Website

All the programs from the examples, case studies, TXT files for the exercises, database files and BMP images can be downloaded by students and instructors at www.prenhall.com/schneider.

Students

The companion website, located at www.prenhall.com/schneider, contains all the programs from the examples and case studies set forth in this textbook, most of the TXT files needed for the exercises, all databases needed for the exercises, and several BMP (picture) files. All these files are contained in the folder "Programs" in the subfolders "Ch03", "Ch04", "Ch05", and so on. Each chapter file contains a subfolder named "Text files for Exercises" which contains TXT files needed for that chapter's exercises. The folder "Ch09" has a subfolder named "Pictures" that contains the BMP files. The folder "Ch10" has a subfolder named "MajorDatabases" containing all the databases needed for the exercises.

Each program is contained in a folder with a name in the for *chapter–section–number*. For instance, the program in Chapter 3, Section 5, Example 2 is contained in the folder "3-5-2". Many of the programs make use of a TXT file in the subfolder of the program's folder named "bin."

Students can access additional Visual Basic 2005 resources via helpful NetSearch Terms and Destination Links located on the companion website.

Instructors

Essential instructor resources including solutions to the exercises, PowerPoint lecture slides, all the example programs and data files used by students throughout the book, and multiple-choice and true/false questions are provided on the Instructor Resource Center. Contact your local Prentice Hall Sales Representative to gain access to the IRC.

Using This Book for a Short or Condensed Course

This book provides more than enough material for a complete semester course. The topics must be trimmed for courses lasting considerably less than a full semester. The following syllabus provides one possible way to present an abbreviated introduction to programming.

1   An Introduction to Computers and Visual Basic 2005

 1.2   Using Windows
 1.3   Files and Folders

3   Fundamentals of Programming in Visual Basic

 3.1   Visual Basic Controls
 3.2   Visual Basic Events
 3.3   Numbers
 3.4   Strings
 3.5   Input and Output

4   Procedures

 4.1   Sub Procedures, Part I
 4.2   Sub Procedures, Part II
 4.3   Functions

5   Decisions

 5.1   Relational and Logical Operators
 5.2   If Blocks
 5.3   Select Case Blocks

6   Repetition

 6.1   Do Loops
 6.2   Processing Lists of Data with Do Loops
 6.3   For . . . Next Loops

7   Arrays

 7.1   Creating and Accessing Arrays
 7.2   Using Arrays (Omit Merging Two Ordered Arrays)
 7.3   Some Additional Types of Arrays (Omit Control Arrays)

9   Additional Controls and Objects

 9.1   List Boxes, Combo Boxes, and the File-Opening Control
 9.2   Seven Elementary Controls

1

An Introduction to Computers and Visual Basic 2005

1.1 **An Introduction to Computers 2**

1.2 **Using Windows 4**
- Mouse Pointers ◆ Mouse Actions ◆ Windows Start Button
- Windows and Its Little Windows ◆ Using Notepad

1.3 **Files and Folders 12**
- Using Windows Explorer ◆ Using the Open and Save As Dialog Boxes ◆ Read-Only Attribute

1.4 **An Introduction to Visual Basic 2005 18**
- Why Windows and Why Visual Basic? ◆ How You Develop a Visual Basic Application ◆ The Different Versions of Visual Basic

1.5 **Biographical History of Computing 21**
- 1800s ◆ 1930s ◆ 1940s ◆ 1950s ◆ 1960s ◆ 1970s
- 1980s ◆ 1990s

1.1   An Introduction to Computers

An Introduction to Programming Using Visual Basic 2005 is a book about problem solving using computers. The programming language used is Visual Basic 2005 (hereafter shortened to Visual Basic), but the principles taught apply to many modern programming languages. The examples and exercises present a sampling of the ways that computers are used in society.

Computers are so common today that you certainly have heard some of the terminology applied to them. Here are some questions that you might have about computers and programming.

Question: *What is meant by a "personal" computer?*

Answer: The word "personal" does not mean that the computer is intended for personal, as opposed to business, purposes. Rather, it indicates that the machine is operated by one person at a time instead of by many people.

Question: *What are the main components of a personal computer?*

Answer: Hidden from view inside the system unit are several components, including the microprocessor, memory, and hard drive of the computer. The *central processing unit* (CPU), sometimes referred to as the *microprocessor*, can be thought of as the computer's brain, which carries out all of the computations. The *memory*, often referred to as *random access memory* (RAM), stores instructions and data while they are being used by the computer. When the computer's power is turned off, the contents of memory are lost. A *hard disk drive* is used to store instructions and data when they are not being used in memory and when the computer is turned off. Inside the system unit there are also device cards, such as a graphics card, sound card, network card, and a modem. A *graphics card* is used to send an image to the monitor, and a *sound card* is used to send audio to a set of speakers attached to the computer. *Network cards* can be used to connect to a *local area network* (LAN) of computers, while a *modem* uses a telephone line to connect to any computer that can be reached by a phone call.

The personal computer also has several *input* and *output devices*, which are used to communicate with the computer. Standard input devices include the keyboard and mouse. Standard output devices include the monitor and printer. Instructions are entered into the computer by typing them on the keyboard, clicking a mouse, or loading them from a file located on a disk drive or downloaded from a network. Information processed by the computer can be displayed on the monitor, printed on the printer, or recorded on a disk drive.

Question: *What are some uses of computers in our society?*

Answer: The dramatic decrease in the cost of hardware and software technology has made computers widely available to consumers and corporations alike. Whenever we make a phone call, a computer determines how to route the call and calculates the cost of the call. Banks store all customer transactions on computers and process these transactions to revise the balance for each customer. Airlines record all reservations with computers. This information, which is stored in a database, can be accessed to determine the status of any flight. NASA uses computers to calculate the trajectories of satellites. Business analysts use computers to create pie and bar charts that give visual impact to data. With the Internet connecting millions of home computers, families and friends can exchange messages, information, and pictures. Consumers can shop from their PCs. Virtually no aspect of modern life is untouched by computer technology.

Question: *What are some topics covered in this text that students could use immediately?*

Answer: Computer files can be created to hold lists of names, addresses, and phone numbers, which can be alphabetized and displayed in their entirety or selectively. Mathematical computations can be carried out for science, business, and engineering courses. Personal financial transactions, such as bank deposits and loans, can be recorded, organized, and analyzed.

Question: *How do we communicate with the computer?*

Answer: Many languages are used to communicate with the computer. At the lowest level, there is machine language, which is understood directly by the microprocessor, but is awkward for humans. Visual Basic is an example of a higher-level language. It consists of instructions to which people can relate, such as Click, If, and Do.

Question: *How do we get computers to perform complicated tasks?*

Answer: Tasks are broken down into a sequence of instructions that can be expressed in a computer language. (This text uses the language Visual Basic.) This sequence of instructions is called a *program*. Programs can range in size from two or three instructions to millions of instructions. Instructions are typed on the keyboard, or read in from a file on a disk, and stored in the computer's memory. The process of executing the instructions is called *running* the program.

Question: *What is a server?*

Answer: Whether a computer is a server depends on how it is being used. A computer that is only used by one person is a computer. A server is a computer that provides resources such as files, printers, or Internet access to other computers. Since a server needs to be continuously available to other computers, additional components are usually added to it to increase its reliability in the event of a power failure or other unexpected event.

Question: *Are there certain features that all programs have in common?*

Answer: Most programs do three things: take in data, manipulate them, and give desired information. These operations are referred to as input, processing, and output. The input data might be held in a portion of the program, reside on a disk drive, or be provided by the computer operator in response to requests made by the computer while the program is running. The processing of the input data occurs inside the computer and can take from a fraction of a second to many hours. The output data are either displayed on the monitor, printed on the printer, or recorded on a disk. As a simple example, consider a program that computes sales tax. An item of input data is the cost of the thing purchased. The processing consists of multiplying the cost by a certain percentage. An item of output data is the resulting product, the amount of sales tax to be paid.

Question: *What are the meanings of the terms "hardware" and "software?"*

Answer: **Hardware** refers to the physical components of the computer, including all peripherals, the central processing unit, disk drives, and all mechanical and electrical devices. Programs are referred to as **software**.

Question: *What are the meanings of the terms "programmer" and "user?"*

Answer: A **programmer** is a person who solves problems by writing programs on a computer. After analyzing the problem and developing a plan for solving it, he or she writes and tests the program that instructs the computer how to carry out the plan. The program might be run many times, either by the programmer or by others. A **user** is any person who uses a program. While working through this text, you will function both as a programmer and as a user.

Question: *What is meant by problem solving?*

Answer: Problems are solved by carefully reading them to determine what data are given and what outputs are requested. Then a step-by-step procedure is devised to process the given data and produce the requested output. This procedure is called an **algorithm**. Finally, a computer program is written to carry out the algorithm. Algorithms are discussed in Section 2.2.

Question: *What types of problems are solved in this text?*

Answer: Carrying out business computations, creating and maintaining records, alphabetizing lists, and displaying tabular data are some of the types of problems we will solve.

Question: *How did Visual Basic 2005 evolve?*

Answer: In the early 1960s, two mathematics professors at Dartmouth College developed BASIC to provide their students with an easily learned language that could tackle complicated programming projects. As the popularity of BASIC grew, refinements were introduced that permitted structured programming, which increases the reliability of programs. Visual Basic 1.0 is a version of BASIC developed in 1991 by the Microsoft Corporation to allow easy, visual-oriented development of Windows applications. Visual Basic 2005 is a language similar to the original Visual Basic, but more powerful. It is targeted for what is known as the .NET run time, which is a program that executes Visual Basic 2005 as well as programs from other languages that are targeted for the .NET run time. This will ultimately allow programs written in Visual Basic to be run on devices other than computers, such as cell phones and handheld devices. Other features of Visual Basic include full object-oriented programming capabilities and the development of Web services. Object-oriented programming is discussed in Chapter 11. The techniques presented in this book can be applied to the development of Web services.

1.2 Using Windows

Programs such as Visual Basic, which are designed for Microsoft Windows, are easy to use—once you learn a little jargon and a few basic techniques. This section explains the jargon, giving you enough understanding of Windows to get you started in Visual Basic. Although Windows may seem intimidating if you've never used it before, you need to learn only a few basic techniques, which are covered in this section.

▓ Mouse Pointers

When you use Windows, think of yourself as the conductor and Windows as the orchestra. The conductor in an orchestra points to various members and does something with his or her baton; then the orchestra members respond in certain ways. For a Windows user, the baton is called the **pointing device**; most often it is a **mouse**. As you move the mouse across your desk, a pointer moves along the screen in sync with your movements. Two basic types of mouse pointers you will see in Windows are an arrow and an hourglass.

The **arrow** is the ordinary mouse pointer you use to point at various Windows objects before activating them. You will usually be told to "Move the pointer to . . . ." This really means "Move the mouse around your desk until the mouse pointer is at . . . ."

The **hourglass** mouse pointer pops up whenever Windows is saying "Wait a minute; I'm thinking." This pointer still moves around when you move the mouse, but you can't tell Windows to do anything until it finishes what it's doing and the mouse pointer no longer resembles an hourglass. (Sometimes you can press the Esc key to tell Windows to stop what it is doing.)

Note: The mouse pointer can take on many other shapes, depending on which application you are using and what task you are performing. For instance, when entering text in a word processor or Visual Basic, the mouse pointer appears as a thin, large, uppercase I (referred to as an I-beam).

▓ Mouse Actions

After you move the (arrow) pointer to a place where you want something to happen, you need to do something with the mouse. There are five basic things you can do with a mouse—point, hover, click, double-click, and drag.

Pointing means moving your mouse across your desk until the mouse pointer is over the desired object on the screen.

Hovering means lingering the mouse at a particular place and waiting for a message or menu to appear.

Clicking (sometimes people say single-clicking) means pressing and releasing the left mouse button once. Whenever a sentence begins "Click on . . . ," you need to

1. move the mouse pointer until it is at the object you are supposed to click on and

2. press and release the left mouse button.

An example of a sentence using this jargon might be "Click on the button marked Yes." You also will see sentences that begin "Click inside the . . . ." This means to move the mouse pointer until it is inside the boundaries of the object, and then click.

Double-clicking means clicking the left mouse button twice in quick succession (that is, pressing it, releasing it, pressing it, and releasing it again quickly so that Windows doesn't think you single-clicked twice). Whenever a sentence begins "Double-click on . . . ", you need to

1. move the mouse pointer until it is at the object you are supposed to double-click on and

2. press and release the left mouse button twice in quick succession.

For example, you might be instructed to "Double-click on the little box at the far left side of your screen."

Note: An important Windows convention is that clicking selects an object so you can give Windows or the document further directions about it, but double-clicking tells Windows to perform a default operation. For example, double-clicking on a folder will open that folder.

Dragging usually moves a Windows object. If you see a sentence that begins "Drag the . . . ", you need to

1. move the mouse pointer until it is at the object,
2. press the left mouse button and hold it down,
3. move the mouse pointer until the object moves to where you want it to be, and
4. finally, release the mouse button.

Sometimes this whole activity is called *drag and drop*.

Windows Start Button

Clicking on the **Start** button at the bottom left corner of the screen displays a menu that you can use to run programs, shut down Windows, and carry out several other tasks. The Start menu also can be accessed by pressing a special key labeled with the Windows logo (located next to the Alt key) or by pressing Ctrl + Esc. (In the notation "key1 + key2", the plus sign (+) instructs you to hold down key1 and then press key2. There are many useful key combinations of this type.)

Windows and Its Little Windows

Windows gets its name from the way it organizes your screen into rectangular regions. When you run a program, the program runs inside a bordered rectangular box. Unfortunately Windows jargon calls all of these windows, so there's only a lowercase "w" to distinguish them from the operating system called Windows.

When Windows' attention is focused on a specific window, the Title bar at the top of the window is blue and the window is said to be **active**. (Inactive windows have a gray Title bar.) The active window is the only one that can be affected by your actions. An example of a sentence you might see is "Make the window active." This means that if the Title bar of the window is gray, click inside the window. At this point, the active window will be responsive to your actions.

Using Notepad

We will explore the Windows application Notepad to illustrate the Windows environment. Notepad is used extensively in this text to create text files for programs. Most of the concepts learned here carry over to Visual Basic and other Windows applications.

To invoke Notepad from Windows, click the Start button, click on Run, type "Notepad" into the box labeled "Name:", and click the OK button. The window in Figure 1.1 will appear. As its name suggests, Notepad is an elementary word processor. You can type text into the Notepad window, edit the text, print the text on the printer, and save the text for later recall.

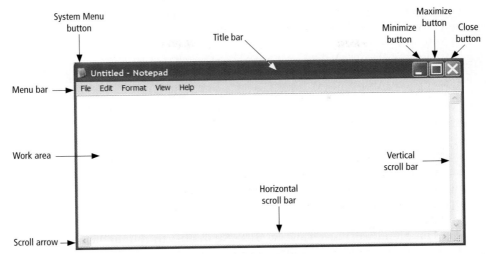

FIGURE 1.1   The Notepad window.

The blinking vertical line is called the **cursor**. Each letter you type will appear at the cursor. The Notepad window is divided into four parts. The part containing the cursor is called the **Work area**. It is the largest and most important part of the window because documents are typed into this window.

The **Title bar** at the top of the screen holds the name of the document currently being written. Until the document is given a name, the document is called "Untitled." The three buttons on the right side of the title bar can be used to maximize, minimize, or close the window. You can click on the **Maximize button** to make the Notepad window fill the entire screen, click on the **Minimize button** to change the Notepad window into a button on the taskbar, or click on the **Close button** to exit Notepad. As long as a window isn't maximized or minimized, you can usually move it around the screen by dragging its title bar. (Recall that this means to move the mouse pointer until it is in the title bar, hold down the left mouse button, move the mouse until the window is where you want it to be, and then release the mouse button.)

Note 1: After you have maximized a window, the Maximize button changes to a pair of rectangles called the **Restore button**. Click on this button to return the window to its previous size.

Note 2: If the Notepad window has been minimized, it can be restored to its previous size by clicking on the button that was created on the task bar when the application was opened. (The three tasks discussed in this paragraph also can be carried out with the **System Menu button** in the upper-left corner of the window.)

You can change the Notepad window to suit your needs. To adjust the size, do the following:

1. Move the mouse pointer until it is at the place on the boundary you want to adjust. The mouse pointer changes to a double-headed arrow.
2. Drag the border to the left or right or up or down to make the window smaller or larger.
3. When you are satisfied with the new size of the window, release the left mouse button.

If the Work area contains more information than can fit on the screen, you need a way to move through this information so you can see it all. For example, you will certainly be writing instructions in Visual Basic that are longer than one screen. You can use the mouse to scroll through your instructions with small steps or giant steps. A **Vertical scroll bar** lets you move from the top to the bottom of the window; a **Horizontal scroll bar** lets you move between the left and right margins of the window. Use this Scroll bar when the contents of the window are too wide to fit on the screen. Figure 1.1 shows both Vertical and Horizontal scroll bars.

A scroll bar has two arrows at the end of a channel and sometimes contains a box called the **Scroll box**. The Scroll box is the key to moving rapidly; the arrows are the key to moving in smaller increments. Dragging the Scroll box enables you to quickly move long distances to an approximate location in your document. For example, if you drag the Scroll box to the middle of the channel, you'll scroll to approximately the middle of your document.

The **Menu bar** just below the Title bar is used to call up menus, or lists of tasks. Several of these tasks are described in this section.

Documents are created from the keyboard in much the same way they would be written with a typewriter. In computerese, writing a document is referred to as editing the document; therefore, Notepad is called a **text editor**.

After Notepad has been invoked, the following routine will introduce you to using Notepad:

1. Click on the Work area of Notepad.

2. Type a few words into Notepad.

3. Press the **Home key** to move the cursor back to the beginning of the line. In general, the Home key moves the cursor to the beginning of the line on which it currently is located.

4. Now press the **End** key. The cursor will move to the end of the line.

5. Type some letters, and then press the **Backspace** key a few times. It will erase letters one at a time. Another method of deleting a letter is to move the cursor to that letter and press the **Del** key. (Del stands for "Delete.") The backspace key erases the character to the left of the cursor, and the Del key erases the character to the right of the cursor.

6. Hold down the **Ctrl** key (Ctrl stands for "Control"), and press the **Del** key. This key combination (denoted Ctrl + Del) erases the portion of the line to the right of the cursor.

7. Type more characters than can fit on one line of the screen. Notice that the left-most characters scroll off the screen to make room for the new characters.

8. Press and release **Alt**, then press and release O, and then press and release W. (This key combination is abbreviated Alt/F̲ormat/W̲ord Wrap or Alt/O/W. The slash character (/), officially called a **solidus**, instructs you to release the character preceding it, before pressing the character following it.) Notice that Notepad divided the long line so that it fits in Notepad's window.

9. Click Format on the Menu bar, and notice that there is a check mark in front of Word Wrap. To remove the check mark, turn the Word Wrap feature off by clicking once on Word Wrap.

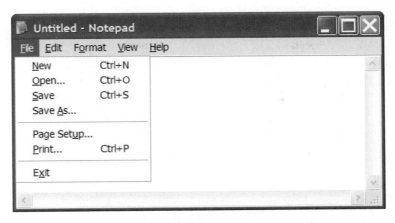

FIGURE 1.2   **A menu and its options.**

10. The **Enter** key is used to begin a new line on the screen.

11. The **Alt** key activates the Menu bar and causes a letter from each menu item to be underlined. Then, pressing one of the underlined letters, such as F, E, O, V, or H, selects a menu. (From the Menu bar, a menu also can be selected by pressing the right arrow key to highlight the name and then pressing the Enter key.) As shown in Figure 1.2, after a menu is opened, each option has one letter underlined. You can press an underlined letter to select an option. (Underlined letters are called **access keys.**) For instance, pressing A from the file menu selects the option "Save As". Selections also can be made with the cursor-movement keys and the Enter key.

    Note 1: You can select menus and options without the use of keys by clicking on them with the mouse.

    Note 2: You can close a menu, without making a selection, by clicking anywhere outside the menu or pressing the Esc key twice.

12. The **Esc** key (Esc stands for "Escape") is used to return to the Work area.

13. Press Alt/F/N. The dialog box in Figure 1.3 will appear and ask you if you want to save the current document. Decline by pressing N or clicking on the No button.

14. Type the following information into Notepad. (It gives the names of employees, their hourly wages, and the number of hours worked in the past week.) This document is used in Section 3.5

    ```
    Mike Jones
    7.35
    35
    John Smith
    6.75
    33
    ```

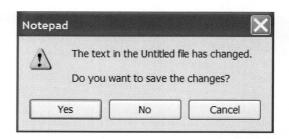

FIGURE 1.3   **A "Do you want to save the changes?" dialog box.**

15. Store the document as a file on a disk. To save the document, press Alt/File/Save As. A dialog box appears, requesting a file name for the document. The cursor is in a narrow rectangular box labeled "File name:". Type a drive letter, a colon, a backslash (\ ), and a name, and then press the Enter key or click on Save. For instance, you might type C:\PAYROLL. The document will then be stored on drive C. This process is called **saving** the document. Notepad automatically adds a period and the extension *txt* to the name. Therefore, the complete file name is PAYROLL.TXT on the disk.

    Note: If you want to save the document in a specific folder (directory) of the disk, include the folder's name. For instance, you might type C:\Myfiles\PAYROLL. See Section 1.3 for a discussion of folders.

16. Press the key combination Alt/File/New to clear PAYROLL.TXT from Notepad.

17. To restore PAYROLL.TXT as the document in Notepad, press Alt/File/Open, type something like C:\PAYROLL in the "File name:" box , and then press the Enter key.

18. Move the cursor to the beginning of the document, and then press Alt/Edit/Find (or Ctrl + F) to invoke the Find dialog box. This dialog box contains several objects that will be discussed in this book. The text to be found should be typed into the rectangle containing the cursor. Such a rectangle is called a text box. The phrase "Find what:", which identifies the type of information that should be placed into the text box, is referred to as the *text* of a *label*.

19. Type "smith" into the text box, and then click on the "Find Next" button. Clicking on it carries out a task. Text boxes, labels, and buttons are discussed in Section 3.2.

20. The small square to the left of the words "Match case" is called a check box. Click on it to see it checked, and then click again to remove the check mark.

21. The object captioned "Direction" is called a group box. It contains a pair of objects called radio buttons. Click on the "Up" radio button to select it, and then click on the "Down" radio button. Only one radio button at a time can be selected. Check boxes, group boxes, and radio buttons are discussed in Section 9.2.

22. Press Alt/File/Exit to exit Notepad.

▨ Comments

1. Two useful key combinations that we have not discussed yet are the following:
    (a) Ctrl + Home moves the cursor to the beginning of the document.
    (b) Ctrl + End moves the cursor to the end of the document.

2. Notepad can perform many of the tasks of word processors, such as search and block operations. However, these features needn't concern us presently. A discussion of them can be found in Appendix B, under "HOW TO: Use the Editor."

Practice Problems 1.2

(Solutions to practice problems always follow the exercises.) Assume that you are using Windows Notepad:

1. Give two ways to open the Edit menu.

2. Assume that the Edit menu has been opened. Give three ways to pick a menu item.

EXERCISES 1.2

1. What does an hourglass pointer mean?

2. Describe "clicking" in your own words.

3. Describe "double-clicking" in your own words.

4. Describe "dragging" in your own words.

5. What is the blinking vertical line in Notepad called, and what is its purpose?

6. How can you tell when a window is active?

7. What is the difference between "Windows" and "windows?"

8. What is the purpose of the vertical scroll bar in Notepad?

9. By what name is a Notepad document known before it is named as part of being saved on disk?

In Exercises 10 through 24, give the key (or key combination) that performs the task in Windows Notepad.

10. Remove a pull-down menu from the screen.

11. Erase the character to the left of the cursor.

12. Access the Start menu.

13. Erase the character to the right of the cursor.

14. Move the cursor to the beginning of the line containing the cursor.

15. Move the cursor to the end of the line containing the cursor.

16. Exit Notepad.

17. Move the cursor to the beginning of the document.

18. Move the cursor to the end of the document.

19. Move from the Work area to the Menu bar.

20. Move from the Menu bar to the Work area.

21. Cancel a dialog box.

22. Move from one option rectangle of a dialog box to another rectangle.

23. Save the current document on a disk.

24. Clear the current document from the Work area and start a new document.

Solutions to Practice Problems 1.2

---

1. Press Alt/Edit, or click on the word Edit in the toolbar to display the Edit menu. The jargon says the menu is "dropped down" or "pulled down."

2. Press the down-arrow key to highlight the item, then press the Enter key. Or, press the underlined letter in the name of the item, or click on the item.

1.3 Files and Folders

Modern computers have a hard disk, a diskette drive, and a CD (or DVD) drive. The hard disk is permanently housed inside the computer. You can read information from all three drives, but can write information easily only to the hard disk and to diskettes. We use the word **disk** to refer to either the hard disk, a diskette, a CD, or DVD. Each drive is identified by a letter. Normally, the hard drive is identified by C, the diskette drive by A, and the CD (or DVD) drive by D or E. Disk management is handled by Windows.

Disks hold not only programs, but also collections of data stored in files. The term **file** refers to either a program file, a text file, or some other kind of data file. We created a text file in Section 1.2. Each file has a name consisting of a base name followed by an optional extension consisting of a period and one or more characters. The term **filename** refers to the combination of the base name, the period, and the extension. A filename can contain up to 215 characters, typically consisting of letters, digits, spaces, periods, and other assorted characters. (The only characters that cannot be used in filenames are \, /, :, *, ?, <, >, ", and |.) Extensions are normally used to identify the type of file. For example, spreadsheets created with Excel have the extension *xls* (eXceL Spreadsheet), documents created with Word have the extension *doc* (DOCument), and files created with Notepad have the extension *txt* (TeXT document). Some examples of filenames are "Annual Sales.xls," "Letter to Mom.doc," and "Phone.txt".

Neither Windows nor Visual Basic distinguishes between uppercase and lowercase letters in folder and filenames. For instance, the names COSTS02.TXT, Costs02.Txt, and costs02.txt are equivalent. We use uppercase letters in this book for filenames.

Because a disk is capable of holding thousands of files, locating a specific file can be quite time consuming. Therefore, related files are grouped into collections called **folders**. For instance, one folder might hold all your Visual Basic programs, and another the documents created with your word processor.

Think of a disk as a large folder, called the **root folder**, that contains several smaller folders, each with its own name. (The naming of folders follows the same rules as the naming of files.) Each of these smaller folders can contain yet other named folders. Any folder contained inside another folder is said to be a **subfolder** of that folder. Each folder is identified by listing its name preceded by the names of the successively larger folders that contain it, with each folder name preceded by a backslash. Such a sequence is called a **path**. For instance, the path \Sales\NY02\July identifies the folder July, contained in the folder NY02, which in turn is contained in the folder Sales. Think of a file, along with its name, as written on a slip of paper that can be placed into either the root folder or one of the smaller folders. The combination of a drive letter followed by a colon, a path, and a filename is called a **filespec**, an abbreviation of "file specification." Some examples of filespecs are C:\VB01\VB.EXE and A:\Personal\INCOME02.TXT.

In early operating systems such as MS-DOS, folders were called **directories**. Many Visual Basic objects and commands still refer to folders as directories. The terms "root folder" and "path" are a reference to the "tree" metaphor commonly used to describe a computer's disk. In this metaphor, the large folder at the lowest level of the disk is called the "root" folder. The smaller folders contained in the root folder can be thought of as "branches" that emanate from the root. Each branch may have smaller branches, which in turn may have their own smaller branches, and so on. Finally, a file in one of these folders can be thought of as a leaf on a branch. The leaf is reached by starting at the root and following a "path" through the branches.

A program called Windows Explorer helps you view, organize, and manage the folders and files on your disks. We will learn how to use Windows Explorer to create, rename, copy, move, and delete folders and files.

■ Using Windows Explorer

To invoke Windows Explorer, click the Windows Start button, click on Run, type in the word "Explorer", and click on the OK button. The appearance of the Explorer window depends on the version of Windows being used and the values of certain settings. Figure 1.4 (on the next page) shows a possible Explorer window for Windows XP. The Folders pane on the left side of the window contains a folder tree with the My Documents folder highlighted. (Only one folder at a time can be highlighted. The icon for a highlighted folder appears to be physically open, and its name appears in the title bar at the top of the Explorer window.) The contents of the highlighted folder are displayed in the right pane of the Explorer window. In Figure 1.4, the highlighted folder contains six subfolders and two files. To highlight a different folder, just click on it with the left mouse button.

In the Folders pane, you can click on a plus box to expand the folder tree so that it reveals the subfolders of the folder next to the plus box. You click on a minus box to reverse the process. This process allows you to locate any file.

In Figure 1.4, the folders and files in the right pane are displayed in the so-called **Details view**. This view is invoked by pressing Alt/V/D. Also, in Figure 1.4, the extensions of the filenames are shown. By default, Windows shows only the base names of files. The following steps get it to also display the extensions:

1. From Windows Explorer, press Alt/T/O to display the Folders Options dialog box.
2. Click on the View tab in the dialog box.
3. If there is a check mark in the box next to "Hide extensions for known file types," click on the box to remove the check mark.
4. Click on the OK button to close the Folders Options dialog box.

To create a new folder:

1. Highlight the folder that is to contain the new folder as a subfolder.
2. On the File menu, point to New, and then click Folder. (Or press Alt/File/New/Folder.) The new folder appears with the temporary name New Folder.
3. Type a name for the folder, and then press the Enter key. (The allowable names for folders are the same as for files. However, folder names do not usually have an extension.)

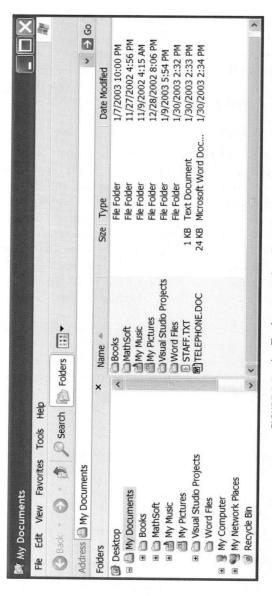

FIGURE 1.4   An Explorer window for Windows XP

To rename a folder or file:

1. Click on the folder or file in the right pane with the right mouse button.
2. In the Context menu that appears, click Rename. The current name will appear highlighted inside a rectangle.
3. Type the new name, and then press the Enter key.

To delete a folder or file:

1. Click on the folder or file with the right mouse button.
2. In the Context menu that appears, click Delete. A "Confirm Folder Delete" or a "Confirm File Delete" dialog box containing the name of the folder or file will appear.
3. Click the Yes button.

Or

1. Click on the file or folder with the left mouse button.
2. Press the Delete key.

To copy a folder or file:

1. Click on the folder or file to be copied with the right mouse button.
2. In the Context menu that appears, click on Copy.
3. Point to the folder where the copy is to be placed.
4. Click on the second folder with the right mouse button.
5. In the Context menu that appears, click on Paste.

To move a folder or file:

1. Click on the folder or file to be moved with the right mouse button.
2. In the Context menu that appears, click on Cut.
3. Point to the folder where the copy is to be moved.
4. Click on the second folder with the right mouse button.
5. In the Context menu that appears, click on Paste.

You also can carry out some of the preceding operations by "drag and drop." For details, see the Help Topics accessed through the Windows Explorer Help menu. For instance, you can delete a folder or file by dragging it to the Recycle Bin and releasing the left mouse button.

▦ Using the Open and Save As Dialog Boxes

In Section 1.2, we used the Open and Save As dialog boxes by just typing in the filespec for the desired file. These dialog boxes provide many features that assist with the locating of folders and files. Figure 1.5 shows an Open dialog box obtained from Windows XP. In the Save As dialog box, "Look in:" is replaced with "Save in:", and "Files of type:" is replaced with "Save as type:".

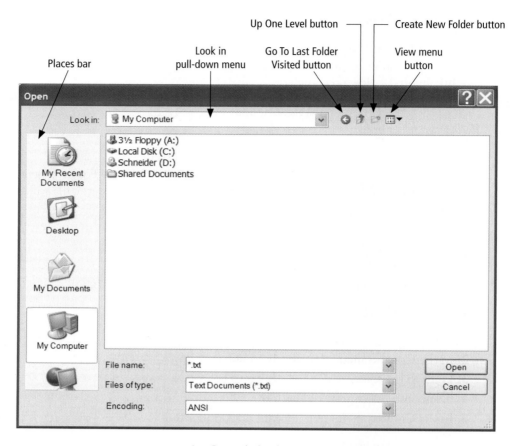

FIGURE 1.5   An Open dialog box from Windows XP.

You can begin the search by clicking on one of the icons in the Places bar. In Figure 1.5, the My Computer icon was pressed. The following steps would be used to locate the file with filespec "C:\VB Programs\3-5-3\bin\Debug\PAYROLL.TXT":

1. Double-click on "Local Disk (C:)" to obtain a list of all the folders and files on the hard drive C:. (The text in the "Look in:" box will now read "Local Disk (C:)".

2. Double-click on the folder named "VB Programs" to obtain a list of its subfolders and files.

3. In succession, double-click on "3-5-3," then on "bin," and finally on "Debug." The subfolders and files in the folder *Debug* will now be displayed. PAYROLL.TXT will be in the list.

4. Double-click on PAYROLL.TXT to open it.

The Save As dialog box operates in a similar way. However, after the desired folder is displayed in the "Save in:" box at the top of the dialog box, you would type the base name of the file into the "File name:" box.

1. Where is the file having filespec "C:\TODAY.TXT" located?
2. Is "C:\Sales\New York" a filespec or a path?

1. Explain why "Who is there?" is not a valid filename.
2. Explain why "FOUR STAR HOTEL ****" is not a valid filename.
3. What is wrong with the filespec "C:/Sports/TENNIS.DOC"?
4. Why do files on CDs usually have their read-only attribute turned on?
5. What is the path for a file whose filespec is "C:\Revenue\Chicago\MAIN.TXT"?
6. What is the filespec for the file PRES.TXT that is contained in the folder InfoUSA, where InfoUSA is a subfolder of the root directory of a diskette in the A drive?
7. Must the two files with filespecs "A:\DATA.TXT" and "A:\Info\DATA.TXT" be identical; that is, copies of one another?
8. What is the difference between a filespec and a filename?

From Windows Explorer, highlight a folder on your computer that contains many files, and then press Alt/V/D to select the Details option from the View menu. In Exercises 9-12, give the effect of clicking on the specified column head in the right-hand pane.

9. Size
10. Type
11. Modified
12. Name
13. The companion website for this book has a folder named Programs\Ch09\Pictures. Use Windows Explorer to obtain a list of the files in this folder, and then press Alt/V/H to select the Thumbnails option from the View menu. Describe what you see in the right pane.
14. Open the folder on your hard disk named My Documents. How many subfolders does the folder contain directly? How many files does the folder contain directly?

In Exercises 15 and 16, carry out the stated tasks.

15. (a) Take a blank diskette, and create two folders named Laurel and Hardy.
    (b) Create a subfolder of Laurel called Stan.
    (c) Use Notepad to create a file containing the sentence "Here's another nice mess you've gotten me into." and save the file with the name QUOTE.TXT in the folder Laurel.
    (d) Copy the file QUOTE.TXT into the folder Hardy.
    (e) Rename the new copy of the file QUOTE.TXT as LINE.TXT.
    (f) Delete the original copy of the file QUOTE.TXT.

16. (a) Take a blank diskette, create a folder named Slogans, and create two subfolders of Slogans named Coke and CocaCola.

(b) Use Notepad to create a file containing the sentence "It's the real thing.", and save the file with the name COKE1970.TXT in the folder Coke.

(c) Use Notepad to create a file containing the phrase "The ideal brain tonic.", and save the file with the name COKE1892.TXT in the folder Coke.

(d) Copy the two files in Coke into the folder CocaCola.

(e) Delete the folder Coke.

(f) Rename the folder CocaCola as Coke.

Solutions to Practice Problems 1.3

1. The file is located in the root folder of the C drive.

2. It could be either. If "New York" is a folder, then it is a path. If "New York" is a file, it is a filespec. In this book, we always give extensions to files and never give extensions to folders. Therefore, by our conventions, "C:\Sales\New York" would be a path.

1.4 An Introduction to Visual Basic 2005

Visual Basic 2005 is one of the most exciting developments in programming in many years. It is the latest generation of Visual Basic, a language used by millions of software developers.

Visual Basic was designed to make user-friendly programs easier to develop. Prior to the creation of Visual Basic, developing a friendly user interface usually required a programmer to use a language such as C or C++, often requiring hundreds of lines of code just to get a window to appear on the screen. Now the same program can be created with much less time and fewer instructions using a language that is a direct descendant of BASIC—the language most accessible to beginning programmers.

Visual Basic requires the Microsoft Windows operating system. Although you don't need to be an expert user of Microsoft Windows, you do need to know the basics before you can master Visual Basic—that is, you need to be comfortable with manipulating a mouse, you need to know how to manipulate a window, and you need to know how to use Notepad and Windows Explorer. However, there is no better way to master Microsoft Windows than to write applications for it—and that is what Visual Basic is all about.

▨ Why Windows and Why Visual Basic?

What people call **graphical user interfaces**, or GUIs (pronounced "gooies"), have revolutionized the computer industry. Instead of the confusing prompts that earlier users once saw, today's users are presented with a desktop filled with little pictures called icons. Icons provide a visual guide to what a program does or is used for.

Accompanying the revolution in how programs look was a revolution in how they feel. Consider a program that requests information for a database. Figure 1.6 shows how a program written before the advent of GUIs got its information. The program requests the six pieces of data one at a time, with no opportunity to go back and alter previously entered information. Then the screen clears and the six inputs are again requested one at a time. Figure 1.7 shows how an equivalent Visual Basic program gets its information.

Enter name (Enter EOD to terminate): <u>Mr. President</u>
Enter Address: <u>1600 Pennsylvania Avenue</u>
Enter City: <u>Washington</u>
Enter State: <u>DC</u>
Enter Zipcode: <u>20500</u>
Enter Phone Number: <u>202-456-1414</u>

FIGURE 1.6   Input screen of a pre-VB program to fill a database.

The boxes may be filled in any order. When the user clicks on a box with the mouse, the cursor moves to that box. The user can either type in new information or edit the existing information. When the user is satisfied that all the information is correct, he or she just clicks on the Write to Database button. The boxes will clear, and the data for another person can be entered. After all names have been entered, the user clicks on the Exit button. In Figure 1.6, the program is in control; in Figure 1.7, the user is in control!

How You Develop a Visual Basic Application

One of the key elements of planning a Visual Basic application is deciding what the user sees—in other words, designing the screen. What data will he or she be entering? How large a window should the application use? Where will you place the buttons the user clicks on to activate the applications? Will the applications have places to enter text (text boxes) and places to display output? What kind of warning boxes (message boxes) should the application use? In Visual Basic, the responsive objects a program designer places on windows are called **controls**. Two features make Visual Basic different from traditional programming tools:

1. You literally draw the user interface, much like using a paint program.
2. Perhaps more important, when you're done drawing the interface, the buttons, text boxes, and other objects that you have placed in a blank window will automatically recognize user actions such as mouse movements and button clicks.

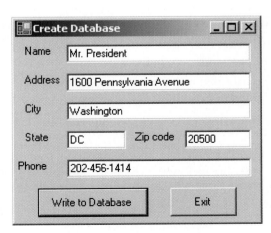

FIGURE 1.7   Input screen of a Visual Basic program to fill a database.

That is, the sequence of procedures executed in your program is controlled by "events" that the user initiates rather than by a predetermined sequence of procedures in your program.

In any case, only after you design the interface does anything like traditional programming occur. Objects in Visual Basic recognize events like mouse clicks; how the objects respond to them depends on the instructions you write. You always need to write instructions in order to make controls respond to events. This makes Visual Basic programming fundamentally different from conventional programming.

Programs in traditional programming languages ran from the top down. For these programming languages, execution started from the first line and moved with the flow of the program to different parts as needed. A Visual Basic program works differently. Its core is a set of independent groups of instructions that are activated by the events they have been told to recognize. This event-driven methodology is a fundamental shift. The user decides the order in which things happen, not the programmer.

Most of the programming instructions in Visual Basic that tell your program how to respond to events like mouse clicks occur in what Visual Basic calls *event procedures*. Essentially, anything executable in a Visual Basic program either is in an event procedure or is used by an event procedure to help the procedure carry out its job. In fact, to stress that Visual Basic is fundamentally different from traditional programming languages, Microsoft uses the term *project*, rather than *program*, to refer to the combination of programming instructions and user interface that makes a Visual Basic application possible.

Here is a summary of the steps you take to design a Visual Basic application:

1. Design the appearance of the window that the user sees.
2. Determine the events that the controls on the window should recognize.
3. Write the event procedures for those events.

Now here is what happens when the program is running:

1. Visual Basic monitors the controls in the window to detect any event that a control can recognize (mouse movements, clicks, keystrokes, and so on).
2. When Visual Basic detects an event, it examines the program to see if you've written an event procedure for that event.
3. If you have written an event procedure, Visual Basic executes the instructions that make up that event procedure and goes back to Step 1.
4. If you have not written an event procedure, Visual Basic ignores the event and goes back to Step 1.

These steps cycle continuously until the application ends. Usually, an event must happen before Visual Basic will do anything. Event-driven programs are reactive more than active—and that makes them more user friendly.

■ The Different Versions of Visual Basic

Visual Basic 1.0 first appeared in 1991. It was followed by version 2.0 in 1992, version 3.0 in 1993, version 4.0 in 1995, version 5.0 in 1997, and version 6.0 in 1998. VB.NET, initially released in February 2002, was not backward compatible with the earlier versions of Visual Basic. It incorporated many features requested by software developers, such as true inheritance and powerful Web capabilities. Visual Basic 2005, released in November 2005, is a significantly improved version of VB.NET.

1.5 Biographical History of Computing

The following people made important contributions to the evolution of the computer and the principles of programming. While we think of the computer as a modern technology, it is interesting to note that many of its technologies and concepts were developed decades before Silicon Valley became an address in American culture.

■ 1800s

George Boole: a self-taught British mathematician; devised an algebra of logic that later became a key tool in computer design. The logical operators presented in Section 5.1 are also known as Boolean operators.

Charles Babbage: a British mathematician and engineer; regarded as the father of the computer. Although the mechanical "analytical engine" that he conceived was never built, it influenced the design of modern computers. It had units for input, output, memory, arithmetic, logic, and control. Algorithms were intended to be communicated to the computer via punched cards, and numbers were to be stored on toothed wheels.

Augusta Ada Byron: a mathematician and colleague of Charles Babbage; regarded as the first computer programmer. She encouraged Babbage to modify the design based on programming considerations. Together they developed the concepts of decision structures, loops, and a library of procedures. Decision structures, loops, and procedures are presented in Chapters 5, 6, and 4 of this text, respectively.

Herman Hollerith: the founder of a company that was later to become IBM; at the age of 20, he devised a computer that made it possible to process the data for the U.S. Census of 1890 in one-third the time required for the 1880 census. His electromagnetic "tabulating machine" passed metal pins through holes in punched cards and into mercury-filled cups to complete an electric circuit. Each location of a hole corresponded to a characteristic of the population.

■ 1930s

Alan Turing: a gifted and far-sighted British mathematician; made fundamental contributions to the theory of computer science, assisted in the construction of some of the early large computers, and proposed a test for detecting intelligence within a machine.

His theoretical "Turing machine" laid the foundation for the development of general-purpose programmable computers. He changed the course of the Second World War by breaking the German "Enigma" code, thereby making secret German messages comprehensible to the Allies.

John V. Atanasoff: a mathematician and physicist at Iowa State University; declared by a federal court in Minnesota to be the inventor of the first electronic digital special-purpose computer. Designed with the assistance of his graduate assistant, Clifford Berry, this computer used vacuum tubes (instead of the less efficient relays) for storage and arithmetic functions.

■ 1940s

Howard Aiken: a professor at Harvard University; built the Mark I, a large-scale digital computer functionally similar to the "analytical engine" proposed by Babbage. This computer took five years to build and used relays for storage and computations. It was technologically obsolete before it was completed.

Grace M. Hopper: retired in 1986 at the age of 79 as a rear admiral in the United States Navy; wrote the first major subroutine (a procedure that was used to calculate sin x on the Mark I computer) and one of the first assembly languages. In 1945, she found that a moth fused onto a wire of the Mark I was causing the computer to malfunction, thus the origin of the term "debugging" for finding errors. As an administrator at Remington Rand in the 1950s, Dr. Hopper pioneered the development and use of COBOL, a programming language for the business community written in English-like notation.

John Mauchley and J. Presper Eckert: electrical engineers working at the University of Pennsylvania; built the first large-scale electronic digital general-purpose computer to be put into full operation. The ENIAC used 18,000 vacuum tubes for storage and arithmetic computations, weighed 30 tons, and occupied 1500 square feet. It could perform 300 multiplications of two 10-digit numbers per second, whereas the Mark I required 3 seconds to perform a single multiplication. Later they designed and developed the UNIVAC I, the first commercial electronic computer.

John von Neumann: a mathematical genius and member of the Institute for Advanced Study in Princeton, New Jersey; developed the stored program concept used in all modern computers. Prior to this development, instructions were programmed into computers by manually rewiring connections. Along with Hermann H. Goldstein, he wrote the first paper on the use of flowcharts.

Maurice V. Wilkes: an electrical engineer at Cambridge University in England and student of von Neumann; built the EDSAC, the first computer to use the stored program concept. Along with D. J. Wheeler and S. Gill, he wrote the first computer-programming text, *The Preparation of Programs for an Electronic Digital Computer* (Addison–Wesley, 1951), which dealt in depth with the use and construction of a versatile subroutine library.

John Bardeen, Walter Brattain, and William Shockley: physicists at Bell Labs; developed the transistor, a miniature device that replaced the vacuum tube and revolutionized computer design. It was smaller, lighter, more reliable, and cooler than the vacuum tube.

1950s

John Backus: a programmer for IBM; in 1953, headed a small group of programmers who wrote the most extensively used early interpretive computer system, the IBM 701 Speedcoding System. An interpreter translates a high-level language program into machine language one statement at a time as the program is executed. In 1957, Backus and his team produced the compiled language Fortran, which soon became the primary academic and scientific language. A compiler translates an entire program into efficient machine language before the program is executed. (Visual Basic combines the best of both worlds. It has the power and speed of a compiled language and the ease of use of an interpreted language.)

Reynold B. Johnson: IBM researcher; invented the computer disk drive. His disk drive, known as the Ramac, weighed a ton and stored five megabytes of data. Mr. Johnson's other inventions included an electromechanical device that can read pencil-marked multiple-choice exams and grade them mechanically, the technology behind children's "Talk to Me Books," and major advances in the quality of tapes used in VCRs. He was a 1986 recipient of the National Medal of Technology.

Donald L. Shell: in 1959, the year that he received his Ph.D. in mathematics from the University of Cincinnati, published an efficient algorithm for ordering (or sorting) lists of data. Sorting often consumes a significant amount of running time on computers. The Shell sort is presented in Chapter 7 of this text.

1960s

John G. Kemeny and Thomas E. Kurtz: professors of mathematics at Dartmouth College and the inventors of BASIC; led Dartmouth to national leadership in the educational uses of computing. Kemeny's distinguished career included serving as an assistant to both John von Neumann and Albert Einstein, serving as president of Dartmouth College, and chairing the commission to investigate the Three Mile Island nuclear power plant accident. In later years, Kemeny and Kurtz devoted considerable energy to the promotion of structured BASIC.

Corrado Bohm and Guiseppe Jacopini: European mathematicians; proved that any program can be written with the three structures discussed in Section 2.2: sequence, decisions, and loops. This result led to the systematic methods of modern program design known as structured programming.

Edsger W. Dijkstra: professor of computer science at the Technological University at Eindhoven, The Netherlands; stimulated the move to structured programming with the publication of a widely read article, "Go To Statement Considered Harmful." In that article, he proposes that GOTO statements be abolished from all high-level languages such as BASIC. The modern programming structures available in Visual Basic do away with the need for GOTO statements.

Harlan B. Mills: IBM Fellow and professor of computer science at the University of Maryland; advocated the use of structured programming. In 1969, Mills was asked to write a program creating an information database for the *New York Times*, a project that was estimated to require 30 person-years with traditional programming techniques. Using structured programming techniques, Mills single-handedly completed the project in six months. The methods of structured programming are used throughout this text.

Donald E. Knuth: professor of computer science at Stanford University; generally regarded as the preeminent scholar of computer science in the world. He is best known for his monumental series of books, *The Art of Computer Programming*, the definitive work on algorithms.

Ted Hoff, Stan Mazer, Robert Noyce, and Federico Faggin: engineers at the Intel Corporation; developed the first microprocessor chip. Such chips, which serve as the central processing units for microcomputers, are responsible for the extraordinary reduction in the size of computers. A computer with greater power than the ENIAC now can be held in the palm of the hand.

Douglas Engelbart: human interface designer at the Stanford Research Institute; inventor of the computer mouse. While most of us would believe that the mouse is a new technology, the prototype was actually developed in the 1960s. Funded by a government project, Engelbert and his team developed the idea of a mouse to navigate a computer screen with pop-up "windows" to present information to the user. In a contest to choose the best navigation tool, the mouse won over the light pen, a joystick, a "nose-pointing" device, and even a knee-pointing device!

1970s

Ted Codd: software architect; laid the groundwork for relational databases in his seminal paper, "A Relational Model of Data for Large Shared Data Banks," which appeared in the June 1970 issue of the *Communications of the* ACM. Relational databases are studied in Chapter 10 of this text.

Paul Allen and Bill Gates: cofounders of Microsoft Corporation; developed languages and the original operating system for the IBM PC. The operating system, known as MS-DOS, is a collection of programs that manage the operation of the computer. In 1974, Gates dropped out of Harvard after one year, and Allen left a programming job with Honeywell to write software together. Their initial project was a version of BASIC for the Altair, the first microcomputer. Microsoft is one of the most highly respected software companies in the World and a leader in the development of applications and programming languages.

Stephen Wozniak and Stephen Jobs: cofounders of Apple Computer Inc.; started the microcomputer revolution. The two had met as teenagers while working summers at Hewlett–Packard. Another summer, Jobs worked in an orchard, a job that inspired the names of their computers. Wozniak designed the Apple computer in Jobs's parents' garage, and Jobs promoted it so successfully that the company was worth hundreds of millions of dollars when it went public. Both men resigned from the company in 1985. Jobs founded a new company that developed the "Next" computer. He later returned to Apple and incorporated aspects of the Next computer into the Apple operating system.

Dan Bricklin and Dan Fylstra: cofounders of Software Arts; wrote VisiCalc, the first electronic spreadsheet program. An electronic spreadsheet is a worksheet divided into rows and columns, which analysts use to construct budgets and estimate costs. A change made in one number results in the updating of all numbers derived from it. For instance, changing a person's housing expenses will immediately produce a change in total expenses. Bricklin got the idea for an electronic spreadsheet after watching one of his professors at Harvard Business School struggle while updating a spreadsheet at the blackboard. VisiCalc became so popular that many people bought personal computers just so they could run the program.

Dennis Ritchie: member of the team at Bell Labs, creator of the C programming language. C is often referred to as a "portable assembly language." Programs developed in C benefit from speed of execution by being fairly low-level and close to assembly language, yet not being tied up in the specifics of a particular hardware architecture. This characteristic was particularly important to the development of the Unix operating system, which occurred around the same time as the development of C. Throughout the 1970s, 1980s, 1990s, and even today, C has been a widely used language, particularly in situations where very fast program execution time is important.

Ken Thompson: member of the team at Bell Labs that created the Unix operating system as an alternative to the operating system for IBM's 360 mainframe computers. Unlike many other earlier operating systems, Unix was written in C instead of assembly language. This allowed it to be adapted to a wide variety of computer architectures. Programmers could then develop programs in C that were intended to run on a Unix operating system, avoiding much of the rewriting involved in porting (adapting) these programs from one type of machine to another. Over the past 30 years, many variants upon Unix have emerged, often referred to as different "flavors" of Unix. Unix and its variants have played a tremendous role in the growth of the Internet, as well as being an operating system used by many commercial, scientific, and academic institutions.

Alan Kay: a brilliant programmer at the University of Utah; crystallized the concept of reuseable building blocks of code to develop software programs. He developed a new language, Smalltalk, a pure object-oriented language, while at Xerox Palo Alto Research Center (PARC) in the 1970s. Most of today's programming languages such as C++, C#, Java, and Visual Basic make use of object-oriented features first developed in Smalltalk. Still, because of its conceptual purity, Kay believes that Smalltalk "is the only real object-oriented language."

Don Chamberlain: a Stanford Ph.D. and National Science Foundation scholar working at IBM; created a database programming language, later known as SQL (Structured Query Language). This innovative language was built on a "relational" model for data, where related data groups could be put into tables, then linked in various ways for easy programming and access. Very few people know that one of the world's largest software companies, Oracle Corporation, was founded on this technology, developed by IBM and published for all to use. SQL is covered in Chapter 10 of this book.

▦ 1980s

Phillip "Don" Estridge: head of a product group at IBM; directly responsible for the success of the personal computer. The ubiquity of the PC today can be attributed to a marketing decision by Estridge to make off-the-shelf, easily producible computers for a mass market, and to back that with IBM's huge marketing resources. Estridge's "skunk-works" group in Boca Raton broke many established IBM rules for product introduction. The IBM PC, introduced in 1981, chose an operating system from Microsoft and a processor chip from Intel over other vendors. This licensing deal opened the way for Microsoft's and Intel's successes today.

Mitchell D. Kapor: cofounder of Lotus Corporation; wrote the business software program Lotus 1-2-3, one of the most successful pieces of software for personal computers in its time. Lotus 1-2-3 is an integrated program consisting of a spreadsheet, a database manager, and a graphics package.

Tom Button: group product manager for applications programmability at Microsoft; headed the team that developed QuickBasic, QBasic, and Visual Basic. These modern, yet easy-to-use, languages greatly increased the productivity of programmers.

Alan Cooper: director of applications software for Coactive Computing Corporation; considered the father of Visual Basic. In 1987, he wrote a program called Ruby that delivered visual programming to the average user. A few years later, Ruby was combined with QuickBasic to produce Visual Basic, the remarkably successful language that allows Windows programs to be written from within Windows easily and efficiently.

Tim Berners–Lee: British computer scientist; father of the World Wide Web. He proposed the Web project in 1989 while working in Switzerland. His brainchild has grown into a global phenomenon. Berners-Lee, currently a senior research scientist at MIT, was awarded the first Millenium Technology Prize in 2004.

Charles Simonyi: a Hungarian programmer; known to the industry as the "father of Word." He left his native Budapest as a 17-year-old prodigy to work at Xerox's prestigious Palo Alto Research Center (PARC), where he developed the capability of "What You See Is What You Get" (WYSIWYG) software. This technology, which allows users to define the fonts and presentations for computer output, opened the door to desktop publishing on the personal computer. In 1980, Simonyi joined a fledgling software company called Microsoft and developed Microsoft Word into one of the most widely used software programs ever.

Bjarne Stroustrup: a native of Denmark; creator of the C++ programming language. Stoustrup came to the United States to work for Bell Labs, during which time he created C++ to extend the C programming language with additional capabilities for object-oriented and generic programming. C++ has been one of the most widely used programming languages, combining the speed and efficiency of C with features that make the development of large-scale programs much simpler. Because of its ability to work at a low level in a manner similar to C, C++ remains the language of choice for many projects where other programming languages such as Java and Visual Basic are not suitable.

Richard M. Stallman: a star programmer at MIT's Artificial Intelligence Lab and a MacArthur Foundation Fellow; founded the Free Software Foundation (FSF). The FSF is an organization dedicated to promoting the free availability of software for public access, modification, and improvement. This philosophy contrasts with that of a large part of the commercial software development world, where software is developed for sale, but the full rights to the source code are maintained by the company writing the software. Among his many technical accomplishments, Stallman created free versions of EMACS (a highly popular text editor on Linux/Unix systems) and GCC (a free C language compiler).

▪ 1990s

Marc Andreessen: a former graduate student at the University of Illinois; inventor of the Web browser. He led a small band of fellow students to develop Mosaic, a program that allowed the user to move around the World Wide Web by clicking on words and symbols. Andreessen went on to cofound NCSA and Netscape Communications Corporation. Netscape's was the leading Web browser throughout the mid 1990s before being surpassed by Microsoft's Internet Explorer.

James Gosling: corporate vice president and Sun Fellow at Sun Microsystems; creator of the Java programming language. What started as an attempt to create a simple language for a networked world, Java, an object-oriented language, became a popular language for Internet programming. Java has become the primary teaching language at many universities. Visual Basic has many of the features and capabilities of Java.

Linus Torvalds: a graduate of the University of Helsinki in Finland; developed the popular Linux operating system. Linux began as a project by Linus to create a Unix operating system that could be used on personal computers. In the early 1990s, he began sharing the Linux source code with other OS programmers over the Internet, allowing them to contribute to and improve it. This philosophy resonated with the Internet culture, and the popularity of Linux grew quickly. Today, Linux is widely used, particularly as an operating system for Web servers. It is an open-source operating system, meaning that the source code (instructions) is made freely available for anyone to obtain, view, modify and use.

2

Problem Solving

2.1   Program Development Cycle 30

◆ Performing a Task on the Computer ◆ Program Planning

2.2   Programming Tools 32

◆ Flowcharts ◆ Pseudocode ◆ Hierarchy Chart ◆ Direction of
Numbered NYC Streets Algorithm ◆ Class Average Algorithm

2.1   Program Development Cycle

We learned in the first chapter that hardware refers to the machinery in a computer system (such as the monitor, keyboard, and CPU) and software refers to a collection of instructions, called a **program**, that directs the hardware. Programs are written to solve problems or perform tasks on a computer. Programmers translate the solutions or tasks into a language the computer can understand. As we write programs, we must keep in mind that the computer will only do what we instruct it to do. Because of this, we must be very careful and thorough with our instructions. **Note:** A program is also known as a **project, application,** or **solution.**

▨ Performing a Task on the Computer

The first step in writing instructions to carry out a task is to determine what the **output** should be—that is, exactly what the task should produce. The second step is to identify the data, or **input**, necessary to obtain the output. The last step is to determine how to **process** the input to obtain the desired output, that is, to determine what formulas or ways of doing things can be used to obtain the output.

   This problem-solving approach is the same as that used to solve word problems in an algebra class. For example, consider the following algebra problem:

How fast is a car traveling if it goes 50 miles in 2 hours?

The first step is to determine the type of answer requested. The answer should be a number giving the speed in miles per hour (the output). (*Speed* is also called *velocity*.) The information needed to obtain the answer is the distance and time the car has traveled (the input). The formula

$$speed = distance/time$$

is used to process the distance traveled and the time elapsed in order to determine the speed. That is,

$$speed = 50 \text{ miles}/2 \text{ hours}$$
$$= 25 \text{ miles/hour}$$

   A pictorial representation of this problem-solving process is

   We determine what we want as output, get the needed input, and process the input to produce the desired output.

   In the following chapters we discuss how to write programs to carry out the preceding operations. But first we look at the general process of writing programs.

▦ Program Planning

A baking recipe provides a good example of a plan. The ingredients and the amounts are determined by what is to be baked. That is, the *output* determines the *input* and the *processing*. The recipe, or plan, reduces the number of mistakes you might make if you tried to bake with no plan at all. Although it's difficult to imagine an architect building a bridge or a factory without a detailed plan, many programmers (particularly students in their first programming course) try to write programs without first making a careful plan. The more complicated the problem, the more complex the plan may be. You will spend much less time working on a program if you devise a carefully thought out step-by-step plan and test it before actually writing the program.

Many programmers plan their programs using a sequence of steps, referred to as the **program development cycle**. The following step-by-step process will enable you to use your time efficiently and help you design error-free programs that produce the desired output.

1. *Analyze:* Define the problem.

   Be sure you understand what the program should do, that is, what the output should be. Have a clear idea of what data (or input) are given and the relationship between the input and the desired output.

2. *Design:* Plan the solution to the problem.

   Find a logical sequence of precise steps that solve the problem. Such a sequence of steps is called an **algorithm**. Every detail, including obvious steps, should appear in the algorithm. In the next section, we discuss three popular methods used to develop the logic plan: flowcharts, pseudocode, and top-down charts. These tools help the programmer break a problem into a sequence of small tasks the computer can perform to solve the problem. Planning also involves using representative data to test the logic of the algorithm by hand to ensure that it is correct.

3. *Choose the interface:* Select the objects (text boxes, buttons, etc.).

   Determine how the input will be obtained and how the output will be displayed. Then create objects to receive the input and display the output. Also, create appropriate buttons and menus to allow the user to control the program.

4. *Code:* Translate the algorithm into a programming language.

   Coding is the technical word for writing the program. During this stage, the program is written in Visual Basic and entered into the computer. The programmer uses the algorithm devised in Step 2 along with a knowledge of Visual Basic.

5. *Test and debug:* Locate and remove any errors in the program.

   Testing is the process of finding errors in a program, and **debugging** is the process of correcting errors that are found. (An error in a program is called a **bug.**) As the program is typed, Visual Basic points out certain types of program errors. Other types of errors will be detected by Visual Basic when the program is executed; however, many errors due to typing mistakes, flaws in the algorithm, or incorrect use of the Visual Basic language rules can be uncovered and corrected only by careful detective work. An example of such an error would be using addition when multiplication was the proper operation.

6. ***Complete the documentation:*** Organize all the material that describes the program.

Documentation is intended to allow another person, or the programmer at a later date, to understand the program. Internal documentation (comments) consists of statements in the program that are not executed, but point out the purposes of various parts of the program. Documentation might also consist of a detailed description of what the program does and how to use the program (for instance, what type of input is expected). For commercial programs, documentation includes an instruction manual and on-line help. Other types of documentation are the flow-chart, pseudocode, and top-down chart that were used to construct the program. Although documentation is listed as the last step in the program development cycle, it should take place as the program is being coded.

2.2 Programming Tools

This section discusses some specific algorithms and develops three tools used to convert algorithms into computer programs: flowcharts, pseudocode, and hierarchy charts.

You use algorithms every day to make decisions and perform tasks. For instance, whenever you mail a letter, you must decide how much postage to put on the envelope. One rule of thumb is to use one stamp for every five sheets of paper or fraction thereof. Suppose a friend asks you to determine the number of stamps to place on an envelope. The following algorithm will accomplish the task.

1. Request the number of sheets of paper; call it Sheets.   (*input*)
2. Divide Sheets by 5.   (*processing*)
3. Round the quotient up to the next highest whole number;
   call it Stamps.   (*processing*)
4. Reply with the number Stamps.   (*output*)

The preceding algorithm takes the number of sheets (Sheets) as input, processes the data, and produces the number of stamps needed (Stamps) as output. We can test the algorithm for a letter with 16 sheets of paper.

1. Request the number of sheets of paper; Sheets = 16.
2. Dividing 5 into 16 gives 3.2.
3. Rounding 3.2 up to 4 gives Stamps = 4.
4. Reply with the answer, 4 stamps.

This problem-solving example can be pictured by

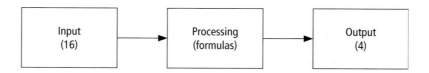

Of the program design tools available, three popular tools are the following:

Flowcharts: Graphically depict the logical steps to carry out a task and show how the steps relate to each other.

Pseudocode: Uses English-like phrases with some Visual Basic terms to outline the task.

Hierarchy charts: Show how the different parts of a program relate to each other.

■ Flowcharts

A flowchart consists of special geometric symbols connected by arrows. Within each symbol is a phrase presenting the activity at that step. The shape of the symbol indicates the type of operation that is to occur. For instance, the parallelogram denotes input or output. The arrows connecting the symbols, called **flowlines**, show the progression in which the steps take place. Flowcharts should "flow" from the top of the page to the bottom. Although the symbols used in flowcharts are standardized, no standards exist for the amount of detail required within each symbol.

Symbol	Name	Meaning
→	*Flowline*	Used to connect symbols and indicate the flow of logic.
	Terminal	Used to represent the beginning (Start) or the end (End) of a task.
	Input/Output	Used for input and output operations, such as reading and displaying. The data to be read or displayed are described inside.
	Processing	Used for arithmetic and data-manipulation operations. The instructions are listed inside the symbol.
	Decision	Used for any logic or comparison operations. Unlike the input/ouput and processing symbols, which have one entry and one exit flowline, the decision symbol has one entry and two exit paths. The path chosen depends on whether the answer to a question is "yes" or "no."
	Connector	Used to joint different flowlines.
	Offpage Connector	Used to indicate that the flowchart continues to a second page.
	Predefined Process	Used to represent a group of statements that perform one processing task.
	Annotation	Used to provide additional information about another flowchart symbol.

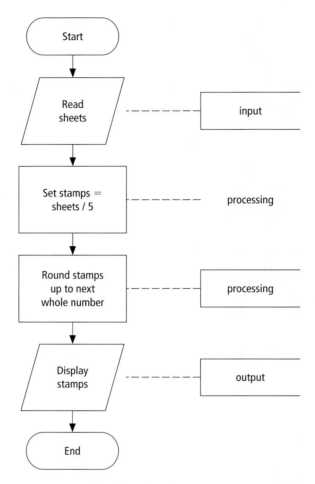

FIGURE 2.1   Flowchart for the postage stamp problem.

The table of the flowchart symbols shown on the previous page has been adopted by the American National Standards Institute (ANSI). Figure 2.1 shows the flowchart for the postage stamp problem.

The main advantage of using a flowchart to plan a task is that it provides a pictorial representation of the task, which makes the logic easier to follow. We can clearly see every step and how each is connected to the next. The major disadvantage with flowcharts is that when a program is very large, the flowcharts may continue for many pages, making them difficult to follow and modify.

◼ Pseudocode

Pseudocode is an abbreviated plain English version of actual computer code (hence, *pseudocode*). The geometric symbols used in flowcharts are replaced by English-like statements that outline the process. As a result, pseudocode looks more like computer code than does a flowchart. Pseudocode allows the programmer to focus on the steps required to solve a problem rather than on how to use the computer language. The programmer can describe the algorithm in Visual Basic-like form without being restricted by the rules of Visual Basic. When the pseudocode is completed, it can be easily translated into the Visual Basic language.

The following is pseudocode for the postage stamp problem:

Program: Determine the proper number of stamps for a letter
Read Sheets   *(input)*
Set the number of stamps to Sheets / 5   *(processing)*
Round the number of stamps up to the next whole number   *(processing)*
Display the number of stamps   *(output)*

Pseudocode has several advantages. It is compact and probably will not extend for many pages as flowcharts commonly do. Also, the plan looks like the code to be written and so is preferred by many programmers.

■ Hierarchy Chart

The last programming tool we'll discuss is the **hierarchy chart**, which shows the overall program structure. Hierarchy charts are also called structure charts, HIPO (Hierarchy plus Input-Process-Output) charts, top-down charts, or VTOC (Visual Table of Contents) charts. All these names refer to planning diagrams that are similar to a company's organization chart.

Hierarchy charts depict the organization of a program but omit the specific processing logic. They describe what each part, or **module**, of the program does and they show how the modules relate to each other. The details on how the modules work, however, are omitted. The chart is read from top to bottom and from left to right. Each module may be subdivided into a succession of submodules that branch out under it. Typically, after the activities in the succession of submodules are carried out, the module to the right of the original module is considered. A quick glance at the hierarchy chart reveals each task performed in the program and where it is performed. Figure 2.2 shows a hierarchy chart for the postage stamp problem.

The main benefit of hierarchy charts is in the initial planning of a program. We break down the major parts of a program so we can see what must be done in general.

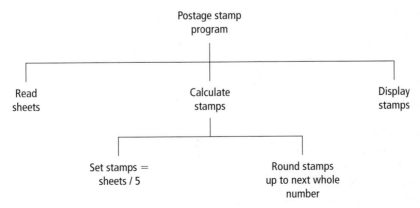

FIGURE 2.2   Hierarchy chart for the postage stamp problem.

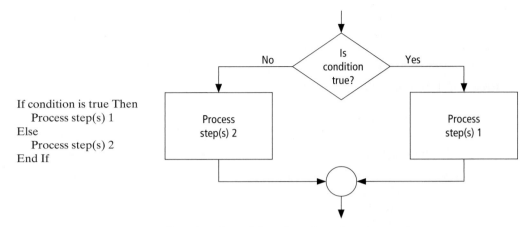

If condition is true Then
        Process step(s) 1
Else
        Process step(s) 2
End If

FIGURE 2.3   Pseudocode and flowchart for a decision structure.

From this point, we can then refine each module into more detailed plans using flow-charts or pseudocode. This process is called the **divide-and-conquer** method.

The postage stamp problem was solved by a series of instructions to read data, per-form calculations, and display results. Each step was in a sequence; that is, we moved from one line to the next without skipping over any lines. This kind of structure is called a **sequence structure**. Many problems, however, require a decision to determine whether a series of instructions should be executed. If the answer to a question is "Yes," then one group of instructions is executed. If the answer is "No," then another is exe-cuted. This structure is called a **decision structure**. Figure 2.3 contains the pseudocode and flowchart for a decision structure.

The sequence and decision structures are both used to solve the following problem.

▨ Direction of Numbered NYC Streets Algorithm

Problem: Given a street number of a one-way street in New York, decide the direction of the street, either eastbound or westbound.

Discussion: There is a simple rule to tell the direction of a one-way street in New York: Even-numbered streets run eastbound.

Input: Street number

Processing: Decide if the street number is divisible by 2.

Output: "Eastbound" or "Westbound"

Figures 2.4 through 2.6 show the flowchart, pseudocode, and hierarchy chart for the New York City numbered streets problem.

The solution to the next problem requires the repetition of a series of instructions. A programming structure that executes instructions many times is called a **loop structure**.

We need a test (or decision) to tell when the loop should end. Without an exit condition, the loop would repeat endlessly (an infinite loop). One way to control the number of times a loop repeats (often referred to as the number of passes or iterations) is to check a condition before each pass through the loop and continue executing the loop as long as the condition is true. See Figure 2.7.

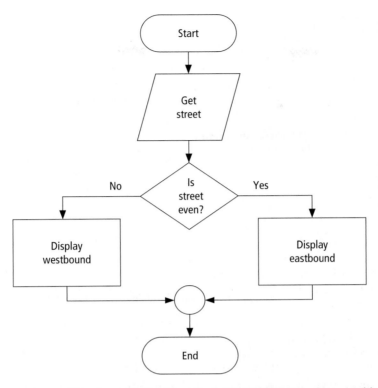

FIGURE 2.4   **Flowchart for the New York City numbered streets problem.**

Program: Determine the direction of a numbered NYC street.
Get street
If street is even Then
    Display Eastbound
Else
    Display Westbound
End If

FIGURE 2.5   **Pseudocode for the New York City numbered streets problem.**

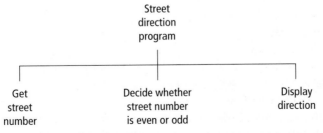

FIGURE 2.6   **Hierarchy chart for the New York City numbered streets problem.**

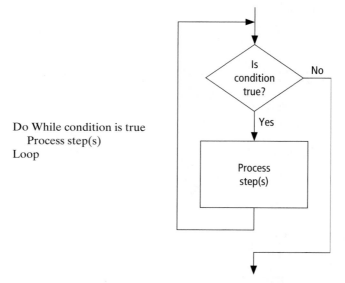

```
Do While condition is true
    Process step(s)
Loop
```

FIGURE 2.7   **Pseudocode and flowchart for a loop.**

■ Class Average Algorithm

Problem: Calculate and report the grade-point average for a class.

Discussion: The average grade equals the sum of all grades divided by the number of students. We need a loop to read and then add (accumulate) the grades for each student in the class. Inside the loop, we also need to total (count) the number of students in the class. See Figures 2.8 to 2.10.

Input: Student grades

Processing: Find the sum of the grades; count the number of students; calculate average grade = sum of grades / number of students.

Output: Average grade

■ Comments

1. Tracing a flowchart is like playing a board game. We begin at the Start symbol and proceed from symbol to symbol until we reach the End symbol. At any time, we will be at just one symbol. In a board game, the path taken depends on the result of spinning a spinner or rolling a pair of dice. The path taken through a flowchart depends on the input.

2. The algorithm should be tested at the flowchart stage before being coded into a program. Different data should be used as input, and the output checked. This process is known as **desk checking**. The test data should include nonstandard data as well as typical data.

3. Flowcharts, pseudocode, and hierarchy charts are universal problem-solving tools. They can be used to construct programs in any computer language, not just Visual Basic.

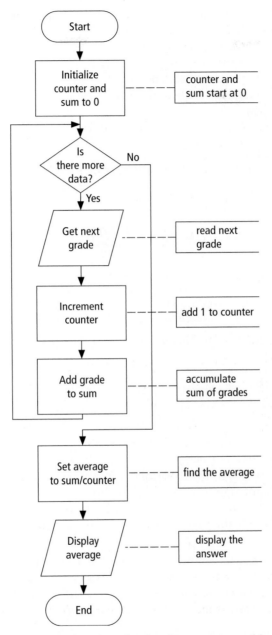

FIGURE 2.8   **Flowchart for the class average problem.**

Program: Calculate and report the average grade of a class.
Initialize Counter and Sum to 0
Do While there is more data
    Get the next Grade
    Increment the Counter
    Add the Grade to the Sum
Loop
Compute Average = Sum/Counter
Display Average

FIGURE 2.9 Pseudocode for the class average problem.

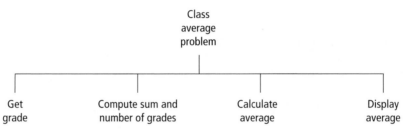

FIGURE 2.10 Hierarchy chart for the class average problem.

4. Flowcharts are used throughout this text to provide a visualization of the flow of certain programming tasks and Visual Basic control structures. Major examples of pseudocode and hierarchy charts appear in the case studies.

5. There are four primary logical programming constructs: sequence, decision, loop, and unconditional branch. Unconditional branch, which appears in some languages as Goto statements, involves jumping from one place in a program to another. Structured programming uses the first three constructs but forbids the fourth. One advantage of pseudocode over flowcharts is that pseudocode has no provision for unconditional branching and thus forces the programmer to write structured programs.

6. Flowcharts are time consuming to write and difficult to update. For this reason, professional programmers are more likely to favor pseudocode and hierarchy charts. Because flowcharts so clearly illustrate the logical flow of programming techniques, however, they are a valuable tool in the education of programmers.

7. There are many styles of pseudocode. Some programmers use an outline form, whereas others use a form that looks almost like a programming language. The pseudocode appearing in the case studies of this text focuses on the primary tasks to be performed by the program and leaves many of the routine details to be completed during the coding process. Several Visual Basic keywords, such as, If, Else, Do, and While, are used extensively in the pseudocode appearing in this text.

8. Many people draw rectangles around each item in a hierarchy chart. In this text, rectangles are omitted in order to make hierarchy charts easier to draw and thereby to encourage their use.

3

Fundamentals of

Programming in Visual Basic

3.1 Visual Basic Controls 42

◆ Starting a New Visual Basic Program ◆ A Text Box Walkthrough ◆ A Button Walkthrough ◆ A Label Walkthrough ◆ A List Box Walkthrough ◆ The Name Property ◆ A Help Walkthrough ◆ Fonts ◆ Auto Hide ◆ Positioning and Aligning Controls

3.2 Visual Basic Events 60

◆ An Event Procedure Walkthrough ◆ Properties and Event Procedures of the Form ◆ The Header of an Event Procedure

3.3 Numbers 73

◆ Arithmetic Operations ◆ Variables ◆ Incrementing the Value of a Variable ◆ Built-In Functions: Math.Sqrt, Int, Math.Round ◆ The Integer Data Type ◆ Multiple Declarations ◆ Parentheses ◆ Three Types of Errors

3.4 Strings 88

◆ Variables and Strings ◆ Using Text Boxes for Input and Output ◆ Concatenation ◆ String Properties and Methods: Length Property and ToUpper, ToLower, Trim, IndexOf, and Substring Methods ◆ The Empty String ◆ Initial Value of a String ◆ Option Strict ◆ Internal Documentation ◆ Line-Continuation Character

3.5 Input and Output 105

◆ Formatting Output with Format Functions ◆ Formatting Output with Zones ◆ Reading Data from Files ◆ Getting Input from an Input Dialog Box ◆ Using a Message Dialog Box for Output ◆ Using a Masked Text Box for Input

Summary 127

Programming Projects 128

3.1 Visual Basic Controls

Visual Basic programs display a Windows-style screen (called a **form**) with boxes into which users type (and in which users edit) information and buttons that they click to initiate actions. The boxes and buttons are referred to as **controls**. In this section, we examine forms and four of the most useful Visual Basic controls.

◼ Starting a New Visual Basic Program

For our purposes, Visual Basic programs are also known as **applications**, **solutions**, or **projects**. Each program is saved (as several files and subfolders) in its own folder. Before starting a new program, you should use Windows Explorer to create a folder to hold the folders for your programs.

The process for invoking Visual Basic varies slightly with the edition of Visual Basic installed on the computer. To invoke Visual Basic from a computer that has Visual Basic Express installed, click the Windows Start button, hover over All Programs, and then click on Microsoft Visual Basic 2005 Express Edition. With the other editions of Visual Basic, hover over All Programs, hover over Microsoft Visual Studio 2005, and then click on Microsoft Visual Studio 2005 in the short list that is revealed.

The window that appears after Visual Basic is invoked has a menu bar whose first item is "File". Click on File, and then click on New Project to produce a New Project input dialog box. Figure 3.1 shows the New Project input dialog box produced by Visual Basic Express. The "Windows Application" icon should be selected as the installed template. If this is not the case, click on "Windows Application" to select it. (The other editions of Visual Basic contain a pane identifying a Project type. You should select "Visual Basic" as the Project type.)

Note: The number of project types and icons showing will vary depending on the version of Visual Basic you are using. Figure 3.1 was created from the Express Edition.

The name of the program, initially set to WindowsApplication1, can be specified at this time. Since we will have a chance to change the name later, let's just call the program WindowsApplication1 for now. Click on the OK button to invoke the Visual Basic programming environment. See Figure 3.2. **Note:** Your screen will resemble, but may differ somewhat from, Figure 3.2. The Visual Basic programming environment is often referred to as the IDE (Integrated Development Environment).

The **Menu bar** of the IDE displays the commands you use to work with Visual Basic. Some of the menus, like File, Edit, View, and Window, are common to most Windows applications. Others, such as Project, Build, and Debug, provide commands specific to programming in Visual Basic.

The **Toolbars** hold a collection of icons that carry out standard operations when clicked. For example, you can use the fifth icon, which looks like a stack of three diskettes, to save the files associated with the current program. To reveal the purpose of a Toolbar icon, hover the mouse pointer over the icon for a few seconds. The little information rectangle that pops up is called a **tooltip**.

In Figure 3.2, the **Main area** currently holds the **Windows Form Designer**. The rectangular **Form window**, or **form** for short, becomes a Windows window when a program

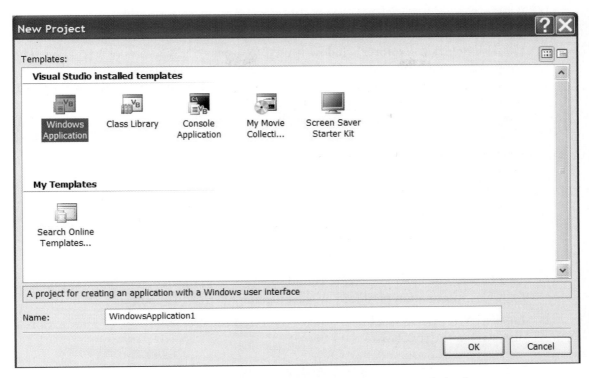

FIGURE 3.1   The Visual Basic Express New Project input dialog box.

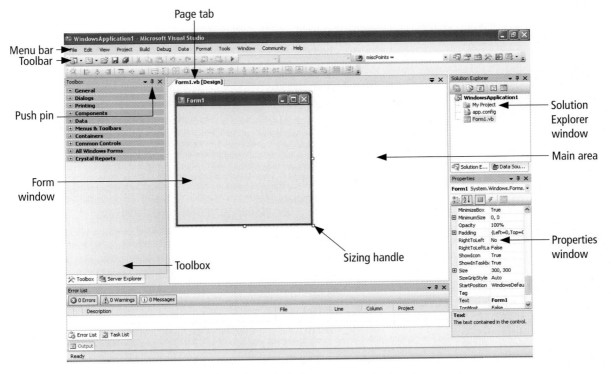

FIGURE 3.2   The Visual Basic programming environment.

is executed. Most information displayed by the program appears on the form. The information usually is displayed in controls that the programmer has placed on the form.

The **Solution Explorer window** is used to display various parts of a program. The **Properties window** is used to change how objects look and react.

The **Toolbox** holds icons representing controls that can be placed on the form. These controls are grouped into categories such as General, Dialogs, Printing, etc. Figure 3.3 shows the Toolbox after the plus sign to the left of "Common Controls" has been clicked. Nearly all the controls discussed in this text can be found in the list of common controls. The four controls discussed in this chapter are text boxes, labels, buttons, and list boxes.

Note: If your screen does not show the Toolbox, move the mouse over the tab marked Toolbox at the left side of the screen. The Toolbox will appear. Then click on the push-pin icon in the title bar of the top of the Toolbox to keep the toolbox from sliding out of the way when the cursor is moved away from the Toolbox.

Text boxes: You use a text box to get information from the user, referred to as **input**, or to display information produced by the program, referred to as **output**.

Labels: You place a label near a text box to tell the user what type of information is displayed in the text box.

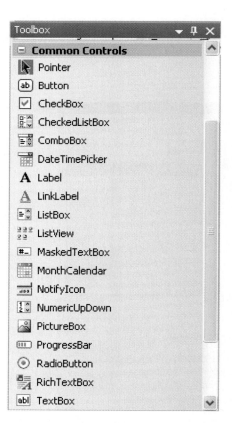

FIGURE 3.3   **The Toolbox's common controls.**

Buttons: The user clicks a button to initiate an action.

List boxes: In the first part of the book, we use list boxes to display tables or several lines of output. Later, we use list boxes to make selections.

▓ A Text Box Walkthrough

1. Double-click on the text box icon in the Common Controls portion of the Toolbox. A rectangle with two small squares, called **sizing handles**, appears at the upper left corner of the form. (You can alter the width of the text box by dragging one of the sizing handles.) Move the mouse arrow to any point of the text box other than a sizing handle, hold down the left mouse button, and drag the text box to the center of the form. See Figure 3.4. **Note:** The Tasks button will be discussed later in this chapter.

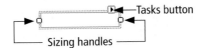

FIGURE 3.4   A text box with sizing handles.

2. Click anywhere on the form outside the rectangle to deselect the text box.
3. Click on the rectangle to restore the handles. An object showing its handles is said to be **selected**. A selected text box can have its width altered, location changed, and other properties modified.
4. Move the mouse arrow to the handle in the center of the right side of the text box. The cursor should change to a double arrow (↔). Hold down the left mouse button, and move the mouse to the right. The text box is stretched to the right. Similarly, grabbing the text box on the left side and moving the mouse to the left stretches the text box to the left. You also can use the handles to make the text box smaller. Steps 1 and 4 allow you to place a text box of any width anywhere on the form. **Note:** The text box should now be selected; that is, its sizing handles should be showing. If not, click anywhere inside the text box to select it.
5. Press the delete key, Del, to remove the text box from the form. Step 6 gives an alternative way to place a text box of any width at any location on the form.
6. Click on the text box icon in the Toolbox. Then move the mouse pointer to any place on the form. (When over the form, the mouse pointer becomes a pair of crossed thin lines.) Hold down the left mouse button, and drag the mouse on a diagonal to generate a rectangle. Release the mouse button to obtain a selected text box. You can now alter the width and location as before. **Note:** The text box should now be selected. If not, click anywhere inside the text box to select it.
7. Press F4 to activate the Properties window. (You also can activate the Properties window by clicking on it, clicking on the Properties window icon in the right part of the Toolbar, selecting Properties Window from the View menu, or clicking on

the text box with the right mouse button and selecting Properties.) See Figure 3.5. The first line of the Properties window (called the **Object box**) reads "TextBox1 etc." TextBox1 is the current name of the text box. The first two buttons below the Object box permit you to view the list of properties either grouped into categories or alphabetically. Use the up- and down-arrow keys (or the up- and down-scroll arrows) to move through the list. The left column gives the property names, and the right column gives the current settings of the properties. We discuss four properties in this walkthrough.

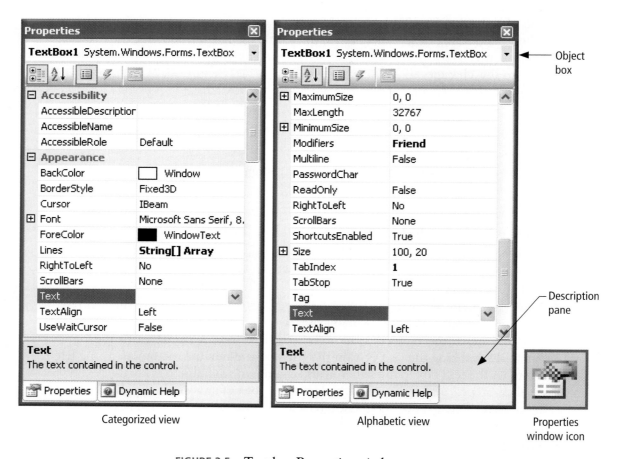

Categorized view   Alphabetic view   Properties window icon

FIGURE 3.5 **Text box Properties window.**

Note: If the Description pane is not visible, right-click on the Properties window, and then click on "Description." The Description pane describes the currently highlighted property.

8. Move to the Text property with the up- and down-arrow keys. (Alternatively, scroll until the property is visible, and click on the property.) The Text property, which determines the words displayed in the text box, is now highlighted. Currently, there is no text displayed in the **Settings box** on the right.

9. Type your first name. Then press the Enter key, or click on another property. Your name now appears in both the Settings box and the text box. See Figure 3.6.

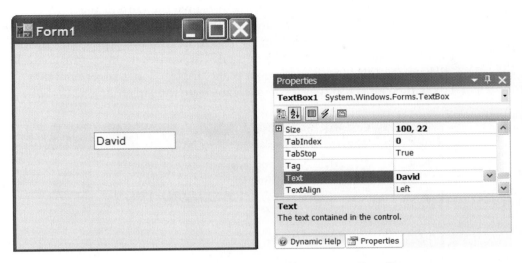

FIGURE 3.6 **Setting the Text property to David.**

10. Click at the beginning of your name in the Text Settings box, and add your title, such as Mr., Ms., or The Honorable. (If you mistyped your name, you can easily correct it now.) Then, press Enter.

11. Use the up-arrow key or the mouse to move to the ForeColor property. This property determines the color of the information displayed in the text box.

12. Click on the down arrow in the right part of the Settings box, and then click on the Custom tab to display a selection of colors. See Figure 3.7. Click on one of the colors, such as *blue* or *red*. Notice the change in the color of your name.

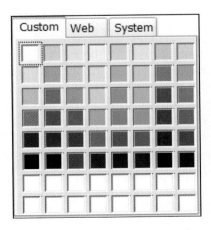

FIGURE 3.7 **Setting the ForeColor property.**

13. Highlight the Font property with a single click of the mouse. The current font is named Microsoft Sans Serif.

14. Click on the ellipsis (...) box in the right part of the Settings box to display a dialog box. See Figure 3.8. The three lists give the current name (Microsoft Sans Serif), current style (Regular), and current size (8) of the font. You can change any of these attributes by clicking on an item in its list or by typing into the box at the top of the list. Click on Bold in the style list, and click on 12 in the size list. Now click on the OK button to see your name displayed in a larger bold font. The text box will be longer so that it can accommodate the larger font.

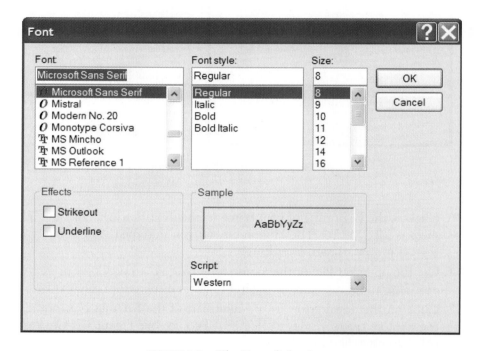

FIGURE 3.8   **The Font dialog box.**

15. Click on the text box and resize it to be about 3 inches wide.

    Visual Basic programs consist of three parts: interface, values of properties, and code. Our interface consists of a form with a single object, a text box. We have set a few properties for the text box—the text (namely, your name), the foreground color, the font style, and the font size. In Section 3.2, we discuss how to place code into a program. Visual Basic endows certain capabilities to programs that are independent of any code that we will write. We will now run the existing program without adding any code in order to experience these capabilities.

16. Press F5 to run the program. (Alternatively, a program can be run from the menu by pressing Alt/D/S or by clicking on the Start Debugging icon, the fourteenth or fifteenth icon on the Toolbar.) After a brief delay, a copy of the form appears that has neither the form or the text box selected.

Note: When a program is run, all the work done so far on the program is automatically saved in a temporary location with the name listed earlier in the New Project input dialog box.

17. Your name is highlighted. Press the End key to move the cursor to the end of your name. Now type in your last name, and then keep typing. Eventually, the words will scroll to the left.

18. Press Home to return to the beginning of the text. You have a miniature word processor at your disposal. You can place the cursor anywhere you like to add or delete text. You can drag the cursor across text to select a block, place a copy of the block in the Clipboard with Ctrl+C, and then duplicate it elsewhere with Ctrl+V.

19. To end the program, press Alt + F4. Alternatively, you can end a program by clicking on the form's Close button at the right corner of the title bar.

20. Select the text box, activate the Properties window, select the ReadOnly property, click on the down-arrow button, and finally click on True. Notice that the background color is now gray.

21. Run the program, and try typing into the text box. You can't. Such a text box is used for output. Only code can display information in the text box.

   Note: In this textbook, whenever a text box will be used only for the purpose of displaying output, we will always set the ReadOnly property to True.

22. End the program.

23. Let's now save the program on a disk. Click on the Save All icon to save the work done so far. (The Save All icon is the fifth or sixth icon on the Toolbar. It shows three fanned diskettes. Alternately, you can press Alt/F/L.) You will be prompted for the name of the program and the path to the folder where you want the program to be saved. Type a name, such as "VBdemo". You can either type a path or use Browse to locate a folder. (This folder will automatically be used the next time you click on the Save All icon while working on this program.) The files for the program will be held in a subfolder of the selected folder.

   Important: If the "Create directory for solution" check box is checked, then click on the check box to uncheck it. Finally, click on the Save button.

24. Create a new program as before by clicking on "New Project" on the File menu. (Or, you can click on the New Project icon, the first icon on the Toolbar.) A New Project dialog box will appear.

25. Give a name to the project, such as My Program, and then click on the OK button.

26. Place three text boxes on the form. (If you use the double-click technique, move the text boxes so that they do not overlap.) Notice that they have the names TextBox1, TextBox2, and TextBox3.

27. Run the program. Notice that the cursor is in TextBox1. We say that TextBox1 has the **focus**. (This means that TextBox1 is the currently selected object and any keyboard actions will be sent directly to this object.) Any text typed will display in that text box.

28. Press Tab once. Now, TextBox2 has the focus. When you type, the characters appear in TextBox2.

29. Press Tab several times, and then press Shift+Tab a few times. With Tab, the focus cycles through the objects on the form in the order the objects were created. With Shift+Tab, the focus cycles in the reverse order.

30. End the program you created.

31. We would now like to reload the first program. Click on "Open Project" from the File menu. An Open Project dialog box will appear stating that "You must choose to either save or discard changes in the current project before opening a project." There is no need to save his program, so click on the Discard button. Then a second Open Project dialog box will appear.

32. Find the folder corresponding to the program you saved earlier, double-click on the folder, and double-click on the file with extension *sln*. You have now recovered the first program.

33. If you do not see the Form Designer for the program, double-click on Form1.vb in the Solution Explorer.

A Button Walkthrough

1. Click on the New Project icon to start a new program. (Give a name, such as ButtonProg, to the program, and click on OK.)

2. Double-click on the Button icon in the Toolbox to place a button on the form. (The Button icon is the second icon in the Common Controls portion of the Toolbox.)

3. Move the button to the center of the form.

4. Activate the Properties window, highlight the Text property, type "Please Push Me," and press Enter. See Figure 3.9. The button is too small.

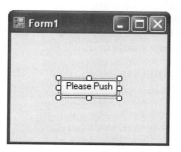 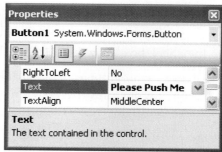

FIGURE 3.9   **Setting the Text property.**

5. Click on the button to select it, and then enlarge it to accommodate the phrase "Please Push Me" on one line.

6. Run the program, and click on the button. The button appears to move in and then out. In Section 3.2, we write code that is executed when a button is pushed.

7. End the program and select the button.

8. From the Properties window, edit the Text setting by inserting an ampersand (&) before the first letter, P. Press the Enter key, and notice that the first letter P on the button is now underlined. See Figure 3.10. Pressing Alt+P while the program is running triggers the same event as clicking the button. However, the button will not appear to move in and out. Here, P is referred to as the **access key** for the button. (The access key is always specified as the character following the ampersand.)

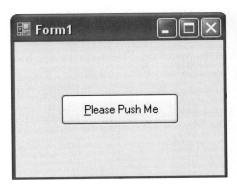 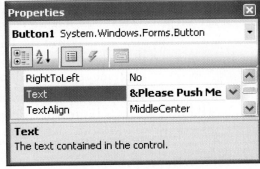

FIGURE 3.10   **Designating P as an access key.**

A Label Walkthrough

1. Click on the New Project icon to start a new program. Feel free to select the default name, such as WindowsApplication1.

2. Double-click on the label icon to place a label on the form. (The label icon is a large letter A.) Move the label to the center of the form.

3. Activate the Properties window, highlight the Text property, type "Enter Your Phone Number:", and press Enter. (Such a label would be placed next to a text box into which the user will type a phone number.) Notice that the label widened to accommodate the text. This happened because the AutoSize property of the label is set to True by default.

4. Change the AutoSize property to False. Press Enter. Notice that the label now has eight sizing handles when selected.

5. Make the label narrower and longer until the words occupy two lines.

6. Activate the Properties window, and click on the down arrow to the right of the setting for the TextAlign property. Experiment by clicking on the various rectangles and observing their effects. The combination of sizing and alignment permits you to design a label easily.

7. Run the program. Nothing happens, even if you click on the label. Labels just sit there. The user cannot change what a label displays unless you write code to make the change.

8. End the program.

▨ A List Box Walkthrough

1. Click on the New Project icon to start a new program. Feel free to select the default name, such as WindowsApplication1.

2. Place a list box on the form. (The list box icon is the ninth icon in the Common Controls group of the Toolbox.)

3. Press F4 to activate the Properties window and notice that the list box does not have a Text property. The word ListBox1 is actually the setting for the Name property.

4. Also place a text box, a button and a label on the form.

5. Click on the Object box of the Properties window. The name of the form and the names of the four controls are displayed. If you click on one of the names, that object will become selected and its properties displayed in the Properties window.

6. Run the program. Notice that the word ListBox1 has disappeared, but the words Button1 and Label1 are still visible. The list box is completely blank. In subsequent sections, we will write code to place information into the list box.

▨ The Name Property

Every control has a Name property. It is used in code to refer to the control. By default, controls are given names like TextBox1 and TextBox2. You can use the Properties window to change the Name property of a control to a more meaningful name. (The Name property is always the third property in the alphabetized list of properties. A control's name must start with a letter and can be a maximum of 215 characters. It can include numbers and underline (_) characters, but cannot include punctuation or spaces.) Also, it is good coding practice to have each name begin with a three- or four-letter prefix that identifies the type of the control. See Table 3.1. The form itself also has a Name property. Beginning with Section 3.2, we will use suggestive names and these prefixes whenever possible.

TABLE 3.1	Some controls and their three-letter prefixes.	
Control	Prefix	Example
form	frm	frmLottery
button	btn	btnComputeTotal
label	lbl	lblInstructions
list box	lst	lstOutput
text box	txt	txtAddress

The Name property of the form itself also can be changed. Suppose you want to change the name of the form from Form1 to frmPayroll. The most efficient way to set the name of the form is to change the name of the file Form1.vb appearing in the Solution Explorer window to frmPayroll.vb. To make the change, right-click on Form1.vb in the Solution Explorer window, click on Rename, type in the new name (frmPayroll.vb), and press Enter.

Important: Make sure that the new filename has the extension "vb".

To display the name of the form, and the names of all the controls on the form, click on the down-arrow icon at the right of the Property window's Object box. You can make one of these items the selected item by clicking on its name.

The Name and Text properties of a button are both initially set to something like Button1. However, changing one of these properties does not affect the setting of the other property, and similarly for the Name and Text properties of forms, text boxes, and labels. The Text property of a form specifies the words appearing in the form's title bar.

■ A Help Walkthrough

Visual Basic has an extensive help system. The following walkthrough demonstrates one of its features—the Help Index. The Help Index presents an alphabetized list of all the help topics available for Visual Basic.

1. Press Alt/H/I to invoke the Index window from the Help menu.
2. If the "Filtered by:" box does not say "Visual Basic" or "Visual Basic Express Edition," click on the down arrow and select one of them from the drop-down list.
3. Type "TextBox class" into the "Look for" box.
4. Click on the last subheading, "Properties." The window that appears contains a list of all the properties of the textbox control, along with their descriptions.
5. Scroll down the list of properties and read the description of the MaxLength property. The MaxLength property is used to limit the number of characters that can be typed into a text box. Think about where this property could be useful.
6. Type "Windows Forms controls" into the "Look for" box, look down about 27 subheadings of "Windows Forms controls" and then click on "list of."
7. The window that appears contains a long list of underlined links. Click on the first underlined link, "Windows Form Controls by Function."
8. Read the description of the four controls we have discussed so far. As a preview of coming attractions, read about some of the controls we will discuss later in the book. They are MaskedTextBox, ComboBox, OpenFileDialog, GroupBox, CheckBox, RadioButton, PictureBox, and DataGridView.

■ Fonts

The default font for controls is Microsoft Sans Serif. Two other useful fonts are Courier New and Wingdings.

Courier New is a fixed-width font; that is, each character has the same width. With such a font, the letter i occupies the same space as the letter m. Fixed-width fonts are used with tables when information is to be aligned in columns.

The Wingdings font consists of assorted small pictures and symbols, each corresponding to a character on the keyboard. For instance if one of the characters %, (, 1, or J is typed into the Text setting of a control whose Font is Wingdings, the control will display a bell, phone, open folder, or smiling face, respectively.

To view the character set for a Windows font, click on the Start button in the Windows task bar and successively select All Programs, Accessories, System Tools, and

Character Map. Then click on Character Map, or press the Enter key. After selecting the font, click on any item to enlarge it. You can insert the keyboard character for the item into the Clipboard by pressing the Select button and then the Copy button. To place the character into the Text property of a control having that font, just move the cursor to the Settings box for the Text property and press Ctrl+V.

▨ Auto Hide

The Auto Hide feature allows you to make more room for the Main area of the screen by minimizing tool windows (such as the Toolbox or Index window). Let's illustrate the feature with a walkthrough using the Toolbox window. We start by discussing the situation where the feature is *disabled*.

1. If the Toolbox window is currently visible and the pushpin icon in the window title is vertical, then the Auto Hide feature is disabled. (If the Toolbox window is not visible, press Alt/V/X to select Toolbox from the View menu. If the pushpin icon is horizontal, then click on the icon to make it vertical.) When the Auto Hide feature is disabled, the Toolbox window stays stationary and is always ready for use.

2. Click the mouse cursor somewhere outside of the Toolbox window and note that the window stays fixed.

3. Click on the pushpin icon to make it horizontal. The Auto Hide feature is now *enabled*.

4. Move the mouse cursor somewhere outside of the Toolbox window and note that the window slides into a tab on the left side of the screen. The name and icon of the Toolbox window appear on the tab.

5. Hover the mouse cursor over the tab. The window slides into view and is ready for use.

6. Place a new control on the form, and then move the cursor away from the Toolbox window. The window automatically slides back to its tab on the edge of the screen.

▨ Positioning and Aligning Controls

Visual Basic provides several tools for positioning and aligning controls on a form. **Proximity lines** are short line segments that help you place controls a comfortable distance from each other and from the sides of the form. **Snap lines** are horizontal and vertical line segments that are help you align controls. The **Format menu** is used to align controls, center controls horizontally and vertically in a form, and make a group of selected controls the same size.

A Positioning and Aligning Walkthrough

1. Start a new program.

2. Place a button near the center of the form.

3. Drag the button toward the upper-right corner of the form until two short line segments appear. See Figure 3.11 (a). The button is now a comfortable distance from the two sides of the form.

4. Place a second button below the first button and drag it upwards until a proximity line appears between the two buttons. The buttons are now a comfortable distance apart.

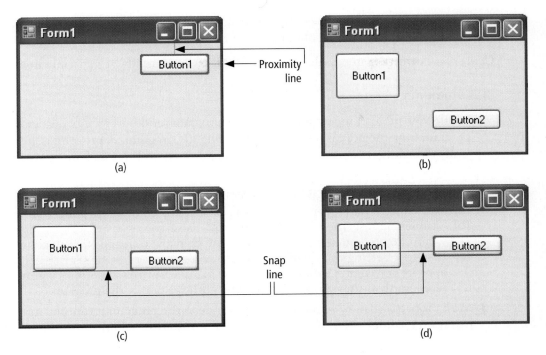

FIGURE 3.11 **Positioning Controls.**

5. Resize and position the two buttons as shown in Figure 3.11(b).

6. Drag Button2 upwards until a blue line appears along the bottoms of the two buttons. See Figure 3.11(c). This blue line is called a *snap line*. The bottoms of the two buttons are now aligned.

7. Continue dragging Button2 upwards until a purple snap line appears just underneath the words Button1 and Button2. See Figure 3.11(d). The middles of the two buttons are now aligned. If we were to continue dragging Button2 upwards, a blue snap line would tell us when the tops are aligned. Steps 8 and 9 show another way to align the tops.

8. Click on Button1 and then hold down the Ctrl key and click on Button2. After the mouse button is released, both buttons will be selected.

   Note: This process can be repeated to select groups of any number of controls.

9. Open the Format menu in the Menu bar, hover over Align, and click on Tops. The tops of the two buttons are now aligned. Precisely, Button1 (the first button selected) will stay fixed, and Button2 will move up so that its top is aligned with the top of Button1.

The most common uses of the submenus of the Format menu are as follows:

Align: Align middles or corresponding sides, of a group of selected controls.

Make Same Size: Make the width and/or height of a group of selected controls the same.

Horizontal Spacing: Equalize the horizontal spacing between a group of three or more selected controls arranged in a row.

Vertical Spacing: Equalize the vertical spacing between a group of three or more selected controls arranged in a column.

Center in Form: Center a selected control either horizontally or vertically in a form.

■ Comments

1. While you are working on a program, the program resides in memory. Removing a program from memory is referred to as **closing** the program. A program is automatically closed then you start a new program. Also, it can be closed directly with the Close Project command from the File menu.

2. Three useful properties that have not been discussed are the following:

    (a) BackColor: This property specifies the background color for the form or a control.

    (b) Visible: Setting the Visible property to False causes an object to disappear when the program is run. The object can be made to reappear with code.

    (c) Enabled: Setting the Enabled property of a control to False restricts its use. It appears grayed and cannot receive the focus. Controls sometimes are disabled temporarily if they do not apply to the current state of the program.

3. Most properties can be set or altered with code as the program is running instead of being preset from the Properties window. For instance, a button can be made to disappear with a line such as `Button1.Visible = False`. The details are presented in Section 3.2.

4. If you inadvertently double-click on a form, a window containing text will appear. (The first line begins Public Class Form1.) This is a Code window, which is discussed in the next section. Press Ctrl+Z to undo the addition of this new code. To return to the Form Designer, click on the page tab above the Main area labeled "Form1.vb [Design]."

5. We have seen two ways to place a control onto a form. A third method is to drag the control from the Toolbox to the form.

Practice Problems 3.1

1. What is the difference between the Text and the Name properties of a button?

2. Give a situation where the MaxLength property of a text box is useful.

EXERCISES 3.1

1. Create a form with two buttons, run the program, and click on each button. Do you notice anything different about a button after it has been clicked?

2. While a program is running, a control is said to lose focus when the focus moves from that control to another control. In what three ways can the user cause a control to lose focus?

In Exercises 3 through 24, carry out the task. Use a new program for each exercise.

3. Place "CHECKING ACCOUNT" in the title bar of a form.

4. Create a text box containing the words "PLAY IT, SAM" in blue letters.

5. Create a text box with a yellow background.

6. Create a text box named txtGreeting and containing the word "HELLO" in large italic letters.

7. Create a label containing the sentence "After all is said and done, more is said than done." The sentence should occupy three lines, and each line should be centered horizontally in the label.

8. Create a read-only text box containing the words "Visual Basic" in bold white letters on a red background.

9. Create a text box named txtLanguage and containing the words "Visual Basic 2005" in Courier New font.

10. Create a yellow button named btnPush and containing the word "PUSH".

11. Create a white button containing the word "PUSH" in large italic letters.

12. Create a button containing the word "PUSH" in bold letters in which the letter P is underlined.

13. Create a button containing the word "PUSH" with the letter H as the access key.

14. Create a label containing the word "ALIAS" in white on a blue background.

15. Create a label named lblAKA and containing the centered italicized word "ALIAS".

16. Place BALANCE SHEET in the title bar of a form, where the form has a yellow background.

17. Create a label containing VISUAL on the first line and BASIC on the second line. Each word should be right justified.

18. Create a form named frmHello whose title bar reads "Hello World".

19. Create a label containing a picture of a diskette. (**Hint:** Use the Wingdings character <.) Make the diskette as large as possible.

20. Create a label containing the bold word "ALIAS" in the Courier New font.

21. Create a list box with a yellow background.

22. Create a list box that will be invisible when the program is run.

23. Create a form named frmYellow having a yellow background.

24. Create a button containing a picture of a red bell. (**Hint:** Use the Wingdings character %.) Make the bell as large as possible.

In Exercises 25 through 30, create the interface shown in that figure. (These exercises give you practice creating controls and assigning properties. The interfaces do not necessarily correspond to actual programs.)

25.

26.

27.

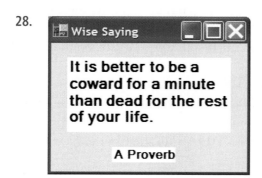

28.

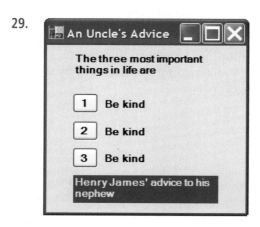

29.

30.

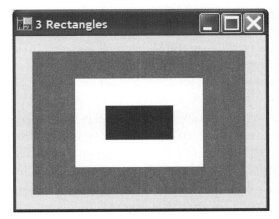

31. Create a replica of your bank check on a form. Words common to all checks, such as "PAY TO THE ORDER OF," should be contained in labels. Items specific to your checks, such as your name at the top left, should be contained in text boxes. Make the check on the screen resemble your personal check as much as possible.

32. Create a replica of your campus ID on a form. Words that are on all student IDs, such as the name of the college, should be contained in labels. Information specific to your ID, such as your name and Social Security number, should be contained in text boxes. Simulate your picture with a text box containing a smiling face—a size 24 Wingdings J.

The following hands-on exercises develop additional techniques for manipulating and accessing controls placed on a form.

33. Place a text box on a form and select the text box. What is the effect of pressing the various arrow keys?

34. Place a text box on a form and select the text box. What is the effect of pressing the various arrow keys while holding down the Shift key?

35. Experiment with the Align command on the Format menu to determine the difference between the *center* and the *middle* of a control.

36. Place four large buttons vertically on a form. Use the Format menu to make them the same size and to make the spacing between them uniform.

37. Place three buttons vertically on a form. Make them different sizes without their left sides aligned. Click on the first button. While holding down the Ctrl key, click on the second button and then the third button. (Notice that the first button has white sizing handles, and the other two buttons have black sizing handles.) This process is referred to as **selecting multiple controls**.

   (a) What is the effect of pressing the left-arrow key?
   (b) What is the effect of pressing the left-arrow key while holding down the Shift key?
   (c) Press F4, set the ForeColor property to Blue, and press Enter. What happens?
   (d) Open the Format menu and experiment with the Align and Make Same Size options. What special role does the control with white sizing handles play?

38. Place a button, a list box, and a text box on a form. Then run the program, and successively press Tab. Notice that the controls receive the focus in the order in which they were created. Invoke the Index from the Help menu and type "Tab order" into the "Look for:" text box. Double-click on the subheading "controls on Windows forms" and read the discussion of how to set the tab order on Windows forms. Then change the tab order for the three controls you placed on the form.

39. Place a text box on a form, select the text box, and open its Properties window. Double-click on the name (not the Settings box) of the ReadOnly property. Double-click again. What is the effect of double-clicking on a property whose possible settings are True and False?

40. Place a button on a form, select the button, and open its Properties window. Double-click on the name (not the Settings box) of the ForeColor property. Double-click repeatedly. Describe what is happening.

Solutions to Practice Problems 3.1

1. The text is the words appearing on the button, whereas the name is the designation used to refer to the button. Initially, they have the same value, such as Button1. However, each can be changed independently of the other.

2. If a text box is intended to hold a telephone number, then you might want to set the MaxLength property to 12. Similarly, text boxes intended for Social Security numbers or state abbreviations might be given maximum lengths of 11 and 2, respectively.

3.2 Visual Basic Events

When a Visual Basic program runs, the form and its controls appear on the screen. Normally, nothing happens until the user takes an action, such as clicking a control or pressing a key. We call such an action an **event**. The programmer writes code that reacts to an event by performing some functionality.

The three steps in creating a Visual Basic program are as follows:

1. Create the interface; that is, generate, position, and size the objects.

2. Set properties; that is, configure the appearance of the objects.

3. Write the code that executes when events occur.

Section 3.1 covered Steps 1 and 2; this section is devoted to Step 3.

Code consists of statements that carry out tasks. In this section, we limit ourselves to statements that change properties of a control or the form while a program is running.

Properties of controls are changed in code with statements of the form

```
controlName.property = setting
```

where *controlName* is the name of the control, *property* is one of the properties of the control, and *setting* is a valid setting for that property. Such statements are called **assignment statements**. They assign values to properties. Three examples of assignment statements are as follows:

1. The statement

```
txtBox.Text = "Hello"
```

displays the word *Hello* in the text box.

2. The statement

```
btnButton.Visible = True
```

makes the button visible.

3. The statement

```
txtBox.ForeColor = Color.Red
```

sets the color of the characters in the text box named txtBox to red.

Most events are associated with controls. The event "click on btnButton" is different from the event "click on lstBox." These two events are specified btnButton.Click and lstBox.Click. The statements to be executed when an event occurs are written in a block of code called an **event procedure**. The first line of an event procedure (called the **header**) has the form

```
Private Sub objectName_event(ByVal sender As System.Object,
        ByVal e As System.EventArgs) Handles objectName.event
```

Since we do not make any use of the lengthy text inside the parentheses in this book, for the sake of readability we replace it with an ellipsis. However, it will automatically appear in our programs each time Visual Basic creates the header for an event procedure. The structure of an event procedure is

```
Private Sub objectName_event(...) Handles objectName.event
  statements
End Sub
```

where the three dots (that is, the ellipsis) represent

```
ByVal sender As System.Object, ByVal e As System.EventArgs
```

Words such as "Private," "ByVal," "As," "Sub," "Handles," and "End" have special meanings in Visual Basic and are referred to as **keywords** or **reserved words**. The Visual Basic editor automatically capitalizes the first letter of a keyword and displays the word in blue. The word "Sub" in the first line signals the beginning of the procedure, and the first line identifies the object and the event occurring to that object. The last line signals the termination of the event procedure. The statements to be executed appear between these two lines. (**Note:** The word "Private" indicates that the event procedure cannot be invoked by another form. This will not concern us until much later in the book. The expression following Handles identifies the object and the event happening to that object. The expression **"objectName_event"** is the default name of the procedure and can be changed if desired. In this book, we always use the default name. The word "Sub" is an abbreviation of *Subroutine*.) For instance, the event procedure

```
Private Sub btnButton_Click(...) Handles btnButton.Click
  txtBox.ForeColor = Color.Red
End Sub
```

changes the color of the words in the text box to red when the button is clicked.

■ An Event Procedure Walkthrough

The form in Figure 3.12, which contains two text boxes and a button, will be used to demonstrate what event procedures are and how they are created. Three event procedures will be used to alter the appearance of a phrase appearing in the text box. The event procedures are named txtFirst_TextChanged, btnRed_Click, and txtFirst_Leave.

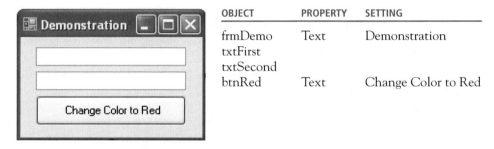

OBJECT	PROPERTY	SETTING
frmDemo	Text	Demonstration
txtFirst		
txtSecond		
btnRed	Text	Change Color to Red

FIGURE 3.12 **The interface for the event procedure walkthrough.**

1. Create the interface in Figure 3.12 in the Form Designer. The Name properties of the form, text boxes, and button should be set as shown in the Object column. The Text property of the form should be set to Demonstration, the Text property of the text boxes should remain blank, and the Text property of the button should be set to Change Color to Red.

2. Click the right mouse button anywhere on the Main area, and select View code. The Form Designer is replaced by the **Code window** (also known as the *Code view* or the *Code editor*). See Figure 3.13.

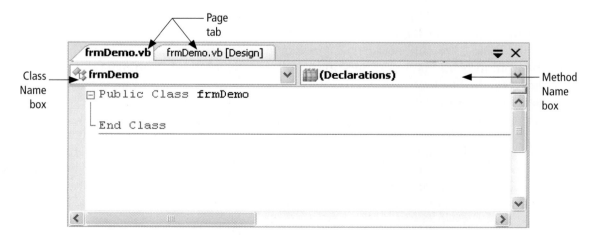

FIGURE 3.13 **The Code window.**

The page tab, labeled frmDemo.vb, corresponds to the Code window. You press the page tab labeled frmDemo.vb [Design], when you want to return to the Form Designer window. Just below the title bar are two drop-down list boxes. The left box is called the **Class Name box**, and the right box is called the **Method Name box**. (When you hover the mouse pointer over one of these list boxes, its type appears in a tooltip.) We will place our program code between the two lines shown. Let's refer to this region as the **program region**.

3. Click on the tab labeled "frmDemo.vb [Design]" to return to the Form Designer.

4. Double-click on the first text box. The Code window reappears, but now the following two lines of code have been added to the program region and the cursor is located on the line between them.

```
Private Sub txtFirst_TextChanged(...) Handles txtFirst.TextChanged

End Sub
```

The first line is the header for the event procedure named txtFirst_TextChanged. This procedure is triggered by the event txtFirst.TextChanged. That is, whenever there is a change in the text displayed in the text box txtFirst, the code between the two lines just shown will be executed.

5. Type the line

```
txtFirst.ForeColor = Color.Blue
```

at the cursor location. When you type the first period, a list containing all the properties of text boxes appears. See Figure 3.14(a). (Each property is preceded by a little Properties window icon. The list also contains something called *methods*, which we will discuss later.) At this point, you can scroll down the list and double-click on ForeColor to automatically enter that property. Or, you can keep typing. After you have typed "For," the list appears as in Figure 3.14(b). At that point, you can press the Tab key to enter the highlighted word "ForeColor." This feature, known as **Member Listing**, is one of the helpful features of Visual Basic that use a Microsoft technology called **IntelliSense**.

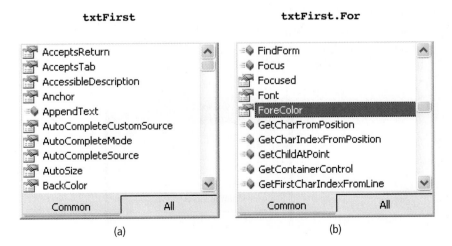

(a)   (b)

FIGURE 3.14   IntelliSense at work.

6. Return to the Form Designer and double-click on the button. The Code window reappears, and the first and last lines of the event procedure btnRed_Click appear in the program region. Type the line that sets the ForeColor property of txtFirst to Red. The event procedure will now appear as follows:

```
Private Sub btnRed_Click(...) Handles btnRed.Click
  txtFirst.ForeColor = Color.Red
End Sub
```

7. Click on the down-arrow button to the right of the Class Name box and on txtFirst in the drop-down list.

8. Click on the down-arrow button to the right of the Method Name box and on Leave in the drop-down list box. (The event txtFirst.Leave is triggered when the focus is removed from the text box.) The first and last lines of the event procedure txtFirst_Leave will be displayed. In this procedure, type the line that sets the ForeColor property of txtFirst to Black. The Code window will now look as follows:

```
Public Class frmDemo
  Private Sub txtFirst_Leave(...) Handles txtFirst.Leave
    txtFirst.ForeColor = Color.Black
  End Sub

  Private Sub txtFirst_TextChanged(...) Handles txtFirst.TextChanged
    txtFirst.ForeColor = Color.Blue
  End Sub

  Private Sub btnRed_Click(...) Handles btnRed.Click
    txtFirst.ForeColor = Color.Red
  End Sub
End Class
```

9. Place the cursor on the word "ForeColor" and press F1. Visual Basic now displays information about the foreground color property. This illustrates another help feature of Visual Basic known as **context-sensitive help**.

10. Now run the program by pressing F5.

11. Type something into the text box. In Figure 3.15, the blue word "Hello" has been typed. (Recall that a text box has the focus whenever it is ready to accept typing—that is, whenever it contains a blinking cursor.)

FIGURE 3.15   Text box containing input.

12. Click on the second text box. The contents of the first text box will become black. When the second text box was clicked, the first text box lost the focus; that is, the event Leave happened to txtFirst. Thus, the event procedure txtFirst_Leave was invoked, and the code inside the procedure was executed.

13. Click on the button. This invokes the event procedure btnRed_Click, which changes the color of the words in txtFirst to Red.

14. Click on the first text box, and type the word "Friend" after the word "Hello." As soon as typing begins, the text in the text box is changed and the TextChanged event is triggered. This event causes the color of the contents of the text box to become blue.

15. You can repeat Steps 11 through 14 as many times as you like. When you are finished, end the program by pressing Alt+F4, clicking the End icon on the Toolbar, or clicking the Close button (X) on the form.

▓ Properties and Event Procedures of the Form

You can assign properties to the Form itself in code. However, a statement such as

```
frmDemo.Text = "Demonstration"
```

will not work. The form is referred to by the keyword *Me*. Therefore, the proper statement is

```
Me.Text = "Demonstration"
```

To display a list of the events associated with frmDemo, select "(frmDemo Events)" from the Class Name box and then open the Method Name box.

▓ The Header of an Event Procedure

As mentioned earlier, in a header for an event procedure such as

```
Private Sub btnOne_Click(...) Handles btnOne.Click
```

btnOne_Click is the name of the event procedure, and btnOne.Click identifies the event that triggers the procedure. The name can be changed at will. For instance, the header can be changed to

```
Private Sub ButtonPushed(...) Handles btnOne.Click
```

Also, an event procedure can be triggered by more than one event. For instance, if the previous line is changed to

```
Private Sub ButtonPushed(...) Handles btnOne.Click, btnTwo.Click
```

the event will be triggered if either btnOne or btnTwo is clicked.

We have been using ellipses (...) as place holders for the phrase

```
ByVal sender As System.Object, ByVal e As System.EventArgs
```

In Chapter 4, we will gain a better understanding of this type of phrase. Essentially, the word "sender" carries a reference to the object that triggered the event, and the letter "e" carries some additional information that the sending object wants to communicate. We will not make use of either "sender" or "e".

▒ Comments

1. The Visual Basic editor automatically indents the statements inside procedures. In this book, we indent by two spaces. To instruct your editor to indent by two spaces, select Options from the Tools menu, and uncheck the "Show all settings" box in the Options window that appears. Expand "Text Editor Basic" or "Text Editor," click on "Editor," enter 2 into the "Indent size:" box, and click on OK.

2. The event *control*.Leave is triggered when the specified control loses the focus. Its counterpart is the event *control*.Enter which is triggered when the specified control gets the focus. A related statement is

   control.Focus()

   which moves the focus to the specified control.

3. We have ended our programs by clicking the End icon or pressing Alt + F4. A more elegant technique is to create a button, call it btnQuit, with caption Quit and the following event procedure:

   ```
   Private Sub btnQuit_Click(...) Handles btnQuit.Click
     End
   End Sub
   ```

4. For statements of the form

   object.Text = setting

   the expression for *setting* must be surrounded by quotes. (For instance, lblName. Text = "Name".) For properties where the proper setting is one of the words True or False, these words should *not* be surrounded by quotation marks.

5. Names of existing event procedures associated with an object are not automatically changed when you rename the object. You must change them yourself. However, the event that triggers the procedure (and all other references to the control) will change automatically. For example, suppose an event procedure is

   ```
   Private Sub btnOne_Click(...) Handles btnOne.Click
     btnOne.Text = "Press Me"
   End Sub
   ```

   and, in the Form Designer, you change the name of btnOne to btnTwo. Then, when you return to the Code window the procedure will be

   ```
   Private Sub btnOne_Click(...) Handles btnTwo.Click
     btnTwo.Text = "Press Me"
   End Sub
   ```

6. Code windows have many features of word processors. For instance, the operations cut, copy, paste, undo, and redo can be carried out with the sixth through tenth icons from the Toolbar. These operations, and several others, also can be initiated from the Edit menu.

7. The code editor can detect certain types of errors. For instance, if you type

```
txtFirst.Text = hello
```

and then move away from the line, the automatic syntax checker will underline the word "hello" with a blue squiggle to indicate that something is wrong. When the mouse cursor is hovered over the offending wording, the editor will display a message explaining what is wrong. If you run the program without correcting the error, the dialog box in Figure 3.16 will appear.

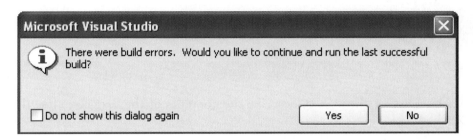

FIGURE 3.16   Error dialog box.

8. When you double-click on a control in the Form Designer, the header for the most used event procedure is placed in the Code window. The event that appears most frequently in this book is the Click event for button controls.

9. Font properties, such as the name, style, and size, are usually specified at design time. The setting of the properties can be displayed in code with statements such as

```
lstBox.Items.Add(txtBox.Font.Name)
lstBox.Items.Add(txtBox.Font.Bold)
lstBox.Items.Add(txtBox.Font.Size)
```

However, a font's name, style, and size properties cannot be altered in code with statements of the form

```
txtBox.Font.Name = "Courier New"
txtBox.Font.Bold = True
txtBox.Font.Size = 16
```

10. When you make changes to a program, asterisks appear as superscripts on the page tabs labeled "frmName.vb [design]" and "frmName.vb." The asterisks disappear when the program is saved or run.

11. Beginning with the next section, each example contains a program. These programs are on the companion website for this book. See the discussion on page xv for details. The process of opening a program stored on a disk is referred to as **loading** the program. You might want to prepare for the next section by loading the program 3-3-1 from the subfolder Ch03 of the Programs folder.

Note: After you load the program with the Open Project command from the File menu, you should see the form designer for the program. If not, double-click on the file in the Solution Explorer with extension "vb", that is, frmArithmetic.vb. If the form designer is still not visible, click on the View Designer icon at the top of the Solution Explorer window.

Practice Problem 3.2

1. What event procedure is displayed when you double-click on each of the following controls in the Form Designer?
   (a) text box
   (b) button
   (c) label
   (d) list box
2. Give a statement that will prevent the user from typing into txtBox.

EXERCISES 3.2

In Exercises 1 through 6, describe the contents of the text box after the button is clicked.

1.
```
Private Sub btnOutput_Click(...) Handles btnOutput.Click
    txtBox.Text = "Hello"
End Sub
```

2.
```
Private Sub btnOutput_Click(...) Handles btnOutput.Click
    txtBox.ForeColor = Color.Red
    txtBox.Text = "Hello"
End Sub
```

3.
```
Private Sub btnOutput_Click(...) Handles btnOutput.Click
    txtBox.BackColor = Color.Orange
    txtBox.Text = "Hello"
End Sub
```

4.
```
Private Sub btnOutput_Click(...) Handles btnOutput.Click
    txtBox.Text = "Goodbye"
    txtBox.Text = "Hello"
End Sub
```

5.
```
Private Sub btnOutput_Click(...) Handles btnOutput.Click
    txtBox.Text = "Hello"
    txtBox.Visible = False
End Sub
```

6.
```
Private Sub btnOutput_Click(...) Handles btnOutput.Click
    txtBox.BackColor = Color.Yellow
    txtBox.Text = "Hello"
End Sub
```

In Exercises 7 through 10, assume that the three objects on the form were created in the order txtFirst, txtSecond, and lblOne. Determine the output displayed in lblOne when the program is run and the Tab key is pressed. *Note:* Initially, txtFirst has the focus.

7.
```
Private Sub txtFirst_Leave(...) Handles txtFirst.Leave
    lblOne.ForeColor = Color.Green
    lblOne.Text = "Hello"
End Sub
```

8.
```
Private Sub txtFirst_Leave(...) Handles txtFirst.Leave
    lblOne.BackColor = Color.White
    lblOne.Text = "Hello"
End Sub
```

9.
```
Private Sub txtSecond_Enter(...) Handles txtSecond.Enter
    lblOne.BackColor = Color.Gold
    lblOne.Text = "Hello"
End Sub
```

10.
```
Private Sub txtSecond_Enter(...) Handles txtSecond.Enter
    lblOne.Visible = False
    lblOne.Text = "Hello"
End Sub
```

In Exercises 11 through 16, determine the errors.

11.
```
Private Sub btnOutput_Click(...) Handles btnOutput.Click
    Form1.Text = "Hello"
End Sub
```

12.
```
Private Sub btnOutput_Click(...) Handles btnOutput.Click
    txtBox.Text = Hello
End Sub
```

13.
```
Private Sub btnOutput_Click(...) Handles btnOutput.Click
    txtFirst.ForeColor = Red
End Sub
```

14.
```
Private Sub btnOutput_Click(...) Handles btnOutput.Click
    txtBox = "Hello"
End Sub
```

15.
```
Private Sub btnOutput_Click(...) Handles btnOutput.Click
    txtBox.Font.Size = 20
End Sub
```

16.
```
Private Sub btnOutput_Click(...) Handles btn1.Click, btn2.Click
    Me.Color = Color.Yellow
End Sub
```

In Exercises 17 through 28, write a line (or lines) of code to carry out the task.

17. Display "E.T. phone home." in lblTwo.

18. Display "Play it, Sam." in lblTwo.

19. Display "The stuff that dreams are made of." in red letters in txtBox.

20. Display "Life is like a box of chocolates." in txtBox with blue letters on a gold background.

21. Disable txtBox.

22. Change the words in the form's title bar to "Hello World."

23. Make lblTwo disappear.

24. Change the color of the letters in lblName to red.

25. Enable the disabled button btnOutcome.

26. Give the focus to btnCompute.

27. Change the background color of the form to White.

28. Give the focus to txtBoxTwo.

29. Describe the Enter event in your own words.

30. Describe the Leave event in your own words.

31. The label control has an event called DoubleClick that responds to a double-clicking of the left mouse button. Write a simple program to test this event. Determine whether you can trigger the DoubleClick event without also triggering the Click event.

32. Write a simple program to demonstrate that a button's Click event is triggered when you press the Enter key while the button has the focus.

In Exercises 33 through 38, the interface and initial properties are specified. Write the program to carry out the stated task.

33. When one of the three buttons is pressed, the words on the button are displayed in the text box with the stated alignment. **Note:** Rely on IntelliSense to provide you with the proper settings for the TextAlign property.

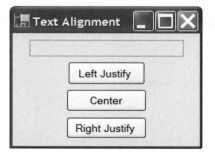

OBJECT	PROPERTY	SETTING
frmAlign	Text	Text Alignment
txtBox	ReadOnly	True
btnLeft	Text	Left Justify
btnCenter	Text	Center
btnRight	Text	Right Justify

34. When one of the buttons is pressed, the face changes to a smiling face (Wingdings character "J") or a frowning face (Wingdings character "L").

OBJECT	PROPERTY	SETTING
frmFace	Text	Face
lblFace	Font Name	Wingdings
	Font Size	24
	Text	K
btnSmile	Text	Smile
btnFrown	Text	Frown

35. Pressing the buttons alters the background and foreground colors in the text box.

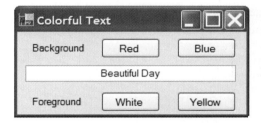

OBJECT	PROPERTY	SETTING
frmColors	Text	Colorful Text
lblBack	Text	Background
btnRed	Text	Red
btnBlue	Text	Blue
txtBox	Text	Beautiful Day
	TextAlign	Center
lblFore	Text	Foreground
btnWhite	Text	White
btnYellow	Text	Yellow

36. When one of the three text boxes receives the focus, its text becomes red. When it loses the focus, the text returns to black. The buttons set the alignment in the text boxes to Left or Right. ***Note:*** Rely on IntelliSense to provide you with the proper settings for the TextAlign property.

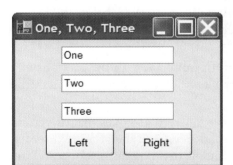

OBJECT	PROPERTY	SETTING
frm123	Text	One, Two, Three
txtOne	Text	One
txtTwo	Text	Two
txtThree	Text	Three
btnLeft	Text	Left
btnRight	Text	Right

37. When the user moves the focus to one of the three small text boxes at the bottom of the form, an appropriate saying is displayed in the large text box. Use the sayings "I like life, it's something to do."; "The future isn't what it used to be."; and "Tell the truth and run."

OBJECT	PROPERTY	SETTING
frmQuote	Text	Sayings
txtQuote	ReadOnly	True
txtLife	Text	Life
txtFuture	Text	Future
txtTruth	Text	Truth

38. The user can disable or enable the text box by clicking on the appropriate button. After the user clicks the Enable button, the text box should receive the focus.

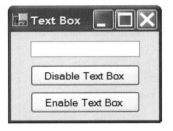

OBJECT	PROPERTY	SETTING
frmTextBox	Text	Text Box
txtBox		
btnDisable	Text	Disable Text Box
btnEnable	Text	Enable Text Box

In Exercises 39 through 44, write a program with a Windows-style interface to carry out the task.

39. The form contains four square buttons arranged in a rectangular array. Each button has the caption "Push Me." When the user clicks on a button, the button disappears and the other three become or remain visible.

40. A form contains two text boxes and one large label between them with no preset caption. When the first text box receives the focus, the label reads "Enter your full name." When the second text box receives the focus, the label reads "Enter your phone number, including area code."

41. Use the same form and properties as in Exercise 34, with the captions for the buttons replaced with Vanish and Reappear. Clicking a button should produce the stated result.

42. Simulate a traffic light with three small square text boxes placed vertically on a form. Initially, the bottom text box is solid green and the other text boxes are dark gray. When the Tab key is pressed, the middle text box turns yellow and the bottom text box turns dark gray. The next time Tab is pressed, the top text box turns red and the middle text box turns dark gray. Subsequent pressing of the Tab key cycles through the three colors. **Hint:** First, place the bottom text box on the form, then the middle text box, and finally the top text box.

43. The form contains a single read-only text box and two buttons. When the user clicks on one of the buttons, the sentence "You just clicked on a button." is displayed in the text box. The program should consist of a single event procedure.

44. The form contains two text boxes into which the user types information. When the user clicks on one of the text boxes, it becomes blank and its contents are displayed in the other text box. **Note:** A text box can be cleared with the statement `txtBox.Clear()` or the statement `txtBox.Text = ""`.

Solutions to Practice Problem 3.2

1. **(a)** TextChanged
   (b) Click
   (c) Click
   (d) SelectedIndexChanged

2. Three possibilities are

   ```
   txtBox.Enabled = False
   txtBox.ReadOnly = True
   txtBox.Visible = False
   ```

3.3 Numbers

Much of the data processed by computers consist of numbers. In computerese, numbers are called **numeric literals**. This section discusses the operations that are performed with numbers and the ways numbers are displayed.

▦ Arithmetic Operations

The five standard arithmetic operations in Visual Basic are addition, subtraction, multiplication, division, and exponentiation. Addition, subtraction, and division are denoted in Visual Basic by the standard symbols +, −, and /, respectively. However, the notations for multiplication and exponentiation differ from the customary mathematical notations as follows:

Mathematical Notation	Visual Basic Notation
$a \cdot b$ or $a \times b$	$a * b$
a^r	$a \wedge r$

(The asterisk [*] is the upper character of the 8 key. The caret [^] is the upper character of the 6 key.)

One way to show a number on the screen is to display it in a list box. If n is a number, then the instruction

```
lstBox.Items.Add(n)
```

displays the number n as the last item in the list box. *Add* is called a **method**. (Generally, a method is a process that performs a task for a particular object.) If the parentheses contain a combination of numbers and arithmetic operations, the *Add* method carries out the operations and displays the result. Another important method is *Clear*. The statement

```
lstBox.Items.Clear()
```

erases all the items displayed in the list box lstBox.

 ████ **Example 1** ████ The following program applies each of the five arithmetic operations. Preceding the program is the form design and a table showing the names of the objects on the form and the settings, if any, for properties of these objects. This form design is also used in the discussion and examples in the remainder of this section.

The word "Run" in the phrasing [Run . . .] indicates that F5 should be pressed to execute the program. Notice that in the output 3 / 2 is displayed in decimal form. Visual Basic never displays numbers as common fractions. In the evaluation of 2 * (3 + 4), the operation inside the parentheses is calculated first.

Note: All programs appearing in examples and case studies are provided on the companion website for this book. See the discussion on page xv for details.

OBJECT	PROPERTY	SETTING
frmArithmetic	Text	3-3-1
lstResults		
btnCompute	Text	Compute

```
Private Sub btnCompute_Click(...) Handles btnCompute.Click
  lstResults.Items.Clear()
  lstResults.Items.Add(3 + 2)
  lstResults.Items.Add(3 - 2)
  lstResults.Items.Add(3 * 2)
  lstResults.Items.Add(3 / 2)
  lstResults.Items.Add(3 ^ 2)
  lstResults.Items.Add(2 * (3 + 4))
End Sub
```

[Run, and then click the button. The output is shown at the top of the next page.]

In Example 1, the words "lstResults.Items" appear seven times. Visual Basic provides a device for both reducing the amount of repetitive typing required and making the program appear less cluttered. The program can be written as

```
Private Sub btnCompute_Click(...) Handles btnCompute.Click
  With lstResults.Items
    .Clear()
    .Add(3 + 2)
    .Add(3 - 2)
    .Add(3 * 2)
    .Add(3 / 2)
    .Add(3 ^ 2)
    .Add(2 * (3 + 4))
  End With
End Sub
```

The nine statements inside the procedure are called a **With block**. Within the block, each expression starting with a period is evaluated as if the expression lstResults.Items preceded it.

■ Variables

In applied mathematics problems, quantities are referred to by names. For instance, consider the following high school algebra problem: "If a car travels at 50 miles per hour, how far will it travel in 14 hours? Also, how many hours are required to travel 410 miles?" The solution to this problem uses the well-known formula

$$\text{distance} = \text{speed} \times \text{time elapsed}$$

Here's how this problem would be solved with a computer program:

```
Private Sub btnCompute_Click(...) Handles btnCompute.Click
  Dim speed As Double
  Dim timeElapsed As Double
  Dim distance As Double
  lstResults.Items.Clear()
  speed = 50
  timeElapsed = 14
  distance = speed * timeElapsed
  lstResults.Items.Add(distance)
```

```
  distance = 410
  timeElapsed = distance / speed
  lstResults.Items.Add(timeElapsed)
End Sub
```

[Run, and then click the button. The following is displayed in the list box.]

700

8.2

Skip the second, third, and fourth lines of the event procedure for now. We will return to them soon. The sixth line sets the speed to 50, and the seventh line sets the time elapsed to 14. The eighth line multiplies the value for the speed by the value for the time elapsed and sets the distance to this product. The next line displays the answer to the distance-traveled question. The three lines before the End Sub statement answer the time-required question in a similar manner.

The names *speed*, *timeElapsed*, and *distance*, which hold numbers, are referred to as **variables.** Consider the variable *timeElapsed*. In the seventh line, its value was set to 14. In the eleventh line, its value was changed as the result of a computation. On the other hand, the variable *speed* had the same value, 50, throughout the program.

In general, a variable is a name that is used to refer to an item of data. The value assigned to the variable may change during the execution of the program. In Visual Basic, variable names can be up to 16,383 characters long, must begin with a letter or an underscore, and can consist only of letters, digits, and underscores. (The shortest variable names consist of a single letter.) Visual Basic does not distinguish between uppercase and lowercase letters used in variable names. Some examples of variable names are *total*, *numberOfCars*, *taxRate_2006*, and *n*. As a convention, we write variable names in lowercase letters except for the first letters of additional words (as in *gradeOnFirstExam*).

If *var* is a variable and *n* is a literal, then the statement

```
var = n
```

assigns the number *n* to the variable *var*. (Such a statement is another example of an **assignment statement**.)

A variable is declared to be of a certain type depending on the sort of data that can be assigned to it. The most versatile type for holding numbers is called **Double**. A variable of type Double can hold whole, fractional, or mixed numbers between about $-1.8 \cdot 10^{308}$ and $1.8 \cdot 10^{308}$. Dim statements (also called **declaration statements**) declare the names and types of the variables to be used in the program. The second, third, and fourth lines of this event procedure declare three variables of type Double and give them the names *speed*, *timeElapsed*, and *distance*.

In general, a statement of the form

```
Dim varName As Double
```

declares a variable named *varName* to be of type Double. Actually, the Dim statement causes the computer to set aside a location in memory with the name *varName*. Since *varName* is a numeric variable, the Dim statement also places the number zero in that memory location. (We say that zero is the **initial value** or **default value** of the variable.) Each subsequent assignment statement having *varName* to the left of the equal sign will change the value of the number.

The initial value can be set to a value other than zero. To specify a nonzero initial value, follow the declaration statement with an equal sign followed by the initial value. The statement

```
Dim varName As Double = 50
```

declares the specified variable as a variable of type Double and gives it the initial value 50.

The statement

```
lstBox.Items.Add(varName)
```

looks into this memory location for the current value of the variable and displays the value in the list box.

A combination of literals, variables, and arithmetic operations that can be evaluated to yield a number is called a **numeric expression**. Expressions are evaluated by replacing each variable by its value and carrying out the arithmetic. Some examples of expressions are $2*\text{distance} + 7$, $n + 1$, and $(a + b)/3$.

 Example 2   The following program displays the default value of a variable and the value of an expression:

```
Private Sub btnCompute_Click(...) Handles btnCompute.Click
  Dim a As Double
  Dim b As Double = 3
  lstResults.Items.Clear()
  lstResults.Items.Add(a)
  lstResults.Items.Add(b)
  a = 5
  lstResults.Items.Add(a * (2 + b))
End Sub
```

[Run, and then click the button. The following is displayed in the list box.]

```
0
3
25
```

If *var* is a variable, then the assignment statement

```
var = expression
```

first evaluates the expression on the right and *then* assigns its value to the variable on the left. For instance, the event procedure in Example 2 can be written as

```
Private Sub btnCompute_Click(...) Handles btnCompute.Click
  Dim a As Double
  Dim b As Double
  Dim c As Double
```

```
    lstResults.Items.Clear()
    a = 5
    b = 3
    c = a * (2 + b)
    lstResults.Items.Add(c)
End Sub
```

The expression $a*(2 + b)$ is evaluated to 25, and then this value is assigned to the variable c.

Incrementing the Value of a Variable

Because the expression on the right side of an assignment statement is evaluated *before* an assignment is made, a statement such as

```
var = var + 1
```

is meaningful. It first evaluates the expression on the right (that is, it adds 1 to the original value of the variable *var*) and then assigns this sum to the variable *var*. The effect is to increase the value of the variable *var* by 1. In terms of memory locations, the statement retrieves the value of *var* from *var*'s memory location, uses it to compute *var* + 1, and then places the sum back into *var*'s memory location. This type of calculation is so common that Visual Basic provides a special operator to carry it out. The statement **var = var + 1** can be replaced with the statement

```
var += 1
```

In general, if n has a numeric value, then the statement

```
var += n
```

adds n to the value of *var*.

Built-In Functions: Math.Sqrt, Int, Math.Round

There are several common operations that we often perform on numbers other than the standard arithmetic operations. For instance, we may take the square root of a number or round a number. These operations are performed by built-in functions. Functions associate with one or more values called the *input*, and a single value called the *output*. The function is said to **return** the output value. The three functions considered here have numeric input and output.

The function Math.Sqrt calculates the square root of a number. The function Int finds the greatest integer less than or equal to a number. Therefore, Int discards the decimal part of positive numbers. The value of Math.Round(n, r) is the number n rounded to r decimal places. The parameter r can be omitted. If so, n is rounded to a whole number. Some examples follow:

Math.Sqrt(9) is 3.	Int(2.7) is 2.	Math.Round(2.7) is 3.
Math.Sqrt(0) is 0.	Int(3) is 3.	Math.Round(2.317, 2) is 2.32.
Math.Sqrt(2) is 1.414214.	Int(−2.7) is −3.	Math.Round(2.317, 1) is 2.3.

The terms inside the parentheses can be numbers (as shown), numeric variables, or numeric expressions. Expressions are first evaluated to produce the input.

 Example 3   The following program evaluates each of the functions for a specific input given by the value of the variable *n*:

```
Private Sub btnCompute_Click(...) Handles btnCompute.Click
  Dim n As Double
  Dim root As Double
  n = 6.76
  root = Math.Sqrt(n)
  With lstResults.Items
    .Clear()
    .Add(root)
    .Add(Int(n))
    .Add(Math.Round(n, 1))
  End With
End Sub
```

[Run, and then click the Compute button. The following is displayed in the list box.]

```
2.6
6
6.8
```

 Example 4   The following program evaluates each of the preceding functions at an expression:

```
Private Sub btnCompute_Click(...) Handles btnCompute.Click
  Dim a As Double
  Dim b As Double
  a = 2
  b = 3
  With lstResults.Items
    .Clear()
    .Add(Math.Sqrt(5 * b + 1))
    .Add(Int(a ^ b + 0.8))
    .Add(Math.Round(a / b, 3))
  End With
End Sub
```

[Run, and then click the button. The following is displayed in the list box.]

```
4
8
0.667
```

The Integer Data Type

In this text, we sometimes need to use variables of type Integer. An Integer variable is declared with a statement of the form

```
Dim varName As Integer
```

and can be assigned only whole numbers from about −2 billion to 2 billion. Integer variables are used primarily for counting.

Multiple Declarations

Several variables of the same type can be declared with a single Dim statement. For instance, the two Dim statements in Example 2 can be replaced by the single statement

```
Dim a, b As Double
```

Two other types of multiple-declaration statement are

```
Dim a As Double, b As Integer
Dim c As Double = 2, b As Integer = 5
```

Parentheses

Parentheses cannot be used to indicate multiplication, as is commonly done in algebra. For instance, the expression $x(y + z)$ is not valid. It must be written as $x*(y + z)$.

Parentheses should be used when necessary to clarify the meaning of an expression. When there are no parentheses, the arithmetic operations are performed in the following order: (1) exponentiations; (2) multiplications and divisions; (3) additions and subtractions. In the event of ties, the leftmost operation is carried out first. Table 3.2 summarizes these rules. **Note:** If you use parentheses liberally, you will not have to remember the precedence table for arithmetic operations.

TABLE 3.2   **Level of precedence for arithmetic operations.**

( )	Inner to outer, left to right
^	Left to right in expression
* /	Left to right in expression
+ −	Left to right in expression

Three Types of Errors

Grammatical errors, such as misspellings, omissions, or incorrect punctuations, are called **syntax errors**. Most syntax errors are spotted by the code editor when they are entered; however, some are not detected until the program is executed. Some incorrect statements and their errors are as follows:

Statement	*Reason for Error*
lstBox.Itms.Add(3)	The word Items is misspelled.
lstBox.Items.Add(2+)	The number following the plus sign is omitted.
Dim m; n As Integer	The semicolon should be a comma.

Errors that occur while a program is running are called **run-time errors**. They usually result from the inability of the computer to carry out the intended task. For instance, if the file DATA.TXT is not in the root folder of the C drive, then a statement that refers to the file by the filespec "C:\DATA.TXT" will cause the program to stop executing and produce a message box with the title

```
FileNotFoundException was unhandled.
```

Also, a yellow arrow will appear at the left side of the line of code that caused the error. At that point, you should end the program.

A third type of error is the so-called **logical error**. Such an error occurs when a program does not perform the way it was intended. For instance, the line

```
average = firstNum + secondNum / 2
```

is syntactically correct. However, the missing parentheses in the line of code are responsible for an incorrect value being generated. Appendix D discusses debugging tools that can be used to detect and correct logical errors.

Comments

1. Declaring variables at the beginning of each event procedure is regarded as good programming practice because it makes programs easier to read and helps prevent certain types of errors.

2. Keywords (reserved words) cannot be used as names of variables. For instance, the statements **Dim private as Double** and **Dim sub As Double** are not valid. To obtain a complete list of Visual Basic reserved keywords, look up *keywords* under Visual Basic in Help's Index.

3. Names given to variables are sometimes referred to as *identifiers*.

4. In math courses, *literals* are referred to as *constants*. However, the word "constant" has a special meaning in programming languages.

5. Numeric constants used in expressions or assigned to variables must not contain commas, dollar signs, or percent signs. Also, mixed numbers, such as 8 1/2, are not allowed.

6. Although requesting the square root of a negative number does not terminate the execution of the program, it can produce unexpected results. For instance, the statement

```
lstBox.Items.Add(Math.Sqrt(-1))
```

displays **NaN**. *Note:* NaN is an abbreviation for "Not a Number."

7. If the value of *numVar* is 0 and *numVar* has type Double, then the statements

```
numVarInv = 1 / numVar
lstBox.Items.Add(numVarInv)
lstBox.Items.Add(1 / numVarInv)
```

cause the following items to be displayed in the list box:

```
Infinity
0
```

8. When *n* is halfway between two successive whole numbers (such as 1.5, 2.5, 3.5, and 4.5), then it rounds to the nearest even number. For instance, Math.Round (2.5) is 2 and Math.Round(3.5) is 4.

9. In addition to the five arithmetic operators discussed at the beginning of this section, the **Mod operator** is another useful operator. If *m* and *n* are positive whole numbers, then *m* Mod *n* is the remainder when *m* is divided by *n*. For instance, 14 Mod 3 is 2, 18 Mod 5 is 3, and 7 Mod 2 is 1.

10. In scientific notation, numbers are written in the form $b \cdot 10^r$, where *b* is a number of magnitude from 1 up to (but not including) 10, and *r* is an integer. Visual Basic displays very large numbers in **scientific notation** where $b \cdot 10^r$ is written as *b*E*r*. (The letter E is an abbreviation for *exponent*.) For instance, when the statement `lstBox.Items.Add(123 * 10 ^ 15)` is executed, 1.23E+17 is displayed in the list box.

Practice Problems 3.3

1. Evaluate 2 + 3 * 4.

2. Explain the difference between the assignment statement

   ```
   var1 = var2
   ```

   and the assignment statement

   ```
   var2 = var1
   ```

3. Complete the table by filling in the value of each variable after each line is executed.

	a	b	c
`Private Sub btnEvaluate_Click(...) Handles btnEvaluate.Click`			
`Dim a, b, c As Double`	0	0	0
`a = 3`	3	0	0
`b = 4`	3	4	0
`c = a + b`			
`a = c * a`			
`lstResults.Items.Add(a - b)`			
`b = b * b`			
`End Sub`			

4. Write a statement that increases the value of the numeric variable *var* by 5%.

EXERCISES 3.3

In Exercises 1 through 6, evaluate the numeric expression without the computer, and then use Visual Basic to check your answer.

1. $3*4$

2. 7^2

3. $1/(2^3)$

4. $3 + (4*5)$

5. $(5 - 3)*4$

6. $3*((-2)^5)$

In Exercises 7 through 10, evaluate the Mod operation.

7. 6 Mod 2

8. 14 Mod 4

9. 7 Mod 3

10. 5 Mod 5

In Exercises 11 through 16, determine whether the name is a valid variable name.

11. sales.2006

12. room&Board

13. fOrM_1040

14. 1040B

15. expenses?

16. INCOME 2006

In Exercises 17 through 22, evaluate the numeric expression where a = 2, b = 3, and c = 4.

17. $(a*b) + c$

18. $a*(b + c)$

19. $(1 + b)*c$

20. a^c

21. $b^{(c - a)}$

22. $(c - a)^b$

In Exercises 23 through 28, write an event procedure to calculate and display the value of the expression.

23. $7 \cdot 8 + 5$

24. $(1 + 2 \cdot 9)^3$

25. 5.5% of 20

26. $15 - 3(2 + 3^4)$

27. $17(3 + 162)$

28. $4\ 1/2 - 3\ 5/8$

In Exercises 29 and 30, complete the table by filling in the value of each variable after each line is executed.

29.

	x	y
`Private Sub btnEvaluate_Click(...) Handles btnEvaluate.Click`		
`Dim x, y As Double`		
`x = 2`		
`y = 3 * x`		
`x = y + 5`		
`lstResults.Items.Clear()`		
`lstResults.Items.Add(x + 4)`		
`y = y + 1`		
`End Sub`		

30.

	bal	inter	withDr
`Private Sub btnEvaluate_Click(...) Handles btnEvaluate.Click`			
`  Dim bal, inter, withDr As Double`			
`  bal = 100`			
`  inter = 0.05`			
`  withDr = 25`			
`  bal += inter * bal`			
`  bal = bal - withDr`			
`End Sub`			

In Exercises 31 through 38, determine the output displayed in the list box by the lines of code.

31.
```
Dim amount As Double
amount = 10
lstOutput.Items.Add(amount - 4)
```

32.
```
Dim a, b As Integer
a = 4
b = 5 * a
lstOutput.Items.Add(a + b)
```

33.
```
Dim n As Integer = 7
n += 1
With lstOutput.Items
  .Add(1)
  .Add(n)
  .Add(n + 1)
End With
```

34.
```
Dim num As Integer = 5
num = 2 * num
lstOutput.Items.Add(num)
```

35.
```
Dim a, b As Integer
lstOutput.Items.Add(a + 1)
a = 4
b = a * a
lstOutput.Items.Add(a * b)
```

36.
```
Dim tax As Double
tax = 200
tax = 25 + tax
lstOutput.Items.Add(tax)
```

37.
```
Dim x As Double = 3
x += 2
lstOutput.Items.Add(x * x)
lstOutput.Items.Add(x + 3 * x)
```

38.
```
Dim n As Double = 2, m As Double = 5
lstOutput.Items.Add(3 * n)
n += n
With lstOutput.Items
  .Add(n + m)
  .Add(n - m)
End With
```

In Exercises 39 through 44, identify the errors.

39.
```
Dim a, b, c As Double
a = 2
b = 3
a + b = c
lstOutput.Items.Add(c)
```

40.
```
Dim a, b, c, d As Double
a = 2
b = 3
c = d = 4
lstOutput.Items.Add(5((a + b) / (c + d)
```

41.
```
Dim balance, deposit As Double
balance = 1,234
deposit = $100
lstOutput.Items.Add(balance + deposit)
```

42.
```
Dim interest, balance As Double
0.05 = interest
balance = 800
lstOutput.Items.Add(interest * balance)
```

43.
```
Dim 9W As Double
9W = 2 * 9W
lstOutput.Add(9W)
```

44.
```
Dim n As Double = 1.2345
lstOutput.Items.Add(Round(n, 2))
```

In Exercises 45 and 46, rewrite the code using one line.

45.
```
Dim quantity As Integer
quantity = 12
```

46.
```
Dim m As Integer
Dim n As Double
m = 2
n = 3
```

In Exercises 47 through 52, find the value of the given function.

47. Int(10.75)   48. Int(9 − 2)   49. Math.Sqrt(3 * 12)

50. Math.Sqrt(64)   51. Math.Round(3.1279, 3)   52. Math.Round(−2.6)

In Exercises 53 through 58, find the value of the given function where *a* and *b* are numeric variables of type Double, a = 5 and b = 3.

53. Int($-a/2$)

54. Math.Round(a / b)

55. Math.Sqrt(a − 5)

56. Math.Sqrt(4 + a)

57. Math.Round(a + .5)

58. Int(b*.5)

In Exercises 59 through 66, write an event procedure starting with a Private Sub btnCompute_Click(...) Handles btnCompute.Click **statement, ending with an** End Sub **statement, and having one line for each step. Lines that display data should use the given variable names.**

59. The following steps calculate a company's profit:

   (a) Declare all variables.
   (b) Assign the value 98456 to the variable *revenue*.
   (c) Assign the value 45000 to the variable *costs*.
   (d) Assign the difference between the variables *revenue* and *costs* to the variable *profit*.
   (e) Display the value of the variable *profit* in a list box.

60. The following steps calculate the amount of a stock purchase:

   (a) Declare all variables.
   (b) Assign the value 25.625 to the variable *costPerShare*.
   (c) Assign the value 400 to the variable *numberOfShares*.
   (d) Assign the product of *costPerShare* and *numberOfShares* to the variable *amount*.
   (e) Display the value of the variable *amount* in a list box.

61. The following steps calculate the price of an item after a 30% reduction:

   (a) Declare all variables.
   (b) Assign the value 19.95 to the variable *price*.
   (c) Assign the value 30 to the variable *discountPercent*.
   (d) Assign the value of (*discountPercent* divided by 100) times *price* to the variable *markDown*.
   (e) Decrease *price* by *markdown*.
   (f) Display the value of *price* in a list box.

62. The following steps calculate a company's break-even point, the number of units of goods the company must manufacture and sell in order to break even:

   (a) Declare all variables.
   (b) Assign the value 5000 to the variable *fixedCosts*.
   (c) Assign the value 8 to the variable *pricePerUnit*.
   (d) Assign the value 6 to the variable *costPerUnit*.
   (e) Assign the value *fixedCosts* divided by (the difference of *pricePerUnit* and *costPerUnit*) to the variable *breakEvenPoint*.
   (f) Display the value of the variable *breakEvenPoint* in a list box.

63. The following steps calculate the balance after three years when $100 is deposited in a savings account at 5% interest compounded annually:

(a) Declare all variables.
(b) Assign the value 100 to the variable *balance*.
(c) Increase the variable *balance* by 5% of its value.
(d) Increase the variable *balance* by 5% of its value.
(e) Increase the variable *balance* by 5% of its value.
(f) Display the value of the variable *balance* in a list box.

64. The following steps calculate the balance at the end of three years when $100 is deposited at the beginning of each year in a savings account at 5% interest compounded annually:

(a) Declare all variables.
(b) Assign the value 100 to the variable *balance*.
(c) Increase the variable *balance* by 5% of its value, and add 100.
(d) Increase the variable *balance* by 5% of its value, and add 100.
(e) Increase the variable *balance* by 5% of its value.
(f) Display the value of the variable *balance* in a list box.

65. The following steps calculate the balance after 10 years when $100 is deposited in a savings account at 5% interest compounded annually:

(a) Declare all variables.
(b) Assign the value 100 to the variable *balance*.
(c) Multiply the variable *balance* by 1.05 raised to the 10th power.
(d) Display the value of the variable *balance* in a list box.

66. The following steps calculate the percentage profit from the sale of a stock:

(a) Declare all variables.
(b) Assign the value 10 to the variable *purchasePrice*.
(c) Assign the value 15 to the variable *sellingPrice*.
(d) Assign, to the variable *percentProfit*, 100 times the value of the difference between *sellingPrice* and *purchasePrice* divided by *purchasePrice*.
(e) Display the value of the variable *percentProfit* in a list box.

In Exercises 67 through 72, write an event procedure to solve the problem and display the answer in a list box. The program should use variables for each of the quantities.

67. Suppose each acre of farmland produces 18 tons of corn. How many tons of corn can be produced on a 30-acre farm?

68. Suppose a ball is thrown straight up in the air with an initial velocity of 50 feet per second and an initial height of 5 feet. How high will the ball be after 3 seconds?

Note: The height after t seconds is given by the expression $-16t^2 + v_0t + h_0$, where v_0 is the initial velocity and h_0 is the initial height.

69. If a car left Washington, D.C., at 2 o'clock and arrived in New York at 7 o'clock, what was its average speed? **Note:** New York is 233 miles from Washington.

70. A motorist wants to determine her gas mileage. At 23,340 miles (on the odometer), the tank is filled. At 23,695 miles the tank is filled again with 14.1 gallons. How many miles per gallon did the car average between the two fillings?

71. A U.S. geological survey showed that Americans use an average of 1600 gallons of water per person per day, including industrial use. How many gallons of water are used each year in the United States? **Note:** The current population of the United States is about 300 million people.

72. According to FHA specifications, each room in a house should have a window area equal to at least 10 percent of the floor area of the room. What is the minimum window area for a 14-ft by 16-ft room?

Solutions to Practice Problems 3.3

1. Multiplications are performed before additions. If the intent is for the addition to be performed first, the expression should be written (2 + 3)*4.

2. The first assignment statement assigns the value of the variable *var2* to the variable *var1*, whereas the second assignment statement assigns *var1*'s value to *var2*.

3.

	a	b	c
`Private Sub btnEvaluate_Click(...) Handles btnEvaluate.Click`			
`Dim a, b, c As Double`	0	0	0
`a = 3`	3	0	0
`b = 4`	3	4	0
`c = a + b`	3	4	7
`a = c * a`	21	4	7
`lstResults.Items.Add(a - b)`	21	4	7
`b = b * b`	21	16	7
`End Sub`			

Each time an assignment statement is executed, only one variable (the variable to the left of the equal sign) has its value changed.

4. Each of the three following statements increases the value of *var* by 5%.

```
var = var + 0.05 * var
var = 1.05 * var
var += 0.05 * var
```

3.4 Strings

The most common types of data processed by Visual Basic are numbers and strings. Sentences, phrases, words, letters of the alphabet, names, telephone numbers, addresses, and Social Security numbers are all examples of strings. Formally, a **string literal** is a sequence of characters that is treated as a single item. String literals can be assigned to variables, displayed in text boxes and list boxes, and combined by an operation called concatenation (denoted by &).

◼ Variables and Strings

A **string variable** is a name used to refer to a string. The allowable names of string variables are the same as those of numeric variables. The value of a string variable is assigned or altered with assignment statements and displayed in a list box like the value of a numeric variable. String variables are declared with statements of the form

```
Dim varName As String
```

 Example 1   The following code shows how assignment statements and the Add method are used with strings. The string variable *today* is assigned a value by the third line and this value is displayed by the seventh line. The quotation marks surrounding each string literal are not part of the literal and are not displayed by the Add method. (The form for this example contains a button and a list box.)

```
Private Sub btnDisplay_Click(...) Handles btnDisplay.Click
  Dim today As String
  today = "Monday"
  With lstOutput.Items
    .Clear()
    .Add("today")
    .Add(today)
  End With
End Sub
```

[Run, and then click the button. The following is displayed in the list box.]

```
today
Monday
```

If $x, y, \ldots, z$ are characters and *strVar* is a string variable, then the statement

```
strVar = "xy...z"
```

assigns the string literal $xy \ldots z$ to the variable and the statement

```
lstBox.Items.Add("xy...z")
```

or

```
lstBox.Items.Add(strVar)
```

displays the string $xy \ldots z$ in a list box. If *strVar2* is another string variable, then the statement

```
strVar2 = strVar
```

assigns the value of the variable *strVar* to the variable *strVar2*. (The value of *strVar* will remain the same.) String literals used in assignment or lstBox.Items.Add statements must be surrounded by quotation marks, but string variables are never surrounded by quotation marks.

▨ Using Text Boxes for Input and Output

The content of a text box is always a string. Therefore, statements such as

```
strVar = txtBox.Text
```

and

```
txtBox.Text = strVar
```

can be used to assign the contents of the text box to the string variable *strVar* and vice versa.

Numbers typed into text boxes are stored as strings. Such strings must be converted to Double or Integer numeric values before they can be assigned to numeric variables or used in numeric expressions. The functions CDbl and CInt convert strings representing numbers into numbers of type Double and Integer, respectively. Going in the other direction, the function CStr converts a number into a string representation of the number. Therefore, statements such as

```
dblVar = CDbl(txtBox.Text)
```

and

```
txtBox.Text = CStr(dblVar)
```

can be used to assign the contents of a text box to the Double variable *numVar* and vice versa. CDbl, CInt, and CStr, which stand for "convert to Double," "convert to Integer," and "convert to String," are referred to as **data-conversion** or **type-casting functions**.

 Example 2   The following program computes the sum of two numbers supplied by the user:

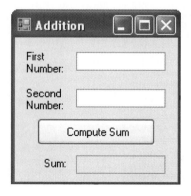

OBJECT	PROPERTY	SETTING
frmAdd	Text	Addition
lblFirstNum	AutoSize	False
	Text	First Number:
txFirstNum		
lblSecondNum	AutoSize	False
	Text	Second Number:
btnCompute	Text	Compute Sum
txtSecondNum		
lblSum	Text	Sum:
txtSum	ReadOnly	True

```
Private Sub btnCompute_Click() Handles btnCompute.Click
  Dim num1, num2, sum As Double
  num1 = CDbl(txtFirstNum.Text)
  num2 = CDbl(txtSecondNum.Text)
  sum = num1 + num2
  txtSum.Text = CStr(sum)
End Sub
```

[Run, type 45 into the first text box, type 55 into the second text box, and click on the button.]

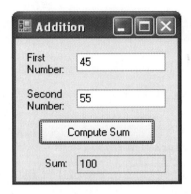

■ Concatenation

Two strings can be combined to form a new string consisting of the strings joined together. The joining operation is called **concatenation** and is represented by an ampersand (&). For instance, "good" & "bye" is "goodbye". A combination of strings and ampersands that can be evaluated to form a string is called a **string expression**. The assignment statement and the Add method evaluate expressions before assigning them or displaying them.

 Example 3 The following program illustrates concatenation. (The form for this example contains a button and a text box.) Notice the space at the end of the string assigned to *quote1*. If that space weren't present, then the statement that assigns a value to *quote* would have to be **quote = quote1 & " " & quote2.**

```
Private Sub btnDisplay_Click(...) Handles btnDisplay.Click
  Dim quote1, quote2, quote As String
  quote1 = "The ballgame isn't over, "
  quote2 = "until it's over."
  quote = quote1 & quote2
  txtOutput.Text = quote & "   Yogi Berra"
End Sub
```

[Run, and then click the button. The following is displayed in the text box.]

```
The ball game isn't over, until it's over.   Yogi Berra
```

Visual Basic also allows strings to be concatenated with numbers and allows numbers to be concatenated with numbers. In each case, the result is a string.

 Example 4 The following program concatenates a string with a number. Notice that a space was inserted after the word "has" and before the word "keys." (The form for this example contains a button and a text box.)

```
Private Sub btnDisplay_Click(...) Handles btnDisplay.Click
  Dim str As String, numOfKeys As Double
  str = "The piano keyboard has "
  numOfKeys = 88
  txtOutput.Text = str & numOfKeys & " keys."
End Sub
```

[Run, and then click the button. The following is displayed in the text box.]

The piano keyboard has 88 keys.

The statement

strVar = strVar & strVar2

will append the value of *strVar2* to the end of the current value of *strVar*. The same result can be accomplished with the statement

strVar &= strVar2

▨ String Properties and Methods: Length Property and ToUpper, ToLower, Trim, IndexOf, and Substring Methods

We have seen that controls, such as text and list boxes, have properties and methods. A control placed on a form is an example of an object. A string is also an object, and, like a control, has both properties and methods that are specified by following the string with a period and the name of the property or method. The Length property gives the number of characters in a string. The ToUpper and ToLower methods return an uppercase and lowercase version of the string. The Trim method returns the string with all leading and trailing spaces deleted. The Substring method returns a sequence of consecutive characters from the string. The IndexOf method searches for the first occurrence of one string in another and gives the position at which the string is found.

If *str* is a string, then

str.Length

is the number of characters in the string,

str.ToUpper

is the string with all its letters capitalized,

str.ToLower

is the string with all its letters in lowercase format, and

str.Trim

is the string with all spaces removed from the front and back of the string. For instance,

```
"Visual".Length is 6.                    "Visual".ToUpper is VISUAL.
"123 Hike".Length is 8.                  "123 Hike".ToLower is 123 hike.
"a" & "  bcd  ".Trim & "efg" is abcdefg.
```

In Visual Basic, the **position** of a character in a string is identified with one of the numbers 0, 1, 2, 3, ... A **substring** of a string is a sequence of consecutive characters from the string. For instance, consider the string "Just a moment". The substrings "Jus", "mom", and "nt" begin at positions 0, 7, and 11, respectively.

If *str* is a string, then

```
str.Substring(m, n)
```

is the substring of *str* consisting of *n* characters beginning with the character in position *m* of *str*. If the comma and the number *n* are omitted, then the substring starts at position *m* and continues until the end of *str*. The value of

```
str.IndexOf(str2)
```

is −1 if *str2* is not a substring of *str*, and otherwise is the beginning position of the first occurrence of *str2* in *str*. Some examples using these two methods are as follows:

```
"fanatic".Substring(0, 3) is "fan".      "fanatic".IndexOf("ati") is 3.
"fanatic".Substring(4, 2) is "ti".       "fanatic".IndexOf("a") is 1.
"fanatic".Substring(4) is "tic".         "fanatic".IndexOf("nt") is −1.
```

The IndexOf method has a useful extension. The value of str.IndexOf(str2, n), where *n* is an integer, is the position of the first occurrence of *str2* in *str* in position *n* or greater. For instance, the value of "Mississippi".IndexOf("ss", 3) is 5.

Like the numeric functions discussed before, string properties and methods also can be applied to variables and expressions.

Example 5   The following program uses variables and expressions with the property and methods just discussed:

```
Private Sub btnEvaluate_Click(...) Handles btnEvaluate.Click
  Dim str1, str2 As String
  str1 = "Quick as "
  str2 = "a wink"
  With lstResults.Items
    .Clear()
    .Add(str1.Substring(0, 7))
    .Add(str1.IndexOf("c"))
    .Add(str1.Substring(0, 3))
    .Add((str1 & str2).Substring(6, 6))
    .Add((str1 & str2).ToUpper)
    .Add(str1.Trim & str2)
    .Add("The average " & str2.Substring(str2.Length - 4) & _
         " lasts .1 second.")
  End With
End Sub
```

[Run, and then click the button. The following is displayed in the list box.]

```
Quick a
3
Qui
as a w
QUICK AS A WINK
Quick asa wink
The average wink lasts .1 second.
```

Note: In Example 5, *c* is in the third position of *str1*, and there are three characters of *str1* to the left of *c*. In general, there are *n* characters to the left of the character in position *n*. This fact is used in Example 6.

Example 6   The following program parses a name. The fifth line locates the position, call it *n*, of the space separating the two names. The first name will contain *n* characters, and the last name will consist of all characters to the right of the *n*th character.

```
Private Sub btnAnalyze_Click(...) Handles btnAnalyze.Click
  Dim fullName, firstName, lastName As String
  Dim n As Integer
  fullName = txtName.Text
  n = fullName.IndexOf(" ")
  firstName = fullName.Substring(0, n)
  lastName = fullName.Substring(n + 1)
  With lstResults.Items
    .Clear()
    .Add("First name: " & firstName)
    .Add("Your last name has " & lastName.Length & " letters.")
  End With
End Sub
```

[Run, type "John Doe" into the text box, and then click the button.]

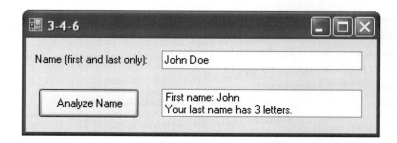

▨ The Empty String

The string "", which contains no characters, is called the **empty string** or the **zero-length string**. It is different from " ", the string consisting of a single space.

The statement **lstBox.Items.Add("")** skips a line in the list box. The contents of a text box can be cleared with either the statement

```
txtBox.Clear()
```

or the statement

```
txtBox.Text = ""
```

▨ Initial Value of a String

When a string variable is declared with a Dim statement, it has the keyword Nothing as its default value. To specify a different initial value, follow the declaration statement with an equal sign followed by the initial value. For instance, the statement

```
Dim today As String = "Monday"
```

declares the variable *today* to be of type String and assigns it the initial value "Monday."

An error occurs whenever an attempt is made to perform an operation on a variable having the value Nothing or to display it in a list box. Therefore, unless a string variable is guaranteed to be assigned a value before being used, you should initialize it—even if you just assign the empty string to it.

▨ Option Strict

Visual Basic allows string variables to be assigned to numeric variables and vice versa. However, doing so is considered poor programming practice, and Visual Basic provides a device, called **Option Strict**, to prevent it. When the statement

```
Option Strict On
```

is placed at the very top of the Code window, Visual Basic requires the use of type-casting functions when assigning string values to numeric variables and assigning numeric values to string variables. In addition, Option Strict On requires type-casting functions when assigning a Double value to an Integer variable.

Visual Basic provides a way to enforce Option Strict for all programs. Press Alt/**T**ools/**O**ptions to open the Options dialog box. In the left pane, click on the + sign to the left of Projects and Solutions to expand this entry. Then click on the subentry VB Defaults. Three default project settings will appear on the right. Set the default for Object Strict to On and then click on the OK button. From now on, all new programs will enforce Object Strict.

When Option Strict is in effect, values of Integer variables can be assigned to Double variables, but not vice versa. Actually, great care must be taken when computing with Integer variables. For instance, the value of an expression involving division or exponentiation has type Double and therefore cannot be assigned to an Integer variable even if the value is a whole number. For instance, none of the four assignment statements that follow is acceptable with Option Strict in effect:

```
Dim m As Integer
Dim n As Double
m = n
m = 2.5
m = 2 ^ 3
m = 6 / 2
```

Throughout this book, we assume that Option Strict is in effect. Therefore, in order to not have to worry about the four occurrences just discussed, we restrict the use of the Integer variables primarily to counting rather than computation.

Internal Documentation

Program documentation is the inclusion of comments that specify the intent of the program, the purpose of the variables, and the tasks performed by individual portions of the program. To create a comment statement, just begin the line with an apostrophe. Such a statement appears green on the screen and is completely ignored when the program is executed. Comment lines appear whenever the program is displayed or printed. Also, a line of code can be documented by adding an apostrophe, followed by the desired information, after the end of the line.

Example 7   The following rewrite of Example 6 uses internal documentation. The first comment describes the entire program, the comment in line 4 gives the meaning of the variable, and the final comment describes the purpose of the With block.

```
Private Sub btnAnalyze_Click(...) Handles btnAnalyze.Click
  'Determine a person's first name and the length of the second name
  Dim fullName, firstName, lastName As String
  Dim n As Integer    'location of the space separating the two names
  fullName = txtName.Text
  n = fullName.IndexOf(" ")
  firstName = fullName.Substring(0, n)
  lastName = fullName.Substring(n + 1)
  'Display the desired information in a list box
  With lstResults.Items
    .Clear()
    .Add("First name: " & firstName)
    .Add("Your last name has " & lastName.Length & " letters.")
  End With
End Sub
```

Some of the benefits of documentation are as follows:

1. Other people can easily understand the program.
2. You can understand the program when you read it later.

3. Long programs are easier to read because the purposes of individual pieces can be determined at a glance.

Even though Visual Basic code is easy to read, it is difficult to understand the programmer's intentions without supporting documentation. Good programming practice dictates that developers document their code at the same time that they are writing it. In fact, many software companies require a certain level of documentation before they release a version, and some judge their programmers' performances on how well their code is documented. A rule of thumb is that 10% of the effort developing a software program is the initial coding, while the remaining 90% is maintenance. Much of the anxiety surrounding the fixing of the "Year 2000" problem was due to the enormous amount of effort required by programmers to read and fix old, undocumented code. The challenge was compounded by the fact that most of the original programmers of the code were retired or could not recall how their code was written.

▇ Line-Continuation Character

Thousands of characters can be typed in a line of code. If you use a statement with more characters than can fit in the window, Visual Basic scrolls the Code window toward the right as needed. However, most programmers prefer having lines that are no longer than the width of the Code window. A long statement can be split across two or more lines by ending each line (except the last) with the underscore character (_) preceded by a space. Make sure the underscore doesn't appear inside quotation marks, though. For instance, the line

```
msg = "640K ought to be enough for anybody. (Bill Gates, 1981)"
```

can be written as

```
msg = "640K ought to be enough for " & _
"anybody. (Bill Gates, 1981)"
```

The line-continuation character does not work with comment statements. That is, each line of a comment statement must be preceded by an apostrophe.

▇ Comments

1. From the Code window, you can determine the type of a variable by letting the mouse cursor hover over the variable name until a tooltip appears.

2. Variable names should describe the role of the variable. Also, some programmers use a prefix, such as *dbl* or *str*, to identify the type of a variable. For example, they would use names like *dblInterestRate* and *strFirstName*. This device is not needed in Visual Basic for the reason mentioned in Comment 1.

3. The functions CInt and CDbl are user friendly. If the user types a number into a text box, but types in a comma as the thousands separator, the values of CInt(txtBox.Text) and CDbl(txtBox.Text) will be the number with the comma removed.

4. The Trim method is useful when reading data from a text box. Sometimes users type spaces at the end of the input. Unless the spaces are removed, they can cause havoc elsewhere in the program.

5. There are several alternatives to CStr for casting a value to a string value. For instance, the statement

```
strVar = CStr(dblVar)
```

can be replaced with any of the following statements:

```
strVar = CType(dblVar, String)
strVar = convert.ToString(dblVar)
strVar = dblVar.ToString
```

6. *Colorization.* You can specify colors for the different elements of a program. For instance, in this book keywords are colored blue, comment statements are colored green, and strings are colored maroon. To specify the color for an element, Click on Options in the Tools menu. Then click on the + sign to the left of Environment to expand this entry, and click on the subentry Fonts and Colors. At this point, you can select an item from the Display list and specify the items foreground and background colors.

Practice Problems 3.4

1. What is the value of "Computer".IndexOf("E")?
2. What is the difference in the output produced by the following two statements? Why is CStr used in the first statement, but not in the second?

```
txtBox.Text = CStr(8 + 8)
txtBox.Text = 8 & 8
```

EXERCISES 3.4

In Exercises 1 through 28, determine the output displayed in the text box or list box by the lines of code.

1. `txtBox.Text = "Visual Basic"`

2. `lstBox.Items.Add("Hello")`

3.
```
Dim var As String
var = "Ernie"
lstBox.Items.Add(var)
```

4.
```
Dim var As String
var = "Bert"
txtBox.Text = var
```

5. `txtBox.Text = "f" & "lute"`

6. `lstBox.Items.Add("a" & "cute")`

7. ```
Dim var As Double
var = 123
txtBox.Text = CStr(var)
```

8. ```
Dim var As Double
var = 3
txtBox.Text = CStr(var + 5)
```

9. ```
txtBox.Text = "Your age is " & 21 & "."
```

10. ```
txtBox.Text = "Fred has " & 2 & " children."
```

11. ```
Dim r, b As String
r = "A ROSE"
b = " IS "
txtBox.Text = r & b & r & b & r
```

12. ```
Dim s As String, n As Integer
s = "trombones"
n = 76
txtBox.Text = n & " " & s
```

13. ```
Dim num As Double
txtBox.Text = "5"
num = 0.5 + CDbl(txtBox.Text)
txtBox.Text = CStr(num)
```

14. ```
Dim num As Integer = 2
txtBox.Text = CStr(num)
txtBox.Text = CStr(1 + CInt(txtBox.Text))
```

15. ```
txtBox.Text = "good"
txtBox.Text &= "bye"
```

16. ```
Dim var As String = "eight"
var &= "h"
txtBox.Text = var
```

17. ```
Dim var As String = "WALLA"
var &= var
txtBox.Text = var
```

18. ```
txtBox.Text = "mur"
txtBox.Text &= txtBox.Text
```

19. ```
With lstBox.Items
    .Add("aBc".ToUpper)
    .Add("Wallless".IndexOf("lll"))
    .Add("five".Length)
    .Add(" 55 ".Trim & " mph")
    .Add("UNDERSTUDY".Substring(5, 3))
End With
```
```

20.
```
With lstBox.Items
    .Add("8 Ball".ToLower)
    .Add("colonel".IndexOf("k"))
    .Add("23.45".Length)
    .Add("revolutionary".Substring(1))
    .Add("whippersnapper".IndexOf("pp", 5))
End With
```

21.
```
Dim a As Integer = 4
Dim b As Integer = 2
Dim c As String = "Municipality"
Dim d As String = "pal"
With lstOutput.Items
    .Add(c.Length)
    .Add(c.ToUpper)
    .Add(c.Substring(a, b) & c.Substring(5 * b))
    .Add(c.IndexOf(d))
End With
```

22.
```
Dim m As Integer = 4
Dim n As Integer = 3
Dim s As String = "Microsoft"
Dim t As String = "soft"
With lstOutput.Items
    .Add(s.Length)
    .Add(s.ToLower)
    .Add(s.Substring(m, n - 1))
    .Add(s.IndexOf(t))
End With
```

23. How many positions does a string of eight characters have?

24. What is the highest numbered position for a string of eight characters?

25. (True or False) If *n* is the length of *str*, then `str.Substring(n - 1)` is the string consisting of the last character of *str*.

26. (True or False) If *n* is the length of *str*, then `str.Substring(n - 2)` is the string consisting of the last two characters of *str*.

In Exercises 27 through 32, identify any errors.

27.
```
Dim phoneNumber As Double
phoneNumber = "234-5678"
txtBox.Text = "My phone number is " & phoneNumber
```

28.
```
Dim quote As String
quote = I came to Casablanca for the waters.
txtBox.Text = quote & ": " & "Bogart"
```

29. ```
    Dim end As String
    end = "happily ever after."
    txtBox.Text = "They lived " & end
    ```

30. ```
    Dim hiyo As String
    hiyo = "Silver"
    txtBox = "Hi-Yo " & hiYo
    ```

31. ```
    Dim num As Double = 1234
    txtBox.Text = Str(num.IndexOf("2"))
    ```

32. ```
    Dim num As Integer = 45
    txtBox.Text = Str(num.Length)
    ```

In Exercises 33 through 34, write an event procedure starting with a Private Sub btnCompute_Click(...) Handles btnCompute.Click **statement, ending with an** End Sub **statement, and having one line for each step. Display each result by assigning it to the txtOutput.Text property. Lines that display data should use the given variable names.**

33. The following steps give the name and birth year of a famous inventor:

    (a) Declare all variables used in steps (b)–(e).
    (b) Assign "Thomas" to the variable *firstName*.
    (c) Assign "Alva" to the variable *middleName*.
    (d) Assign "Edison" to the variable *lastName*.
    (e) Assign 1847 to the variable *yearOfBirth*.
    (f) Display the inventor's full name followed by a comma and his year of birth.

34. The following steps compute the price of ketchup:

    (a) Declare all variables used in steps (b)–(d).
    (b) Assign "ketchup" to the variable *item*.
    (c) Assign 1.80 to the variable *regularPrice*.
    (d) Assign .27 to the variable *discount*.
    (e) Display the phrase "1.53 is the sale price of ketchup."

35. The following steps display a copyright statement:

    (a) Declare the variable used in step (b).
    (b) Assign "Prentice Hall, Inc." to the variable *publisher*.
    (c) Display the phrase "(c) Prentice Hall, Inc."

36. The following steps give advice:

    (a) Declare the variable used in step (b).
    (b) Assign "Fore" to the variable *prefix*.
    (c) Display the phrase "Forewarned is Forearmed."

In Exercises 37 through 40, the interface is specified. Write the code to carry out the stated task.

37. If *n* is the number of seconds between lightning and thunder, the storm is *n*/5 miles away. Write a program that requests the number of seconds between lightning and thunder and reports the distance of the storm. A sample run is shown in Figure 3.17.

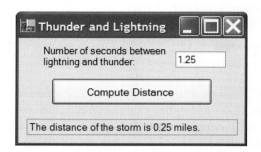

FIGURE 3.17　**Sample output of Exercise 37.**

38. The American College of Sports Medicine recommends that you maintain your *training heart rate* during an aerobic workout. Your training heart rate is computed as $.7*(220 - a) + .3*r$, where *a is* your age and *r is* your resting heart rate (your pulse when you first awaken). Write a program to request a person's age and resting heart rate and then calculate the training heart rate. (Determine your training heart rate.) A sample run is shown in Figure 3.18.

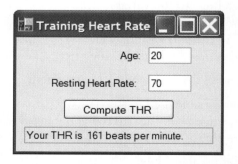

FIGURE 3.18　**Sample output of Exercise 38.**

39. The number of calories burned per hour by bicycling, jogging, and swimming are 200, 475, and 275, respectively. A person loses 1 pound of weight for each 3500 calories burned. Write a program that allows the user to input the number of hours spent at each activity and then calculates the number of pounds worked off. A sample run is shown in Figure 3.19.

FIGURE 3.19   **Sample output of Exercise 39.**

40. Write a program to request the name of a baseball team, the number of games won, and the number of games lost as input, and then display the name of the team and the percentage of games won. A sample run is shown in Figure 3.20.

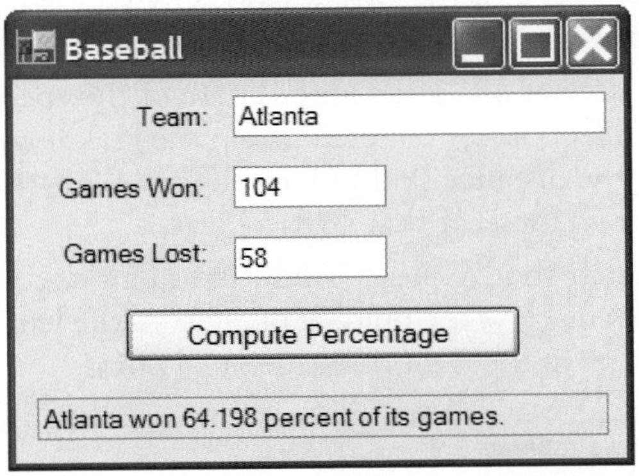

FIGURE 3.20   **Sample output of Exercise 40.**

In Exercises 41 through 46, write a program with a Windows-style interface to carry out the task. The program should use variables for each of the quantities and display the outcome in a text box with a label as in Example 6.

41. Request a company's annual revenue and expenses as input, and display the company's net income (revenue minus expenses). (Test the program with the amounts $550,000 and $410,000.)

42. Request a company's earnings-per-share for the year and the price of one share of stock as input, and then display the company's price-to-earnings ratio (that is, price/earnings). (Test the program with the amounts $5.25 and $68.25.)

43. Calculate the amount of a waiter's tip, given the amount of the bill and the percentage tip as input. (Test the program with $20 and 15 percent.)

44. Calculate a baseball player's batting average, given his times at bat and number of hits as input. **Note:** Batting averages are displayed to three decimal places.

45. Write a program that contains a button and a read-only text box on the form, with the text box initially containing 0. Each time the button is pressed, the number in the text box should increase by 1.

46. Write a program that requests a (complete) phone number in a text box and then displays the area code in another text box when a button is pressed.

47. Write a program that requests a sentence, a word in the sentence, and another word and then displays the sentence with the first word replaced by the second. For example, if the user responds by typing "What you don't know won't hurt you." into the first text box and *know* and *owe* into the second and third text boxes, then the message "What you don't owe won't hurt you." is displayed.

48. Write a program that requests a letter, converts it to uppercase, and gives its first position in the sentence "THE QUICK BROWN FOX JUMPS OVER A LAZY DOG." For example, if the user responds by typing *b* into the text box, then the message "B first occurs in position 10." is displayed.

49. The formula $s = \sqrt{24d}$ gives an estimate of the speed of a car in miles per hour that skidded d feet on dry concrete when the brakes were applied. Write a program that requests the distance skidded and then displays the estimated speed of the car. (Try the program for a car that skids 54 feet.)

50. Write a program that requests a positive number containing a decimal point as input and then displays the number of digits to the left of the decimal point and the number of digits to the right of the decimal point.

Solutions to Practice Problems 3.4

1. −1. There is no uppercase letter E in the string "Computer". IndexOf distinguishes between uppercase and lowercase.

2. The first statement displays 16 in the text box, whereas the second statement displays 88. With Option Strict in effect, the first statement would not be valid if CStr were missing, since 8 + 8 is a number and txtBox.Text is a string. Visual Basic treats the second statement as if it were

```
txtBox.Text = CStr(8) & CStr(8)
```

3.5   Input and Output

■ Formatting Output with Format Functions

The Format functions are used to display numbers in familiar forms and to align numbers. Here are some examples of how numbers are converted to strings with Format functions:

FUNCTION	STRING VALUE
FormatNumber(12345.628, 1)	12,345.6
FormatCurrency(12345.628, 2)	$12,345.63
FormatPercent(0.185, 2)	18.50%

The value of FormatNumber(n, r) is the string containing the number n rounded to r decimal places and displayed with commas as thousands separators. The value of FormatCurrency(n, r) is the string consisting of a dollar sign followed by the value of FormatNumber(n, r). FormatCurrency uses the accountant's convention of denoting negative amounts with surrounding parentheses. The value of FormatPercent(n, r) is the string consisting of the number n displayed as a percent and rounded to r decimal places. With all three functions, r can be omitted. If so, the number is rounded to two decimal places. Strings corresponding to numbers less than one in magnitude have a zero to the left of the decimal point. Also, n can be a number, a numeric expression, or even a string corresponding to a number.

FUNCTION	STRING VALUE
FormatNumber(1 + Math.Sqrt(2), 3)	2.414
FormatCurrency(−1000)	($1,000.00)
FormatPercent(".05")	5.00%

■ Formatting Output with Zones

Data can be displayed in tabular form in a list box. In order to have the items line up nicely in columns, you must

1. use a fixed-width font such as Courier New so that each character will have the same width;
2. divide the line into zones with a format string.

Figure 3.21 (on the next page) shows a line of a list box divided into zones of widths 15 characters, 10 characters, and 8 characters. The leftmost zone is referred to as zone 0, the next zone is zone 1, and so on. These zones are declared in a string with the statement

```
Dim fmtStr As String = "{0, 15}{1, 10}{2, 8}"
```

Note: The pairs of numbers are surrounded by curly brackets, not parentheses.

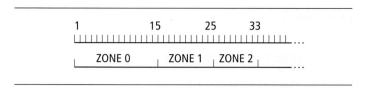

FIGURE 3.21   Zones.

If *data0*, *data1*, and *data2* are strings or numbers, the statement

```
lstOutput.Items.Add(String.Format(fmtStr, data0, data1, data2))
```

displays the pieces of data right justified into the zones. If any of the width numbers 15, 10, or 8 is preceded with a minus sign, the data placed into the corresponding zone will be left justified.

 Example 1   The following program displays information about two colleges in the United States. *Note:* The endowments are in billions of dollars. The final column tells what fraction of the student body attended public secondary schools.

OBJECT	PROPERTY	SETTING
frmColleges	Text	College Data
lstColleges	Font	Courier New
btnDisplay	Text	Display Table

```
Private Sub btnDisplay_Click(...) Handles btnDisplay.Click
  Dim fmtStr As String = "{0,-10}{1,12}{2,14}{3,12}"
  With lstColleges.Items
    .Clear()
    .Add(String.Format(fmtStr, "College", "Enrollment", _
                    "Endowment", "Public SS"))
    .Add(String.Format(fmtStr, "Harvard", 6660, 19.2, 0.659))
    .Add(String.Format(fmtStr, "Yale", 5278, 10.1, 0.532))
  End With
End Sub
```

[Run, and click on the button.]

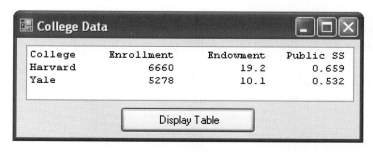

There is no limit to the number of zones, and the zones can be of any widths. In addition, by placing a colon and formatting symbols after the width, you can instruct Visual Basic to specially format numeric data. (String data are not affected.) The most used formatting symbols consist of a letter (*N* for number, *C* for currency, or *P* for percent) followed by a digit specifying the number of decimal places. If there is no digit after the letter, two decimal places are displayed. Here are some examples of such formatting:

ZONE FORMAT TERM	NUMBER TO BE FORMATTED	NUMBER DISPLAYED
{1, 12 : N3}	1234.5679	1,234.568
{1, 12 : N0}	34.6	34
{1, 12 : C1}	1234.567	$1,234.6
{1, 12 : P}	0.569	56.90%

If the second line of the program in Example 1 is replaced with

```
Dim fmtStr As String = "{0,-10}{1,12:N0}{2,14:C}{3,12:P0}"
```

the output will be as follows.

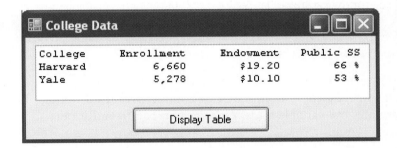

The format strings considered so far consist of a sequence of pairs of curly brackets. We also can insert spaces between successive pairs of brackets. If so, the corresponding zones in the output will be separated by those spaces. The lines of code

```
Dim fmtStr As String = "{0, 5}  {1, -5}"   'Two spaces after the
                                           'first right curly bracket
With lstOutput.Items
  .Add("12345678901234567890")
  .Add(String.Format(fmtStr, 1, 2))
End With
```

produce the output

```
12345678901234567890
    1  2
```

▥ Reading Data from Files

So far, we have relied on assignment statements and text box controls to assign data to variables. Data also can be stored in files and accessed with a StreamReader object or supplied by the user with an input dialog box.

In Chapter 1, we saw how to create text files with Windows Notepad. We will assume that the files created with Notepad have one item of information per line. Figure 3.22 shows a sample file giving payroll information. Each set of three lines gives the name of a person, their hourly wage, and the number of hours that person worked during the week.

Mike Jones
7.35
35
John Smith
6.75
33

FIGURE 3.22   Contents of PAYROLL.TXT.

Data stored in a file can be read in order (that is, sequentially) and assigned to variables with the following steps:

1. Execute a statement of the form

   ```
   Dim readerVar As IO.StreamReader
   ```

   A StreamReader is an object from the Input/Output class that can read a stream of characters coming from a disk or coming over the Internet. The Dim statement declares the variable *readerVar* to be of type StreamReader.

2. Execute a statement of the form

   ```
   readerVar = IO.File.OpenText(filespec)
   ```

   where *filespec* identifies the file to be read. This statement establishes a communications link between the computer and the disk drive for reading data *from* the disk. Data then can be input from the specified file and assigned to variables in the program. This assignment statement is said to "open the file for input."

   Just as with other variables, the declaration and assignment statements in Steps 2 and 3 can be combined into the single statement

   ```
   Dim readerVar As IO.StreamReader = IO.File.OpenText(filespec)
   ```

3. Read items of data in order, one at a time, from the file with the ReadLine method. Each datum is retrieved as a string. A statement of the form

   ```
   strVar = readerVar.ReadLine
   ```

causes the program to look in the file for the next unread line of data and assign it to the variable *strVar*. The data can be assigned to a numeric variable if it is first converted to a numeric type with a statement such as

numVar = CDbl(*readerVar*.ReadLine)

Note: If all the data in a file have been read by ReadLine statements and another item is requested by a ReadLine statement, the item retrieved will have the value Nothing.

4. After the desired items have been read from the file, terminate the communications link set in Step 3 with the statement

readerVar.Close()

 Example 2   Consider the following program that displays the address of the White House. (The form design for all examples in this section consists of a button and a text or list box.)

```
Private Sub btnDisplay_Click(...) Handles btnDisplay.Click
  Dim houseNumber As Double
  Dim street, address As String
  houseNumber = 1600
  street = "Pennsylvania Ave."
  address = houseNumber & " " & street
  txtAddr.Text = "The White House is located at " & address
End Sub
```

[Run, and then click the button. The following is displayed in the text box.]

The White House is located at 1600 Pennsylvania Ave.

Let's now rewrite this program so that it uses a file for input and produces the same output. First, use Windows Notepad to create the file DATA.TXT containing the following two lines:

1600
Pennsylvania Ave.

In the following code, the fifth line of the event procedure reads the first row of data as the string "l600", converts its type to Double, and assigns it to the variable *houseNumber*. (Visual Basic records that this row of data has been used.) The sixth line looks for the next available line of data, "Pennsylvania Ave.", and assigns it to the string variable *street*.

Note: You will have to alter the information inside the parentheses in the second line to tell Visual Basic where the file DATA.TXT is located. For instance, if the file is in the root folder of a diskette in drive A, then the parentheses should contain the string "A:\DATA.TXT". If the file is located in the subfolder My Programs of the C drive, then the parentheses should contain the string "C:\My Programs\DATA.TXT". In this book, we will always write just the name of the file and leave it up to you to add an appropriate path.

```
Private Sub btnDisplay_Click(...) Handles btnDisplay.Click
  Dim sr As IO.StreamReader = IO.File.OpenText("DATA.TXT")
  Dim houseNumber As Double
  Dim street, address As String
  houseNumber = CDbl(sr.ReadLine)
  street = sr.ReadLine
  sr.Close()
  address = houseNumber & " " & street
  txtAddr.Text = "The White House is located at " & address
End Sub
```

Each Visual Basic program is contained in a folder with the name you specified in the Save Project window. This folder holds the files for the program and contains three subfolders named *bin*, My Project, and *obj*. The folder *bin* contains two subfolders named *Debug* and *Release*. If no path is specified for a text file, Visual Basic will look for the file in the *Debug* subfolder for the program. Every program from the companion website for this book that reads a file assumes that the file is located in the *Debug* subfolder for the program. Therefore, even after you copy the contents of the Programs folder onto a hard drive, the programs will continue to execute properly without your having to alter any paths.

 Example 3   The following program uses the file PAYROLL.TXT shown in Figure 3.22.

```
Private Sub btnCompute_Click(...) Handles btnCompute.Click
  Dim sr As IO.StreamReader = IO.File.OpenText("PAYROLL.TXT")
  'The file PAYROLL.TXT is in the Debug subfolder
  'of the bin subfolder of the folder 3-5-3.
  Dim name As String
  Dim hourlyWage, hoursWorked, salary As Double
  name = sr.ReadLine
  hourlyWage = CDbl(sr.ReadLine)
  hoursWorked = CDbl(sr.ReadLine)
  salary = hourlyWage * hoursWorked
  lstPayroll.Items.Add(name & "    " & FormatCurrency(salary))
  name = sr.ReadLine
  hourlyWage = CDbl(sr.ReadLine)
  hoursWorked = CDbl(sr.ReadLine)
  sr.Close()
  salary = hourlyWage * hoursWorked
  lstPayroll.Items.Add(name & "    " & FormatCurrency(salary))
End Sub
```

[Run, and then click the button. The following is displayed in the list box.]

```
Mike Jones    $257.25
John Smith    $222.75
```

In certain situations, we must read the data in a file more than once. This is accomplished by reopening the file with a second assignment statement of the form **sr = IO.File.OpenText(*filespec*)**. This statement sets a pointer to the first line of data in the specified file. Each time a ReadLine method is executed, the line pointed to is read, and the pointer in then moved to the next line. After the last line of data is read, the pointer is said to be at the end of the file.

Example 4   The following program takes the average annual amounts of money spent by single-person households for several categories and converts these amounts to percentages. The data are read once to compute the total amount of money spent and then read again to calculate the percentage for each category. ***Note:*** These figures were compiled for a recent year by the Bureau of Labor Statistics.

The file COSTS.TXT consists of the following eight lines:

Transportation
4251
Housing
8929
Food
3414
Other
8829

```
Private Sub btnCompute_Click(...) Handles btnCompute.Click
  Dim sr As IO.StreamReader = IO.File.OpenText("COSTS.TXT")
  Dim total As Double              'Total annual amount spent
  Dim category As String
  Dim amount As Double             'Amount spent on category
  Dim fmtStr As String = "{0,-15}{1,8:P}"
  category = sr.ReadLine           'Read the first category from the file
  total += CDbl(sr.ReadLine)       'Increment total by the amount
                                   'associated with the category
  category = sr.ReadLine           'Read the next category from the file
  total += CDbl(sr.ReadLine)
  category = sr.ReadLine
  total += CDbl(sr.ReadLine)
  category = sr.ReadLine
  total += CDbl(sr.ReadLine)
  sr.Close()
```

```
    sr = IO.File.OpenText("COSTS.TXT")   'Open the file anew
    category = sr.ReadLine
    amount = CDbl(sr.ReadLine)
    lstPercent.Items.Add(String.Format(fmtStr, category, amount / total))
    category = sr.ReadLine
    amount = CDbl(sr.ReadLine)
    lstPercent.Items.Add(String.Format(fmtStr, category, amount / total))
    category = sr.ReadLine
    amount = CDbl(sr.ReadLine)
    lstPercent.Items.Add(String.Format(fmtStr, category, amount / total))
    category = sr.ReadLine
    amount = CDbl(sr.ReadLine)
    lstPercent.Items.Add(String.Format(fmtStr, category, amount / total))
    sr.Close()
End Sub
```

[Run, and then click the button. The following is displayed in the list box.]

```
Transportation         16.72 %
Housing                34.12 %
Food                   13.43 %
Other                  34.73 %
```

▣ Getting Input from an Input Dialog Box

Normally, a text box is used to obtain input, where the type of information requested is specified in a label adjacent to the text box. Sometimes, we want just one piece of input and would rather not have a text box and label stay on the screen forever. The problem can be solved with an **input dialog box**. When a statement of the form

stringVar = InputBox(*prompt*, *title*)

is executed, an input dialog box similar to the one shown in Figure 3.23 pops up on the screen. After the user types a response into the text box at the bottom of the screen and presses Enter (or clicks OK), the response is assigned to the string variable. The *title* argument is optional and provides the text that appears in the Title bar. The *prompt* argument is a string that tells the user what information to type into the text box.

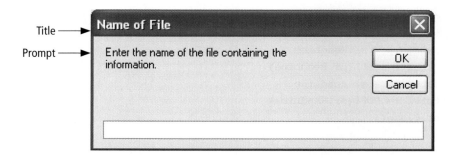

FIGURE 3.23   Sample input dialog box.

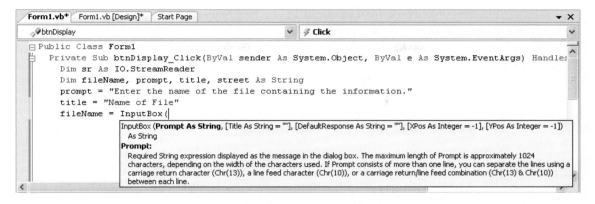

FIGURE 3.24   Parameter Info feature of IntelliSense.

When you type the opening parenthesis following the word InputBox, the editor displays a line containing the general form of the InputBox statement. See Figure 3.24. This feature of IntelliSense is called **Parameter Info**. Optional parameters are surrounded by square brackets. All the parameters in the general form of the InputBox statement are optional except for *prompt*.

Example 5   In the following enhancement to Example 2, the file name is provided by the user in an input dialog box. We assume that the program is contained in the subfolder *Debug* of the program folder.

```
Private Sub btnDisplay_Click(...) Handles btnDisplay.Click
  Dim sr As IO.StreamReader
  Dim fileName, prompt, title, street As String
  Dim houseNumber As Double
  prompt = "Enter the name of the file containing the information."
  title = "Name of File"
  fileName = InputBox(prompt, title)
  'We assume the file is located in the subfolder Debug
  'of the bin subfolder of the folder 3-5-5.
  sr = IO.File.OpenText(fileName)
  houseNumber = CDbl(sr.ReadLine)
  street = sr.ReadLine
  sr.Close()
  txtAddr.Text = "The White House is located at " & _
                  houseNumber & " " & street & "."
End Sub
```

[Run, and then click the button. The input dialog box of Figure 3.23 appears on the screen. Type "DATA.TXT" into the input dialog box, and click on OK. The input dialog box disappears, and the following appears in the text box.]

The White House is located at 1600 Pennsylvania Ave.

The response typed into an input dialog box is treated as a single string value, no matter what is typed. (Quotation marks are not needed and, if included, are considered as part of the string.) Numeric data typed into an input dialog box should be converted to a number with CDbl or CInt before being assigned to a numeric variable or used in a calculation. Just as with a text box or file, the typed data must be a literal. It cannot be a variable or an expression. For instance, *num*, 1/2, and 2 + 3 are not acceptable.

■ Using a Message Dialog Box for Output

Sometimes you want to grab the user's attention with a brief message such as "Correct" or "Nice try, but no cigar." You want this message only to appear on the screen until the user has read it. This task is easily accomplished with a **message dialog box** such as the one shown in Figure 3.25. When a statement of the form

FIGURE 3.25 Sample message dialog box.

```
MsgBox(prompt, 0, title)
```

is executed, where *prompt* and *title* are strings, a message dialog box appears with *prompt* displayed and the Title bar caption *title* and stays on the screen until the user presses Enter, clicks on the box in the upper-right corner, or clicks OK. For instance, the statement

```
MsgBox("Nice try, but no cigar.", 0, "Consolation")
```

produces Figure 3.25. You can omit the zero and a value for *title* and just execute MsgBox(*prompt*). If you do, the Title bar will contain the name of the program and the rest of the message dialog box will appear as before.

■ Using a Masked Text Box for Input

Problems can arise when the wrong type of data is entered as input into a text box. For instance, if the user replies to the request for an age by entering "twenty-one" into a text box, the program can easily crash. Sometimes this type of predicament can be avoided by using a masked text box for input. (In later chapters, we will consider other ways of insuring the integrity of input.)

In the Toolbox, the icon for the MaskedTextBox control consists of a rectangle containing the two characters # and _. The most important property of a masked text box is the Mask property that can be used to restrict the characters entered into the box. Also, the Mask property can be used to show certain characters in the control—to give users a visual cue that they should be entering a phone number or a social security number, for example. Some possible settings for the Mask property are shown in Table 3.3. The first two settings can be selected from a list of specified options. The last three settings generalize to any number of digits, letters, or ampersands. If the Mask property is left blank, then the MaskedTextBox control is nearly identical to the TextBox control.

TABLE 3.3   Some settings for the Mask property.

Setting	Effect
000-00-0000	The user can only enter a social security number.
000-0000	The user can only enter a phone number (without an area code).
(000)000-0000	The user can only enter a phone number (with an area code).
00/00/0000	The user can only enter a date.
0000000	The user can only enter a positive integer consisting of 7 digits.
LLLLL	The user can only enter a string consisting of 5 letters.
&&&&&&&&	The user can only enter a string consisting of 8 characters.

Suppose a form contains a masked text box whose Mask property has the setting 000-00-0000. When the program is run, the string "___-__-____" will appear in the masked text box. The user will be allowed to type a digit in place of each of the eight underscore characters. The hyphens cannot be altered, and no characters can be typed anywhere else in the masked text box.

During run time, the characters 0, L, and & in the setting for a Mask property are replaced by underscore characters that are place holders for digits, letters, and letters and/or spaces, respectively. When the characters "-", "(", ")", or "/" appear in a characters for a Mask property, they appear as themselves in the masked text box and cannot be altered. There are some other mask settings, but these seven will suffice for our purposes.

Figure 3.26 (a) shows a masked text box during design time. It looks like an ordinary text box. However, the Tasks button for the masked text box is used to set the Mask property rather than the Multiline property. Figure 3.26 (b) shows the result of clicking on the Tasks button. Then, clicking on "Set mask …" brings up the Input Mask dialog box shown in Figure 3.27. (This input dialog box is the same input dialog box that is invoked when you click on the ellipses in the Mask property's setting box.) You can use this input dialog box to select a commonly used value for the Mask property, such as the social security number or phone number mask, or set and test a custom-designed mask you create with characters such as 0, &, and L. We will use the prefix *mtxt* for the names of masked dialog boxes.

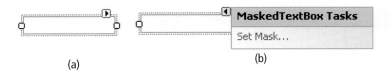

(a)   (b)

FIGURE 3.26   The Masked TextBox control.

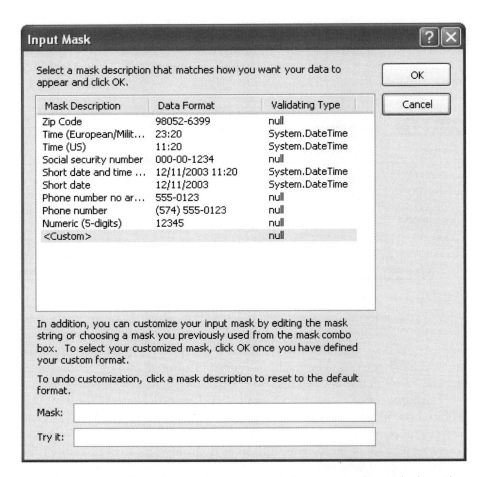

FIGURE 3.27 Input dialog box used to set the Mask property of a masked text box.

■ Comments

The statement `Dim sr As IO.StreamReader = IO.File.OpenText("DATA.TXT")` will be used frequently in this book, albeit with a different file name each time. You can store this line of code (or any frequently used fragment of code) for later reuse by highlighting it and dragging it from the Code window into the Toolbox. To reuse the code, just drag it back from the Toolbox to the Code window. A copy of the code will remain in the Toolbox for further use. Alternately, you can click on the location in the Code window where you want the code to be inserted, and then double-click on the code in the Toolbox.

Practice Problems 3.5

1. Is the statement

```
txtOutput.Text = FormatNumber(12345.628, 1)
```

correct, or should it be written

```
txtOutput.Text = CStr(FormatNumber(12345.628, 1))
```

2. What is the difference in the outcomes of the following two sets of code?

```
strVar = InputBox("How old are you?", "Age")
numVar = CDbl(strVar)
txtOutput.Text = numVar

numVar = CDbl(InputBox("How old are you?", "Age")
txtOutput.Text = numVar
```

EXERCISES 3.5

In Exercises 1 through 30, determine the output produced by the lines of code.

1. `txtOutput.Text = FormatNumber(1234.56, 0)`

2. `txtOutput.Text = FormatNumber(-12.3456, 3)`

3. `txtOutput.Text = FormatNumber(1234, 1)`

4. `txtOutput.Text = FormatNumber(12345)`

5. `txtOutput.Text = FormatNumber(0.012, 1)`

6. `txtOutput.Text = FormatNumber(5 * (10 ^ -2), 1)`

7. `txtOutput.Text = FormatNumber(-2/3)`

8. `Dim numVar As Double = Math.Round(1.2345, 1)`
`   txtOutput.Text = FormatNumber(numVar)`

9. `Dim numVar As Double = Math.Round(12345.9)`
`   txtOutput.Text = FormatNumber(numVar, 3)`

10. `Dim numVar As Double = Math.Round(12.5)`
`    txtOutput.Text = FormatNumber(numVar, 0)`

11. `Dim numVar As Double = Math.Round(11.5)`
`    txtOutput.Text = FormatNumber(numVar, 0)`

12. `txtOutput.Text = FormatCurrency(1234.5)`

13. `txtOutput.Text = FormatCurrency(12345.67, 0)`

14. `txtOutput.Text = FormatCurrency(-1234567)`

15. `txtOutput.Text = FormatCurrency(-0.225)`

16. `txtOutput.Text = FormatCurrency(32 * (10 ^ 2))`

17. `txtOutput.Text = FormatCurrency(4 / 5)`

18. `txtOutput.Text = FormatPercent(0.04, 0)`

19. `txtOutput.Text = FormatPercent(0.075)`

20. `txtOutput.Text = FormatPercent(-.05, 3)`

21. `txtOutput.Text = FormatPercent(1)`

22. `txtOutput.Text = FormatPercent(0.01)`

23. `txtOutput.Text = FormatPercent(2 / 3)`

24. `txtOutput.Text = FormatPercent(3 / 4, 1)`

25. `txtOutput.Text = "Pay to France " & FormatCurrency(27267622)`

26. `txtOutput.Text = "Manhattan was purchased for " & FormatCurrency(24)`

27.
```
Dim popUSover24 As Double = 177.6        'Million
Dim collegeGrads As Double = 45.5        'Million
                                         '45.5/177.6 = 0.2561937
txtOutput.Text = FormatPercent(collegeGrads / popUSover24, 1) & _
   " of the U.S. population 25+ years old are college graduates."
```

28.
```
Dim degrees As String = FormatNumber(1711500, 0)
txtOutput.Text = degrees & " degrees were conferred."
```

29.
```
txtOutput.Text = "The likelihood of Heads is " & _
                 FormatPercent(1 / 2, 0)
```

30.
```
txtOutput.Text = "Pi = " & FormatNumber(3.1415926536, 4)
```

In Exercises 31 through 40, determine the output produced by the lines of code. Assume that Courier New is the font for the list box.

31.
```
Dim fmtStr As String = "{0,-5}{1,5}"
With lstOutput.Items
  .Add("12345678901234567890")
  .Add(String.Format(fmtStr, 1, 2))
End With
```

32.
```
Dim fmtStr As String = "{0,5}{1,5}"
With lstOutput.Items
  .Add("12345678901234567890")
  .Add(String.Format(fmtStr, 1, 2))
End With
```

33.
```
Dim fmtStr As String = "{0,5}{1,-5}"
With lstOutput.Items
  .Add("12345678901234567890")
  .Add(String.Format(fmtStr, 1, 2))
End With
```

34.
```
Dim fmtStr As String = "{0,-5}{1,-5}"
With lstOutput.Items
  .Add("12345678901234567890")
  .Add(String.Format(fmtStr, 1, 2))
End With
```

35.
```
Dim fmtStr As String = "{0,3}{1,10}"
With lstOutput.Items
  .Add("12345678901234567890")
  .Add(String.Format(fmtStr, "A", "Alice"))
End With
```

36.
```
Dim fmtStr As String = "{0,-13}{1,-10}{2,-7:N0}"
With lstOutput.Items
    .Add("12345678901234567890123456789012345678901234567890")
    .Add(String.Format(fmtStr, "Mountain", "Place", "Ht (ft)"))
    .Add(String.Format(fmtStr, "K2", "Kashmir", 28250))
End With
```

37.
```
Dim fmtStr As String = "{0,11}   {1,-11}"  'Three spaces
With lstOutput.Items
    .Add("12345678901234567890")
    .Add(String.Format(fmtStr, "College", "Mascot"))
    .Add(String.Format(fmtStr, "Univ. of MD", "Terrapins"))
    .Add(String.Format(fmtStr, "Duke", "Blue Devils"))
End With
```

38.
```
'Toss coin twice
Dim fmtStr As String = "{0,8}  {1,-7:P0}"  'Two spaces
With lstOutput.Items
    .Clear()
    .Add("12345678901234567890")
    .Add(String.Format(fmtStr, "Number", "Percent"))
    .Add(String.Format(fmtStr, "of Heads", "of time"))
    .Add(String.Format(fmtStr, 0, 1 / 4))
    .Add(String.Format(fmtStr, 1, 1 / 2))
    .Add(String.Format(fmtStr, 2, 1 / 4))
End With
```

39.
```
'Elements in a 150 Pound Person
Dim fmtStr As String = "{0,-7}   {1,-7:N1}   {2,-7:P1}"  '2 spaces
With lstOutput.Items
    .Clear()
    .Add("12345678901234567890")
    .Add(String.Format(fmtStr, "Element", "Weight", "Percent"))
    .Add(String.Format(fmtStr, "Oxygen", 97.5, 97.5 / 150))
    .Add(String.Format(fmtStr, "Carbon", 27, 27 / 150))
End With
```

40.
```
Dim fmtStr As String = "{0,10}   {1,-10:C0}"  'Three spaces
With lstOutput.Items
    .Clear()
    .Add("12345678901234567890")
    .Add(String.Format(fmtStr, "", "Tuition"))
    .Add(String.Format(fmtStr, "College", "& Fees"))
    .Add(String.Format(fmtStr, "Stanford", 24441))
    .Add(String.Format(fmtStr, "Harvard", 25128))
End With
```

In Exercises 41 through 52, assume that the file DATA.TXT (shown to the right of the code) has been accessed with the statement `Dim sr As IO.StreamReader = IO.File.OpenText("DATA.TXT")` and closed afterwards with the statement `sr.Close()`. Determine the output displayed by the lines of code.

41.
```
Dim num As Double
num = CDbl(sr.ReadLine)
txtOutput.Text = CStr(num * num)
```
DATA.TXT

4

42.
```
Dim word As String
word = sr.ReadLine
txtOutput.Text = "un" & word
```
DATA.TXT

speakable

43.
```
Dim str1, str2 As String
str1 = sr.ReadLine
str2 = sr.ReadLine
txtOutput.Text = str1 & str2
```
DATA.TXT

base

ball

44.
```
Dim num1, num2, num3 As Double
num1 = CDbl(sr.ReadLine)
num2 = CDbl(sr.ReadLine)
num3 = CDbl(sr.ReadLine)
txtOutput.Text = CStr((num1 + num2) * num3)
```
DATA.TXT

3

4

5

45.
```
Dim yrOfBirth, curYr As Double
yrOfBirth = CDbl(sr.ReadLine)
curYr = CDbl(sr.ReadLine)  'Current year
txtOutput.Text = "Age: " & curYr - yrOfBirth
```
DATA.TXT

1986

2006

46.
```
Dim str1, str2 As String
str1 = sr.ReadLine
str2 = sr.ReadLine
txtOutput.Text = str1 & " " & str2
```
DATA.TXT

A, my name is

Alice

47.
```
Dim building As String
Dim numRooms As Double
building = sr.ReadLine
numRooms = CDbl(sr.ReadLine)
txtOutput.Text = "The " & building " has " & numRooms & " rooms."
```
DATA.TXT

White House

132

48.
```
Dim major As String
Dim percent As Double
major = sr.ReadLine
percent = CDbl(sr.ReadLine)
txtOutput.Text = "In 2004, " & percent & _
      "% of entering college freshmen majored in " & major & "."
```
DATA.TXT

Computer Science

1.4

49.
```
Dim num, sum As Double
sum = 0
num = CDbl(sr.ReadLine)
sum += num
num = CDbl(sr.ReadLine)
sum += num
txtOutput.Text = "Sum: " & sum
```
DATA.TXT

123

321

50.
```
Dim grade, total, average As Double          DATA.TXT
Dim numGrades As Integer                     85
total = 0                                    95
numGrades = 0
grade = CDbl(sr.ReadLine)
total += grade        'Increase value of total by value of grade
numGrades += 1          'Increase value of numGrades by 1
grade = CDbl(sr.ReadLine)
total += grade    'Increase value of total by value of grade
numGrades += 1    'Increase value of numGrades by 1
average = total / numGrades
txtOutput.Text = "Average grade: " & average
```

51.
```
Dim college As String                        DATA.TXT
college = sr.ReadLine                         Harvard
lstOutput.Items.Add(college)                  Yale
sr.Close()
sr = IO.File.OpenText("DATA.TXT")
college = sr.ReadLine
lstOutput.Items.Add(college)
```

52.
```
Dim num As Integer, str As String            DATA.TXT
num = CInt(sr.ReadLine)                       4
str = sr.ReadLine                            calling birds
lstOutput.Items.Add(num & " " & str)          3
sr.Close()                                   French hens
sr = IO.File.OpenText("DATA.TXT")
num = CInt(sr.ReadLine)
str = sr.ReadLine
lstOutput.Items.Add(num & " " & str)
```

In Exercises 53 through 58, determine the output displayed.

53.
```
Dim bet As Double                     'Amount bet at roulette
bet = CDbl(InputBox("How much do you want to bet?", "Wager"))
txtOutput.Text = "You might win " & 36 * bet & " dollars."
```

(Assume that the response is 10.)

54.
```
Dim word As String
word = InputBox("Word to negate:", "Negatives")
txtOutput.Text = "un" & word
```

(Assume that the response is "tied".)

55.
```
Dim lastName, message, firstName As String
lastName = "Jones"
message = "What is your first name Mr. " & lastName & "?"
firstName = InputBox(message, "Name")
txtOutput.Text = "Hello " & firstName & " " & lastName
```

(Assume that the response is "John".)

56.
```
Dim intRate, doublingTime As Double 'Current interest rate, time to double
intRate = CDbl(InputBox("Current interest rate?", "Interest"))
doublingTime = 72 / intRate
lstOutput.Items.Add("At the current interest rate, money will")
lstOutput.Items.Add("double in " & doublingTime & " years.")
```

(Assume that the response is 4.)

In Exercises 57 and 58, write a line of code to carry out the task.

57. Pop up a message dialog box with "Good Advice" in the title bar and the message "Keep cool, but don't freeze."

58. Pop up a message dialog box with "Taking Risks Proverb" in the title bar and the message "You can't steal second base and keep one foot on first."

In Exercises 59 through 66, identify any errors. If the code refers to a file, assume that DATA.TXT (on the right of the code) already has been opened for input.

59.
```
Dim num As Double
num = CDbl(sr.ReadLine)
txtOutput.Text = CStr(3 * num)
```
DATA.TXT

1 + 2

60.
```
'Each line triplet of DATA.TXT contains
'building, height, # of stories
Dim building As String
Dim ht As Double
Dim numStories As Integer
lstOutput.Items.Clear()
building = sr.ReadLine
ht = CDbl(sr.ReadLine)
lstOutput.Items.Add(building & " is " & ht & " feet tall.")
building = sr.ReadLine
ht = CDbl(sr.ReadLine)
lstOutput.Items.Add(building & " is " & ht & " feet tall.")
```
DATA.TXT

Sears Tower
1454
110
Empire State Building
1250
102

61.
```
Dim num As Double
num = InputBox("Pick a number from 1 to 10.")
txtOutput.Text = "Your number is " & num
```

62.
```
info = InputBox()
```

63.
```
Dim num As Double = FormatNumber(123456)
lstOutput.Items.Add(num)
```

64.
```
txtOutput.Text = FormatCurrency($1234)
```

65.
```
Dim fmtStr As String = "{0,20}{1,10}"
lstOutput.Items.Add(fmtStr, "Washington", "George")
```

66.
```
MsgBox("Proof", "Pulitzer Prize for Drama")
```

In Exercises 67 through 70, write an event procedure starting with a `Private Sub btnCompute_Click(. . .) Handles btnCompute.Click` statement, ending with an `End Sub` statement, and having one, two, or three lines for each step. Lines that display data should use the given variable names.

67. The following steps display information about Americans' eating habits. Assume that the three lines of the file SODA.TXT contain the following data: soft drinks, million gallons, 23.

    (a) Declare all variables used in step (c).
    (b) Open the file SODA.TXT for input.
    (c) Use ReadLine statements to assign values to the variables *food*, *units*, and *quantityPerDay*.
    (d) Display a sentence giving the quantity of a food item consumed by Americans in one day.

68. The following steps display the changes in majors for first-year college students from 2003 to 2004. Assume that file MAJORS.TXT consists of six lines containing the following data: Elementary Education, 4.9, 4.6, Psychology, 4.7, 4.6.

    (a) Declare all variables used in the steps that follow.
    (b) Open the file MAJORS.TXT for input.
    (c) Use ReadLine statements to assign values to the variables *major*, *percent03*, and *percent04*.
    (d) Display a sentence giving the change in the percentage of students majoring in a certain subject.
    (e) Repeat steps (c) and (d).

69. The following steps calculate the percent increase in a typical grocery basket of goods:

    (a) Declare all variables used in the steps that follow.
    (b) Assign 200 to the variable *begOfYearPrice*.
    (c) Request the price at the end of the year with an input dialog box, and assign it to the variable *endOfYearPrice*.
    (d) Assign 100*(*endOfYearPrice* − *begOfYearPrice*) / *begOfYearPrice* to the variable *percentIncrease*.
    (e) Display a sentence giving the percent increase for the year.

    (Test the program with a $215 end-of-year price.)

70. The following steps calculate the amount of money earned in a walk-a-thon:

    (a) Declare all variables used in the steps that follow.
    (b) Request the amount pledged per mile from an input dialog box, and assign it to the variable *pledge*.
    (c) Request the number of miles walked from an input dialog box, and assign it to the variable *miles*.
    (d) Display a sentence giving the amount to be paid.

    (Test the program with a pledge of $2.00 and a 15-mile walk.)

In Exercises 71 through 76, give a setting for the Mask property of a masked text box used to input the stated information.

71. A number from 100 to 999.

72. A word of ten letters.

73. A Maryland license plate consisting of three letters followed by three digits. (*Example:* BHC365)

74. A California license plate consisting of a digit followed by three letters and then three digits. (*Example:* 7BHC365)

75. An ISBN number. [Every book is identified by a ten-character International Standard Book Number (ISBN). The first nine characters are digits and the last character is either a digit or the letter X.] (*Example:* 0-32-108599-X).

76. A two-letter state abbreviation. (*Example:* CA)

77. Table 3.4 summarizes the month's activity of three checking accounts. Write a program that displays the account number and the end-of-month balance for each account and then displays the total amount of money in the three accounts. Assume that the data are stored in a text file.

TABLE 3.4	**Checking account activity.**		
Account Number	Beginning of Month Balance	Deposits	Withdrawals
AB4057	1234.56	345.67	100.00
XY4321	789.00	120.00	350.00
GH2222	321.45	143.65	0.00

78. Table 3.5 contains a list of colleges with their student enrollments and faculty sizes. Write a program to display the names of the colleges and their student/faculty ratios, and the ratio for the total collection of students and faculty. Assume that the data for the colleges are stored in a text file.

TABLE 3.5	**Colleges.**	
	Enrollment	Faculty
Ohio State	50721	3657
Univ. of MD, College Park	35262	2087
Princeton	6849	1015

Source: The World Almanac, 2005.

79. Write a program to compute semester averages. Each set of five lines in a text file should contain a student's Social Security number and the grades for three hourly exams and the final exam. (The final exam counts as two hourly exams.) The program should display each student's Social Security number and semester average, and then the class average. Use the data in Table 3.6.

TABLE 3.6	Student grades.			
Soc. Sec. No.	Exam 1	Exam 2	Exam 3	Final Exam
123-45-6789	67	85	90	88
111-11-1111	93	76	82	80
123-32-1234	85	82	89	84

80. Table 3.7 gives the year 2003 populations of three New England states. Write a program that calculates the average population and then displays the name of each state and the difference between its population and the average population. The states and their populations should be stored in a text file.

TABLE 3.7	2003 population (in thousands) of three New England states.	
State	Population	
Maine	1305	
Massachusetts	6433	
Connecticut	3483	

81. Design a form with two text boxes labeled "Name" and "Phone number". Then write an event procedure that shows a message dialog box stating "Be sure to include the area code!" when the second text box receives the focus.

82. Write a program to calculate the amount of a waiter's tip given the amount of the bill and the percentage tip obtained via input dialog boxes. The output should be a complete sentence that reiterates the inputs and gives the resulting tip, as shown in Figure 3.28.

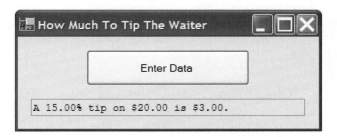

FIGURE 3.28 Sample output for Exercise 82.

83. When P dollars are deposited in a savings account at interest rate r compounded annually, the balance after n years is $P(1 + r)^n$. Write a program to request the principal P and the interest rate r as input, and compute the balance after 10 years, as shown in Figure 3.29 (on the next page).

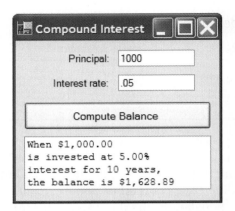

FIGURE 3.29   Sample output for Exercise 83.

In Exercises 84 and 85, write lines of code corresponding to the given flowchart. Assume that the data needed are contained in a file.

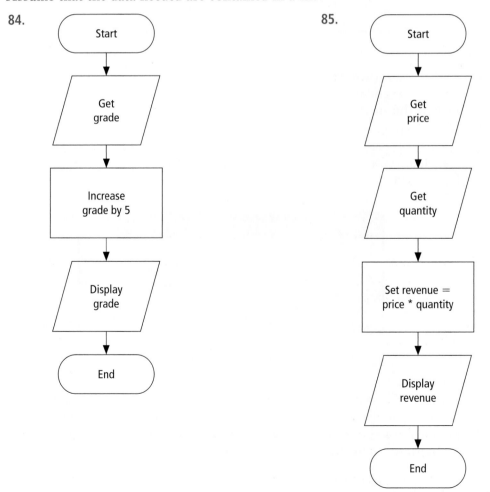

Solutions to Practice Problems 3.5

1. The first statement is correct, since FormatNumber evaluates to a string. Although the second state- ment is not incorrect, the use of CStr is redundant.

2. The outcomes are identical. In this text, we primarily use the second style.

CHAPTER 3   SUMMARY

1. The Visual Basic window consists of a form holding a collection of *controls* for which various properties can be set. Some examples of controls are text boxes, labels, buttons, and list boxes. Some useful properties are Text (sets the text dis- played in a control), Name (used to give a meaningful name to a control), Font.Name (selects the name of the font used), Font.Size (sets the size of the char- acters displayed), Font.Bold (displays boldface text), Font.Italic (displays italic text), BackColor (sets the background color), ForeColor (sets the color of the text), ReadOnly (determines whether text can be typed into the text box), TextAlign (sets the type of alignment for the text in a control), and Visible (shows or hides an object). The With block is a useful device for setting properties at run time.

2. An *event procedure* is executed when something happens to a specified object. Some events are *object*.Click (*object* is clicked), *object*.TextChanged (a change occurred in the value of the object's Text property), *object*.Leave (*object* loses the focus), and *object*.Enter (*object* receives the focus). **Note:** The statement *object*.Focus() moves the focus to the specified object.

3. Two types of *literals* that can be stored and processed by Visual Basic are numbers and strings.

4. Many Visual Basic tasks are carried out by methods such as Clear (erases the con- tents of a text box or list box), Add (places an item into a list box), ToUpper (con- verts a string to uppercase), ToLower (converts a string to lowercase), Trim (removes leading and trailing spaces from a string), IndexOf (searches for a speci- fied character in a string and gives its position if found), and SubString (returns a sequence of consecutive characters from a string).

5. The standard *arithmetic operations* are +, −, *, /, and ^. The only string operation is &, concatenation. An *expression* is a combination of literals, variables, functions, and operations that can be evaluated.

6. A *variable* is a name used to refer to data. Variable names must begin with a letter or an underscore and may contain letters, digits, and underscores. Dim statements explicitly declare variables, specify the data types of the variables, and assign initial values to the variables. In this book, most variables have data types Double, Integer, or String.

7. Values are assigned to variables by *assignment statements*. The values appearing in assignment statements can be literals, variables, or expressions. String literals used in assignment statements must be surrounded by quotation marks.

8. *Comment statements* are used to explain formulas, state the purposes of variables, and articulate the purposes of various parts of a program.

9. *Format strings* can be used to line up data in tables uniformly and display them with dollar signs, commas, percent signs, and a specified number of decimal places.

10. A *StreamReader* object allows us to read data from a file that is specified with an OpenText method. The ReadLine method reads the next unread line from a file.

11. *Functions* can be thought of as accepting numbers or strings as input and returning numbers or strings as output.

FUNCTION	INPUT	OUTPUT
CDbl	string or number	number
CInt	string or number	number
CStr	number	string
FormatCurrency	number	string
FormatNumber	number	string
FormatPercent	number	string
InputBox	string, string	string
Int	number	number
Math.Round	number, number	number
Math.Sqrt	number	number

12. Masked text boxes are useful for input since they have a Mask property that specifies the type of data that can be typed into them.

CHAPTER 3   PROGRAMMING PROJECTS

1. Write a program that allows the user to specify two numbers and then adds, subtracts, or multiplies them when the user clicks on the appropriate button. The output should give the type of arithmetic performed and the result.

2. Suppose automobile repair customers are billed at the rate of $35 per hour for labor. Also, costs for parts and supplies are subject to a 5% sales tax. Write a program to display a simplified bill. The customer's name, the number of hours of labor, and the cost of parts and supplies should be entered into the program via text boxes. When a button is clicked, the customer's name (indented) and the three costs should be displayed in a list box, as shown in the sample run in Figure 3.30.

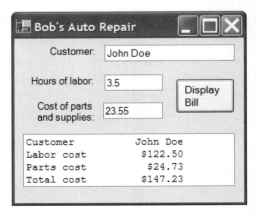

FIGURE 3.30   Sample run for Programming Project 2.

3. At the end of each month, a credit card company constructs the table in Figure 3.31 to summarize the status of the accounts. Write a program to produce this table. The first four pieces of information for each account should be read from a text file. The program should compute the finance charges (1.5% of the unpaid past due amount) and the current amount due.

FIGURE 3.31   Status of credit card accounts.

4. Table 3.8 gives the projected 2005 distribution of the U.S. population (in thousands) by age group and sex. Write a program to produce the table shown in Figure 3.32. For each age group, the column labeled "%Males" gives the percentage of the people in that age group who are male, and the column labeled "%Females" gives this information about the female population. The last column gives the percentage of the total population in each age group. **Note:** Store the information in Table 3.8 in a text file. For instance, the first three lines in the file should contain the following data: Under 25, 51210, 48905. Read and add up the data once to obtain the total population, and then read the data again to produce the table.

TABLE 3.8   Projected U.S. population (2005).

Age Group	Males	Females
Under 25	51,210	48,905
25–64	74,169	77,059
65+	15,319	21,051

2005 U.S. Population

Display Population Distribution Table

Age group	Males	Females	%Males	%Females	%Total
Under 25	51,210	48,905	51.15 %	48.85 %	34.80 %
25-64	74,169	77,059	49.04 %	50.96 %	52.56 %
65+	15,319	21,051	42.12 %	57.88 %	12.64 %

FIGURE 3.32   Output of Programming Project 4.

5. Write a program to convert a U.S. Customary System length in miles, yards, feet, and inches to a Metric System length in kilometers, meters, and centimeters. A sample run is shown in Figure 3.33. After the numbers of miles, yards, feet, and inches are read from the text boxes, the length should be converted entirely to inches and then divided by 39.37 to obtain the value in meters. The Int function should be used to break the total number of meters into a whole number of kilometers and meters. The number of centimeters should be displayed to one decimal place. Some of the needed formulas are as follows:

total inches = 63360 * miles + 36 * yards + 12 * feet + inches

total meters = total inches/39.37

kilometers = Int(meters/1000)

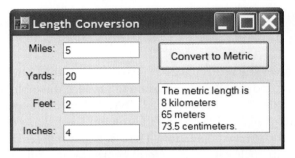

FIGURE 3.33   **Sample run for Programming Project 5.**

4

General Procedures

4.1 Sub Procedures, Part I 132

◆ Variables and Expressions as Arguments ◆ Sub Procedures Calling Other Sub Procedures

4.2 Sub Procedures, Part II 154

◆ Passing by Value ◆ Passing by Reference ◆ Local Variables ◆ Class-Level Variables ◆ Debugging

4.3 Function Procedures 169

◆ User-Defined Functions Having Several Parameters ◆ User-Defined Functions Having No Paramenters ◆ Comparing Function Procedures with Sub Procedures ◆ Collapsing a Procedure with a Region Directive

4.4 Modular Design 183

◆ Top-Down Design ◆ Structured Programming ◆ Advantages of Structured Programming ◆ Object-Oriented Programming ◆ A Relevant Quote

Summary 188

Programming Projects 188

4.1 Sub Procedures, Part I

Visual Basic has two devices, **Sub procedures** and **Function procedures**, that are used to break complex problems into small problems to be solved one at a time. To distinguish them from event procedures, Sub and Function procedures are referred to as **general procedures**. General procedures also eliminate repetitive code and can be reused in other programs.

In this section, we show how Sub procedures are defined and used. The programs in this section are designed to demonstrate the use of Sub procedures rather than to accomplish sophisticated programming tasks. Later chapters of the book use them for more substantial programming efforts.

A **Sub procedure** is a part of a program that performs one or more related tasks, has its own name, and is written as a separate part of the program. The simplest sort of Sub procedure has the form

```
Sub ProcedureName()
  statement(s)
End Sub
```

A Sub procedure is invoked with a statement consisting only of the name of the procedure, that is, a statement of the form

```
ProcedureName()
```

Such a statement is said to *call* the Sub procedure and is referred to as a **call statement**.

The rules for naming general procedures are identical to the rules for naming variables. The name chosen for a Sub procedure should describe the task it performs. Sub procedures are typed directly into the Code window.

Consider the following program that calculates the sum of two numbers. This program will be revised to incorporate Sub procedures.

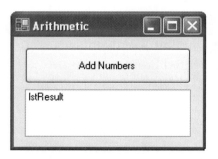

OBJECT	PROPERTY	SETTING
frmAdd	Text	Arithmetic
btnAdd	Text	Add Numbers
lstResult		

```
Private Sub btnAdd_Click(...) Handles btnAdd.Click
  'Display the sum of two numbers
  Dim num1, num2 As Double
  lstResult.Items.Clear()
  lstResult.Items.Add("This program displays a sentence")
  lstResult.Items.Add("identifying two numbers and their sum.")
  lstResult.Items.Add("")
  num1 = 2
  num2 = 3
```

```
lstResult.Items.Add("The sum of " & num1 & " and " _
                    & num2 & " is " & num1 + num2 & ".")
End Sub
```

[Run, and then click the button. The following is displayed in the list box:]

This program displays a sentence
identifying two numbers and their sum.
The sum of 2 and 3 is 5.

The tasks performed by this program can be summarized as follows:

Task #1: Explain purpose of program.

Task #2: Display numbers and their sum.

Sub procedures allow us to write and read a program in such a way that we first focus on the tasks and later on how to accomplish each task.

Example 1   The following program uses a Sub procedure to accomplish the first task of the preceding program. When the statement **ExplainPurpose()** is reached, execution jumps to the **Sub ExplainPurpose()** statement. The lines between **Sub ExplainPurpose()** and **End Sub** are executed, and then execution continues with the line following the call statement.

```
Private Sub btnAdd_Click(...) Handles btnAdd.Click
  'Display the sum of two numbers
  Dim num1, num2 As Double
  lstResult.Items.Clear()
  ExplainPurpose()
  lstResult.Items.Add("")
  num1 = 2
  num2 = 3
  lstResult.Items.Add("The sum of " & num1 & " and " _
                      & num2 & " is " & num1 + num2 & ".")
End Sub

Sub ExplainPurpose()
  'Explain the task performed by the program
  lstResult.Items.Add("This program displays a sentence")
  lstResult.Items.Add("identifying two numbers and their sum.")
End Sub
```

Note: When you type **Sub ExplainPurpose** and then press the Enter key, the editor automatically inserts the parentheses, the line **End Sub**, and a blank line separating the two lines of code. Also, the smart indenting feature of the editor automatically indents all lines in the block of code between the Sub and End Sub statements.

In Example 1, the btnAdd_Click event procedure is referred to as the **calling procedure** and the ExplainPurpose Sub procedure is referred to as the **called procedure**. The second task performed by the addition program also can be handled by a Sub procedure. The values of the two numbers, however, must be transmitted to the Sub procedure. This transmission is called **passing**.

Example 2 The following revision of the program in Example 1 uses a Sub procedure to accomplish the second task. The statement `DisplaySum(2, 3)` causes execution to jump to the `Sub DisplaySum(ByVal num1 As Double, ByVal num2 As Double)` statement, which assigns the number 2 to *num1* and the number 3 to *num2*.

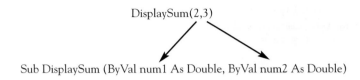

DisplaySum(2,3)

Sub DisplaySum (ByVal num1 As Double, ByVal num2 As Double)

After the lines between `Sub DisplaySum(ByVal num1 As Double, ByVal num2 As Double)` and `End Sub` are executed, execution continues with the line following `DisplaySum(2, 3)`, namely, the `End Sub` statement in the event procedure. ***Note:*** If you don't type in the word *ByVal* from the Sub DisplaySum line, the editor will automatically insert it when you either press the Enter key or move the cursor away from the line. In the next section, we consider an alternative to the keyword *ByVal*. For now we needn't be concerned with *ByVal*.

```
Private Sub btnAdd_Click(...) Handles btnAdd.Click
  'Display the sum of two numbers
  lstResult.Items.Clear()
  ExplainPurpose()
  lstResult.Items.Add("")
  DisplaySum(2, 3)
End Sub

Sub DisplaySum(ByVal num1 As Double, ByVal num2 As Double)
  'Display numbers and their sum
  lstResult.Items.Add("The sum of " & num1 & " and " _
                      & num2 & " is " & (num1 + num2) & ".")
End Sub

Sub ExplainPurpose()
  'Explain the task performed by the program
  lstResult.Items.Add("This program displays a sentence")
  lstResult.Items.Add("identifying two numbers and their sum.")
End Sub
```

Sub procedures make a program easy to read, modify, and debug. The event procedure gives a description of what the program does, and the Sub procedures fill in the details. Another benefit of Sub procedures is that they can be called several times during the execution of the program. This feature is especially useful when there are many statements in the Sub procedure.

Example 3 The following extension of the program in Example 2 displays several sums:

```
Private Sub btnAdd_Click(...) Handles btnAdd.Click
  'Display the sum of two numbers
  lstResult.Items.Clear()
```

```
  ExplainPurpose()
  lstResult.Items.Add("")
  DisplaySum(2, 3)
  DisplaySum(4, 6)
  DisplaySum(7, 8)
End Sub

Sub DisplaySum(ByVal num1 As Double, ByVal num2 As Double)
  'Display numbers and their sum
  lstResult.Items.Add("The sum of " & num1 & " and " _
                      & num2 & " is " & num1 + num2 & ".")
End Sub

Sub ExplainPurpose()
  'Explain the task performed by the program
  lstResult.Items.Add("This program displays sentences")
  lstResult.Items.Add("identifying two numbers and their sum.")
End Sub
```

[Run, and then click the button. The following is displayed in the list box.]

```
This program displays sentences
identifying pairs of numbers and their sums.

The sum of 2 and 3 is 5.
The sum of 4 and 6 is 10.
The sum of 7 and 8 is 15.
```

The variables *num1* and *num2* appearing in the Sub procedure DisplaySum are called **parameters**. They are merely temporary place holders for the numbers passed to the Sub procedure; their names are not important. The only essentials are their type, quantity, and order. In this DisplaySum Sub procedure, the parameters must be numeric variables of type Double and there must be two of them. For instance, the Sub procedure could have been written

```
Sub DisplaySum(ByVal this As Double, ByVal that As Double)
  'Display numbers and their sum
  lstResult.Items.Add("The sum of " & this & " and " _
                      & that & " is " & this + that & ".")
End Sub
```

When a parameter is defined in a Sub procedure, it is automatically available to the code between the Sub and End Sub lines. That is, the code "this As Double" that defines a parameter behaves similarly to the "Dim this As Double" code that defines a variable. A string also can be passed to a Sub procedure. In this case, the receiving parameter in the Sub procedure must be followed by the type declaration "As String".

   Example 4   The following program passes a string and two numbers to a Sub procedure. When the Sub procedure is first called, the string parameter *state* is assigned the value "Hawaii", and the numeric parameters *pop* and *area* are assigned the values 1257608 and 6471, respectively. The Sub procedure then uses these parameters to carry

out the task of calculating the population density of Hawaii. The second call statement assigns different values to the parameters.

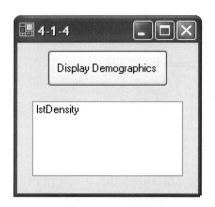

OBJECT	PROPERTY	SETTING
frmDensities	Text	4-1-4
btnDisplay	Text	Display Demographics
lstDensity		

```
Private Sub btnDisplay_Click(...) Handles btnDisplay.Click
  'Calculate the population densities of states
  lstDensity.Items.Clear()
  CalculateDensity("Hawaii", 1257608, 6471)
  lstDensity.Items.Add("")
  CalculateDensity("Alaska", 648818, 591000)
End Sub

Sub CalculateDensity(ByVal state As String, _
                 ByVal pop As Double, ByVal area As Double)
  Dim rawDensity, density As Double
  'The density (number of people per square mile)
  'will be displayed rounded one decimal place
  rawDensity = pop / area
  density = Math.Round(rawDensity, 1)      'Round to one decimal place
  lstDensity.Items.Add("The density of " & state & " is " & density)
  lstDensity.Items.Add("people per square mile.")
End Sub
```

[Run, and then click the button. The following is displayed in the list box.]

```
The density of Hawaii is 194.3
people per square mile.

The density of Alaska is 1.1
people per square mile.
```

The parameters in the density program can have any valid variable names, as with the parameters in the addition program of Example 3. The only restriction is that the first parameter be a string variable and that the last two parameters have type Double. For instance, the Sub procedure could have been written

```
Sub CalculateDensity(ByVal x As String, _
                 ByVal y As Double, ByVal z As Double)
  'The density (number of people per square mile)
  'will be displayed rounded to a whole number
```

```
   Dim rawDensity, density As Double
   rawDensity = y / z
   density = Math.Round(rawDensity, 1)    'Round to one decimal place
   lstDensity.Items.Add("The density of " & x & " is " & density)
   lstDensity.Items.Add("people per square mile.")
End Sub
```

When nondescriptive names are used for parameters, the Sub procedure should contain comments giving the meanings of the variables. Possible comments for the preceding program are

```
'x     name of the state
'y     population of the state
'z     area of the state
```

■ Variables and Expressions as Arguments

The items appearing in the parentheses of a call statement are called **arguments**. These should not be confused with parameters, which appear in the header of a Sub procedure. Each parameter defined for a Sub procedure corresponds to an argument passed in a call statement for that procedure. In Example 3, the arguments of the DisplaySum statements were literals. These arguments also could have been variables or expressions. For instance, the event procedure could have been written as follows. See Figure 4.1.

```
Private Sub btnAdd_Click(...) Handles btnAdd.Click
   'Display the sum of two numbers
   Dim x, y As Double
   lstResult.Items.Clear()
   ExplainPurpose()
   lstResult.Items.Add("")
   x = 2
   y = 3
   DisplaySum(x, y)
   DisplaySum(x + 2, 2 * y)
   z = 7
   DisplaySum(z, z + 1)
End Sub
```

This feature allows values obtained as input from the user to be passed to a Sub procedure.

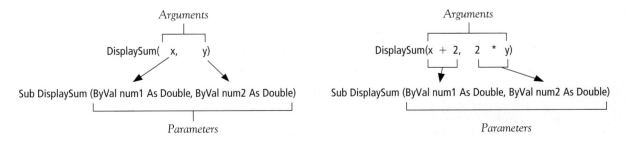

FIGURE 4.1   **Passing arguments to parameters.**

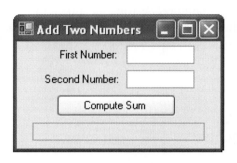

Example 5   The following variation of the addition program requests the two numbers as input from the user. Notice that the names of the arguments, *x* and *y*, are different from the names of the parameters. The names of the arguments and parameters may be the same or different; what matters is that the *order, number,* and *types* of the arguments and parameters match.

OBJECT	PROPERTY	SETTING
frmAdd	Text	Add Two Numbers
lblFirstNum	Text	First Number:
txtFirstNum		
lblSecondNum	Text	Second Number:
txtSecondNum		
btnCompute	Text	Compute Sum
txtResult	ReadOnly	True

```
Private Sub btnCompute_Click(...) Handles btnCompute.Click
  'This program requests two numbers and
  'displays the two numbers and their sum.
  Dim x, y As Double
  x = CDbl(txtFirstNum.Text)
  y = CDbl(txtSecondNum.Text)
  DisplaySum(x, y)
End Sub

Sub DisplaySum(ByVal num1 As Double, ByVal num2 As Double)
  'Display numbers and their sum
  txtResult.Text = "The sum of " & num1 & " and " & num2 _
                   & " is " & (num1 + num2) & "."
End Sub
```

[Run, type 23 and 67 into the text boxes, and then click the button.]

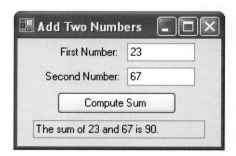

Example 6   The following variation of Example 4 obtains its input from the file DEMOGRAPHICS.TXT. The second call statement uses different variable names for the arguments to show that using the same argument names is not necessary. See Figure 4.2.

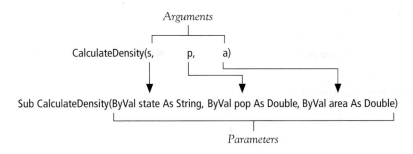

FIGURE 4.2   Passing arguments to parameters in Example 6.

DEMOGRAPHICS.TXT contains the following lines:

Hawaii
1257608
6471
Alaska
648818
591000

```
Private Sub btnDisplay_Click(...) Handles btnDisplay.Click
   'Calculate the population densities of states
   Dim state As String, pop, area As Double
   Dim s As String, p, a As Double
   Dim sr As IO.StreamReader = IO.File.OpenText("DEMOGRAPHICS.TXT")
   lstDensity.Items.Clear()
   state = sr.ReadLine
   pop = CDbl(sr.ReadLine)
   area = CDbl(sr.ReadLine)
   CalculateDensity(state, pop, area)
   lstDensity.Items.Add("")
   s = sr.ReadLine
   p = CDbl(sr.ReadLine)
   a = CDbl(sr.ReadLine)
   sr.Close()
   CalculateDensity(s, p, a)
End Sub

Sub CalculateDensity(ByVal state As String, _
                     ByVal pop As Double, ByVal area As Double)
   'The density (number of people per square mile)
   'will be displayed rounded to one decimal place
   Dim rawDensity, density As Double
   rawDensity = pop / area
   density = Math.Round(rawDensity, 1)     'Round to one decimal place
   lstDensity.Items.Add("The density of " & state & " is " & density)
   lstDensity.Items.Add("people per square mile.")
End Sub
```

[Run, and then click the button. The following is displayed in the list box.]

```
The density of Hawaii is 194.3
people per square mile.

The density of Alaska is 1.1
people per square mile.
```

▨ Sub Procedures Calling Other Sub Procedures

A Sub procedure can call another Sub procedure. If so, after the End Sub of the called Sub procedure is reached, execution continues with the line in the calling Sub procedure that follows the call statement.

 Example 7   In the following program, the Sub procedure FirstPart calls the Sub procedure SecondPart. After the statements in SecondPart are executed, execution continues with the remaining statements in the Sub procedure FirstPart before returning to the event procedure. The form contains a button and a list box.

```
Private Sub btnDisplay_Click(...) Handles btnDisplay.Click
  'Demonstrate Sub procedure calling other Sub procedures
  FirstPart()
  lstOutput.Items.Add(4)
End Sub

Sub FirstPart()
  lstOutput.Items.Add(1)
  SecondPart()
  lstOutput.Items.Add(3)
End Sub

Sub SecondPart()
  lstOutput.Items.Add(2)
End Sub
```

[Run, and click the button. The following is displayed in the list box.]

```
1
2
3
4
```

Arguments and parameters also can be used to pass values from Sub procedures back to event procedures or other Sub procedures. This important property is explored in detail in the next section.

▨ Comments

1. Sub procedures allow programmers to focus on the main flow of a complex task and defer the details of implementation. Modern programs use them liberally. This method of program construction is known as **modular** or **top-down** design. As a rule, a Sub procedure should perform only one task, or several closely related tasks, and should be kept relatively small.

2. In this text, Sub procedure names begin with uppercase letters in order to distinguish them from variable names. Like variable names, however, they can be written with any combination of upper- and lowercase letters. **Note:** Parameters appearing in a Sub statement are not part of the Sub procedure name.

3. The first line inside a Sub procedure is often a comment statement describing the task performed by the Sub procedure. If necessary, several comment statements are devoted to this purpose. Conventional programming practice also recommends that all variables used by the Sub procedure be listed in comment statements with their meanings. In this text, we give several examples of this practice, but adhere to it only when the variables are especially numerous or lack descriptive names.

4. After a Sub procedure has been defined, Visual Basic automatically reminds you of the Sub procedure's parameters when you type in a call statement. As soon as you type in the left parenthesis of a call statement, a Parameter Info banner appears giving the names and types of the parameters. See Figure 4.3.

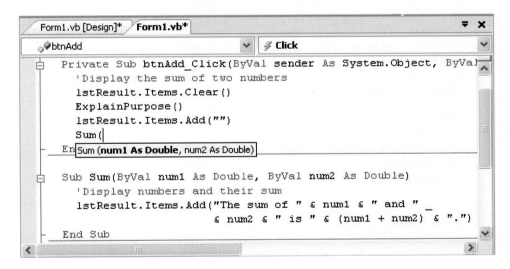

FIGURE 4.3 **The Parameter Info help feature.**

Practice Problems 4.1

1. What is the difference between an event procedure and a Sub procedure?

2. What is wrong with the following code?

```
Private Sub btnDisplay_Click(...) Handles btnDisplay.Click
  Dim phone As String
  phone = mtxtPhoneNum.Text
  AreaCode(phone)
End Sub

Sub AreaCode()
  txtOutput.Text = "Your area code is " & phone.Substring(1, 3)
End Sub
```

EXERCISES 4.1

In Exercises 1 through 34, determine the output displayed when the button is clicked

1. ```
Private Sub btnDisplay_Click(...) Handles btnDisplay.Click
    'Quote from Kermit
    Quotation()
    lstOutput.Items.Add ("Kermit the frog")
End Sub

Sub Quotation()
    'Display a quotation
    lstOutput.Items.Add("Time's fun when you're having flies.")
End Sub
```

2. ```
Private Sub btnDisplay_Click(...) Handles btnDisplay.Click
    lstOutput.Items.Add("Today")
    WhatDay()
    lstOutput.Items.Add("of the rest of your life.")
End Sub

Sub WhatDay()
    lstOutput.Items.Add("is the first day")
End Sub
```

3. ```
Private Sub btnDisplay_Click(...) Handles btnDisplay.Click
    Question()
    Answer()
End Sub

Sub Answer()
    lstOutput.Items.Add("Since they were invented in the northern")
    lstOutput.Items.Add("hemisphere where sundials go clockwise.")
End Sub

Sub Question()
    lstOutput.Items.Add("Why do clocks run clockwise?")
    lstOutput.Items.Add("")
End Sub
```

4. ```
Private Sub btnDisplay_Click(...) Handles btnDisplay.Click
    FirstName()
    lstOutput.Items.Add("How are you today?")
End Sub

Sub FirstName()
    Dim name As String
    name = InputBox("What is your first name?", "Name")
    lstOutput.Items.Add("Hello " & name.ToUpper)
End Sub
```

(Assume that the response is *George*.)

5.
```
Private Sub btnDisplay_Click(...) Handles btnDisplay.Click
    'The fates of Henry the Eighth's six wives
    CommonFates()
    lstOutput.Items.Add("died,")
    CommonFates()
    lstOutput.Items.Add("survived")
End Sub

Sub CommonFates()
    'The most common fates
    lstOutput.Items.Add("divorced")
    lstOutput.Items.Add("beheaded")
End Sub
```

6.
```
Private Sub btnDisplay_Click(...) Handles btnDisplay.Click
    lstOutput.Items.Add("a rose")
    Rose()
    Rose()
End Sub

Sub Rose()
    lstOutput.Items.Add("is a rose")
End Sub
```

7.
```
Private Sub btnDisplay_Click(...) Handles btnDisplay.Click
    'Good advice to follow
    Advice()
End Sub

Sub Advice()
    lstOutput.Items.Add("Keep cool, but don't freeze.")
    Source()
End Sub

Sub Source()
    lstOutput.Items.Add("Source: A jar of mayonnaise.")
End Sub
```

8.
```
Private Sub btnDisplay_Click(...) Handles btnDisplay.Click
    Answer()
    Question()
End Sub

Sub Answer()
    lstOutput.Items.Add("The answer is 9W.")
    lstOutput.Items.Add("What is the question?")
End Sub

Sub Question()
    'Note: "Wagner" is pronounced "Vagner"
    lstOutput.Items.Add("Do you spell your name with a V,")
    lstOutput.Items.Add("Mr. Wagner?")
End Sub
```

9.
```
Private Sub btnDisplay_Click(...) Handles btnDisplay.Click
    Piano(88)
End Sub

Sub Piano(ByVal num As Integer)
    txtOutput.Text = num & " keys on a piano"
End Sub
```

10.
```
Private Sub btnDisplay_Click(...) Handles btnDisplay.Click
    'Opening line of Moby Dick
    FirstLine("Ishmael")
End Sub

Sub FirstLine(ByVal name As String)
    'Display first line
    txtOutput.Text = "Call me " & name & "."
End Sub
```

11.
```
Private Sub btnDisplay_Click(...) Handles btnDisplay.Click
    'Beginning of Tale of Two Cities
    Times("best")
    Times("worst")
End Sub

Sub Times(ByVal word As String)
    'Display sentence
    lstOutput.Items.Add("It was the " & word & " of times.")
End Sub
```

12.
```
Private Sub btnDisplay_Click(...) Handles btnDisplay.Click
    Potato(1)
    Potato(2)
    Potato(3)
    lstOutput.Items.Add(4)
End Sub

Sub Potato(ByVal quantity As Integer)
    lstOutput.Items.Add(quantity & " potato")
End Sub
```

13.
```
Private Sub btnDisplay_Click(...) Handles btnDisplay.Click
    'Analyze a name
    Dim name As String = "Gabriel"
    AnalyzeName(name)
End Sub

Sub AnalyzeName(ByVal name As String)
    'Display length and first letter
    lstBox.Items.Add("Your name has " & name.Length & " letters.")
    lstBox.Items.Add("The first letter is " & name.Substring(0, 1))
End Sub
```

14.
```
Private Sub btnDisplay_Click(...) Handles btnDisplay.Click
    Dim color As String
    color = InputBox("What is your favorite color?")
    Flattery(color)
End Sub

Sub Flattery(ByVal color As String)
    txtOutput.Text = "You look dashing in " & color & "."
End Sub
```

(Assume that the response is *blue*.)

15.
```
Private Sub btnDisplay_Click(...) Handles btnDisplay.Click
    Dim num As Integer
    num = CInt(InputBox("Give a number from 1 to 26."))
    Alphabet(num)
End Sub

Sub Alphabet(ByVal num As Integer)
    txtOutput.Text = "abcdefghijklmnopqrstuvwxyz".Substring(0, num)
End Sub
```

(Assume that the response is *5*.)

16.
```
Private Sub btnDisplay_Click(...) Handles btnDisplay.Click
    Dim size As Double
    size = 435
    House(size)
    lstOutput.Items.Add("of Representatives")
End Sub

Sub House(ByVal size As Double)
    lstOutput.Items.Add(size & " members in the House")
End Sub
```

17.
```
Private Sub btnDisplay_Click(...) Handles btnDisplay.Click
    Dim num As Double
    num = 144
    Gross(num)
End Sub

Sub Gross(ByVal amount As Double)
    txtOutput.Text = amount & " items in a gross"
End Sub
```

18.
```
Private Sub btnDisplay_Click(...) Handles btnDisplay.Click
    Dim a As String = "mile"
    Acres(a)
End Sub

Sub Acres(ByVal length As String)
    txtOutput.Text = "640 acres in a square " & length
End Sub
```

19.
```
Private Sub btnDisplay_Click(...) Handles btnDisplay.Click
    Dim candy As String
    candy = "M&M's Plain Chocolate Candies"
    Brown(candy)
End Sub

Sub Brown(ByVal item As String)
    txtOutput.Text = "30% of " & item & " are brown."
End Sub
```

20.
```
Private Sub btnDisplay_Click(...) Handles btnDisplay.Click
    Dim annualRate As Double = 0.08
    Balance(annualRate)
End Sub

Sub Balance(ByVal r As Double)
    Dim p As Double
    p = CDbl(InputBox("What is the principal?"))
    txtOutput.Text = "The balance after 1 year is " & (1 + r) * p
End Sub
```
(Assume that the response is *100*.)

21.
```
Private Sub btnDisplay_Click(...) Handles btnDisplay.Click
    Dim hours As Double
    hours = 24
    Minutes(60 * hours)
End Sub

Sub Minutes(ByVal num As Double)
    txtOutput.Text = num & " minutes in a day"
End Sub
```

22.
```
Private Sub btnDisplay_Click(...) Handles btnDisplay.Click
    Dim a, b As String
    a = "United States"
    b = "acorn"
    Display(a.Substring(0, 3) & b.Substring(1, 4))
End Sub

Sub Display(ByVal word As String)
    txtOutput.Text = word
End Sub
```

23.
```
Private Sub btnDisplay_Click(...) Handles btnDisplay.Click
    Dim word As String
    word = InputBox("Enter a word.")
    T(word.IndexOf("t"))
End Sub

Sub T(ByVal num As Integer)
    txtBox.Text = "t is the " & (num + 1) & "th letter of the word."
End Sub
```
(Assume that the response is *computer*.)

24. ```
Private Sub btnDisplay_Click(...) Handles btnDisplay.Click
    Dim states, senators As Double
    states = 50
    senators = 2
    Senate(states * senators)
End Sub

Sub Senate(ByVal num As Double)
    txtBox.Text = "The number of U.S. Senators is " & num
End Sub
```

25. ```
Private Sub btnDisplay_Click(...) Handles btnDisplay.Click
    DisplaySource()
    Database("Sybase SQL Server", 75633)
    Database("Oracle", 73607)
    Database("Windows CE", 73375)
    Database("Microsoft SQL Server", 68295)
End Sub

Sub DisplaySource()
    lstOutput.Items.Add("A recent salary survey of readers of")
    lstOutput.Items.Add("Visual Basic Programmer's Journal gave")
    lstOutput.Items.Add("average salaries of database developers")
    lstOutput.Items.Add("according to the database used.")
    lstOutput.Items.Add("")
End Sub

Sub Database(ByVal db As String, ByVal salary As Double)
    lstOutput.Items.Add(db & " programmers earned " & _
            FormatCurrency(salary, 0) & ".")
End Sub
```

26. ```
Private Sub btnDisplay_Click(...) Handles btnDisplay.Click
    'Sentence using number, thing, and place
    Sentence(168, "hour", "a week")
    Sentence(76, "trombone", "the big parade")
End Sub

Sub Sentence(ByVal num As Double, ByVal thing As String, _
            ByVal where As String)
    lstOutput.Items.Add(num & " " & thing & "s in " & where)
End Sub
```

27. ```
Private Sub btnDisplay_Click(...) Handles btnDisplay.Click
    Dim pres, college As String
    Dim sr As IO.StreamReader = IO.File.OpenText("CHIEF.TXT")
    pres = sr.ReadLine
    college = sr.ReadLine
    PresAlmaMater(pres, college)
    pres = sr.ReadLine
    college = sr.ReadLine
```

```
    PresAlmaMater(pres, college)
    sr.Close()
End Sub

Sub PresAlmaMater(ByVal pres As String, ByVal college As String)
    lstBox.Items.Add("President " & pres & " is a graduate of " _
                        & college & ".")
End Sub
```

(Assume that the four lines of the file CHIEF.TXT contain the following data: Clinton, Georgetown University, Bush, Yale University.)

28.
```
Private Sub btnDisplay_Click(...) Handles btnDisplay.Click
    Dim name As String, yob As Integer
    name = InputBox("Name?")
    yob = CInt(InputBox("Year of birth?"))
    AgeIn2010(name, yob)
End Sub

Sub AgeIn2010(ByVal name As String, ByVal yob As Integer)
    txtBox.Text = name & ", in the year 2010 your age will be " _
            & (2010 − yob) & "."
End Sub
```

(Assume that the responses are *Gabriel* and *1980*.)

29.
```
Private Sub btnDisplay_Click(...) Handles btnDisplay.Click
    Dim word As String, num As Integer
    word = "Visual Basic"
    num = 6
    FirstPart(word, num)
End Sub

Sub FirstPart(ByVal term As String, ByVal digit As Integer)
    txtOutput.Text = "The first " & digit & " letters are " _
                        & term.Substring(0, digit) & "."
End Sub
```

30.
```
Private Sub btnDisplay_Click(...) Handles btnDisplay.Click
    Dim statue As String, tons As Double
    statue = "The Statue of Liberty"
    tons = 250
    HowHeavy(statue, tons)
End Sub

Sub HowHeavy(ByVal what As String, ByVal weight As Double)
    txtOutput.Text = what & " weighs " & weight & " tons."
End Sub
```

31.
```
Private Sub btnDisplay_Click(...) Handles btnDisplay.Click
    Dim word As String
    word = "worldly"
    Negative("un" & word, word)
End Sub
```

```
Sub Negative(ByVal neg As String, ByVal word As String)
  txtOutput.Text = "The negative of " & word & " is " & neg
End Sub
```

32.
```
Private Sub btnDisplay_Click(...) Handles btnDisplay.Click
  Dim age, yrs As Integer, major As String
  age = CInt(InputBox("How old are you?"))
  yrs = CInt(InputBox("In how many years will you graduate?"))
  major = InputBox("What sort of major do you have " & _
                   "(Arts or Sciences)?")
  Graduation(age + yrs, major.Substring(0, 1))
End Sub

Sub Graduation(ByVal num As Integer, ByVal letter As String)
  txtOutput.Text = "You will receive a B" & letter.ToUpper & _
                   " degree at age " & num
End Sub
```

(Assume that the responses are *19*, *3*, and *arts*.)

33.
```
Private Sub btnDisplay_Click(...) Handles btnDisplay.Click
  HowMany(24)
  lstOutput.Items.Add("a pie.")
End Sub

Sub HowMany(ByVal num As Integer)
  What(num)
  lstOutput.Items.Add("baked in")
End Sub

Sub What(ByVal num As Integer)
  lstOutput.Items.Add(num & " blackbirds")
End Sub
```

34.
```
Private Sub btnDisplay_Click(...) Handles btnDisplay.Click
  txtOutput.Text = "All's"
  PrintWell()
  PrintWords(" that ends")
  PrintWell()
  txtOutput.Text &= "."
End Sub

Sub PrintWell()
  txtOutput.Text &= " well"
End Sub

Sub PrintWords(ByVal words As String)
  txtOutput.Text &= words
End Sub
```

In Exercises 35 through 38, find the errors.

35.
```
Private Sub btnDisplay_Click(...) Handles btnDisplay.Click
    Dim n As Integer = 5
    Alphabet()
End Sub

Sub Alphabet(ByVal n As Integer)
    txtOutput.Text = "abcdefghijklmnopqrstuvwxyz".Substring(0, n)
End Sub
```

36.
```
Private Sub btnDisplay_Click(...) Handles btnDisplay.Click
    Dim word As String, number As Double
    word = "seven"
    number = 7
    Display(word, number)
End Sub

Sub Display(ByVal num As Double, ByVal term As String)
    txtOutput.Text = num & " " & term
End Sub
```

37.
```
Private Sub btnDisplay_Click(...) Handles btnDisplay.Click
    Dim name As String
    name = InputBox("Name")
    Handles(name)
End Sub

Sub Handles(ByVal moniker As String)
    txtOutput.Text = "Your name is " & moniker
End Sub
```

38.
```
Private Sub btnDisplay_Click(...) Handles btnDisplay.Click
    Dim num As Integer = 2
    Tea(num)
End Sub

Sub Tea()
    txtOutput.Text = "Tea for " & num
End Sub
```

In Exercises 39 through 42, rewrite the program with the output performed by a call to a Sub procedure.

39.
```
Private Sub btnDisplay_Click(...) Handles btnDisplay.Click
    'Display a lucky number
    Dim num As Integer = 7
    txtOutput.Text = num & " is a lucky number."
End Sub
```

40.
```
Private Sub btnDisplay_Click(...) Handles btnDisplay.Click
    'Greet a friend
    Dim name As String = "Jack"
    txtOutput.Text = "Hi, " & name
End Sub
```

41.
```
Private Sub btnDisplay_Click(...) Handles btnDisplay.Click
    'Information about trees
    Dim tree As String, ht As Double
    Dim sr As IO.StreamReader = IO.File.OpenText("TREES.TXT")
    lstBox.Items.Clear()
    tree = sr.ReadLine
    ht = CDbl(sr.ReadLine)
    lstBox.Items.Add("The tallest " & tree & " in the U.S. is " _
                    & ht & " feet.")
    tree = sr.ReadLine
    ht = CDbl(sr.ReadLine)
    lstBox.Items.Add("The tallest " & tree & " in the U.S. is " _
                    & ht & " feet.")
    sr.Close()
End Sub
```
(Assume that the four lines of the file TREES.TXT contain the following data: redwood, 362, pine, 223.)

42.
```
Private Sub btnDisplay_Click(...) Handles btnDisplay.Click
    Dim city As String, salary As Double
    Dim sr As IO.StreamReader = IO.File.OpenText("DATA.TXT")
    lstBox.Items.Clear()
    city = sr.ReadLine
    salary = CDbl(sr.ReadLine)
    lstBox.Items.Add("In 2000, the average salary for " & city & _
                    " residents was " & FormatCurrency(salary, 0))
    city = sr.ReadLine
    salary = CDbl(sr.ReadLine)
    lstBox.Items.Add("In 2000, the average salary for " & city & _
                    " residents was " & FormatCurrency(salary, 0))
    sr.Close()
End Sub
```
(Assume that the four lines of the file DATA.TXT contain the following data: San Jose, 76076, Hartford, 42349.) **Note:** San Jose is located in Silicon Valley, and Hartford is the center of the insurance industry.

43. Write a program that requests a number as input and displays three times the number. The output should be produced by a call to a Sub procedure named Triple.

44. Write a program that requests a word as input and displays the word followed by the number of letters in the word. The output should be produced by a call to a Sub procedure named HowLong.

45. Write a program that requests a word of at most ten letters and a width from 10 through 20 as input and displays the word right-justified in a zone having the specified width. The output should be produced by a call to a Sub procedure named PlaceNShow.

46. Write a program that requests three numbers as input and displays the average of the three numbers. The output should be produced by a call to a Sub procedure named Average.

In Exercises 47 through 50, write a program that, when btnDisplay is clicked, will display in lstOutput the output shown. The last two lines of the output should be displayed by one or more Sub procedures using data passed by variables from an event procedure.

47. (Assume that the following is displayed.)

```
According to a 2004 survey of college freshmen
taken by the Higher Educational Research Institute:

16 percent said they intend to major in business.
1.4 percent said they intend to major in computer science.
```

48. (Assume that the current date is 12/31/2006, the label for txtBox reads "What is your year of birth?", and the user types 1980 into txtBox before btnDisplay is clicked.)

```
You are now 26 years old.
You have lived for more than 9490 days.
```

49. (Assume that the label for txtBox reads "What is your favorite number?", and the user types 7 into txtBox before btnDisplay is clicked.)

```
The sum of your favorite number with itself is 14.
The product of your favorite number with itself is 49.
```

50. (Assume that the following is displayed.)

```
In a recent year,
657 thousand college students took a course in Spanish
199 thousand college students took a course in French
```

51. Write a program to display three verses of "Old McDonald Had a Farm." The primary verse, with variables substituted for the animals and sounds, should be contained in a Sub procedure. The program should use the file FARM.TXT. The eight lines of the file FARM.TXT contain the following data: lamb, baa, firefly, blink, computer, beep.

    The first verse of the output should be

```
Old McDonald had a farm. Eyi eyi oh.
And on his farm he had a lamb. Eyi eyi oh.
With a baa baa here, and a baa baa there.
Here a baa, there a baa, everywhere a baa baa.
Old McDonald had a farm. Eyi eyi oh.
```

52. Write a program that displays the word WOW vertically in large letters. Each letter should be drawn in a Sub procedure. For instance, the Sub procedure for the letter W follows. **Hint:** Use the font *Courier New* in the list box.

```
Sub DrawW()
  'Draw the letter W
  lstWOW.Items.Add("**        **")
  lstWOW.Items.Add(" **        **")
  lstWOW.Items.Add("  **  **  **")
  lstWOW.Items.Add("   **    **")
  lstWow.Items.Add("")
End Sub
```

53. Write a program to display the data from Table 4.1. The occupations and numbers of jobs for 2000 and 2012 should be contained in the file GROWTH.TXT. A Sub procedure, to be called four times, should read the first three pieces of data for an occupation, calculate the percent increase from 2000 to 2012, and display the four items. **Note:** The percent increase is calculated as (2012 value − 2000 value)/(2000 value).

TABLE 4.1   Occupations projected to experience the largest job growth, 2000–2012 (numbers in thousands of jobs).

Occupation	2000	2012	Increase
Medical assistant	365	579	59%
Home health aide	580	859	48%
Software engineer	394	573	45%
Systems analyst	468	653	40%

Source: U.S. Department of Labor.

54. Write a program to compute tips for services rendered. The program should request the person's occupation, the amount of the bill, and the percentage tip as input and pass this information to a Sub procedure to display the person and the tip. A sample run is shown in the following figure:

Solutions to Practice Problems 4.1

1. An event procedure always has the two parameters *sender* and *e* and ends with a phrase of the form "Handles *object.event.*" It is triggered when the specified object experiences the specified event. On the other hand, a Sub procedure is triggered by a line of code containing the name of the Sub procedure.

2. The statement **Sub AreaCode()** must be replaced by **Sub AreaCode(ByVal phone As String)**. Whenever a value is passed to a Sub procedure, the Sub statement must provide a parameter to receive the value.

4.2   Sub Procedures, Part II

The previous section introduced the concept of a Sub procedure, but left some questions unanswered. Why can't the value of a variable be passed from an event procedure to a Sub procedure by just using the variable in the Sub procedure? How do Sub procedures pass values back to an event procedure? The answers to these questions provide a deeper understanding of the workings of Sub procedures and reveal their full capabilities.

■ Passing by Value

In Section 4.1, all parameters appearing in Sub procedures were preceded by the word ByVal, which stands for "By Value." When a variable is passed to such a parameter, we say that the variable is "passed by value." A variable that is passed by value will retain its original value after the Sub procedure terminates—regardless of what was done to the corresponding parameter inside the Sub procedure. Example 1 illustrates this feature.

 Example 1   The following program illustrates the fact that changes to the value of a parameter passed by value have no effect on the value of the calling argument:

```
Private Sub btnDisplay_Click(...) Handles btnDisplay.Click
  'Illustrate that a change in value of parameter does not alter the
  'value of the argument
  Dim amt As Double = 2
  lstResults.Items.Add(amt)
  Triple(amt)
  lstResults.Items.Add(amt)
End Sub

Sub Triple(ByVal num As Double)
  'Triple a number
  lstResults.Items.Add(num)
  num = 3 * num
  lstResults.Items.Add(num)
End Sub
```

[Run, and then click the button. The following is displayed in the list box.]

```
2
2
6
2
```

When a variable is passed by value, two memory locations are involved. At the time the Sub procedure is called, a temporary second memory location for the parameter is set aside for the Sub procedure's use and the value of the argument is copied into that location. After the completion of the Sub procedure, the temporary memory location is released, and the value in it is lost. So, for instance, the outcome in Example 1 would be the same even if the name of the parameter were *amt*.

▣ Passing by Reference

Another way to pass a variable to a Sub procedure is "By Reference." In this case the parameter is preceded by the reserved word ByRef. Suppose a variable, call it *arg*, appears as an argument in a call statement, and its corresponding parameter in the Sub procedure's header, call it *par*, is preceded by ByRef. After the Sub procedure is executed, *arg* will have whatever value *par* had in the Sub procedure. Hence, not only is the value of *arg* passed to *par*, but the value of *par* is passed back to *arg*.

In Example 1, if the first line of the Sub procedure is changed to

```
Sub Triple(ByRef num As Double)
```

then the last number of the output will be 6.

Although this feature may be surprising at first glance, it provides a vehicle for passing values from a Sub procedure back to the place from which the Sub procedure was called. Different names may be used for an argument and its corresponding parameter, but only one memory location is involved. Initially, the btnDisplay_Click() event procedure allocates a memory location to hold the value of *amt* (Figure 4.4(a)). When the Sub procedure is called, the parameter *num* becomes the Sub procedure's name for this memory location (Figure 4.4(b)). When the value of *num* is tripled, the value in the memory location becomes 6 (Figure 4.4(c)). After the completion of the Sub procedure, the parameter name *num* is forgotten; however, its value lives on in *amt* (Figure 4.4(d)). The variable *amt* is said to be **passed by reference**.

amt	amt	amt	amt
2	2	6	6
	num	num	
(a)	(b)	(c)	(d)

FIGURE 4.4   **Passing a variable by reference to a Sub procedure.**

Passing by reference has a wide variety of uses. In the next example, it is used as a vehicle to transport a value from a Sub procedure back to an event procedure.

Example 2   The following variation of Example 5 from the previous section uses a Sub procedure to acquire the input. The variables *x* and *y* are not assigned values prior to the execution of the first call statement. Therefore, before the call statement is executed, they have the value 0. After the call statement is executed, however, they have the values entered into the text boxes. These values then are passed by the second call statement to the Sub procedure DisplaySum.

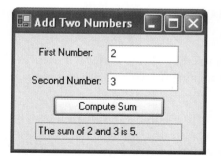

OBJECT	PROPERTY	SETTING
frmAdd	Text	Add Two Numbers
lblFirstNum	Text	First Number:
txtFirstNum		
lblSecondNum	Text	Second Number:
txtSecondNum		
btnCompute	Text	Compute Sum
txtResult	ReadOnly	True

```
Private Sub btnCompute_Click(...) Handles btnCompute.Click
  'This program requests two numbers and
  'displays the two numbers and their sum.
  Dim x, y As Double
  GetNumbers(x, y)
  DisplaySum(x, y)

End Sub

Sub GetNumbers(ByRef x As Double, ByRef y As Double)
  'Record the two numbers in the text boxes
  x = CDbl(txtFirstNum.Text)
  y = CDbl(txtSecondNum.Text)

End Sub

Sub DisplaySum(ByVal num1 As Double, ByVal num2 As Double)
  'Display numbers and their sum
  txtResult.Text = "The sum of " & num1 & " and " & num2 _
                   & " is " & (num1 + num2) & "."
End Sub
```

[Run, type 2 and 3 into the text boxes, and then click the button.]

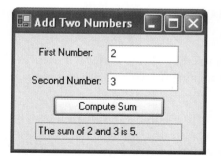

In most situations, a variable with no preassigned value is used as an argument of a call statement for the sole purpose of carrying back a value from the Sub procedure.

 Example 3 The following variation of Example 2 allows the btnCompute_Click event procedure to be written in the input-process-output style. Just before the call

statement **CalculateSum (x, y, t)** is executed, the value of *t* is 0. After the call, the value of *t* will be the sum of the two numbers in the text boxes.

```
Private Sub btnCompute_Click(...) Handles btnCompute.Click
    'This program requests two numbers and
    'displays the two numbers and their sum.
    Dim x As Double       'First number
    Dim y As Double       'Second number
    Dim t As Double       'Total
    GetNumbers(x, y)
    CalculateSum(x, y, t)
    DisplayResult(x, y, t)
End Sub

Sub GetNumbers(ByRef num1 As Double, ByRef num2 As Double)
    'Retrieve the two numbers in the text boxes
    num1 = CDbl(txtFirstNum.Text)
    num2 = CDbl(txtSecondNum.Text)
End Sub

Sub CalculateSum(ByVal num1 As Double, ByVal num2 As Double, _
                 ByRef total As Double)
    'Add the values of num1 and num2
    total = num1 + num2
End Sub

Sub DisplayResult(ByVal num1 As Double, ByVal num2 As Double, _
                  ByVal total As Double)
    txtResult.Text = "The sum of " & num1 & " and " & num2 _
                     & " is " & total & "."
End Sub
```

Visual Basic provides a way to override passing by reference, even if the ByRef keyword precedes the parameter. If you enclose the variable in the call statement in an extra pair of parentheses, then the variable will be passed by value.

For instance, in Example 1, if you change the call statement to

```
Triple((amt))
```

then the fourth number of the output will be 2 even if the parameter *num* is preceded with ByRef.

▥ Local Variables

When a variable is declared in an event or Sub procedure with a Dim statement, a portion of memory is set aside to hold the value of the variable. As soon as the End Sub statement for the procedure executes, the memory location is freed up; that is, the variable ceases to exist. The variable is said to be **local** to the procedure.

When variables of the same name are declared with Dim statements in two different procedures (either event or Sub), Visual Basic gives the variables separate identities and treats them as two different variables. A value assigned to a variable in one part of the program will not affect the value of the like-named variable in the other part of the program.

Example 4   The following program illustrates the fact that each time a Sub procedure is called, its variables are set to their initial values; that is, numerical variables are set to 0 and string variables are set to the keyword Nothing.

```
Private Sub btnDisplay_Click(...) Handles btnDisplay.Click
  'Demonstrate that variables declared in a Sub procedure
  'do not retain their values in subsequent calls
  Three()
  Three()
End Sub

Sub Three()
  'Display the value of num and assign it the value 3
  Dim num As Double
  lstResults.Items.Add(num)
  num = 3
End Sub
```

[Run, and then click the button. The following is displayed in the list box.]

```
0
0
```

 Example 5   The following program illustrates the fact that variables are local to the part of the program in which they reside. The variable *x* in the event procedure and the variable *x* in the Sub procedure are treated as different variables. Visual Basic handles them as if their names were separate, such as xbtnDisplay_Click and xTrivial. Also, each time the Sub procedure is called, the value of variable *x* inside the Sub procedure is reset to 0.

```
Private Sub btnDisplay_Click(...) Handles btnDisplay.Click
  'Demonstrate the local nature of variables
  Dim x As Double = 2
  lstResults.Items.Clear()
  lstResults.Items.Add(x)
  Trivial()
  lstResults.Items.Add(x)
  Trivial()
  lstResults.Items.Add(x)
End Sub

Sub Trivial()
  'Do something trivial
  Dim x As Double
  lstResults.Items.Add(x)
  x = 3
  lstResults.Items.Add(x)
End Sub
```

[Run, and then click the button. The following is displayed in the list box.]

2
0
3
2
0
3
2

Class-Level Variables

Visual Basic provides a way to make a variable visible to every procedure in a form's code without being passed. Such a variable is called a **class-level variable**. The Dim statement for a class-level variable can be placed anywhere between the statements **Public Class formName** and **End Class**, provided that the Dim statement is not inside a procedure. Normally, we place the Dim statement just after the **Public Class formName** statement (We refer to this region as the **Declarations section** of the Code window.) A class-level variable is visible to every procedure. When a class-level variable has its value changed by a procedure, the value persists even after the procedure has finished executing. We say that such a variable has **class-level scope**. Variables declared inside a procedure are said to have **local scope**.

In general, the **scope** of a variable is the portion of the program that can refer to it. Class-level scope also is referred to as **module-level scope**, and local scope also is referred to as **procedure-level scope**. If a procedure declares a local variable with the same name as a class-level variable, then the name refers to the local variable for code inside the procedure.

 Example 6   The following program contains the class-level variables *num1* and *num2*. Their Dim statement does not appear inside a procedure. It appears immediately following the statement **Public Class frmAdd**.

```
Dim num1, num2 As Double      'Class-level variables

Private Sub btnDisplay_Click(...) Handles btnDisplay.Click
  'Display the sum of two numbers
  num1 = 2
  num2 = 3
  lstResults.Items.Clear()
  AddAndIncrement()
  lstResults.Items.Add("")
  lstResults.Items.Add("num1 = " & num1)
  lstResults.Items.Add("num2 = " & num2)
End Sub

Sub AddAndIncrement()
  'Display numbers and their sum
  lstResults.Items.Add("The sum of " & num1 & " and " & _
                  num2 & " is " & (num1 + num2) & ".")
  num1 += 1      'Add 1 to the value of num1
  num2 += 1      'Add 1 to the value of num2
End Sub
```

[Run, and click the button. The following is displayed in the list box.]

The sum of 2 and 3 is 5.

num1 = 3
num2 = 4

In the preceding example, we had to click a button to assign values to the class-level variables. In some situations, we want to assign a value immediately to a class-level variable, without requiring the user to perform some specific action. This can be accomplished by declaring each class-level variable with a statement of the type

```
Dim variableName As varType = value
```

 Example 7 The following program assigns a value to a class-level variable as soon as it is created:

```
Dim pi As Double = 3.14159

Private Sub btnCompute_Click(...) Handles btnCompute.Click
  'Display the area of a circle of radius 5
  txtArea.Text = "The area of a circle of radius 5 is " & (pi * 5 * 5)
End Sub
```

[Run, and then click the button. The following is displayed in the text box.]

The area of a circle of radius 5 is 78.53975

Debugging

Programs with Sub procedures are easier to debug. Each Sub procedure can be checked individually before being placed into the program.

In Appendix D, the section "Stepping through a Program Containing a General Procedure: Chapter 4" uses the Visual Basic debugger to trace the flow through a program and observe the interplay between arguments and parameters.

Practice Problems 4.2

1. What does the following code display in the list box when the button is clicked?

```
Private Sub btnDisplay_Click(...) Handles btnDisplay.Click
  Dim b As Integer = 1, c As Integer = 2
  Rhyme()
  lstOutput.Items.Add(b & " " & c)
End Sub

Sub Rhyme()
  Dim b, c As Integer
  lstOutput.Items.Add(b & " " & c & " buckle my shoe.")
  b = 3
End Sub
```

2. Determine the output displayed in the list box when the button is clicked.

```
Private Sub btnDisplay_Click(...) Handles btnDisplay.Click
  Dim amt1 As Integer = 1, amt2 As Integer = 2
  lstOutput.Items.Add(amt1 & " " & amt2)
  Swap(amt1, amt2)
  lstOutput.Items.Add(amt1 & " " & amt2)
End Sub

Sub Swap(ByRef num1 As Integer, ByRef num2 As Integer)
  'Interchange the values of num1 and num2
  Dim temp As Integer
  temp = num1
  num1 = num2
  num2 = temp
  lstOutput.Items.Add(num1 & " " & num2)
End Sub
```

3. In Problem 2, change the Sub statement to

```
Sub Swap(ByRef num1 As Integer, ByVal num2 As Integer)
```

and determine the output.

4. In Problem 2, change the calling statement to

```
Swap((amt1), (amt2))
```

and determine the output.

EXERCISES 4.2

In Exercises 1 through 18, determine the output displayed when the button is clicked.

1.
```
Private Sub btnDisplay_Click(...) Handles btnDisplay.Click
  Dim num As Double = 7
  AddTwo(num)
  txtOutput.Text = CStr(num)
End Sub

Sub AddTwo(ByRef num As Double)
  'Add 2 to the value of num
  num += 2
End Sub
```

2.
```
Private Sub btnDisplay_Click(...) Handles btnDisplay.Click
  Dim term As String
  term = "Fall"
  Plural(term)
  txtOutput.Text = term
End Sub
```

```
Sub Plural(ByRef term As String)
  'Concatenate the letter "s" to the value of term
  term &= "s"
End Sub
```

3.
```
Private Sub btnDisplay_Click(...) Handles btnDisplay.Click
  Dim dance As String
  dance = "Can "
  Twice(dance)
  txtOutput.Text = dance
End Sub

Sub Twice(ByRef dance As String)
  'Concatenate the value of dance to itself
  dance &= dance
End Sub
```

4.
```
Private Sub btnCompute_Click(...) Handles btnCompute.Click
  Dim a As Integer = 1, b As Integer = 3
  lstOutput.Items.Add(a & " " & b)
  Combine(a, b)
  lstOutput.Items.Add(a & " " & b)
  Combine((a), b)
  lstOutput.Items.Add(a & " " & b)
End Sub

Sub Combine(ByRef x As Integer, ByVal y As Integer)
  x = y - x
  y = x + y
  lstOutput.Items.Add(x & " " & y)
End Sub
```

5.
```
Private Sub btnDisplay_Click(...) Handles btnDisplay.Click
  Dim a As Double = 5
  Square(a)
  txtOutput.Text = CStr(a)
End Sub

Sub Square(ByRef num As Double)
  num = num * num
End Sub
```

6.
```
Private Sub btnDisplay_Click(...) Handles btnDisplay.Click
  Dim state As String = "NEBRASKA"
  Abbreviate(state)
  txtOutput.Text = state
End Sub

Sub Abbreviate(ByRef a As String)
  a = a.SubString(0, 2)
End Sub
```

7.
```
Private Sub btnDisplay_Click(...) Handles btnDisplay.Click
   Dim word As String = " "
   GetWord(word)
   txtOutput.Text = "Less is " & word & "."
End Sub

Sub GetWord(ByRef w As String)
   W = "more"
End Sub
```

8.
```
Private Sub btnDisplay_Click(...) Handles btnDisplay.Click
   Dim hourlyWage, annualWage As Double
   hourlyWage = 10
   CalcAnnualWage(hourlyWage, annualWage)
   txtOutput.Text = "Approximate Annual Wage: " & _
                    FormatCurrency(annualWage)
End Sub

Sub CalcAnnualWage(ByVal hWage As Double, ByRef aWage As Double)
   aWage = 2000 * hWage
End Sub
```

9.
```
Private Sub btnDisplay_Click(...) Handles btnDisplay.Click
   Dim name As String = "", yob As Integer
   GetVita(name, yob)
   txtOutput.Text = name & " was born in the year " & yob
End Sub

Sub GetVita(ByRef name As String, ByRef yob As Integer)
   name = "Gabriel"
   yob = 1980    'Year of birth
End Sub
```

10.
```
Private Sub btnDisplay_Click(...) Handles btnDisplay.Click
   Dim word1, word2 As String
   word1 = "fail"
   word2 = "plan"
   txtOutput.Text = "If you "
   Sentence(word1, word2)
   txtOutput.Text &= ","
   Exchange(word1, word2)
   txtOutput.Text &= " then you "
   Sentence(word1, word2)
   txtOutput.Text &= "."
End Sub

Sub Exchange(ByRef word1 As String, ByRef word2 As String)
   Dim temp As String
   temp = word1
   word1 = word2
   word2 = temp
End Sub
```

```
Sub Sentence(ByVal word1 As String, ByVal word2 As String)
  txtOutput.Text &= word1 & " to " & word2
End Sub
```

11.
```
Private Sub btnDisplay_Click(...) Handles btnDisplay.Click
   Dim state As String = "Ohio "
   Team()
End Sub

Sub Team()
  Dim state As String
  txtOutput.Text = state
  txtOutput.Text &= "Buckeyes"
End Sub
```

12.
```
Private Sub btnDisplay_Click(...) Handles btnDisplay.Click
   Dim a As Double = 5
   Multiply(7)
   lstOutput.Items.Add(a * 7)
End Sub

Sub Multiply(ByRef num As Double)
  Dim a As Double
  a = 11
  lstOutput.Items.Add(a * num)
End Sub
```

13.
```
Private Sub btnDisplay_Click(...) Handles btnDisplay.Click
   Dim a As Double = 5
   Multiply(7)
End Sub

Sub Multiply(ByVal num As Double)
  Dim a As Double
  txtOutput.Text = CStr(a * num)
End Sub
```

14.
```
Private Sub btnDisplay_Click(...) Handles btnDisplay.Click
   Dim name, n As String
   name = "Ray"
   Hello(name)
   lstOutput.Items.Add(n & " and " & name)
End Sub

Sub Hello(ByRef name As String)
  Dim n As String
  n = name
  name = "Bob"
  lstOutput.Items.Add("Hello " & n & " and " & name)
End Sub
```

15. ```
    Private Sub btnDisplay_Click(...) Handles btnDisplay.Click
        Dim num As Double = 1
        Amount(num)
        Amount(num)
    End Sub

    Sub Amount(ByVal num As Double)
      Dim total As Double
      total += num 'Add the value of num to the value of total
      lstOutput.Items.Add(total)
    End Sub
    ```

16. ```
    Private Sub btnDisplay_Click(...) Handles btnDisplay.Click
        Dim river As String
        river = "Wabash"
        Another()
        lstOutput.Items.Add(river & " River")
        Another()
    End Sub

    Sub Another()
      Dim river As String
      lstOutput.Items.Add(river & " River")
      river = "Yukon"
    End Sub
    ```

17. ```
    Private Sub btnCompute_Click(...) Handles btnCompute.Click
        Dim n As Integer = 4, word As String = "overwhelming"
        lstOutput.Items.Add(n & " " & word)
        Crop(n, word)
        lstOutput.Items.Add(n & " " & word)
        Crop(n, (word))
        lstOutput.Items.Add(n & " " & word)
    End Sub

    Sub Crop(ByVal n As Integer, ByRef word As String)
      n = word.Length - n
      word = word.Substring(word.Length - n)
      lstOutput.Items.Add(n & " " & word)
    End Sub
    ```

18. ```
    Private Sub btnCompute_Click(...) Handles btnCompute.Click
        Dim tax, price, total As Double
        tax = 0.05
        GetPrice("bicycle", price)
        ProcessItem(price, tax, total)
        DisplayResult(total)
    End Sub

    Sub DisplayResult(ByVal total As Double)
      txtOutput.Text = "With tax, price is " & FormatCurrency(total)
    End Sub
    ```

```
Sub GetPrice(ByVal item As String, ByRef price As Double)
  Dim strVar As String
  strVar = InputBox("What is the price of a " & item & "?")
  price = CDbl(strVar)
End Sub

Sub ProcessItem(ByVal price As Double, ByVal tax As Double, _
                ByRef total As Double)
  total = (1 + tax) * price
End Sub
```

(Assume that the cost of the bicycle is $200.)

In Exercises 19 and 20, find the errors.

19.
```
Private Sub btnCompute_Click(...) Handles btnCompute.Click
  Dim a, b, c As Double
  a = 1
  b = 2
  Sum(a, b, c)
  txtOutput.Text = "The sum is " & c
End Sub

Sub Sum(ByVal x As Double, ByVal y As Double)
  Dim c As Double
  c = x + y
End Sub
```

20.
```
Private Sub btnDisplay_Click(...) Handles btnDisplay.Click
  Dim ano As String = ""
  GetYear(ano)
  txtOutput.Text = ano
End Sub

Sub GetYear(ByRef yr As Double)
  yr = 2006
End Sub
```

In Exercises 21 through 24, rewrite the program so input, processing, and output are each performed by calls to Sub procedures.

21.
```
Private Sub btnCompute_Click(...) Handles btnCompute.Click
  'Calculate sales tax
  Dim price, tax, cost As Double
  lstOutput.Items.Clear()
  price = CDbl(InputBox("Enter the price of the item:"))
  tax = .05 * price
  cost = price + tax
  lstOutput.Items.Add("Price:  " & price)
  lstOutput.Items.Add("Tax:    " & tax)
  lstOutput.Items.Add("-------")
  lstOutput.Items.Add("Cost:   " & cost)
End Sub
```

22.
```
Private Sub btnDisplay_Click(...) Handles bnDisplay.Click
    'Letter of acceptance
    Dim name, firstName As String, n As Integer
    lstOutput.Items.Clear()
    name = InputBox("What is your full name?")
    n = name.IndexOf(" ")
    firstName = name.Substring(0, n)
    lstOutput.Items.Add("Dear " & firstName & ",")
    lstOutput.Items.Add("")
    lstOutput.Items.Add("We are proud to accept you to Yale.")
End Sub
```

23.
```
Private Sub btnDisplay_Click(...) Handles bnDisplay.Click
    'Determine the area of a rectangle
    Dim length, width, area As Double
    length = CDbl(txtLength.Text)
    width = CDbl(txtWidth.Text)
    area = length * width
    txtOutput.Text = "The area of the rectangle is " & area
End Sub
```

24.
```
Private Sub btnCompute_Click(...) Handles btnCompute.Click
    'Convert feet and inches to centimeters
    Dim str As String
    Dim feet, inches, totalInches, centimeters As Double
    str = "Give the length in feet and inches. "
    feet = CDbl(InputBox(str & "Enter the number of feet."))
    inches = CDbl(InputBox(str & "Enter the number of inches. "))
    totalInches = 12 * feet + inches
    centimeters = 2.54 * totalInches
    txtOutput.Text = "The length in centimeters is " & centimeters
End Sub
```

In Exercises 25 and 26, write a line of code to carry out the task. Specify where in the program the line of code would occur.

25. Declare the variable *str* as a string variable visible to all parts of the program.

26. Declare the variable *str* as a string variable visible only to the btnTest_Click event procedure.

In Exercises 27 through 32, write a program to perform the stated task. The input, processing, and output should be performed by calls to Sub procedures.

27. Request a person's first name and last name as input and display the corresponding initials.

28. Request the amount of a restaurant bill as input and display the amount, the tip (15 percent), and the total amount.

29. Request the cost and selling price of an item of merchandise as input and display the percentage markup. Test the program with a cost of $4 and a selling price of $6. *Note:* The percentage markup is (selling price − cost) / cost.

30. Read the number of students in public colleges (12.1 million) and private colleges (3.7 million) from a file, and display the percentage of college students attending public colleges.

31. Read a baseball player's name (Sheffield), times at bat (557), and hits (184) from a file and display his name and batting average. **Note:** Batting average is calculated as (hits)/(times at bat).

32. Request three numbers as input, and then calculate and display the average of the three numbers.

33. The Hat Rack is considering locating its new branch store in one of three malls. The following file gives the monthly rent per square foot and the total square feet available at each of the three locations. Write a program to display a table exhibiting this information along with the total monthly rent for each mall.

    (Assume the nine lines of the file MALLS.TXT contain the following data: Green Mall, 6.50, 583, Red Mall, 7.25, 426, Blue Mall, 5.00, 823.)

34. Write a program that uses the data in the file CHARGES.TXT to display the end-of-month credit-card balances of three people. (Each set of four lines gives a person's name, beginning balance, purchases during month, and payment for the month.) The end-of-month balance is calculated as [finance charges] + [beginning-of-month balance] + [purchases] − [payment], where the finance charge is 1.5 percent of the beginning-of-month balance.

    (Assume the 12 lines of the file CHARGES.TXT contain the following data: John Adams, 125.00, 60.00, 110.00, Sue Jones, 0, 117.25, 117.25, John Smith, 350.00, 200.50, 300.00.)

35. Write a program to produce a sales receipt. Each time the user clicks on a button, an item and its price should be read from a pair of text boxes and displayed in a list box. Use a class-level variable to track the sum of the prices. When the user clicks on a second button (after all the entries have been made), the program should display the sum of the prices, the sales tax (5 percent of total), and the total amount to be paid. Figure 4.5 shows a sample output of the program.

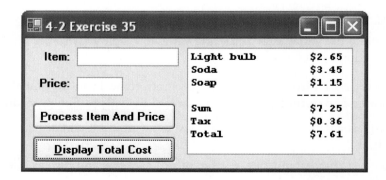

FIGURE 4.5   Sample output for Exercise 35.

Solutions to Practice Problems 4.2

1. **0 0 buckle my shoe.**
   1 2

   This program illustrates the local nature of the variables in a Sub procedure. Notice that the variables *b* and *c* appearing in the Sub procedure have no relationship whatsoever to the variables of the same name in the event procedure. In a certain sense, the variables inside the Sub procedure can be thought of as having alternate names, such as *bRhyme* and *cRhyme*.

2. **1 2**
   2 1
   2 1

   Both variables are passed by reference and so have their values changed by the Sub procedure.

3. **1 2**
   2 1
   2 2

   Here *amt1* is passed by reference and *amt2* is passed by value. Therefore, only *amt1* has its value changed by the Sub procedure.

4. **1 2**
   2 1
   1 2

   Both variables are passed by value, so their values are not changed by the Sub procedure.

4.3 Function Procedures

Visual Basic has many built-in functions. In one respect, functions are like miniature programs. They use input, they process the input, and they have output. Some functions we encountered earlier are listed in Table 4.2.

TABLE 4.2 **Some Visual Basic built-in functions.**

Function	Example	Input	Output
Int	Int(2.6) is 2	number	number
Chr	Chr(65) is "A"	number	string
Asc	Asc("Apple") is 65	string	number
FormatNumber	FormatNumber(12345.628, 1) is 12,345.6	number, number	string

Although the input can involve several values, the output always consists of a single value. The items inside the parentheses can be literals (as in Table 4.2), variables, or expressions.

In addition to using built-in functions, we can define functions of our own. These new functions, called **Function procedures** or **user-defined functions**, are defined in much the same way as Sub procedures and are used in the same way as built-in functions. Like built-in functions, Function procedures have a single output that can be of any data type. Function procedures can be used in expressions in exactly the same way as built-in functions. Programs refer to them as if they were literals, variables, or expressions. Function procedures are defined by function blocks of the form

```
Function FunctionName(ByVal var1 As Type1, _
                      ByVal var2 As Type2, ...) As DataType
    statement(s)
    Return expression
End Function
```

The variables appearing in the top line are called **parameters**. Variables declared by statements inside the function block have local scope. Function names should be suggestive of the role performed and must conform to the rules for naming variables. The type *DataType*, which specifies the type of the output, will be one of String, Integer, Double, and so on. In the preceding general code, the next-to-last line specifies the output, which must be of type *DataType*. Like Sub procedures, Function procedures are typed directly into the Code window. (The last line, End Function, will appear automatically after the first line is entered into the Code window.) A variable passed to a Function procedure is normally passed by value. It can also be passed by reference and thereby possibly have its value changed by the Function procedure. However, passing a variable by reference violates good design principles, since a function is intended to only create a single result and not cause any other changes.

Two examples of Function procedures are as follows:

```
Function FtoC(ByVal t As Double) As Double
    'Convert Fahrenheit temperature to Celsius
    Return (5 / 9) * (t - 32)
End Function

Function FirstName(ByVal name As String) As String
    'Extract the first name from a full name
    Dim firstSpace As Integer
    firstSpace = name.IndexOf(" ")
    Return name.Substring(0, firstSpace)
End Function
```

The value of each of the preceding functions is assigned by a statement of the form **Return** *expression*. The variables *t* and *name* appearing in the preceding functions are parameters. They can be replaced with any variable of the same type without affecting the function definition. For instance, the function FtoC could have been defined as

```
Function FtoC(ByVal temp As Double) As Double
    'Convert Fahrenheit temperature to Celsius
    Return (5 / 9) * (temp - 32)
End Function
```

Example 1 The following program uses the function FtoC.

OBJECT	PROPERTY	SETTING
frmConvert	Text	Convert Fahrenheit to Celsius
lblTempF	Text	Temperature (Fahrenheit)
txtTempF		
btnConvert	Text	Convert to Celsius
lblTempC	Text	Temperature (Celsius)
txtTempC	ReadOnly	True

```
Private Sub btnConvert_Click(...) Handles btnConvert.Click
  Dim fahrenheitTemp, celsiusTemp As Double
  fahrenheitTemp = CDbl(txtTempF.Text)
  celsiusTemp = FtoC(fahrenheitTemp)
  txtTempC.Text = CStr(celsiusTemp)
  'Note: The above four lines can be replaced with the single line
  'txtTempC.Text = CStr(FtoC(CDbl(txtTempF.Text)))
End Sub

Function FtoC(ByVal t As Double) As Double
  'Convert Fahrenheit temperature to Celsius
  Return (5 / 9) * (t - 32)
End Function
```

[Run, type 212 into the text box, and then click the button.]

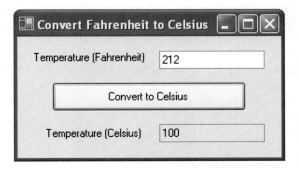

 Example 2 The following program uses the function FirstName.

OBJECT	PROPERTY	SETTING
frmFirstName	Text	Extract First Name
lblName	Text	Name
txtFullName		
btnDetermine	Text	Determine First Name
txtFirstName	ReadOnly	True

```vb
Private Sub btnDetermine_Click(...) Handles btnDetermine.Click
  'Determine a person's first name
  Dim name As String
  name = txtFullName.Text
  txtFirstName.Text = FirstName(name)
End Sub

Function FirstName(ByVal name As String) As String
  'Extract the first name from a full name
  Dim firstSpace As Integer
  firstSpace = name.IndexOf(" ")
  Return name.Substring(0, firstSpace)
End Function
```

[Run, type Thomas Woodrow Wilson into the text box, and then click the button.]

User-Defined Functions Having Several Parameters

The input to a user-defined function can consist of one or more values. Two examples of functions with several parameters follow. One-letter variable names have been used so the mathematical formulas will look familiar and be readable. Because the names are not descriptive, the meanings of these variables are carefully spelled out in comment statements.

```vb
Function Hypotenuse(ByVal a As Double, ByVal b As Double) As Double
  'Calculate the hypotenuse of a right triangle
  'having sides of lengths a and b
  Return Math.Sqrt(a ^ 2 + b ^ 2)
End Function

Function FutureValue(ByVal p As Double, ByVal r As Double, _
          ByVal c As Double, ByVal n As Double) As Double
  'Find the future value of a bank savings account
  'p principal, the amount deposited
  'r annual rate of interest
  'c number of times interest is compounded per year
  'n number of years
  Dim i As Double  'interest rate per period
  Dim m As Double  'total number of times interest is compounded
  i = r / c
  m = c * n
  Return p * ((1 + i) ^ m)
End Function
```

Example 3 The following program uses the Hypotenuse function.

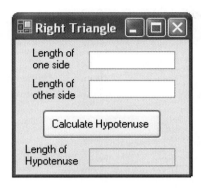

OBJECT	PROPERTY	SETTING
frmPythagoras	Text	Right Triangle
lblSideOne	AutoSize	False
	Text	Length of one side
txtSideOne		
lblSideTwo	AutoSize	False
	Text	Length of other side
txtSideTwo		
btnCalculate	Text	Calculate Hypotenuse
lblHyp	AutoSize	False
	Text	Length of Hypotenuse
txtHyp	ReadOnly	True

```
Private Sub btnCalculate_Click(...) Handles btnCalculate.Click
    'Calculate the length of the hypotenuse of a right triangle
    Dim a, b As Double
    a = CDbl(txtSideOne.Text)
    b = CDbl(txtSideTwo.Text)
    txtHyp.Text = CStr(Hypotenuse(a, b))
End Sub

Function Hypotenuse(ByVal a As Double, ByVal b As Double) As Double
    'Calculate the hypotenuse of a right triangle
    'having sides of lengths a and b
    Return Math.Sqrt(a ^ 2 + b ^ 2)
End Function
```

[Run, type 3 and 4 into the text boxes, and then click the button.]

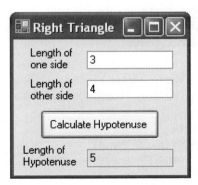

 Example 4 The following program uses the future value function. With the responses shown, the program computes the balance in a savings account when $100 is deposited for five years at 4% interest compounded quarterly. Interest is earned four times per year at the rate of 1% per interest period. There will be 4 * 5, or 20, interest periods.

OBJECT	PROPERTY	SETTING
frmBank	Text	Bank Deposit
lblAmount	Text	Amount of bank deposit:
txtAmount		
lblRate	Text	Annual rate of interest:
txtRate		
lblNumComp	AutoSize	False
	Text	Number of times interest is compounded per year:
txtNumComp		
lblNumYrs	Text	Number of years:
txtNumYrs		
btnCompute	Text	Compute Balance
lblBalance	Text	Balance:
txtBalance	ReadOnly	True

```
Private Sub btnCompute_Click(...) Handles btnCompute.Click
  'Find the future value of a bank deposit
  Dim p As Double    'principal, the amount deposited
  Dim r As Double    'annual rate of interest
  Dim c As Double    'number of times interest is compounded per year
  Dim n As Double    'number of years
  InputData(p, r, c, n)
  DisplayBalance(p, r, c, n)
End Sub

Sub InputData(ByRef p As Double, ByRef r As Double, _
              ByRef c As Double, ByRef n As Double)
    'Get the four values from the text boxes
    p = CDbl(txtAmount.Text)
    r = CDbl(txtRate.Text)
    c = CDbl(txtNumComp.Text)
    n = CDbl(txtNumYrs.Text)
End Sub

Sub DisplayBalance(ByVal p As Double, ByVal r As Double, _
                   ByVal c As Double, ByVal n As Double)
  'Display the balance in a text box
  Dim balance As Double
  balance = FutureValue(p, r, c, n)
  txtbalance.Text = FormatCurrency(balance)
End Sub

Function FutureValue(ByVal p As Double, ByVal r As Double, _
                     ByVal c As Double, ByVal n As Double) As Double
  'Find the future value of a bank savings account
  'p  principal, the amount deposited
  'r  annual rate of interest
  'c  number of times interest is compounded per year
  'n  number of years
```

```
    Dim i As Double      'interest rate per period
    Dim m As Double      'total number of times interest is compounded
    i = r / c
    m = c * n
    Return p * ((1 + i) ^ m)
End Function
```

[Run, type 100, .04, 4, and 5 into the text boxes, then click the button.]

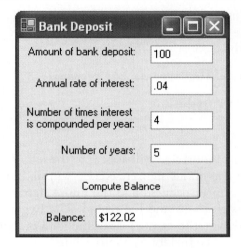

User-Defined Functions Having No Parameters

Function procedures, like Sub procedures, need not have any parameters.

 Example 5   The following program uses a parameterless function.

```
Private Sub btnDisplay_Click(...) Handles btnDisplay.Click
    'Request and display a saying
    txtBox.Text = Saying()
End Sub

Function Saying() As String
    'Retrieve a saying from the user
    Return InputBox("What is your favorite saying?")
End Function
```

[Run, click the button, and then type "Less is more." into the message box.]
   The saying "Less is more." is displayed in the text box.

Comparing Function Procedures with Sub Procedures

Function procedures differ from Sub procedures in the way they are accessed. Sub procedures are invoked with call statements, whereas functions are invoked by placing them where you would otherwise expect to find a literal, variable, or expression. Unlike a Function procedure, a Sub procedure can't be used in an expression.

   Function procedures can perform the same tasks as Sub procedures. For instance, they can request input and display text. However, Function procedures are primarily used to calculate a single value. Normally, Sub procedures are used to carry out other tasks.

The Sub procedures considered in this book terminate only when End Sub is reached. On the other hand, Function procedures terminate as soon as the first Return statement is executed. For instance, if a Return statement is followed by a sequence of statements and the Return statement is executed, then the sequence of statements will not be executed.

■ Collapsing a Procedure with a Region Directive

A group of procedures or class-level variables can be collapsed behind a captioned rectangle. This task is carried out with a so-called **Region directive**. To specify a region, precede the code to be collapsed with a line of the form

```
#Region "Text to be displayed in the rectangle."
```

and follow the code with the line

```
#End Region
```

A tiny box holding a minus sign will appear to the left of the #Region line. To collapse the code, click on the minus sign. The code will be hidden behind a rectangle captioned with the text you specified and the minus sign will be replaced by a plus sign. Click on the plus sign to expand the region. The Region directive is used to make a program more readable or to create an outline for a program. In Figure 4.6(a), Region directives have been specified for each procedure in Example 5. In Figure 4.6(b), these two regions have been collapsed.

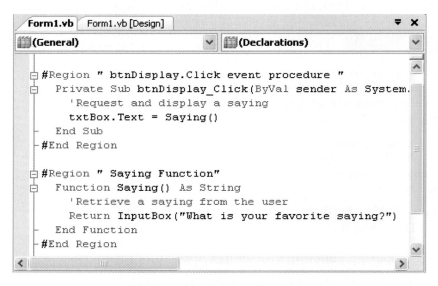

FIGURE 4.6(a)   Region directives.

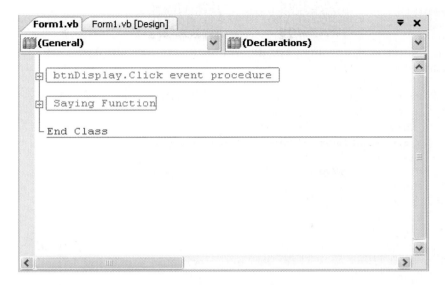

FIGURE 4.6(b) Collapsed regions.

Practice Problems 4.3

1. Suppose a program contains the lines

```
Dim n As Double, x As String
lstOutput.Items.Add(Arc(n, x))
```

What types of inputs (numeric or string) and output does the function Arc have?

2. What is displayed in the text box when btnCompute is clicked?

```
Private Sub btnCompute_Click(...) Handles btnCompute.Click
  'How many gallons of apple cider can we make?
  Dim gallonsPerBushel, apples As Double
  GetData(gallonsPerBushel, apples)
  DisplayNumOfGallons(gallonsPerBushel, apples)
End Sub

Function Cider(ByVal g As Double, ByVal x As Double) As Double
  Return g * x
End Function

Sub DisplayNumOfGallons(ByVal galPerBu As Double, _
                        ByVal apples As Double)
  txtOutput.Text = "You can make " & Cider(galPerBu, apples) _
                 & " gallons of cider."
End Sub

Sub GetData(ByRef gallonsPerBushel As Double, _
            ByRef apples As Double)
  'gallonsPerBushel Number of gallons of cider one bushel
  'of apples makes
  'apples          Number of bushels of apples available
  gallonsPerBushel = 3
  apples = 9
End Sub
```

EXERCISES 4.3

In Exercises 1 through 10, determine the output displayed when the button is clicked.

1.
```
Private Sub btnConvert_Click(...) Handles btnConvert.Click
    'Convert Celsius to Fahrenheit
    Dim temp As Double = 95
    txtOutput.Text = CStr(CtoF(temp))
End Sub

Function CtoF(ByVal t As Double) As Double
  Return (9 / 5) * t + 32
End Function
```

2.
```
Private Sub btnDisplay_Click(...) Handles btnDisplay.Click
    Dim acres As Double 'Number of acres in a parking lot
    acres = 5
    txtOutput.Text = "You can park about " & Cars(acres) & " cars."
End Sub

Function Cars(ByVal x As Double) As Double
  'Number of cars that can be parked
  Return 100 * x
End Function
```

3.
```
Private Sub btnDisplay_Click(...) Handles btnDisplay.Click
    'Rule of 72
    Dim p As Double
    p = CDbl(txtPopGr.Text) 'Population growth as a percent
    txtOutput.Text = "The population will double in " & _
                     DoublingTime(p) & " years."
End Sub

Function DoublingTime(ByVal x As Double) As Double
  'Estimate time required for a population to double
  'at a growth rate of x percent
  Return 72 / x
End Function
```

(Assume the text box txtPopGr contains the number 3.)

4.
```
Private Sub btnDisplay_Click(...) Handles btnDisplay.Click
    'Calculate max. ht. of a ball thrown straight up in the air
    Dim initVel, initHt As Double
    initVel = CDbl(txtVel.Text) 'Initial velocity of ball
    initHt = CDbl(txtHt.Text)    'Initial height of ball
    txtOutput.Text = CStr(MaximumHeight(initVel, initHt))
End Sub
```

```
Function MaximumHeight(ByVal v As Double, ByVal h As Double) _
                    As Double
    Return h + (v ^ 2 / 64)
End Function
```

(Assume the text boxes contain the values 96 and 256.)

5.
```
Private Sub btnDisplay_Click(...) Handles btnDisplay.Click
    'Compute volume of a cylinder
    Dim r As Double = 1    'Radius
    Dim h As Double = 2    'Height
    DisplayVolume(r, h)
    r = 3
    h = 4
    DisplayVolume(r, h)
End Sub

Function Area(ByVal r As Double) As Double
    'Compute area of a circle of radius r
    Return 3.14159 * r ^ 2
End Function

Sub DisplayVolume(ByVal r As Double, ByVal h As Double)
    lstBox.Items.Add("Volume of cylinder having base area " & _
        Area(r) & " and height " & h & " is " & (h * Area(r)))
End Sub
```

6.
```
Private Sub btnDisplay_Click(...) Handles btnDisplay.Click
    'Determine the day of the week from its number
    Dim days As String, num As Integer
    days = "SunMonTueWedThuFriSat"
    num = CInt(InputBox("Enter the number of the day."))
    txtOutput.Text = "The day is " & DayOfWk(days, num) & "."
End Sub

Function DayOfWk(ByVal x As String, ByVal n As Integer) As String
    'x String containing 3-letter abbreviations of days
    'n The number of the day
    Dim position As Integer
    position = 3 * n - 3
    Return x.Substring(position, 3)
End Function
```

(Assume the response is 4.)

7.
```
Private Sub btnDisplay_Click(...) Handles btnDisplay.Click
    'Demonstrate local variables
    Dim word As String = "Choo "
    txtOutput.Text = TypeOfTrain()
End Sub
```

```
Function TypeOfTrain() As String
  'Concatenate the value of word with itself
  Dim word As String
  word &= word
  Return word & "train"
End Function
```

8.
```
Private Sub btnDisplay_Click(...) Handles btnDisplay.Click
  'Triple a number
  Dim num As Double = 5
  lstOutput.Items.Add(Triple(num))
  lstOutput.Items.Add(num)
End Sub

Function Triple(ByVal x As Double) As Double
  Dim num As Double = 3
  Return num * x
End Function
```

9.
```
Private Sub btnDisplay_Click(...) Handles btnDisplay.Click
  Dim word As String
  word = "moral"
  Negative(word)
  word = "political"
  Negative(word)
End Sub

Function AddA(ByVal word As String) As String
  Return "a" & word
End Function

Sub Negative(ByVal word As String)
  lstOutput.Items.Add(word & " has the negative " & AddA(word))
End Sub
```

10.
```
Private Sub btnDisplay_Click(...) Handles btnDisplay.Click
  Dim city As String, pop, shrinks As Double
  Dim sr As IO.StreamReader = IO.File.OpenText("DOCS.TXT")
  city = sr.ReadLine
  pop = CDbl(sr.ReadLine)
  shrinks = CDbl(sr.ReadLine)
  DisplayData(city, pop, shrinks)
  city = sr.ReadLine
  pop = CDbl(sr.ReadLine)
  shrinks = CDbl(sr.ReadLine)
  sr.Close()
  DisplayData(city, pop, shrinks)
End Sub

Sub DisplayData(ByVal city As String, ByVal pop As Double, _
            ByVal shrinks As Double)
  lstBox.Items.Add(city & " has " & ShrinkDensity(pop, shrinks) _
                & " psychiatrists per 100,000 people.")
End Sub
```

```
Function ShrinkDensity(ByVal pop As Double, _
                       ByVal shrinks As Double) As Double
  Return Int(100000 * (shrinks / pop))
End Function
```

(Assume the six lines of the file DOCS.TXT contain the following data: Boston, 2824000, 8602, Denver, 1633000, 3217.)

In Exercises 11 and 12, identify the errors.

11.
```
Private Sub btnDisplay_Click(...) Handles btnDisplay.Click
    'Select a greeting
    Dim answer As Integer
    answer = CInt(InputBox("Enter 1 or 2."))
    txtOutput.Text = CStr(Greeting(answer))
End Sub

Function Greeting(ByVal x As Integer) As Integer
  Return "hellohi ya".Substring(5 * (x − 1), 5)
End Function
```

12.
```
Private Sub btnDisplay_Click(...) Handles btnDisplay.Click
    Dim word As String
    word = InputBox("What is your favorite word?")
    txtOutput.Text = "When the word is written twice, " & _
                    Twice(word) & " letters are used."
End Sub

Function Twice(ByVal w As String) As Integer
  'Compute twice the length of a string
  Dim len As Integer
  Return len = 2 * w.Length
End Function
```

In Exercises 13 through 21, construct user-defined functions to carry out the primary task(s) of the program.

13. To determine the number of square centimeters of tin needed to make a tin can, add the square of the radius of the can to the product of the radius and height of the can, and then multiply this sum by 6.283. Write a program that requests the radius and height of a tin can in centimeters as input and displays the number of square centimeters required to make the can.

14. According to Plato, a man should marry a woman whose age is half his age plus seven years. Write a program that requests a man's age as input and gives the ideal age of his wife.

15. The federal government developed the body mass index (BMI) to determine ideal weights. Body mass index is calculated as 703 times the weight in pounds, divided by the square of the height in inches, and then rounded to the nearest whole number. Write a program that accepts a person's weight and height as input and gives the person's body mass index. **Note:** A BMI of 19 to 25 corresponds to a healthy weight.

16. In order for exercise to be beneficial to the cardiovascular system, the heart rate (number of heart beats per minute) must exceed a value called the *training heart rate*, THR. A person's THR can be calculated from his age and resting heart rate (pulse when first awakening) as follows:

(a) Calculate the maximum heart rate as 220 − age.
(b) Subtract the resting heart rate from the maximum heart rate.
(c) Multiply the result in step (b) by 60%, and then add the resting heart rate.

Write a program to request a person's age and resting heart rate as input and display their THR. (Test the program with an age of 20 and a resting heart rate of 70, and then determine *your* training heart rate.)

17. The three ingredients for a serving of popcorn at a movie theater are popcorn, butter substitute, and a bucket. Write a program that requests the cost of these three items and the price of the serving as input and then displays the profit. (Test the program where popcorn costs 5 cents, butter substitute costs 2 cents, the bucket costs 25 cents, and the selling price is $5.)

18. Rewrite the population-density program from Example 4 of Section 4.1 using a function to calculate the population density.

19. The original cost of airmail letters was 5 cents for the first ounce and 10 cents for each additional ounce. Write a program to compute the cost of a letter whose weight is given by the user in a text box. Use a function called Ceil that rounds noninteger numbers up to the next integer. The function Ceil can be defined by Ceil(x) = −Int(−x). (Test the program with the weights 4, 1, 2.5, and .5 ounces.)

20. Suppose a fixed amount of money is deposited at the beginning of each month into a savings account paying 6% interest compounded monthly. After each deposit is made, [new balance] = 1.005 * [previous balance one month ago] + [fixed amount]. Write a program that requests the fixed amount of the deposits as input and displays the balance after each of the first four deposits. A sample outcome when 800 is typed into the text box for the amount deposited each month follows.

```
Month 1      800.00
Month 2    1,604.00
Month 3    2,412.02
Month 4    3,224.08
```

21. Write a program to request the name of a United States senator as input and display the address and greeting for a letter to the senator. Assume the name has two parts, and use a function to determine the senator's last name. A sample outcome when Robert Smith is typed into the input dialog box requesting the senator's name follows.

```
The Honorable Robert Smith
United States Senate
Washington, DC 20001

Dear Senator Smith,
```

Solutions to Practice Problems 4.3

1. The first argument, *n*, takes a value of type Double and the second argument, *x*, takes a String value; therefore, the input consists of a number and a string. From the two lines shown here, there is no way to determine the type of the output. This can be determined only by looking at the definition of the function.

2. **You can make 27 gallons of cider** In this program, the function was called by a Sub procedure rather than by an event procedure.

4.4 Modular Design

▨ Top-Down Design

Full-featured software usually requires large programs. Writing the code for an event procedure in such a Visual Basic program might pose a complicated problem. One method programmers use to make a complicated problem more understandable is to divide it into smaller, less complex subproblems. Repeatedly using a "divide-and-conquer" approach to break up a large problem into smaller subproblems is called **stepwise refinement**. Stepwise refinement is part of a larger methodology of writing programs known as **top-down design.** The term top-down refers to the fact that the more general tasks occur near the top of the design and tasks representing their refinement occur below. Top-down design and structured programming emerged as techniques to enhance programming productivity. Their use leads to programs that are easier to read and maintain. They also produce programs containing fewer initial errors, with these errors being easier to find and correct. When such programs are later modified, there is a much smaller likelihood of introducing new errors.

The goal of top-down design is to break a problem into individual tasks, or modules, that can easily be transcribed into pseudocode, flowcharts, or a program. First, a problem is restated as several simpler problems depicted as modules. Any modules that remain too complex are broken down further. The process of refining modules continues until the smallest modules can be coded directly. Each stage of refinement adds a more complete specification of what tasks must be performed. The main idea in top-down design is to go from the general to the specific. This process of dividing and organizing a problem into tasks can be pictured using a hierarchy chart. When using top-down design, certain criteria should be met:

1. The design should be easily readable and emphasize small module size.
2. Modules proceed from general to specific as you read down the chart.
3. The modules, as much as possible, should be single minded. That is, they should only perform a single well-defined task.
4. Modules should be independent of each other as much as possible, and any relationships among modules should be specified.

This process is illustrated with the following example.

Example 1   The chart in Figure 4.7 is a hierarchy chart for a program that gives certain information about a car loan. The inputs are the amount of the loan, the duration (in years), and the interest rate. The output consists of the monthly payment and the amount of interest paid during the first month. In the broadest sense, the program calls for obtaining the input, making calculations, and displaying the output. Figure 4.7 shows these tasks as the first row of a hierarchy chart.

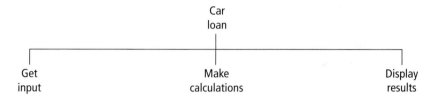

FIGURE 4.7   Beginning of a hierarchy chart for the car loan program.

Each of these tasks can be refined into more specific subtasks. (See Figure 4.8 for the final hierarchy chart.) Most of the subtasks in the third row are straightforward and so do not require further refinement. For instance, the first month's interest is computed by multiplying the amount of the loan by one-twelfth of the annual rate of interest. The most complicated subtask, the computation of the monthly payment, has been broken down further. This task is carried out by applying a standard formula found in finance books; however, the formula requires the number of payments.

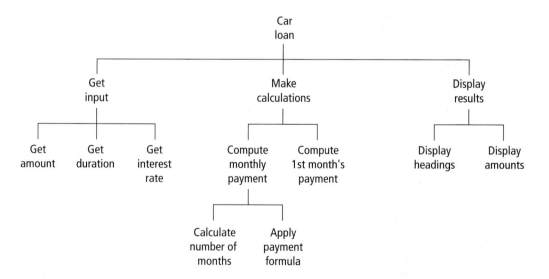

FIGURE 4.8   Hierarchy chart for the car loan program.

It is clear from the hierarchy chart that the top modules manipulate the modules beneath them. While the higher-level modules control the flow of the program, the lower-level modules do the actual work. By designing the top modules first, specific processing decisions can be delayed.

▦ Structured Programming

A program is said to be **structured** if it meets modern standards of program design. Although there is no formal definition of the term **structured program**, computer scientists are in uniform agreement that such programs should have modular design and use only the three types of logical structures discussed in Chapter 2: sequences, decisions, and loops.

Sequences: Statements are executed one after another.

Decisions: One of several blocks of program code is executed based on a test for some condition.

Loops (iteration): One or more statements are executed repeatedly as long as a specified condition is true.

Chapters 5 and 6 are devoted to decisions and loops, respectively.

One major shortcoming of the earliest programming languages was their reliance on the GoTo statement. This statement was used to branch (that is, jump) from one line of a program to another. It was common for a program to be composed of a convoluted tangle of branchings that produced confusing code referred to as spaghetti code. At the heart of structured programming is the assertion of E. W. Dijkstra that GoTo statements should be eliminated entirely because they lead to complex and confusing programs. Two Italians, C. Bohm and G. Jacopini, were able to prove that GoTo statements are not needed and that any program can be written using only the three types of logic structures discussed before.

Structured programming requires that all programs be written using sequences, decisions, and loops. Nesting of such statements is allowed. All other logical constructs, such as GoTos, are not allowed. The logic of a structured program can be pictured using a flowchart that flows smoothly from top to bottom without unstructured branching (GoTos). The portion of a flowchart shown in Figure 4.9(a) (on the next page) contains the equivalent of a GoTo statement and, therefore, is not structured. A correctly structured version of the flowchart in which the logic flows from the top to the bottom appears in Figure 4.9(b).

▦ Advantages of Structured Programming

The goal of structured programming is to create correct programs that are easy to write, understand, and change. Let us now take a closer look at the way modular design, along with a limited number of logical structures, contributes to attaining these goals.

1. *Easy to write.*

    Modular design increases the programmer's productivity by allowing him or her to look at the big picture first and focus on the details later. During the actual coding, the programmer works with a manageable chunk of the program and does not have to think about an entire complex program.

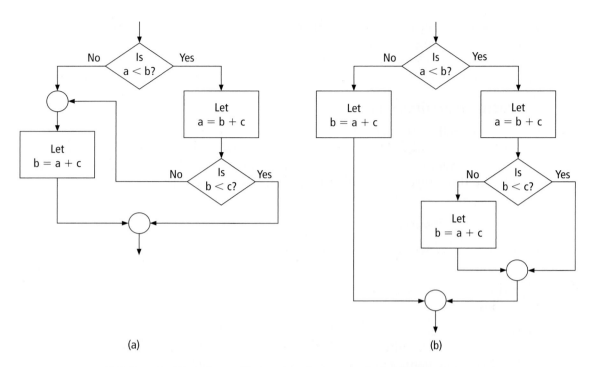

(a)   (b)

FIGURE 4.9   **Flowcharts illustrating the removal of a GoTo statement.**

Several programmers can work on a single large program, each taking responsibility for a specific module.

Studies have shown structured programs require significantly less time to write than standard programs.

Often, procedures written for one program can be reused in other programs requiring the same task. Not only is time saved in writing a program, but reliability is enhanced, because reused procedures will already be tested and debugged. A procedure that can be used in many programs is said to be **reusable**.

2. *Easy to debug.*

Because each procedure is specialized to perform just one task or several related tasks, a procedure can be checked individually to determine its reliability. A dummy program, called a **driver**, is set up to test the procedure. The driver contains the minimum definitions needed to call the procedure to be tested. For instance, if the procedure to be tested is a function, the driver program assigns diverse values to the arguments and then examines the corresponding function return values. The arguments should contain both typical and special-case values.

The program can be tested and debugged as it is being designed with a technique known as **stub programming**. In this technique, the key event procedures and perhaps some of the smaller procedures are coded first. Dummy procedures, or stubs, are written for the remaining procedures. Initially, a stub procedure might consist of a message box to indicate that the procedure has been called, and thereby confirm that the procedure was called at the right time. Later, a stub might simply display values passed to it in order to confirm not only that the procedure was called, but also that it received the correct values from the calling procedure. A stub also can assign new values to one or more of its parameters to simulate either input or computation. This provides greater control of the conditions being tested. The stub procedure is always simpler than the actual procedure it represents. Although the stub program is only a skeleton of the final program, the program's structure can still be debugged and tested. (The stub program consists of some coded procedures and the stub procedures.)

Old-fashioned unstructured programs consist of a sequence of instructions that are not grouped for specific tasks. The logic of such a program is cluttered with details and therefore difficult to follow. Needed tasks are easily left out and crucial details easily neglected. Tricky parts of the program cannot be isolated and examined. Bugs are difficult to locate because they might be present in any part of the program.

3. *Easy to understand.*

The interconnections of the procedures reveal the modular design of the program.

The meaningful procedure names, along with relevant comments, identify the tasks performed by the modules.

The meaningful variable names help the programmer to recall the purpose of each variable.

4. *Easy to change.*

Because a structured program is self-documenting, it can easily be deciphered by another programmer.

Modifying a structured program often amounts to inserting or altering a few procedures rather than revising an entire complex program. The programmer does not even have to look at most of the program.

▓ Object-Oriented Programming

An object is an encapsulation of data and code that operates on the data. Like controls, objects have properties, respond to methods, and raise events. The most effective type of programming for complex problems is called **object-oriented** design. An object-oriented program can be viewed as a collection of cooperating objects. Most modern programmers use a blend of traditional structured programming along with object-oriented design.

Visual Basic.NET was the first version of Visual Basic that was truly object-oriented; in fact, every element such as a control or a String is actually an object. This book illustrates the building blocks of Visual Basic in the initial chapters and then puts them together using object-oriented techniques in Chapter 11. Throughout the book, an object-oriented approach is taken whenever feasible.

■ A Relevant Quote

We end this section with a few paragraphs from *Dirk Gently's Holistic Detective Agency*, by Douglas Adams, Pocketbooks, 1987:

"What really is the point of trying to teach anything to anybody?"

This question seemed to provoke a murmur of sympathetic approval from up and down the table.

Richard continued, "What I mean is that if you really want to understand something, the best way is to try and explain it to someone else. That forces you to sort it out in your own mind. And the more slow and dim-witted your pupil, the more you have to break things down into more and more simple ideas. And that's really the essence of programming. By the time you've sorted out a complicated idea into little steps that even a stupid machine can deal with, you've certainly learned something about it yourself. The teacher usually learns more than the pupil. Isn't that true?"

CHAPTER 4   SUMMARY

1. A *general procedure* is a portion of a program that is accessed by event procedures or other general procedures. The two types of general procedures are *Sub procedures* and *Function procedures*.

2. *Sub procedures* are defined in blocks beginning with Sub statements and ending with End Sub statements. A Sub procedure is accessed (called) by a statement consisting of the name of the procedure.

3. *Function procedures* are defined in blocks beginning with Function statements and ending with End Function statements. A function is invoked by a reference in an expression and returns a value.

4. In any procedure, the *arguments* appearing in the calling statement must match the *parameters* of the Sub or Function statement in number, type, and order. They need not match in name.

5. A variable declared in the Declarations section of the Code window is *class-level*. Such a variable is available to every procedure in the form's code and retains its value from one procedure invocation to the next.

6. Variables declared with a Dim statement inside a procedure are *local* to the procedure. The values of these variables are reinitialized each time the procedure is called. A variable with the same name appearing in another part of the program is treated as a different variable.

7. *Structured programming* uses modular design to refine large problems into smaller subproblems. Programs are coded using the three logical structures of sequences, decisions, and loops.

CHAPTER 4   PROGRAMMING PROJECTS

1. The numbers of calories per gram of carbohydrate, fat, and protein are 4, 9, and 4, respectively. Write a program that requests the nutritional content of a serving of food and displays the number of calories in the serving. The input and output should be handled by Sub procedures and the calories computed by a function. A sample run for a typical breakfast cereal is shown in Figure 4.10.

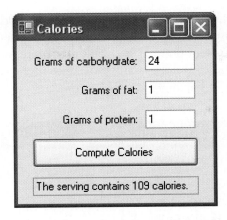

FIGURE 4.10   **Sample run for Programming Project 1.**

2. Annually, 1.7 billion dollars worth of toothpaste are sold each year in the United States. Table 4.3 gives the market share for the four top brands. Write a program that displays the annual sales (in millions of dollars) for each of the top four. The input and output should be handled by Sub procedures and the annual sales calculated by a Function procedure.

TABLE 4.3   **2001 market shares of the top-selling toothpaste brands.**

Company	Market Share
Crest	19.4%
Colgate	17.2%
Aquafresh	8.0%
Colgate Total	6.6%

Source: The World Almanac and Book of Facts 2002.

3. Table 4.4 gives the research and development budgets (in billions of dollars) for four departments of the federal government for the years 2004 and 2005. Write a program that displays the percentage change in the budget for each department. Sub procedures should be used for input and output, and the percentage change should be computed with a Function procedure. **Note:** The percentage change is ([2005 budget] − [2004 budget])/[2004 budget].

TABLE 4.4   **Research and development budget for several departments.**

Department	2004 Budget	2005 Budget
Defense	65.6	70.3
Health and Human Services	28.5	29.1
NASA	10.9	11.1
Homeland Security	1.0	1.2

Source: American Association for the Advancement of Science.

4. A fast-food vendor sells pizza slices ($1.25), fries ($1.00), and soft drinks ($.75). Write a program to compute a customer's bill. The program should request the quantity of each item ordered in a Sub procedure, calculate the total cost with a Function procedure, and use a Sub procedure to display an itemized bill. A sample output is shown in Figure 4.11.

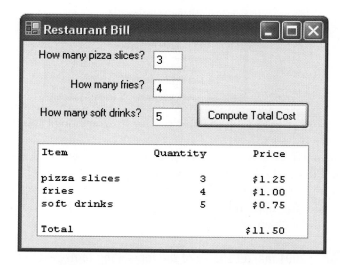

FIGURE 4.11   Sample run for Programming Project 4.

5. Write a program to generate a business travel expense attachment for an income-tax return. The program should request as input the name of the organization visited, the date and location of the visit, and the expenses for meals and entertainment, airplane fare, lodging, and taxi fares. (Only 50% of the expenses for meals and entertainment are deductible.) A possible form layout and run are shown in Figures 4.12 and 4.13, respectively. The output is displayed in a list box that becomes visible when the button is clicked. Sub procedures should be used for the input and output.

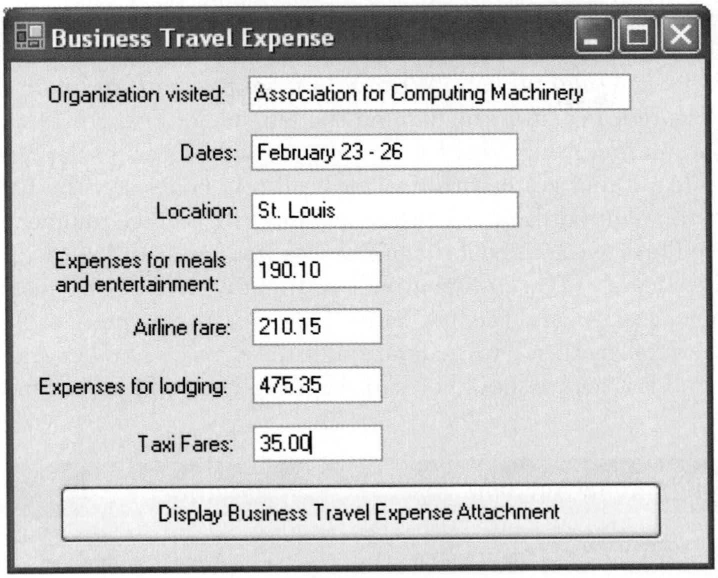

FIGURE 4.12   Form with sample data for Programming Project 5.

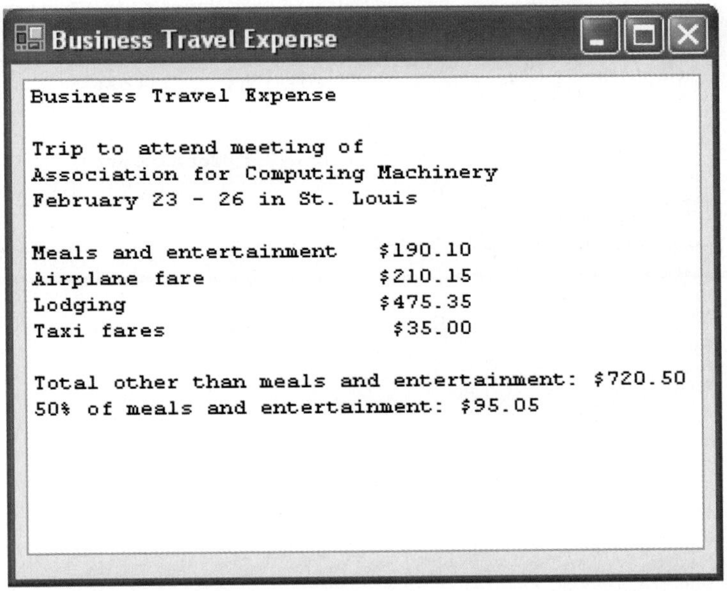

FIGURE 4.13   Output in list box for sample run of Programming Project 5.

6. A furniture manufacturer makes two types of furniture—chairs and sofas. The file PRICE&TAXDATA.TXT contains three numbers giving the cost per chair, cost per sofa, and sales tax rate. Write a program to create an invoice form for an order. See Figure 4.14. After the data on the left side of Figure 4.14 are entered, you can display an invoice in a list box by pressing the Process Order button. You can press the Clear Order Form button to clear all text boxes and the list box, and you can press the Quit button to exit the program. The invoice number consists of the capitalized first two letters of the customer's last name, followed by the last four digits of the zip code. The customer name is input with the last name first, followed by a comma, a space, and the first name. However, the name is displayed in the invoice in the proper order. The generation of the invoice number and the reorder of the first and last names should be carried out in Function procedures.

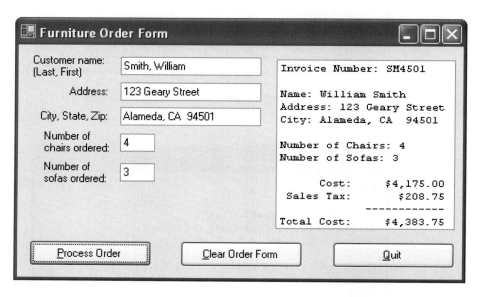

FIGURE 4.14   **Sample run for Programming Project 6.**

5

Decisions

5.1 Relational and Logical Operators 194

 ◆ ANSI Values ◆ Logical Operators ◆ Boolean Data Type

5.2 If Blocks 201

 ◆ If Block ◆ ElseIf Clauses

5.3 Select Case Blocks 218

5.4 A Case Study: Weekly Payroll 235

 ◆ Designing the Weekly Payroll Program ◆ Pseudocode for the
 Display Payroll Event ◆ Writing the Weekly Payroll Program
 ◆ The Program and the User Interface

Summary 243

Programming Projects 243

5.1   Relational and Logical Operators

In Chapter 2, we discussed the two logical programming constructs *decision* and *loop*. In order to make a decision or control a loop, you need to specify a condition that determines the course of action.

A **condition** is an expression involving relational operators (such as < and =) that is either true or false. Conditions also may incorporate logical operators (such as And, Or, and Not). ANSI values determine the order used to compare strings with the relational operators. Boolean variables and literals can assume the values True or False.

▧ ANSI Values

Each of the 47 different keys in the center typewriter portion of the keyboard can produce two characters, for a total of 94 characters. Adding 1 for the space character produced by the space bar makes 95 characters. These characters have numbers ranging from 32 to 126 associated with them. These values, called the ANSI (or ASCII) values of the characters, are given in Appendix A. Table 5.1 shows a few of the values.

TABLE 5.1   A few ANSI values.

32 (space)	48 0	66 B	122 z
33 !	49 1	90 Z	123 {
34 "	57 9	97 a	125 }
35 #	65 A	98 b	126 ~

Most of the best known fonts, such as Courier New, Microsoft San Serif, and Times New Roman, are essentially governed by the ANSI standard, which assigns characters to the numbers from 0 to 255. Table 5.2 shows a few of the higher ANSI values.

TABLE 5.2   A few higher ANSI values.

162 ¢	177 ±	181 μ	190 $^3/_4$
169 ©	178 ^{2}	188 $^1/_4$	247 ÷
176 °	179 ^{3}	189 $^1/_2$	248 ϕ

If *n* is a number between 0 and 255, then

`Chr(n)`

is the string consisting of the character with ANSI value *n*. If *str* is any string, then

`Asc(str)`

is the ANSI value of the first character of *str*. For instance, the statement

`txtBox.Text = Chr(65)`

displays the letter A in the text box, and the statement

`lstBox.Items.Add(Asc("Apple"))`

displays the number 65 in the list box.

Concatenation can be used with Chr to obtain strings using the higher ANSI characters. For instance, with one of the fonts that conforms to the ANSI standard, the statement

```
txtBox.Text = "32" & Chr(176) & " Fahrenheit"
```

displays 32° Fahrenheit in the text box.

The quotation-mark character (") can be placed into a string by using Chr(34). For example, after the statement

```
txtBox.Text = "George " & Chr(34) & "Babe" & Chr(34) & " Ruth"
```

is executed, the text box contains

```
George "Babe" Ruth
```

The relational operator *less than* (<) can be applied to both numbers and strings. The number a is said to be less than the number b if a lies to the left of b on the number line. For instance, $2 < 5$, $-5 < -2$, and $0 < 3.5$.

The string a is said to be less than the string b if a precedes b alphabetically when using the ANSI table to alphabetize their values. For instance, "cat" < "dog", "cart" < "cat", and "cat" < "catalog". Digits precede uppercase letters, which precede lowercase letters. Two strings are compared working from left to right, character by character, to determine which one should precede the other. Therefore, "9W" < "bat", "Dog" < "cat", and "Sales-99" < "Sales-retail".

Table 5.3 shows the different mathematical relational operators, their representations in Visual Basic, and their meanings.

TABLE 5.3   Relational operators.

Mathematical Notation	Visual Basic Notation	Numeric Meaning	String Meaning
=	=	equal to	identical to
≠	<>	not equal to	different from
<	<	less than	precedes alphabetically
>	>	greater than	follows alphabetically
≤	<=	less than or equal to	precedes alphabetically or is identical to
≥	>=	greater than or equal to	follows alphabetically or is identical to

Example 1   Determine whether each of the following conditions is true or false.

(a) $1 <= 1$

(b) $1 < 1$

(c) "car" < "cat"

(d) "Dog" < "dog"

SOLUTION

(a) True. The notation <= means "less than *or* equal to." That is, the condition is true provided either of the two circumstances holds. The second one (equal to) holds.

(b) False. The notation < means "strictly less than" and no number can be strictly less than itself.

(c) True. The characters of the strings are compared one at a time working from left to right. Because the first two match, the third character decides the order.

(d) True. Because uppercase letters precede lowercase letters in the ANSI table, the first character of "Dog" precedes the first character of "dog".

Conditions also can involve variables, numeric operators, and functions. To determine whether a condition is true or false, first compute the numeric or string values and then decide if the resulting assertion is true or false.

 Example 2   Suppose the numeric variables *a* and *b* have values 4 and 3, and the string variables *c* and *d* have values "hello" and "bye". Are the following conditions true or false?

(a) (a + b) < 2*a

(b) (c.Length − b) = (a/2)

(c) c < ("good" & d)

SOLUTION

(a) The value of a + b is 7 and the value of 2*a is 8. Because 7 < 8, the condition is true.

(b) True, because the value of c.Length − b is 2, the same as (a / 2).

(c) The condition "hello" < "goodbye" is false, because "h" follows "g" in the ANSI table.

◼ Logical Operators

Programming situations often require more complex conditions than those considered so far. For instance, suppose we would like to state that the value of a numeric variable, *n*, is strictly between 2 and 5. The proper Visual Basic condition is

$$(2 < n) \text{ And } (n < 5)$$

The condition (2 < n) And (n < 5) is a combination of the two conditions 2 < n and n < 5 with the logical operator And.

The three main logical operators are And, Or, and Not. If *cond1* and *cond2* are conditions, then the condition

cond1 And cond2

is true if both *cond1* and *cond2* are true. Otherwise, it is false. The condition

cond1 Or cond2

is true if either *cond1* or *cond2* (or both) is true. Otherwise, it is false. The condition

Not cond1

is true if *cond1* is false, and is false if *cond1* is true.

Example 3   Suppose the numeric variable *n* has value 4 and the string variable *answ* has value "Y". Determine whether each of the following conditions is true or false.

(a) $(2 < n)$ And $(n < 6)$

(b) $(2 < n)$ Or $(n = 6)$

(c) Not $(n < 6)$

(d) $(answ = "Y")$ Or $(answ = "y")$

(e) $(answ = "Y")$ And $(answ = "y")$

(f) Not $(answ = "y")$

(g) $((2 < n)$ And $(n = 5 + 1))$ Or $(answ = "No")$

(h) $((n = 2)$ And $(n = 7))$ Or $(answ = "Y")$

(i) $(n = 2)$ And $((n = 7)$ Or $(answ = "Y"))$

SOLUTION

(a) True, because the conditions $(2 < 4)$ and $(4 < 6)$ are both true.

(b) True, because the condition $(2 < 4)$ is true. The fact that the condition $(4 = 6)$ is false does not affect the conclusion. The only requirement is that at least one of the two conditions be true.

(c) False, because $(4 < 6)$ is true.

(d) True, because the first condition becomes $("Y" = "Y")$ when the value of *answ* is substituted for *answ*.

(e) False, because the second condition is false. Actually, this compound condition is false for every value of *answ*.

(f) True, because $("Y" = "y")$ is false.

(g) False. In this logical expression, the compound condition $((2 < n)$ And $(n = 5 + 1))$ and the simple condition $(answ = "No")$ are joined by the logical operator Or. Because both of these conditions are false, the total condition is false.

(h) True, because the second Or clause is true.

(i) False. Comparing (h) and (i) shows the necessity of using parentheses to specify the intended grouping.

▓ Boolean Data Type

A statement of the form

```
txtBox.Text = condition
```

will display either True or False in the text box, depending on the truth value of the condition. Any variable or expression that evaluates to either True or False is said to have a **Boolean data type**. The following lines of code display False in the text box.

```
Dim x As Integer = 5
txtBox.Text = (3 + x) < 7
```

A variable is declared to be of type Boolean with a statement of the form

```
Dim varName As Boolean
```

The following lines of code will display True in the text box.

```
Dim boolVar as Boolean
Dim x As Integer = 2
Dim y As Integer = 3
boolVar = x < y
txtBox.Text = boolVar
```

The answer to part (i) of Example 3 can be confirmed to be "false" by executing the following lines of code.

```
Dim n as Integer = 4
Dim answ as String = "Y"
txtBox.Text = (n = 2) And ((n = 7) Or (answ = "Y"))
```

▨ Comments

1. A condition involving numeric variables is different from an algebraic truth. The assertion $(a + b) < 2*a$, considered in Example 2, is not a valid algebraic truth because it isn't true for all values of a and b. When encountered in a Visual Basic program, however, it will be considered true if it is correct for the current values of the variables.

2. Conditions evaluate to either true or false. These two values often are called the possible **truth values** of the condition.

3. A condition such as $2 < n < 5$ should never be used, because Visual Basic will not evaluate it as intended. The correct condition is $(2 < n)$ And $(n < 5)$.

4. A common error is to replace the condition Not $(n < m)$ by the condition $(n > m)$. The correct replacement is $(n >= m)$.

Practice Problems 5.1

1. Is the condition "Hello " = "Hello" true or false?

2. Complete Table 5.4.

TABLE 5.4 **Truth values of logical operators.**

cond1	cond2	cond1 And cond2	cond1 Or cond2	Not cond2
True	True	True		
True	False		True	
False	True			False
False	False			

EXERCISES 5.1

In Exercises 1 through 6, determine the output displayed in the text box.

1. `txtBox.Text = Chr(104) & Chr(105)`

2. `txtBox.Text = "C" & Chr(35)`

3. `txtBox.Text = "The letter before G is" & Chr(Asc("G") - 1)`

4. `txtBox.Text = Chr(Asc("B"))` `'The ANSI value of B is 66`

5. ```
Dim quote, person, qMark As String
quote = "We're all in this alone."
person = "Lily Tomlin"
qMark = Chr(34)
txtBox.Text = qMark & quote & qMark & "-" & person
```

6. ```
Dim letter As String
letter = "D"
txtBox.Text = letter & " is the " & (Asc(letter) - Asc("A") + 1) & _
              "th letter of the alphabet."
```

In Exercises 7 through 18, determine whether the condition is true or false. Assume $a = 2$ and $b = 3$.

7. $3 * a = 2 * b$

8. $(5 - a) * b < 7$

9. $b <= 3$

10. $a^b = b^a$

11. $a^{(5 - 2)} > 7$

12. $3E-02 < .01 * a$

13. $(a < b)$ Or $(b < a)$

14. $(a * a < b)$ Or Not $(a * a < a)$

15. Not $((a < b)$ And $(a < (b + a)))$

16. Not $(a < b)$ Or Not $(a < (b + a))$

17. $((a = b)$ And $(a * a < b * b))$ Or $((b < a)$ And $(2 * a < b))$

18. $((a = b)$ Or Not $(b < a))$ And $((a < b)$ Or $(b = a + 1))$

In Exercises 19 through 30, determine whether the condition is true or false.

19. "9W" <> "9w"

20. "Inspector" < "gadget"

21. "Car" < "Train"

22. "J" >= "J"

23. "99" > "ninety-nine"

24. "B" > "?"

25. ("Duck" < "pig") And ("pig" < "big")

26. "Duck" < "Duck" & "Duck"

27. Not (("B" = "b") Or ("Big" < "big"))

28. Not ("B" = "b") And Not ("Big" < "big")

29. (("Ant" < "hill") And ("mole" > "hill")) Or Not (Not ("Ant" < "hill") Or Not ("Mole" > "hill"))

30. (7 < 34) And ("7" > "34")

In Exercises 31 through 40, determine whether or not the two conditions are equivalent—that is, whether they will be true or false for exactly the same values of the variables appearing in them.

31. a <= b; (a < b) Or (a = b)

32. Not (a < b); a > b

33. (a = b) And (a < b); a <> b

34. Not ((a = b) Or (a = c)); (a <> b) And (a <> c)

35. (a < b) And ((a > d) Or (a > e)); ((a < b) And (a > d)) Or ((a < b) And (a > e))

36. Not ((a = b + c) Or (a = b)); (a <> b) Or (a <> b + c)

37. (a < b + c) Or (a = b + c); Not ((a > b) Or (a > c))

38. Not (a >= b); (a <= b) Or Not (a = b)

39. Not (a >= b); (a <= b) And Not (a = b)

40. (a = b) And ((b = c) Or (a = c)); (a = b) Or ((b = c) And (a = c))

In Exercises 41 through 45, write a condition equivalent to the negation of the given condition. (For example, a <> b is equivalent to the negation of a = b.)

41. a > b

42. (a = b) Or (a = d)

43. (a < b) And (c <> d)

44. Not ((a = b) Or (a > b))

45. (a <> "") And (a < b) And (a.Length < 5)

46. Rework Exercise 20 by evaluating a Boolean expression.

47. Rework Exercise 21 by evaluating a Boolean expression.

48. Rework Exercise 22 by evaluating a Boolean expression.

49. Rework Exercise 23 by evaluating a Boolean expression.

Solutions to Practice Problems 5.1

1. False. The first string has six characters, whereas the second has five. Two strings must be 100% identical to be called equal.

2.

cond1	cond2	cond1 And cond2	cond1 Or cond2	Not cond2
True	True	True	True	False
True	False	False	True	True
False	True	False	True	False
False	False	False	False	True

5.2   If Blocks

An **If block** allows a program to decide on a course of action based on whether certain conditions are true or false.

■ If Block

A block of the form:

```
If condition Then
    action1
Else
    action2
End If
```

causes the program to take *action1* if *condition* is true and *action2* if *condition* is false. Each action consists of one or more Visual Basic statements. After an action is taken, execution continues with the line after the If block. Figure 5.1 contains the pseudocode and flowchart for an If block.

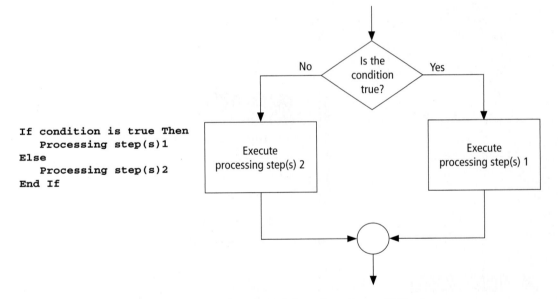

```
If condition is true Then
    Processing step(s)1
Else
    Processing step(s)2
End If
```

FIGURE 5.1   **Pseudocode and flowchart for an If block.**

 Example 1   The following program finds the larger of two numbers input by the user. The condition is

```
num1 > num2
```

and each action consists of a single assignment statement. With the inputs 3 and 7, the condition is false, and so the second action is taken.

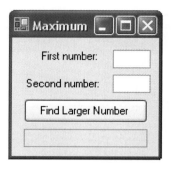

OBJECT	PROPERTY	SETTING
frmMaximum	Text	Maximum
lblFirstNum	Text	First Number:
txtFirstNum		
lblSecondNum	Text	Second Number:
txtSecondNum		
btnFindLarger	Text	Find Larger Number
txtResult	ReadOnly	True

```
Private Sub btnFindLarger_Click(...) Handles btnFindLarger.Click
  Dim num1, num2, largerNum As Double
  num1 = CDbl(txtFirstNum.Text)
  num2 = CDbl(txtSecondNum.Text)
  If num1 > num2 Then
    largerNum = num1
  Else
    largerNum = num2
  End If
  txtResult.Text = "The larger number is " & largerNum
End Sub
```

[Run, type 3 and 7 into the text boxes, and press the button.]

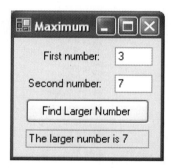

 Example 2   The following program requests the costs and revenue for a company and displays the message "Break even" if the costs and revenue are equal; otherwise, it displays the profit or loss. The action following Else is another If block.

OBJECT	PROPERTY	SETTING
frmStatus	Text	Profit/Loss
lblCosts	Text	Costs:
txtCosts		
lblRev	Text	Revenue:
txtRev		
btnShow	Text	Show Financial Status
txtResult	ReadOnly	True

```
Private Sub btnShow_Click(...) Handles btnShow.Click
  Dim costs, revenue, profit, loss As Double
  costs = CDbl(txtCosts.Text)
  revenue = CDbl(txtRev.Text)
  If costs = revenue Then
    txtResult.Text = "Break even"
  Else
    If costs < revenue Then
      profit = revenue - costs
      txtResult.Text = "Profit is " & FormatCurrency(profit)
    Else
      loss = costs - revenue
      txtResult.Text = "Loss is " & FormatCurrency(loss)
    End If
  End If
End Sub
```

[Run, type 9500 and 8000 into the text boxes, and press the button.]

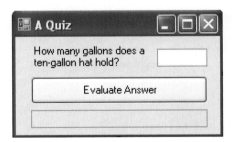

 Example 3   The If block in the following program has a logical operator in its condition.

OBJECT	PROPERTY	SETTING
frmQuiz	Text	A Quiz
lblQuestion	Text	How many gallons does a ten-gallon hat hold?
txtAnswer		
btnEvaluate	Text	Evaluate Answer
txtSolution	ReadOnly	True

```
Private Sub btnEvaluate_Click(...) Handles btnEvaluate.Click
  'Evaluate answer
  Dim answer As Double
  answer = CDbl(txtAnswer.Text)
  If (answer >= 0.5) And (answer <= 1) Then
    txtSolution.Text = "Good, "
  Else
```

```
          txtSolution.Text = "No, "
       End If
       txtSolution.Text &= "it holds about 3/4 of a gallon."
    End Sub
```

[Run, type 10 into the text box, and press the button.]

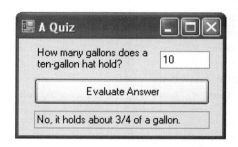

The Else part of an If block can be omitted. This important type of If block appears in the next example.

 Example 4 The following program offers assistance to the user before presenting a quotation.

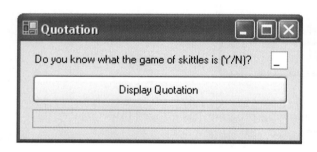

OBJECT	PROPERTY	SETTING
frmQuotation	Text	Quotation
lblQuestion	Text	Do you know what the game of skittles is (Y/N)?
mtxtAnswer	Mask	L
btnDisplay	Text	Display Quotation
txtQuote	ReadOnly	True

```
Private Sub btnDisplay_Click(...) Handles btnDisplay.Click
   Dim message As String
   message = "Skittles is an old form of bowling in which a wooden " & _
             "disk is used to knock down nine pins arranged in a square."
   If mtxtAnswer.Text.ToUpper = "N" Then
      MsgBox(message, 0, "")
   End If
   txtQuote.Text = "Life ain't all beer and skittles." & _
                   " - Du Maurier (1894)"
End Sub
```

[Run, type "N" into the masked text box, and press the button.]

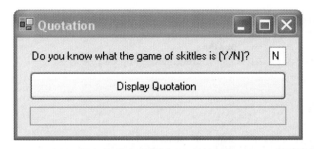

[Press OK.]

Note: Rerun the program, type "Y" into the masked text box, press the button, and observe that the description of the game is skipped.

ElseIf Clauses

An extension of the If block allows for more than two possible alternatives with the inclusion of ElseIf clauses. A typical block of this type is

```
If condition1 Then
  action1
ElseIf condition2 Then
  action2
ElseIf condition3 Then
  action3
Else
  action4
End If
```

This block searches for the first true condition, carries out its action, and then skips to the statement following End If. If none of the conditions is true, then Else's action is carried out. Execution then continues with the statement following the block. In general, an If block can contain any number of ElseIf clauses. As before, the Else clause is optional.

Example 5   The following program redoes Example 1 so that if the two numbers are equal, the program so reports:

```
Private Sub btnFindLarger_Click(...) Handles btnFindLarger.Click
  Dim num1, num2 As Double
  num1 = CDbl(txtFirstNum.Text)
  num2 = CDbl(txtSecondNum.Text)
  If (num1 > num2) Then
     txtResult.Text = "The larger number is " & num1
  ElseIf (num2 > num1) Then
     txtResult.Text = "The larger number is " & num2
  Else
     txtResult.Text = "The two numbers are equal."
  End If
End Sub
```

[Run, type 7 into both text boxes, and press the button.]

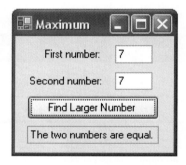

If blocks allow us to define functions whose values are not determined by a simple formula. The function in Example 6 uses an If block.

Example 6   The Social Security or FICA tax has two components—the Social Security benefits tax, which in 2005 is 6.2 percent on the first $90,000 of earnings for the year, and the Medicare tax, which is 1.45 percent of earnings. The following program calculates an employee's FICA tax for the current pay period.

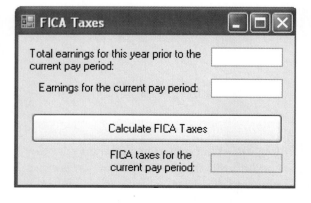

OBJECT	PROPERTY	SETTING
frmFICA	Text	FICA Taxes
lblToDate	Text	Total earnings for this year prior to the current pay period:
txtToDate		
lblCurrent	Text	Earnings for the current pay period:
txtCurrent		
btnCalculate	Text	Calculate FICA Taxes
lblTax	Text	FICA taxes for the current pay period:
txtTax	ReadOnly	True

```
Private Sub btnCalculate_Click(...) Handles btnCalculate.Click
  Dim ficaTaxes As Double
  ficaTaxes = CalcFICA(CDbl(txtToDate.Text), CDbl(txtCurrent.Text))
  txtTax.Text = FormatCurrency(ficaTaxes)
End Sub

Function CalcFICA(ByVal ytdEarnings As Double, _
                  ByVal curEarnings As Double) As Double
  'Calculate Social Security benefits tax and Medicare tax
  'for a single pay period in 2005
  Dim socialSecurityBenTax, medicareTax As Double
  If (ytdEarnings + curEarnings) <= 90000 Then
    socialSecurityBenTax = 0.062 * curEarnings
  ElseIf ytdEarnings < 90000 Then
    socialSecurityBenTax = 0.062 * (90000 - ytdEarnings)
  End If
  medicareTax = 0.0145 * curEarnings
  Return socialSecurityBenTax + medicareTax
End Function
```

[Run, type 12345.67 and 543.21 into the top two text boxes, and press the button. The following is displayed in txtTax.]

$41.56

▧ Comments

1. Constructs in which an If block is contained inside another If block are referred to as **nested** If blocks.

2. Care should be taken to make If blocks easy to understand. For instance, in Figure 5.2, the block on the left is difficult to follow and should be replaced by the clearer block on the right.

```
If cond1 Then              If cond1 And cond2 Then
  If cond2 Then              action
    action                 End If
  End If
End If
```

FIGURE 5.2   A confusing If block and an improvement.

3. In Appendix C, the section "Stepping through Programs Containing Decision Structures: Chapter 5" uses the Visual Basic debugging tools to trace the flow through an If block.

4. Some programs call for selecting among many possibilities. Although such tasks can be accomplished with complicated If blocks, the Select Case block (discussed in the next section) is often a better alternative.

Practice Problems 5.2

1. Suppose the user is asked to input a number into txtNumber for which the square root is to be taken. Fill in the If block so that the lines of code that follow will display either the message "Number can't be negative." or the square root of the number.

```
Private Sub btnSqrt_Click(...) Handles btnSqrt.Click
  'Check reasonableness of data
  Dim num As Double
  num = CDbl(txtNumber.Text)
  If


  End If
End Sub
```

2. Improve the block

```
If a < b Then
  If c < 5 Then
    txtBox.Text = "hello"
  End If
End If
```

EXERCISES 5.2

In Exercises 1 through 12, determine the output displayed in the text box when the button is clicked.

1.
```
Private Sub btnDisplay_Click(...) Handles btnDisplay.Click
  Dim num As Double = 4
  If num <= 9 Then
    txtOutput.Text = "Less than ten."
  Else
    If num = 4 Then
      txtOutput.Text = "Equal to four."
    End If
  End If
End Sub
```

2.
```
Private Sub btnDisplay_Click(...) Handles btnDisplay.Click
  Dim gpa As Double = 3.49
  txtOutput.Clear()
  If gpa >= 3.5 Then
    txtOutput.Text = "Honors "
  End If
  txtOutput.Text &= "Student"
End Sub
```

3. ```
Private Sub btnDisplay_Click(...) Handles btnDisplay.Click
    Dim a As Double = 5
    txtOutput.Clear()
    If (3 * a - 4) < 9 Then
        txtOutput.Text = "Remember, "
    End If
    txtOutput.Text &= "tomorrow is another day."
End Sub
```

4. ```
Private Sub btnDisplay_Click(...) Handles btnDisplay.Click
    Dim change As Double = 356    'Amount of change in cents
    If change >= 100 Then
        txtOutput.Text = "Your change contains "  & _
                        Int(change / 100) & " dollars."
    Else
        txtOutput.Text = "Your change contains no dollars."
    End If
End Sub
```

5. ```
Private Sub btnDisplay_Click(...) Handles btnDisplay.Click
    Dim a as Double = 2
    Dim b As Double = 3
    Dim c As Double = 5
    If a * b < c Then
        b = 7
    Else
        b = c * a
    End If
    txtOutput.Text = CStr(b)
End Sub
```

6. ```
Private Sub btnDisplay_Click(...) Handles btnDisplay.Click
    Dim a, b As Double
    a = CDbl(InputBox("Enter a number."))
    b = CDbl(InputBox("Enter another number."))
    If a > b Then
        a += 1
    Else
        b += 1
    End If
    txtOutput.Text = a & "   " & b
End Sub
```
(Assume the responses are *7* and *11*.)

7. ```
Private Sub btnDisplay_Click(...) Handles btnDisplay.Click
    'Cost of phone call from New York to London
    Dim length As Double
    InputLength(length)
    DisplayCost(length)
End Sub
```
```

```
Function Cost(ByVal length As Double) As Double
   If length < 1 Then
      Return .46
   Else
      Return .46 + (length - 1) * .36
   End If
End Function
Sub DisplayCost(ByVal length As Double)
  'Display the cost of a call
  txtBox.Text = "Cost of call: " & FormatCurrency(Cost(length))
End Sub

Sub InputLength(ByRef length As Double)
  'Request the length of a phone call
  length = CDbl(InputBox("Duration of the call in minutes?"))
End Sub
```

(Assume the response is 31.)

8.
```
Private Sub btnDisplay_Click(...) Handles btnDisplay.Click
   Dim letter As String
   letter = InputBox("Enter A, B, or C.")
   If letter = "A" Then
     DisplayAmessage()
   ElseIf letter = "B" Then
     DisplayBmessage()
   ElseIf letter = "C" Then
     DisplayCmessage()
   Else
      txtOutput.Text = "Not a valid letter."
   End If
End Sub

Sub DisplayAmessage()
   txtOutput.Text = "A, my name is Alice."
End Sub

Sub DisplayBmessage()
   txtOutput.Text = "To be, or not to be."
End Sub

Sub DisplayCmessage()
   txtOutput.Text = "Oh, say, can you see."
End Sub
```

(Assume the response is B.)

9.
```
Private Sub btnDisplay_Click(...) Handles btnDisplay.Click
   Dim vowels As Integer     'Number of vowels
   ExamineLetter(vowels)
```

```
        ExamineLetter(vowels)
        ExamineLetter(vowels)
        txtOutput.Text = "The number of vowels is " & vowels
    End Sub

    Sub ExamineLetter(ByRef vowels As Integer)
        Dim ltr As String
        ltr = InputBox("Enter a letter.")
        ltr = ltr.ToUpper
        If (ltr = "A") Or (ltr = "E") Or (ltr = "I") Or _
           (ltr = "O") Or (ltr = "U") Then
            vowels += 1
        End If
    End Sub
```

(Assume the three responses are *U*, *b*, and *a*.)

10.
```
    Private Sub btnDisplay_Click(...) Handles btnDisplay.Click
        Dim a As Double = 5
        If (a > 2) And ((a = 3) Or (a < 7)) Then
            txtOutput.Text = "Hi"
        End If
    End Sub
```

11.
```
    Private Sub btnDisplay_Click(...) Handles btnDisplay.Click
        Dim num As Double = 5
        If num < 0 Then
            txtOutput.Text = "neg"
        Else
            If num = 0 Then
                txtOutput.Text = "zero"
            Else
                txtOutput.Text = "positive"
            End If
        End If
    End Sub
```

12.
```
    Private Sub btnDisplay_Click(...) Handles btnDisplay.Click
        Dim msg As String, age As Integer
        msg = "You are eligible to vote"
        age = CInt(InputBox("Enter your age."))
        If age >= 18 Then
            txtOutput.Text = msg
        Else
            txtOutput.Text = msg & " in " & (18 - age) &  " years."
        End If
    End Sub
```

(Assume the response is *16*.)

In Exercises 13 through 20, identify the errors.

13. ```
Private Sub btnDisplay_Click(...) Handles btnDisplay.Click
    Dim num As Double = 0.5
    If (1 < num < 3) Then
      txtOutput.Text = "Number is between 1 and 3."
    End If
End Sub
```

14. ```
Private Sub btnDisplay_Click(...) Handles btnDisplay.Click
    Dim num As Double = 6
    If num > 5 And < 9 Then
      txtOutput.Text = "Yes"
    Else
      txtOutput.Text = "No"
    End If
End Sub
```

15. ```
Private Sub btnDisplay_Click(...) Handles btnDisplay.Click
    If (2 <> 3)
      txtOutput.Text = "Numbers are not equal"
    End If
End Sub
```

16. ```
Private Sub btnDisplay_Click(...) Handles btnDisplay.Click
    Dim major As String
    major = "Computer Science"
    If major = "Business" Or "Computer Science" Then
      txtOutput.Text = "Yes"
    End If
End Sub
```

17. ```
Private Sub btnDisplay_Click(...) Handles btnDisplay.Click
    Dim numName As String, num As Double
    numName = "Seven"
    num = CDbl(InputBox("Enter a number."))
    If num < numName Then
      txtOutput.Text = "Less than"
    Else
      txtOutput.Text = "Greater than"
    End If
End Sub
```

18. ```
Private Sub btnDisplay_Click(...) Handles btnDisplay.Click
    'Change switch from "on" to "off", or from "off" to "on"
    Dim switch As String
    switch = InputBox("Enter On or Off.")
    If switch = "Off" Then
      switch = "On"
    End If
```

```
        If switch = "On" Then
            switch = "Off"
        End If
        txtOutput.Text = switch
    End Sub
```

19.
```
    Private Sub btnDisplay_Click(...) Handles btnDisplay.Click
        'Display "OK" if either j or k equals 4
        Dim j As Double = 2
        Dim k As Double = 3
        If j Or k = 4 Then
            txtOutput.Text = "OK"
        End If
    End Sub
```

20.
```
    Private Sub btnDisplay_Click(...) Handles btnDisplay.Click
        'Is your program correct?
        Dim query, answer1, answer2 As String
        query = "Are you sure everything in your program is correct?"
        answer1 = InputBox(query)
        answer1 = answer1.ToUpper.Substring(0, 1)
        If answer1 = "N" Then
            txtOutput.Text = "Don't patch bad code, rewrite it."
        Else
            query = "Does your program run correctly?"
            answer2 = InputBox(query)
            answer2 = answer2.ToUpper.Substring(0, 1)
            If answer2 = "Y" Then
                txtOutput.Text = "Congratulations."
            Else
                txtOutput.Text = "Something you are sure about is wrong."
            End If
        End If
    End Sub
```

In Exercises 21 through 26, simplify the code.

21.
```
    If (a = 2) Then
        a = 3 + a
    Else
        a = 5
    End If
```

22.
```
    If Not (answer <> "y") Then
        txtOutput.Text = "YES"
    Else
        If (answer = "y") Or (answer = "Y") Then
            txtOutput.Text = "YES"
        End If
    End If
```

23.
```
If (j = 7) Then
    b = 1
Else
    If (j <> 7) Then
        b = 2
    End If
End If
```

24.
```
If (a < b) Then
    If (b < c) Then
        txtOutput.Text = b & " is between " & a & " and " & c
    End If
End If
```

25.
```
message = "Is Alaska bigger than Texas and California combined?"
answer = InputBox(message)
If (answer.Substring(0, 1) = "Y") Then
    answer = "YES"
End If
If (answer.Substring(0, 1) = "y") Then
    answer = "YES"
End If
If (answer = "YES") Then
    txtOutput.Text = "Correct"
Else
    txtOutput.Text = "Wrong"
End If
```

26.
```
message = "How tall (in feet) is the Statue of Liberty?"
feet = CDbl(InputBox(message))
If (feet <= 141) Then
    lstOutput.Items.Add("Nope")
End If
If (feet > 141) Then
    If (feet < 161) Then
        lstOutput.Items.Add("Close")
    Else
        lstOutput.Items.Add("Nope")
    End If
End If
lstOutput.Items.Add("The statue is 151 feet from base to torch.")
```

27. Write a program to determine how much to tip the server in a restaurant. The tip should be 15 percent of the check, with a minimum of $1.

28. A bagel shop charges 75 cents per bagel for orders of less than a half-dozen bagels and charges 60 cents per bagel for orders of a half-dozen or more bagels. Write a program that requests the number of bagels ordered and displays the total cost. (Test the program for orders of four bagels and a dozen bagels.)

29. A computer store sells diskettes at 25 cents each for small orders or at 20 cents each for orders of 100 diskettes or more. Write a program that requests the number of diskettes ordered and displays the total cost. (Test the program for purchases of 5 and 200 diskettes.)

30. A copy center charges 5 cents per copy for the first 100 copies and 3 cents per copy for each additional copy. Write a program that requests the number of copies as input and displays the total cost. (Test the program with the quantities 25 and 125.)

31. Write a quiz program to ask "Who was the first Ronald McDonald?" The program should display "Correct." if the answer is "Willard Scott" and "Nice try" for any other answer.

32. Suppose a program has a button with the caption "Quit." Suppose also that the Name property of this button is btnQuit. Write a btnQuit_Click event procedure that gives the user a second chance before ending the program. The procedure should use an input box to request that the user confirm that the program should be terminated, and then end the program only if the user responds in the affirmative.

33. Write a program to handle a savings-account withdrawal. The program should request the current balance and the amount of the withdrawal as input and then display the new balance. If the withdrawal is greater than the original balance, the program should display "Withdrawal denied." If the new balance is less than $150, the message "Balance below $150" should be displayed.

34. Write a program that requests three scores as input and displays the average of the two highest scores. The input and output should be handled by Sub procedures, and the average should be determined by a user-defined function.

35. A grocery store sells apples for 79 cents per pound. Write a cashier's program that requests the number of pounds and the amount of cash tendered as input and displays the change from the transaction. If the cash is not enough, the message "I need $x.xx more." should be displayed, where $x.xx is the difference between the cash and the total cost. (Test the program with six pounds and $5, and four pounds and $3.)

36. Federal law requires hourly employees be paid "time-and-a-half" for work in excess of 40 hours in a week. For example, if a person's hourly wage is $8 and he works 60 hours in a week, his gross pay should be

$$(40 \times 8) + (1.5 \times 8 \times (60 - 40)) = \$560$$

Write a program that requests as input the number of hours a person works in a given week and his hourly wage, and then displays his gross pay.

37. Write a program that requests a word (with lowercase letters) as input and translates the word into pig latin. The rules for translating a word into pig latin are as follows:

   (a) If the word begins with a consonant, move the first letter to the end of the word and add *ay*. For instance, *chip* becomes *hipcay*.
   (b) If the word begins with a vowel, add *way* to the end of the word. For instance, *else* becomes *elseway*.

38. The current calendar, called the Gregorian calendar, was introduced in 1582. Every year divisible by four was declared to be a leap year, with the exception of the years ending in 00 (that is, those divisible by 100) and not divisible by 400. For

instance, the years 1600 and 2000 are leap years, but 1700, 1800, and 1900 are not. Write a program that requests a year as input and states whether it is a leap year. (Test the program on the years 1994, 1995, 1900, and 2000.)

39. Create a form with a text box and two buttons captioned Bogart and Raines. When Bogart is first pressed, the sentence "I came to Casablanca for the waters." is displayed in the text box. The next time Bogart is pressed, the sentence "I was misinformed." is displayed. When Raines is pressed, the sentence "But we're in the middle of the desert." is displayed. Run the program and then press Bogart, Raines, and Bogart to obtain a dialogue.

40. Write a program that allows the user to use a button to toggle the color of the text in a text box between black and red.

41. Write a program that allows the user ten tries to answer the question, "Which U.S. President was born on July 4?" After three incorrect guesses, the program should display the hint, "He once said, 'If you don't say anything, you won't be called upon to repeat it.'" in a message box. After seven incorrect guesses, the program should give the hint, "His nickname was 'Silent Cal.'" The number of guesses should be displayed in a text box. **Note:** Calvin Coolidge was born on July 4, 1872.

42. Write a program that reads a test score from a text box each time a button is clicked and then displays the two highest scores whenever a second button is clicked. Use two class-level variables to track the two highest scores.

43. The flowchart in Figure 5.3 (on the next page) calculates New Jersey state income tax. Write a program corresponding to the flowchart. (Test the program with taxable incomes of $15,000, $30,000, and $60,000.)

44. Write a program to play "Hide and Seek" with the name of our programming language. When the button is pressed, the name should disappear and the caption on the button should change to "Show Name of Language." The next time the button is pressed, the name should reappear and the caption should revert to "Hide Name of Language," and so on.

OBJECT	PROPERTY	SETTING
frmHideSeek	Text	Hide and Seek
lblLanguage	Text	VB 2005
	Font.Size	26
btnDisplay	Text	Hide Name of Language

Solutions to Practice Problems 5.2

```
1. If (num < 0) Then
     MsgBox("Number can't be negative.", 0, "Input Error")
     txtNumber.Clear()
     txtNumber.Focus()
   Else
     txtSquareRoot.Text = CStr(Math.Sqrt(num))
   End If
```

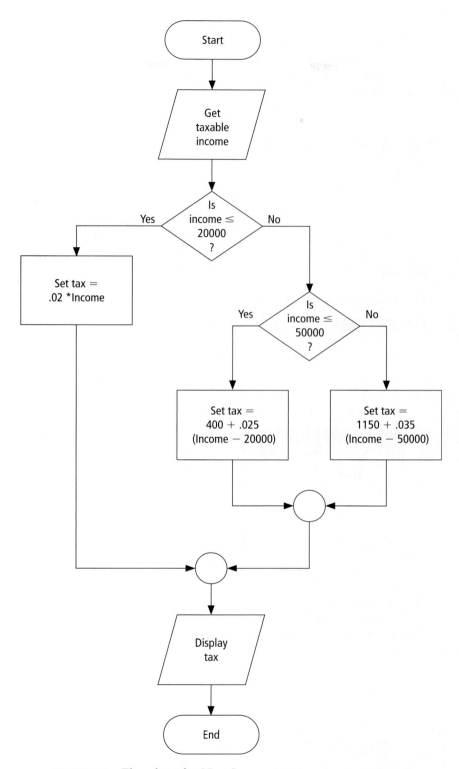

FIGURE 5.3   Flowchart for New Jersey state income tax program.

2. The word "hello" will be displayed when (a < b) is true and (c < 5) is also true. That is, it will be displayed when both of these two conditions are true. The clearest way to write the block is

```
If (a < b) And (c < 5) Then
   txtBox.Text = "hello"
End If
```

5.3   Select Case Blocks

A Select Case block is an efficient decision-making structure that simplifies choosing among several actions. It avoids complex If constructs. If blocks make decisions based on the truth value of a condition; Select Case choices are determined by the value of an expression called a **selector**. Each of the possible actions is preceded by a clause of the form

Case *valueList*

where *valueList* itemizes the values of the selector for which the action should be taken.

  Example 1   The following program converts the finishing position in a horse race into a descriptive phrase. After the variable *position* is assigned a value from txtPosition, Visual Basic searches for the first Case clause whose value list contains that value and executes the succeeding statement. If the value of *position* is greater than 5, then the statement following Case Else is executed.

OBJECT	PROPERTY	SETTING
frmRace	Text	Horse Race
lblPosition	AutoSize	False
	Text	Finishing position (1, 2, 3, . . .):
txtPosition		
btnEvaluate	Text	Evaluate Position
txtOutcome	ReadOnly	True

```
Private Sub btnEvaluate_Click(...) Handles btnEvaluate.Click
   Dim position As Integer    'selector
   position = CInt(txtPosition.Text)
   Select Case position
     Case 1
       txtOutcome.Text = "Win"
     Case 2
       txtOutcome.Text = "Place"
     Case 3
       txtOutcome.Text = "Show"
```

```
    Case 4, 5
        txtOutcome.Text = "You almost placed in the money."
    Case Else
        txtOutcome.Text = "Out of the money."
    End Select
End Sub
```

[Run, type 2 into the text box, and press the button.]

 Example 2 In the following variation of Example 1, the value lists specify ranges of values. The first value list provides another way to stipulate the numbers 1, 2, and 3. The second value list covers all numbers from 4 on.

```
Private Sub btnEvaluate_Click(...) Handles btnEvaluate.Click
    'Describe finishing positions in a horse race
    Dim position As Integer
    position = CInt(txtPosition.Text)
    Select Case position
        Case 1 To 3
            txtOutcome.Text = "In the money. Congratulations."
        Case Is >= 4
            txtOutcome.Text = "Not in the money."
    End Select
End Sub
```

[Run, type 2 into the text box, and press the button.]

A typical form of the Select Case block is

```
Select Case selector
  Case valueList1
    action1
  Case valueList2
    action2
  Case Else
    action of last resort
End Select
```

where Case Else (and its action) is optional, and each value list contains one or more of the following types of items:

1. a literal;

2. a variable;

3. an expression;

4. an inequality sign preceded by Is and followed by a literal, variable, or expression;

5. a range expressed in the form **a To b**, where *a* and *b* are literals, variables, or expressions.

Different items appearing in the same list must be separated by commas. Each action consists of one or more statements. After the selector is evaluated, Visual Basic looks for the first value-list item including the value of the selector and carries out its associated action. (If the value of the selector appears in two different value lists, only the action associated with the first value list will be carried out.) If the value of the selector does not appear in any of the value lists and there is no Case Else clause, execution of the program will continue with the statement following the Select Case block.

Figure 5.4 (on the next page) contains the flowchart for a Select Case block. The pseudocode for a Select Case block is the same as for the equivalent If block.

 Example 3 The following program uses several different types of value lists. With the response shown, the second action was selected.

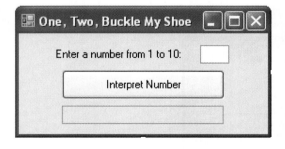

OBJECT	PROPERTY	SETTING
frmRhyme	Text	One, Two, Buckle My Shoe
lblEnterNum	Text	Enter a number from 1 to 10:
txtNumber		
btnInterpret	Text	Interpret Number
txtPhrase	ReadOnly	True

```
Private Sub btnInterpret_Click(...) Handles btnInterpret.Click
    'One, Two, Buckle My Shoe
    Dim x As Integer = 2, y As Integer = 3
    Dim num As Integer
    num = CInt(txtNumber.Text)
```

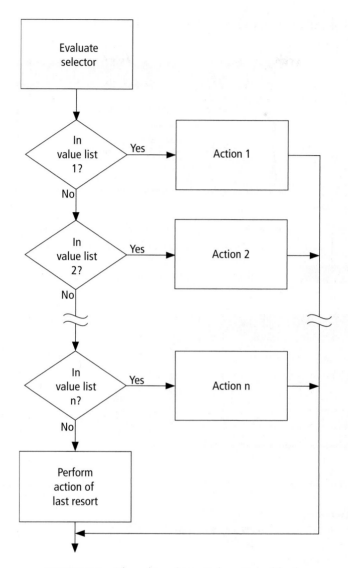

FIGURE 5.4   Flowchart for a Select Case block.

```
Select Case num
  Case y - x, x
    txtPhrase.Text = "Buckle my shoe."
  Case Is <= 4
    txtPhrase.Text = "Shut the door."
  Case x + y To x * y
    txtPhrase.Text = "Pick up sticks."
  Case 7, 8
    txtPhrase.Text = "Lay them straight."
  Case Else
    txtPhrase.Text = "Start all over again."
  End Select
End Sub
```

[Run, type 4 into the text box, and press the button.]

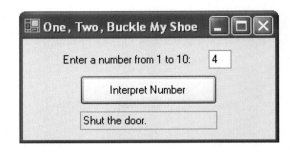

In each of the three preceding examples, the selector was a numeric variable; however, the selector also can be a string variable or an expression.

 Example 4 The following program has the string variable *firstName* as a selector.

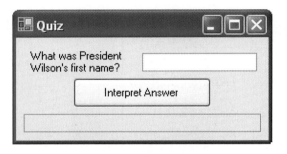

OBJECT	PROPERTY	SETTING
frmQuiz	Text	Quiz
lblQuestion	AutoSize	False
	Text	What was President Wilson's first name?
txtName		
btnInterpret	Text	Interpret Answer
txtReply	ReadOnly	True

```
Private Sub btnInterpret_Click(...) Handles btnInterpret.Click
  'Quiz
  Dim firstName As String
  firstName = txtName.Text.ToUpper
  Select Case firstName
    Case "THOMAS"
      txtReply.Text = "Correct."
    Case "WOODROW"
      txtReply.Text = "Sorry, his full name was " & _
                      "Thomas Woodrow Wilson."
    Case "PRESIDENT"
      txtReply.Text = "Are you for real?"
    Case Else
      txtReply.Text = "Nice try, but no cigar."
  End Select
End Sub
```

[Run, type "Woodrow" into the text box, and press the button.]

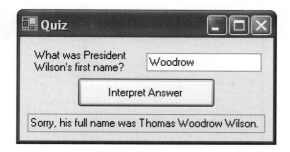

✓ **Example 5**   The following program has the string selector *anyString.Substring (0, 1)*. In the sample run, only the first action was carried out, even though the value of the selector was in both of the first two value lists. Visual Basic stops looking as soon as it finds the value of the selector.

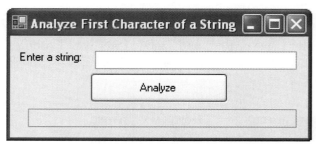

OBJECT	PROPERTY	SETTING
frmAnalyze	Text	Analyze First Character of a String
lblEnter	Text	Enter a string:
txtString		
btnAnalyze	Text	Analyze
txtResult	ReadOnly	True

```vb
Private Sub btnAnalyze_Click(...) Handles btnAnalyze.Click
    'Analyze the first character of a string
    Dim anyString As String
    anyString = txtString.Text.ToUpper
    Select Case anyString.Substring(0, 1)
      Case "S", "Z"
        txtResult.Text = "The string begins with a sibilant."
      Case "A" To "Z"
        txtResult.Text = "The string begins with a nonsibilant."
      Case "0" To "9"
        txtResult.Text = "The string begins with a digit."
      Case Is < "0"
        txtResult.Text = "The string begins with a character of " & _
                         "ANSI value less than 48."
      Case Else
        txtResult.Text = "The string begins with : ; < = > " & _
                         " ? @ [ \ ] ^ _ or ' . "
    End Select
End Sub
```

[Run, type "Sunday" into the text box, and press the button.]

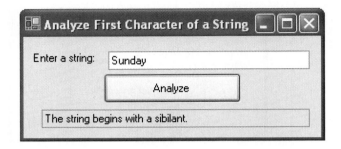

 Example 6   The color of the beacon light atop Boston's John Hancock Building forecasts the weather according to the following rhyme:

Steady blue, clear view.
Flashing blue, clouds due.
Steady red, rain ahead.
Flashing red, snow instead.

The following program requests a color (Blue or Red) and a mode (Steady or Flashing) as input and displays the weather forecast. The program contains a Select Case block with a string expression as selector.

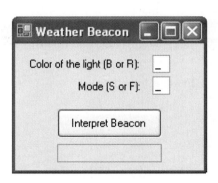

OBJECT	PROPERTY	SETTING
frmWeather	Text	Weather Beacon
lblColor	Text	Color of the light (B or R):
mtxtColor	Mask	L
lblMode	Text	Mode (S or F):
mtxtMode	Mask	L
btnInterpret	Text	Interpret Beacon
txtForecast	ReadOnly	True

```
Private Sub btnInterpret_Click(...) Handles btnInterpret.Click
  'Interpret a weather beacon
  Dim color, mode As String
  color = mtxtColor.Text
  mode = mtxtMode.Text
  Select Case mode.ToUpper & color.ToUpper
    Case "SB"
      txtForecast.Text = "CLEAR VIEW"
    Case "FB"
      txtForecast.Text = "CLOUDS DUE"
    Case "SR"
      txtForecast.Text = "RAIN AHEAD"
```

```
    Case "FR"
      txtForecast.Text = "SNOW AHEAD"
   End Select
End Sub
```

[Run, type "R" and "S" into the masked text boxes, and press the button.]

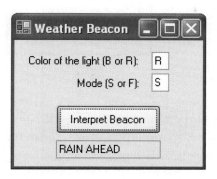

 Example 7 Select Case is useful in defining functions that are not determined by a formula. The following program assumes that the current year is not a leap year:

OBJECT	PROPERTY	SETTING
frmSeasons	Text	Seasons
lblSeason	Text	Season:
txtSeason		
btnNumber	Text	Number of Days
txtNumDays	ReadOnly	True

```
Private Sub btnNumber_Click(...) Handles btnNumber.Click
   'Determine the number of days in a season
   Dim season As String
   season = txtSeason.Text
   txtNumDays.Text = season & " has " & NumDays(season) & " days."
End Sub

Function NumDays(ByVal season As String) As Integer
   'Look up the number of days in a given season
   Select Case season.ToUpper
     Case "WINTER"
       Return 87
     Case "SPRING"
       Return 92
     Case "SUMMER", "AUTUMN", "FALL"
       Return 93
   End Select
End Function
```

[Run, type "Summer" into the text box, and press the button.]

▨ Comments

1. In a Case clause of the form **Case b To c**, the value of *b* should be less than or equal to the value of *c*. Otherwise, the clause is meaningless.

2. If the word **Is**, which should precede an inequality sign in a value list, is accidentally omitted, the editor will automatically insert it when checking the line.

3. The items in the value list must evaluate to a literal of the same type as the selector. For instance, if the selector evaluated to a string value, as in

```
Dim firstName As String
firstName = txtBox.Text
Select Case firstName
```

then the clause

```
Case firstName.Length
```

would be meaningless.

4. Variables are rarely declared inside an If . . . Then block or a Select Case block. If so, such a variable has **block-level scope**; that is, the variable cannot be referred to by code outside of the block.

5. In Appendix D, the section "Stepping through Programs Containing Selection Structures: Chapter 5" uses the Visual Basic debugging tools to trace the flow through a Select Case block.

Practice Problems 5.3

1. Suppose the selector of a Select Case block is the numeric variable *num*. Determine whether each of the following Case clauses is valid.

   (a) `Case 1, 4, Is < 10`
   (b) `Case Is < 5, Is >= 5`
   (c) `Case num = 2`

2. Do the following two programs always produce the same output for a whole-number grade from 0 to 100?

```
grade = CDbl(txtBox.Text)            grade = CDbl(txtBox.Text)
Select Case grade                    Select Case grade
  Case Is >= 90                        Case Is >= 90
    txtOutput.Text = "A"                 txtOutput.Text = "A"
  Case Is >= 60                        Case 60 To 89
    txtOutput.Text = "Pass"              txtOutput.Text = "Pass"
  Case Else                            Case 0 To 59
    txtOutput.Text = "Fail"              txtOutput.Text = "Fail"
End Select                           End Select
```

EXERCISES 5.3

In Exercises 1 through 8, for each of the responses shown in the parentheses, determine the output displayed in the text box when the button is clicked.

1.
```
Private Sub btnDisplay_Click(...) Handles btnDisplay.Click
    Dim age, price As Double
    age = CDbl(InputBox("What is your age?"))
    Select Case age
      Case Is < 6
        price = 0
      Case 6 To 17
        price = 3.75
      Case Is >= 17
        price = 5
    End Select
    txtOutput.Text = "The price is " & FormatCurrency(price)
End Sub
```
   (8.5, 17)

2.
```
Private Sub btnDisplay_Click(...) Handles btnDisplay.Click
    Dim n As Double
    n = CDbl(InputBox("Enter a number from 5 to 12"))
    Select Case n
      Case 5
        txtOutput.Text = "case 1"
      Case 5 To 7
        txtOutput.Text = "case 2"
      Case 7 To 12
        txtOutput.Text = "case 3"
    End Select
End Sub
```
   (7, 5, 11.2)

3.
```
Private Sub btnDisplay_Click(...) Handles btnDisplay.Click
    Dim age As Integer
    age = CDbl(InputBox("Enter age (in millions of years)"))
```

```
    Select Case age
      Case Is < 70
        txtOutput.Text = "Cenozoic Era"
      Case Is < 225
        txtOutput.Text = "Mesozoic Era"
      Case Is <= 600
        txtOutput.Text = "Paleozoic Era"
      Case Else
        txtOutput.Text = "?"
    End Select
  End Sub
```

(100, 600, 700)

4.
```
Private Sub btnDisplay_Click(...) Handles btnDisplay.Click
    Dim yearENIAC As Integer
    AskQuestion(yearENIAC)
    ProcessAnswer(yearENIAC)
  End Sub

  Sub AskQuestion(ByRef yearENIAC As Integer)
    'Ask question and obtain answer
    Dim message As String
    message = "In what year was the ENIAC computer completed?"
    yearENIAC = CInt(InputBox(message))
  End Sub

  Sub ProcessAnswer(ByVal yearENIAC As Integer)
    'Respond to answer
    Select Case yearENIAC
      Case 1945
        txtOutput.Text = "Correct."
      Case 1943 To 1947
        txtOutput.Text = "Close, 1945."
      Case Is < 1943
        txtOutput.Text = "Sorry, 1945. Work on the ENIAC " & _
                         "began in June 1943."
      Case Is > 1947
        txtOutput.Text = "No, 1945. By then IBM had built " & _
                         "a stored-program computer."
    End Select
  End Sub
```

(1940, 1945, 1950)

5.
```
Private Sub btnDisplay_Click(...) Handles btnDisplay.Click
    Dim name As String
    name = InputBox("Who developed the stored-program concept?")
    Select Case name.ToUpper
      Case "JOHN VON NEUMANN", "VON NEUMANN"
        txtOutput.Text = "Correct."
```

```vbnet
      Case "JOHN MAUCHLY", "MAUCHLY", "J. PRESPER ECKERT", "ECKERT"
        txtOutput.Text = "He worked with the developer, " & _
                         "von Neumann, on the ENIAC."
      Case Else
        txtOutput.Text = "Nope."
    End Select
  End Sub
```

(Grace Hopper, Eckert, John von Neumann)

6.
```vbnet
  Private Sub btnDisplay_Click(...) Handles btnDisplay.Click
    Dim message As String, a, b, c As Double
    message = "Analyzing solutions to the quadratic equation "
    message &= "AX^2 + BX + C = 0.  Enter the value for "
    a = CDbl(InputBox(message & "A"))
    b = CDbl(InputBox(message & "B"))
    c = CDbl(InputBox(message & "C"))
    Select Case (b ^ 2) — (4 * a * c)
      Case Is < 0
        txtOutput.Text = "The equation has no real solutions."
      Case 0
        txtOutput.Text = "The equation has exactly one solution."
      Case Is > 0
        txtOutput.Text = "The equation has two solutions."
    End Select
  End Sub
```

(1,2,3; 1,5,1; 1,2,1)

7.
```vbnet
  Private Sub btnDisplay_Click(...) Handles btnDisplay.Click
    'State a quotation
    Dim num1, num2 As Double
    Dim word As String = "hello"
    num1 = 3
    num2 = CDbl(InputBox("Enter a number"))
    Select Case (2 * num2 - 1)
      Case num1 * num1
        txtBox.Text = "Less is more."
      Case Is > word.Length
        txtBox.Text = "Time keeps everything from happening at once."
      Case Else
        txtBox.Text = "The more things change, the less " & _
                      "they remain the same."
    End Select
  End Sub
```

(2, 5, 6)

8.
```vbnet
  Private Sub btnDisplay_Click(...) Handles btnDisplay.Click
    Dim whatever As Double
    whatever = CDbl(InputBox("Enter a number:"))
```

```
      Select Case whatever
        Case Else
          txtOutput.Text = "Hi"
      End Select
    End Sub
```

$(7, -1)$

In Exercises 9 through 16, identify the errors.

9.
```
Private Sub btnDisplay_Click(...) Handles btnDisplay.Click
  Dim num As Double = 2
  Select Case num
    txtOutput.Text = "Two"
  End Select
End Sub
```

10.
```
Private Sub btnDisplay_Click(...) Handles btnDisplay.Click
  Dim num1 As Double = 5
  Dim num2 As Double = 2
  Select Case num1
    Case 3 <= num1 <= 10
      txtOutput.Text = "between 3 and 10."
    Case num2 To 5; 4
      txtOutput.Text = "near 5."
  End Select
End Sub
```

11.
```
Private Sub btnDisplay_Click(...) Handles btnDisplay.Click
  Dim a As String
  a = InputBox("What is your name?")
  Select Case a
    Case a = "Bob"
      txtOutput.Text = "Hi, Bob."
    Case Else
  End Select
End Sub
```

12.
```
Private Sub btnDisplay_Click(...) Handles btnDisplay.Click
  Dim word As String = "hello"
  Select Case word.Substring(0,1)
    Case h
      txtOutput.Text = "begins with h."
  End Select
End Sub
```

13.
```
Private Sub btnDisplay_Click(...) Handles btnDisplay.Click
  Dim word As String
  word = InputBox("Enter a word from the United States motto.")
  Select Case word.ToUpper
    Case "E"
      txtOutput.Text = "This is the first word of the motto."
```

```
        Case word.Substring(0,1) = "P"
          txtOutput.Text = "The second word is PLURIBUS."
        Case Else
          txtOutput.Text = "The third word is UNUM."
      End Select
    End Sub
```

14.
```
  Private Sub btnDisplay_Click(...) Handles btnDisplay.Click
    Dim num As Double = 5
    Select Case num
      Case 5, Is <> 5
        txtOutput.Text = "five"
      Case Is > 5
        txtOutput.Text = "greater than five"
    End Sub
```

15.
```
  Private Sub btnDisplay_Click(...) Handles btnDisplay.Click
    Dim fruit As String = "Peach"
    Select Case fruit.ToUpper
      Case Is >= "Peach"
        txtOutput.Text = "Georgia"
      Case "ORANGE To PEACH"
        txtOutput.Text = "Ok"
     End Select
    End Sub
```

16.
```
  Private Sub btnDisplay_Click(...) Handles btnDisplay.Click
    Dim purchase As Double
    purchase = CDbl(InputBox("Quantity purchased?"))
    Select Case purchase
      Case purchase < 10000
        txtOutput.Text = "Five dollars per item."
      Case Is 10000 To 30000
        txtOutput.Text = "Four dollars per item."
      Case Is > 30000
        txtOutput.Text = "Three dollars per item."
    End Select
    End Sub
```

In Exercises 17 through 22, suppose the selector of a Select Case block, *word*, evaluates to a String value. Determine whether the Case clause is valid.

17. `Case "un" & "til"`

18. `Case "hello", Is < "goodbye"`

19. `Case 0 To 9`

20. `Case word <> "No"`

21. `Case "abc".Substring(0, 1)`

22. `Case Is <> "No"`

In Exercises 23 through 26, rewrite the code using a Select Case block.

23.
```
If a = 1 Then
    txtOutput.Text = "one"
Else
  If a > 5 Then
     txtOutput.Text = "two"
  End If
End If
```

24.
```
If a = 1 Then
   lstOutput.Items.Add("lambs")
End If
If ((a <= 3) And (a < 4)) Then
  lstOutput.Items.Add("eat")
End If
If ((a = 5) Or (a > 7)) Then
  lstOutput.Items.Add("ivy")
End If
```

25.
```
If a < 5 Then
  If a = 2 Then
     txtOutput.Text = "yes"
  Else
     txtOutput.Text = "no"
  End If
Else
  If a = 2 Then
   txtOutput.Text = "maybe"
  End If
End If
```

26.
```
If a = 3 Then
  a = 1
End If
If a = 2 Then
  a = 3
End If
If a = 1 Then
  a = 2
End If
```

27. Table 5.5 gives the terms used by the National Weather Service to describe the degree of cloudiness. Write a program that requests the percentage of cloud cover as input and then displays the appropriate descriptor.

28. Table 5.6 shows the location of books in the library stacks according to their call numbers. Write a program that requests the call number of a book as input and displays the location of the book.

TABLE 5.5	Cloudiness descriptors.	
	Percentage of Cloud Cover	Descriptor
	0–30	clear
	31–70	partly cloudy
	71–99	cloudy
	100	overcast

TABLE 5.6	Location of library books.	
	Call Numbers	Location
	100 to 199	basement
	200 to 500 and over 900	main floor
	501 to 900 except 700 to 750	upper floor
	700 to 750	archives

29. Write a program that requests a month of the year and then gives the number of days in the month. If the month is February, the user should be asked whether the current year is a leap year.

30. Figure 5.5 shows some geometric shapes and formulas for their areas. Write a program that requests the user to select one of the shapes, requests the appropriate lengths, and then gives the area of the figure. The areas should be computed by Function procedures.

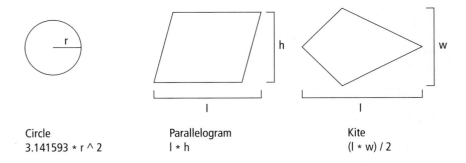

Circle	Parallelogram	Kite
3.141593 * r ^ 2	l * h	(l * w) / 2

FIGURE 5.5 Areas of geometric shapes.

31. Write a program that requests an exam score and assigns a letter grade with the scale 90–100 (A), 80–89 (B), 70–79 (C), 60–69 (D), 0–59 (F). The computation should be carried out in a Function procedure. (Test the program with the grades 84, 100, and 57.)

32. Computerized quiz show. Write a program that asks the contestant to select one of the numbers 1, 2, or 3 and then calls a Sub procedure that asks the question and requests the answer. The program should then tell the contestant if the answer is correct. Use the following three questions:

1. Who was the only living artist to have his work displayed in the Grand Gallery of the Louvre?
2. Who said, "Computers are useless. They can only give you answers."?
3. By what name is Pablo Blasio better known?

Note: These questions have the same answer, Pablo Picasso.

33. IRS informants are paid cash awards based on the value of the money recovered. If the information was specific enough to lead to a recovery, the informant receives 10 percent of the first $75,000, 5 percent of the next $25,000, and 1 percent of the remainder, up to a maximum award of $50,000. Write a program that requests the amount of the recovery as input and displays the award. (Test the program on the amounts $10,000, $125,000, and $10,000,000.)(**Note:**The source of this formula is *The Book of Inside Information*, Boardroom Books, 1993.)

34. Table 5.7 contains information on several states. Write a program that requests a state and category (flower, motto, and nickname) as input and displays the requested information. If the state or category requested is not in the table, the program should so inform the user.

TABLE 5.7   **State flowers, nicknames, and mottoes.**

State	Flower	Nickname	Motto
California	Golden Poppy	Golden State	Eureka
Indiana	Peony	Hoosier State	Crossroads of America
Mississippi	Magnolia	Magnolia State	By valor and arms
New York	Rose	Empire State	Ever upward

35. Write a program that, given the last name of one of the five most recent presidents, displays his state and a colorful fact about him. (**Hint:** The program might need to request further information.) **Note**: Carter: Georgia; The only soft drink served in the Carter White House was Coca-Cola. Reagan: California; His Secret Service code name was Rawhide. George H. W. Bush: Texas; He was the third left-handed president. Clinton: Arkansas; In college he did a good imitation of Elvis Presley. George W. Bush: Texas; He once owned the Texas Rangers baseball team.

36. Table 5.8 contains the meanings of some abbreviations doctors often use for prescriptions. Write a program that requests an abbreviation and gives its meaning. The user should be informed if the meaning is not in the table.

TABLE 5.8   **Physicians' abbreviations.**

Abbreviation	Meaning
ac	before meals
ad lib	freely as needed
bid	twice daily
gtt	a drop
hs	at bedtime
qid	four times a day

37. The user enters a number into a masked text box and then clicks on the appropriate button to have either one of three pieces of humor or one of three insults displayed in a text box below the buttons. Place the humor and insults in Function procedures, with Select Case statements in each to return the appropriate phrase. Also, if the number entered is not between 1 and 3, the masked text box should be cleared. Note: Some possible bits of humor are "I can resist everything except temptation," "I just heard from Bill Bailey. He's not coming home," and "I have enough money to last the rest of my life, unless I buy something." Some possible insults are "How much would you charge to haunt a house?" "I bet you have no more friends than an alarm clock," and "When your IQ rises to 30, sell."

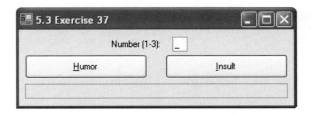

OBJECT	PROPERTY	SETTING
frmExercise 37		
lblNumber	Text	Number (1–3):
mtxtNumber	Mask	0
btnHumor	Text	&Humor
btnInsult	Text	&Insult
txtSentence	ReadOnly	True

Solutions to Practice Problems 5.3

1. (a) Valid. These items are redundant because 1 and 4 are just special cases of `Is < 10`. However, this makes no difference in Visual Basic.

(b) Valid. These items are contradictory. However, Visual Basic looks at them one at a time until it finds an item containing the value of the selector. The action following this Case clause will always be carried out.

(c) Not valid. It should be `Case 2`.

2. Yes. However, the program on the right is clearer and therefore preferable.

5.4   A Case Study: Weekly Payroll

This case study processes a weekly payroll using the 2005 Employer's Tax Guide. Table 5.9 shows typical data used by a company's payroll office. These data are processed to produce

TABLE 5.9   Employee data.

Name	Hourly Wage	Hours Worked	Withholding Exemptions	Marital Status	Previous Year-to-Date Earnings
Al Clark	$45.50	38	4	Married	$88,600.00
Ann Miller	$44.00	35	3	Married	$68,200.00
John Smith	$17.95	50	1	Single	$30,604.75
Sue Taylor	$25.50	43	2	Single	$36,295.50

the information in Table 5.10 that is supplied to each employee along with his or her paycheck. The program should request the data from Table 5.9 for an individual as input and produce output similar to that in Table 5.10.

TABLE 5.10	Payroll information.				
Name	Current Earnings	Yr. to Date Earnings	FICA Taxes	Income Tax Wh.	Check Amount
Al Clark	$1,729.00	$90,329.00	$111.87	$206.26	$1,410.87

The items in Table 5.10 should be calculated as follows:

Current Earnings: hourly wage times hours worked (with time-and-a-half after 40 hours)

Year-to-Date Earnings: previous year-to-date earnings plus current earnings

FICA Taxes: sum of 6.2 percent of first $90,000 of earnings (Social Security benefits tax) and 1.45 percent of total wages (Medicare tax)

Federal Income Tax Withheld: subtract $61.54 from the current earnings for each withholding exemption and use Table 5.11 or Table 5.12, depending on marital status

Check Amount: [current earnings] − [FICA taxes] − [income tax withheld]

TABLE 5.11	2005 Federal income tax withheld for a single person paid weekly.
Adjusted Weekly Income	Income Tax Withheld
$0 to $51	$0
Over $51 to $188	10% of amount over $51
Over $188 to $606	$13.70 + 15% of amount over $188
Over $606 to $1,341	$76.40 + 25% of amount over $606
Over $1,341 to $2,922	$260.15 + 28% of amount over $1,341
Over $2,922 to $6,313	$702.83 + 33% of amount over $2,922
Over $6,313	$1,821.86 + 35% of amount over $6,313

TABLE 5.12	2005 Federal income tax withheld for a married person paid weekly.
Adjusted Weekly Income	Income Tax Withheld
$0 to $154	$0
Over $154 to $435	10% of amount over $154
Over $435 to $1,273	$28.10 + 15% of amount over $435
Over $1,273 to $2,322	$153.80 + 25% of amount over $1,273
Over $2,322 to $3,646	$416.05 + 28% of amount over $2,322
Over $3,646 to $6,409	$786.77 + 33% of amount over $3,646
Over $6,409	$1,698.56 + 35% of amount over $6,409

▧ Designing the Weekly Payroll Program

After the data for an employee have been gathered from the text boxes, the program must compute the five items appearing in Table 5.10 and then display the payroll information. The five computations form the basic tasks of the program:

1. Compute current earnings.

2. Compute year-to-date earnings.

3. Compute FICA tax.

4. Compute federal income tax withheld.

5. Compute paycheck amount (that is, take-home pay).

Tasks 1, 2, 3, and 5 are fairly simple. Each involves applying a formula to given data. (For instance, if hours worked are at most 40, then [Current Earnings] = [Hourly Wage] times [Hours Worked].) Thus, we won't break down these tasks any further. Task 4 is more complicated, so we continue to divide it into smaller subtasks.

4. *Compute Federal Income Tax Withheld.* First, the employee's pay is adjusted for exemptions, and then the amount of income tax to be withheld is computed. The computation of the income tax withheld differs for married and single individuals. Task 4 is, therefore, divided into the following subtasks:

4.1. Compute pay adjusted by exemptions.

4.2. Compute income tax withheld for single employee.

4.3. Compute income tax withheld for married employee.

The hierarchy chart in Figure 5.6 shows the stepwise refinement of the problem.

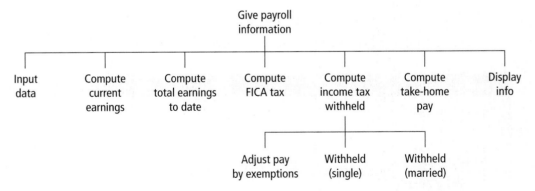

FIGURE 5.6   Hierarchy chart for the weekly payroll program.

▧ Pseudocode for the Display Payroll Event

INPUT employee data (Sub procedure InputData)
COMPUTE CURRENT GROSS PAY (Function Gross_Pay)
COMPUTE TOTAL EARNINGS TO DATE (Function Total_Pay)
COMPUTE FICA TAX (Function FICA_Tax)
COMPUTE FEDERAL TAX (Function Fed_Tax)

Adjust pay for exemptions
If employee is single Then
   COMPUTE INCOME TAX WITHHELD (Function TaxSingle)
Else
   COMPUTE INCOME TAX WITHHELD (Function TaxMarried)
End If
   COMPUTE PAYCHECK AMOUNT (Function Net_Check)
DISPLAY PAYROLL INFORMATION (Sub procedure ShowPayroll)

▨ Writing the Weekly Payroll Program

The btnDisplay_Click event procedure calls a sequence of seven procedures. Table 5.13 shows the tasks and the procedures that perform the tasks.

TABLE 5.13   **Tasks and their procedures.**

Task	Procedure
0. Input employee data.	InputData
1. Compute current earnings.	Gross_Pay
2. Compute year-to-date earnings.	Total_Pay
3. Compute FICA tax.	FICA_Tax
4. Compute federal income tax withheld.	Fed_Tax
4.1 Compute adjusted pay.	Fed_Tax
4.2 Compute amount withheld for single employee.	TaxSingle
4.3 Compute amount withheld for married employee.	TaxMarried
5. Compute paycheck amount.	Net_Check
6. Display payroll information.	ShowPayroll

▨ The Program and the User Interface

Figure 5.7 and Table 5.14 define the user interface for the Weekly Payroll Program.

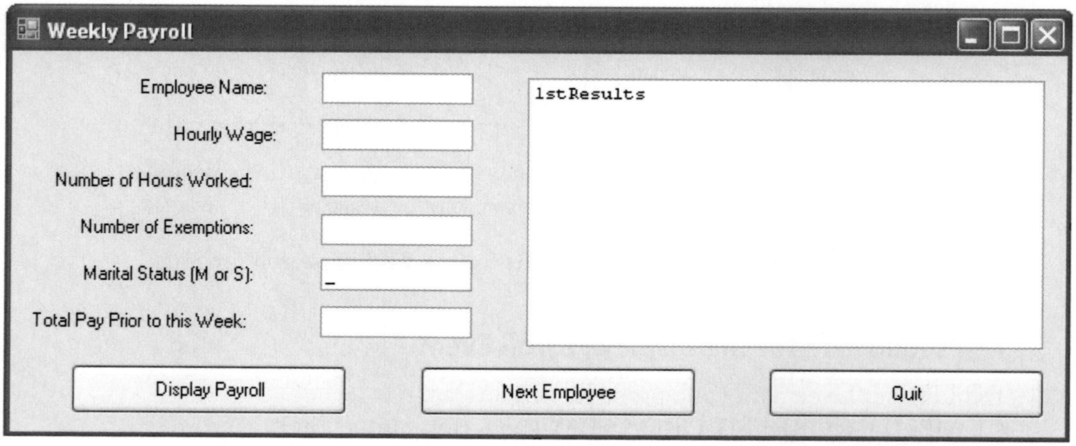

FIGURE 5.7   **Template for entering payroll data.**

TABLE 5.14	Objects and initial properties for the weekly payroll program.		
Object		**Property**	**Setting**
frmPayroll		Text	Weekly Payroll
lblName		Text	Employee Name:
txtName			
lblWage		Text	Hourly Wage:
txtWage			
lblHours		Text	Number of Hours Worked:
txtHours			
lblExempts		Text	Number of Exemptions:
txtExempts			
lblMarital		Text	Marital Status (M or S):
mtxtMarital		Mask	L
lblPriorPay		Text	Total Pay Prior to this Week:
txtPriorPay			
btnDisplay		Text	Display Payroll
btnNext		Text	Next Employee
btnQuit		Text	Quit
lstResults			

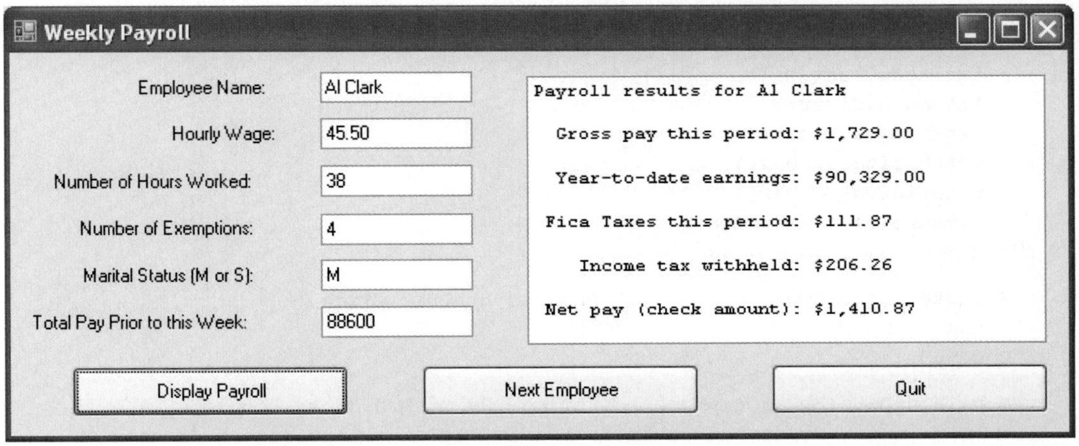

FIGURE 5.8   Sample run of weekly payroll program.

```
Private Sub btnDisplay_Click(...) Handles btnDisplay.Click
  Dim empName As String = ""   'Name of employee
  Dim hrWage As Double         'Hourly wage
  Dim hrsWorked As Double      'Hours worked this week
  Dim exemptions As Integer    'Number of exemptions for employee
  Dim mStatus As String = ""   'Marital status: S - Single; M - Married
  Dim prevPay As Double        'Total pay for year excluding this week
  Dim pay As Double            'This week's pay before taxes
  Dim totalPay As Double       'Total pay for year including this week
  Dim ficaTax As Double        'FICA taxes for this week
  Dim fedTax As Double         'Federal income tax withheld this week
  Dim check As Double          'Paycheck this week (take-home pay)
  'Obtain data, compute payroll, display results
  InputData(empName, hrWage, hrsWorked, exemptions, _
                                mStatus, prevPay)      'Task 0
  pay = Gross_Pay(hrWage, hrsWorked)                   'Task 1
  totalPay = Total_Pay(prevPay, pay)                   'Task 2
  ficaTax = FICA_Tax(pay, prevPay, totalPay)           'Task 3
  fedTax = Fed_Tax(pay, exemptions, mStatus)           'Task 4
  check = Net_Check(pay, ficaTax, fedTax)              'Task 5
  ShowPayroll(empName, pay, totalPay, ficaTax, fedTax, check)  'Task 6
End Sub

Private Sub btnNext_Click(...) Handles btnNext.Click
  'Clear all masked text boxes for next employee's data
  txtName.Clear()
  txtWage.Clear()
  txtHours.Clear()
  txtExempts.Clear()
  mtxtMarital.Clear()
  txtPriorPay.Clear()
  lstResults.Items.Clear()
End Sub

Private Sub btnQuit_Click(...) Handles btnQuit.Click
  End
End Sub

Sub InputData(ByRef empName As String, ByRef hrWage As Double, _
              ByRef hrsWorked As Double, ByRef exemptions As Integer, _
              ByRef mStatus As String, ByRef prevPay As Double)
  'Task 0: Get payroll data for employee
  empName = txtName.Textd
  hrWage = CDbl(txtWage.Text)
  hrsWorked = CDbl(txtHours.Text)
  exemptions = CInt(txtExempts.Text)
  mStatus = mtxtMarital.Text.ToUpper.Substring(0, 1)   'M or S
  prevPay = CDbl(txtPriorPay.Text)
End Sub

Function Gross_Pay(ByVal hrWage As Double, ByVal hrsWorked As Double) _
         As Double
  'Task 1: Compute weekly pay before taxes
  If hrsWorked <= 40 Then
    Return hrsWorked * hrWage
```

```
    Else
      Return 40 * hrWage + (hrsWorked - 40) * 1.5 * hrWage
    End If
End Function

Function Total_Pay(ByVal prevPay As Double, _
                   ByVal pay As Double) As Double
    'Task 2: Compute total pay before taxes
    Return prevPay + pay
End Function

Function FICA_Tax(ByVal pay As Double, ByVal prevPay As Double, _
                  ByVal totalPay As Double) As Double
    'Task 3: Compute social security and medicare tax
    Dim socialSecurity As Double    'Social Security tax for this week
    Dim medicare As Double          'Medicare tax for this week
    Dim sum As Double               'Sum of above two taxes
    If totalPay <= 90000 Then
      socialSecurity = 0.062 * pay
    ElseIf prevPay < 90000 Then
      socialSecurity = 0.062 * (90000 - prevPay)
    End If
    medicare = 0.0145 * pay
    sum = socialSecurity + medicare
    Return Math.Round(sum, 2)       'Round to nearest cent
End Function

Function Fed_Tax(ByVal pay As Double, ByVal exemptions As Integer, _
                 ByVal mStatus As String) As Double
    'Task 4.1: Compute federal income tax rounded to two decimal places
    Dim adjPay As Double
    Dim tax As Double               'Unrounded federal tax
    adjPay = pay - (61.54 * exemptions)
    If adjPay < 0 Then
      adjPay = 0
    End If
    If mStatus = "S" Then
      tax = TaxSingle(adjPay)       'Task 4.2
    Else
      tax = TaxMarried(adjPay)      'Task 4.3
    End If
    Return Math.Round(tax, 2)       'Round to nearest cent
End Function

Function TaxSingle(ByVal adjPay As Double) As Double
    'Task 4.2: Compute federal tax withheld for single person
    Select Case adjPay
      Case 0 To 51
        Return 0
      Case 51 To 188
        Return 0.1 * (adjPay - 51)
      Case 188 To 606
        Return 13.7 + 0.15 * (adjPay - 188)
      Case 606 To 1341
        Return 76.4 + 0.25 * (adjPay - 606)
```

```
      Case 1341 To 2922
        Return 260.15 + 0.28 * (adjPay - 1341)
      Case 2922 To 6313
        Return 702.83 + 0.33 * (adjPay - 2922)
      Case Is > 6313
        Return 1821.86 + 0.35 * (adjPay - 6313)
    End Select
  End Function

  Function TaxMarried(ByVal adjPay As Double) As Double
    'Task 4.3: Compute federal tax withheld for married person
    Select Case adjPay
      Case 0 To 154
        Return 0
      Case 154 To 435
        Return 0.1 * (adjPay - 154)
      Case 435 To 1273
        Return 28.1 + 0.15 * (adjPay - 435)
      Case 1273 To 2322
        Return 153.8 + 0.25 * (adjPay - 1273)
      Case 2322 To 3646
        Return 416.05 + 0.28 * (adjPay - 2322)
      Case 3646 To 6409
        Return 786.77 + 0.33 * (adjPay - 3646)
      Case Is > 6409
        Return 1698.56 + 0.35 * (adjPay - 6409)
    End Select
  End Function

  Function Net_Check(ByVal pay As Double, ByVal ficaTax As Double, _
                     ByVal fedTax As Double) As Double
    'Task 5: Compute amount of money given to employee
    Return pay - ficaTax - fedTax
  End Function

  Sub ShowPayroll(ByVal empName As String, ByVal pay As Double, _
                  ByVal totalPay As Double, ByVal ficaTax As Double, _
                  ByVal fedTax As Double, ByVal check As Double)
    'Task 6: Display results of payroll computations
    Dim fmtStr As String = "{0,24} {1,-10:C}"
    With lstResults.Items
      .Clear()
      .Add("Payroll results for " & empName)
      .Add("")
      .Add(String.Format(fmtStr, "Gross pay this period:", pay))
      .Add("")
      .Add(String.Format(fmtStr, "Year-to-date earnings:", totalPay))
      .Add("")
      .Add(String.Format(fmtStr, "Fica Taxes this period:", ficaTax))
      .Add("")
      .Add(String.Format(fmtStr, "Income tax withheld:", fedTax))
      .Add("")
      .Add(String.Format(fmtStr, "Net pay (check amount):", check))
    End With
  End Sub
```

Comments

1. In the function FICA_Tax, care has been taken to avoid computing Social Security benefits tax on income in excess of $90,000 per year. The logic of the program makes sure an employee whose income crosses the $90,000 threshold during a given week is taxed only on the difference between $90,000 and his previous year-to-date income.

2. The two functions TaxMarried and TaxSingle use Select Case blocks to incorporate the tax brackets given in Tables 5.11 and 5.12 for the amount of federal income tax withheld. The upper limit of each Case clause is the same as the lower limit of the next Case clause. This ensures that fractional values for *adjPay*, such as 61.54 in the TaxSingle function, will be properly treated as part of the higher salary range.

CHAPTER 5 SUMMARY

1. The function Chr associates a character with each number from 0 through 255 as determined by the ANSI table. The function Asc is the inverse of the Chr function.

2. The *relational operators* are $<$, $>$, $=$, $<>$, $<=$, and $>=$.

3. The principal *logical operators* are And, Or, and Not.

4. A *condition* is an expression involving literals, variables, functions, and operators (arithmetic, relational, or logical) that can be evaluated as either True or False.

5. The value of a variable or expression of Boolean data type is either True or False.

6. An *If block* decides what action to take depending on the truth values of one or more conditions. To allow several courses of action, the If, ElseIf, and Else parts of an If statement can contain other If statements.

7. A *Select Case block* selects from one of several actions depending on the value of an expression, called the *selector*. The entries in the *value lists* should have the same type as the selector.

CHAPTER 5 PROGRAMMING PROJECTS

1. Table 5.15 gives the price schedule for Eddie's Equipment Rental. Full-day rentals cost one-and-a-half times half-day rentals. Write a program that displays Table 5.15 in a list box when an appropriate button is clicked and displays a bill in another list box based on the item number and time period chosen by a customer. The bill

TABLE 5.15 **Price schedule for Eddie's Equipment Rental.**

Piece of Equipment	Half-Day	Full-Day
1. Rug cleaner	$16.00	$24.00
2. Lawn mower	$12.00	$18.00
3. Paint sprayer	$20.00	$30.00

should include a $30.00 deposit. A possible form layout and sample run are shown in Figure 5.9.

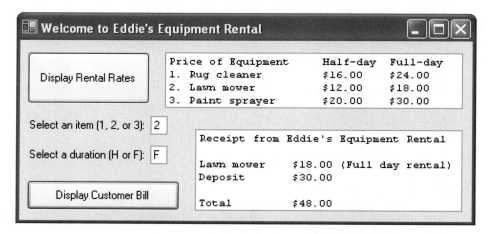

FIGURE 5.9   **Form layout and sample run for Programming Project 1.**

2. The American Heart Association suggests that at most 30 percent of the calories in our diet come from fat. Although food labels give the number of calories and amount of fat per serving, they often do not give the percentage of calories from fat. This percentage can be calculated by multiplying the number of grams of fat in one serving by 9, dividing that number by the total number of calories per serving, and multiplying the result by 100. Write a program that requests the name, number of calories per serving, and the grams of fat per serving as input, and tells us whether the food meets the American Heart Association recommendation. A sample run is as in Figure 5.10.

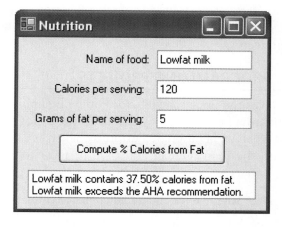

FIGURE 5.10   **Sample run of Programming Project 2.**

3. Table 5.16 gives the 2004 federal income tax rate schedule for single taxpayers. Write a program that requests taxable income and calculates federal income tax. Use a Sub procedure for the input and a Function procedure to calculate the tax.

TABLE 5.16 **2004 federal income tax rates for single tax payers.**

Taxable Income Over	But Not Over	Your Tax Is	Of Amount Over
$0	$7,150	10%	$0
$7,150	$29,050	$715.00 + 15%	$7,150
$29,050	$70,350	$4,000.00 + 25%	$29,050
$70,350	$146,750	$14,325.00 + 28%	$70,350
$146,750	$319,100	$35,717.00 + 33%	$146,750
$319,100		$92,592.50 + 35%	$319,100

4. Write a program to determine the real roots of the quadratic equation $ax^2 + bx + c = 0$ (where $a \neq 0$) after requesting the values of a, b, and c. Use a Sub procedure to ensure that a is nonzero. **Note:** The equation has 2, 1, or 0 solutions depending on whether the value of $b^2 - 4*a*c$ is positive, zero, or negative. In the first two cases, the solutions are given by the quadratic formula $(-b \pm \text{Sqrt}(b^2 - 4*a*c))/(2*a)$. Test the program with the following sets of coefficients:

$a = 1 \quad b = -11 \quad c = 28 \quad$ Solutions are 4 and 7
$a = 1 \quad b = -6 \quad c = 9 \quad$ Solution is 3
$a = 1 \quad b = 4 \quad c = 5 \quad$ No solution

5. Table 5.17 contains seven proverbs and their truth values. Write a program that presents these proverbs one at a time and asks the user to evaluate them as true or false. The program should then tell the user how many questions were answered correctly and display one of the following evaluations: Perfect (all correct), Excellent (5 or 6 correct), You might consider taking Psychology 101 (less than 5 correct).

TABLE 5.17 **Seven proverbs.**

Proverb	Truth Value
The squeaky wheel gets the grease.	True
Cry and you cry alone.	True
Opposites attract.	False
Spare the rod and spoil the child.	False
Actions speak louder than words.	True
Familiarity breeds contempt.	False
Marry in haste, repent at leisure.	True

Source: "You Know What They Say …," by Alfie Kohn, *Psychology Today*, April 1988.

6. Write a program to analyze a mortgage. The user should enter the amount of the loan, the annual rate of interest, and the duration of the loan in months. When the user clicks on the button, the information that was entered should be checked to make sure it is reasonable. If bad data have been supplied, the user should be so advised. Otherwise, the monthly payment and the total amount of interest paid should be displayed. The formula for the monthly payment is

$$payment = p*r/(1 - (1 + r)^{\wedge}(-n)),$$

where p is the amount of the loan, r is the monthly interest rate (annual rate divided by 12) given as a number between 0 (for 0 percent) and 1 (for 100 percent), and n is the duration of the loan in months. The formula for the total interest paid is

$$total\ interest = n*payment - p.$$

(Test the program for a mortgage of $240,000 at 6% annual rate of interest, and duration 360 months. Such a mortgage will have a monthly payment of $1,438.92 and total interest of $278,011.65.)

7. *Five, Six, Pick up Sticks.*

Write a program that allows the user to challenge the computer to a game of Pick-up-Sticks. Here is how the game works. The user chooses the number of matchsticks (from 5 to 50) to place in a pile. Then, the computer chooses who will go first. At each turn, the contestant can remove one, two, or three matchsticks from the pile. The contestant who chooses the last matchstick loses.

The computer should make the user always select from a pile where the number of matchsticks has a remainder of 1 when divided by 4. For instance, if the user initially chooses a number of matchsticks that has a remainder of 1 when divided by 4, then the computer should have the user go first. Otherwise, the computer should go first and remove the proper number of matchsticks. [**Note:** The remainder when n is divided by 4 is (n Mod 4).] After writing the program, play a few games with the computer and observe that the computer always wins.

FIGURE 5.11   **A possible outcome of Programming Project 7.**

6

Repetition

6.1 Do Loops 248

6.2 Processing Lists of Data with Do Loops 261
   ◆ Peek Method ◆ Counters and Accumulators ◆ Flags
   ◆ Nested Loops

6.3 For . . . Next Loops 277
   ◆ Declaration of Control Variables ◆ Nested For . . . Next Loops

6.4 A Case Study: Analyze a Loan 291
   ◆ Designing the Analyze-a-Loan Program ◆ The User Interface
   ◆ Writing the Analyze-a-Loan Program ◆ Pseudocode for the
   Analyze-a-Loan Program

Summary 301

Programming Projects 301

247

6.1 Do Loops

A **loop**, one of the most important structures in Visual Basic, is used to repeat a sequence of statements a number of times. At each repetition, or **pass**, the statements act upon variables whose values are changing.

The **Do loop** repeats a sequence of statements either as long as or until a certain condition is true. A Do statement precedes the sequence of statements, and a Loop statement follows the sequence of statements. The condition, preceded by either the word "While" or the word "Until", follows the word "Do" or the word "Loop". When Visual Basic executes a Do loop of the form

```
Do While condition
  statement(s)
Loop
```

it first checks the truth value of *condition*. If *condition* is false, then the statements inside the loop are not executed, and the program continues with the line after the Loop statement. If *condition* is true, then the statements inside the loop are executed. When the statement Loop is encountered, the entire process is repeated, beginning with the testing of *condition* in the Do While statement. In other words, the statements inside the loop are repeatedly executed only as long as (that is, while) the condition is true. Figure 6.1 contains the pseudocode and flowchart for this loop.

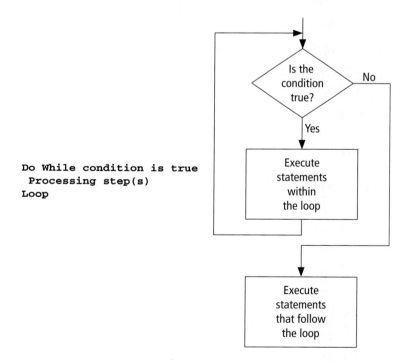

```
Do While condition is true
  Processing step(s)
Loop
```

FIGURE 6.1 Pseudocode and flowchart for a Do While loop.

Example 1   The following program, in which the condition in the Do loop is "num <= 7", displays the numbers from 1 through 7. (After the Do loop executes, the value of *num* will be 8.)

```
Private Sub btnDisplay_Click(...) Handles btnDisplay.Click
  'Display the numbers from 1 to 7
  Dim num As Integer = 1
  Do While num <= 7
    lstNumbers.Items.Add(num)
    num += 1     'Add 1 to the value of num
  Loop
End Sub
```

[Run, and click the button. The following is displayed in the list box.]

```
1
2
3
4
5
6
7
```

Do loops are commonly used to ensure that a proper response is received from the InputBox function.

 Example 2   The following program requires the user to enter a number from 1 through 3. The Do loop repeats the request until the user gives a proper response.

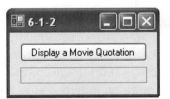

OBJECT	PROPERTY	SETTING
frmMovie	Text	6-1-2
btnDisplay	Text	Display a Movie Quotation
txtQuotation	ReadOnly	True

```
Private Sub btnDisplay_Click(...) Handles btnDisplay.Click
  Dim response As Integer, quotation As String = ""
  response = CInt(InputBox("Enter a number from 1 to 3."))
  Do While (response < 1) Or (response > 3)
    response = CInt(InputBox("Enter a number from 1 to 3."))
  Loop
  Select Case response
    Case 1
      quotation = "Plastics."
    Case 2
      quotation = "Rosebud."
```

```
   Case 3
      quotation = "That's all folks."
   End Select
   txtQuotation.Text = quotation
End Sub
```

[Run, and click the button.]

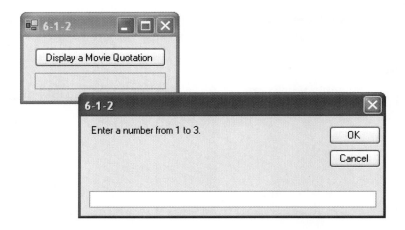

[Type 3 into the box and press the OK button.]

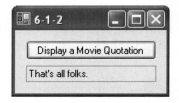

In Examples 1 and 2, the condition was checked at the top of the loop—that is, before the statements were executed. Alternatively, the condition can be checked at the bottom of the loop when the statement Loop is reached. When Visual Basic encounters a Do loop of the form

```
Do
   statement(s)
Loop Until condition
```

it executes the statements inside the loop and then checks the truth value of *condition*. If *condition* is true, then the program continues with the line after the Loop statement. If *condition* is false, then the entire process is repeated beginning with the Do statement. In other words, the statements inside the loop are executed once and then are repeatedly executed *until* the condition is true. Figure 6.2 shows the pseudocode and flowchart for this type of Do loop.

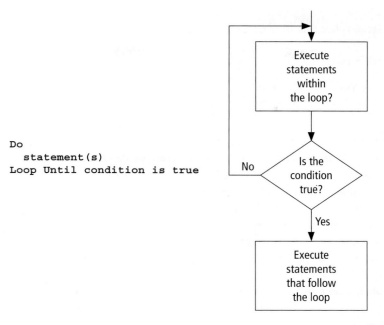

```
Do
    statement(s)
Loop Until condition is true
```

FIGURE 6.2   Pseudocode and flowchart for a Do loop with condition tested at the bottom.

 Example 3   The following program is equivalent to Example 2, except that the condition is tested at the bottom of the loop:

```
Private Sub btnDisplay_Click(...) Handles btnDisplay.Click
  Dim response As Integer, quotation As String = ""
  Do
    response = CInt(InputBox("Enter a number from 1 to 3."))
  Loop Until (response >= 1) And (response <= 3)
  Select Case response
    Case 1
      quotation = "Plastics."
    Case 2
      quotation = "Rosebud."
    Case 3
      quotation = "That's all folks."
  End Select
  txtQuotation.Text = quotation
End Sub
```

Do loops allow us to calculate useful quantities for which we might not know a simple formula.

 Example 4   Suppose you deposit money into a savings account and let it accumulate at 6 percent interest compounded annually. The following program determines when you will be a millionaire:

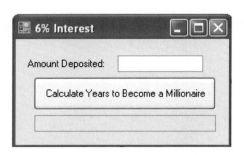

OBJECT	PROPERTY	SETTING
frmMillionaire	Text	6% Interest
lblAmount	Text	Amount Deposited:
txtAmount		
btnCalculate	Text	Calculate Years to Become a Millionaire
txtWhen	ReadOnly	True

```
Private Sub btnYears_Click(...) Handles btnYears.Click
  'Compute years required to become a millionaire
  Dim balance As Double, numYears As Integer
  balance = CDbl(txtAmount.Text)
  Do While balance < 1000000
    balance += 0.06 * balance
    numYears += 1
  Loop
  txtWhen.Text = "In " & numYears & _
                 " years you will have a million dollars."
End Sub
```

[Run, type 100000 into the text box, and press the button.]

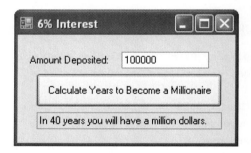

Comments

1. Be careful to avoid infinite loops—that is, loops that are never exited. The following loop is infinite, because the condition "balance < 1000" will always be true.

   Note: Click on the form's Close button at the upper right corner of the title bar to end the program.

   ```
   Private Sub btnButton_Click(...) Handles btnlick
     'An infinite loop
     Dim balance As Double = 100, intRate As Double
     Do While balance < 1000
       balance = (1 + intRate) * balance
     Loop
     txtBalance.Text = FormatCurrency(balance)
   End Sub
   ```

   Notice that this slip-up can be avoided by adding something like **= 0.04** to the end of the Dim statement.

2. Visual Basic allows the use of the words "While" and "Until" at either the top or bottom of a Do loop. In this text, the usage of these words is restricted for the following reasons:

(a) Because any While statement can be easily converted to an Until statement and vice versa, the restriction produces no loss of capabilities and the programmer has one less matter to think about.

(b) Restricting the use simplifies reading the program. The word "While" proclaims testing at the top, and the word "Until" proclaims testing at the bottom.

(c) Certain other major structured languages only allow "While" at the top and "Until" at the bottom of a loop. Therefore, following this convention will make life easier for people already familiar with or planning to learn one of these languages.

(d) Standard pseudocode uses the word "While" to denote testing a loop at the top and the word "Until" to denote testing at the bottom.

Practice Problems 6.1

1. How do you decide whether a condition should be checked at the top of a loop or at the bottom?

2. Change the following code segment so it will be executed at least once:

```
Do While continue = "Yes"
  answer = InputBox("Do you want to continue? (Y or N)")
  If answer.ToUpper = "Y" Then
    continue = "Yes"
  Else
    continue = "No"
  End If
Loop
```

EXERCISES 6.1

In Exercises 1 through 6, determine the output displayed when the button is clicked.

```
1. Private Sub btnDisplay_Click(...) Handles btnDisplay.Click
     Dim q As Double
     q = 3
     Do While q < 15
       q = 2 * q - 1
     Loop
     txtOutput.Text = CStr(q)
   End Sub
```

2. ```
Private Sub btnDisplay_Click(...) Handles btnDisplay.Click
    Dim balance As Double = 1000
    Dim interest As Double = 0.1
    Dim n As Integer = 0   'Number of years
    Do
       lstOutput.Items.Add(n & " " & balance)
       balance = (1 + interest) * balance
       n += 1
    Loop Until (balance > 1200)
    lstOutput.Items.Add(n)
End Sub
```

3. ```
Private Sub btnDisplay_Click(...) Handles btnDisplay.Click
    'Display a message
    Dim num As Double = 4
    Dim message As String = ""
    Do
       Select Case num
          Case 1
             message = "grammer!"
             num = -1
          Case 2
             message = "re a su"
             num = (5 - num) * (3 - num)
          Case 3
             message = "per pro"
             num = 4 - num
          Case 4
             message = "You a"
             num = 2 * num - 6
       End Select
       txtOutput.Text &= message
    Loop Until (num = -1)
End Sub
```

4. ```
Private Sub btnQuiz_Click(...) Handles btnQuiz.Click
    Dim prompt As String, firstYear As Integer
    'Computer-assisted instruction
    prompt = "In what year was the IBM PC first produced?"
    lstQuiz.Items.Clear()
    Do
       firstYear = CInt(InputBox(prompt))
       Select Case firstYear
          Case 1981
             lstQuiz.Items.Add("Correct. The computer was an instant")
             lstQuiz.Items.Add("success. By the end of 1981, there")
             lstQuiz.Items.Add("was such a backlog of orders that buyers")
             lstQuiz.Items.Add("had a three-month waiting period.")
```
```

```
      Case Is < 1981
        lstQuiz.Items.Add("Later. The Apple II, which preceded")
        lstQuiz.Items.Add("the IBM PC, appeared in 1977.")
      Case Is > 1981
        lstQuiz.Items.Add("Earlier. The first successful IBM PC")
        lstQuiz.Items.Add("clone, the Compaq Portable, ")
        lstQuiz.Items.Add("appeared in 1983.")
    End Select
    lstQuiz.Items.Add("")
  Loop Until firstYear = 1981
End Sub
```

(Assume that the first response is 1980 and the second response is 1981.)

5.
```
Private Sub btnDisplay_Click(...) Handles btnDisplay.Click
   'Calculate the remainder in long division
   txtOutput.Text = CStr(Remainder(3, 17))
End Sub

Function Remainder(ByVal divisor As Double, _
                   ByVal dividend As Double) As Double
  Dim sum As Double = 0
  Do While sum <= dividend
    sum += divisor
  Loop
  Return (dividend - sum + divisor)
End Function
```

6.
```
Private Sub btnDisplay_Click(...) Handles btnDisplay.Click
   'Simulate IndexOf; search for the letter t
   Dim info As String = "Potato"
   Dim letter As String = "t"
   Dim answer As Integer
   answer = IndexOf(info, letter)
   txtOutput.Text = CStr(answer)
End Sub

Function IndexOf(ByVal word As String, ByVal letter As String) _
               As Integer
  Dim counter As Integer = 0
  Dim current As String = ""
  Do While counter < word.Length
    current = word.Substring(counter, 1)
    If letter = current Then
      Return counter
    End If
    counter += 1 'Add 1 to the value of counter
  Loop
  'If not found then the answer is -1
  Return -1
End Function
```

In Exercises 7 through 10, identify the errors.

7.
```
Private Sub btnDisplay_Click(...) Handles btnDisplay.Click
    Dim q As Double
    q = 1
    Do While q > 0
        q = 3 * q - 1
        lstOutput.Items.Add(q)
    Loop
End Sub
```

8.
```
Private Sub btnDisplay_Click(...) Handles btnDisplay.Click
    'Display the numbers from 1 to 5
    Dim num As Integer
    Do While num <> 6
        num = 1
        lstOutput.Items.Add(num)
        num += 1
    Loop
End Sub
```

9.
```
Private Sub btnDisplay_Click(...) Handles btnDisplay.Click
    'Repeat until a yes response is given
    Dim answer As String = "N"
    Loop
        answer = InputBox("Did you chop down the cherry tree (Y/N)?")
    Do Until (answer.ToUpper = "Y")
End Sub
```

10.
```
Private Sub btnDisplay_Click(...) Handles btnDisplay.Click
    'Repeat as long as desired
    Dim n As Integer, answer As String = ""
    Do
        n += 1
        lstOutput.Items.Add(n)
        answer = InputBox("Do you want to continue (Y/N)?")
    Until answer.ToUpper = "N"
End Sub
```

In Exercises 11 through 20, replace each phrase containing "Until" with an equivalent phrase containing "While", and vice versa. For instance, the phrase (Until sum = 100) would be replaced by (While sum <> 100).

11. `Until num < 7`
12. `Until name = "Bob"`
13. `While response = "Y"`
14. `While total = 10`
15. `While name <> ""`
16. `Until balance >= 100`

17. `While (a > 1) And (a < 3)`
18. `Until (ans = "") Or (n = 0)`
19. `Until Not (n = 0)`
20. `While (ans = "Y") And (n < 7)`

In Exercises 21 and 22, write simpler and clearer code that performs the same task as the given code.

21.
```
Private Sub btnDisplay_Click(...) Handles btnDisplay.Click
    Dim name As String
    name = InputBox("Enter a name:")
    lstOutput.Items.Add(name)
    name = InputBox("Enter a name:")
    lstOutput.Items.Add(name)
    name = InputBox("Enter a name:")
    lstOutput.Items.Add(name)
End Sub
```

22.
```
Private Sub btnDisplay_Click(...) Handles btnDisplay.Click
    Dim loopNum As Integer, answer As String = ""
    Do
      If loopNum >= 1 Then
        answer = InputBox("Do you want to continue (Y/N)?")
        answer = answer.ToUpper
      Else
        answer = "Y"
      End If
      If (answer = "Y") Or (loopNum = 0) Then
        loopNum += 1
        txtOutput.Text = CStr(loopNum)
      End If
    Loop Until (answer <> "Y")
End Sub
```

23. Write a program that displays a Celsius-to-Fahrenheit conversion table. Entries in the table should range from -40 to 40 degrees Celsius in increments of 5 degrees. **Note:** The formula $f = (9/5)*c + 32$ converts Celsius to Fahrenheit.

24. The world population doubled from 3 billion in 1959 to 6 billion in 1999. Assuming that the world population has been doubling every 40 years, write a program to determine when in the past the world population was less than 6 million.

25. The world population reached 6.5 billion people in 2006 and was growing at the rate of 1.2 percent each year. Assuming that the population will continue to grow at the same rate, write a program to determine when the population will reach 10 billion.

26. Write a program to display all the numbers between 1 and 100 that are perfect squares. (A perfect square is an integer that is the square of another integer; 1, 4, 9, and 16 are examples of perfect squares.)

27. Write a program to display all the numbers between 1 and 100 that are part of the Fibonacci sequence. The Fibonacci sequence begins 1, 1, 2, 3, 5, 8, ..., where each new number in the sequence is found by adding the previous two numbers in the sequence.

28. Write a program to request positive numbers one at a time from the user in an input dialog box. The user should be instructed to enter −1 after all the positive numbers have been supplied. At that time, the program should display the sum of the numbers.

29. An old grandfather clock reads 6:00 p.m. Sometime not too long after 6:30 p.m., the minute hand will pass directly over the hour hand. Write a program using a loop to make better and better guesses as to what time it is when the hands exactly overlap. Keep track of the positions of both hands using the minutes at which they are pointing. (At 6:00 p.m., the minute hand points at 0 while the hour hand points at 30.) You will need to use the fact that when the minute hand advances m minutes, the hour hand advances $m/12$ minutes. (For example, when the minute hand advances 60 minutes, the hour hand advances 5 minutes from one hour mark to the next.) To make an approximation, record how far the minute hand is behind the hour hand, then advance the minute hand by this much and the hour hand by $1/12$ this much. The loop should terminate when the resulting positions of the minute and hour hands differ by less than .0001 minute. (The exact answer is 32 and 8/11 minutes after 6.)

30. Write a program that requests a word containing the two letters r and n as input and determines which of the two letters appears first. If the word does not contain both of the letters, the program should so advise the user. (Test the program with the words "colonel" and "merriment.")

31. The coefficient of restitution of a ball, a number between 0 and 1, specifies how much energy is conserved when a ball hits a rigid surface. A coefficient of .9, for instance, means a bouncing ball will rise to 90 percent of its previous height after each bounce. Write a program to input a coefficient of restitution and an initial height in meters, and report how many times a ball bounces when dropped from its initial height before it rises to a height of less than 10 centimeters. Also report the total distance traveled by the ball before this point. The coefficients of restitution of a tennis ball, basketball, super ball, and softball are .7, .75, .9, and .3, respectively.

In Exercises 32 through 35, write a program to solve the stated problem.

32. *Savings Account.* $15,000 is deposited into a savings account paying 5 percent interest and $1000 is withdrawn from the account at the end of each year. Approximately how many years are required for the savings account to be depleted?

   Note: If at the end of a certain year the balance is $1000 or less, then the final withdrawal will consist of that balance and the account will be depleted.

33. Rework Exercise 32 so that the amount of money deposited initially is input by the user and the program computes the number of years required to deplete the account. **Note:** Be careful to avoid an infinite loop.

34. Consider an account in which $1000 is deposited upon opening the account and an additional $1000 is deposited at the end of each year. If the money earns interest at the rate of 5 percent, how long will it take before the account contains at least $1 million?

35. A person born in 1980 can claim, "I will be x years old in the year x squared." Write a program to determine the value of x.

36. Illustrate the growth of money in a savings account. When the user presses the button, values for Amount and Interest Rate are obtained from text boxes and used to calculate the number of years until the money doubles and the number of years until the money reaches a million dollars. Use the form design shown below.

Note: The balance at the end of each year is $(1 + r)$ times the previous balance, where r is the annual rate of interest in decimal form.

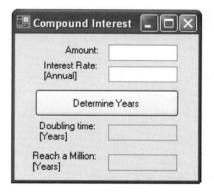

OBJECT	PROPERTY	SETTING
frmInterest	Text	Compound Interest
lblAmount	Text	Amount:
txtAmount		
lblRate	AutoSize	False
	Text	Interest Rate: [Annual]
txtRate		
btnDetermine	Text	Determine Years
lblDouble	AutoSize	False
	Text	Doubling Time: [Years]
txtDouble	ReadOnly	True
lblMillion	AutoSize	False
	Text	Reach a Million: [Years]
txtMillion	ReadOnly	True

37. Allow the user to enter a sentence. Then, depending on which button the user clicks, display the sentence entirely in capital letters or with just the first letter of each word capitalized.

In Exercises 38 and 39, write a program corresponding to the flowchart.

38. The flowchart in Figure 6.3 (on the next page) requests a whole number greater than 1 as input and factors it into a product of prime numbers. **Note:** A number is prime if its only factors are 1 and itself. Test the program with the numbers 660 and 139.

39. The flowchart in Figure 6.4 (on page 261) finds the greatest common divisor (the largest integer that divides both) of two positive integers input by the user. Write a program that corresponds to the flowchart. Use the Visual Basic operator Mod. The value of m Mod n is the remainder when m is divided by n.

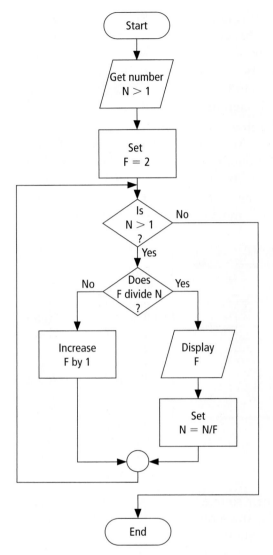

FIGURE 6.3 **Prime factors.**

Solutions to Practice Problems 6.1

1. As a rule of thumb, the condition is checked at the bottom if the loop should be executed at least once.

2. Either precede the loop with the statement **continue = "Yes"**, or change the first line to **Do** and replace the Loop statement with **Loop Until continue <> "Yes"**.

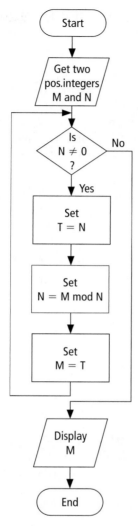

FIGURE 6.4   Greatest common divisor.

6.2   Processing Lists of Data with Do Loops

One of the main applications of programming is the processing of lists of data. Do loops are used to display all or selected items from lists, search lists for specific items, and perform calculations on the numerical entries of a list. This section introduces several devices that facilitate working with lists. **Counters** calculate the number of elements in lists, **accumulators** sum numerical values in lists, **flags** record whether certain events have occurred, and the **Peek method** can be used to determine when the end of a text file has been reached. **Nested loops** add yet another dimension to repetition.

■ Peek Method

Data to be processed are often retrieved from a file by a Do loop. Visual Basic has a useful method that will tell us if we have reached the end of the file from which we are reading. Suppose a file has been opened with a StreamReader object named *sr*. At any time, the value of

sr.Peek

is the ANSI value of the first character of the line about to be read with ReadLine. If the end of the file has been reached, the value of **sr.Peek** is −1.

One of the programs I wrote when I got my first personal computer in 1982 stored a list of names and phone numbers and displayed a phone directory. I stored the names in a file so I could easily add, change, or delete entries.

 Example 1   The following program displays the contents of a telephone directory. The names and phone numbers are contained in the file PHONE.TXT. The loop will repeat as long as there is still data in the file.

PHONE.TXT contains the following eight lines:

Bert
123-4567
Ernie
987-6543
Grover
246-8321
Oscar
135-7900

OBJECT	PROPERTY	SETTING
frmPhone	Text	Directory
btnDisplay	Text	Display Phone Numbers
lstNumbers		

```
Private Sub btnDisplay_Click(...) Handles btnDisplay.Click
  Dim name, phoneNum As String
  Dim sr As IO.StreamReader = IO.File.OpenText("PHONE.TXT")
  lstNumbers.Items.Clear()
  Do While sr.Peek <> -1
    name = sr.ReadLine
    phoneNum = sr.ReadLine
    lstNumbers.Items.Add(name & "    " & phoneNum)
  Loop
  sr.Close()
End Sub
```

[Run, and press the button.]

The program in Example 1 illustrates the proper way to process a list of data contained in a file. The Do loop should be tested at the top with an end-of-file condition. (If the file is empty, no attempt is made to input data from the file.) The first set of data should be input after the Do statement, and then the data should be processed. Figure 6.5 contains the pseudocode and flowchart for this technique.

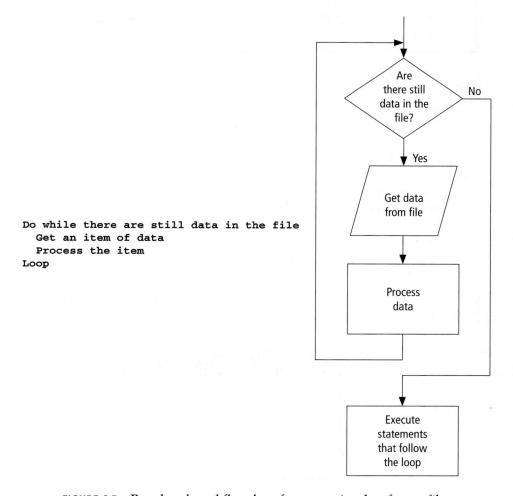

```
Do while there are still data in the file
   Get an item of data
   Process the item
Loop
```

FIGURE 6.5   Pseudocode and flowchart for processing data from a file.

Text files can be quite large. Rather than list the entire contents, we typically search the file for a specific piece of information.

Example 2   The following program modifies the program in Example 1 to search the telephone directory for a name specified by the user. If the name does not appear in the directory, the user is so notified. We want to keep searching as long as there is no match and we have not reached the end of the list. Therefore, the condition for the Do While statement is a compound logical expression with the operator And. After the last pass through the loop, we will know whether the name was found and will be able to display the requested information.

OBJECT	PROPERTY	SETTING
frmPhone	Text	Phone Number
lblName	Text	Name to look up:
txtName		
btnDisplay	Text	Display Phone Number
txtNumber	ReadOnly	True

```
Private Sub btnDisplay_Click(...) Handles btnDisplay.Click
  Dim name As String = "",  phoneNum As String = ""
  Dim sr As IO.StreamReader = IO.File.OpenText("PHONE.TXT")
  Do While (name <> txtName.Text) And (sr.Peek <> -1)
    name = sr.ReadLine
    phoneNum = sr.ReadLine
  Loop
  If (name = txtName.Text) Then
    txtNumber.Text = name & "    " & phoneNum
  Else
    txtNumber.Text = "Name not found."
  End If
  sr.Close()
End Sub
```

[Run, type "Grover" into the text box, and press the button.]

Counters and Accumulators

A **counter** is a numeric variable that keeps track of the number of items that have been processed. An **accumulator** is a numeric variable that totals numbers.

Example 3   The following program counts and finds the value of coins listed in a file. The file COINS.TXT contains the following entries, one per line: 1, 1, 5, 10, 10, 25. The fifth and sixth lines of the event procedure are not needed, since the counter *numCoins* and the accumulator *sum* have the initial value 0 by default. However, since these default values show the starting points for the two variables, the two assignment statements add clarity to the program.

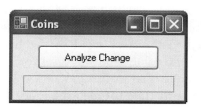

OBJECT	PROPERTY	SETTING
frmCoins	Text	Coins
btnAnalyze	Text	Analyze Change
txtValue	ReadOnly	True

```
Private Sub btnAnalyze_Click(...) Handles btnAnalyze.Click
  Dim numCoins As Integer, coin As String
  Dim sum As Double
  Dim sr As IO.StreamReader = IO.File.OpenText("COINS.TXT")
  numCoins = 0
  sum = 0
  Do While (sr.Peek <> -1)
    coin = sr.ReadLine
    numCoins += 1        'Add 1 to the value of numCoins
    sum += CDbl(coin)    'Add the value of the current coin to the sum
  Loop
  sr.Close()
  txtValue.Text = "The value of the " & numCoins & _
                  " coins is " & sum & " cents."
End Sub
```

[Run, and press the button.]

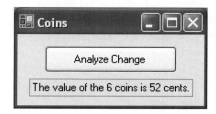

The value of the counter, *numCoins*, was initially 0 and changed on each execution of the loop to 1, 2, 3, 4, 5, and finally 6. The accumulator, *sum*, initially had the value 0 and increased with each execution of the loop to 1, 2, 7, 17, 27, and finally 52.

▦ Flags

A **flag** is a variable that keeps track of whether a certain situation has occurred. The data type most suited to flags is the **Boolean data type**. Variables of type Boolean can assume just two values: True and False. (As a default, Boolean variables are initialized to False.) Flags are used within loops to provide information that will be utilized after the loop terminates. Flags also provide an alternative method of terminating a loop.

Example 4   The following program counts the number of words in the file WORDS.TXT and then reports whether the words are in alphabetical order. In each execution of the loop, a word is compared to the next word in the list. The flag variable, called *orderFlag*, is initially assigned the value True and is set to False if a pair of adjacent words is out of order. The technique used in this program will be used in Chapter 7 when we study sorting. *Note:* The first time through the loop, the value of *word1* is the empty string. Each word must first be read into the variable *word2*.

WORDS.TXT contains the following winning words from the U.S. National Spelling Bee, one word per line: cambist, croissant, deification, hydrophyte, incisor, maculature, macerate, narcolepsy, shallon.

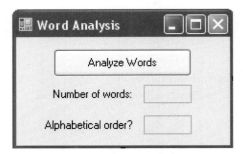

OBJECT	PROPERTY	SETTING
frmWords	Text	Word Analysis
btnAnalyze	Text	Analyze Words
lblNumber	Text	Number of words:
txtNumber	ReadOnly	True
lblAlpha	Text	Alphabetical order?
txtAlpha	ReadOnly	True

```
Private Sub btnAnalyze_Click(...) Handles btnAnalyze.Click
  'Count words.  Are they in alphabetical order?
  Dim orderFlag As Boolean, wordCounter As Integer
  Dim word1 As String = "", word2 As String
  Dim sr As IO.StreamReader = IO.File.OpenText("WORDS.TXT")
  orderFlag = True
  Do While (sr.Peek <> -1)
    word2 = sr.ReadLine
    wordCounter += 1          'Increment the word count by 1
    If word1 > word2 Then     'Two words are out of order
      orderFlag = False
    End If
    word1 = word2
  Loop
  sr.Close()
  txtNumber.Text = CStr(wordCounter)
```

```
  If orderFlag = True Then
    txtAlpha.Text = "YES"
  Else
    txtAlpha.Text = "NO"
  End If
End Sub
```

[Run, and press the button.]

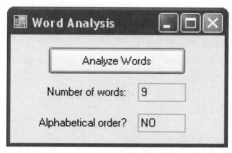

▦ Nested Loops

The statements within a Do loop can contain another Do loop. Such a configuration is referred to as **nested loops** and is useful in repeating a single data-processing routine several times.

 Example 5 The following program allows the user to look through several lists of names. Suppose we have several different phone directories, the names of which are listed in the file LISTS.TXT. (For instance, the file LISTS.TXT might contain the entries CLIENTS.TXT, FRIENDS.TXT, and KINFOLK.TXT.) A sought-after name might be in any one of the files. The statements in the inner Do loop will be used to look up names as before. At least one pass through the outer Do loop is guaranteed, and passes will continue as long as the name is not found and phone lists remain to be examined.

OBJECT	PROPERTY	SETTING
frmPhone	Text	Phone Number
lblName	Text	Name to look up:
txtName		
btnDisplay	Text	Display Phone Number
txtNumber	ReadOnly	True

```
Private Sub btnDisplay_Click(...) Handles btnDisplay.Click
  Dim foundFlag As Boolean
  Dim fileName As String
  Dim name As String = ""
  Dim phoneNum As String = ""
  Dim sr1 As IO.StreamReader = IO.File.OpenText("LISTS.TXT")
```

```
'The next line is not needed. It is added for clarity.
foundFlag = False
Do While (foundFlag = False) And (sr1.Peek <> -1)
  fileName = sr1.ReadLine
  Dim sr2 As IO.StreamReader = IO.File.OpenText(fileName)
  Do While (name <> txtName.Text) And (sr2.Peek <> -1)
    name = sr2.ReadLine
    phoneNum = sr2.ReadLine
  Loop
  sr2.Close()
  If name = txtName.Text Then
    txtNumber.Text = name & "      " & phoneNum
    foundFlag = True
  End If
Loop
sr1.Close()
If foundFlag = False Then
  txtNumber.Text = "Name not found."
End If
End Sub
```

Comments

1. In Appendix D, the section "Stepping through a Program Containing a Do Loop: Chapter 6" uses the Visual Basic debugging tools to trace the flow through a Do loop.

2. When *flagVar* is a variable of Boolean type, the statements

   If flagVar = True Then and **If flagVar = False Then**

   can be replaced by

   If flagVar Then and **If Not flagVar Then**

   Similarly, the statements

   Do While flagVar = True and **Do While flagVar = False**

   can be replaced by

   Do While flagVar and **Do While Not flagVar**

Practice Problems 6.2

1. Determine the output of the following program, where the three lines of the file SCORES.TXT contain the scores 150, 200, and 300:

```
Private Sub btnCompute_Click(...) Handles btnCompute.Click
  'Find the sum of a collection of bowling scores
  Dim sum, score As Double
```

```
Dim sr As IO.StreamReader = IO.File.OpenText("SCORES.TXT")
sum = 0
score = CDbl(sr.ReadLine)
Do While (sr.Peek <> -1)
  sum += score    'Add value of score to value of sum
  score = CDbl(sr.ReadLine)
Loop
sr.Close()
txtTotal.Text = CStr(sum)
End Sub
```

2. Why didn't the preceding program produce the intended output?

3. Correct the preceding program so it has the intended output.

EXERCISES 6.2

In Exercises 1 through 10, determine the output displayed when the button is clicked.

1.
```
Private Sub btnDisplay_Click(...) Handles btnDisplay.Click
    Dim flag As Boolean, word As String
    Dim sr As IO.StreamReader = IO.File.OpenText("DATA.TXT")
    Do While (sr.Peek <> -1)
      word = sr.ReadLine
      If word.IndexOf("A") <> -1 Then
        flag = True
      End If
    Loop
    sr.Close()
    If flag Then
      txtOutput.Text = "At least one word contains the letter A."
    Else
      txtOutput.Text = "No word contains the letter A."
    End If
End Sub
```
(Assume that the four lines of the file DATA.TXT have the following entries: AL, GORE, VIDAL, SASSOON.)

2.
```
Private Sub btnDisplay_Click(...) Handles btnDisplay.Click
    Dim name As String
    Dim sr As IO.StreamReader = IO.File.OpenText("DATA.TXT")
    Do While (sr.Peek <> -1)
      name = sr.ReadLine
      txtOutput.Text &= name
    Loop
    sr.Close()
End Sub
```
(Assume that the two lines of the file DATA.TXT contain the following entries: Ben, son.)

3.
```
Private Sub btnDisplay_Click(...) Handles btnDisplay.Click
  'Display list of desserts
  Dim dessert As String
  Dim sr As IO.StreamReader = IO.File.OpenText("DESSERTS.TXT")
  Do While (sr.Peek <> -1)
    dessert = sr.ReadLine
    lstOutput.Items.Add(dessert)
  Loop
  sr.Close()
End Sub
```
(Assume that the three lines of the file DESSERTS.TXT contain the following entries: pie, cake, melon.)

4.
```
Private Sub btnDisplay_Click(...) Handles btnDisplay.Click
  Dim city As String, pop As Double
  Dim sr As IO.StreamReader = IO.File.OpenText("CITYPOPS.TXT")
  Do While (sr.Peek <> -1)
    city = sr.ReadLine
    pop = CDbl(sr.ReadLine)
    If pop >= 3 Then
      lstOutput.Items.Add(city & "   " & pop)
    End If
  Loop
  sr.Close()
End Sub
```
(Assume that the eight lines of the file CITYPOPS.TXT contain the following data, where each pair of lines gives a city and its population in millions: New York, 8.1, Los Angeles, 3.8, Chicago, 2.9, Houston, 2.0.)

5.
```
Private Sub btnDisplay_Click(...) Handles btnDisplay.Click
  Dim firstLetter As String = "", fruit As String = ""
  Dim sr As IO.StreamReader = IO.File.OpenText("DATA.TXT")
  Do While (sr.Peek <> -1)
    fruit = sr.ReadLine
    If fruit.Substring(0, 1) <> firstLetter Then
      If firstLetter <> "" Then
        lstOutput.Items.Add("")
      End If
      firstLetter = fruit.Substring(0, 1)
      lstOutput.Items.Add("   " & firstLetter)
    End If
    lstOutput.Items.Add(fruit)
  Loop
  sr.Close()
End Sub
```
(Assume that the eight lines of the file FRUITS.TXT contain the following entries: Apple, Apricot, Avocado, Banana, Blueberry, Grape, Lemon, Lime.)

6.
```
Private Sub btnDisplay_Click(...) Handles btnDisplay.Click
  'Display list of numbers
  Dim num As Double
  Dim sr As IO.StreamReader = IO.File.OpenText("DATA.TXT")
  num = CDbl(sr.ReadLine)
  Do While (sr.Peek <> -1)
    lstOutput.Items.Add(num)
    num = CDbl(sr.ReadLine)
  Loop
  sr.Close()
End Sub
```
(Assume the four lines of the file DATA.TXT contain the entries 2, 3, 8, 5.)

7.
```
Private Sub btnDisplay_Click(...) Handles btnDisplay.Click
  Dim animal As String = "", groupName As String = ""
  InputAnimal(animal)
  If animal <> "" Then
    SearchList(animal, groupName)
    DisplayResult(animal, groupName)
  End If
End Sub

Sub DisplayResult(ByVal anml As String, ByVal gName As String)
  If gName = "" Then
    txtOutput.Text = "Animal not found."
  Else
    txtOutput.Text = "A " & gName & " of " & anml & "s."
  End If
End Sub

Sub InputAnimal(ByRef anml As String)
  'Request the name of an animal as input
  anml = InputBox("Please enter the name of an animal.")
End Sub

Sub SearchList(ByVal anml As String, ByRef gName As String)
  Dim creature, groupName As String
  creature = ""
  Dim sr As IO.StreamReader = IO.File.OpenText("ANIMALS.TXT")
  Do While (creature <> anml) And (sr.Peek <> -1)
    creature = sr.ReadLine
    groupName = sr.ReadLine
  Loop
  If (sr.Peek = -1) Then
    gName = ""
  Else
    gName = groupName
  End If
  sr.Close()
End Sub
```

(The six lines of the file ANIMALS.TXT contain the following entries: lion, pride, duck, brace, bee, swarm. Each pair of lines give an animal and the name of a group of those animals. Assume that the response is "duck".)

8.
```
Private Sub btnDisplay_Click(...) Handles btnDisplay.Click
  Dim excerpt As String
  excerpt = "I think I can. "
  Duplicate30(excerpt)
  excerpt = "We're off to see the wizard, " & _
            "the wonderful wizard of Oz."
  Duplicate30(excerpt)
End Sub

Sub Duplicate30(ByVal sentence As String)
  Dim flag As Boolean
  flag = False    'Flag tells whether loop has been executed
  Do While sentence.Length < 30
    flag = True
    sentence &= sentence
  Loop
  If flag = True Then
    lstOutput.Items.Add(sentence)
  Else
    lstOutput.Items.Add("Loop not executed.")
  End If
End Sub
```

9.
```
Private Sub btnDisplay_Click(...) Handles btnDisplay.Click
  Dim word As String = "", cWord As String = ""
  Dim sr As IO.StreamReader = IO.File.OpenText("WORDS.TXT")
  Do While (sr.Peek <> -1)
    word = sr.ReadLine
    If word.Substring(0, 1) = "c" Then
      cWord = word
    End If
  Loop
  sr.Close()
  txtOutput.Text = cWord
End Sub
```

(Assume that the 11 lines of the file WORDS.TXT contain the following items: time, is, a, child, idly, moving, counters, in, a, game, Heraclitus.)

10.
```
Private Sub btnDisplay_Click(...) Handles btnDisplay.Click
  Dim max, value, rowMax As Double
  Dim sr As IO.StreamReader = IO.File.OpenText("DATA.TXT")
  Do While (sr.Peek <> -1)
    value = CDbl(sr.ReadLine)
    rowMax = 0
```

```
      Do While value <> -2
        If value > rowMax Then
          rowMax = value
        End If
        value = CDbl(sr.ReadLine)
      Loop
      lstOutput.Items.Add(rowMax)
      If rowMax > max Then
        max = rowMax
      End If
    Loop
    sr.Close()
    lstOutput.Items.Add(max)
  End Sub
```

(Assume that the 12 lines of the file DATA.TXT contain the following entries: 5, 7, 3, −2, 10, 12, 6, 4, −2, 1, 9, −2.)

In Exercises 11 through 14, identify the errors.

11.
```
Private Sub btnDisplay_Click(...) Handles btnDisplay.Click
    Dim num As Double
    Dim sr As IO.StreamReader = IO.File.OpenText("DATA.TXT")
    Do While (sr.Peek <> -1) And (num > 0)
      num = CDbl(sr.ReadLine)
      lstOutput.Items.Add(num)
      sr.Close()
  End Sub
```

(Assume that the five lines of the file DATA.TXT contain the following entries: 7, 6, 0, −1, 2.)

12.
```
Private Sub btnDisplay_Click(...) Handles btnDisplay.Click
    Dim flag As Boolean, num, sum As Double
    Do While flag = False
      num = CDbl(InputBox("Enter a number"))
      sum += num
      If num * num < 0 Then
        flag = True
      End If
    Loop
    txtOutput.Text = CStr(num)
  End Sub
```

13.
```
Private Sub btnDisplay_Click(...) Handles btnDisplay.Click
    'Display names of four U.S. Presidents
    Dim president As String
    Dim sr As IO.StreamReader = IO.File.OpenText("PRES.TXT")
    president = sr.ReadLine
```

```
    Do
      lstOutput.Items.Add(president)
      president = sr.ReadLine
    Loop Until (sr.Peek = -1)
    sr.Close()
  End Sub
```

(Assume that the lines of the file PRES.TXT contain the following entries: Lincoln, Washington, Kennedy, Jefferson.)

14.
```
Private Sub btnDisplay_Click(...) Handles btnDisplay.Click
  Dim num As Double
  Dim sr As IO.StreamReader = IO.File.OpenText("DATA.TXT")
  If (sr.Peek = -1) Then
    num = 0
  Else
    num = CDbl(sr.ReadLine)
  End If
  Do While 1 < num < 5
    lstOutput.Items.Add(num)
    If (sr.Peek = -1) Then
      num = 0
    Else
      num = CDbl(sr.ReadLine)
    End If
  Loop
  sr.Close()
End Sub
```

(Assume that the five lines of the file DATA.TXT contain the following entries: 3, 2, 4, 7, 2.)

15. Write a program to find and display the largest of a collection of positive numbers contained in a text file. (Test the program with the collection of numbers 89, 77, 95, and 86.)

16. Write a program to find and display those names that are repeated in a text file. Assume that the file has already been sorted into alphabetical order. When a name is found to be repeated, display it only once.

17. Suppose that the file FINAL.TXT contains student grades on a final exam. Write a program that displays the average grade on the exam and the percentage of grades that are above average.

18. Suppose that the file BIDS.TXT contains a list of bids on a construction project. Write a program to analyze the list and report the two highest bids.

19. Suppose that the file USPRES.TXT contains the names of the United States presidents in order from George Washington to George W. Bush. Write a program that asks the user to type a number from 1 to 43 into a text box and then, when the user clicks a button, displays the name of the president corresponding to that number.

20. Table 6.1 shows the different grades of eggs and the minimum weight required for each classification. Write a program that processes the text file EGGS.TXT containing a list of the weights of a sample of eggs. The program should report the number of eggs in each grade and the weight of the lightest and heaviest egg in the sample. Figure 6.6 shows a possible output of the program. **Note:** Eggs weighing less than 1.5 ounces cannot be sold in supermarkets.

TABLE 6.1	Grades of eggs.
Grade	**Weight (in ounces)**
Jumbo	2.5
Extra Large	2.25
Large	2
Medium	1.75
Small	1.5

```
57 Jumbo eggs
95 Extra Large eggs
76 Large eggs
96 Medium eggs
77 Small eggs
Lightest egg: 1 ounces
Heaviest egg: 2.69 ounces
```

FIGURE 6.6   Possible output for Exercise 20.

21. Write a program to request a positive integer as input and carry out the following algorithm. If the number is even, divide it by 2. Otherwise, multiply the number by 3 and add 1. Repeat this process with the resulting number and continue repeating the process until the number 1 is reached. After the number 1 is reached, the program should display how many iterations were required. **Note:** A number is even if Int(num/2) = num/2. (Test the program with the numbers 9, 21, and 27.)

22. Suppose that the file USPRES.TXT contains the names of all United States Presidents, and the file USSENATE.TXT contains the names of all former and present U.S. Senators. Write a program with nested loops that uses these files to display the names of all Presidents who served in the Senate.

23. Suppose that the file SONNET.TXT contains Shakespeare's Sonnet #18. Each entry in the file consists of a line of the sonnet. Write a program using nested loops to analyze this file line by line and report the average number of words in a line and the total number of words in the sonnet.

24. Suppose that the file SALES.TXT contains information on the sales during the past week at a new car dealership. The file contains the following information for each salesperson at the dealership: the name of the salesperson, pairs of numbers giving the final sales price and the dealer cost for each sale made by that salesperson, and a pair of zeros to indicate the end of data for that salesperson. The first fourteen lines of the file contain the following data: Tom Jones, 18100, 17655, 22395, 21885, 15520, 14895, 0, 0, Bill Smith, 16725, 16080, 0, 0. Write a program to display the name of each salesperson and the commission earned for the week. Assume that the commission is 15% of the profit on each sale.

25. Write a program that uses a flag and does the following:

    (a) Ask the user to input a sentence containing parentheses. **Note:** The closing parenthesis should not directly precede the period.

    (b) Display the sentence with the parentheses and their contents removed. Test the program with the following sentence as input: BASIC (Beginners All-purpose Symbolic Instruction Code) was the world's most widely known computer language.

26. The salespeople at a health club keep track of the members who have joined in the last month. Their names and types of membership (Bronze, Silver, or Gold) are stored in the text file NEWMEMBERS.TXT. Write a program that displays all the Bronze members, then the Silver members, and finally the Gold members.

27. Table 6.2 gives the prices of various liquids. Write a program that requests an amount of money as input and displays the names of all liquids for which a gallon could be purchased with that amount of money. The information from the table should be read from a file. As an example, if the user has $2.35, then the following should be displayed in the list box:

```
You can purchase one gallon of any of the following liquids:
Bleach
Gasoline
Milk
```

TABLE 6.2 Some comparative prices per gallon of various liquids.

Liquid	Price	Liquid	Price
Apple Cider	2.60	Milk	2.30
Beer	6.00	Gatorade	4.20
Bleach	1.40	Perrier	6.85
Coca-Cola	2.55	Pancake Syrup	15.50
Gasoline	2.25	Spring Water	4.10

Solutions to Practice Problems 6.2

1. 350

2. When the third score was read from the file, sr.Peek assumed the value −1. With sr.Peek = −1, the loop terminated and the third score was never added to *sum*.

3. ```
   Private Sub btnCompute_Click(...) Handles btnCompute.Click
       'Find the sum of a collection of bowling scores
       Dim sum, score As Double
       Dim sr As IO.StreamReader = IO.File.OpenText("SCORE.TXT")
       Do While (sr.Peek <> −1)
         score = CDbl(sr.ReadLine)
         sum += score
   ```
   ```

```
   Loop
   sr.Close()
   txtTotal.Text = CStr(sum)
End Sub
```

6.3   For . . . Next Loops

When we know exactly how many times a loop should be executed, a special type of loop, called a For . . . Next loop, can be used. For . . . Next loops are easy to read and write, and have features that make them ideal for certain common tasks. The following code uses a For . . . Next loop to display a table:

```
Private Sub btnDisplayTable_Click(...) Handles btnDisplayTable.Click
  'Display a table of the first 5 numbers and their squares
  'Assume the font for lstTable is Courier New
  Dim i As Integer
  For i = 1 To 5
    lstTable.Items.Add(i & "   " & i ^ 2)
  Next
End Sub
```

[Run, and click on btnDisplayTable. The following is displayed in the list box.]

```
1   1
2   4
3   9
4   16
5   25
```

The equivalent program written with a Do loop is as follows.

```
Private Sub btnDisplayTable_Click(...) Handles btnDisplayTable.Click
  'Display a table of the first 5 numbers and their squares
  Dim i As Integer
  i = 1
  Do While i <= 5
    lstTable.Items.Add(i & "   " & i ^ 2)
    i += 1     'Add 1 to i
  Loop
End Sub
```

In general, a portion of a program of the form

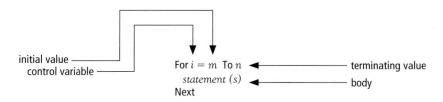

constitutes a For ... Next loop. The pair of statements For and Next cause the statements between them to be repeated a specified number of times. The For statement designates a numeric variable, called the **control variable**, that is initialized and then automatically changes after each execution of the loop. Also, the For statement gives the range of values this variable will assume. The Next statement increments the control variable. If $m \leq n$, then i is assigned the values $m, m + 1, \ldots, n$ in order, and the body is executed once for each of these values. If $m > n$, then the body is skipped and execution continues with the statement after the For ... Next loop.

```
For i = m to n
  Processing steps(s)
Next
```

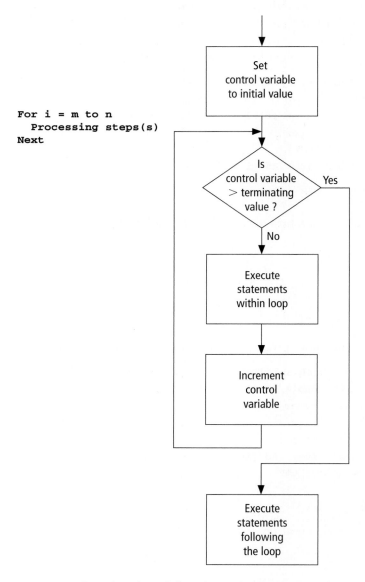

FIGURE 6.7   Pseudocode and flowchart of a For ... Next loop.

When program execution reaches a For . . . Next loop, such as the one shown previously, the For statement assigns to the control variable i the initial value m and checks to see whether i is greater than the terminating value n. If so, then execution jumps to the line following the Next statement. If $i <= n$, the statements inside the loop are executed. Then, the Next statement increases the value of i by 1 and checks this new value to see if it exceeds n. If not, the entire process is repeated until the value of i exceeds n. When this happens, the program moves to the line following the loop. Figure 6.7 contains the pseudocode and flowchart of a For . . . Next loop.

The control variable can be any numeric variable. The most common single-letter names are i, j, and k; however, if appropriate, the name should suggest the purpose of the control variable.

Example 1   Suppose the population of a city is 300,000 in the year 2006 and is growing at the rate of 3 percent per year. The following program displays a table showing the population each year until 2010.

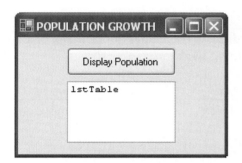

OBJECT	PROPERTY	SETTING
frmPopulation	Text	POPULATION GROWTH
btnDisplay	Text	Display Population
lstTable		

```
Private Sub btnDisplay_Click(...) Handles btnDisplay.Click
  'Display population from 2006 to 2010
  Dim pop As Double = 300000, yr As Integer
  Dim fmtStr As String = "{0,4}{1,12:N0}"
  For yr = 2006 To 2010
    lstTable.Items.Add(String.Format(fmtStr, yr, pop))
    pop += 0.03 * pop
  Next
End Sub
```

[Run, and click the button.]

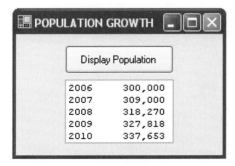

The initial and terminating values can be literals, variables, or expressions. For instance, the For statement in the preceding program can be replaced by

```
Dim firstYr As Integer = 2006
Dim lastYr As Integer = 2010
For yr = firstYr To lastYr
```

In Example 1, the control variable was increased by 1 after each pass through the loop. A variation of the For statement allows any number to be used as the increment. The statement

```
For i = m To n Step s
```

instructs the Next statement to add *s* to the control variable instead of 1. The numbers *m*, *n*, and *s* do not have to be whole numbers. The number *s* is called the **step value** of the loop. **Note:** If the control variable will assume values that are not whole numbers, then the variable must be of type Double.

 Example 2 The following program displays the values of the index of a For . . . Next loop for terminating and step values input by the user:

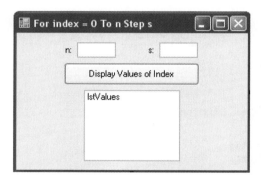

OBJECT	PROPERTY	SETTING
frmIndex	Text	For index = 0 To n Step s
lblN	Text	n:
txtEnd		
lblS	Text	s:
txtStep		
btnDisplay	Text	Display Values of Index
lstValues		

```
Private Sub btnDisplay_Click(...) Handles btnDisplay.Click
  'Display values of index ranging from 0 to n Step s
  Dim n, s, As Double
  Dim index As Double
  n = CDbl(txtEnd.Text)
  s = CDbl(txtStep.Text)
  lstValues.Items.Clear()
  For index = 0 To n Step s
    lstValues.Items.Add(index)
  Next
End Sub
```

[Run, type 3.2 and .5 into the text boxes, and click the button.]

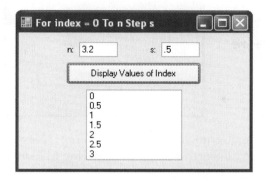

In the examples considered so far, the control variable was successively increased until it reached the terminating value. However, if a negative step value is used and the initial value is greater than the terminating value, then the control value is decreased until reaching the terminating value. In other words, the loop counts backward or downward.

 Example 3 The following program accepts a word as input and displays it backwards:

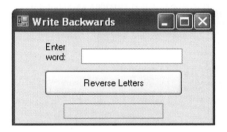

OBJECT	PROPERTY	SETTING
frmBackwards	Text	Write Backwards
lblWord	AutoSize	False
	Text	Enter word:
txtWord		
btnReverse	Text	Reverse Letters
txtBackwards	ReadOnly	True

```
Private Sub btnReverse_Click(...) Handles btnReverse.Click
  txtBackwards.Text = Reverse(txtWord.Text)
End Sub

Function Reverse(ByVal info As String) As String
  Dim m, j As Integer, temp As String = ""
  m = info.Length
  For j = m - 1 To 0 Step -1
    temp &= info.Substring(j, 1)
  Next
  Return temp
End Function
```

[Run, type "SUEZ" into the text box, and click the button.]

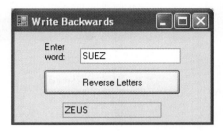

Note: The initial and terminating values of a For . . . Next loop can be expressions. For instance, the third and fourth lines of the function in Example 3 can be consolidated to

```
For j = info.Length - 1 To 0 Step -1
```

▣ Declaration of Control Variables

The control variable of a For . . . Next loop can be declared directly in the For statement. A statement of the form

```
For i As DataType = m to n
```

(possibly with a Step clause) both declares the control variable *i* and specifies its initial and terminating values. In this case, however, the scope of the control variable *i* is limited to the body of the For . . . Next loop. For instance, in Example 1, the two statements

```
Dim yr As Integer
For yr = 2006 to 2010
```

can be replaced by the single statement

```
For yr As Integer = 2006 to 2010
```

In Example 2, the two statements

```
Dim index as Double
For index = 0 to n Step s
```

can be replaced by the single statement

```
For index As Double = 0 to n Step s
```

This feature is new to Visual Basic 2005 and is the preferred way to declare control variables of For . . . Next loops.

▣ Nested For . . . Next Loops

The body of a For . . . Next loop can contain any sequence of Visual Basic statements. In particular, it can contain another For . . . Next loop. However, the second loop must be completely contained inside the first loop and must have a different control variable. Such a configuration is called **nested For . . . Next loops**. Figure 6.8 shows several examples of valid nested loops.

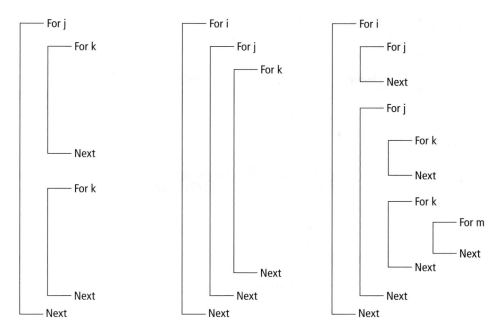

FIGURE 6.8   Nested For . . . Next loops.

Example 4   The following program displays a multiplication table for the integers from 1 to 3. Here *j* denotes the left factors of the products, and *k* denotes the right factors. Each factor takes on a value from 1 to 3. The values are assigned to *j* in the outer loop and to *k* in the inner loop. Initially, *j* is assigned the value 1, and then the inner loop is traversed three times to produce the first row of products. At the end of these three passes, the value of *j* will still be 1, and the value of *k* will have been incremented to 4. The first execution of the outer loop is then complete. Following this, the statement Next increments the value of *j* to 2. The statement beginning "For k" is then executed. It resets the value of *k* to 1. The second row of products is displayed during the next three executions of the inner loop and so on.

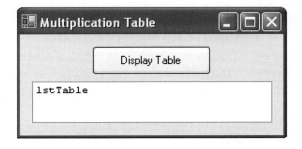

OBJECT	PROPERTY	SETTING
frmTable	Text	Multiplication Table
btnDisplay	Text	Display Table
lstTable	Font	Courier New

```
Private Sub btnDisplay_Click(...) Handles btnDisplay.Click
  Dim row, entry As String
  lstTable.Items.Clear()
  For j As Integer = 1 To 3
    row = ""
```

```
    For k As Integer = 1 To 3
        entry = j & " x " & k & " = " & (j * k)
        row &= entry & "      "
      Next
      lstTable.Items.Add(row)
  Next
End Sub
```

[Run, and press the button.]

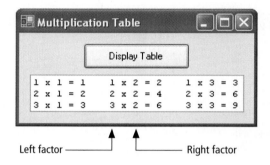

Left factor ——————— ⌐ —— Right factor

Comments

1. For and Next statements must be paired. If one is missing, the automatic syntax checker will complain with a wavy underline and a message such as "A 'For' must be paired with a 'Next'."

2. Consider a loop beginning with For $i = m$ To n Step s. The loop will be executed exactly once if m equals n no matter what value s has. The loop will not be executed at all if m is greater than n and s is positive, or if m is less than n and s is negative.

3. The value of the control variable should not be altered within the body of the loop; doing so might cause the loop to repeat indefinitely or have an unpredictable number of repetitions.

4. Noninteger step values can lead to roundoff errors with the result that the loop is not executed the intended number of times. For instance, a loop beginning with **For i As Double = 1 To 2 Step .1** will be executed only 10 times instead of the intended 11 times. It should be replaced with **For i As Double = 1 To 2.01 Step .1**.

5. Visual Basic provides a way to skip an iteration in a For...Next loop. When the statement **Continue For** is encountered in the body of the loop, execution immediately jumps to the Next statement. An analogous statement **Continue Do** is available for Do loops. This feature is new in Visual Basic 2005.

6. Visual Basic provides a way to back out of a For...Next loop. When the statement **Exit For** is encountered in the body of the loop, execution jumps immediately to the statement following the Next statement. An analogous statement **Exit Do** is available for Do loops.

Practice Problems 6.3

1. Why won't the following lines of code work as intended?

```
For i As Integer = 15 To 1
  lstBox.Items.AddItem(i)
Next
```

2. When is a For . . . Next loop more appropriate than a Do loop?

EXERCISES 6.3

In Exercises 1 through 12, determine the output displayed in the list box when the button is clicked.

1. ```
Private Sub btnDisplay_Click(...) Handles btnDisplay.Click
  For i As Integer = 1 To 4
    lstBox.Items.Add("Pass #" & i)
  Next
End Sub
```

2. ```
Private Sub btnDisplay_Click(...) Handles btnDisplay.Click
  For i As Integer = 3 To 6
    lstBox.Items.Add(2 * i)
  Next
End Sub
```

3. ```
Private Sub btnDisplay_Click(...) Handles btnDisplay.Click
  For j As Integer = 2 To 8 Step 2
    lstBox.Items.Add(j)
  Next
  lstBox.Items.Add("Who do we appreciate?")
End Sub
```

4. ```
Private Sub btnDisplay_Click(...) Handles btnDisplay.Click
  For countdown As Integer = 10 To 1 Step -1
    lstBox.Items.Add(countdown)
  Next
  lstBox.Items.Add("blastoff")
End Sub
```

5. ```
Private Sub btnDisplay_Click(...) Handles btnDisplay.Click
  Dim num As Integer
  num = 5
  For i As Integer = num To (2 * num - 3)
    lstBox.Items.Add(i)
  Next
End Sub
```
```

6.
```
Private Sub btnDisplay_Click(...) Handles btnDisplay.Click
    For i As Double = 3 To 5 Step .25
        lstBox.Items.Add(i)
    Next
    lstBox.Items.Add(i)
End Sub
```

7.
```
Private Sub btnDisplay_Click(...) Handles btnDisplay.Click
    'First entry in text file is number of records in file
    Dim recCount As Integer
    Dim name, mileTime As String
    Dim sr As IO.StreamReader = IO.File.OpenText("MILER.TXT")
    recCount = CInt(sr.Readline)
    For miler As Integer = 1 To recCount
        name = sr.Readline
        mileTime = sr.Readline
        lstBox.Items.Add(name & "   " & mileTime)
    Next
    sr.Close()
End Sub
```
(Assume that the seven lines of the file MILER.TXT contain the following entries: 3, Steve Cram, 3:46.31, Steve Scott, 3:51.6, Mary Slaney, 4:20.5.)

8.
```
Private Sub btnDisplay_Click(...) Handles btnDisplay.Click
    'First entry in text file is number of records in file
    Dim recCount, total, score As Integer
    Dim sr As IO.StreamReader = IO.File.OpenText("SCORES.TXT")
    recCount = CInt(sr.Readline)
    For i As Integer = 1 To recCount
        score = CInt(sr.Readline)
        total += score 'Add the value of score to the value of total
    Next
    sr.Close()
    lstBox.Items.Add("Average = " & total / recCount)
End Sub
```
(Assume the file SCORES.TXT contains the entries 4, 89, 85, 88, 98.)

9.
```
Private Sub btnDisplay_Click(...) Handles btnDisplay.Click
    Dim row, entry As String
    For i As Integer = 0 To 2
        row = ""
        For j As Integer = 0 To 3
            entry = CStr(i + (3 * j) + 1)
            row &= entry & "     "
        Next
        lstBox.Items.Add(row)
    Next
End Sub
```

10.
```
Private Sub btnDisplay_Click(...) Handles btnDisplay.Click
    Dim row As String
    For i As Integer = 1 To 5
      row = ""
      For j As Integer = 1 To i
        row &= "*"
      Next
      lstBox.Items.Add(row)
    Next
End Sub
```

11.
```
Private Sub btnDisplay_Click(...) Handles btnDisplay.Click
    Dim word As String
    Dim num1, num2 As Integer
    word = InputBox("Please enter a word.")
    num1 = CInt(Int((20 - word.Length) / 2))
    num2 = 20 - num1 - word.Length
    lstBox.Items.Add(Asterisks(num1) & word & Asterisks(num2))
End Sub

Function Asterisks(ByVal num As Integer) As String
    Dim chain As String = ""
    For i As Integer = 1 To num
      chain &= "*"
    Next
    Return chain
End Function
```
(Assume that the response is *Hooray*.)

12.
```
Private Sub btnDisplay_Click(...) Handles btnDisplay.Click
    'Display an array of letters
    Dim info As String, letter As String
    info = "DATA"
    For i As Integer = 1 To info.Length
      letter = info.Substring(i - 1, 1)
      lstBox.Items.Add(RepeatFive(letter))
    Next
End Sub

Function RepeatFive(ByVal letter As String) As String
    Dim chain As String = ""
    For i As Integer = 1 To 5
      chain &= letter
    Next
    Return chain
End Function
```

In Exercises 13 through 16, identify the errors.

13.
```
Private Sub btnDisplay_Click(...) Handles btnDisplay.Click
    For j As Double = 1 To 25.5 Step -1
        lstBox.Items.Add(j)
    Next
End Sub
```

14.
```
Private Sub btnDisplay_Click(...) Handles btnDisplay.Click
    For i As Integer = 1 To 3
        lstBox.Items.Add(i & " " & 2 ^ i)
End Sub
```

15.
```
Private Sub btnDisplay_Click(...) Handles btnDisplay.Click
    'Display all numbers from 0 through 20 except for 13
    For i As Double = 20 To 0
        If i = 13 Then
            i = 12
        End If
        lstBox.Items.Add(i)
    Next
End Sub
```

16.
```
Private Sub btnDisplay_Click(...) Handles btnDisplay.Click
    For j As Integer = 1 To 4 Step 0.5
        lstBox.Items.Add(j)
    Next
End Sub
```

In Exercises 17 and 18, rewrite the program using a For … Next loop.

17.
```
Private Sub btnDisplay_Click(...) Handles btnDisplay.Click
    Dim num As Integer = 1
    Do While num <= 9
        lstBox.Items.Add(num)
        num += 2     'Add 2 to value of num
    Loop
End Sub
```

18.
```
Private Sub btnDisplay_Click(...) Handles btnDisplay.Click
    lstBox.Items.Add("hello")
    lstBox.Items.Add("hello")
    lstBox.Items.Add("hello")
    lstBox.Items.Add("hello")
End Sub
```

In Exercises 19 through 38, write a program to complete the stated task.

19. Display a row of 10 stars (asterisks).

20. Request a number from 1 to 20 and display a row of that many stars (asterisks).

21. Display a 10-by-10 array of stars.

22. Request a number and call a Sub procedure to display a square having that number of stars on each side.

23. Find the sum $1 + 1/2 + 1/3 + 1/4 + \cdots + 1/100$.

24. Find the sum of the odd numbers from 1 through 99.

25. You are offered two salary options for ten days of work. Option 1: $100 per day. Option 2: $1 the first day, $2 the second day, $4 the third day, and so on, with the amount doubling each day. Write a program to determine which option pays better.

26. When $1000 is deposited at 5 percent simple interest, the amount grows by $50 each year. When money is invested at 5 percent compound interest, then the amount at the end of each year is 1.05 times the amount at the beginning of that year. Write a program to display the amounts for 10 years for a $1000 deposit at 5 percent simple and compound interest. The first few lines displayed in the list box should appear as in Figure 6.9.

Year	Amount Simple Interest	Amount Compound Interest
1	$1,050.00	$1,050.00
2	$1,100.00	$1,102.50
3	$1,150.00	$1,157.63

FIGURE 6.9   Growth of $1000 at simple and compound interest.

27. According to researchers at Stanford Medical School (as cited in *Medical Self Care*), the ideal weight for a woman is found by multiplying her height in inches by 3.5 and subtracting 108. The ideal weight for a man is found by multiplying his height in inches by 4 and subtracting 128. Request a lower and upper bound for heights and then produce a table giving the ideal weights for women and men in that height range. For example, when a lower bound of 62 and an upper bound of 65 are specified, Figure 6.10 shows the output displayed in the list box.

Height	Wt–Women	Wt–Men
62	109	120
63	112.5	124
64	116	128
65	119.5	132

FIGURE 6.10   Output for Exercise 27.

28. Table 6.3 (on the next page) gives data (in millions) on personal computer sales and revenues. Read the data from the file PC.TXT, and generate an extended table with two additional columns, Pct Foreign (percent of personal computers sold outside the United States) and Avg Rev (average revenue per computer sold in the United States).

29. Request a sentence, and display the number of sibilants (that is, letters *S* or *Z*) in the sentence. The counting should be carried out by a function.

30. Request a number, *n*, from 1 to 30 and one of the letters *S* or *P*. Then, depending upon whether *S* or *P* was selected, calculate the sum(s) or product(s) of the numbers from 1 to *n*. The calculations should be carried out in Function procedures.

TABLE 6.3	Personal computer sales and revenues (in millions).			
	Year	U.S. Sales	Worldwide Sales	U.S. Revenues
	1998	34.6	98.4	74,920
	1999	40.1	116.2	80,200
	2000	46.0	128.5	88,110
	2001	43.5	132.0	77,000

31. Suppose $800 is deposited into a savings account earning 4 percent interest compounded annually, and $100 is added to the account at the end of each year. Calculate the amount of money in the account at the end of 10 years. (Determine a formula for computing the balance at the end of one year based on the balance at the beginning of the year. Then write a program that starts with a balance of $800 and makes 10 passes through a loop containing the formula to produce the final answer.)

32. A TV set is purchased with a loan of $563 to be paid off with five monthly payments of $116. The interest rate is 1 percent per month. Display a table giving the balance on the loan at the end of each month.

33. *Radioactive Decay.* Cobalt 60, a radioactive form of cobalt used in cancer therapy, decays or dissipates over a period of time. Each year, 12 percent of the amount present at the beginning of the year will have decayed. If a container of cobalt 60 initially contains 10 grams, determine the amount remaining after five years.

34. *Supply and Demand.* This year's level of production and price (per bushel) for most agricultural products greatly affects the level of production and price next year. Suppose the current crop of soybeans in a certain country is 80 million bushels and experience has shown that for each year,

$$[\text{price this year}] = 20 - .1 * [\text{quantity this year}]$$

$$[\text{quantity next year}] = 5 * [\text{price this year}] - 10,$$

where quantity is measured in units of millions of bushels. Generate a table to show the quantity and price for each of the next 12 years.

35. Request a number greater than 3, and display a hollow rectangle similar to the one in Figure 6.11(a) with each outer row and column having that many stars. Use a fixed-width font such as Courier New so that the spaces and asterisks will have the same width.

(a)   (b)

FIGURE 6.11 **Outputs for Exercises 35 and 36.**

36. Request an odd number, and display a triangle similar to the one in Figure 6.11(b) with the input number of stars in the top row.

37. A man pays $1 to get into a gambling casino. He loses half of his money there and then has to pay $1 to leave. He goes to a second casino, pays another $1 to get in, loses half of his money again, and pays another $1 to leave. Then, he goes to a third casino, pays another $1 to get in, loses half of his money again, and pays another $1 to get out. After this, he's broke. Write a program to determine the amount of money he began with by testing $5, then $6, and so on.

38. Create the histogram in Figure 6.12. A file should hold the years and values. The first line in the file could be used to hold the title for the histogram.

```
1999    * * * * *   5
2000    * * * * * * * * * *   11
2001    * * * * * * * * * * * * *   15
2002    * * * * * * * * * * * * * * * * * * *   21
2003    * * * * * * * * * * * * * * * * * * * * * * * * *   27
```

Worldwide PDA Sales in Millions

FIGURE 6.12   **Histogram for Exercise 38.**

39. Write a program to estimate how much a young worker will make before retiring at age 65. Request the worker's name, age, and starting salary as input. Assume the worker receives a 5 percent raise each year. For example, if the user enters Helen, 25, and 20000, then the text box should display the following:

Helen will earn about $2,415,995

40. Write a program that accepts a word as input and determines if its letters are in alphabetical order. (Test the program with the words "almost," "imply," and "biopsy.")

Solutions to Practice Problems 6.3

1. The loop will never be entered because 15 is greater than 1. The intended first line might have been

```
For i = 15 To 1 Step -1
```
or
```
For i = 1 To 15
```

2. If the exact number of times the loop will be executed is known before entering the loop, then a For...Next loop should be used. Otherwise, a Do loop is more appropriate.

6.4   A Case Study: Analyze a Loan

This case study develops a program to analyze a loan. Assume the loan is repaid in equal monthly payments and interest is compounded monthly. The program should request the amount (principal) of the loan, the annual rate of interest, and the number of years over which the loan is to be repaid. The four options to be provided by buttons are as follows:

1. Calculate the monthly payment. The formula for the monthly payment is

$$\text{payment} = p*r/(1 - (1 + r)^{\wedge}(-n)),$$

where p is the principal of the loan, r is the monthly interest rate (annual rate divided by 12) given as a number between 0 (for 0 percent) and 1 (for 100 percent), and n is the number of months over which the loan is to be repaid. Because a payment computed in this manner can be expected to include fractions of a cent, the value should be rounded up to the next nearest cent. This corrected payment can be achieved using the formula

$$\text{correct payment} = \text{Math.Round(payment} + .005, 2).$$

2. Display an amortization schedule, that is, a table showing the balance on the loan at the end of each month for any year over the duration of the loan. Also show how much of each monthly payment goes toward interest and how much is used to repay the principal. Finally, display the total interest paid over the duration of the loan. The balances for successive months are calculated with the formula

$$\text{balance} = (1 + r)*b - m,$$

where r is the monthly interest rate (annual rate / 12, a fraction between 0 and 1), b is the balance for the preceding month (amount of loan left to be paid), and m is the monthly payment.

3. Show the effect of changes in the interest rate. Display a table giving the monthly payment for each interest rate from 1 percent below to 1 percent above the specified annual rate in steps of one-eighth of a percent.

4. Quit.

▨ Designing the Analyze-a-Loan Program

For each of the tasks described in preceding options 1 to 4, the program must first look at the text boxes to obtain the particulars of the loan to be analyzed. Thus, the first division of the problem is into the following tasks:

1. Input the principal, interest, and duration.
2. Calculate the monthly payment.
3. Calculate the amortization schedule.
4. Display the effects of interest-rate changes.
5. Quit.

Task 1 is a basic input operation and Task 2 involves applying the formula given in Option 1; therefore, these tasks need not be broken down any further. The demanding work of the program is done in Tasks 3 and 4, which can be divided into smaller subtasks.

3. *Calculate amortization schedule.* This task involves simulating the loan month by month. First, the monthly payment must be computed. Then, for each month, the new balance must be computed together with a decomposition of the monthly payment into the amount paid for interest and the amount going toward repaying the principal. That is, Task 3 is divided into the following subtasks:

3.1 Calculate monthly payment.

3.2 Calculate new balance.

3.3 Calculate amount of monthly payment for principal.

3.4 Calculate amount of monthly payment for interest.

3.5 Calculate total interest paid.

4. ***Display the effects of interest-rate changes.*** A table is needed to show the effects of changes in the interest rate on the size of the monthly payment. First, the interest rate is reduced by one percentage point and the new monthly payment is computed. Then the interest rate is increased by regular increments until it reaches one percentage point above the original rate, with new monthly payment amounts computed for each intermediate interest rate. The subtasks for this task are then as follows:

4.1 Reduce the interest rate by 1 percent.

4.2 Calculate the monthly payment.

4.3 Increase the interest rate by 1/8 percent.

4.4 Repeat until a certain condition is met.

The hierarchy chart in Figure 6.13 shows the stepwise refinement of the problem.

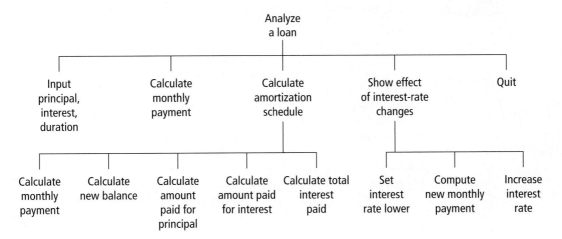

FIGURE 6.13   Hierarchy chart for the Analyze-a-Loan Program.

■ The User Interface

Figure 6.14 shows a possible form design and Table 6.4 gives the initial settings for the form and its controls. Figures 6.15, 6.16, and 6.17 (following the program) show possible runs of the program for each task available through the buttons. The width and height of the list box were adjusted by trial and error to handle the extensive output generated.

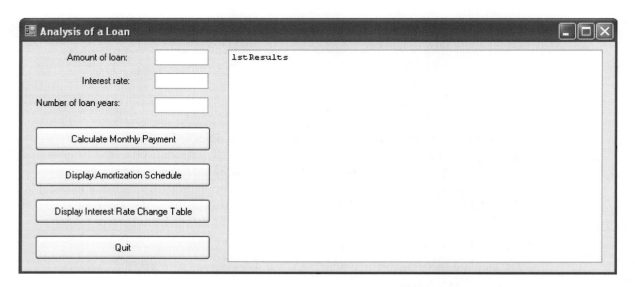

FIGURE 6.14 **Template for the Analyze-a-Loan program.**

TABLE 6.4 **Objects and initial properties for the Analyze-a-Loan program.**

Object	Property	Setting
frmLoan	Text	Analysis of a Loan
lblPrincipal	Text	Amount of loan:
txtPrincipal		
lblYearly Rate	Text	Interest rate:
txtYearly Rate		
lblNumYears	Text	Number of loan years:
txtNumYears		
btnPayment	Text	Calculate Monthly Payment
btnAmort	Text	Display Amortization Schedule
btnRateTable	Text	Display Interest Rate Change Table
btnQuit	Text	Quit
lstResults		

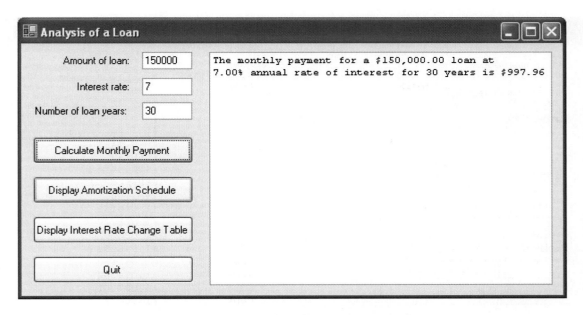

FIGURE 6.15   Monthly payment on a 30-year loan.

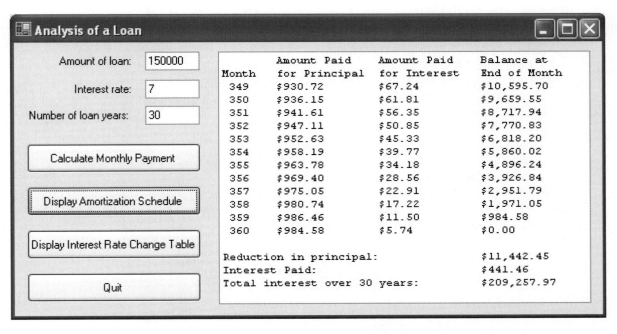

FIGURE 6.16   Amortization for year 30 of a loan.

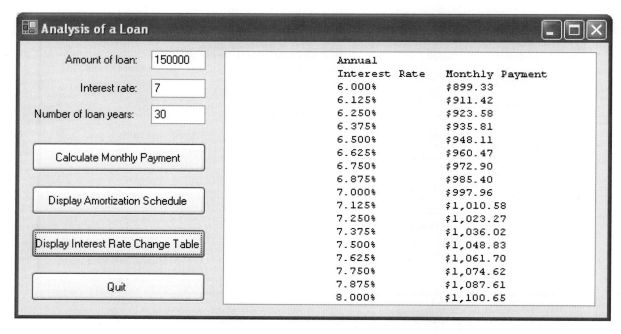

FIGURE 6.17   Interest-rate-change table for a 30-year loan.

▓ Pseudocode for the Analyze-a-Loan Program

Calculate Monthly Payment button:
    INPUT LOAN DATA (Sub procedure InputData)
    COMPUTE MONTHLY PAYMENT (Function Payment)
    DISPLAY MONTHLY PAYMENT (Sub procedure ShowPayment)

Display Amortization Schedule button:
    INPUT LOAN DATA (Sub procedure InputData)
    DISPLAY AMORTIZATION SCHEDULE (Sub procedure ShowAmortSched)
    Compute monthly interest rate
    COMPUTE MONTHLY PAYMENT (Function Payment)
    Calculate and display amortization table
    Display total interest paid

Display Interest Rate Change Table button:
    INPUT LOAN DATA (Sub procedure InputData)
    DISPLAY INTEREST RATE CHANGE TABLE
      (Sub procedure ShowInterestChanges)

    Decrease annual rate by .01
    Do
      Display monthly interest rate
      COMPUTE AND DISPLAY MONTHLY PAYMENT (Function Payment)
      Increase annual rate by .00125
    Loop Until annual rate > original annual rate + .01

Writing the Analyze-a-Loan Program

Table 6.5 shows each task discussed before and the procedure that carries out the task.

TABLE 6.5   Tasks and their procedures.

Task	Procedure
1. Input principal, interest, and duration.	InputData
2. Calculate monthly payment.	ShowPayment
3. Calculate amortization schedule.	ShowAmortizationSchedule
3.1 Calculate monthly payment.	Payment
3.2 Calculate new balance.	Balance
3.3 Calculate amount paid for principal.	ShowAmortizationSchedule
3.4 Calculate amount paid for interest.	ShowAmortizationSchedule
3.5 Calculate total interest paid.	ShowAmortizationSchedule
4. Show effect of interest-rate changes.	ShowInterestChanges
4.1 Reduce interest rate.	ShowInterestChanges
4.2 Compute new monthly payment.	Payment
4.3 Increase interest rate.	ShowInterestChanges
4.4 Repeat until a certain condition is met.	ShowInterestChanges

```
Private Sub btnPayment_Click(...) Handles btnPayment.Click
   Dim principal As Double        'Amount of loan
   Dim yearlyRate As Double       'Annual rate of interest
   Dim numMonths As Integer       'Number of months to repay loan
   InputData(principal, yearlyRate, numMonths)
   ShowPayment(principal, yearlyRate, numMonths)
End Sub

Private Sub btnAmort_Click(...) Handles btnAmort.Click
   Dim principal As Double        'Amount of loan
   Dim yearlyRate As Double       'Annual rate of interest
   Dim numMonths As Integer       'Number of months to repay loan
   InputData(principal, yearlyRate, numMonths)
   ShowAmortizationSchedule(principal, yearlyRate, numMonths)
End Sub

Private Sub btnRateTable_Click(...) Handles btnRateTable.Click
   Dim principal As Double        'Amount of loan
   Dim yearlyRate As Double       'Annual rate of interest
   Dim numMonths As Integer       'Number of months to repay loan
   InputData(principal, yearlyRate, numMonths)
   ShowInterestChanges(principal, yearlyRate, numMonths)
End Sub

Private Sub btnQuit_Click(...) Handles btnQuit.Click
   End
End Sub
```

```vb
Sub InputData(ByRef principal As Double, _
              ByRef yearlyRate As Double, ByRef numMonths As Integer)
    'Input the loan amount, yearly rate of interest, and duration
    Dim percentageRate As Double, numYears As Integer
    principal = CDbl(txtPrincipal.Text)
    percentageRate = CDbl(txtYearlyRate.Text)
    yearlyRate = percentageRate / 100
    numYears = CInt(txtNumYears.Text)
    numMonths = numYears * 12
End Sub

Sub ShowPayment(ByVal principal As Double, _
                ByVal yearlyRate As Double, ByVal numMonths As Integer)
    Dim monthlyRate As Double = yearlyRate / 12
    Dim monthlyPayment As Double
    'Calculate monthly payment
    monthlyPayment = Payment(principal, monthlyRate, numMonths)
    'Display results
    lstResults.Items.Clear()
    lstResults.Items.Add("The monthly payment for a " & _
              FormatCurrency(principal) & " loan at")
    lstResults.Items.Add(FormatNumber(yearlyRate * 100) & _
              "% annual rate of interest for " _
       & FormatNumber(numMonths / 12, 0) & " years is " & _
              FormatCurrency(monthlyPayment))
End Sub

Sub ShowAmortizationSchedule(ByVal principal As Double, _
          ByVal yearlyRate As Double, ByVal numMonths As Integer)
    Dim questionYear As String
    Dim startMonth As Integer
    Dim monthlyRate As Double = yearlyRate / 12
    Dim monthlyPayment As Double
    Dim totalInterest As Double = 0
    Dim yearInterest As Double = 0
    Dim oldBalance, newBalance As Double
    Dim numYears As Double = numMonths / 12
    Dim principalPaid, interestPaid As Double
    Dim principalReduced As Double
    Dim fmtStr As String
    'Ask for the year to display
    questionYear = "Please enter year (1-" & numYears & _
                   ") for which amortization is to be shown:"
    startMonth = 12 * CInt(InputBox(questionYear, "Which Year?")) - 11
    'Display column headings
    lstResults.Items.Clear()
    fmtStr = "{0,-8}{1,-15}{2,-15}{3,-15}"
    lstResults.Items.Add(String.Format(fmtStr, "", "Amount Paid", _
                                       "Amount Paid", "Balance at"))
```

```vb
  lstResults.Items.Add(String.Format(fmtStr, "Month", _
                   "for Principal", "for Interest", "End of Month"))
  monthlyPayment = Payment(principal, monthlyRate, numMonths)
  oldBalance = principal
  fmtStr = "{0,4}      {1,-15:C}{2,-15:C}{3,-15:C}"
  'Loop for each month of the loan period
  For monthNum As Integer = 1 To numMonths
    'Calculate the relevant figures
    newBalance = Balance(monthlyPayment, oldBalance, monthlyRate)
    principalPaid = oldBalance - newBalance
    interestPaid = monthlyPayment - principalPaid
    totalInterest = totalInterest + interestPaid
    'Display results if current year is the desired year to display
    If (monthNum >= startMonth) And (monthNum < startMonth + 12) Then
      lstResults.Items.Add(String.Format(fmtStr, monthNum, _
                     principalPaid, interestPaid, newBalance))
      yearInterest = yearInterest + interestPaid
    End If
    'Update the old balance for the next pass through the For loop
    oldBalance = newBalance
  Next
  'Display totals
  principalReduced = 12 * monthlyPayment - yearInterest
  fmtStr = "{0,-38}{1,-15:C}"
  lstResults.Items.Add("")
  lstResults.Items.Add(String.Format(fmtStr, _
                   "Reduction in principal:", principalReduced))
  lstResults.Items.Add(
     String.Format(fmtStr, "Interest Paid:", yearInterest))
  lstResults.Items.Add(String.Format(fmtStr, "Total interest over " & _
                   numYears & " years:", totalInterest))
End Sub

Function Balance(ByRef payment As Double, _
  ByVal principal As Double, ByVal monthlyRate As Double) As Double
  'Compute balance at end of month
  Dim newBalance As Double
  newBalance = (1 + monthlyRate) * principal
  'If balance is less than payment, then this
  'payment is the last one for this loan
  If newBalance <= payment Then
    payment = newBalance
    Return 0
  Else
    Return newBalance - payment
  End If
End Function
```

```vb
Function Payment(ByVal principal As Double, _
      ByVal monthlyRate As Double, ByVal numMonths As Integer) As Double
   Dim estimate As Double              'Estimate of monthly payment
   If numMonths = 0 Then
      'If no months then the loan must be repaid immediately
      estimate = principal
   ElseIf monthlyRate = 0 Then
      'If loan has no interest then just repay the principal over time
      estimate = principal / numMonths
   Else
      'Otherwise, use the formula for determining the monthly payment
      estimate = principal * monthlyRate / (1 - _
            (1 + monthlyRate) ^ (-numMonths))
   End If
   'Round the payment up if it there are fractions of a cent
   If estimate = Math.Round(estimate, 2) Then
      Return estimate
   Else
      Return Math.Round(estimate + 0.005, 2)
   End If
End Function

Sub ShowInterestChanges(ByVal principal As Double, _
               ByVal yearlyRate As Double, ByVal numMonths As Integer)
   Dim newRate As Double, monthlyRate As Double, monthlyPayment As Double
   Dim fmtStr As String = "{0,15} {1,-15} {2,-15}"
   'Display effect of interest changes
   lstResults.Items.Clear()
   lstResults.Items.Add(String.Format(fmtStr, "", "Annual", ""))
   lstResults.Items.Add(String.Format(fmtStr, "", _
            "Interest Rate", "Monthly Payment"))
   'Set the annual rate's lower limit for the table
   newRate = yearlyRate - 0.01
   fmtStr = "{0,15} {1,-15} {2,-15:C}"
   'Loop the annual rate from its lower limit to its upper limit
   Do
      'Calculate the monthly payment for the corresponding monthly rate
      monthlyRate = newRate / 12
      monthlyPayment = Payment(principal, monthlyRate, numMonths)
      lstResults.Items.Add(String.Format(fmtStr, "", _
         FormatPercent(newRate, 3), monthlyPayment))
      newRate = newRate + 0.00125    'Increment by 1/8 of one percent for
      'the next pass through the loop
      'To avoid rounding errors, add 0.001 to the upper-limit condition
   Loop Until newRate > yearlyRate + 0.01 + 0.001
End Sub
```

▓ Comments

1. Tasks 3.1 and 3.2 are performed by functions. Using functions to compute these quantities simplifies the computations in ShowAmortizationSchedule.

2. Because the payment was rounded up to the nearest cent, it is highly likely that the payment needed in the final month to pay off the loan will be less than the normal payment. For this reason, ShowAmortizationSchedule checks if the balance of the loan (including interest due) is less than the regular payment and, if so, makes appropriate adjustments.

3. The standard formula for computing the monthly payment cannot be used if either the interest rate is zero percent or the loan duration is zero months. Although both of these situations do not represent reasonable loan parameters, provisions are made in the function Payment so that the program can handle these esoteric situations.

CHAPTER 6   SUMMARY

1. A *Do loop* repeatedly executes a block of statements either as long as or until a certain condition is true. The condition can be checked either at the top of the loop or at the bottom.

2. The Peek method can be used to tell us if we have read to the end of a file.

3. As various items of data are processed by a loop, a *counter* can be used to keep track of the number of items, and an *accumulator* can be used to sum numerical values.

4. A *flag* is a Boolean variable, used to indicate whether a certain event has occurred.

5. A *For...Next loop* repeats a block of statements a fixed number of times. The *control variable* assumes an initial value and increments by one after each pass through the loop until it reaches the terminating value. Alternative increment values can be specified with the Step keyword.

CHAPTER 6   PROGRAMMING PROJECTS

1. Write a program to display a company's payroll report in a list box. The program should read each employee's name, hourly rate, and hours worked from a file and produce a report in the form of the sample run shown in Figure 6.18. Employees should be paid time-and-a-half for hours in excess of 40.

```
Payroll Report for week ending 11/17/06

Employee          Hourly Rate      Hours Worked      Gross Pay

Al Adams            $6.50              38            $247.00
Bob Brown           $5.70              50            $313.50
Carol Coe           $7.00              40            $280.00

Final Total                                          $840.50
```

FIGURE 6.18   Sample output from Programming Project 1.

2. Table 6.6 shows the standard prices for items in a department store. Suppose prices will be reduced for the annual President's Day Sale. The new price will be computed by reducing the old price by 10 percent, rounding up to the nearest dollar, and subtracting 1 cent. If the new price is greater than the old price, the old price is used as the sale price. Write a program to display in a list box the output shown in Figure 6.19.

TABLE 6.6   President's Day sale.

Item	Original Price
GumShoes	39.00
SnugFoot Sandals	21.00
T-Shirt	7.75
Maine Handbag	33.00
Maple Syrup	6.75
Flaked Vest	24.00
Nightshirt	26.00

Item	Sale Price
GumShoes	35.99
SnugFoot Sandals	18.99
T-Shirt	6.99
Maine Handbag	29.99
Maple Syrup	6.75
Flaked Vest	21.99
Nightshirt	23.99

FIGURE 6.19   Output of Programming Project 2.

3. The Rule of 72 is used to make a quick estimate of the time required for prices to double due to inflation. If the inflation rate is r percent, then the Rule of 72 estimates that prices will double in $72/r$ years. For instance, at an inflation rate of 6 percent, prices double in about $72/6$ or 12 years. Write a program to test the accuracy of this rule. The program should display a table showing, for each value of r from 1 to 20, the rounded value of $72/r$ and the actual number of years required for prices to double at an r percent inflation rate. (Assume prices increase at the end of each year.) Figure 6.20 shows the first few rows of the output.

Interest Rate (%)	Rule of 72	Actual
1	72	70
2	36	36
3	24	24

FIGURE 6.20   Rule of 72 used in Programming Project 3.

4. Table 6.7 shows the number of bachelor degrees conferred in 1980 and 2002 in certain fields of study. Tables 6.8 and 6.9 show the percentage change and a histogram of 2002 levels, respectively. Write a program that allows the user to display any one of these tables as an option and quit as a fourth option.

TABLE 6.7 **Bachelor degrees conferred in certain fields.**

Field of Study	1980	2002
Business and management	184,867	281,330
Computer and info. science	11,154	47,299
Education	118,038	106,383
Engineering	68,893	59,481
Social sciences	103,662	132,874

Source: U.S. National Center of Educational Statistics

TABLE 6.8 **Percentage change in bachelor degrees conferred.**

Field of Study	% Change (1980–2002)
Business and management	52.2
Computer and info. science	324.1
Education	−9.9
Engineering	−13.7
Social sciences	28.2

TABLE 6.9 **Bachelor degrees conferred in 2002 in certain fields.**

Business and management	*****************************	281,330
Computer and info. science	*****	47,299
Education	***********	106,383
Engineering	******	59,481
Social sciences	*************	132,874

5. *Least-Squares Approximation.* Table 6.10 shows the 1988 prices of a gallon of gasoline and the amounts of fuel consumed for several countries. Figure 6.21 displays the data as points in the xy plane. For instance, the point with coordinates $(1, 1400)$ corresponds to the USA. Figure 6.21 also shows the straight line that best fits these data in the least-squares sense. (The sum of the squares of the distances of the 11 points from this line is as small as possible.) In general, if (x_1, y_1), (x_2, y_2), ...,(x_n, y_n) are n points in the xy coordinate system, then the least-squares approximation to these points is the line $y = mx + b$, where

$$m = \frac{n*(\text{sum of } x_i * y_i) - (\text{sum of } x_i)*(\text{sum of } y_i)}{n*(\text{sum of } x_i * x_i) - (\text{sum of } x_i)^2}$$

and

$$b = ((\text{sum of } y_i) - m*(\text{sum of } x_i))/n.$$

Write a program that calculates and displays the equation of the least-squares line. The program should then allow the user to enter a gasoline price and use the equation of the line to predict the corresponding consumption of fuel. (Place the numeric data from the table in a text file.) A sample run is shown in Figure 6.22.

| TABLE 6.10 | A comparison of 1988 gasoline prices and per capita fuel use. | | | | |

Country	Price per gallon in U.S. Dollars	Tons of Fuel per 1000 Persons	Country	Price per gallon in U.S. Dollars	Tons of Fuel per 1000 Persons
USA	$1.00	1400	France	$3.10	580
W. Ger.	$2.20	620	Norway	$3.15	600
England	$2.60	550	Japan	$3.60	410
Austria	$2.75	580	Denmark	$3.70	570
Sweden	$2.80	700	Italy	$3.85	430
Holland	$3.00	490			

Source: World Resources Institute

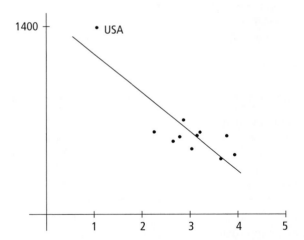

FIGURE 6.21   Least-squares fit to data from Table 6.10.

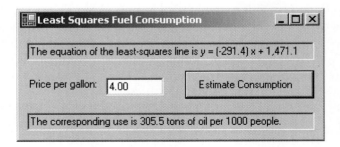

FIGURE 6.22   Sample run of Programming Project 5.

6. Write a program to provide information on the height of a ball thrown straight up into the air. The program should request the initial height, *h* feet, and the initial velocity, *v* feet per second, as input. The four options to be provided by buttons are as follows:

(a) Determine the maximum height of the ball. **Note:** The ball will reach its maximum height after $v/32$ seconds.

(b) Determine approximately when the ball will hit the ground. **Hint:** Calculate the height after every .1 second and observe when the height is no longer a positive number.

(c) Display a table showing the height of the ball every quarter second for five seconds or until it hits the ground.

(d) Quit.

The formula for the height of the ball after *t* seconds, $h + v*t - 16*t*t$, should be specified in a user-defined function. (Test the program with $v = 148$ and $h = 0$. This velocity is approximately the top speed clocked for a ball thrown by a professional baseball pitcher.)

7. *Depreciation to a Salvage Value of 0.* For tax purposes an item may be depreciated over a period of several years, *n*. With the *straight-line* method of depreciation, each year the item depreciates by 1/nth of its original value. With the *double-declining-balance* method of depreciation, each year the item depreciates by 2/nths of its value at the beginning of that year. (In the last year, it is depreciated by its value at the beginning of the year.) Write a program that performs the following tasks:

(a) Requests a description of the item, the year of purchase, the cost of the item, the number of years to be depreciated (estimated life), and the method of depreciation. The method of depreciation should be chosen by clicking one of two buttons.

(b) Displays a depreciation schedule for the item similar to the schedule shown in Figure 6.23.

```
Description: Computer
Year of purchase: 2002
Cost: $2,000.00
Estimated life: 5
Method of depreciation: double-declining-balance
```

Year	Value at Beg of Yr	Amount Deprec During Year	Total Depreciation to End of Year
2002	2,000.00	800.00	800.00
2003	1,200.00	480.00	1,280.00
2004	720.00	288.00	1,568.00
2005	432.00	172.80	1,740.80
2006	259.20	259.20	2,000.00

FIGURE 6.23   Depreciation schedule for Programming Project 7.

8. *The Twelve Days of Christmas.* Each year, PNC Advisors of Pittsburgh publishes a Christmas price list. See Table 6.11. Write a program that requests an integer from 1 through 12 and then lists the gifts for that day along with that day's cost. On the *n*th day, the *n* gifts are 1 partridge in a pear tree, 2 turtle doves, ..., *n* of the *n*th item. The program also should give the total cost of all twelve days. As an example, Figure 6.24 shows the output in the list box when the user enters 3.

TABLE 6.11   **Christmas price list for 2005.**

Item	Cost	Item	Cost
partridge in a pear tree	104.99	swan-a-swimming	600.00
turtle dove	20.00	maid-a-milking	5.15
French hen	15.00	lady dancing	508.46
calling bird	99.99	lord-a-leaping	403.91
gold ring	65.00	piper piping	186.65
geese-a-laying	50.00	drummer drumming	185.36

```
The gifts for day 3 are
1 partridge in a pear tree
2 turtle doves
3 french hens
Cost: $189.99
Total cost for the twelve days: $72,608.00
```

FIGURE 6.24   Sample output for Programming Project 8.

7
Arrays

7.1   Creating and Accessing Arrays 308

- Declaring an Array Variable ◆ The Load Event Procedure
- The GetUpperBound Method ◆ ReDim Statement
- Using an Array as a Frequency Table

7.2   Using Arrays 326

- Ordered Arrays ◆ Using Part of an Array
- Merging Two Ordered Arrays ◆ Passing Arrays to Procedures

7.3   Some Additional Types of Arrays 341

- Control Arrays ◆ Structures

7.4   Sorting and Searching 356

- Bubble Sort ◆ Shell Sort ◆ Searching

7.5   Two-Dimensional Arrays 377

7.6   A Case Study: A Sophisticated Cash Register 392

- The Design of the Program ◆ The User Interface
- The Data Structures ◆ Coding the Program

Summary 401

Programming Projects 402

7.1 Creating and Accessing Arrays

A **variable** (or simple variable) is a name to which Visual Basic can assign a single value. An **array variable** is a collection of simple variables of the same type to which Visual Basic can efficiently assign a list of values.

Consider the following situation: Suppose that you want to evaluate the exam grades for 30 students. Not only do you want to compute the average score, but you also want to display the names of the students whose scores are above average. You might place the 30 pairs of student names and scores in a text file and run the program outlined:

```
Private Sub btnDisplay_Click(...) Handles btnDisplay.Click
  Dim student1 As String, score1 As Double
  Dim student2 As String, score2 As Double
  Dim student3 As String, score3 As Double
     .
     .
  Dim student30 As String, score30 As Double
  'Analyze exam grades
  Dim sr As IO.StreamReader = IO.File.OpenText("SCORES.TXT")
  student1 = sr.ReadLine
  score1 = CDbl(sr.ReadLine)
  student2 = sr.ReadLine
  score2 = CDbl(sr.ReadLine)
     .
     .
  student30 = sr.ReadLine
  score30 = CDbl(sr.ReadLine)
  sr.Close()
  'Compute the average grade
     .
     .
  'Display names of above average students
     .
     .

End Sub
```

This program is going to be uncomfortably long. What's most frustrating is that the 30 Dim statements and 30 pairs of statements reading from the file are very similar and look as if they should be condensed into a short loop. A shorthand notation for the many related variables would be welcome. It would be nice if we could just write

```
For i As Integer = 1 To 30
  studenti = sr.ReadLine
  scorei = CDbl(sr.ReadLine)
Next
```

Of course, this will not work. Visual Basic will treat *studenti* and *scorei* as two variables and keep reassigning new values to them. At the end of the loop, they will have the values of the thirtieth student.

■ Declaring an Array Variable

Visual Basic provides a data structure called an **array** that lets us do what we tried to accomplish in the loop. The variable names, similar to those in the preceding program, will be

```
student(0), student(1), student(2), student(3), ..., student(29)
```

and

```
score(0), score(1), score(2), score(3), ..., score(29)
```

We refer to these collections of variables as the array variables *student*() and *score*(). The numbers inside the parentheses of the individual variables are called **subscripts**, and each individual variable is called a **subscripted variable** or **element** . For instance, *student*(3) is the fourth subscripted variable of the array *student*(), and *score*(20) is the 21st subscripted variable of the array *score*(). The elements of an array are assigned successive memory locations. Figure 7.1 shows the memory locations for the array *score*().

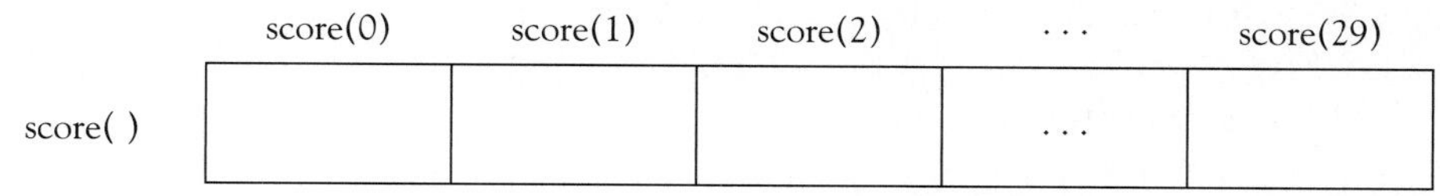

	score(0)	score(1)	score(2)	⋯	score(29)
score( )				⋯	

FIGURE 7.1   The array *score*().

Array variables have the same kinds of names as simple variables. If *arrayName* is the name of an array variable and *n* is an Integer literal, variable, or expression, then the declaration statement

```
Dim arrayName(n) As varType
```

reserves space in memory to hold the values of the subscripted variables *arrayName*(0), *arrayName*(1), *arrayName*(2), ..., *arrayName*(n). The value of *n* is called the **upper bound** of the array. The number of elements in the array, $n + 1$, is called the **size** of the array. The subscripted variables will all have the same data type; namely, the type specified by *varType*. For instance, they could be all String variables or all Integer variables. In particular, the statements

```
Dim student(29) As String
Dim score(29) As Double
```

declare the arrays needed for the preceding program.

Values can be assigned to individual subscripted variables with assignment statements and displayed in text boxes and list boxes just as values of ordinary variables. The default initial value of each subscripted variable is the same as with an ordinary variable; that is, the keyword Nothing for String types and 0 for numeric types. The statement

```
Dim score(29) As Double
```

sets aside a portion of memory for the Integer array *score*( ) and assigns the default value 0 to each element.

	score(0)	score(1)	score(2)	· · ·	score(29)
score( )	0	0	0	· · ·	0

The statements

```
score(0) = 87
score(1) = 92
```

assign values to the zeroth and first elements.

	score(0)	score(1)	score(2)	· · ·	score(29)
score( )	87	92	0	· · ·	0

The statements

```
For i As Integer = 0 To 2
  lstBox.Items.Add(score(i))
Next
```

then produce the following output in the list box:

87
92
0

As with an ordinary variable, an array declared in the Declarations section of the Code window is class-level. That is, it will be visible to all procedures in the form, and any value assigned to it in a procedure will persist when the procedure terminates. Array variables declared inside a procedure are local to that procedure and cease to exist when the procedure is exited.

  Example 1   The following program creates a string array consisting of the names of the first four Super Bowl winners. Figure 7.2 shows the array created by the program.

	teamName(0)	teamName(1)	teamName(2)	teamName(3)
teamName( )	Packers	Packers	Jets	Chiefs

FIGURE 7.2   The array *teamName*( ) of Example 1.

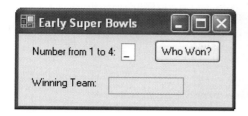

OBJECT	PROPERTY	SETTING
frmBowl	Text	Early Super Bowls
lblNumber	Text	Number from 1 to 4:
mtxtNumber	Mask	0
btnWhoWon	Text	Who Won?
lblWinner	Text	Winning Team:
txtWinner	ReadOnly	True

```
Private Sub btnWhoWon_Click(...) Handles btnWhoWon.Click
  Dim teamName(3) As String
  Dim n As Integer
  'Place Super Bowl Winners into the array
  teamName(0) = "Packers"
  teamName(1) = "Packers"
  teamName(2) = "Jets"
  teamName(3) = "Chiefs"
  'Access array
  n = CInt(mtxtNumber.Text)
  txtWinner.Text = teamName(n - 1)
End Sub
```

[Run, type 2 into the masked text box, and click the button.]

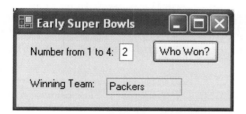

■ The Load Event Procedure

In Example 1, the array *teamName* was assigned values within the btnWhoWon_Click event procedure. Every time the button is clicked, the values are reassigned to the array. This manner of assigning values to an array can be very inefficient, especially in programs with large arrays where the task of the program (in Example 1, looking up a fact) may be repeated numerous times for different user input. When, as in Example 1, the data to be placed in an array are known at the time the program begins to run, a more efficient location for the statements that fill the array is in the form's Load event procedure. The Load event occurs automatically when the form is loaded into memory, before it becomes visible on the screen. The header and End Sub statements for the Load event procedure are placed in the Code window when you double-click on the form. A typical header looks like

```
Private Sub frmName_Load(...) Handles MyBase.Load
```

The keyword MyBase is similar to the Me keyword and refers to the form being loaded. Example 2 uses the frmBowl_Load procedure to improve on Example 1.

Example 2 The following improvement on Example 1 makes *teamName*() a class-level array and assigns values to the elements of the array in the frmBowl_Load procedure:

```
Dim teamName(3) As String
Private Sub btnWhoWon_Click(...) Handles btnWhoWon.Click
  Dim n As Integer
  n = CInt(mtxtNumber.Text)
  txtWinner.Text = teamName(n - 1)
End Sub

Private Sub frmBowl_Load(...) Handles MyBase.Load
  'Place Super Bowl Winners into the array
  teamName(0) = "Packers"
  teamName(1) = "Packers"
  teamName(2) = "Jets"
  teamName(3) = "Chiefs"
End Sub
```

Like ordinary variables, array variables can be declared and assigned initial values at the same time. A statement of the form

```
Dim arrayName() As varType = {value0, value1, value2, ..., valueN}
```

declares an array having upper bound N and assigns *value0* to *arrayName*(0), *value1* to *arrayName*(1), *value2* to *arrayName*(2), ..., and *valueN* to *arrayName*(N). For instance, in Example 4, the Dim statement and frmBowl_Load event procedure can be replaced by the single line

```
Dim teamName() As String = {"Packers", "Packers", "Jets", "Chiefs"}
```

▨ The GetUpperBound Method

The value of *arrayName*.GetUpperBound(0) is the upper bound of the array. For instance, in Example 1, the value of `teamName.GetUpperBound(0)` is 3.

▨ ReDim Statement

After an array has been declared, its size (but not its type) can be changed with a statement of the form

```
ReDim arrayName(m)
```

where *arrayName* is the name of the already declared array and *m* is an Integer literal, variable, or expression. **Note:** Since the type cannot be changed, there is no need for an "As *dataType*" clause at the end of the ReDim statement.

Visual Basic allows you to declare an array without specifying an upper bound with a statement of the form

```
Dim arrayName() As varType
```

Later, the size of the array can be stipulated with a ReDim statement.

The ReDim statement has one shortcoming: It causes the array to lose its current contents. That is, it resets all String values to Nothing and resets all numeric values to 0. This situation can be remedied by following ReDim with the word Preserve. The general form of a ReDim Preserve statement is

```
ReDim Preserve arrayName(m)
```

Of course, if you make an array smaller than it was, data in the eliminated elements will be lost.

 Example 3   The following program reads the names of the winners of Super Bowl games from a file and places them into an array. The user can type a team's name into a text box and then display the numbers of the Super Bowl games won by that team. The user has the option of adding winners of subsequent games to the array of winners. The program uses the text file SBWINNERS.TXT whose lines contain the names of the winners in order. That is, the first four lines of the file contain the names Packers, Packers, Jets, and Chiefs.

```
Dim teamName() As String
Dim upperBound As Integer

Private Sub frmBowl_Load(...) Handles MyBase.Load
  Dim sr As IO.StreamReader = IO.File.OpenText("SBWINNERS.TXT")
  Dim name As String, numLines As Integer
  'Count number of lines in the file and assign it minus one to upperBound
  numLines = 0
  Do While (sr.Peek <> -1)
    name = sr.ReadLine
    numLines += 1
  Loop
  upperBound = numLines - 1
  sr.Close()
  'Specify the title bar of the form
  Me.Text = "First " & upperBound + 1 & " Super Bowls"
  'Specify the caption of the Next Winner button
  btnNextWinner.Text = "Add Winner of Game " & upperBound + 2
  'Specify the size of the array and fill it with the entries of the file
  ReDim teamName(upperBound)
  sr = IO.File.OpenText("SBWINNERS.TXT")
  For i As Integer = 0 To upperBound
    teamName(i) = sr.ReadLine
  Next
  sr.Close()
End Sub
```

```
Private Sub btnDisplay_Click(...) Handles btnDisplay.Click
  'Display the numbers of the games won by the team in the text box
  lstGamesWon.Items.Clear()
  For i As Integer = 0 To upperBound
    If teamName(i) = txtName.Text Then
      lstGamesWon.Items.Add(i + 1)
    End If
  Next
End Sub

Private Sub btnNextWinner_Click(...) Handles btnNextWinner.Click
  'Add winner of next Super Bowl to the array
  Dim prompt As String
  upperBound += 1
  'Add one more element to the array
  ReDim Preserve teamName(upperBound)
  'Request the name of the next winner
  prompt = "Enter winner of game #" & upperBound + 1
  teamName(upperBound) = InputBox(prompt, , "")
  'Update the title bar of the form and the caption of the button
  'Note: "Me" refers to the form.
  Me.Text = "First " & upperBound + 1 & " Super Bowls"
  btnNextWinner.Text = "Add Winner of Game " & upperBound + 2
End Sub
```

[Run, type "49ers" into the text box, and press the Display button. Then, feel free to add subsequent winners. Your additions will be taken into account when you next press the Display button.]

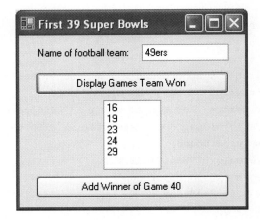

▨ Using an Array as a Frequency Table

An array can be used as either a checklist or a frequency table, as in the next example.

Example 4   The following program requests a sentence as input and records the frequencies of the letters occurring in the sentence. The first element of the array *charCount*() holds the frequency with which the letter A occurs in the sentence, and so on. Recall that the function Asc associates each character with its position in the ANSI table.

```
Private Sub btnAnalyze_Click(...) Handles btnAnalyze.Click
  'Count occurrences of the various letters in a sentence
  Dim index As Integer
  Dim sentence, letter As String
  Dim charCount(25) As Integer
  'Examine and tally each letter of the sentence
  sentence = (txtSentence.Text).ToUpper
  For letterNum As Integer = 1 To sentence.Length
    letter = sentence.Substring(letterNum - 1, 1)
    If (letter >= "A") And (letter <= "Z") Then
      index = Asc(letter) - 65   'The ANSI value of "A" is 65
      charCount(index) += 1
    End If
  Next
  'List the tally for each letter of alphabet
  lstCount.Items.Clear()
  For i As Integer = 0 To 25
    letter = Chr(i + 65)
    If charCount(i) > 0 Then
      lstCount.Items.Add(letter & "   " & charCount(i))
    End If
  Next
End Sub
```

[Run, type a sentence into the text box, and press the button.]

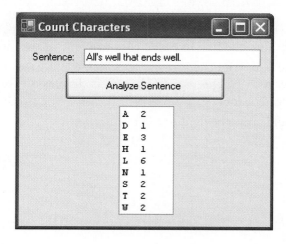

■ Comments

1. Using a subscript greater than the upper bound of an array is not allowed. For instance, the following lines of code produce the error dialog box shown immediately thereafter:

```
Dim trees() As String = {"Sequoia", "Redwood", "Spruce"}
txtBox.Text = trees(5)
```

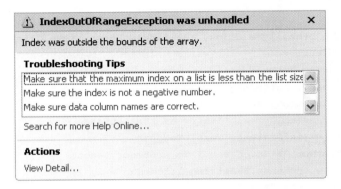

2. If *arrayOne*() and *arrayTwo*() have been declared with the same data type, then the statement

```
arrayOne = arrayTwo
```

makes *arrayOne*() an exact duplicate of *arrayTwo*(). It will have the same size and contain the same information.

3. An array can require a large block of memory. After the array is no longer needed, the statement

```
Erase arrayname
```

can be executed to release all memory allocated to the array.

Practice Problems 7.1

1. Write code to declare an array with upper bound 10 and place the names of the five Great Lakes into the first five elements. Use one or two lines of code.

2. In Example 3, rewrite the btnDisplay_Click event procedure so that only the first Super Bowl won by the requested team is displayed. The loop should terminate when the team is found.

3. When should arrays be used to hold data?

1. What is the size of an array whose upper bound is 100?
2. What is the upper bound of an array whose size is 100?

In Exercises 3 through 12, determine the output displayed when the button is clicked.

3.
```
Private Sub btnDisplay_Click(...) Handles btnDisplay.Click
    Dim num As Integer = 2
    Dim spoon(num) As String
    spoon(0) = "soup"
    spoon(1) = "dessert"
    spoon(2) = "coffee"
    txtOutput.Text = "Have a " & spoon(num - 1) & " spoon."
End Sub
```

4.
```
Private Sub btnDisplay_Click(...) Handles btnDisplay.Click
    Dim a(20) As Integer
    a(5) = 1
    a(10) = 2
    a(15) = 7
    lstOutput.Items.Add(a(5) + a(10))
    lstOutput.Items.Add(a(5 + 10))
    lstOutput.Items.Add(a(20))
End Sub
```

5.
```
Dim sq(5) As Integer
Private Sub btnDisplay_Click(...) Handles btnDisplay.Click
    Dim t As Integer
    For i As Integer = 0 To 5
        sq(i) = i * i
    Next
    lstOutput.Items.Add(sq(3))
    t = 3
    lstOutput.Items.Add(sq(5 - t))
End Sub
```

6.
```
Dim fh(3) As String
Private Sub btnDisplay_Click(...) Handles btnDisplay.Click
    Dim n As Integer
    Dim sr As IO.StreamReader = IO.File.OpenText("HORSEMEN.TXT")
    For i As Integer = 0 To 3
        fh(i) = sr.ReadLine
    Next
```

```
      sr.Close()
      lstOutput.Items.Add(fh(fh.GetUpperBound(0)))
      n = 1
      lstOutput.Items.Add(fh(2 * n))
    End Sub
```

(Assume that the four lines of the file HORSEMEN.TXT contain the following entries: Miller, Layden, Crowley, Stuhldreher.)

7.
```
    Dim s(3) As Integer
    Private Sub btnDisplay_Click(...) Handles btnDisplay.Click
      Dim t As Integer
      Dim sr As IO.StreamReader = IO.File.OpenText("DATA.TXT")
      t = 0
      For k As Integer = 0 To 3
        s(k) = CInt(sr.ReadLine)
        t += s(k)
      Next
      txtOutput.Text = CStr(t)
      sr.Close()
    End Sub
```

(Assume that the four lines of the file DATA.TXT contain the following entries: 3, 5, 2, 1.)

8.
```
    Dim a(3), b(3) As Integer
    Dim c(3) As Double
    Private Sub btnDisplay_Click(...) Handles btnDisplay.Click
      Dim sr As IO.StreamReader = IO.File.OpenText("DATA.TXT")
      For i As Integer = 0 To 3
        a(i) = CInt(sr.ReadLine)
        b(i) = CInt(sr.ReadLine)
      Next
      sr.Close()
      For i As Integer = 0 To c.GetUpperBound(0)
        c(i) = a(i) * b(i)
        lstOutput.Items.Add(c(i))
      Next
    End Sub
```

(Assume that the eight lines of the file DATA.TXT contain the following entries: 2, 5, 3, 4, 1, 3, 7, 2.)

9.
```
    Private Sub btnDisplay_Click(...) Handles btnDisplay.Click
      'Compare the values of two chess pieces
      Dim chess() As string = {"king", "queen", ""}
      chess(2) = "rook"
      ReDim Preserve chess(6)
      chess(3) = "bishop"
      txtOutput.Text = "A " & chess(2) & " is worth more than a " _
                    & chess(3)
    End Sub
```

10.
```
Dim grade(1) As Double
Private Sub btnDisplay_Click(...) Handles btnDisplay.Click
  Dim average As Double
  ReDim grade(3)
  grade(2) = 70
  grade(3) = 80
  average = (grade(0) + grade(1) + grade(2) + grade(3)) / 4
  txtOutput.Text = "Your average is " & average
End Sub
Private Sub frmGrades_Load(...) Handles MyBase.Load
  grade(0) = 89
  grade(1) = 91
End Sub
```

11.
```
Dim score() As Double = {71, 68, 69}
Private Sub btnDisplay_Click(...) Handles btnDisplay.Click
  'Find the sum of four scores
  Dim total As Double
  ReDim Preserve score(3)
  score(3) = 72
  total = score(0) + score(1) + score(2) + score(3)
  txtOutput.Text = "Your total is " & total & "."
End Sub
```

12.
```
Dim band() As String = {"soloist", "duet", "trio", "quartet"}
Private Sub btnDisplay_Click(...) Handles btnDisplay.Click
  Dim num As Integer
  ReDim Preserve band(9)
  band(4) = "quintet"
  band(5) = "sextet"
  band(6) = InputBox("What do you call a group of 7 musicians?")
  num = CInt(InputBox("How many musicians are in your group?"))
  txtOutput.Text = "You have a " & band(num - 1) & "."
End Sub
```

(Assume that the first response is *septet* and the second response is 3.)

In Exercises 13 through 18, identify the errors.

13.
```
Dim companies(100) As String
Private Sub frmFirms_Load(...) Handles MyBase.Load
  Dim recCount Integer
  Dim sr As IO.StreamReader = IO.File.OpenText("FIRMS.TXT")
  recCount = CInt(sr.ReadLine)
  ReDim companies(recCount - 1) As String
  For i As Integer = 0 To recCount - 1
    companies(i) = sr.ReadLine
  Next
  sr.Close()
End Sub
```

(Assume that the file FIRMS.TXT contains a list of companies and the first line of the file gives the number of companies.)

14.
```
Dim p(100) As Double
Private Sub btnDisplay_Click(...) Handles btnDisplay.Click
  For i As Integer = 0 To 200
    p(i) = i / 2
  Next
End Sub
```

15.
```
Dim a(10) As Integer
Private Sub btnDisplay_Click(...) Handles btnDisplay.Click
  Dim sr As IO.StreamReader = IO.File.OpenText("DATA.TXT")
  For i As Integer = 0 To 8
    a(i) = CInt(sr.ReadLine)
  Next
  sr.Close()
  For k As Integer = 0 To 8
    a(k) = a(5 - k)
  Next
End Sub
```

(Assume that the nine lines of the file DATA.TXT contain the following entries: 1, 2, 3, 4, 5, 6, 7, 8, 9.)

16.
```
Private Sub btnDisplay_Click(...) Handles btnDisplay.Click
  Dim films() As String = {"Gladiator", "Titanic"}
  lstOutput.Items.Add(films)
End Sub
```

17.
```
Private Sub btnDisplay_Click(...) Handles btnDisplay.Click
  Dim amount(2) As Integer = {7, 11, 14}
  Dim total As Integer = 0
  For i As Integer = 0 To 2
    total += amount(i)
  Next
  txtOutput.Text = CStr(total)
End Sub
```

18.
```
Private Sub frmNames_Load(...) Handles MyBase.Load
  Dim recCount As Integer
  Dim sr As IO.StreamReader = IO.File.OpenText("DATA.TXT")
  recCount = CInt(sr.ReadLine)
  ReDim names(recCount - 1) As String
  For i As Integer = 0 to recCount - 1
    names(i) = sr.ReadLine
  Next
  sr.Close()
End Sub
```

(Assume that the four lines of the file DATA.TXT contain the following entries: 3, Tom, Dick, Harry.)

19. Assuming that the array *river*( ) is as follows, fill in the empty rectangles to illustrate the progressing status of *river*( ) after the execution of each program segment:

	river(0)	river(1)	river(2)	river(3)	river(4)
river( )	Nile	Ohio	Amazon	Volga	Thames

```
temp = river(0)
river(0) = river(4)
river(4) = temp
```

	river(0)	river(1)	river(2)	river(3)	river(4)
river( )					

```
temp = river(0)
For i As Integer = 0 To 3
  river(i) = river(i + 1)
Next
river(4) = temp
```

	river(0)	river(1)	river(2)	river(3)	river(4)
river( )					

20. Assuming the array *cat*( ) is as follows, fill in the empty rectangles (on the next page) to show the final status of *cat*( ) after executing the nested loops:

	cat(0)	cat(1)	cat(2)	cat(3)
cat( )	Morris	Garfield	Socks	Felix

```
For i As Integer = 0 To 2
  For j As Integer = 0 To 3 - i
    If cat(j) > cat(j + 1) Then
     temp = cat(j)
     cat(j) = cat(j + 1)
     cat(j + 1) = temp
    End If
  Next
Next
```

	cat(0)	cat(1)	cat(2)	cat(3)
cat( )				

```
Dim gap As Integer = 2
Do While gap >= 1
  Do
    doneFlag = True
    For i As Integer = 0 To 3 - gap
      If cat(i) > cat(i + gap) Then
        temp = cat(i)
        cat(i) = cat(i + gap)
        cat(i + gap) = temp
        doneFlag = False
      End If
    Next
  Loop Until doneFlag = True
  gap = CInt(gap / 2)
Loop
```

	cat(0)	cat(1)	cat(2)	cat(3)
cat( )				

21. The subscripted variables of the array a() have the following values: a(0) = 4, a(1) = 6, a(2) = 3, a(3) = 1, a(4) = 2, a(5) = 5, a(6) = 8, a(7) = 7. Suppose $i = 2, j = 4$, and $k = 5$. What values are assigned to n when the following assignment statements are executed?

    (a) n = a(k) − a(i)   (c) n = a(k) * a(i + 2)
    (b) n = a(k − i) + a(k − j)   (d) n = a(j − i) * a(i)

22. The array *monthName*( ) holds the following three-character strings:

    ```
    monthName(0)="Jan", monthName(1)="Feb", ..., monthName(11)="Dec"
    ```

    (a) What is displayed by the following statement?

    ```
    txtMonth.Text = monthName(3) & " " & monthName(8)
    ```

    (b) What value is assigned to *fall* by the following statement?

    ```
    fall = monthName(8) & ", " & monthName(9) & ", " & monthName(10)
    ```

23. Modify the program in Example 3 to display "Never Won a Super Bowl" if the specified team has never won a Super Bowl game.

24. Modify the program in Example 3 so that the text file SBWINNERS.TXT is only read once.

In Exercises 25 through 36, write a line of code or program segment to complete the stated task.

25. Suppose the Integer array *quantities*() has been declared with an upper bound of 100 and data have been placed into several elements of the array. Write one line of code that will restore the values of all the elements to their default value of 0.

26. Write code to declare an array of size 20 and place the names Jerry, George, Elaine, and Kramer into the first four elements. Use one or two lines of code.

27. Declare the string array *marx*() with upper bound 3 so that the array is visible to all parts of the program. Assign the four values Chico, Harpo, Groucho, and Zeppo to the array before any buttons are pressed.

28. Declare the string array *stooges*() to have size 3 so that the array is local to the event procedure btnStooges_Click. Assign the three values Moe, Larry, and Curly to the array as soon as the button is clicked.

29. The arrays *a*() and *b*() have been declared to have upper bound 4, and values have been assigned to *a*(0) through *a*(4). Store these values in array *b*() in reverse order.

30. Given two arrays of type Double, *p*() and *q*(), each with upper bound 20, compute the sum of the products of the corresponding array elements, that is,

```
p(0)*q(0) + p(1)*q(1) + p(2)*q(2) + ... + p(20)*q(20)
```

31. Display the values of the array *a*() having upper bound 29 in five columns, like the following:

$$
\begin{array}{ccccc}
a(0) & a(1) & a(2) & a(3) & a(4) \\
a(5) & a(6) & a(7) & a(8) & a(9) \\
\cdot & \cdot & \cdot & \cdot & \cdot \\
\cdot & \cdot & \cdot & \cdot & \cdot \\
\cdot & \cdot & \cdot & \cdot & \cdot \\
a(25) & a(26) & a(27) & a(28) & a(29)
\end{array}
$$

32. A list of 20 digits, all between 0 and 9, is contained in a text file. Display the frequency of each digit.

33. Compare two arrays *a*() and *b*() of size 10 to see if they hold identical values, that is, if $a(i) = b(i)$ for all *i* from 0 through 9.

34. Calculate the sum of the entries with odd subscripts in an integer array *a*() of size 10.

35. Twelve exam grades are stored in the array *grades*(). Curve the grades by adding 7 points to each grade.

36. Read 10 digits contained in a text file into an array and then display three columns in a list box as follows: column 1 should contain the original 10 digits, column 2 should contain these digits in reverse order, and column 3 should contain the averages of the corresponding digits numbers in columns 1 and 2.

37. Thirty scores, each lying between 0 and 49, are given in a text file. Write a program that uses these scores to create an array *frequency*( ) as follows:

$$frequency(0) = \# \text{ of scores} < 10$$
$$frequency(1) = \# \text{ of scores such that } 10 <= score < 20$$
$$frequency(2) = \# \text{ of scores such that } 20 <= score < 30$$
$$frequency(3) = \# \text{ of scores such that } 30 <= score < 40$$
$$frequency(4) = \# \text{ of scores such that } 40 <= score < 50$$

The program should then display the results in tabular form as follows:

INTERVAL	FREQUENCY
0 to 9	frequency(0)
10 to 19	frequency(1)
20 to 29	frequency(2)
30 to 39	frequency(3)
40 to 49	frequency(4)

38. Write a program that asks the user for a month by number and then displays the name of that month. For instance, if the user inputs 2, the program should display February. **Hint:** Create an array of 12 strings, one for each month of the year.

39. The file USPRES.TXT contains the names of the 43 U.S. Presidents in the order they served. Write a program that places the names in an array, supplies all presidents having a requested first name, and supplies all presidents for a requested range of numbers. The following is one possible outcome:

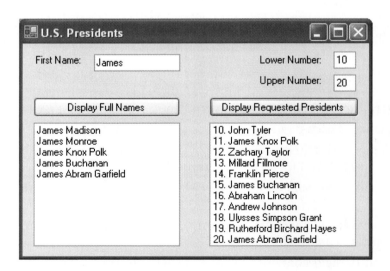

40. The file COLORS.TXT contains the names of the colors of Crayola®* crayons in alphabetical order. Write a program to read the colors into an array and then

---

*Crayola® is a registered trademark of Binney & Smith.

display the colors beginning with a specified letter. The program should declare an array with upper bound 50 and then increase the size of the array by 10 elements whenever it runs out of space to store the colors. One possible outcome is the following:

41. An *anagram* of a word or phrase is another word or phrase that uses the same letters with the same frequency. Punctuation marks and spaces are ignored. Write a program that requests two words or phases as input and determines if they are anagrams of each other. (Test the program with the pair of phrases DWIGHT DAVID EISENHOWER and HE DID VIEW THE WAR DOINGS.)

Solutions to Practice Problems 7.1

1. Two possible answers are as follows:

```
Dim lakes() As String = {"Huron", "Ontario", "Michigan", _
                "Erie", "Superior", "", "", "", "", "", ""}

Dim lakes() As String = {"Huron", "Ontario", "Michigan", _
                "Erie", "Superior"}
ReDim Preserve lakes(10)
```

2. This task consists of searching through an array and is carried out just like the task of searching a text file for a specified item. Replace the For loop with the following code:

```
Do While (teamName(i) <> txtName.Text) And (i < upperBound)
  i += 1
Loop
If teamName(i) = txtName.Text Then
  lstGamesWon.Items.Add(i + 1)
End If
```

3. Arrays should be used when

   (a) several pieces of data of the same type will be entered by the user; or
   (b) computations must be made on the items in a text file after all of the items have been read.

7.2 Using Arrays

This section considers three aspects of the use of arrays: processing ordered arrays, reading part of an array, and passing arrays to procedures.

▧ Ordered Arrays

An array is said to be **ordered** if its values are in either ascending or descending order. The following arrays illustrate the different types of ordered and unordered arrays. In an ascending ordered array, the value of each element is less than or equal to the value of the next element. That is,

$$[\text{each element}] \leq [\text{next element}].$$

For string arrays, the ANSI table is used to evaluate the "less than or equal to" condition.

Ordered Ascending Numeric Array

dates()	1492	1776	1812	1929	1969

Ordered Descending Numeric Array

discov()	1610	1541	1513	1513	1492

Ordered Ascending String Array

king()	Edward	Henry	James	John	Kong

Ordered Descending String Array

lake()	Superior	Ontario	Michigan	Huron	Erie

Unordered Numeric Array

rates()	8.25	5.00	7.85	8.00	6.50

Unordered String Array

char()	G	R	E	A	T

Ordered arrays can be searched more efficiently than unordered arrays. In this section, we use their order to shorten the search. The technique used here is applied to searching text files in Chapter 8.

 Example 1 The following program places an ordered list of names into an array, requests a name as input, and informs the user if the name is in the list. Because the list is ordered, the search of the array ends when an element is reached whose value is

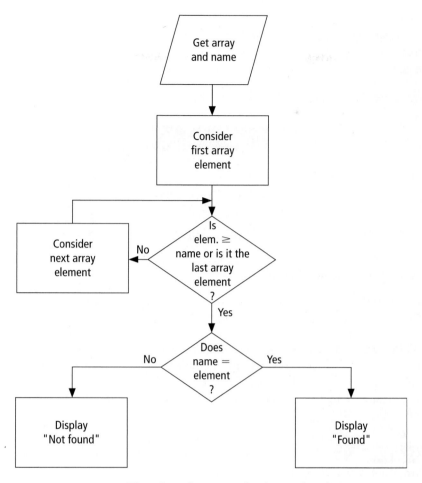

FIGURE 7.3 Flowchart for a search of an ordered array.

greater than or equal to the input name. On average, only half the ordered array will be searched. Figure 7.3 shows the flowchart for this search.

```
'Create array to hold 10 strings
Dim nom() As String = {"AL", "BOB", "CARL", "DON", "ERIC", _
                       "FRED", "GREG", "HERB", "IRA", "JACK"}
Private Sub btnSearch_Click(...) Handles btnSearch.Click
  'Search for a name in an ordered list
  Dim name2Find As String
  Dim n As Integer = -1
  name2Find = txtName.Text.ToUpper
  Do
    n += 1    'Add 1 to n
  Loop Until (nom(n) >= name2Find) Or (n = 9)
  'Interpret result of search
  If nom(n) = name2Find Then
    txtResult.Text = "Found."
```

```
    Else
      txtResult.Text = "Not found."
    End If
End Sub
```

[Run, type "Don" into the text box, and click the button.]

Using Part of an Array

In some programs, we must dimension an array before knowing how many pieces of data are to be placed into it. In these cases, we dimension the array large enough to handle all reasonable contingencies. For instance, if the array is to hold exam grades, and class sizes are at most 100 students, we use a statement such as **Dim grades(99) As Integer**. In such situations, we must employ a **counter variable** to keep track of the number of values actually stored in the array. We create this counter variable using a Dim statement in the Declarations section of the program so that all procedures will have access to it.

 Example 2 The following program requests a list of companies and then displays them along with a count:

```
'Demonstrate using part of an array
Dim stock(99) As String
Dim counter As Integer

Private Sub btnRecord_Click(...) Handles btnRecord.Click
  If (counter < 99) Then
    counter += 1   'Increment counter by 1
    stock(counter - 1) = txtCompany.Text
    txtCompany.Clear()
    txtCompany.Focus()
    txtNumber.Text = CStr(counter)
  Else
    MsgBox("No space to record additional companies.", 0, "")
    txtCompany.Clear()
    btnSummarize.Focus()
  End If
End Sub
```

```
Private Sub btnSummarize_Click(...) Handles btnSummarize.Click
  'List stock companies that have been recorded
  lstStocks.Items.Clear()
  For i As Integer = 0 To counter - 1
    lstStocks.Items.Add(stock(i))
  Next
End Sub
```

[Run, type in the seven companies shown (press Record Name after each company name is typed), and press Summarize.]

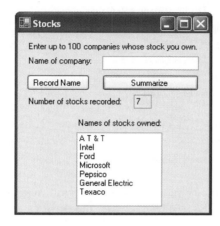

■ Merging Two Ordered Arrays

Suppose that you have two ordered lists of customers (possibly with some customers on both lists) and you want to consolidate them into a single ordered list. The technique for creating the third list, called the **merge algorithm**, is as follows:

1. Compare the two names at the top of the first and second lists.
  (a) If one name alphabetically precedes the other, copy it onto the third list and cross it off its original list.
  (b) If the names are the same, copy the name onto the third list and cross out the name from the first and second lists.
2. Repeat Step 1 with the current top names until you reach the end of either list.
3. Copy the names from the remaining list onto the third list.

 Example 3 The following program stores two lists of names in arrays and merges them into a third list. At most 10 names will be placed into the third array; duplicates will reduce this number. Because the variable r identifies the next position to insert a name in the third array, $r - 1$ is the number of names in the array.

```
Private Sub btnMerge_Click(...) Handles btnMerge.Click
  'Create arrays to hold list of names
  Dim list1() As String = {"Al", "Carl", "Don", "Greg", "Jack"}
  Dim list2() As String = {"Bob", "Carl", "Eric", "Greg", "Herb"}
```

```
    Dim newList(9) As String
    Dim m, n, r, numNames As Integer
    'Merge two lists of names
    m = 0     'Subscript for first array
    n = 0     'Subscript for second array
    r = 0     'Subscript and counter for third array
    Do While (m <= 4) And (n <= 4)
      Select Case list1(m)
        Case Is < list2(n)
          newList(r) = list1(m)
          m += 1      'Increase m by 1
        Case Is > list2(n)
          newList(r) = list2(n)
          n += 1      'Increase n by 1
        Case list2(n)
          newList(r) = list1(m)
          m += 1
          n += 1
      End Select
      r += 1          'Increase r by 1
    Loop
    'If one of the lists has items left over, copy them into the third list.
    'At most one of the following two loops will be executed.
    Do While m <= 4        'Copy rest of first array into third
      newList(r) = list1(m)
      r += 1
      m += 1
    Loop
    Do While n <= 4        'Copy rest of second array into third
      newList(r) = list2(n)
      r += 1
      n += 1
    Loop
    numNames = r - 1
    'Show result of merging lists
    lstMergedList.Items.Clear()
    For i As Integer = 0 To numNames
      lstMergedList.Items.Add(newList(i))
    Next
End Sub
```

[Run, and click the button.]

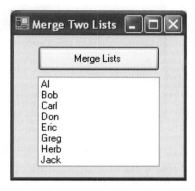

Passing Arrays to Procedures

An array that is not declared in the Declarations section, but rather is declared in a procedure, is local to that procedure and unknown in all other procedures. However, an entire local array can be passed to another procedure. The argument in the calling statement consists of the name of the array, written *without* a trailing empty set of parentheses. The corresponding parameter in the header for the procedure must consist of an array name *with* a trailing empty set of parentheses. Like all other parameters, the array parameter must be preceded with ByVal or ByRef and followed with an "As varType" clause. The method GetUpperBound simplifies working with arrays that have been passed to a procedure.

  Example 4 The following program illustrates passing an array to a Function procedure. Notice that the function call is written Sum(score), not Sum(score()), and that the parameter declaration is written **ByVal s() As Integer**, not **ByVal s As Integer**.

```
Private Sub btnCompute_Click(...) Handles btnCompute.Click
  'Pass array to Function procedure
  Dim score() As Integer = {85, 92, 75, 68, 84, 86, 94, 74, 79, 88}
  txtAverage.Text = CStr(Sum(score) / 10)
End Sub

Function Sum(ByVal s() As Integer) As Integer
  'Add up scores
  Dim total As Integer
  total = 0
  For index As Integer = 0 To s.GetUpperBound(0)    'The upper bound is 9
    total += s(index)    'Add the value of s(index) to the value of total
  Next
  Return total
End Function
```

[Run, and click the button.]

Sometimes it is also necessary to pass a class-level array from one procedure to another. For example, you might have a sorting procedure (discussed in Section 7.3) and three class-level arrays to be sorted. The sorting procedure would be called three times, each time passing a different class-level array. The method for passing a class-level array to another procedure is the same as the method for passing a local array.

 Example 5   The following program incorporates all three topics discussed in this section. It places ordered lists of computer languages and spoken languages into class-level arrays, requests a new language as input, and inserts the language into its proper array position (avoiding duplication). The language arrays are declared to hold up to 21 names; the variables *numCompLangs* and *numSpokLangs* record the actual number of languages in each of the ordered arrays.

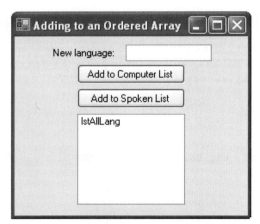

OBJECT	PROPERTY	SETTING
frmAdding	Text	Adding to an Ordered Array
lblLang	Text	New language:
txtLang		
btnAddComp	Text	Add to Computer List
btnAddSpok	Text	Add to Spoken List
lstAllLang		

```
Dim compLang() As String = {"ADA", "C++", "Cobol", _
                            "Fortran", "Java", "Visual Basic"}
Dim spokLang() As String = {"Cantonese", "English", "French", _
                            "Mandarin", "Russian", "Spanish"}
Dim numCompLangs As Integer = 6, numSpokLangs As Integer = 6
Private Sub frmAdding_Load(...) Handles MyBase.Load
  ReDim Preserve compLang(20)
  ReDim Preserve spokLang(20)
End Sub
```

```
Private Sub btnAddComp_Click(...) Handles btnAddComp.Click
  'Insert language into ordered array of computer languages
  AddALang(compLang, numCompLangs)
  DisplayArray(compLang, numCompLangs)
  txtLang.Clear()
  txtLang.Focus()
End Sub

Private Sub btnAddSpok_Click(...) Handles btnAddSpok.Click
  'Insert language into ordered array of spoken languages
  AddALang(spokLang, numSpokLangs)
  DisplayArray(spokLang, numSpokLangs)
  txtLang.Clear()
  txtLang.Focus()
End Sub

Sub AddALang(ByRef lang() As String, ByRef langCount As Integer)
  'Insert a language into an ordered array of languages
  Dim language As String
  Dim n As Integer = -1
  language = txtLang.Text.Trim
  Do
    n += 1     'Increase n by 1
  Loop Until ((lang(n).ToUpper >= language.ToUpper) Or (n = langCount - 1))
  If lang(n).ToUpper < language.ToUpper Then          'Insert language at end
    lang(langCount) = language
    langCount += 1
  ElseIf lang(n).ToUpper > language.ToUpper Then    'Insert before item n
    For i As Integer = (langCount - 1) To n Step -1
      lang(i + 1) = lang(i)
    Next
    lang(n) = language
    langCount += 1
  End If
End Sub

Sub DisplayArray(ByVal lang() As String, ByVal howMany As Integer)
  'Display the languages in the array
  lstAllLang.Items.Clear()
  For i As Integer = 0 To howMany - 1
    lstAllLang.Items.Add(lang(i))
  Next
End Sub
```

[Run, type "German," and click "Add to Spoken List."]

[Type "Fortran," and click "Add to Computer List."]

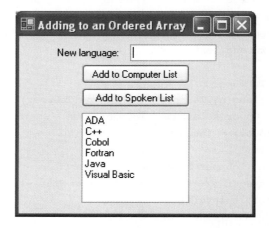

▓ Comments

1. In Examples 1 and 5, we searched successive elements of an ordered list beginning with the first element. This is called a **sequential search**. An efficient alternative to the sequential search is the **binary search**, which is considered in Section 7.4.

2. A single element of an array can be passed to a procedure just like any ordinary numeric or string variable.

```
Private Sub btnDisplay_Click(...) Handles btnDisplay.Click
  Dim num(20) As Integer
  num(5) = 10
  lstOutput.Items.Add(Triple(num(5)))
End Sub

Function Triple(ByVal x As Integer) As Integer
  Return 3 * x
End Function
```

When the program is run and the button clicked, 30 will be displayed.

Practice Problems 7.2

1. Can an array be in both ascending and descending order at the same time?
2. How can the Select Case block in Example 3 be changed so all entries of both arrays (including duplicates) are merged into the third array?

EXERCISES 7.2

In Exercises 1 and 2, decide whether the array is ordered.

1. month()

January	February	March	April	May

2. pres()

Adams	Adams	Bush	Johnson	Johnson

In Exercises 3 through 8, determine the output displayed when the button is clicked.

3.
```
Private Sub btnDisplay_Click(...) Handles btnDisplay.Click
    Dim lake(4) As String
    lake(2) = "Michigan"
    DisplayThird(lake)
End Sub


Sub DisplayThird(ByVal lake() As String)
  'Display the third element of an array
  txtOutput.Text = lake(2)
End Sub
```

4.
```
Private Sub btnDisplay_Click(...) Handles btnDisplay.Click
    Dim num As Integer
    Dim square(20) As Double
    num = CInt(InputBox("Enter a number from 1 to 20:"))
    For i As Integer = 0 To num
      square(i) = i ^ 2
    Next
    Total(square, num)
End Sub

Sub Total(ByVal list() As Double, ByVal n As Integer)
  Dim sum As Double = 0
  For i As Integer = 0 To n
    sum += list(i)
  Next
  txtOutput.Text = "The sum of the " & n + 1 & " numbers is " & sum
End Sub
```

(Assume that the response is 4.)

5.
```
Private Sub btnDisplay_Click(...) Handles btnDisplay.Click
    Dim value(4) As Integer
    FillArray(value)
    For i As Integer = 0 To 3
      Select Case value(i)
        Case Is < value(i + 1)
          lstOutput.Items.Add("less than")
        Case Is > value(i + 1)
          lstOutput.Items.Add("greater than")
        Case Else
          lstOutput.Items.Add("equals")
      End Select
    Next
End Sub

Private Sub FillArray(ByRef list() As Integer)
    'Place values into an array of five elements
    Dim sr As IO.StreamReader = IO.File.OpenText("DATA.TXT")
    For i As Integer = 0 To 4
      list(i) = CInt(sr.ReadLine)
    Next
    sr.Close()
End Sub
```

(Assume that the five lines of the file DATA.TXT contain the following entries: 3, 7, 1, 1, 17.)

6.
```
Private Sub btnDisplay_Click(...) Handles btnDisplay.Click
    Dim ocean(5) As String
    ocean(1) = "Pacific"
    Musical(ocean(1))
End Sub

Sub Musical(ByVal sea As String)
    txtOutput.Text = "South " & sea
End Sub
```

7.
```
Private Sub btnDisplay_Click(...) Handles btnDisplay.Click
    Dim rain(11) As Double
    rain(0) = 2.4
    rain(1) = 3.6
    rain(2) = 4.0
    txtOutput.Text = "total rainfall for first quarter: " & _
                    Total(rain, 2) & " inches"
End Sub

Function Total(ByVal rain() As Double, n As Integer) As Double
    Dim sum As Double = 0
```

```
    For i As Integer = 0 To n
      sum += rain(i)
    Next
    Return sum
  End Function
```

8.
```
Private Sub btnDisplay_Click(...) Handles btnDisplay.Click
    Dim num(7) As Integer
    Dim sr As IO.StreamReader = IO.File.OpenText("DATA.TXT")
    For i As Integer = 0 To 7
      num(i) = CInt(sr.ReadLine)
    Next
    sr.Close()
    txtOutput.Text = "The array has " & Nonzero(num) & _
                     " nonzero entries."
  End Sub

  Function Nonzero(ByVal digit() As Integer) As Integer
    Dim count As Integer
    count = 0
    For i As Integer = 0 To 7
      If digit(i) <> 0 Then
        count += 1
      End If
    Next
    Return count
  End Function
```

(Assume that the eight lines of the file DATA.TXT contain the following data: 5, 0, 2, 1, 0, 0, 7, 7.)

In Exercises 9 through 14, identify the error.

9.
```
Private Sub btnDisplay_Click(...) Handles btnDisplay.Click
    Dim city(3) As String
    Assign(city)
    txtOutput.Text = city
  End Sub

  Sub Assign(ByRef town() As String)
    town(1) = "Chicago"
  End Sub
```

10.
```
Private Sub btnDisplay_Click(...) Handles btnDisplay.Click
    Dim planet(8) As String
    Assign(planet)
    txtOutput.Text = planet(1)
  End Sub

  Sub Assign(ByRef planet As String)
    planet(1) = "Venus"
  End Sub
```

11. ```
Private Sub btnDisplay_Click(...) Handles btnDisplay.Click
    'Multiply several positive numbers together
    Dim prompt As String
    Dim number, product, num(4) As Double
    Dim n As Integer = -1
    prompt = "Enter a positive number to multiply by, or, "
    prompt &= "to see the product, Enter a negative number. "
    prompt &= "(Five numbers maximum can be specified.)"
    Do
      n += 1
      number = CDbl(InputBox(prompt))
      If number > 0 Then
        num(n) = number
      End If
    Loop Until (number < 0) Or (n = 4)
    product = 1
    For i As Integer = 0 To n
      product = product * num(i)
    Next
    txtOutput.Text = "The product of the numbers entered is " _
                     & product & "."
End Sub
```

12. ```
Private Sub btnDisplay_Click(...) Handles btnDisplay.Click
    Dim hue(15) As String
    hue(1) = "Blue"
    Favorite(hue())
End Sub

Sub Favorite(ByVal tone() As String)
    tone(1) = hue(1)
    txtOutput.Text = tone
End Sub
```

13. ```
Private Sub btnDisplay_Click(...) Handles btnDisplay.Click
    Dim a(10), b(10) As Double
    For i As Integer = 0 To 10
      a(i) = i ^ 2
    Next
    CopyArray(a, b)
    txtOutput.Text = CStr(b(10))
End Sub

Sub CopyArray(ByRef a() As Double, ByRef b() As Double)
    'Place a's values in b
    b() = a()
End Sub
```
```

14.
```
Private Sub btnDisplay_Click(...) Handles btnDisplay.Click
    Dim a(2) As Integer
    a(0) = 42
    a(1) = 7
    a(2) = 11
    FlipFirstTwo(a)
    txtOutput.Text = a(0) & " " & a(1) & " " & a (2)
End Sub

Sub FlipFirstTwo(ByRef a() As Integer)
    'Swap first two elements
    a(1) = a(0)
    a(0) = a(1)
End Sub
```

Suppose an array has been declared in the Declarations section of the Code window with the statement **Dim scores(50) As Double** and numbers assigned to the elements having subscripts 0 to 50 by the frmOrder_Load event procedure. In Exercises 15 through 18, write a procedure to perform the stated task.

15. Determine whether the array is in ascending order.

16. Determine whether the array is in descending order.

17. With a single loop, determine whether the array is in ascending order, descending order, both, or neither.

18. Assuming that the array is in ascending order, determine how many numbers appear more than once in the array.

In Exercises 19 and 20, suppose arrays $a()$, $b()$, and $c()$ are class-level and that arrays $a()$ and $b()$ have each been assigned 20 numbers in ascending order (duplications may occur) by a frmNumbers_Load event procedure. For instance, array $a()$ might hold the numbers 1, 3, 3, 3, 9, 9, ...

19. Write a procedure to place all the 40 numbers from arrays $a()$ and $b()$ into $c()$ so that $c()$ is also in ascending order. The array $c()$ could contain duplications.

20. Write a procedure to place the numbers from $a()$ and $b()$ into $c()$ so that $c()$ also has ascending order, but contains no duplications.

21. Write a program to declare an array with the statement **Dim state(49) As String** and maintain a list of certain states. The list of states should always be in alphabetical order and occupy consecutive elements of the array. The buttons in the program should give the user the following options:

(a) Take the state specified by the user in a text box and insert it into its proper position in the array. (If the state is already in the array, so report.)

(b) Take the state specified by the user in a text box and delete it from the array. If the state is not in the array, so report.

(c) Display the states in the array.

22. Write a program that requests a sentence one word at a time from the user and then checks whether the sentence is a *word palindrome*. A word palindrome sentence reads the same, word by word, backward and forward (ignoring punctuation and capitalization). An example is "You can cage a swallow, can't you, but you can't swallow a cage, can you?" The program should hold the words of the sentence in an array and use procedures to obtain the input, analyze the sentence, and declare whether the sentence is a word palindrome. (Test the program with the sentences, "Monkey see, monkey do." and "I am; therefore, am I?")

23. Write a program to display the average score and the number of above-average scores on an exam. Each time the user clicks a "Record Score" button, a grade should be read from a text box. The average score and the number of above-average scores should be displayed in a list box whenever the user clicks on a "Display Average" button. (Assume that the class has at most 100 students.) Use a function to calculate the average and another function to determine the number of above-average scores. **Note:** Pass the functions an array argument for the grades and a numeric argument for the number of elements of the array that have been assigned values.

24. Suppose that an array of 100 names is in ascending order. Write a procedure to search for a name input by the user. If the first letter of the name is found in N through Z, then the search should begin with the 100th element of the array and proceed backward.

25. At the beginning of 1990, a complete box of Crayola crayons had 72 colors (in the file PRE1990COLORS.TXT). During the 1990's, 8 colors were retired (in the file RETIREDCOLORS.TXT) and 56 new colors were added (in the file ADDED-COLORS.TXT). Each of the three files is in alphabetical order. Write a program that reads the text files into the arrays *colors*( ), *retired*( ), and *added*( ), and then uses the arrays *retired*( ) and *added*( ) to update the array *colors*( ) so that it contains the current 120 colors.

Solutions to Practice Problems 7.2

1. Yes, provided each element of the array has the same value.

2. The third Case tests for duplicates and assigns only one array element to the third array if duplicates are found in the two arrays. Thus, we remove the third Case and change the first Case so it will process any duplicates. A situation where you would want to merge two lists while retaining duplications is the task of merging two ordered arrays of test scores.

```
Select Case list1(m)
  Case Is <= list2(n)
    newList(r) = list1(m)
    m += 1
  Case Is > list2(n)
    newList(r) = list2(n)
    n += 1
End Select
```

7.3   Some Additional Types of Arrays

So far, the array elements have been standard data types. This section considers arrays of controls and arrays of a new compound data type designed by the programmer.

■ Control Arrays

We have seen many examples of the usefulness of subscripted variables. They are essential for writing concise solutions to many programming problems. Because of the utility that subscripts provide, Visual Basic also provides for arrays of labels, text boxes, and buttons. Since labels, text boxes, and buttons are referred to generically in Visual Basic as controls, arrays of these objects (or of any other control) are called **control arrays**. **Note:** Since Visual Basic does not provide for arrays of masked text boxes, we will only use ordinary text boxes for input.

Control arrays are created in much the same way as any other array; that is, with a statement of the form

```
Dim arrayName(n) As ControlType
```

or

```
Dim arrayName() As ControlType
```

For instance, the following statements declare control arrays.

```
Dim lblTitle(10) As Label
Dim txtNumber(8) As TextBox
Dim btnAmount() As Button
```

 Example 1   A department store has five departments. The following program requests the amount of sales for each department and displays the total sales for the store. The five labels identifying the departments are grouped into an array of labels and the five text boxes for the individual amounts are grouped into an array of text boxes. The initial settings for these labels are specified at run time in the frmSales_Load event procedure instead of being specified at design time. The Text properties of the labels are set to be "Department 1", "Department 2", and so on.

OBJECT	PROPERTY	SETTING
frmSales	Text	Daily Sales:
Label1–Label5		
TextBox1–TextBox5		
btnCompute	Text	Compute Total Sales
lblTotal	Text	Total Sales:
txtTotal	ReadOnly	True

```
Dim lblDept(4) As Label
Dim txtDept(4) As TextBox

Private Sub frmSales_Load(...) Handles MyBase.Load
  lblDept(0) = Label1
  lblDept(1) = Label2
  lblDept(2) = Label3
  lblDept(3) = Label4
  lblDept(4) = Label5
  txtDept(0) = TextBox1
  txtDept(1) = TextBox2
  txtDept(2) = TextBox3
  txtDept(3) = TextBox4
  txtDept(4) = TextBox5
  'Set the labels' Text property to the corresponding department
  'Set the text boxes' Text property to the empty string
  For depNum As Integer = 1 To 5
    lblDept(depNum - 1).Text = "Department " & depNum & ":"
  Next
End Sub

Private Sub btnCompute_Click(...) Handles btnCompute.Click
  Dim totalSales As Double = 0
  For depNum As Integer = 1 To 5
    totalSales += CDbl(txtDept(depNum - 1).Text)
  Next
  txtTotal.Text = FormatCurrency(totalSales)
End Sub
```

[Run, enter amounts into the text boxes, and then click the button.]

■ Structures

Some of the data types we have worked with so far are Double, Integer, String, and Boolean. A **structure** provides a convenient way of packaging as a single unit several related variables of different types. In previous versions of Visual Basic a structure was called a user-defined type (UDT).

Three pieces of related information about colleges are "name," "state," and "year founded." A structure type capable of holding this data is defined by the following block of statements located in the Declarations section of the Code window.

```
Structure College
  Dim name As String
  Dim state As String
  Dim yearFounded As Integer
End Structure
```

Each of the three subvariables of the structure type is called a **member**. A structure variable of the type College is declared by a statement such as

```
Dim college1 As College
```

Each member is accessed by giving the name of the structure variable and the member, separated by a period. For instance, the three members of the structure variable *college1* are accessed as *college1.name*, *college1.state*, and *college1.yearFounded*.

In general, a structure type is defined by a Structure block of the form

```
Structure StructureType
  Dim memberName1 As MemberType1
  Dim membername2 As MemberType2
    .
    .
    .
End Structure
```

where *StructureType* is the name of the user-defined data type; *memberName1*, *memberName2*, . . . , are the names of the members of the structure; and *MemberType1*, *MemberType2*, . . . , are the corresponding member types, such as String, Integer, Double, or Boolean.

A structure variable, *structureVar*, is declared to be of the user-defined type by a statement of the form

```
Dim structureVar As StructureType
```

Example 2 The following program stores information about two colleges into structure variables of type College and uses the variables to determine which college is older. *Note:* In the third line of the btnOlder_Click event procedure, all the member values of *college1* are assigned simultaneously to *collegeOlder*.

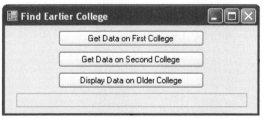

OBJECT	PROPERTY	SETTING
frmFirst	Text	Find Earlier College
btnFirst	Text	Get Data on First College
btnSecond	Text	Get Data on Second College
btnOlder	Text	Display Data on Older College
txtResult	ReadOnly	True

```
Structure College
   Dim name As String
   Dim state As String
   Dim yearFounded As Integer
End Structure

Dim college1, college2, collegeOlder As College

Private Sub btnFirst_Click(...) Handles btnFirst.Click
   Dim prompt As String
   college1.name = InputBox("Enter name of first college.", "Name")
   college1.state = InputBox("Enter state of first college.", "State")
   prompt = "Enter the year the first college was founded."
   college1.yearFounded = CInt(InputBox(prompt, "Year"))
End Sub

Private Sub btnSecond_Click(...) Handles btnSecond.Click
   Dim prompt As String
   college2.name = InputBox("Enter name of second college.", "Name")
   college2.state = InputBox("Enter state of second college.", "State")
   prompt = "Enter the year the second college was founded."
   college2.yearFounded = CInt(InputBox(prompt, "Year"))
End Sub

Private Sub btnOlder_Click(...) Handles btnOlder.Click
   If (college1.yearFounded < college2.yearFounded) Then
     collegeOlder = college1
   Else
     collegeOlder = college2
   End If
   txtResult.Text = collegeOlder.name & " was founded in " & _
           collegeOlder.state & " in " & collegeOlder.yearFounded & "."
End Sub
```

[Run, click the first button, and respond to the input boxes with Princeton University, New Jersey, 1746. Click the second button; respond to the input boxes with Yale University, Connecticut, 1701. Finally, click the third button.]

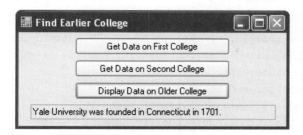

 Example 3   The file COLLEGES.TXT holds the name, state, and year founded for each of the 27 colleges in the United States founded before 1800. The first three lines of the file contain the data Harvard University, MA, 1636. The following program places the information about the colleges into an array of structures. The array is then used to display the names of the colleges in a specified state. *Note:* The masked text box has Mask "LL".

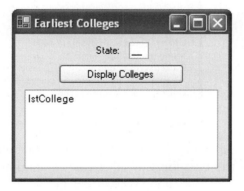

```
Structure College
  Dim name As String
  Dim state As String
  Dim yearFounded As Integer
End Structure

Dim school(26) As College

Private Sub frmColleges_Load(...) Handles MyBase.Load
  'Place the data for each college into the array school()
  Dim i As Integer = -1
  Dim sr As IO.StreamReader = IO.File.OpenText("COLLEGES.TXT")
  Do While (sr.Peek <> -1)
    i += 1
    school(i).name = sr.ReadLine
```

```
        school(i).state = sr.ReadLine
        school(i).yearFounded = CInt(sr.ReadLine)
    Loop
    sr.Close()
End Sub

Private Sub btnDisplay_Click(...) Handles btnDisplay.Click
    'Display the colleges in COLLEGES.TXT located in the given state
    lstCollege.Items.Clear()
    For i As Integer = 0 To 26
        If (school(i).state = mtxtState.Text) Then
            lstCollege.Items.Add(school(i).name, & " " & _
                            school(i).yearFounded)
        End If
    Next
End Sub
```

[Run, type the name of a state into the masked text box, and click the button.]

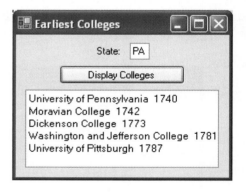

So far, the members of structures have had elementary types; such as String or Integer. However, the type for a member can be another structure or an array type. When a member is given an array type, the defining Dim statement must not specify the upper bound; this task must be left to a ReDim statement. Example 4 demonstrates the use of both of these nonelementary types of members. In addition, the example shows how to pass a structure variable to a Sub procedure.

 Example 4 The following program totals a person's college credits and determines whether they have enough credits for graduation. **Notes:** The structure variable *person* is local to the btnGet_Click event procedure. In the fourth line of the procedure, **person.name.firstName** should be thought of as **(person.name).firstName**.

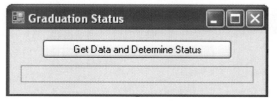

OBJECT	PROPERTY	SETTING
frmStatus	Text	Graduation Status
btnGet	Text	Get Data and Determine Status
txtResult	ReadOnly	True

```
Structure FullName
  Dim firstName As String
  Dim lastName As String
End Structure

Structure Student
  Dim name As FullName
  Dim credits() As Integer
End Structure

Private Sub btnGet_Click(...) Handles btnGet.Click
  Dim numYears As Integer
  Dim person As Student
  txtResult.Clear()
  person.name.firstName = InputBox("First Name:")
  person.name.lastName = InputBox("Second Name:")
  numYears = CInt(InputBox("Number of years completed:"))
  ReDim person.credits(numYears - 1)
  For i As Integer = 0 To numYears - 1
    person.credits(i) = CInt(InputBox("Credits in year " & i + 1))
  Next
  DetermineStatus(person)
End Sub

Sub DetermineStatus(ByVal person As Student)
  Dim total As Integer = 0
  For i As Integer = 0 To person.credits.GetUpperBound(0)
    total += person.credits(i)
  Next
  If (total >= 120) Then
    txtResult.Text = person.name.firstName & " " & _
            person.name.lastName & " has enough credits to graduate."
  Else
    txtResult.Text = person.name.firstName & " " & _
                person.name.lastName & " needs " & _
                (120 - total) & " more credits to graduate."
  End If
End Sub
```

[Run, click the button, and respond to requests for input with Miranda, Smith, 3, 34, 33, 34.]

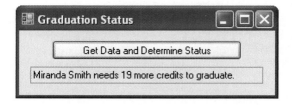

▨ Comments

1. Structures are similar to arrays in that they both store and access data items using a common name. However, the elements in an array must be of the same data type, whereas the members in a structure can be a mixture of different data types. Also, the different elements of an array are identified by their indices, whereas the members of a structure are identified by a name following a period.

2. Statements of the form

   lstBox.Items.Add(structureVar)

   where *structureVar* is a structure variable, do not perform as intended. Each member of a structure should appear separately in a lstBox.Items.Add statement. Also, comparisons involving structures using the relational operators $<$, $>$, $=$, $<>$, $<=$, and $>=$ are valid only with individual members of the structure, not with the structures themselves.

1. Find the errors in the following event procedure.

```
Sub btnDisplay_Click(...) Handles btnDisplay.Click
   Structure Team
      Dim school As String
      Dim mascot As String
   End Structure
   Team.school = "Rice"
   Team.mascot = "Owls"
   txtOutput.Text = Team.school & " " & Team.mascot
End Sub
```

2. Correct the code in Practice Problem 1.

In Exercises 1 through 4, use the following form (already filled in by the user) to determine the output displayed in the read-only text box at the bottom of the form when the button is clicked. The rectangular group of text boxes on the form consist of four arrays of text boxes—*txtWinter()*, *txtSpring()*, *txtSummer()*, and *txtFall()*—with each array having indexes ranging from 0 to 3.

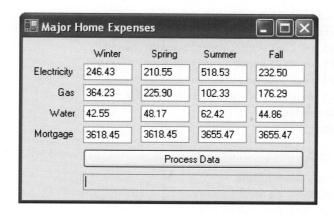

1. ```
Private Sub btnProcess_Click(...) Handles btnProcess.Click
    Dim total As Double = 0
    For itemNum As Integer = 0 To 3
      total += CDbl(txtWinter(itemNum).Text)
    Next
    txtBox.Text = "Expenses for winter: " & FormatCurrency(total)
End Sub
```

2. ```
Private Sub btnProcess_Click(...) Handles btnProcess.Click
    Dim total As Double = 0
    total += CDbl(txtWinter(2).Text)
    total += CDbl(txtSpring(2).Text)
    total += CDbl(txtSummer(2).Text)
    total += CDbl(txtFall(2).Text)
    txtBox.Text = "Annual water bill: " & FormatCurrency(total)
End Sub
```

3. ```
Private Sub btnProcess_Click(...) Handles btnProcess.Click
    Dim diff As Double
    Dim total As Double = 0
    For i As Integer = 0 To 3
      diff = CDbl(txtSummer(i).Text) - CDbl(txWinter(i).Text)
      total += diff
    Next
    txtBox.Text = "Summer bills top winter bills by " & _
                 FormatCurrency(total)
End Sub
```

4. ```
Private Sub btnProcess_Click(...) Handles btnProcess.Click
    Dim total As Double = 0
    For itemNum As Integer = 0 To 3
      total += TotalCateg(itemNum)
    Next
    txtBox.Text = "Total major expenses: " & FormatCurrency(total)
End Sub
```

```
Function TotalCateg(ByVal itemNum As Integer) As Double
   Dim total As Double = 0
   total += CDbl(txtWinter(itemNum).Text)
   total += CDbl(txtSpring(itemNum).Text)
   total += CDbl(txtSummer(itemNum).Text)
   total += CDbl(txtFall(itemNum).Text)
   Return total
End Function
```

In Exercises 5 through 8, determine the output displayed when the button is clicked.

5.
```
Structure Appearance
   Dim height As Double
   Dim weight As Double
End Structure

Private Sub btnDisplay_Click(...) Handles btnDisplay.Click
   Dim person1, person2 As Appearance
   person1.height = 72
   person1.weight = 170
   person2.height = 12 * 6
   If person1.height = person2.height Then
      lstOutput.Items.Add("heights are same")
   End If
   person2 = person1
   lstOutput.Items.Add(person2.weight)
End Sub
```

6.
```
Structure TestData
   Dim name As String
   Dim score As Double
End Structure

Dim sr As IO.StreamReader = IO.File.OpenText("SCORES.TXT")

Private Sub btnDisplay_Click(...) Handles btnDisplay.Click
   Dim student As TestData
   For i As Integer = 1 to 3
      GetScore(student)
      DisplayScore(student)
   Next
   sr.Close()
End Sub

Sub GetScore(ByRef student As TestData)
   student.name = sr.ReadLine
   student.score = CDbl(sr.ReadLine)
End Sub

Sub DisplayScore(ByVal student As testData)
   lstOutput.Items.Add(student.name & " " & student.score)
End Sub
```

(Assume that the six lines of the file SCORES.TXT contain the following data: Joe, 18, Moe, 20, Roe, 25.)

7.
```
Structure Address
    Dim street As String
    Dim city As String
    Dim state As String
End Structure

Structure Citizen
    Dim name As String
    Dim residence As Address
End Structure

Private Sub btnDisplay_Click(...) Handles btnDisplay.Click
    Dim person As Citizen
    person.name = "Mr. President"
    person.residence.street = "1600 Pennsylvania Avenue"
    person.residence.city = "Washington"
    person.residence.state = "DC"
    txtOutput.Text = person.name & " lives in " & _
            person.residence.city & ", " & person.residence.state
End Sub
```

8.
```
Structure TaxData
    Dim socSecNum As String
    Dim numExem As Integer 'Number of exemptions
    Dim maritalStat As String
    Dim hourlyWage As Double
End Structure

Structure Employee
    Dim name As String
    Dim hrsWorked As Double
    Dim taxInfo as TaxData
End Structure

Private Sub btnDisplay_Click(...) Handles btnDisplay.Click
    Dim worker as Employee
    worker.name = "Hannah Jones"
    worker.hrsWorked = 40
    worker.taxInfo.hourlyWage = 20
    txtOutput.Text = worker.name " & earned " & _
        FormatCurrency(worker.hrsWorked * worker.taxInfo.hourlyWage)
End Sub
```

In Exercises 9 through 11, determine the errors.

9.
```
Structure Nobel
    Dim peace as String
    Dim year as Integer
End Structure

Private Sub btnDisplay_Click(...) Handles btnDisplay.Click
    Dim prize As Nobel
    peace = "International Atomic Energy Agency"
```

```
    year = 2005
    txtBox.Text = peace & " won the " & year & " Nobel Peace Prize."
End Sub
```

10.
```
Structure Vitamins
    Dim a As Double
    Dim b As Double
End Structure

Private Sub btnDisplay_Click(...) Handles btnDisplay.Click
    Dim minimum As Vitamins
    minimum.b = 200
    minimum.a = 500
    lstOutput.Items.Add(minimum)
End Sub
```

11.
```
Structure BallGame
    Dim hits As Double
    Dim runs As Double
End Structure

Private Sub btnDisplay_Click(...) Handles btnDisplay.Click
    Dim game1, game2 As BallGame
    game1.hits = 15
    game1.runs = 8
    game2.hits = 17
    game2.runs = 10
    If game1 > game2 Then
      txtOutput.Text = "The first game was better."
    Else
      txtOutput.Text = "The second game was at least as good."
    End If
End Sub
```

12. Write a line or lines of code as instructed in Steps (a) through (e) to fill in the missing lines in the following program.

```
Structure Appearance
    Dim height As Double  'Inches
    Dim weight As Double  'Pounds
End Structure

Structure Person
    Dim name As String
    Dim stats As Appearance
End Structure

Private Sub btnDisplay_Click(...) Handles btnDisplay.Click
    Dim person1, person2 As Person
    (missing lines)
End Sub
```

(a) Give *person1* the name Michael.

(b) Set Michael's height and weight to 71 and 190, respectively.

(c) Give *person2* the name Jacob.

(d) Set Jacob's height and weight to 70 and 175, respectively.

(e) If one person is both taller and heavier than the other, display a sentence of the form "[name of bigger person] is bigger than [name of smaller person]."

A campus club has 10 members. The following program stores information about the students into an array of structures. Each structure contains the student's name and a list of the courses he or she is currently taking. Exercises 13 through 16 request that an additional event procedure be written for this program.

```
Structure Student
    Dim name As String
    Dim courses() As String
End Structure

Dim club(9) As Student

Private Sub frmStudents_Load(...) Handles MyBase.Load
    Dim pupil As student
    'Enter data for first student
    pupil.name = "Juan Santana"
    ReDim pupil.courses(2)
    pupil.courses(0) = "CMSC 100"
    pupil.courses(1) = "PHIL 200"
    pupil.courses(2) = "ENGL 120"
    club(0) = pupil
    'Enter data for second student
    pupil.name = "Mary Carlson"
    ReDim pupil.courses(3)
    pupil.courses(0) = "BIOL 110"
    pupil.courses(1) = "PHIL 200"
    pupil.courses(2) = "CMSC 100"
    pupil.courses(3) = "MATH 220"
    club(1) = pupil
    'Enter names and courses for remaining 8 people in the club
End Sub
```

13. Write the code for a btnDisplay_Click event procedure that will display the names of all the students in the club in a list box.

14. Write the code for a btnDisplay_Click event procedure that will display the names of all the students in the club who are registered for three courses.

15. Write the code for a btnDisplay_Click event procedure that will display the names of all the students in the club who are enrolled in CMSC 100.

16. Write the code for a btnDisplay_Click event procedure that will display the names of all the students in the club who are *not* enrolled in CMSC 100.

17. Write a program to compute a student's grade-point average for a semester. Allow for as many as six courses. For each course, the grades (*A*, *B*, ...) should be entered in an element of an array of six text boxes, and the semester hours credits entered into another array of six text boxes. After the student fills in the grades and clicks on a button, a Function procedure should compute the GPA. Then a Sub procedure should display the GPA along with one of two messages. A student with a GPA of 3 or more should be informed that he or she has made the honor roll. Otherwise, the student should be congratulated on having completed the semester.

18. Table 7.1 gives the U.S. Census Bureau projections for the populations (in millions) of the states predicted to be the most populous in the year 2025. Write a program that allows the user to enter the current populations of the states into an array of text boxes, computes the projected population growths for the states in an array of text boxes, and gives the percentage growth for the collection of five states. The growth is calculated with the formula

$$growth = (projected\ pop. - current\ pop.)/current\ pop$$

TABLE 7.1	State populations in the year 2025.
State	**Population in 2025**
California	49.3
Texas	27.2
New York	19.8
Illinois	13.4
Florida	20.7

Percentage growth can be displayed as FormatPercent(growth). Test the program with the current populations shown in Figure 7.4.

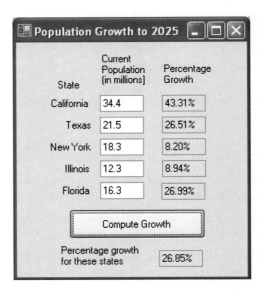

FIGURE 7.4 Sample run for Exercise 18.

19. Write a program to look up data on notable tall buildings. The program should declare a user-defined data type named "Building" with the members "name", "city", "height", and "stories". This interactive program should allow the user to type the name of a building into a text box and then search through an array of structures to determine the city, height, and number of stories of the building when a button is pressed. If the building is not in the array, then the program should so report. Place the information in Table 7.2 into a text file, and read it into the array.

TABLE 7.2   **Tallest buildings.**

Building	City	Height (ft)	Stories
Empire State	New York	1250	102
Sears Tower	Chicago	1454	110
Texas Commerce Tower	Houston	1002	75
Transamerica Pyramid	San Francisco	853	48

20. Given the following flight schedule, write a program to load this information into an array of structures, and ask the user to specify a flight number. Have the computer find the flight number and display the information corresponding to that flight. Account for the case where the user requests a nonexistent flight.

FLIGHT #	ORIGIN	DESTINATION	DEPARTURE TIME
117	Tucson	Dallas	8:45 a.m.
239	LA	Boston	10:15 a.m.
298	Albany	Reno	1:35 p.m.
326	Houston	New York	2:40 p.m.
445	New York	Tampa	4:20 p.m.

21. Table 7.3 contains the names and number of stores of the top 10 pizza chains in 2003. Write a program to place these data into an array of structures, compute the total number of stores for these 10 chains, and display a table giving the name and percentage of total stores for each of the companies.

TABLE 7.3   **Top 10 pizza chains as of July 1, 2003 (and numbers of stores).**

Name	Stores	Name	Stores
1. Pizza Hut	7,523	6. Papa Murphy's	750
2. Domino's	4,904	7. Godfather's	566
3. Little Caesar's	2,850	8. Round Table	485
4. Papa John's	2,574	9. CiCi's Pizza	465
5. Sbarro	790	10. Chuck E. Cheese's	460

Source: Pizza Marketing Quarterly, Summer 2003

22. A retail store has five bins, numbered 1 to 5, each containing a different commodity. At the beginning of a particular day, each bin contains 45 items. Table 7.4 shows the cost per item for each of the bins and the quantity sold during that day.

Write a program to

(a) place the cost per item and the quantity sold from each bin into an array of structures;

TABLE 7.4 Costs of items and quantities sold for Exercise 22.

Bin	Cost per Item	Quantity Sold
1	3.00	10
2	12.25	30
3	37.45	9
4	7.49	42
5	24.95	17

(b) display a table giving the inventory at the end of the day and the amount of revenue obtained from each bin;

(c) compute the total revenue for the day;

(d) list the number of each bin that contains fewer than 20 items at the end of the day.

Solutions to Practice Problems 7.3

1. The event procedure contains two errors. First, the definition of a structure cannot be inside a procedure; it must be typed into the Declarations section of the Code window. Second, the statements **Team.school = "Rice"** and **Team.mascot = "Owls"** are not valid. Team.school and Team.mascot are not valid. "Team" should be replaced by a variable of type Team that has previously been declared.

2.
```
Structure Team
    Dim school As String
    Dim mascot As String
End Structure

Private Sub btnDisplay_Click(...) Handles btnDisplay.Click
    Dim squad As Team
    squad.school = "Rice"
    squad.mascot = "Owls"
    txtOutput.Text = squad.school & " " & squad.mascot
End Sub
```

7.4 Sorting and Searching

A **sort** is an algorithm for ordering an array. Of the many different techniques for sorting an array we discuss two, the **bubble sort** and the **Shell sort**. Both require the interchange of values stored in a pair of variables. If *var1*, *var2*, and *temp* are all variables of the same data type (such as all String), then the statements

```
temp = var1
var1 = var2
var2 = temp
```

assign *var1*'s value to *var2* and *var2*'s value to *var1*.

Example 1   The following program alphabetizes two words supplied in text boxes:

```
Private Sub btnAlphabetize_Click(...) Handles btnAlphabetize.Click
  'Alphabetize two words
  Dim firstWord, secondWord, temp As String
  firstWord = txtFirstWord.Text
  secondWord = txtSecondWord.Text
  If (firstWord > secondWord) Then    'Swap the two words
    temp = firstWord
    firstWord = secondWord
    secondWord = temp
  End If
  txtResult.Text = firstWord & " before " & secondWord
End Sub
```

[Run, type "beauty" and "age" into the text boxes, and click the button.]

Bubble Sort

The bubble sort is an algorithm that compares adjacent items and swaps those that are out of order. If this process is repeated enough times, the list will be ordered. Let's carry out this process on the list Pebbles, Barney, Wilma, Fred, and Dino. The steps for each pass through the list are as follows:

1. Compare the first and second items. If they are out of order, swap them.

2. Compare the second and third items. If they are out of order, swap them.

3. Repeat this pattern for all remaining pairs. The final comparison and possible swap are between the next-to-last and last items.

   The first time through the list, this process is repeated to the end of the list. This is called the first pass. After the first pass, the last item (Wilma) will be in its proper position. Therefore, the second pass does not have to consider it and so requires one less comparison. At the end of the second pass, the last two items will be in their proper position. (The items that must have reached their proper position have been underlined.) Each successive pass requires one less comparison. After four passes, the last four items will be in their proper positions, and hence, the first will be also.

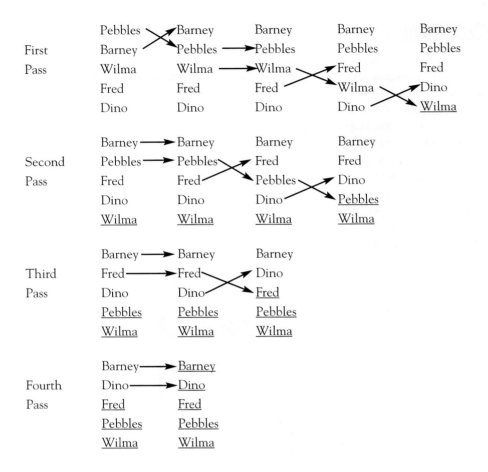

✓ **Example 2**   The following program alphabetizes the names Pebbles, Barney, Wilma, Fred, and Dino. Sorting the list requires a pair of nested loops. The inner loop performs a single pass, and the outer loop controls the number of passes.

```
Dim person() As String = {"Pebbles", "Barney", "Wilma", "Fred", "Dino"}

Private Sub frmFlintstones_Load(...) Handles MyBase.Load
  'Display unsorted list
  For i As Integer = 0 To 4
    lstPeople.Items.Add(person(i))
  Next
End Sub

Private Sub btnSort_Click(...) Handles btnSort.Click
  'Bubble sort names
  Dim temp As String
```

```
For passNum As Integer = 1 To 4      'Number of passes is 1 less than
  'number of items
    For i As Integer = 1 To 5 - passNum   'Each pass needs 1 less comparison
      If (person(i - 1) > person(i)) Then
        temp = person(i - 1)
        person(i - 1) = person(i)
        person(i) = temp
      End If
    Next
  Next
  'Display alphabetized list
  lstPeople.Items.Clear()
  For i As Integer = 0 To 4
    lstPeople.Items.Add(person(i))
  Next
End Sub
```

[Run, and click the button.]

 Example 3   Table 7.5 contains facts about the 10 most populous states with listings in ascending order by state abbreviation. The following program sorts the table in descending order by population. Data are read from a file into an array of structures by the form's Load event procedure. When btnDisplayStats is clicked, the array is sorted based on the population field.

TABLE 7.5   The 10 most populous states.

State	Per Capita Income	% College Graduates	Population in Millions
CA	$32,678	27.5	33.9
FL	$28,493	22.8	16.0
GA	$28,438	23.1	8.2
IL	$32,755	27.1	12.4
MI	$29,538	23.0	9.9
NJ	$38,153	30.1	8.4
NY	$35,884	28.7	19.0
OH	$28,619	24.6	11.4
PA	$30,617	24.3	12.3
TX	$28,486	23.9	20.9

Note: Column 3 gives the percentage of residents age 25 or older with a college degree.

```
Structure District
  Dim name As String
  Dim income As Double
  Dim collegeGrad As Double
  Dim population As Double
End Structure

Dim state(9) As District

Private Sub frmStates_Load(...) Handles MyBase.Load
  'Assume the data for state name, income, % college grads,
  'and population in millions are in the file "STATES.TXT"
  'First four lines of file contain the data CA, 32678, 27.5, 33.9
  Dim sr As IO.StreamReader = IO.File.OpenText("STATES.TXT")
  For i As Integer = 0 To 9
    state(i).name = sr.ReadLine
    state(i).income = CDbl(sr.ReadLine)
    state(i).collegeGrad = CDbl(sr.ReadLine)
    state(i).population = CDbl(sr.ReadLine)
  Next
  sr.Close()
End Sub

Private Sub btnDisplayStats_Click(...) Handles btnDisplayStats.Click
  SortData()
  ShowData()
End Sub

Sub ShowData()
  'Display ordered table
  Dim fmtStr As String = "{0,-4}{1,11:C0}{2,8:N1}{3,9:N1}"
  lstStats.Items.Clear()
  For i As Integer = 0 To 9
    lstStats.Items.Add(String.Format(fmtStr, state(i).name, _
      state(i).income, state(i).collegeGrad, state(i).population))
  Next
End Sub

Sub SortData()
  'Bubble sort table in descending order by population
  For passNum As Integer = 1 To 9
    For index As Integer = 1 To 10 - passNum
      If (state(index - 1).population < state(index).population) Then
        SwapData(index)
      End If
    Next
  Next
End Sub
```

```
Sub SwapData(ByVal index As Integer)
  'Swap entries
  Dim temp As District
  temp = state(index - 1)
  state(index - 1) = state(index)
  state(index) = temp
End Sub
```

[Run, and click the button.]

State Statistics

Display Statistics of Ten Most Populous States

State	Per Capita Income	% College Grads	Pop. in millions
CA	$32,678	27.5	33.9
TX	$28,486	23.9	20.9
NY	$35,884	28.7	19.0
FL	$28,493	22.8	16.0
IL	$32,755	27.1	12.4
PA	$30,617	24.3	12.3
OH	$28,619	24.6	11.4
MI	$29,538	23.0	9.9
NJ	$38,153	30.1	8.4
GA	$28,438	23.1	8.2

▨ Shell Sort

The bubble sort is easy to understand and program. However, it is too slow for really long lists. The Shell sort, named for its inventor, Donald L. Shell, is much more efficient in such cases. It compares distant items first and works its way down to nearby items. The interval separating the compared items is called the **gap**. The gap begins at one-half the length of the list and is successively halved until eventually each item is compared with its neighbor as in the bubble sort. The algorithm for a list of $n + 1$ items referred to as item 0 through item n is as follows.

1. Begin with a gap of $g = \text{Int}([n + 1]/2)$.
2. Compare items 0 and g, items 1 and $1 + g$, 2 and $2 + g, \ldots, n - g$ and n. Swap any pairs that are out of order.
3. Repeat Step 2 until no swaps are made for gap g.
4. Halve the value of g.
5. Repeat Steps 2, 3, and 4 until the value of g is 0.

The Shell sort is illustrated in what follows, in which crossing arrows indicate that a swap occurred:

$$\text{Initial Gap} = \text{Int}([\text{Number of Items}]/2) = \text{Int}(5/2) = 2$$

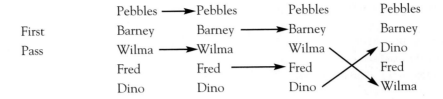

Because there was a swap, use the same gap for the second pass.

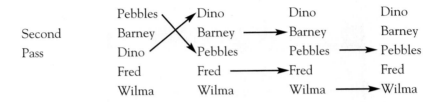

Again, there was a swap, so keep the current gap.

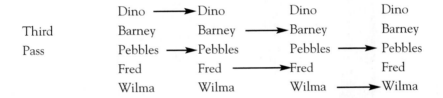

There were no swaps for the current gap of 2, so

$$\text{Next Gap} = \text{Int}([\text{Previous Gap}]/2) = \text{Int}(2/2) = 1.$$

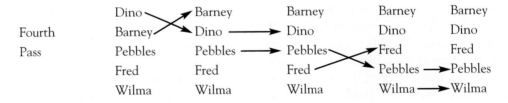

Because there was a swap (actually two swaps), keep the same gap.

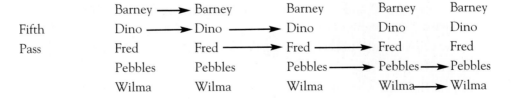

Because there were no swaps for the current gap, then

$$\text{Next Gap} = \text{Int}([\text{Previous Gap}]/2) = \text{Int}(1/2) = 0,$$

and the Shell sort is complete.

Notice that the Shell sort required 17 comparisons to sort the list, whereas the bubble sort required only 10 comparisons for the same list. This illustrates the fact that for very short lists, the bubble sort is preferable; however, for lists of 30 items or more, the Shell sort will consistently outperform the bubble sort. Table 7.6 shows the average number of comparisons required to sort arrays of varying sizes.

TABLE 7.6   Efficiency of bubble and Shell sorts.

Array Elements	Bubble Sort Comparisons	Shell Sort Comparisons
5	10	15
10	45	57
15	105	115
20	190	192
25	300	302
30	435	364
50	1225	926
100	4950	2638
500	124,750	22,517
1000	499,500	58,460

Example 4   The following program uses the Shell sort to alphabetize the parts of a running shoe. (See Figure 7.5.) The data are read into an array whose size is large enough to guarantee sufficient space. In the form's Load event procedure, the variable *numParts* provides the subscripts for the array and serves as a counter. The final value of *numParts* is available to all procedures because the variable was created in the Declarations section of the Code window. The Sub procedure SortData uses a flag to indicate if a swap has been made during a pass.

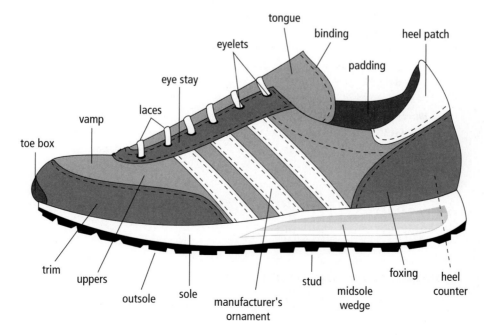

FIGURE 7.5   Running shoe.

```
Dim part(50) As String
Dim numParts As Integer

Private Sub frmShoe_Load(...) Handles MyBase.Load
  'Read names of parts
  numParts = 0          'Number of parts
  Dim sr As IO.StreamReader = IO.File.OpenText("SHOEPART.TXT")
  Do While (sr.Peek <> -1) And (numParts < part.GetUpperBound(0))
    part(numParts) = sr.ReadLine
    numParts += 1
  Loop
  sr.Close()
End Sub

Private Sub btnDisplay_Click(...) Handles btnDisplay.Click
  'Sort and display parts of running shoe
  SortData()
  ShowData()
End Sub

Sub SortData()
  'Shell sort shoe parts
  Dim gap As Integer, doneFlag As Boolean
  Dim temp As String
  gap = CInt(Int(numParts / 2))
  Do While gap >= 1
    Do
      doneFlag = True
      For index As Integer = 0 To numParts - 1 - gap
        If part(index) > part(index + gap) Then
          temp = part(index)
          part(index) = part(index + gap)
          part(index + gap) = temp
          doneFlag = False
        End If
      Next
    Loop Until doneFlag = True    'Also can be Loop Until doneFlag
    gap = CInt(Int(gap / 2))      'Halve the length of the gap
  Loop
End Sub

Sub ShowData()
  'Display sorted list of parts
  lstParts.Items.Clear()
  For i As Integer = 0 To numParts - 1
    lstParts.Items.Add(part(i))
  Next
End Sub
```

[Run, and click the button.]

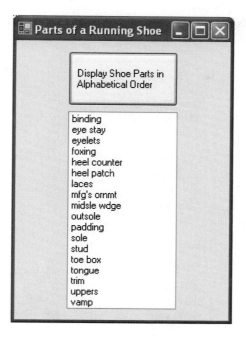

■ Searching

Suppose we had an array of 1000 names in alphabetical order and wanted to locate a specific person in the list. One approach would be to start with the first name and consider each name until a match was found. This process is called a **sequential search.** We would find a person whose name begins with "A" rather quickly, but 1000 comparisons might be necessary to find a person whose name begins with "Z." For much longer lists, searching could be a time-consuming matter. However, there is a method, called a **binary search,** that shortens the task considerably.

Let us refer to the sought item as *quarry*. The binary search looks for *quarry* by determining in which half of the list it lies. The other half is then discarded, and the retained half is temporarily regarded as the entire list. The process is repeated until the item is found. A flag can indicate if *quarry* has been found.

The algorithm for a binary search of an ascending list is as follows (Figure 7.6 shows the flowchart for a binary search):

1. At each stage, denote the subscript of the first item in the retained list by *first* and the subscript of the last item by *last*. Initially, the value of *first* is 0, the value of *last* is one less than the number of items in the list, and the value of *flag* is False.

2. Look at the middle item of the current list, the item having the subscript $middle = \text{Int}((first + last)/2)$.

3. If the middle item is *quarry*, then *flag* is set to True and the search is over.

4. If the middle item is greater than *quarry*, then *quarry* should be in the first half of the list. So the subscript of *quarry* must lie between *first* and $middle - 1$. That is, the new value of *last* is $middle - 1$.

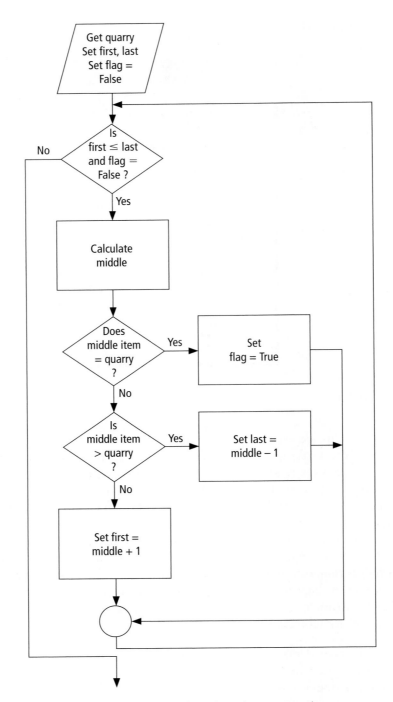

FIGURE 7.6 **Flowchart for a binary search.**

5. If the middle item is less than *quarry*, then *quarry* should be in the second half of the list of possible items. So the subscript of *quarry* must lie between *middle* +1 and *last*. That is, the new value of *first* is *middle* +1.

6. Repeat Steps 2 through 5 until *quarry* is found or until the halving process uses up the entire list. (When the entire list has been used up, *first* > *last.*) In the second case, *quarry* was not in the original list.

Example 5   In the following program the array *firm*() contains the alphabetized names of up to 100 corporations. The program requests the name of a corporation as input and uses a binary search to determine whether the corporation is in the array.

```
Dim firm(99) As String
Dim numFirms As Integer

Private Sub frmCompanies_Load(...) Handles MyBase.Load
  'Fill array with data from FIRMS.TXT, which contains
  'the names of up to 100 companies
  Dim sr As IO.StreamReader = IO.File.OpenText("FIRMS.TXT")
  numFirms = 0
  Do While (sr.Peek <> -1) And (numFirms < firm.GetUpperBound(0))
    firm(numFirms) = sr.ReadLine
    numFirms += 1
  Loop
  sr.Close()
End Sub

Private Sub btnSearch_Click(...) Handles btnSearch.Click
  Dim corp, result As String
  corp = txtCorporation.Text.ToUpper
  result = ""
  BinarySearch(corp, result)
  'Display results of search
  txtResult.Text = corp & " " & result
End Sub

Sub BinarySearch(ByVal corp As String, ByRef result As String)
  'Array firm() assumed already ordered alphabetically
  'Binary search of firm() for corp
  Dim first, middle, last As Integer
  Dim foundFlag As Boolean = False
  first = 0
  last = numFirms - 1
  Do While (first <= last) And (Not foundFlag)
    middle = CInt(Int((first + last) / 2))
    Select Case firm(middle).ToUpper
      Case corp
        foundFlag = True
```

```
      Case Is > corp
        last = middle - 1
      Case Is < corp
        first = middle + 1
    End Select
  Loop
  If foundFlag Then
    result = "found"
  Else
    result = "not found"
  End If
End Sub
```

[Run, type "IBM" into the text box, and click the button.]

Suppose the array contains 100 corporations and the corporation input in Example 5 is in the second half of the array. On the first pass, *middle* would be assigned Int((0 + 99)/2) = Int(49.5) = 49 and then *first* would be altered to 49 + 1 = 50. On the second pass, *middle* would be assigned Int((50 + 99)/2) = Int(74.5) = 74. If the corporation is not the array element with subscript 74, then either *last* would be assigned 73 or *first* would be assigned 75, depending on whether the corporation appears before or after the 74th element. Each pass through the loop halves the range of subscripts containing the corporation until the corporation is located.

In Example 5, the binary search merely reported whether an array contained a certain item. After finding the item, its array subscript was not needed. However, if the search had been carried out on an array of structures (as in Table 7.5), the subscript of the found item could be used to retrieve the related information for the other members. This process, called a **table lookup**, is used in the following example.

 Example 6 The following program uses a binary search procedure to locate the data for a state from Example 3 requested by the user. The program does not include a sort of the text file STATES.TXT, because the file is already ordered alphabetically by city name.

```
Structure District
  Dim name As String
  Dim income As Double
  Dim collegeGrad As Double
  Dim population As Double
End Structure
```

```
Dim state(9) As District

Private Sub frmStates_Load(...) Handles MyBase.Load
  'Assume that the data for state name, per capita income,
  '% college grads, and population in millions
  'have been placed in the file "STATES.TXT"
  'First four lines of file contain the data CA, 32678,27.5,33.9
  Dim sr As IO.StreamReader = IO.File.OpenText("STATES.TXT")
  For i As Integer = 0 To 9
    state(i).name = sr.ReadLine
    state(i).income = CDbl(sr.ReadLine)
    state(i).collegeGrad = CDbl(sr.ReadLine)
    state(i).population = CDbl(sr.ReadLine)
  Next
  sr.Close()
End Sub

Private Sub btnDisplayStats_Click(...) Handles btnDisplayStats.Click
  'Search for state in the populous states table
  Dim searchState As String, result As Integer
  searchState = mtxtState.Text.ToUpper
  result = FindState(searchState)
  If result >= 0 Then
    ShowData(result)
  Else
    MsgBox(searchState & " not in file", 0, "Not Found")
  End If
End Sub

Function FindState(ByVal searchState As String) As Integer
  'Binary search table for state name
  Dim first, middle, last As Integer
  first = 0
  last = 9
  Do While (first <= last)
    middle = CInt(Int((first + last) / 2))
    Select Case city(middle).name.ToUpper
      Case searchState
        Return middle
      Case Is > searchState
        last = middle - 1
      Case Is < searchState
        first = middle + 1
    End Select
  Loop
  Return -1
End Function
```

```
Sub ShowData(ByVal result As Integer)
  'Display the data for the specified state
  Dim fmtStr As String = "{0,-4}{1,11:C0}{2,8:N1}{3,9:N1}"
  txtStats.text = String.Format(fmtStr, state(result).name, _
                  state(result).income, state(result).collegeGrad, _
                  state(result).population.)
End Sub
```

[Run, type "OH" into the masked text box, and click the button.]

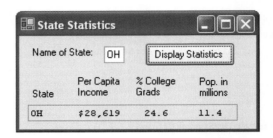

▣ Comments

1. Suppose that our bubble sort algorithm is applied to an ordered list. The algorithm will still make $n - 1$ passes through the list. The process could be shortened for some lists by flagging the presence of out-of-order items as in the Shell sort.

2. In Example 3, an array of structures already ordered by one member was sorted by another member. Usually, an array of structures is sorted by the member to be searched when accessing the member. This member is called the **key member**.

3. Suppose that an array of 2000 items is searched sequentially—that is, one item after another—in order to locate a specific item. The number of comparisons would vary from 1 to 2000, with an average of 1000. With a binary search, the number of comparisons would be at most 11, because $2^{11} > 2000$.

4. The method ToUpper converts all the characters in a string to uppercase. ToUpper is useful in sorting and searching arrays of strings when the alphabetic case (upper or lower) is unimportant. For instance, Example 5 includes ToUpper in the Select Case comparisons, and so the binary search will locate "Mobil" in the array even if the user entered "MOBIL".

5. Visual Basic has a built-in sort routine that can be used to sort arrays. The statement

```
       Array.Sort(arrayName)
```

sorts *arrayName* into ascending order. For instance, in Example 2 the event procedure can be replaced with the following code.

```
Private Sub btnSort_Click(...) Handles btnSort.Click
  Dim name() As String = {"Pebbles", "Barney", "Wilma", _
                          "Fred", "Dino"}
  Array.Sort(name)
  'Display alphabetized list
  lstNames.Items.Clear()
```

```
     For i As Integer = 0 To 4
       lstNames.Items.Add(name(i))
     Next
   End Sub
```

Array.Sort cannot be used with arrays of structures and therefore is not adequate for our purposes.

Practice Problems 7.4

1. The pseudocode for a bubble sort of an array of n items follows. Why is the terminating value of the outer loop $n - 1$ and the terminating value of the inner loop $n - j$?

```
For j As Integer = 1 To n - 1
  For k As Integer = 1 To n - j
    If [(k-1)st and kth items are out of order] Then [swap them]
  Next
Next
```

2. Complete the table that follows by filling in the values of each variable after successive passes of a binary search of an array of 20 items, where the sought item is in the position 13.

FIRST	LAST	MIDDLE
0	19	9
10	19	

EXERCISES 7.4

In Exercises 1 through 4, determine the output displayed in the list box when the button is clicked.

1.
```
Private Sub btnDisplay_Click(...) Handles btnDisplay.Click
    Dim p As Integer = 100
    Dim q As Integer = 200
    Dim temp As Integer = p
    p = q
    q = temp
    lstOutput.Items.Add(p)
    lstOutput.Items.Add(q)
End Sub
```

2.
```
Dim gag() As String = {"Stan", "Oliver"}

Private Sub btnDisplay_Click(...) Handles btnDisplay.Click
  Dim temp As String
    If gag(1) < gag(0) Then
      temp = gag(1)
```

```
        gag(1) = gag(0)
        gag(0) = temp
      End If
    lstOutput.Items.Add(gag(0))
    lstOutput.Items.Add(gag(1))
  End Sub
3. Private Sub btnDisplay_Click(...) Handles btnDisplay.Click
    Dim x, y, temp As Double
    Dim swappedFlag As Boolean = False
    x = 7
    y = 11
    If y > x Then
      temp = x
      x = y
      y = temp
      swappedFlag = True
    End If
    lstOutput.Items.Add(x)
    lstOutput.Items.Add(y)
    If swappedFlag Then
      lstOutput.Items.Add("Numbers interchanged.")
    End If
  End Sub
4. Dim a(2) As Integer

  Private Sub btnDisplay_Click(...) Handles btnDisplay.Click
    Dim temp As Integer
    For j As Integer = 0 To 1
      For k As Integer = 0 To 2 - j
        If a(k) > a(k + 1) Then
          temp = a(k)
          a(k) = a(k + 1)
          a(k + 1) = temp
        End If
      Next
    Next
    For j As Integer = 0 To 2
      lstOutput.Items.Add(a(j))
    Next
  End Sub

  Private Sub frmNumbers_Load(...) Handles MyBase.Load
    Dim sr As IO.StreamReader = IO.File.OpenText("DATA.TXT")
    For j As Integer = 0 To 2
      a(j) = CInt(sr.ReadLine)
    Next
    sr.Close()
  End Sub
```

(Assume that the three lines of the file DATA.TXT contain the following entries: 7, 4, 3.)

In Exercises 5 and 6, identify the errors.

5.
```
Dim c(3), d(3) As Integer

Private Sub btnDisplay_Click(...) Handles btnDisplay.Click
  'Swap two items
  c(3) = d(3)
  d(3) = c(3)
  lstOutput.Items.Add(c(3))
  lstOutput.Items.Add(d(3))
End Sub

Private Sub frmNumbers_Load(...) Handles MyBase.Load
  Dim sr As IO.StreamReader = IO.File.OpenText("DATA.TXT")
  For i As Integer = 0 To 3
    c(i) = CInt(sr.ReadLine)
    d(i) = CInt(sr.ReadLine)
  Next
  sr.Close()
End Sub
```

(Assume that the eight lines of the file DATA.TXT contain the following entries:1, 2, 3, 4, 5, 6, 7, 8.)

6.
```
Dim a(2), b(2) As Integer

Private Sub btnDisplay_Click(...) Handles btnDisplay.Click
  'Swap the two arrays
  Dim temp(2) As Integer
  a = b
  b = a
End Sub

Private Sub frmNumbers_Load(...) Handles MyBase.Load
  Dim sr As IO.StreamReader = IO.File.OpenText("DATA.TXT")
  For i As Integer = 0 To 2
    a(i) = CInt(sr.ReadLine)
    b(i) = CInt(sr.ReadLine)
  Next
  sr.Close()
End Sub
```

(Assume that the six lines of the file DATA.TXT contain the following entries:1, 3, 5, 7, 9, 11.)

7. Which type of search would be best for the following array?

0	1	2	3	4
Paul	Ringo	John	George	Pete

8. Which type of search would be best for the following array?

0	1	2	3	4
Beloit	Green Bay	Madison	Milwaukee	Oshkosh

9. Consider the items Tin Man, Dorothy, Scarecrow, and Lion in that order. After how many swaps in a bubble sort will the list be in alphabetical order?

10. How many comparisons will be made in a bubble sort of six items?

11. How many comparisons will be made in a bubble sort of n items?

12. Modify the program in Example 2 so that it will keep track of the number of swaps and comparisons and display these numbers before ending.

13. Rework Exercise 9 using the Shell sort.

14. How many comparisons would be made in a Shell sort of six items if the items were originally in descending order and were sorted in ascending order?

15. If a list of six items is already in the proper order, how many comparisons will be made by a Shell sort?

16. Suppose a list of 5000 numbers is to be sorted, but the numbers consist of only 1, 2, 3, and 4. Describe a method of sorting the list that would be much faster than either the bubble or Shell sort.

17. What is the maximum number of comparisons required to find an item in a sequential search of 16 items? What is the average number of comparisons? What is the maximum number of comparisons required to find an item in a binary search of 16 items?

18. Redo Exercise 17 with 2^n items, where n is any positive integer.

In Exercises 19 through 26, write a program (or procedure) to complete the stated task.

19. Exchange the values of the variables x, y, and z so that x has y's value, y has z's value, and z has x's value.

20. Display the names of the seven dwarfs in alphabetical order. For the contents of a text file use Doc, Grumpy, Sleepy, Happy, Bashful, Sneezy, and Dopey.

21. The nation's capital has long been a popular staging area for political, religious, and other large public rallies, protest marches, and demonstrations. The events in Table 7.7 have drawn the largest crowds, according to estimates from D.C., U.S. Park, or Capitol police. Read the data into an array of structures and display a similar table with the event names in alphabetical order. **Note:** The data is contained in the file EVENTS.TXT.

22. Table 7.8 presents statistics on the five leading sneaker brands. Read the data into an array of structures, and display a similar table with wholesale revenue in descending order.

23. Accept 10 words to be input in alphabetical order, and store them in an array. Then accept an 11th word as input, and store it in the array in its correct alphabetical position.

TABLE 7.7	Large Public Displays of Emotion in Washington, D.C.
Event	Crowd Estimate (in thousands)
Lyndon Johnson inauguration (1/23/65)	1,200
Bicentennial fireworks (7/4/76)	1,000
Desert Storm rally (6/8/91)	800
Bill Clinton inauguration (l/20/93)	800
Beach Boys concert (7/4/85)	625
Washington Redskins victory parade (2/3/88)	600
Vietnam moratorium rally (11/15/69)	600
Ronald Reagan inauguration (1/20/81)	500
U.S. Iran hostage motorcade (l/28/81)	500

TABLE 7.8	2004 U.S. market share in sneakers.	
Brand	Wholesale Revenue (in millions)	Percentage Share of U.S. Market
Adidas USA	792	8.9
Fila	392	4.4
New Balance	1024	11.5
Nike	3231	36.3
Reebok	1086	12.1

Source: Morgan Stanley Dean Witter Research.

24. An airline has a list of 200 flight numbers (between 1 and 1000) in ascending order in the file FLIGHTS.TXT. Accept a number as input and do a binary search of the list to determine if the flight number is valid.

25. Allow a number *n* to be input by the user. Then accept as input a list of *n* numbers. Place the numbers into an array and apply a bubble sort.

26. Rework Exercise 25, but use a flag to detect the presence of out-of-order items as in the Shell sort.

27. Write a program that accepts a word as input and converts it into Morse code. The dots and dashes corresponding to each letter of the alphabet are as follows:

```
A .-        H ....      O ---       V ...-
B -...      I ..        P .--.      W .--
C -.-.      J .---      Q --.-      X -..-
D -..       K -.-       R .-.       Y -.--
E .         L .-..      S ...       Z --..
F ..-.      M --        T -
G --.       N -.        U ..-
```

28. Write a program that accepts an American word as input and performs a binary search to translate it into its British equivalent. Use the following list of words for data, and account for the case when the word requested is not in the list:

AMERICAN	BRITISH	AMERICAN	BRITISH
attic	loft	ice cream	ice
business suit	lounge suit	megaphone	loud hailer
elevator	lift	radio	wireless
flashlight	torch	sneakers	plimsolls
french fries	chips	truck	lorry
gasoline	petrol	zero	nought

29. Write a program that accepts a student's name and seven test scores as input and calculates the average score after dropping the two lowest scores.

30. Suppose letter grades are assigned as follows:

97 and above	A+	74–76	C
94–96	A	70–73	C−
90–93	A−	67–69	D+
87–89	B+	64–66	D
84–86	B	60–63	D−
80–83	B−	0–59	F
77–79	C+		

Write a program that accepts a grade as input and displays the corresponding letter.

Hint: This problem shows that when you search an array, you don't always look for equality. Set up an array of structures with the member *range* containing the values 97, 94, 90, 87, 84, ..., 0 and the member *letter* containing A+, A, A−, B+,..., F. Next, perform a sequential search to find the first structure such that the value of the *range* member is less than or equal to the input grade.

31. The *median* of a set of n measurements is a number such that half the n measurements fall below the median, and half fall above. If the number of measurements n is odd, the median is the middle number when the measurements are arranged in ascending or descending order. If the number of measurements n is even, the median is the average of the two middle measurements when the measurements are arranged in ascending or descending order. Write a program that requests a number n and a set of n measurements as input and then displays the median.

32. Write a program with two buttons labeled Ascending Order and Descending Order that displays the eight vegetables in V8® in either ascending or descending alphabetic order. The vegetables (tomato, carrot, celery, beet, parsley, lettuce, watercress, and spinach) should be stored in a class-level array.

Solutions to Practice Problems 7.4

1. The outer loop controls the number of passes, one less than the number of items in the list. The inner loop performs a single pass, and the jth pass consists of $n - j$ comparisons.

2. FIRST	LAST	MIDDLE
0	19	9
10	19	14
10	13	11
12	13	12
13	13	13

7.5 Two-Dimensional Arrays

Each array discussed so far held a single list of items. Such array variables are called **one-dimensional arrays** or **single-subscripted variables.** An array can also hold the contents of a table with several rows and columns. Such arrays are called **two-dimensional arrays** or **double-subscripted variables.** Two tables follow. Table 7.9 gives the road mileage between certain cities. It has four rows and four columns. Table 7.10 shows the leading universities in three disciplines. It has three rows and five columns.

Two-dimensional array variables store the contents of tables. They have the same types of names as other array variables. The only difference is that they have two subscripts, each with its own upper bound. The first subscript is determined by the number of rows in the table, and the second subscript is determined by the number of columns. The statement

```
Dim arrayName(m, n) As varType
```

declares an array of type *varType* corresponding to a table with rows labeled from 0 to m and columns labeled from 0 to n. The entry in the jth row, kth column is *arrayName(j, k)*. For instance, the data in Table 7.9 can be stored in an array named *rm()*. The statement

```
Dim rm(3, 3) As Double
```

TABLE 7.9 Road mileage between selected U.S. cities.

	Chicago	Los Angeles	New York	Philadelphia
Chicago	0	2054	802	738
Los Angeles	2054	0	2786	2706
New York	802	2786	0	100
Philadelphia	738	2706	100	0

TABLE 7.10 University rankings.

	1	2	3	4	5
Business	U of PA	U of IN	U of MI	UC Berk	U of VA
Comp Sci.	MIT	Cng-Mellon	UC Berk	Cornell	U of IL
Engr/Gen.	U of IL	U of OK	U of MD	Cng-Mellon	CO Sch. of Mines

Source: A Rating of Undergraduate Programs in American and International Universities, Dr. Jack Gourman, 1998.

will declare the array. Each element of the array has the form *rm*(row, column). The values of the elements of the array we use will be

rm(0, 0) = 0	rm(0, 1) = 2054	rm(0, 2) = 802	rm(0, 3) = 738
rm(1, 0) = 2054	rm(1, 1) = 0	rm(1, 2) = 2786	rm(1, 3) = 2706
rm(2, 0) = 802	rm(2, 1) = 2786	rm(2, 2) = 0	rm(2, 3) = 100
rm(3, 0) = 738	rm(3, 1) = 2706	rm(3, 2) = 100	rm(3, 3) = 0

The data in Table 7.10 can be stored in a two-dimensional string array named *univ*(). The appropriate array is declared with the statement

```
Dim univ(2, 4) As String
```

Some of the entries of the array are

univ(0, 0) = "U of PA"

univ(1, 2) = "UC Berk"

univ(2, 4) = "CO Sch. of Mines"

Example 1 The following program stores and accesses the data from Table 7.9. Data are read from the text file DISTANCE.TXT into a two-dimensional class-level array using a pair of nested loops. The outer loop controls the rows, and the inner loop controls the columns.

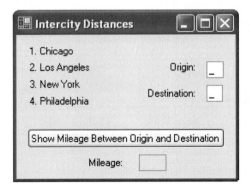

OBJECT	PROPERTY	SETTING
frmDistances	Text	Intercity Distances
lblCh	Text	1. Chicago
lblLA	Text	2. Los Angeles
lblNY	Text	3. New York
lblPh	Text	4. Philadelphia
lblOrig	Text	Origin:
mtxtOrig	Mask	0
lblDest	Text	Destination:
mtxtDest	Mask	0
btnShow	Text	Show Mileage Between Origin and Destination
lblMiles	Text	Mileage:
txtMiles	ReadOnly	True

```
Dim rm(3, 3) As Double

Private Sub frmDistances_Load(...) Handles MyBase.Load
  'Fill two-dimensional array with intercity mileages
  'Assume the data has been placed in the file "DISTANCE.TXT"
  '(First four lines of the file contain the numbers 0, 2054, 802, 738)
  Dim sr As IO.StreamReader = IO.File.OpenText("DISTANCE.TXT")
```

```
    For row As Integer = 0 To 3
      For col As Integer = 0 To 3
        rm(row, col) = CDbl(sr.ReadLine)
      Next
    Next
    sr.Close()
End Sub

Private Sub btnShow_Click(...) Handles btnShow.Click
  'Determine road mileage between cities
  Dim row, col As Integer
  row = CInt(mtxtOrig.Text)
  col = CInt(mtxtDest.Text)
  If (row >= 1 And row <= 4) And (col >= 1 And col <= 4) Then
    txtMiles.Text = CStr(rm(row - 1, col - 1))
  Else
    MsgBox("Origin and Dest. must be numbers from 1 to 4", 0, "Error")
  End If
End Sub
```

[Run, type 3 into the Origin box, type 1 into the Destination box, and click the button.]

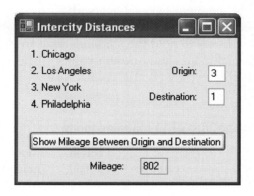

An unsized two-dimensional array can be declared with a statement of the form

```
Dim arrayName(,) As varType
```

and a two-dimensional array can be declared and initialized at the same time with a statement of the form

```
Dim arrayName(,) As varType = {{ROW0}, {ROW1},... {ROWm}}
```

where ROW0 consists of the entries in the top row of the corresponding table separated by commas, ROW1 consists of the entries in the next row of the corresponding table separated by commas, and so on. For instance, in Example 1, the declaration statement and frmDistances_Load event procedure can be replaced by the single statement

```
Dim rm(,) As Double = {{0, 2054, 802, 738}, _
          {2054, 0, 2786, 2706}, {802, 2786, 0, 100}, _
          {738, 2706, 100, 0}}
```

An already-created array can be resized with

```
ReDim arrayName(r, s)
```

which loses the current contents, or with

```
ReDim Preserve arrayName(r, s)
```

which keeps the current values. However, when the keyword Preserve is used, only the last coordinate can be resized. The upper bound of the first coordinate of the array is given by `arrayName.GetUpperBound(0),` and the upper bound of the second coordinate is given by `arrayName.GetUpperBound(1).`

So far, two-dimensional arrays have been used only to store data for convenient lookup. In the next example, an array is used to make a valuable computation.

Example 2   The Center for Science in the Public Interest publishes *The Nutrition Scorebook*, a highly respected rating of foods. The top two foods in each of five categories are shown in Table 7.11 along with some information on their composition. The following program computes the nutritional content of a meal. The table is read into an array, and then the program requests the quantities of each food item that is part of the meal. The program then computes the amounts of each nutritional component consumed by summing each column with each entry weighted by the quantity of the food item. Coding is simplified by using an array of labels to hold the food names and an array of text boxes to hold the amounts input by the user. The five nutrients of interest and the actual names and nutrient values of the foods to be used in building a meal are read from the text file NUTTABLE.TXT.

TABLE 7.11   Composition of 10 top-rated foods.

	Calories	Protein (grams)	Fat (grams)	Vit A (IU)	Calcium (mg)
Spinach (1 cup)	23	3	0.3	8100	93
Sweet potato (1 med.)	160	2	1	9230	46
Yogurt (8 oz.)	230	10	3	120	343
Skim milk (1 cup)	85	8	0	500	302
Whole wheat bread (1 slice)	65	3	1	0	24
Brown rice (1 cup)	178	3.8	0.9	0	18
Watermelon (1 wedge)	110	2	1	2510	30
Papaya (1 lg.)	156	2.4	0.4	7000	80
Tuna in water (1 lb)	575	126.8	3.6	0	73
Lobster (1 med.)	405	28.8	26.6	984	190

OBJECT	PROPERTY	SETTING
frmNutrition	Text	Nutrition in a Meal
Label1–Label10		
lblQnty	Text	Quantity in Meal
TextBox1–TextBox10		
btnAnalyze	Text	Analyze Meal Nutrition
lblStatement	AutoSize	False
	Text	This meal contains the following quantities of these nutritional components:
	Visible	False
lstAnalysis	Visible	False

```
Dim lblarrayFood(9) As Label
Dim txtarrayQnty(9) As TextBox
Dim nutName(4) As String          'Nutrient names
Dim nutTable(9, 4) As Double      'Nutrient values for each food

Private Sub frmNutrition_Load(...) Handles MyBase.Load
  'Fill arrays, set text for labels
  lblarrayFood(0) = Label1
  lblarrayFood(1) = Label2
  lblarrayFood(2) = Label3
  lblarrayFood(3) = Label4
  lblarrayFood(4) = Label5
  lblarrayFood(5) = Label6
  lblarrayFood(6) = Label7
  lblarrayFood(7) = Label8
  lblarrayFood(8) = Label9
  lblarrayFood(9) = Label10
  txtarrayQnty(0) = TextBox1
  txtarrayQnty(1) = TextBox2
  txtarrayQnty(2) = TextBox3
  txtarrayQnty(3) = TextBox4
  txtarrayQnty(4) = TextBox5
  txtarrayQnty(5) = TextBox6
  txtarrayQnty(6) = TextBox7
  txtarrayQnty(7) = TextBox8
  txtarrayQnty(8) = TextBox9
  txtarrayQnty(9) = TextBox10
```

```
   Dim foodName As String
    'Fill arrays; assign label captions
   Dim sr As IO.StreamReader = IO.File.OpenText("NUTTABLE.TXT")
   For i As Integer = 0 To 4
     nutName(i) = sr.ReadLine
   Next
   For i As Integer = 0 To 9
     foodName = sr.ReadLine
     lblarrayFood(i).Text = foodName
     For j As Integer = 0 To 4
       nutTable(i, j) = CDbl(sr.ReadLine)
     Next
   Next
   sr.Close()
 End Sub

 Private Sub btnAnalyze_Click(...) Handles btnAnalyze.Click
    'Determine the nutritional content of a meal
   Dim quantity(9) As Double    'amount of food in meal
   GetAmounts(quantity)
   lblStatement.Visible = True
   lstAnalysis.Visible = True
   ShowData(quantity)
 End Sub

 Sub GetAmounts(ByRef quantity() As Double)
    'Obtain quantities of foods consumed
   For i As Integer = 0 To 9
     If txtarrayQnty(i).Text <> "" Then
       quantity(i) = CDbl(txtarrayQnty(i).Text)
     Else
       quantity(i) = 0
     End If
   Next
 End Sub

 Sub ShowData(ByVal quantity() As Double)
    'Display amount of each component
   Dim amount As Double
   Dim fmtStr As String = "{0,-15}{1,8}"
   lstAnalysis.Items.Clear()
   For col As Integer = 0 To 4
     amount = 0
     For row As Integer = 0 To 9
       amount = amount + quantity(row) * nutTable(row, col)
     Next
     lstAnalysis.Items.Add(String.Format(fmtStr, nutName(col), amount))
   Next
 End Sub
```

[Run, type quantities into the text boxes, and press the button.]

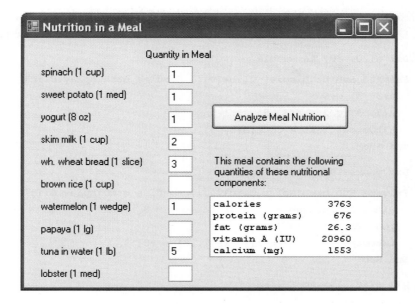

Comments

1. We can define three- (or higher-) dimensional arrays much as we do two-dimensional arrays. A three-dimensional array uses three subscripts, and the assignment of values requires a triple-nested loop. As an example, a meteorologist might use a three-dimensional array to record temperatures for various dates, times, and elevations. The array might be created by the statement

```
Dim temps(31, 24, 14) As Double
```

2. A ReDim statement cannot change the number of dimensions of an array. For instance, it cannot change a one-dimensional array into a two-dimensional array.

Practice Problems 7.5

1. Consider the road-mileage program in Example 1. How can the program be modified so the actual names of the cities can be supplied by the user?
2. In what types of problems are two-dimensional arrays superior to arrays of structures?

In Exercises 1 through 8, determine the output displayed when the button is clicked. All Dim statements for arrays are in the Declarations section of the Code window.

1.
```
Dim a(20, 30) As Double

Private Sub btnDisplay_Click(...) Handles btnDisplay.Click
  a(3, 5) = 6
  a(5, 3) = 2 * a(3, 5)
  txtOutput.Text = CStr(a(5, 3))
End Sub
```

2.
```
Dim years(100, 50) As Double

Private Sub btnDisplay_Click(...) Handles btnDisplay.Click
  Dim x As Integer = 7, y As Integer = 8
  years(x, y) = 1937
  txtOutput.Text = CStr(years(7, 8) + 60)
End Sub
```

3.
```
Dim w(10, 15) As String

Private Sub btnDisplay_Click(...) Handles btnDisplay.Click
  Dim d As String = "Dorothy", n As Integer = 1
  w(1, 1) = d
  txtOutput.Text = w(n, n)
End Sub
```

4.
```
Dim actor(5, 5) As String

Private Sub btnDisplay_Click(...) Handles btnDisplay.Click
  Dim a As Integer = 2, b As Integer = 3, temp As Integer
  actor(a, b) = "Bogart"
  temp = a
  a = b
  b = temp
  lstOutput.Items.Add("1. " & actor(a, b))
  lstOutput.Items.Add("2. " & actor(b, a))
End Sub
```

5.
```
Dim a(,) As Integer

Private Sub btnDisplay_Click(...) Handles btnDisplay.Click
  Dim p, q, sum As Integer
  Dim sr As IO.StreamReader = IO.File.OpenText("DATA.TXT")
  p = CInt(sr.ReadLine)
  q = CInt(sr.ReadLine)
  ReDim a(p, q)
  For j As Integer = 0 To p
    sum = 0
```

```
    For k As Integer = 0 To q
      a(j, k) = CInt(sr.ReadLine)
      sum += a(j, k)
    Next
    lstOutput.Items.Add(sum)
  Next
  sr.Close()
End Sub
```

(Assume that the eight lines of the file DATA.TXT contain the following data: 1, 2, 4, 1, 6, 5, 8, 2.)

6.
```
Dim a(3, 4) As Integer

Private Sub btnDisplay_Click(...) Handles btnDisplay.Click
  Dim row As String
  For j As Integer = 0 To 3
    row = ""
    For k As Integer = 0 To 4
      a(j, k) = j + k
      row &= a(j, k) & "   "
    Next
    lstOutput.Items.Add(row)
  Next
End Sub
```

7.
```
Dim s(2, 2) As Double

Private Sub btnDisplay_Click(...) Handles btnDisplay.Click
  Dim sr As IO.StreamReader = IO.File.OpenText("DATA.TXT")
  For j As Integer = 0 To 2
    For k As Integer = 0 To 2
      s(j, k) = CDbl(sr.ReadLine)
    Next
  Next
  sr.Close()
  For j As Integer = 0 To 2
    lstOutput.Items.Add(s(j, j))
  Next
End Sub
```

(Assume that the nine lines of the file DATA.TXT contain the following entries: 1, 2, 3, 4, 3, 2, 3, 4, 5.)

8.
```
Dim m(,) As Integer

Private Sub btnDisplay_Click(...) Handles btnDisplay.Click
  Dim x, y As Integer
  Dim sr As IO.StreamReader = IO.File.OpenText("DATA.TXT")
  x = CInt(sr.ReadLine)
  y = CInt(sr.ReadLine)
  ReDim m(x, y)
```

```
      For j As Integer = 0 To x
        For k As Integer = 0 To y - j
          m(j, k) = CInt(sr.ReadLine)
          lstOutput.Items.Add(m(j, k) - k)
        Next
      Next
      sr.Close()
End Sub
```

(Assume that the 10 lines of the file DATA.TXT contain the following entries: 1, 2, 6, 3, 2, 1, 3, 4, 9, 8.)

In Exercises 9 and 10, identify the errors.

9.
```
Dim a(2, 3) As Integer
Private Sub btnDisplay_Click(...) Handles btnDisplay.Click
  'Fill an array
  Dim sr As IO.StreamReader = IO.File.OpenText("DATA.TXT")
  For j As Integer = 0 To 3
    For k As Integer = 0 To 2
      a(j, k) = CInt(sr.ReadLine)
    Next
  Next
  sr.Close()
End Sub
```

(Assume that the 12 lines of the file DATA.TXT contain the following entries: 1, 2, 3, 4, 5, 6, 7, 8, 9, 0, 1, 2.)

10.
```
Dim score(2, 2) As Integer
Private Sub frmScores_Load(...) Handles MyBase.Load
  'Fill array from text file
  Dim student As Integer
  Dim sr As IO.StreamReader = IO.File.OpenText("SCORES.TXT")
  For j As Integer = 0 To 2
    student = CInt(sr.ReadLine)
    For k As Integer = 0 To 2
      score(k, j) = CInt(sr.ReadLine)
    Next
  Next
End Sub

Private Sub btnDisplay_Click(...) Handles btnDisplay.Click
  'Report individual scores
  Dim student, exam As Integer
  student = CInt(txtStudent.Text)
  exam = CInt(txtExam.Text)
  If (student>=0 And student<=2) And (exam>=0 And exam<=2) Then
    txtOutput.Text = CStr(score(student, exam))
  End If
End Sub
```

(Assume that the 12 lines of the file SCORES.TXT contain the following data: 0, 80, 85, 90, 1, 72, 80, 88, 2, 87, 93, 90.)

In Exercises 11 through 14, write a procedure to perform the stated task.

11. Given an array declared with the statement `Dim a(10, 10) As Double`, set the entries in the *j*th column to *j* (for *j* = 0, ..., 10).

12. Given an array declared with the statement `Dim a(10, 10) As Double`, and values assigned to each entry, compute the sum of the values in row 10.

13. Given an array declared with the statement `Dim a(10, 10) As Double`, and values assigned to each entry, interchange the values in rows 2 and 3.

14. Given an array declared with the statement `Dim a(3, 45) As Double`, and values assigned to each entry, find the greatest value and the places (possibly more than one) at which it occurs.

In Exercises 15 through 25, write a program to perform the stated task.

15. A company has two stores (1 and 2), and each store sells three items (1, 2, and 3). The following tables give the inventory at the beginning of the day and the amount of each item sold during that day.

Beginning Inventory

		ITEM		
		1	2	3
Store	1	25	64	23
	2	12	82	19

Sales for Day

		ITEM		
		1	2	3
Store	1	7	45	11
	2	4	24	8

(a) Record the values of each table in an array.
(b) Adjust the values in the first array to hold the inventories at the end of the day and display these new inventories.
(c) Calculate and display the number of items in each store at the end of the day.

16. Table 7.12 gives the results of a survey on the uses of computers in the workplace. Each entry shows the percentage of respondents from the age category that use the computer for the indicated purpose.

TABLE 7.12 Workers Using Computers on the job.

Age	Word Processing	Spreadsheets	Internet/ e-mail	Calendar/ schedule	Programming
18–24	55.1	53.7	58.2	47.5	12.7
25–29	67.5	65.9	73.7	54.9	17.2
30–39	69.5	66.5	75.0	56.6	17.4
40–49	68.8	63.6	73.5	54.9	15.9
50–59	69.1	61.2	74.0	51.3	12.5
60 and older	61.0	50.1	65.7	40.2	12.3

Source: U.S. Center of Educational Statistics, Digest of Educational Statistics, 2001

(a) Place the data from the table in an array. (Use 7-5-E16.TXT.)
(b) Determine the average of the percentages in the Spreadsheets column.

17. A university offers 10 courses at each of three campuses. The number of students enrolled in each is presented in Table 7.13.

(a) Find the total number of course enrollments on each campus.
(b) Find the total number of students taking each course.

TABLE 7.13   **Number of students enrolled in courses.**

		Course									
		1	2	3	4	5	6	7	8	9	10
	1	5	15	22	21	12	25	16	11	17	23
Campus	2	11	23	51	25	32	35	32	52	25	21
	3	2	12	32	32	25	26	29	12	15	11

18. Table 7.14 gives the 2002 and 2003 U.S. sales for the five top restaurant chains.

(a) Place the data into an array.
(b) Calculate the total change in sales for these five restaurant chains.

TABLE 7.14   **Top restaurant chains.**

	2002 Sales $MM	2003 Sales $MM
1. McDonald's	20.3	22.1
2. Burger King	8.7	7.9
3. Wendy's	7.1	7.5
4. Subway	5.2	5.7
5. Taco Bell	5.2	5.3

Source: QSR Magazine, Dec. 2004

19. The scores for the top three golfers at the 2005 Buick Invitational are shown in Table 7.15.

(a) Place the data into an array.
(b) Compute the total score for each player.
(c) Compute the average score for each round.

TABLE 7.15   **2005 Buick Invitational.**

	Round			
	1	2	3	4
Tiger Woods	69	63	72	68
Luke Donald	68	67	67	73
Bernhard Langer	69	69	67	72

20. Table 7.16 contains part of the pay schedule for federal employees in Washington, D.C. Table 7.17 gives the number of employees of each classification in a certain division. Place the data from each table into an array and compute the amount of money this division pays for salaries during the year.

TABLE 7.16   **2005 pay schedule for federal white-collar workers.**

	Step			
	1	**2**	**3**	**4**
GS-1	16,016	16,550	17,083	17,613
GS-2	18,007	18,435	19,031	19,537
GS-3	19,647	20,302	20,957	21,612
GS-4	22,056	22,791	23,526	24,261
GS-5	24,677	25,500	26,323	27,146
GS-6	27,507	28,424	29,341	30,258
GS-7	30,567	31,586	32,605	33,624

TABLE 7.17   **Number of employees in each category.**

	1	2	3	4
GS-1	0	0	2	1
GS-2	2	3	0	1
GS-3	4	2	5	7
GS-4	12	13	8	3
GS-5	4	5	0	1
GS-6	6	2	4	3
GS-7	8	1	9	2

21. Consider Table 7.10, the rankings of three university departments. Write a program that places the data into an array, allows the name of a college to be input, and gives the categories in which it appears. Of course, a college might appear more than once or not at all.

22. Table 7.18 gives the monthly precipitation for a typical Nebraska city during a five-year period. Write a program that reads the table from a text file into an array and then displays in a list box the output on the next page.

TABLE 7.18   **Monthly precipitation (in inches) for a typical Nebraska city.**

	Jan.	Feb.	Mar.	Apr.	May	June	July	Aug.	Sept.	Oct.	Nov.	Dec.
1986	0.88	1.11	2.01	3.64	6.44	5.58	4.23	4.34	4.00	2.05	1.48	0.77
1987	0.76	0.94	2.09	3.29	4.68	3.52	3.52	4.82	3.72	2.21	1.24	0.80
1988	0.67	0.80	1.75	2.70	4.01	3.88	3.72	3.78	3.55	1.88	1.21	0.61
1989	0.82	0.80	1.99	3.05	4.19	4.44	3.98	4.57	3.43	2.32	1.61	0.75
1990	0.72	0.90	1.71	2.02	2.33	2.98	2.65	2.99	2.55	1.99	1.05	0.92

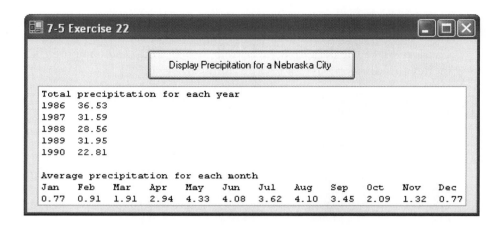

23. Suppose that a course has 15 students enrolled and that five exams are given during the semester. Write a program that accepts each student's name and grades as input and places the names in a one-dimensional array and the grades in a two-dimensional array. The program should then display each student's name and semester average. Also, the program should display the median for each exam. (For an odd number of grades, the median is the middle grade. For an even number of grades, it is the average of the two middle grades.)

24. An n-by-n array is called a magic square if the sums of each row, each column, and each diagonal are equal. Write a program to determine if an array is a magic square and use it to determine if either of the following arrays is a magic square. **Hint:** If, at any time, one of the sums is not equal to the others, the search is complete.

(a)	1	15	15	4	(b)	11	10	4	23	17
	12	6	7	9		18	12	6	5	24
	8	10	11	5		25	19	13	7	1
	13	3	2	16		2	21	20	14	8
						9	3	22	16	15

25. A company has three stores (1, 2, and 3), and each store sells five items (1, 2, 3, 4, and 5). The following tables give the number of items sold by each store and category on a particular day, and the cost of each item.

(a) Place the data from the left-hand table in a two-dimensional array and the data from the right-hand table in a one-dimensional array.

(b) Compute and display the total dollar amount of sales for each store and for the entire company.

Number of Items Sold During Day

		1	2	3	4	5		ITEM	COST PER ITEM
				ITEM				1	$12.00
	1	25	64	23	45	14		2	$17.95
Store	2	12	82	19	34	63		3	$95.00
	3	54	22	17	43	35		4	$86.50
								5	$78.00

Solutions to Practice Problems 7.5

1. Replace the masked text boxes with ordinary text boxes to hold city names. The function FindCityNum can be used to determine the subscript associated with each city. This function and the modified event procedure btnShow_Click are as follows:

```
Function FindCityNum(ByVal city As String) As Integer
  Select Case city.ToUpper
    Case "CHICAGO"
      Return 1
    Case "LOS ANGELES"
      Return 2
    Case "NEW YORK"
      Return 3
    Case "PHILADELPHIA"
      Return 4
    Case Else
      Return 0
  End Select
End Function

Private Sub btnShow_Click(...) Handles btnShow.Click
  Dim orig, dest As String
  Dim row, col As Integer 'Determine road mileage between cities
  orig = txtOrig.Text
  dest = txtDest.Text
  row = FindCityNum(orig)
  col = FindCityNum(dest)
  If (row < 1) Or (row > 4) Then
    MsgBox("City of origin not available", 0, "Error")
  ElseIf (col < 1) Or (col > 4) Then
    MsgBox("Destination city not available", 0, "Error")
  Else
    txtMiles.Text = CStr(rm(row, col))
  End If
End Sub
```

2. Both arrays of structures and two-dimensional arrays are used to hold related data. If some of the data are numeric and some are string, then structures must be used, because all entries of a two-dimensional array must be of the same type. Arrays of structures should also be used if the data will be sorted. Two-dimensional arrays are best suited to tabular data.

7.6   A Case Study: A Sophisticated Cash Register

One of the most prevalent types of computer equipment today is the cash register. This machine has evolved considerably from the time when it functioned like an old-fashioned mechanical typewriter, recording the amount of each sale on a strip of paper and keeping a running sum. Today, cash registers are located not only in stores, but also within gasoline pumps and airport kiosks, performing many functions above and beyond printing receipts. The data from customers' purchases can be stored on a central computer and analyzed to determine trends in buying behavior. For example, a grocery store may glean from cash register transactions that customers who purchase potato chips are likely to also purchase soft drinks. This might lead the store to stock soft drinks in the same aisle as snacks. In the retail industry, the location of a cash register is called the "point of sale" (abbreviated as "POS").

■ The Design of the Program

This case study develops a sophisticated cash register that supports three main features: First, it accepts user input for the quantity, price, and department of a particular article. Second, it calculates the totals including sales tax and stores those data along with the payment method into an array. Finally, the program generates a report on the stored data. Each of these features is a task that is executed by clicking on a button:

1. Enter the price, quantity, and department of a new article to purchase. Display the article's data.

2. Display the subtotal, sales tax, and total, and record the purchase and payment method in an array.

3. Generate a report showing (a) the quantity and sales for each department and (b) the number of receipts and amounts for each payment method.

■ The User Interface

Two text boxes are used to collect input for quantity and price. Buttons that represent each department are used to record and display this data in an output list box. Each payment type is represented by a button that finalizes the purchase and displays the totals. A report button is enabled after a purchase is finalized and, when pressed, generates the report in the same list box. See Figure 7.7 and Table 7.19.

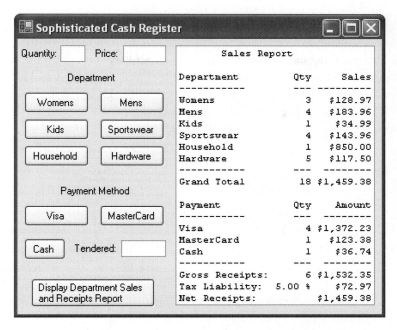

FIGURE 7.7 **Sample output after pressing the bottom button.**

TABLE 7.19 Controls that comprise the user interface.

Object	Property	Setting
frmCashRegister	Text	Sophisticated Cash Register
lblQuantity	Text	Quantity:
txtQuantity		
lblPrice	Text	Price:
txtPrice		
lblDepartment	Text	Department
btnWomens	Text	Womens
btnMens	Text	Mens
btnKids	Text	Kids
btnSportswear	Text	Sportswear
btnHousehold	Text	Household
btnHardware	Text	Hardware
lblMethod	Text	Payment Method
btnVisa	Text	Visa
btnMasterCard	Text	MasterCard
btnCash	Text	Cash
lblCash	Text	Tendered:
txtCash		
btnReport	Enabled	False
	Text	Display Department Sales and Receipts Report
lstOutput		

The Data Structures

The cash register inputs, stores, and processes data. These data are organized into related fields that lend themselves to structure data types. The program employs an Article structure that stores the data for each article that is purchased and a Purchase structure that stores all of the articles and the totals on one receipt. An array of Purchase structures is declared as a class-level variable and holds all of the data for the store. Figure 7.8 shows a representation of the way the structures are organized.

Article

1
2
$23.99

Article.department
Article.quantity
Article.price

Purchase

articles()
2
$23.99
$23.99
$23.99

Purchase.articles
Purchase.articleCount
Purchase.subtotal
Purchase.total
Purchase.method

FIGURE 7.8   Structures used in the Sophisticated Cash Register program.

Coding the Program

The top row of Figure 7.9 shows the different events to which the program must respond. Table 7.20 identifies the corresponding event procedures and the general procedures they call. Let's examine each event procedure:

1. **frmCashRegister_Load** initializes the first Purchase structure by dimensioning its *articles* array to an initial upper bound of 5. It is necessary to do this in the Load procedure because arrays cannot be sized within the structure definition block, yet they must be dimensioned before they are accessed.

2. **RingupArticle** is called by the event procedures connected to the buttons that represent the department names (Womens, Mens, Kids, etc.). It takes as its parameter the number of the department that was clicked. The procedure stores the de-

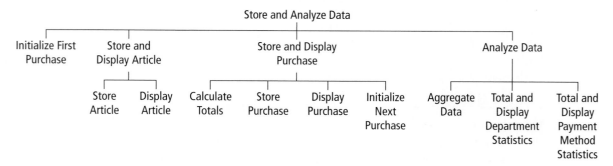

FIGURE 7.9   Hierarchy chart for Sophisticated Cash Register program.

TABLE 7.20	Tasks and their procedures.
1. Initialize First Purchase	frmCashRegister_Load
2. Store and Display Article	RingupArticle
2.1 Store Article	RingupArticle
2.2 Display Article	DisplayArticle
3. Store and Display Purchase	TotalPurchase
3.1 Calculate Totals	TotalPurchase
3.2 Store Purchase	TotalPurchase
3.3 Display Purchase	DisplayTotals
3.4 Initialize Next Purchase	TotalPurchase
4. Analyze Data	btnReport_Click
4.1 Aggregate Data	btnReport_Click
4.2 Total and Display Department Statistics	btnReport_Click
4.2 Total and Display Payment Method Statistics	btnReport_Click

partment, quantity, and price of the article into a new Article structure. If the quantity and price are valid (that is, they are greater than zero), then the new article is stored into the array that is a member of the current Purchase structure. If that array does not have room to accommodate the new article, the array is enlarged using a ReDim Preserve statement. Finally, the procedure calls the Display-Article procedure and resets the quantity to 1 for the next article.

The DisplayArticle procedure displays the quantity, department, price, and total (that is, quantity times price) for an article in the output list box. A heading is displayed along with the first purchase on the receipt. The department names are stored in a string array called *department()* that is declared as a class-level variable. The procedure displays the article's department name by using its department number as the subscript in the *department()* array.

3. TotalPurchase is called by the event procedures that are connected to the buttons representing the methods of payment (Visa, MasterCard, Cash). It takes as its parameter the number of the payment method that was clicked. The procedure first checks to see if any articles have been stored. If not, a message box is displayed. Otherwise, the articles are totaled, and sales tax is applied to calculate the purchase's subtotal and total. If the payment method is Cash, the procedure verifies that the amount tendered by the customer is at least the total amount. If it isn't, a message box is displayed. Otherwise, the purchase is stored, the DisplayTotals procedure is called, and the *articles* array in the next purchase structure is ReDimmed to the default upper bound of 4.

The technique used to store a purchase requires elaboration. The class-level array *purchases()* is declared in the class with an initial upper bound of 30. The integer counter *count* keeps track of the number of stored purchases and is initialized to the default value of zero. New articles are stored in the *purchases()* element with subscript *count*. When a payment method is clicked, the purchase is finalized. The action that does this is the line *count += 1*, which increments the counter by one. Therefore, the new purchase is stored in the *purchases()* array all along, but it is only recognized as "stored" when its index is less than the counter.

The DisplayTotals procedure displays the subtotal, applicable sales tax, and total for the purchase. It also displays the payment method in the following manner: If the payment method is Cash (method #3), it displays the cash tendered and the change due. Otherwise it displays the type of credit card used.

4. **btnReport_Click** aggregates the data in the *purchases*() array and displays the resulting analysis. It first declares the arrays and variables that are used for the results. It then loops through all of the articles for each purchase (using a nested loop) to aggregate each article into a department result and a payment method result. It uses the department and payment method numbers as subscripts for the result arrays, the four arrays declared at the top of the procedure. The department statistics are totaled and displayed, then the payment method statistics are totaled and displayed.P

```
'Define the Purchase and Article structures
Structure Article
   Dim department As Integer    'Department number, see department() below
   Dim quantity As Integer      'Quantity of articles purchased
   Dim price As Double          'Price of each article
End Structure

Structure Purchase
   Dim articles() As Article    'Articles purchased
   Dim articleCount As Integer  'Number of articles purchased
   Dim subtotal As Double       'Subtotal of articles' prices times quantities
   Dim total As Double          'Total of purchase including tax
   Dim method As Integer        'Method of payment, see method() below
End Structure

'Declare the class-level variables
Dim purchases(30) As Purchase    'Array that holds all purchases
Dim count As Integer             'Number of completed purchases
Dim taxRate As Double = 0.05     '5% sales tax
Dim department() As String = {"Womens", "Mens", "Kids", _
    "Sportswear", "Household", "Hardware"}
Dim method() As String = {"Visa", "MasterCard", "Cash"}

Private Sub frmCashRegister_Load(...) Handles MyBase.Load
   'Initialize the first purchase
   ReDim purchases(0).articles(4)
End Sub

Sub RingupArticle(ByVal dept As Integer)
   'Store the user's input into a new article
   Dim newArticle As Article        'New article to hold user input
   Dim size As Integer              'Size of the articles array
   With newArticle
     .department = dept
     .quantity = CInt(txtQuantity.Text)
```

```vbnet
      'If blank price then use default of 0
      If txtPrice.Text = "" Then
        .price = 0
      Else
        .price = CDbl(txtPrice.Text)
      End If
    End With
    'If price and quantity are valid, then store and display article
    If (newArticle.quantity > 0) And (newArticle.price > 0) Then
      'Increment the number of articles in the current purchase
      purchases(count).articleCount += 1
      'Ensure the Purchase's articles array has room for the new article
      size = purchases(count).articles.GetUpperBound(0)
      If purchases(count).articleCount >= size Then
        'If not enough room, increase the array size by 5
        ReDim Preserve purchases(count).articles(size + 5)
      End If
      'Store the new article into the purchase
      purchases(count).articles(purchases(count).articleCount - 1) = _
                      newArticle
      'Display the article in the receipt
      DisplayArticle()
      'Clear the quantity and price for the next article
      txtQuantity.Clear()
      txtPrice.Clear()
    End If
    'Disable the report button until the article is paid for
    btnReport.Enabled = False
    txtQuantity.Focus()     'Focus on the quantity for the next article
  End Sub

  Private Sub btnWomens_Click(...) Handles btnWomens.Click
    RingupArticle(0)
  End Sub

  Private Sub btnMens_Click(...) Handles btnMens.Click
    RingupArticle(1)
  End Sub

  Private Sub btnKids_Click(...) Handles btnKids.Click
    RingupArticle(2)
  End Sub

  Private Sub btnSportswear_Click(...) Handles btnSportswear.Click
    RingupArticle(3)
  End Sub

  Private Sub btnHousehold_Click(...) Handles btnHousehold.Click
    RingupArticle(4)
  End Sub
```

```vb
Private Sub btnHardware_Click(...) Handles btnHardware.Click
  RingupArticle(5)
End Sub

Sub DisplayArticle()
  Dim cost As Double
  Dim fmtStr As String = "{0,3} {1,-12} {2,7:C} {3,7:C}"
  'If article is the first, clear the display and display the header
  If purchases(count).articleCount = 1 Then
    lstOutput.Items.Clear()
    lstOutput.Items.Add("       Customer Receipt")
    lstOutput.Items.Add("")
    lstOutput.Items.Add(String.Format(fmtStr, "Qty", "Dept", _
                                      "  Price", "  Total"))
    lstOutput.Items.Add(String.Format(fmtStr, "---", "------------", _
                                      "-------", "-------"))
  End If
  'Display the article's information
  With purchases(count).articles(purchases(count).articleCount - 1)
    cost = .quantity * .price
    lstOutput.Items.Add(String.Format(fmtStr, .quantity, _
                        department(.department), .price, cost))
  End With
End Sub

Sub TotalPurchase(ByVal meth As Integer)
  Dim cash As Double          'Amount of cash tendered
  Dim flag As Boolean = True   'If purchase is valid
  With purchases(count)
    'If no articles purchased then display message and exit
    If .articleCount < 1 Then
      MsgBox("No articles purchased.", 0, "No sale")
      txtQuantity.Focus()
      flag = False
    End If
    'Calculate and store totals
    .subtotal = 0
    For i As Integer = 0 To .articleCount - 1
      .subtotal += .articles(i).price * .articles(i).quantity
    Next
    'Add sales tax to get total
    .total = (1 + taxRate) * .subtotal
    'Store the method of payment
    .method = meth
    'If cash method, then get the amount tendered by customer
    If .method = 2 Then
      If txtCash.Text = "" Then
        cash = 0
```

```vbnet
      Else
        cash = CDbl(txtCash.Text)
      End If
      'If tendered amount is not enough, then display message
      If (cash < .total) Then
        MsgBox("Not enough cash tendered (need " & _
          FormatCurrency(.total) & ")", 0, "Insufficient Cash")
        txtCash.Focus()    'Focus on cash for reinput
        flag = False
      End If
    End If
  End With
  'If purchase is valid, then store and display it
  If flag Then
    'Increment the counter so the latest purchase is considered stored
    count += 1
    'Display purchase totals
    DisplayTotals()
    'Make sure there is room for the next purchase and initialize it
    If purchases.GetUpperBound(0) <= count Then
      ReDim purchases(count + 5)
    End If
    ReDim purchases(count).articles(4)
  End If
  'Enable the report button
  btnReport.Enabled = True
End Sub

Sub DisplayTotals()
  'Display subtotal, tax, and total
  Dim prompt As String = "Tax: (" & FormatPercent(taxRate) & ")"
  Dim cash As Double
  Dim fmtStr As String = "{0,3} {1,-12} {2,7} {3,7:C}"
  With purchases(count - 1)
    lstOutput.Items.Add(String.Format(fmtStr, "", "", "", "-------"))
    lstOutput.Items.Add(String.Format(fmtStr, "", "Sub Total:", "", _
                                .subtotal))
    lstOutput.Items.Add(String.Format(fmtStr, "", prompt, "", _
                                .total - .subtotal))
    lstOutput.Items.Add(String.Format(fmtStr, "", "", "", "-------"))
    lstOutput.Items.Add(String.Format(fmtStr, "", "Total:", "", .total))
    'If cash purchase, then display amount tendered and change
    If .method = 2 Then
      cash = CDbl(txtCash.Text)
      lstOutput.Items.Add("")
      lstOutput.Items.Add(String.Format(fmtStr, "", "Cash:", "", cash))
      lstOutput.Items.Add(String.Format(fmtStr, "", "Change:", "", _
                                cash - .total))
```

```vb
    Else
      'If not cash, mention how tendered
        lstOutput.Items.Add("  Charged to " & method(.method))
      End If
    End With
    'Clear the cash, and set focus to quantity for the next purchase
    txtCash.Clear()
    txtQuantity.Focus()
  End Sub

  Private Sub btnVisa_Click(...) Handles btnVisa.Click
    TotalPurchase(0)
  End Sub

  Private Sub btnMasterCard_Click(...) Handles btnMasterCard.Click
    TotalPurchase(1)
  End Sub

  Private Sub btnCash_Click(...) Handles btnCash.Click
    TotalPurchase(2)
  End Sub

  Private Sub btnReport_Click(...) Handles btnReport.Click
    Dim deptQuant(5), deptQuantT As Integer    'Quantity per department
    Dim deptSales(5), deptSalesT As Double     'Sales per department
    Dim methQuant(2), methQuantT As Integer    'Quantity per method
    Dim methAmnt(2), methAmntT As Double       'Sales per method
    Dim liability As Double                    'Amount of tax liability
    Dim fmtStr1 As String = "{0,-15} {1,6} {2,9:C}"
    Dim fmtStr2 As String = "{0,-15} {1,6:P} {2,9:C}"
    'Sum quantity and total amounts per department, without tax
    For i As Integer = 0 To count - 1
      'Sum quantity and total amounts per payment method
      methQuant(purchases(i).method) += 1
      methAmnt(purchases(i).method) += purchases(i).total
      For j As Integer = 0 To purchases(i).articleCount - 1
        With purchases(i).articles(j)
          deptQuant(.department) += .quantity
          deptSales(.department) += .price * .quantity
        End With
      Next
    Next
    'Display the quantity and sales per department
    lstOutput.Items.Clear()
    lstOutput.Items.Add("       Sales Report")
    lstOutput.Items.Add("")
    lstOutput.Items.Add(String.Format(fmtStr1, "Department ", "Qty", _
                                  "    Sales"))
    lstOutput.Items.Add(String.Format(fmtStr1, "-----------", "---", _
                                  "---------"))
```

```
    For i As Integer = 0 To 5
      lstOutput.Items.Add(String.Format(fmtStr1, department(i), _
                          deptQuant(i), deptSales(i)))
      deptQuantT += deptQuant(i)
      deptSalesT += deptSales(i)
    Next
    lstOutput.Items.Add(String.Format(fmtStr1, "-----------", "---", _
                                      "--------"))
    lstOutput.Items.Add(String.Format(fmtStr1, "Grand Total", _
                                      deptQuantT, deptSalesT))
    'Display the quantity and sales per payment method
    lstOutput.Items.Add("")
    lstOutput.Items.Add(String.Format(fmtStr1, "Payment     ", "Qty", _
                                      "  Amount"))
    lstOutput.Items.Add(String.Format(fmtStr1, "-----------", "---", _
                                      "--------"))
    For i As Integer = 0 To 2
      lstOutput.Items.Add(String.Format(fmtStr1, method(i), _
                                        methQuant(i), methAmnt(i)))
      methQuantT += methQuant(i)
      methAmntT += methAmnt(i)
    Next
    'Calculate the total amount of sales tax
    liability = methAmntT - deptSalesT
    lstOutput.Items.Add(String.Format(fmtStr1, "-----------", "---", _
                                      "--------"))
    lstOutput.Items.Add(String.Format(fmtStr1, "Gross Receipts:", _
                                      methQuantT, methAmntT))
    lstOutput.Items.Add(String.Format(fmtStr2, "Tax Liability:", _
                                      taxRate, liability))
    lstOutput.Items.Add(String.Format(fmtStr1, "Net Receipts:", "", _
                                      deptSalesT))
    txtQuantity.Focus()        'Focus on quantity for next article
End Sub
```

CHAPTER 7 Summary

1. For programming purposes, tabular data are most efficiently processed if stored in an *array*. An array is declared with a *Dim* statement, which also can specify its *size* and initial values. The size of an already declared array can be specified or changed with a *ReDim* or *ReDim Preserve* statement. The highest subscript of the array is called its *upper bound* and is returned with the *GetUpperBound*(0) method. The *Clear* statement releases all memory allocated to an array.

2. An array of labels, text boxes, or buttons is referred to as a *control array*.

3. A *structure* is a composite programmer-designed data type with a fixed number of fields, each of which can be of any data type.

4. Two of the best-known methods for ordering (or *sorting*) arrays are the *bubble sort* and the *Shell sort*.

5. Any array can be searched *sequentially* to find the subscript associated with a sought-after value. Ordered arrays can be searched most efficiently by a *binary search*.

6. A table can be effectively stored in a *two-dimensional array*.

CHAPTER 7   Programming Projects

1. Table 7.21 contains some lengths in terms of feet. Write a program that displays the nine different units of measure; requests the unit to convert from, the unit to convert to, and the quantity to be converted, and then displays the converted quantity. A typical outcome is shown in Figure 7.10.

TABLE 7.21	Equivalent lengths.	
1 inch = .0833 foot		1 rod = 16.5 feet
1 yard = 3 feet		1 furlong = 660 feet
1 meter = 3.28155 feet		1 kilometer = 3281.5 feet
1 fathom = 6 feet		1 mile = 5280 feet

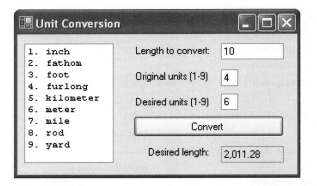

FIGURE 7.10   Possible outcome of Programming Project 1.

2. Statisticians use the concepts of **mean and standard deviation** to describe a collection of data. The mean is the average value of the items, and the standard deviation measures the spread or dispersal of the numbers about the mean. Formally, if $x_1, x_2, x_3, \ldots, x_n$, is a collection of data, then

$$\text{mean} = m = \frac{x_1 + x_2 + x_3 + \cdots + x_n}{n}$$

standard deviation =

$$s = \sqrt{\frac{(x_1 - m)^2 + (x_2 - m)^2 + (x_3 - m)^2 + \cdots + (x_n - m)^2}{n - 1}}$$

Write a computer program to

(a) place the exam scores 59, 60, 65, 75, 56, 90, 66, 62, 98, 72, 95, 71, 63, 77, 65, 77, 65, 50, 85, and 62 into an array;

(b) calculate the mean and standard deviation of the exam scores;

(c) assign letter grades to each exam score, ES, as follows:

$$ES \geq m + 1.5s \qquad\qquad A$$
$$m + .5s \leq ES < m + 1.5s \quad B$$
$$m - .5s \leq ES < m + .5s \quad C$$
$$m - 1.5s\, ES \leq m - .5s \qquad D$$
$$ES < m - 1.5s \qquad\qquad F$$

For instance, if m were 70 and s were 12, then grades of 88 or above would receive A's, grades between 76 and 87 would receive B's, and so on. A process of this type is referred to as *curving grades*.

(d) Display a list of the exam scores along with their corresponding grades as shown in Figure 7.11.

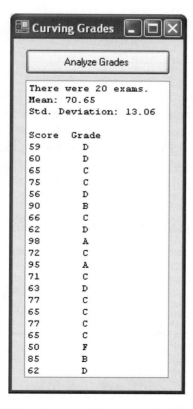

FIGURE 7.11 Output of Programming Project 2.

3. *Rudimentary Translator.* Table 7.22 gives English words and their French and German equivalents. Store these words in a text file and read them into a structure having a member for each language. Write a program that sorts arrays according to the English words. The program should then request an English sentence as input from the keyboard and translate it into French and German. For example, if the English sentence given is MY PENCIL IS ON THE TABLE, then the French translation will be MON CRAYON EST SUR LA TABLE, and the German translation will be MEIN BLEISTIFT IST AUF DEM TISCH.

   Note: Assume that the only punctuation in the sentence is a period at the end of the sentence. Use a binary search to locate each English word.

TABLE 7.22 **English words and their French and German equivalents.**

English	French	German	English	French	German
YES	OUI	JA	LARGE	GROS	GROSS
TABLE	TABLE	TISCH	NO	NON	NEIN
THE	LA	DEM	HAT	CHAPEAU	HUT
IS	EST	IST	PENCIL	CRAYON	BLEISTIFT
YELLOW	JAUNE	GELB	RED	ROUGE	ROT
FRIEND	AMI	FREUND	ON	SUR	AUF
SICK	MALADE	KRANK	AUTO	AUTO	AUTO
MY	MON	MEIN	OFTEN	SOUVENT	OFT

4. Write a program that allows a list of no more than 50 soft drinks and their percent changes in sales volume for a particular year to be input and displays the information in two lists titled *gainers* and *losers*. Each list should be sorted by the *amount* of the percent change. Try your program on the data for the seven soft drinks in Table 7.23.

   Note: You will need to store the data initially in an array to determine the number of gainers and losers.

TABLE 7.23 **Changes in sales volume from 2002 to 2003 of leading soft-drink brands.**

Brand	% Change in Volume	Brand	% Change in Volume
Coke Classic	−3.0	Sprite	−5.0
Pepsi-Cola	−4.5	Dr. Pepper	−3.9
Diet Coke	5.0	Diet Pepsi	6.1
Mt. Dew	−1.5		

Source: Beverage Digest, 2004

5. Each team in a six-team soccer league played each other team once. Table 7.24 shows the winners. Write a program to

   (a) Place the team names in an array of structures that also holds the number of wins.

   (b) Place the data from Table 7.24 in a two-dimensional array.

TABLE 7.24	Soccer league winners.					
	Jazz	Jets	Owls	Rams	Cubs	Zips
Jazz	—	Jazz	Jazz	Rams	Cubs	Jazz
Jets	Jazz	—	Jets	Jets	Cubs	Zips
Owls	Jazz	Jets	—	Rams	Owls	Owls
Rams	Rams	Jets	Rams	—	Rams	Rams
Cubs	Cubs	Cubs	Owls	Rams	—	Cubs
Zips	Jazz	Zips	Owls	Rams	Cubs	—

(c) Place the number of games won by each team in the array of structures.

(d) Display a listing of the teams giving each team's name and number of games won. The list should be in decreasing order by the number of wins.

6. A poker hand can be stored in a two-dimensional array. The statement

```
Dim hand(3, 12) As Integer
```

declares an array with 52 elements, where the first subscript ranges over the four suits and the second subscript ranges over the thirteen denominations. A poker hand is specified by placing ones in the elements corresponding to the cards in the hand. See Figure 7.12.

	A	2	3	4	5	6	7	8	9	10	J	Q	K
Club ♣	0	0	0	0	0	0	0	0	1	0	0	0	0
Diamond ♦	1	0	0	0	0	0	0	0	0	0	0	0	0
Heart ♥	1	0	0	0	0	0	0	0	0	0	0	1	0
Spade ♠	0	0	0	0	1	0	0	0	0	0	0	0	0

FIGURE 7.12   Array for the poker hand A ♥ A ♦ 5 ♠ 9 ♣ Q ♥.

Write a program that requests the five cards as input from the user, creates the related array, and passes the array to procedures to determine the type of the hand: flush (all cards have the same suit), straight (cards have consecutive denominations—ace can come either before 2 or after King), straight flush, four-of-a-kind, full house (3 cards of one denomination, 2 cards of another denomination), three-of-a-kind, two pairs, one pair, or none of the above.

7. *Airline Reservations.* Write a reservation system for an airline flight. Assume the airplane has 10 rows with 4 seats in each row. Use a two-dimensional array of strings to maintain a seating chart. In addition, create an array to be used as a waiting list in case the plane is full. The waiting list should be "first come, first served," that is, people who are added early to the list get priority over those added later. Allow the user the following three options:

(a) Add a passenger to the flight or waiting list.

    1. Request the passenger's name.
    2. Display a chart of the seats in the airplane in tabular form.
    3. If seats are available, let the passenger choose a seat. Add the passenger to the seating chart.
    4. If no seats are available, place the passenger on the waiting list.

(b) Remove a passenger from the flight.

    1. Request the passenger's name.
    2. Search the seating chart for the passenger's name and delete it.
    3. If the waiting list is empty, update the array so the seat is available.
    4. If the waiting list is not empty, remove the first person from the list, and give him or her the newly vacated seat.

(c) Quit.

8. The Game of Life was invented by John H. Conway to model some genetic laws for birth, death, and survival. Consider a checkerboard consisting of an n-by-n array of squares. Each square can contain one individual (denoted by 1) or be empty (denoted by –). Figure 7.13(a) shows a 6-by-6 board with four of the squares occupied. The future of each individual depends on the number of his neighbors. After each period of time, called a *generation*, certain individuals will survive, others will die due to either loneliness or overcrowding, and new individuals will be born. Each nonborder square has eight neighboring squares. After each generation, the status of the squares changes as follows:

(a) An individual *survives* if there are two or three individuals in neighboring squares.
(b) An individual *dies* if he has more than three individuals or less than two in neighboring squares.
(c) A new individual *is born* into each empty square with exactly three individuals as neighbors.

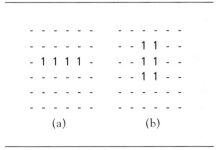

(a)   (b)

FIGURE 7.13 **Two generations.**

Figure 7.13(b) shows the status after one generation. Write a program to do the following:

1. Declare a two-dimensional array of size n, where n is input by the user, to hold the status of each square in the current generation. To specify the initial configuration, have the user input each row as a string of length n, and break the row into 1's or dashes with the Substring method.

2. Declare a two-dimensional array of size n to hold the status of each square in the next generation. Compute the status for each square and produce the display in Figure 7.13(b). **Note:** The generation changes all at once. Only current cells are used to determine which cells will contain individuals in the next generation.

3. Assign the next-generation values to the current generation and repeat as often as desired.

4. Display the individuals in each generation. **Hint:** The hardest part of the program is determining the number of neighbors a cell has. In general, you must check a 3-by-3 square around the cell in question. Exceptions must be made when the cell is on the edge of the array. Don't forget that a cell is not a neighbor of itself.

(Test the program with the initial configuration shown in Figure 7.14. It is known as the figure-eight configuration and repeats after eight generations.)

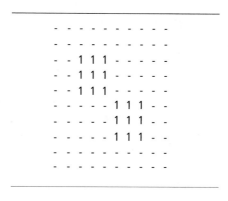

FIGURE 7.14   The figure eight.

9. Every book is identified by a ten-character International Standard Book Number (ISBN) that is usually printed on the back cover of the book. The first nine characters are digits and the last character is either a digit or the letter X (which stands for ten). Three examples of ISBN numbers are 0-13-030657-6, 0-32-108599-X, and 0-471-58719-2. The hyphens separate the characters into four blocks. The first block usually consists of a single digit and identifies the language (0 for English, 2 for French, 3 for German, etc.). The second block identifies the publisher (for example, 13 for Prentice Hall, 32 for Addison-Wesley-Longman, and 471 for Wiley); The third block is the number the publisher has chosen for the book. The fourth block, which always consists of a single character called the **check digit**, is used

to test for errors. Let's refer to the ten characters of the ISBN as $d_1, d_2, d_3, d_4, d_5, d_6, d_7, d_8, d_9$, and d_{10}. The check digit is chosen so that the sum

$$10 \cdot d_1 + 9 \cdot d_2 + 8 \cdot d_3 + 7 \cdot d_4 + 6 \cdot d_5 + 5 \cdot d_6 + 4 \cdot d_7 + 3 \cdot d_8 + 2 \cdot d_9$$
$$+ 1 \cdot d_{10} \tag{$*$}$$

is a multiple of 11. **Note:** A number is a multiple of 11 if it is exactly divisible by 11.). If the last character of the ISBN is an X, then in the sum ($*$), d_{10} is replaced with 10. For example, with the ISBN 0-32-108599-X, the sum would be

$$10 \cdot 0 + 9 \cdot 3 + 8 \cdot 2 + 7 \cdot 1 + 6 \cdot 0 + 5 \cdot 8 + 4 \cdot 5$$
$$+ 3 \cdot 9 + 2 \cdot 9 + 1 \cdot 10 = 165$$

Since 165/11 is 15, the sum is a multiple of 11. This checking scheme will detect every single-digit and transposition-of-adjacent-digits error. That is, if while coping an IBSN number you miscopy a single character or transpose two adjacent characters, then the sum ($*$) will no longer be a multiple of 11.

(a) Write a program to accept an ISBN type number (including the hyphens) as input, calculate the sum ($*$), and tell if it is a valid ISBN number. (**Hint:** The number n is divisible by 11 if n Mod 11 is 0.) Before calculating the sum, the program should check that each of the first nine characters is a digit and that the last character is either a digit or an X.

(b) Write a program that begins with a valid ISBN number (such as 0-13-030657-6) and then confirms that the checking scheme described above detects every single-digit and transposition-of-adjacent-digits error by testing every possible error. [**Hint:** If d is a digit to be replaced, then the nine possibilities for the replacements are $(d + 1)$ Mod 10, $(d + 2)$ Mod 10, $(d + 3)$ Mod 10, $\ldots, (d + 9)$ Mod 10.]

10. *User-Operated Directory Assistance.* Have you ever tried to call a person at their business and been told to type in some of the letters of their name on your telephone's keypad in order to obtain their extension? Write a program to simulate this type of directory assistance. Suppose the names and telephone extensions of all the employees of a company are contained in the text file EMPLOYEES.TXT. Each set of three lines of the file has the three pieces of information: last name, first and middle name(s), and telephone extension. (We have filled the file with the names of the U.S. Presidents so that the names will be familiar.) The user should be asked to press buttons for the first three letters of the person's last name followed by the first letter of the first name. For instance, if the person's name is Gary Land, the user would type in 5264. The number 5264 is referred to as the "push-button encoding" of the name. (**Note:** People with different names can have the same push-button encoding— for instance, Herb James and Gary Land.)

The program should declare an array of structures to hold full names, extensions, and push-button encodings. The arrays should be filled while making a single pass through the file and then sorted by push-button encoding. After the user presses four keys on the keypad, the program should display the names and extensions of all the employees having the specified push-button encoding. See Figure 7.15.

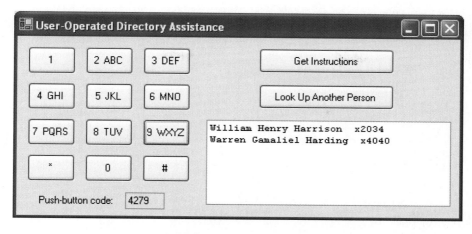

FIGURE 7.15   Sample run of Programming Project 10.

8

Sequential Files

8.1 Sequential Files 412

  ◆ Creating a Sequential File ◆ Adding Items to a Sequential File
  ◆ Structured Exception Handling

8.2 Using Sequential Files 430

  ◆ Sorting Sequential Files ◆ CSV Format
  ◆ Merging Sequential Files ◆ Control Break Processing

8.3 A Case Study: Recording Checks and Deposits 442

  ◆ Design of the Program ◆ User Interface
  ◆ Coding the Program

Summary 454

Programming Projects 454

8.1   Sequential Files

Throughout this text, we have processed data from files created with Windows Notepad and saved on a disk. Such files are stored on disk as a sequence of characters. (Two special characters, called "carriage return" and "line feed", are inserted at the end of each line to indicate where new lines should be started.) These files are called **sequential files** or **text files**. In this section, we create sequential files with Visual Basic programs and develop techniques for using sequential files.

■ Creating a Sequential File

There are many ways to organize data in a sequential file. As done throughout the book so far, we will continue to have each line contain just one piece of data. The following steps create a new sequential file and write data to it:

1. Choose a filename. The first part of a filename can contain up to 156 characters consisting of letters, digits, and other assorted characters (including spaces and periods). The second part of the filename is usually a three-character extension identifying the file type.

2. Choose the path for the folder to contain the file. The *filespec* is the full name of the file; that is, the string consisting of the path to the folder containing the file, followed by a backslash (\ ) and the filename (including the extension). An example of a filespec is "C:\Text files\INCOME FOR APRIL.TXT".

3. Execute a statement of the form

   ```
   Dim sw As IO.StreamWriter = IO.File.CreateText(filespec)
   ```

   where *sw* is a variable name. This process is referred to as **opening a file for output**. It establishes a communications link between the program and the disk drive for storing data onto the disk. It allows data to be output from the program and recorded in the specified file. (Visual Basic takes as the default path the *Debug* subfolder of the *bin* subfolder of the current project. Therefore, if the filename alone is used, the file will be placed in the *Debug* subfolder.) **Note:** The statement

   ```
   Dim sr As IO.StreamReader = IO.File.OpenText(filespec)
   ```

   used earlier in the book is said to **open a file for input**.

4. Place data into the file with the WriteLine method. If *datum* is either a piece of string or numeric data, then the statement

   ```
   sw.WriteLine(datum)
   ```

   writes the information into a new line of the file.

5. After all the data have been recorded in the file, execute

   ```
   sw.Close()
   ```

This statement breaks the communications link with the file and frees up space in memory.

Once a sequential file has been created, you can look at it with Notepad. Alternatively, the entire file can be displayed in a list box.

Example 1   The following program creates a sequential file consisting of several names and then displays the entire contents of the file in a list box. If the list box is too short to display all the items from the file, Visual Basic automatically places a vertical scroll bar on the right side of the list box. The user can then scroll to see the remaining items.

```
Private Sub btnCreateFile_Click(...) Handles btnCreateFile.Click
  'Create the file PIONEERS.TXT
  Dim sw As IO.StreamWriter = IO.File.CreateText("PIONEERS.TXT")
  With sw
    .WriteLine("Atanasoff")
    .WriteLine("Babbage")
    .WriteLine("Codd")
    .WriteLine("Dijkstra")
    .WriteLine("Eckert")
    .WriteLine("Faggin")
    .WriteLine("Gates")
    .WriteLine("Hollerith")
    .Close()
  End With
  Msgbox("The file has been created.", 0, "File Status")
End Sub

Private Sub btnDisplayFile_Click(...) Handles btnDisplayFile.Click
  'Display the contents of the file PIONEERS.TXT in a list box
  Dim sr As IO.StreamReader = IO.File.OpenText("PIONEERS.TXT")
  lstNames.Items.Clear()
  Do While sr.Peek <> -1
    lstNames.Items.Add(sr.ReadLine)
  Loop
  sr.Close()
End Sub
```

[Run, click the first button, and then click the second button.]

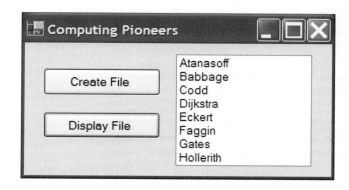

Caution: If an existing file is opened for output, Visual Basic will erase the existing file and create a new empty file.

The WriteLine method allows us to create files just like the Notepad files that appear throughout this text. We already know how to read such files with the ReadLine method. The remaining major task is adding data to the end of a sequential file.

▓ Adding Items to a Sequential File

Data can be added to the end of an existing sequential file with the following steps:

1. Execute the statement

```
Dim sw As IO.StreamWriter = IO.File.AppendText(filespec)
```

where *sw* is a variable name and *filespec* identifies the file. This procedure is called **opening a file for append**. It allows data to be output and recorded at the end of the specified file.

2. Place data into the file with the WriteLine method.

3. After all the data have been recorded into the file, close the file with the statement

```
sw.Close()
```

The IO.File.AppendText option is used to add data to an existing file. However, it also can be used to create a new file. If the file does not exist, then the IO.File.AppendText option creates the file.

The three options, CreateText, OpenText, and AppendText, are referred to as **modes**. A file should not be open in two modes at the same time. For instance, after a file has been opened for output and data have been written to the file, the file should be closed before being opened for input. For instance, had the statement **sw.Close()** in Example 1 been omitted, then the program would have crashed when the second button was clicked.

An attempt to open a nonexistent file for input terminates the program with a FileNotFoundException message box stating that the file could not be found. There is a method that tells us whether a certain file already exists. If the value of

```
IO.File.Exists(filespec)
```

is True, then the specified file exists. Therefore, prudence dictates that files be opened for input with code such as

```
Dim sr As IO.StreamReader
If IO.File.Exists(filespec) Then
  sr = IO.File.OpenText(filespec)
Else
  message = "Either no file has yet been created or the file "
  message &= filespec & " is not where expected."
  MsgBox(message, 0, "File Not Found")
End If
```

There is one file-management operation that we have yet to discuss: changing or deleting an item of information from a sequential file. An individual item of a file cannot be changed or deleted directly. A new file must be created by reading each item from the original file and recording it, with the single item changed or deleted, into the new file. The old file is then erased, and the new file renamed with the name of the original file. Regarding these last two tasks, the Visual Basic statement

```
IO.File.Delete(filespec)
```

removes the specified file from the disk, and the statement

```
IO.File.Move(oldfilespec, newfilespec)
```

changes the filespec of a file. (**Note:** The IO.File.Delete and IO.File.Move methods cannot be used with open files; doing so generates an error message.)

Creating a program that has extensive file handling can be simplified by placing the statement

```
Imports System.IO
```

at the top of the Code window, before the Class frmName statement. Then, there is no need to insert the prefix "IO." before the words StreamReader, StreamWriter, and File.

 Example 2 The following program manages a file of names and years of birth:

OBJECT	PROPERTY	SETTING
frmYOB	Text	Access YOB.TXT
lblName	Text	Name:
txtName		
lblYOB	Text	Year of Birth:
mtxtYOB	Mask	0000
btnAdd	Text	Add Above Person to File
btnLookUp	Text	Look up Year of Birth
btnDelete	Text	Delete Above Person from File

```
Imports System.IO      'Appears at top of code window

Private Sub btnAdd_Click(...) Handles btnAdd.Click
  'Add a person's name and year of birth to file
  Dim message As String
  If (txtName.Text <> "") And (mtxtYOB.Text <> "") Then
    Dim sw As StreamWriter = File.AppendText("YOB.TXT")
    sw.WriteLine(txtName.Text)
    sw.WriteLine(mtxtYOB.Text)
```

```
      sw.Close()
      txtName.Clear()
      mtxtYOB.Clear()
      txtName.Focus()
    Else
      message = "You must enter a name and year of birth."
      MsgBox(message, 0, "Information Incomplete")
    End If
End Sub

Private Sub btnLookUp_Click(...) Handles btnLookUp.Click
  'Determine a person's year of birth
  Dim message As String
  If txtName.Text <> "" Then
    If File.Exists("YOB.TXT") Then
      DisplayYearOfBirth()
    Else
      message = "Either no file has yet been created or "
      message = message & "the file is not where expected."
      MsgBox(message, 0, "File Not Found")
    End If
  Else
    MsgBox("You must enter a name.", 0, "Information Incomplete")
  End If
  txtName.Focus()
End Sub

Private Sub btnDelete_Click(...) Handles btnDelete.Click
  'Remove a person from the file
  Dim message As String
  If txtName.Text <> "" Then
    If File.Exists("YOB.TXT") Then
      DeletePerson()
    Else
      message = "Either no file has yet been created or "
      message = message & "the file is not where expected."
      MsgBox(message, 0, "File Not Found.")
    End If
  Else
    MsgBox("You must enter a name.", 0, "Information Incomplete")
  End If
  txtName.Focus()
End Sub
```

```
Sub DisplayYearOfBirth()
  'Find the year of birth for the person in txtName
  Dim name As String, yob As Integer
  mtxtYOB.Clear()
  Dim sr As StreamReader = File.OpenText("YOB.TXT")
  Do While (name <> txtName.Text) And (sr.Peek <> -1)
    name = sr.ReadLine
    yob = CInt(sr.ReadLine)
  Loop
  If name = txtName.Text Then
    MsgBox(name & " was born in " & yob, 0, "Name Found")
    txtName.Clear()
    mtxtYOB.Clear()
  Else
    MsgBox("Person is not in file.", 0, "")
    txtName.Clear()
  End If
  sr.Close()
End Sub

Sub DeletePerson()
  'Remove the person in txtName from the file
  Dim name As String, yob As Integer
  Dim foundFlag As Boolean = False
  Dim sr As StreamReader = File.OpenText("YOB.TXT")
  Dim sw As StreamWriter = File.CreateText("TEMP.TXT")
  Do While (sr.Peek <> -1)
    name = sr.ReadLine
    yob = CInt(sr.ReadLine)
    If (name <> txtName.Text) Then
      sw.WriteLine(name)
      sw.WriteLine(yob)
    Else
      foundFlag = True
    End If
  Loop
  sr.Close()
  sw.Close()
  File.Delete("YOB.TXT")
  File.Move("TEMP.TXT", "YOB.TXT")    'Rename "TEMP.TXT" As "YOB.TXT"
  If Not foundFlag Then
    MsgBox("The name was not found.", 0, "")
  Else
    txtName.Clear()
    mtxtYOB.Clear()
  End If
End Sub
```

[Run. After several names have been added, the file might look as shown in Figure 8.1.]

```
Barbra
1942
Ringo
1940
Sylvester
1946
```

FIGURE 8.1   **Sample contents of YOB.TXT.**

▨ Structured Exception Handling

There are two main types of problems that a software program might encounter when it executes. The first is a *bug*, which is caused by incorrect or faulty code. Common examples of bugs are typos, using the wrong formula, and accessing the wrong property value. The second type is an *exception*, which, as the term suggests, is a situation that happens occasionally, but not all the time. Two situations where exceptions occur are when invalid data are input and when a file cannot be accessed.

The fundamental difference between bugs and exceptions is that bugs are totally caused by the programmer while exceptions are caused by events beyond the programmer's control. For example, if a user enters a word when the program prompts for a number, an exception is generated and the program terminates abruptly. In this situation, the programmer did not employ faulty logic or mistype. If the user had followed the directions, no problem would have occurred. Even though the user is at fault, however, it is still the programmer's responsibility to anticipate exceptions and to include code to work around their occurrence.

The Visual Studio environment contains powerful tools that programmers can use to find and correct bugs. These debugging tools are discussed extensively in Appendix D. This section describes the techniques used to anticipate and deal with exceptions (in programming terms, called "handling exceptions").

An unexpected problem causes Visual Basic first to throw an exception and then to handle it. If the programmer does not explicitly include exception-handling code in the program, then Visual Basic handles an exception with a default handler. This handler terminates execution, displays the exception's message in a window and highlights the line of code where the exception occurred. Consider a program that contains the following code:

```
Dim taxCredit As Double

Private Sub btnCompute_Click(...) Handles btnCompute.Click
  Dim numDependents As Integer
  numDependents = CInt(InputBox("How many dependents?"))
  taxCredit = 1000 * numDependents
End Sub
```

A user with no dependents might just leave the input dialog box blank and press the OK button. If so, Visual Basic terminates the program and displays the window

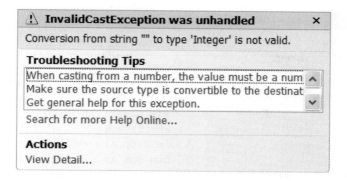

FIGURE 8.2   Exception handled by Visual Basic.

shown in Figure 8.2. (The problem was caused by the fact that the default value in an input dialog box, the empty string, cannot be converted to an integer. Text boxes also have the empty string as their default value.) It also highlights the fourth line of code since the exception was thrown while executing the CInt function. The program also would have crashed had the user typed in an answer like "TWO".

A robust program explicitly handles the previous exception by *protecting* the code in a Try-Catch-Finally block. This allows the program to continue regardless of whether an exception was thrown. The computer tries to execute the code in the Try block. As soon as an exception occurs, execution jumps to the code in the Catch block. Regardless of whether an exception occurred, the code in the Finally block is then executed. The following code is illustrative:

```
Dim taxCredit As Double

Private Sub btnCompute_Click(...) Handles btnCompute.Click
  Dim numDependents As Integer, message As String
  Try
    numDependents = CInt(InputBox("How many dependents?"))
  Catch
    message = "You did not answer the question with an " & _
              "integer value. We will assume your answer is zero."
    MsgBox(message)
    numDependents = 0
  Finally
    taxCredit = 1000 * numDependents
  End Try
End Sub
```

This type of exception handling is known as **data validation**. It catches situations where invalid data cannot be converted to a particular type. An exception is thrown if the user enters data that cannot be converted to an integer using the CInt function. Table 8.1 lists several exceptions and descriptions of why they are thrown.

This Catch block will be executed whenever *any* exception occurs. Visual Basic also allows Try-Catch-Finally blocks to have one or more specialized Catch clauses that only handle a specific type of exception. The general form of a specialized Catch clause is

```
Catch exc As ExceptionName
```

| TABLE 8.1 | Some common exceptions. |

Exception Name	Description and Example
ArgumentOutOfRangeException	An argument to a method is out of range. ```str = "Goodbye".Substring(12,3)```

IndexOutOfRangeException	An array's subscript is out of range.
	```Dim arr(3) As Integer```
	```arr(5) = 2```

InvalidCastException	A value cannot be converted to another type. ```Dim num As Integer = CInt("one")```

NullReferenceException	A method is called on a variable that is set to Nothing.
	```Dim str As String, len As Integer```
	```len = str.Length```

OverflowException	A number too big for the data type is stored.
	```Dim num As Integer = 2000000000```
	```num = 2 * num```

IO.DirectoryNotFoundException	A file within a missing folder is accessed.
	```Dim sr As IO.StreamReader = _```
	``` IO.File.OpenText("C:\BadDir\FILE.TXT")```

IO.FileNotFoundException	A missing file is accessed.
	```Dim sr As IO.StreamReader = _```
	``` IO.File.OpenText("MISSING.TXT")```

IO.EndOfStreamException	Takes place when an attempt to read beyond the end of the file has been made.
	```Dim sr As StreamReader = _```
	``` IO.File.OpenText("NAMES.TXT") 'Empty file```
	```Dim name as String```
	```name = sr.ReadLine```

IO.IOException	Any file handling exception, including those mentioned above. For instance, an attempt is made to delete or re-name an open file, to change the name of a closed file to an already used name, or when a disk drive specified contains no disk. **Note:** If a series of IO exceptions is being tested with Catch clauses, this exception should be the last one tested. ```IO.File.Move(filespec, AlreadyExistingName)```

where the variable *exc* will be assigned the name of the exception. The code in this block will be executed only when the specified exception occurs.

The general form of a Try-Catch-Finally block is

```
Try
  normal code
Catch exc1 As FirstException
  exception-handling code for FirstException
Catch exc2 As SecondException
  exception-handling code for SecondException
  .
  .
```

```
Catch
   exception-handling code for any remaining exceptions
Finally
   clean-up code
End Try
```

The *normal code* is the code that you want to monitor for exceptions. If an exception occurs during execution of any of the statements in this section, Visual Basic transfers control to the code in one of the Catch blocks. As with a Select Case block, the Catch clauses are considered one at a time until the proper exception is located. The last Catch clause in the preceding code functions like the Case Else clause. The *clean-up code* in the Finally block always executes last regardless of whether any *exception-handling code* has executed. In most situations, this code *cleans up* any resources such as files that were opened during the *normal code*. If clean-up is not necessary, then the Finally statement and its corresponding code can be omitted. However, to complete a Try block, a Catch block or a Finally block must appear.

In addition to data validation, a popular use of exception handling is to account for errors when accessing files. Visual Basic has the capability to access files stored on distant servers via the Internet. An exception is thrown if a desired file is missing (IO.FileNotFoundException) or if the file cannot be read because the Internet connection between the computer and the server is broken (IO.IOException).

Example 3   The following program reads the first line from a file on a diskette. The program expects the file to reside in the root directory of a floppy disk. Note that the clean-up code, **sr.Close()**, in the Finally block is enclosed in a Try-Catch block of its own. This protects the Close method from any exceptions that might occur.

```
Private Sub btnDisplay_Click(...) Handles btnDisplay.Click
  Dim sr As IO.StreamReader
  Dim message As String
  Try
     sr = IO.File.OpenText("A:\DataFiles\USPRES.TXT")
     message = "The first President was " & sr.ReadLine & "."
     MsgBox(message, 0, "President")
  Catch exp As IO.DirectoryNotFoundException
     message = "The requested folder is not on the diskette."
     MsgBox(message, 0, "Error")
  Catch exp As IO.FileNotFoundException
     message = "File not in specified folder of diskette."
     MsgBox(exp.Message, 0, "Error")
  Catch exp As IO.IOException
     message = "Check to see if there is a diskette in drive A:."
     MsgBox(message, 0, "Error")
  Finally
     Try
        sr.Close()
```

```
    Catch
        'Disregard any exceptions during the Close() method
    End Try
  End Try
End Sub
```

[Remove the diskette from the A: drive, run the program, and then click on the button.]

[Insert a diskette containing the file USPRES.TXT (in the folder DataFiles) into the A: drive]

▦ Comments

1. Sequential files make efficient use of disk space and are easy to create and use. Their disadvantages are as follows:

   (a) Often a large portion of the file must be read in order to find one specific item.
   (b) An individual item of the file cannot be changed or deleted easily.

   Another type of file, known as a **database**, has neither of the disadvantages of sequential files; however, databases use more disk space, and require greater effort to program. Databases are discussed in Chapter 10.

2. Consider the sequential file shown at the end of Example 2. This file is said to consist of three records of two fields each. A **record** holds all the data about a single individual. Each item of data is called a **field**. The three records are

Barbra	Ringo	Sylvester
1942	1940	1946

   and the two fields are the name field and the year-of-birth field.

3. Any variable declared within a Try-Catch-Finally block has block-level scope. That is, it will not be available after the block terminates.

1. Compose a Sub procedure RemoveDups that could be used in Example 2 to delete from YOB.TXT all repeated records except the first instance of a name matching the name in txtName. (Assume that the existence of YOB.TXT is checked prior to the execution of this Sub procedure.)

2. Compose a Sub procedure AddNoDuplicate to add a name and year of birth to the end of the file YOB.TXT only if the name to be added is not already present in the file. (Assume that the existence of YOB.TXT is checked prior to the execution of this Sub procedure.)

In Exercises 1 through 10, determine the output displayed in the text box when the button is clicked.

1.
```
Private Sub btnDisplay_Click(...) Handles btnDisplay.Click
    Dim salutation As String
    Dim sw As IO.StreamWriter = IO.File.CreateText("GREETINGS.TXT")
    sw.WriteLine("Hello")
    sw.WriteLine("Aloha")
    sw.Close()
    Dim sr As IO.StreamReader = IO.File.OpenText("GREETINGS.TXT")
    salutation = sr.ReadLine
    txtOutput.Text = salutation
    sr.Close()
End Sub
```

2.
```
Private Sub btnDisplay_Click(...) Handles btnDisplay.Click
    Dim salutation, welcome As String
    Dim sw As IO.StreamWriter = IO.File.CreateText("GREETINGS.TXT")
    sw.WriteLine("Hello")
    sw.WriteLine("Aloha")
    sw.Close()
    Dim sr As StreamReader = IO.File.OpenText("GREETINGS.TXT")
    salutation = sr.ReadLine
    welcome = sr.ReadLine
    txtOutput.Text = welcome
    sr.Close()
End Sub
```

3.
```
Private Sub btnDisplay_Click(...) Handles btnDisplay.Click
    Dim salutation As String
    Dim sw As IO.StreamWriter = IO.File.CreateText("GREETINGS.TXT")
    sw.WriteLine("Hello")
    sw.WriteLine("Aloha")
    sw.WriteLine("Bon Jour")
```

```
      sw.Close()
      Dim sr As IO.StreamReader = IO.File.OpenText("GREETINGS.TXT")
      Do While (sr.Peek <> -1)
        salutation = sr.ReadLine
        txtOutput.Text = salutation
      Loop
      sr.Close()
    End Sub
```

4. Assume that the contents of the file GREETING.TXT are as shown in Figure 8.3.

```
                    Hello
                    Aloha
                    Bon Jour
```

FIGURE 8.3   Contents of the file GREETING.TXT.

```
    Private Sub btnDisplay_Click(...) Handles btnDisplay.Click
      Dim file, welcome As String
      file = "GREETING.TXT"
      Dim sw As IO.StreamWriter = IO.File.AppendText(file)
      sw.WriteLine("Buenos Dias")
      sw.Close()
      Dim sr As IO.StreamReader = IO.File.OpenText(file)
      For salutation As Integer = 1 To 4
        welcome = sr.ReadLine
        txtOutput.Text = welcome
      Next
      sr.Close()
    End Sub
```

5.
```
    Private Sub btnDisplay_Click(...) Handles btnDisplay.Click
      Dim num As Integer
      'Assume that txtBox is empty
      Try
        num = CInt(txtBox.Text)
        txtOutput.Text = "Your number is " & num
      Catch
        txtOutput.Text = "You must enter a number."
      End Try
    End Sub
```

6.
```
    Private Sub btnDisplay_Click(...) Handles btnDisplay.Click
      Dim nafta() As String = {"Canada", "United States", "Mexico"}
      Try
        txtOutput.Text = "The third member of NAFTA is " & nafta(3)
      Catch exc As IndexOutOfRangeException
        txtOutput.Text = "Error occurred."
      End Try
    End Sub
```

7.
```
Private Sub btnDisplay_Click(...) Handles btnDisplay.Click
  Try
    Dim usPop As Integer = 300000000      'Approx population of U.S.
    Dim worldPop As Integer
    worldPop = 21 * usPop
    txtOutput.Text = CStr(worldPop)
  Catch exc As ArgumentOutOfRange
    txtOutput.Text = "Oops"
  Catch exc As OverflowException
    txtOutput.Text = "Error occurred."
  End Try
End Sub
```

8.
```
Private Sub btnDisplay_Click(...) Handles btnDisplay.Click
  Dim flower As String = "Bougainvillaea", lastLetter As String
  Try
    lastLetter = flower.Substring(14, 1)
    txtOutput.Text = lastLetter
  Catch exc As InvalidCastException
    txtOutput.Text = "Oops"
  Catch exc As ArgumentOutOfRangeException
    txtOutput.Text = "Error occurred."
  End Try
End Sub
```

9. Assume that the file AGES.TXT is located in the *Debug* subfolder of the project folder *bin* and the first line of the file is "Twenty-one".

```
Private Sub btnDisplay_Click(...) Handles btnDisplay.Click
  Dim sr As IO.StreamReader
  Dim age As Integer
  Try
    sr = IO.File.OpenText("AGES.TXT")     'FileNotFound if fails
    age = CInt(sr.ReadLine)               'InvalidCast if fails
    txtOutput.Text = "Age is " & age
  Catch exc As IO.FileNotFoundException
    txtOutput.Text = "File AGES.TXT not found"
  Catch exc As InvalidCastException
    txtOutput.Text = "File AGES.TXT contains an invalid age."
  Finally
    Try
      sr.Close() 'This code executes no matter what happens above
    Catch
      'Disregard any exceptions thrown during the Close() method
    End Try
  End Try
End Sub
```

10. Redo Exercise 9 with the assumption that the file AGES.TXT is not located in the *Debug* subfolder of the project folder *bin*.

11. Assume that the contents of the file GREETING.TXT are as shown in Figure 8.3. What is the effect of the following program?

```
Private Sub btnDisplay_Click(...) Handles btnDisplay.Click
  Dim g As String
  Dim sr As IO.StreamReader = IO.File.OpenText("GREETING.TXT")
  Dim sw As IO.StreamWriter = IO.File.CreateText("WELCOME.TXT")
  Do While (sr.Peek <> -1)
    g = sr.ReadLine
    If (g <> "Aloha") Then
      sw.WriteLine(g)
    End If
  Loop
  sr.Close()
  sw.Close()
End Sub
```

12. Assume that the contents of the file YOB.TXT are as shown in Figure 8.1 (on page 418). What is the effect of the following program?

```
Private Sub btnDisplay_Click(...) Handles btnDisplay.Click
  Dim flag As Boolean, name As String, year As Integer
  Dim sr As IO.StreamReader = IO.File.OpenText("YOB.TXT")
  Dim sw As IO.StreamWriter = IO.File.CreateText("YOB2.TXT")
  flag = False
  name = ""
  Do While (name < "Clint") And (sr.Peek <> -1)
    name = sr.ReadLine
    year = CInt(sr.ReadLine)
    If name >= "Clint" Then
      sw.WriteLine("Clint")
      sw.WriteLine(1930)
      flag = True
    End If
    sw.WriteLine(name)
    sw.WriteLine(year)
  Loop
  Do While (sr.Peek <> -1)
    name = sr.ReadLine
    year = CInt(sr.ReadLine)
    sw.WriteLine(name)
    sw.WriteLine(year)
  Loop
  If Not flag Then
    sw.WriteLine("Clint")
    sw.WriteLine(1930)
  End If
  sr.Close()
  sw.Close()
End Sub
```

In Exercises 13 through 18, identify any errors. Assume that the contents of the files YOB.TXT and GREETING.TXT are as shown in Figures 8.1 and 8.3.

13.
```
Private Sub btnDisplay_Click(...) Handles btnDisplay.Click
    Dim sw As IO.StreamWriter = IO.File.AppendText(YOB.TXT)
    sw.WriteLine("Michael")
    sw.WriteLine(1965)
    sw.Close()
End Sub
```

14.
```
Private Sub btnDisplay_Click(...) Handles btnDisplay.Click
    Dim name As String, yr As Integer
    Dim sw As IO.StreamWriter = IO.File.CreateText("YOB.TXT")
    name = sw.Readline
    yr = CInt(sw.ReadLine)
    txtOutput.Text = name
    sw.Close()
End Sub
```

15.
```
Private Sub btnDisplay_Click(...) Handles btnDisplay.Click
    'Copy the contents of the file GREETING.TXT into the file NEWGREET.TXT
    Dim name, greeting As String
    Dim sr As IO.StreamReader = IO.File.OpenText("GREETING.TXT")
    name = "NEWGREET.TXT"
    Dim sw As IO.StreamWriter = IO.File.CreateText("name")
    Do While (sr.Peek <> -1)
      greeting = sr.ReadLine
      sw.WriteLine(greeting)
    Loop
    sr.Close()
    sw.Close()
End Sub
```

16.
```
Private Sub btnDisplay_Click(...) Handles btnDisplay.Click
    Dim sw As IO.StreamReader = IO.File.CreateText("GREETING.TXT")
    "GREETING.TXT".Close()
End Sub
```

17.
```
Private Sub btnDisplay_Click(...) Handles btnDisplay.Click
    Try
      Dim age As Integer
      age = CInt(InputBox("Enter your age."))
    Catch
      MsgBox("Invalid age.")
    End Try
    MsgBox("You are " & age & " years old")
End Sub
```

18.
```
Private Sub btnDisplay_Click(...) Handles btnDisplay.Click
    Dim sw As IO.StreamWriter
    Try
      sw = IO.File.CreateFile("A:\LAKES.TXT")
```

```
Catch IO.IOException
  MsgBox("Is there a diskette in the A: drive?")
End Try
sw.Close()
End Sub
```

Exercises 19 through 24 are related and use the data in Table 8.2. The file created in Exercise 19 should be used in Exercises 20 through 24.

19. Write a program to create the sequential file COWBOY.TXT containing the information in Table 8.2.

TABLE 8.2	Prices paid by cowboys for certain items in mid-1800s.	
	Colt Peacemaker	12.20
	Holster	2.00
	Levi Strauss Jeans	1.35
	Saddle	40.00
	Stetson	10.00

20. Suppose the price of saddles is reduced by 20%. Use the file COWBOY.TXT to create a sequential file, COWBOY3.TXT, containing the new price list.

21. Write a program to add the data Winchester rifle, 20.50 to the end of the file COWBOY.TXT.

22. Suppose an order is placed for 3 Colt Peacemakers, 2 Holsters, 10 pairs of Levi Strauss Jeans, 1 saddle, and 4 Stetsons. Write a program to perform the following tasks:

    (a) Create the sequential file ORDER.TXT to hold the numbers 3, 2, 10, 1, and 4.

    (b) Use the files COWBOY.TXT and ORDER.TXT to display a sales receipt with three columns giving the name of each item, the quantity ordered, and the cost for that quantity.

    (c) Compute the total cost of the items and display it at the end of the sales receipt.

23. Write a program to request an additional item and price from the user. Then create a sequential file called COWBOY2.TXT containing all the information in the file COWBOY.TXT with the additional item (and price) inserted in its proper alphabetical sequence. Run the program for both of the following data items: Boots, 20 and Horse, 35.

24. Write a program to allow additional items and prices to be input by the user and added to the end of the file COWBOY.TXT. Include a method to terminate the process.

25. Suppose that the file YOB.TXT contains many names and years and that the names are in alphabetical order. Write a program that requests a name as input and either gives the person's age in 2006 or reports that the person is not in the file. **Note:** Because the names are in alphabetical order, usually there is no need to search to the end of the file.

26. Suppose the file YOBS.TXT contains many names and years. Write a program that creates two files, called SENIORS.TXT and JUNIORS.TXT, and copies all the data on people born before 1940 into the file SENIORS.TXT and the data on the others into the file JUNIORS.TXT.

27. A publisher maintains two sequential files, HARDBACK.TXT and PAPER-BACK.TXT. Each record consists of the name of a book and the quantity in stock. Write a program to access these files. (The program should allow for the case when the book is not in the file.) A run of the program might look as follows:

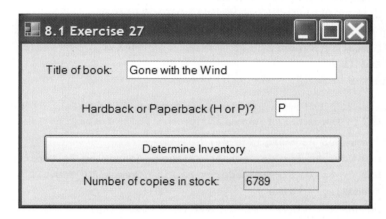

28. Visual Basic cannot erase a file that is open. Attempting to do so generates an exception. Write a short program that uses structured exception handling to handle such an exception.

Solutions to Practice Problems 8.1

1. A record in YOB.TXT is kept if the name in the record does not match the search name, or if the name in the record matches the search name and a flag indicates that the search name has not been found previously.

```
Private Sub RemoveDups()
  Dim name As String, yob As Integer, foundFlag As Boolean
  foundFlag = False
  Dim sr As IO.StreamReader = IO.File.OpenText("YOB.TXT")
  Dim sw As IO.StreamWriter = IO.File.CreateText("TEMP.TXT")
  Do While sr.Peek <> -1
    name = sr.ReadLine
    yob = CInt(sr.ReadLine)
    If name <> txtName.Text Then
      sw.WriteLine(name)
      sw.WriteLine(yob)
    Else
      If Not foundFlag Then
        sw.WriteLine(name)
        sw.WriteLine(yob)
      End If
```

```
        foundFlag = True
      End If
  Loop
  sr.Close()
  sw.Close()
  IO.File.Delete("YOB.TXT")
  IO.File.Move("TEMP.TXT", "YOB.TXT")
  If foundFlag = False Then
    MsgBox("The name was not found.", 0, "")
  Else
    txtName.Clear()
    mtxtYOB.Clear()
  End If
End Sub
```

2. The file YOB.TXT is first opened for input and scanned for the new name. If the name is not found, YOB.TXT is reopened for Append and the name and year of birth are added to the end of the file.

```
Private Sub AddNoDuplicate()
  Dim name As String, yob As Integer, foundFlag As Boolean
  Dim sr As IO.StreamReader = IO.File.OpenText("YOB.TXT")
  foundFlag = False
  Do While (sr.Peek <> -1) And (Not foundFlag)
    name = sr.ReadLine
    yob = CInt(sr.ReadLine)
    If name = txtName.Text Then
      foundFlag = True
    End If
  Loop
  sr.Close()
  If Not foundFlag Then
    Dim sw As IO.StreamWriter = IO.File.AppendText("YOB.TXT")
    sw.WriteLine(txtName.Text)
    sw.WriteLine(mtxtYOB.Text)
    sw.Close()
  End If
End Sub
```

8.2   Using Sequential Files

In addition to being accessed for information, sequential files are regularly updated by modifying certain pieces of data, removing some records, and adding new records. These tasks can be performed most efficiently if the files are first sorted.

▨ Sorting Sequential Files

The records of a sequential file can be sorted on any field by first reading the data into an array of structures and then sorting on an individual element.

Example 1   The following program sorts the sequential file YOB.TXT of the previous section by year of birth:

```
Structure Individual
  Dim name As String
  Dim yearBorn As Integer
End Structure

Private Sub btnSort_Click(...) Handles btnSort.Click
  'Sort data from YOB.TXT file by year of birth
  Dim numPeople As Integer
  numPeople = NumberOfRecords("YOB.TXT")
  Dim person(numPeople - 1) As Individual
  ReadData(person, numPeople)
  SortData(person, numPeople)
  ShowData(person, numPeople)
  WriteData(person, numPeople)
End Sub

Function NumberOfRecords(ByVal filespec As String) As Integer
  Dim name As String, yearBorn As Integer
  Dim n As Integer      'Used to count records
  n = 0
  Dim sr As IO.StreamReader = IO.File.OpenText(filespec)
  Do While (sr.Peek <> -1)
    name = sr.ReadLine
    yearBorn = CInt(sr.ReadLine)
    n += 1      'Increase n by 1
  Loop
  sr.Close()
  Return n
End Function

Sub ReadData(ByRef person() As Individual, ByVal numPeople As Integer)
  'Read data from file into arrays
  Dim sr As IO.StreamReader = IO.File.OpenText("YOB.TXT")
  For index As Integer = 0 To numPeople - 1
    person(index).name = sr.ReadLine
    person(index).yearBorn = CInt(sr.ReadLine)
  Next
  sr.Close()
End Sub

Sub SortData(ByRef person() As Individual, ByVal numPeople As Integer)
  'Bubble sort arrays by year of birth
  For passNum As Integer = 1 To numPeople - 1
    For index As Integer = 1 To numPeople - passNum
      If person(index - 1).yearBorn > person(index).yearBorn Then
        SwapData(person, index - 1)
```

```
        End If
     Next
  Next
End Sub

Sub ShowData(ByVal person() As Individual, ByVal numPeople As Integer)
  'Display the sorted list
  lstShowData.Items.Clear()
  For index As Integer = 0 To numPeople - 1
    lstShowData.Items.Add(person(index).name & "      " & _
                          person(index).yearBorn)
  Next
End Sub

Sub SwapData(ByRef person() As Individual, ByVal index As Integer)
  Dim temp As Individual
  temp = person(index)
  person(index) = person(index + 1)
  person(index + 1) = temp
End Sub

Sub WriteData(ByVal person() As Individual, ByVal numPeople As Integer)
  'Write data back into file
  Dim sw As IO.StreamWriter = IO.File.CreateText("YOB2.TXT")
  For index As Integer = 0 To numPeople - 1
    sw.WriteLine(person(index).name)
    sw.WriteLine(person(index).yearBorn)
  Next
  sw.Close()
End Sub
```

[Run, and then click the button.]

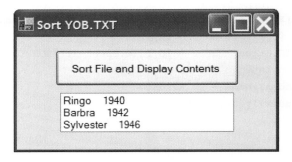

▨ CSV Format

One common way to store data in a text file is to place each record on a single line with the fields separated by commas. This design is known as **CSV format**. (**Note:** CSV is an abbreviation for *Comma Separated Values*.) For example, the YOB.TXT file of the previous section would appear as follows in CSV format:

```
Barbra,1942
Ringo,1940
Sylvester,1946
```

Let's refer to the text file design we have been using as **LSV format**, where LSV stands for Line Separated Values. Also, let's make the convention of placing the prefix *csv* in front of the name of every file using CSV format. For instance, the preceding file would be named "csvYOB.TXT".

Visual Basic has a function called Split that facilitates working with CSV formatted files. Split can convert a line containing commas into a String array where the 0th element contains the text preceding the first comma, the 1st element contains the text between the first and second commas, ..., and the last element contains the text following the last comma. For instance, suppose the String array *employees*() has been declared without an upper bound, and the String variable *line* has the value "Bob, 23.50, 45". Then the statement

```
employees = line.Split(",","c)
```

sets the size of *employees*() to 3 and sets *employees*(0) = "Bob", *employees*(1) = "23.50", and *employees*(2) = "45". In the previous line of code, the character comma is called the **delimiter** for the Split function, and the letter *c* specifies that the comma have data type Character instead of String. (If Option Strict is Off, the letter *c* can be omitted.) Any character can be used as a delimiter. If no character is specified, the Split function will use the space character as delimiter.

Example 2   The following program illustrates the use of the Split function:

```
Private Sub btnRead_Click(...) Handles btnRead.Click
  Dim stateData(), line As String
  line = "California, 1850, Sacramento, Eureka"
  stateData = line.Split(",","c)
  For i As Integer = 0 To stateData.GetUpperBound(0)
    stateData(i) = stateData(i).Trim    'Get rid of extraneous spaces
    lstOutput.Items.Add(stateData(i))
  Next
End Sub
```

[Run, and then click the button. The following is displayed in the list box.]

```
California
1850
Sacramento
Eureka
```

Sequential files created with Visual Basic 6.0 are usually in CSV format. However, they can be converted easily to LSV format if desired.

Example 3   The following program converts any CSV file to an LSV file and then displays the contents of the new file. We will assume that the file to be converted is located in the *Debug* subfolder for the program.

```
Private Sub btnConvert_Click(...) Handles btnConvert.Click
  Dim line, fields(), fromFile, toFile As String
  Dim sr As IO.StreamReader
  Dim sw As IO.StreamWriter
  fromFile = InputBox("Name of original file:", "Convert CSV to LSV")
  toFile = InputBox("Name of converted file:", "Convert CSV to LSV")
  sr = IO.File.OpenText(fromFile)
  sw = IO.File.CreateText(toFile)
  Do While (sr.Peek <> -1)
    line = sr.ReadLine
    fields = line.Split(","c)
    For i As Integer = 0 To fields.GetUpperBound(0)
      sw.WriteLine(fields(i).Trim)
    Next
  Loop
  sr.Close()
  sw.Close()
  sr = IO.File.OpenText(toFile)
  Do While (sr.Peek <> -1)
    lstFile.Items.Add(sr.ReadLine)
  Loop
  sr.Close()
End Sub
```

[Run, press the button, and respond to the two requests with csvSTATES.TXT and STATES.TXT. Assume that the file csvSTATES.TXT contains the two lines "California, 1850, Sacramento, Eureka" and "New York, 1788, Albany, Excelsior". The following will be displayed in the list box.]

```
California
1850
Sacramento
Eureka
New York
1788
Albany
Excelsior
```

The reverse of the Split function is the Join function, which concatenates the elements of a string array into a string containing the elements separated by a specified delimiter. For instance, the code

```
Dim greatLakes() As String = _
    {"Huron", "Ontario", "Michigan", "Erie", "Superior"}
Dim lakes As String
lakes = Join(greatLakes, ",")
txtOutput.Text = lakes
```

produces the output

```
Huron,Ontario,Michigan,Erie,Superior
```

▨ Merging Sequential Files

In Section 7.2, we considered an algorithm for merging two ordered arrays. This same algorithm can be applied to merging two ordered files.

Suppose you have two ordered LSV files (possibly with certain items appearing in both files), and you want to merge them into a third ordered file (without duplications). The technique for creating the third file is as follows:

1. Open the two ordered files for input, and open a third file for output.

2. Try to get an item of data from each file.

3. Repeat the following steps until an item of data is not available in one of the files:

   (a) If one item precedes the other, write it into the third file and try to get another item of data from its file.

   (b) If the two items are identical, write one into the third file and try to get another item of data from each of the two ordered files.

4. At this point, an item of data has most likely been retrieved from one of the files and not yet written to the third file. In this case, write that item and all remaining items in that file to the third file.

5. Close the three files.

 Example 4 The following program merges two ordered files of numbers into a third ordered file:

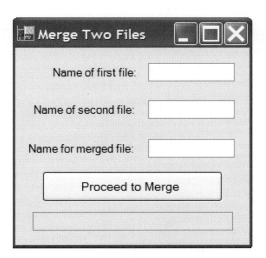

OBJECT	PROPERTY	SETTING
frmMerge	Text	Merge Two Files
lblNameFirst	Text	Name of first file:
txtNameFirst		
lblNameSecond	Text	Name of second file:
txtNameSecond		
lblNameMerged	Text	Name for merged file:
txtNameMerged		
btnProceed	Text	Proceed to Merge
txtProgress	ReadOnly	True

```
Private Sub btnProceed_Click(...) Handles btnProceed.Click
  'Merge two ordered files
  Dim file1, file2, file3 As String
  Dim have1data, have2data As Boolean
  Dim num1, num2 As Double
  Dim recCount As Integer     'Number of records in merged file
```

```
      file1 = txtNameFirst.Text
      file2 = txtNameSecond.Text
      file3 = txtNameMerged.Text
      Dim sr1 As IO.StreamReader = IO.File.OpenText(file1)
      Dim sr2 As IO.StreamReader = IO.File.OpenText(file2)
      Dim sw As IO.StreamWriter = IO.File.CreateText(file3)
      have1data = Get1data(num1, sr1)
      have2data = Get2data(num2, sr2)
      recCount = 0
      Do While (have1data And have2data)
        Select Case num1
          Case Is < num2
            sw.WriteLine(num1)
            have1data = Get1data(num1, sr1)
          Case Is > num2
            sw.WriteLine(num2)
            have2data = Get2data(num2, sr2)
          Case num2
            sw.WriteLine(num1)
            have1data = Get1data(num1, sr1)
            have2data = Get2data(num2, sr2)
        End Select
        recCount += 1
      Loop
      Do While have1data
        sw.WriteLine(num1)
        recCount += 1
        have1data = Get1data(num1, sr1)
      Loop
      Do While have2data
        sw.WriteLine(num2)
        recCount += 1
        have2data = Get2data(num2, sr2)
      Loop
      sr1.Close()
      sr2.Close()
      sw.Close()
      txtProgress.Text = recCount & " numbers written to " & file3
    End Sub

    Function Get1data(ByRef num1 As Double, ByVal sr1 As IO.StreamReader) _
          As Boolean
      'If possible, read next value from file 1
      'Return value of True when new data are read; False if data
      'not available
      If (sr1.Peek <> -1) Then
        num1 = CDbl(sr1.ReadLine)
        Return True
```

```
    Else
      Return False
    End If
End Function

Function Get2data(ByRef num2 As Double, ByVal sr2 As IO.StreamReader) _
        As Boolean
  'If possible, read next value from file 2
  'Return value True when new data are read; False if data not available
  If (sr2.Peek <> -1) Then
    num2 = CDbl(sr2.ReadLine)
    Return True
  Else
    Return False
  End If
End Function
```

▇ Control Break Processing

Suppose a small real estate company stores its sales data for a year in a sequential file in which each record contains four fields: month of sale, day of sale (1 through 31), address, and price. Typical data for the sales of the first quarter of a year are shown in Figure 8.4. The records are ordered by date of sale.

Month	Day	Address	Price
January	9	102 Elm Street	$203,000
January	20	1 Main Street	$315,200
January	25	5 Maple Street	$123,450
February	15	1 Center Street	$100,000
February	23	2 Vista Drive	$145,320
March	15	205 Rodeo Circle	$389,100

FIGURE 8.4   Real estate sales for first quarter of year.

Figure 8.5 shows the output of a program that displays the total sales for the quarter year, with a subtotal for each month.

A program to produce the output of Figure 8.5 must calculate a subtotal at the end of each month. The variable holding the month triggers a subtotal whenever its value changes. Such a variable is called a **control variable**, and each change of its value is called a **break**.

Example 5   The following program produces the output of Figure 8.5. The data of Figure 8.4 are stored in the sequential file HOMESALE.TXT. The program allows for months with no sales. Because monthly subtotals will be displayed, the variable holding the current month is an appropriate control variable.

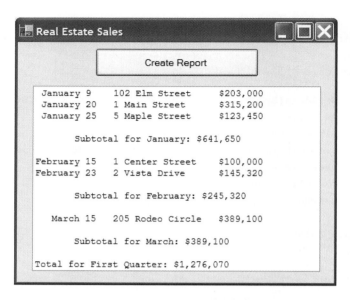

FIGURE 8.5   Output of Example 5.

```
Private Sub btnCreateReport_Click(...) Handles btnCreateReport.Click
  'Display home sales by month
  Dim currentMonth As String = "", newMonth As String = ""
  Dim address As String = "", subtotalText As String = ""
  Dim dayNum As Integer, doneFlag As Boolean
  Dim price, monthTotal, yearTotal As Double
  Dim fmtStr As String = "{0,8} {1,-5}{2,-17}{3,10:C0}"
  Dim sr As IO.StreamReader = IO.File.OpenText("HOMESALE.TXT")
  doneFlag = False          'Flag to indicate end of list
  Do While (Not doneFlag)
    If (sr.Peek <> -1) Then
      newMonth = sr.ReadLine
      dayNum = CInt(sr.ReadLine)
      address = sr.ReadLine
      price = CDbl(sr.ReadLine)
    Else
      doneFlag = True                    'End of list
    End If
    If (newMonth <> currentMonth) Or doneFlag Then    'Ctrl break processing
      If currentMonth <> "" Then          'Don't print subtotal before 1st month
        lstReport.Items.Add("")
        subtotalText = "Subtotal for " & currentMonth & ": "
        lstReport.Items.Add("        " & subtotalText & _
                        FormatCurrency(monthTotal, 0))
        lstReport.Items.Add("")
      End If
      currentMonth = newMonth
      monthTotal = 0
    End If
```

```
    If (Not doneFlag) Then
      lstReport.Items.Add(String.Format(fmtStr, newMonth, dayNum, _
                          address, price))
      yearTotal += price
    End If
    monthTotal += price
  Loop
  sr.Close()
  lstReport.Items.Add("Total for First Quarter: " & _
                FormatCurrency(yearTotal, 0))
End Sub
```

▦ Comment

In the examples of this and the previous section, the files to be processed have been opened and closed within a single procedure. However, the solution to some programming problems requires that a file be opened just once the instant the program is run and stay open until the program is terminated. This is easily accomplished by opening the file in the form's Load event procedure and coding the Close method and End statement in the click event procedure for a button labeled "Quit."

Practice Problems 8.2

1. The program in Example 4 contains three Do loops. Explain why at most one of the last two loops will be executed. Under what circumstances will neither of the last two loops be executed?

2. Modify the program in Example 4 so that duplicate items will be repeated in the merged file.

EXERCISES 8.2

In Exercises 1 through 4, determine the output produced by the lines of code.

1.
```
Dim allVowelWords(), line As String
line = "abstemious,dialogue,facetious,sequoia,education"
allVowelWords = line.Split(","c)
txtOutput.Text = allVowelWords(2)
```

2.
```
Dim orderWords() As String   'Letters in alphabetical order
Dim line As String = "bijoux, biopsy, almost"
orderWords = line.Split(","c)
txtOutput.Text = orderWords(orderWords.GetUpperBound(0)).Trim
```

3.
```
Dim notes() As String = {"A","B","C","D","E","F","G"}
txtOutput.Text = Join(notes, ",")
```

4. ```
Dim line As String = "I came, I saw, I conquered"
Dim temp() As String
temp = line.Split(",","c)
txtOutput.Text = Join(temp, ",")
```

**Exercises 5 through 8 are related. They create and maintain the sequential file AVERAGE.TXT to hold batting averages of baseball players.**

5. Suppose the season is about to begin. Compose a program to create the sequential file containing the name of each player, his times at bat, and his number of hits. The program should allow the user to type a name into a text box and then click a button to add a record to the file. The times at bat and number of hits initially should be set to 0. (**Hint:** Open the file for Output in the form's Load event procedure and Close the file when a "Quit" button is clicked.)

6. Each day, the statistics from the previous day's games should be used to update the file. Write a program to read the records one at a time and allow the user to enter the number of times at bat and the number of hits in yesterday's game for each player in appropriate text boxes on a form. When a button is clicked, the program should update the file by adding these numbers to the previous figures. **Hint:** Open files in the form's Load event procedure. Close the files and end the program when all data have been processed.

7. Several players are added to the league. Compose a program to update the file.

8. Compose a program to sort the file AVERAGE.TXT with respect to batting averages and display the players with the top 10 batting averages. **Hint:** The file should be read once to determine the number of players and again to load the players into an array.

9. Write a program to convert any LSV file into a CSV file. **Note:** In addition to supplying the filenames, the user also must provide the number of fields in each record of the LSV file.

10. The file csvAgeAtInaugural.TXT contains the name and age at inaugural for each of the first 43 U.S. Presidents. (The first record is "George Washington, 57".) Write a program that requests an age as input and then displays in a list box the names of all U.S. Presidents of that age at their inaugurals.

11. Each record of the file csvUSSTATES.TXT has five fields: state name, abbreviation, when it entered the union, area (in square miles), population in 2000. The file is ordered by when the states entered the union. (The first record is "Delaware, DE, Dec. 1787, 2489, 759000".) Write a program to create a new file containing the same records, but ordered alphabetically by the state's abbreviation. The program also should display the contents of the new file, neatly formatted into columns, in a list box.

12. A sentence is called a *chain-link* sentence if the last two letters of each word are the same as the first two letters of the next word, for instance, "The head administrator organized education on online networks." Write a program that accepts a sentence as input and determines whether it is a chain-link sentence. **Hint:** Use the space character as a delimiter for the Split method. To be robust, you can first remove commas by executing the statement `sentence = sentence.Replace(",", "")`,
```

which replaces all commas in *sentence* with the empty string. Test the program with the sentence "Broadcast station, once certified, educates estimable legions."

Exercises 13 and 14 refer to the ordered file BLOCK.TXT containing the names of people on your block and the ordered file TIMES.TXT containing the names of all people who subscribe to the *New York Times*.

13. Write a program that creates a file consisting of the names of all people on your block who subscribe to the *New York Times*.

14. Write a program that creates a file consisting of the names of all *New York Times* subscribers who do not live on your block.

15. Suppose that a file of positive integers is in ascending order. Write a program to determine the maximum number of times any integer is repeated in the file. (For instance, if the entries in the file are 5, 5, 6, 6, 6, and 10, then the output is 3.)

16. Suppose that each record of the file SALES.TXT contains a salesperson's name and the dollar amount of a sale, and the records are ordered by the names. Write a program to display the name, number of sales, and average sale amount for each salesperson. For instance, if the first eight lines of the file contain the data: Adams, 123.45, Adams, 432.15, Brown, 89.95, Cook, 500.00, then the first two entries of the output would be

Salesperson	Number of Sales	Average Sale Amount
Adams	2	$277.80
Brown	1	$89.95

17. An elementary school holds a raffle to raise funds. Suppose that each record of the file RAFFLE.TXT contains a student's grade (1 through 6), name, and the number of raffle tickets sold and that the records are ordered by grade. Write a program using a control break to display the number of tickets sold by each grade and the total number of tickets sold.

18. *Multiple Control Breaks.* Suppose the sorted sequential file CENSUS.TXT contains names of all residents of a state, where each record consists of two lines of the form "last Name", "first Name". Write a program to determine, in one pass through the file, the most common last name and most common full name. (**Note:** In the unlikely event of a tie, the program should display the first occurring name.) For instance, the output in the list box might be as follows:

```
The most common last name is Brown.
The most common full name is John Smith.
```

In Exercises 19 and 20, suppose that the file MASTER.TXT contains the names and phone numbers of all members of an organization, where the records are ordered by name.

19. Suppose that the ordered file MOVED.TXT contains the names and new phone numbers of all members who have changed their phone numbers. Write a program to update the file MASTER.TXT.

20. Suppose that the ordered file QUIT.TXT contains the names of all members who have left the organization. Write a program to update the file MASTER.TXT.

Solutions to Practice Problems 8.2

1. Execution proceeds beyond the first Do loop only when the Peek method returns −1 for one of the input files. Because each of the last two Do loops executes only if the Peek method does not return −1, at most one loop can execute. Neither of the last two loops will be executed if each input file is empty or if the last entries of the files are the same.

2. Change the Select Case block to the following:

```
Select Case num1
  Case Is <= num2
    sw.WriteLine(num1)
    have1data = Get1data(num1, sr1)
  Case Is > num2
    sw.WriteLine(num2)
    have2data = Get2data(num2, sr2)
End Select
```

8.3 A Case Study: Recording Checks and Deposits

The purpose of this section is to take you through the design and implementation of a quality program for personal checkbook management. Nothing in this chapter shows off the power of Visual Basic better than the program in this section. That a user-friendly checkbook management program can be written in less than seven pages of code clearly shows Visual Basic's ability to improve the productivity of programmers. It is easy to imagine an entire finance program, similar to programs that have generated millions of dollars of sales, being written in only a few weeks by using Visual Basic!

■ Design of the Program

Though there are many commercial programs available for personal financial management, they include so many bells and whistles that their original purposes—keeping track of transactions and reporting balances—have become obscured. The program in this section was designed specifically as a checkbook program. It keeps track of expenditures and deposits and produces a report. Adding a reconciliation feature would be easy enough, although we did not include one.

The program is supposed to be user friendly. Therefore, it showcases many of the techniques and tools available in Visual Basic.

The general design goals for the program included the following abilities:

- Automatically enter the user's name on each check and deposit slip.
- Automatically provide the next consecutive check or deposit slip number. (The user can override this feature if necessary.)
- Automatically provide the date. (Again, this feature can be overridden.)
- For each check, record the payee, the amount, and optionally a memo.
- For each deposit slip, record the source, the amount, and optionally a memo.
- Display the current balance at all times.
- Produce a report detailing all transactions.

User Interface

With Visual Basic, we can place a replica of a check or deposit slip on the screen and let the user supply the information as if actually filling out a check or deposit slip. Figure 8.6 shows the form in its check mode. At the bottom of the check are a label and a check box for the current balance and four buttons.

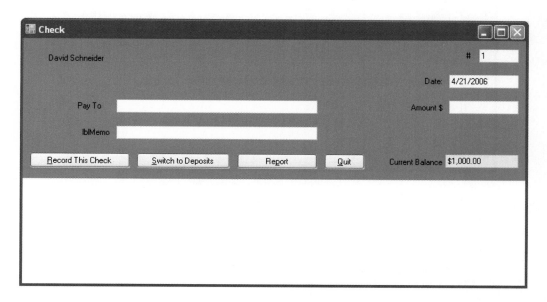

FIGURE 8.6   Template for entering a check.

The first time the program is run, the user is asked for his or her name, the starting balance, and the numbers of the first check and deposit slip. Suppose the user's name is David Schneider, the starting balance is $1000, and both the first check number and deposit slip number are 1. Figure 8.6 shows the form after the four pieces of input. The upper part of the form looks like a check. The form has a color of light turquoise blue (or cyan) when in check mode. The Date box is automatically set to today's date, but can be altered by the user. The user fills in the payee, amount, and optionally a memo. When the user pushes the Record This Check button, the information is written to a file, the balance is updated, and check number 2 appears.

To record a deposit, the user pushes the Switch to Deposits button. The form then appears as in Figure 8.7. The form's title bar now reads Deposit Slip, the words Pay To change to Source, and the color of the form changes to yellow. Also, in the buttons at the bottom of the slip, the words Check and Deposit are interchanged. A deposit is recorded in much the same way as a check. When the Report button is pushed, a report similar to the one in Figure 8.8 is displayed below the buttons.

The common design for the check and deposit slip allows one set of controls to be used for both items. The text of the label lblName is set to the user's name, while the text of the label lblToFrom will change back and forth between Pay To and Source.

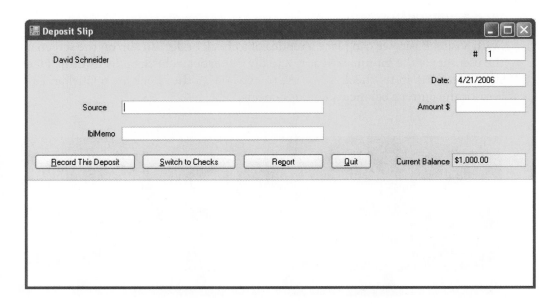

FIGURE 8.7   **Template for entering a deposit.**

Name: David Schneider	Starting balance: $1, 000.00		5/6/2006
Date	Transaction	Amount	Balance
4/21/2006	Check #: 1 Paid to: Land's End Memo: shirts	$75.95	$924.05
4/29/2006	Check #: 2 Paid to: Bethesda Coop Memo: groceries	$125.00	$799.05
5/5/2006	Deposit #: 1 Source: Prentice Hall Memo: typing expenses	$245.00	$1,044.05
	Ending Balance: $1,044.05		

FIGURE 8.8   **Sample transaction report.**

Table 8.3 lists the objects and their initial property settings. Because the program will always begin by displaying the next check, all the text for the labels and the BackColor property of the form could have been set at design time. We chose instead to leave these assignments to the SetupCheck method, which is normally used to switch from deposit entry to check entry, but also can be called by the form's Load event procedure to prepare the initial mode (check or deposit) for the form.

TABLE 8.3   Objects and initial property settings for the checkbook management program.

Object	Property	Setting
frmAccount		
lblName	Font Size	10pt
lblNum	Text	#
txtNum		
lblDate	Text	Date:
txtDate		
lblToFrom		
txtToFrom		
lblAmount	Text	Amount $
txtAmount		
lblMemo	Text	Memo
txtMemo		
btnRecord	Text	&Record This Check
btnMode	Text	&Switch to Deposits
btnReport	Text	&Report
btnQuit	Text	&Quit
lblCurBal	Text	Current Balance
txtBalance	ReadOnly	True
lstTransactions	Font	Courier New

The transactions are stored in CSV format in a text file named CHECKBOOK.TXT. The first line of the file contains four entries: the name to appear on the check and deposit slip, the starting balance, the number of the first check, and the number of the first deposit slip. After that, each transaction is recorded on one line as a sequence of eight items: the type of transaction, the contents of txtToFrom, the current balance, the number of the last check, the number of the last deposit slip, the amount of money, the memo, and the date.

■ Coding the Program

The second row of Figure 8.9 identifies the different events to which the program must respond. Table 8.4 lists the corresponding event procedures and the general procedures they call.

Let's examine each event procedure:

1. *frmAccount_Load* first calls the InitializeData Sub procedure to process the text file. This procedure first looks to see if the file CHECKBOOK.TXT exists. The function IO.File.Exists returns True if the file exists and False otherwise. If CHECKBOOK.TXT does exist, the procedure reads through the entire file to determine all information needed to proceed. If CHECKBOOK.TXT does not exist, the Sub procedure prompts the user for the name to appear on the checks and deposit slips, the starting balance, and the numbers of the first check and deposit slip and then writes these items to the text file. The event procedure calls the SetupCheck Sub procedure next to set the transaction type to Check and sets the appropriate text

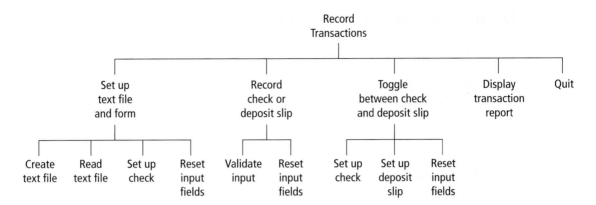

FIGURE 8.9 Hierarchy chart for checkbook management program.

TABLE 8.4		Tasks and their procedures.
	Task	Procedure
1.	Set up text file and form	frmAccount_Load
	1.1 Create text file	InitializeData
	1.2 Read text file	InitializeData
	1.3 Set up check	SetupCheck
	1.4 Reset input fields	ResetInput
2.	Record check or deposit slip	btnRecord_Click
	2.1 Validate input	DataValid
	2.2 Reset input fields	ResetInput
3.	Toggle between check & deposit slip	btnMode_Click
	3.1 Set up check	SetupCheck
	3.2 Set up deposit slip	SetupDeposit
	3.3 Reset input fields	ResetInput
4.	Display transaction report	btnReport_Click
5.	Quit	btnQuit_Click

and background color for a check. The event procedure then calls ResetInput, which initializes all the text boxes.

The InitializeData Sub procedure employs structured exception handling to protect the code from four possible failures: The text file cannot be read, the text file has an invalid format, the user's input cannot be stored in a new file, and the user's input is invalid. In the first two situations, the program works around the exception by creating a new text file. In the third and fourth situation, the program displays an error message and terminates.

2. ***btnRecord_Click*** first confirms that the required fields contain valid entries. This is accomplished by calling the function DataValid. If the value returned is True, then btnRecord_Click updates the current balance, opens the text file in append mode, writes eight pieces of data to the file, and then closes the file. When DataValid returns False, the function itself pops up a message box to tell the user where information is needed or invalid. The user must type in the information and then press the Record button again. Both procedures employ structured exception

handling to protect their code from failures. The btnRecord_Click procedure ensures that the new data can be stored in the file. If it can't, then an error message is displayed and the program terminates. The DataValid function ensures that the user's input is valid. If either the amount or number field is not a number, the InvalidCastException is thrown. The Catch block handles this exception by displaying an appropriate message asking the user to reenter the information.

3. *btnMode_Click* toggles back and forth from a check to a deposit slip. It calls SetupCheck, or its analog SetupDeposit, and then calls ResetInput.

4. *btnReport_Click* displays a complete history of all transactions as shown in Figure 8.8. This procedure reads the text file and displays each entry along with the beginning and ending balances. This procedure employs structured exception handling to protect its code from IO failures when the text file cannot be read correctly or has an invalid format.

5. *btnQuit_Click* ends the program.

```
#Region "Class-level variables"
  'Text file that stores information
  Dim fileName As String = "CHECKBOOK.TXT"
  'Variables used for each entry
  Dim mode As Boolean          'Mode: check = True, deposit slip = False
  Dim nameOnChk As String      'Name to appear on checks
  Dim lastCkNum As Integer     'Number of last check written
  Dim lastDpNum As Integer     'Number of last deposit slip processed
  Dim curBal As Double         'Current balance in account
#End Region


Private Sub frmAccount_Load(...) Handles MyBase.Load
  'Sets the class variables from a new or existing text file
  InitializeData()
  'Set name and balance labels
  lblName.Text = nameOnChk
  txtBalance.Text = FormatCurrency(curBal)
  'Set the date field to the current date
  'The value of CStr(Now) is a string consisting of the current
  'date (m/d/yr) followed by a space and the current time. The current
  'date is the substring consisting of the characters preceding the space
  Dim curDateTime As String = CStr(Now)
  txtDate.Text = curDateTime.Substring(0, curDateTime.IndexOf(" "))
  'Setup the form for a check
  SetupCheck()
  'Reset the input fields
  ResetInput()
End Sub


Private Sub InitializeData()
  'Reads or creates the file and sets the class-level variables
  Dim sr As IO.StreamReader
  Dim exists As Boolean = False   'Set to True if text file exists
```

```
Try
    'If text file exists, then read it.
    If IO.File.Exists(fileName) Then
        Dim data() As String   'Holds the data read from the file
        sr = IO.File.OpenText(fileName)
        'Split the first line of the text file using the separator
        data = sr.ReadLine.Split(","c)
        'Recover name to appear on checks, current balance, number of
        'last check written and number of last deposit slip processed
        nameOnChk = data(0)
        curBal = CDbl(data(1))
        lastCkNum = CInt(data(2))
        lastDpNum = CInt(data(3))
        Do While (sr.Peek <> -1)
            data = sr.ReadLine.Split(","c)
            curBal = CDbl(data(2))
            lastCkNum = CInt(data(3))
            lastDpNum = CInt(data(4))
        Loop
        exists = True
    End If
Catch exc As IO.IOException
    'Display error message and set flag to False
    MsgBox("Could not read " & fileName & _
            ", will create a new file.", 0, "Error")
    exists = False
Catch
    'Display error message and set flag to False
    MsgBox("File " & fileName & _
            " is invalid, will create a new one.", 0, "Error")
    exists = False
Finally
    'Close the reader no matter what happens above
    Try
        sr.Close()
    Catch
    End Try
End Try
'If the file doesn't exist, then create one.
If Not exists Then
    Dim sw As IO.StreamWriter
    Try
        'Text file does not exist, so get initial data from user
        nameOnChk = InputBox("Name to appear on checks:")
        curBal = CDbl(InputBox("Starting Balance:"))
```

```
      'Get numbers of last check and deposit slip
      lastCkNum = CInt(InputBox("Number of first check:")) - 1
      lastDpNum = CInt(InputBox("Number of first deposit slip:")) - 1
      'First record in text file records name to appear on checks
      'plus initial data for account
      Dim outputLine() As String = {nameOnChk, CStr(curBal), _
                                   CStr(lastCkNum), CStr(lastDpNum)}
      sw = IO.File.CreateText(fileName)
      sw.WriteLine(Join(outputLine, ","))
    Catch exc As IO.IOException
      'If an exception occurs then display message and quit
      MsgBox("Cannot store data into file " & fileName & _
             ". Program terminating.", 0, "Error")
      End
    Catch
      'If a number cannot be converted then display message and quit
      MsgBox("Invalid number. Program terminating.", 0, "Error")
      End
    Finally
      'Close the writer no matter what happens above
      Try
        sw.Close()
      Catch
      End Try
    End Try
  End If
End Sub

Private Sub btnRecord_Click(...) Handles btnRecord.Click
  'Store the input into the text file
  Dim amt As Double
  Dim transType As String
  'Only store if all required fields are filled and valid
  If DataValid() Then
    amt = CDbl(txtAmount.Text)
    'Adjust balance by amount depending on check or deposit slip mode
    If mode Then
      curBal = curBal - amt
      lastCkNum = CInt(txtNum.Text)
      transType = "Check"
    Else
      curBal += amt
      lastDpNum = CInt(txtNum.Text)
      transType = "Deposit"
    End If
    txtBalance.Text = FormatCurrency(curBal)
```

```
          'String array contains info to be stored
          Dim transOutput() As String = {transType, txtToFrom.Text, _
            CStr(curBal), CStr(lastCkNum), CStr(lastDpNum), CStr(amt), _
            txtMemo.Text, txtDate.Text}
          Dim sw As IO.StreamWriter
          Try
             'Append the info to the text file, separated by the separator
             sw = IO.File.AppendText(fileName)
             sw.WriteLine(Join(transOutput, ","))
          Catch
             'Display error message and quit
             MsgBox("Could not store data into file " & fileName & _
                   ". Program terminating.", 0, "Error")
             End
          Finally
             'Close writer no matter what happens above
             Try
                sw.Close()
             Catch
             End Try
          End Try
          'Reset input controls to blank for next entry
          ResetInput()
        End If
      End Sub


      Function DataValid() As Boolean
        'Returns True if all data are valid, or displays a message if not
        Dim errorMessage As String
        'If one of the four required pieces of information
        'is missing, assign its name to errorMessage
        errorMessage = ""
        If txtToFrom.Text.Trim = "" Then
          If mode Then
            errorMessage = "Pay To"
          Else
            errorMessage = "Source"
          End If
          txtToFrom.Focus()
        ElseIf txtAmount.Text.Trim = "" Then
          errorMessage = "Amount"
          txtAmount.Focus()
        End If
        'If no errors yet then check syntax of the two numerical fields
        If errorMessage = "" Then
          'Check syntax of the amount field (Double)
          Try
            If CDbl(txtAmount.Text) <= 0 Then
              errorMessage = "The amount must be greater than zero."
```

```
            txtAmount.Focus()
         End If
      Catch exc As InvalidCastException
         errorMessage = "The amount " & txtAmount.Text & " is invalid."
         txtAmount.Focus()
      End Try
   Else
      errorMessage = "The '" & errorMessage & "' field must be filled."
   End If
   'Display error message if available
   If errorMessage = "" Then
      'All required data fields have been filled; recording can proceed
      Return True
   Else
      'Advise user of invalid data
      MsgBox(errorMessage & " Please try again.", 0, "")
      Return False
   End If
End Function

Private Sub btnMode_Click(...) Handles btnMode.Click
   'Toggle mode between Check and Deposit Slip
   If mode Then
      SetupDeposit()
   Else
      SetupCheck()
   End If
   'Set fields for next entry
   ResetInput()
End Sub

Sub SetupCheck()
   'Prepare form for the entry of a check
   mode = True
   Me.Text = "Check"    'Sets the title bar of the form
   lblToFrom.Text = "Pay To"
   btnRecord.Text = "&Record This Check"
   btnMode.Text = "&Switch to Deposits"
   Me.BackColor = Color.Cyan
End Sub

Sub SetupDeposit()
   'Prepare form for the entry of a deposit
   mode = False
   Me.Text = "Deposit Slip"    'Sets the title bar of the form
   lblToFrom.Text = "Source"
   btnRecord.Text = "&Record This Deposit"
   btnMode.Text = "&Switch to Checks"
   Me.BackColor = Color.Yellow
End Sub
```

```
Sub ResetInput()
  'Reset report listing
  lstTransactions.Items.Clear()
  'Reset all text entry fields except date
  txtToFrom.Clear()
  txtAmount.Clear()
  txtMemo.Clear()
  If mode Then
    'Make txtNum reflect next check number
    txtNum.Text = CStr(lastCkNum + 1)
  Else
    'Make txtNum reflect next deposit slip number
    txtNum.Text = CStr(lastDpNum + 1)
  End If
  'Set focus on to/from control for the next entry
  txtToFrom.Focus()
End Sub

Private Sub btnReport_Click(...) Handles btnReport.Click
  'Display report of all transactions in the text file
  Dim fmtStr As String = "{0, -18} {1, -35} {2, -12} {3, -12}"
  Dim data() As String      'Holds the data for each entry
  Dim balance As String
  Dim sr As IO.StreamReader
  Dim curDateTime As String = CStr(Now)
  curDateTime = curDateTime.Substring(0, curDateTime.IndexOf(" "))
  lstTransactions.Items.Clear()
  Try
    'Display headings for the transaction data
    sr = IO.File.OpenText(fileName)
    data = sr.ReadLine.Split(","c)
    balance = data(1)
    'Display the name, starting balance, and today's date
    lstTransactions.Items.Add(String.Format(fmtStr, data(0), _
        "Starting Balance: " & FormatCurrency(balance), "", curDateTime))
    lstTransactions.Items.Add("")
    lstTransactions.Items.Add(String.Format(fmtStr, "Date", _
            "Transaction", "Amount", "Balance"))
    fmtStr = "{0,-18} {1,-35} {2,-12:C} {3,-12:C}"
    'Loop until the end of file is reached
    Do While (sr.Peek <> -1)
      'Add a blank line in between entries
      lstTransactions.Items.Add("")
```

```vb
      'Fields are separated by a separator on one line for each entry
      data = sr.ReadLine.Split(","c)
      If data(0) = "Check" Then    'The entry is a check
        lstTransactions.Items.Add(String.Format(fmtStr, data(7), _
          "Check #: " & data(3), CDbl(data(5)), CDbl(data(2))))
        lstTransactions.Items.Add(String.Format(fmtStr, "", _
          "Paid to: " & data(1), "", ""))
        lstTransactions.Items.Add(String.Format(fmtStr, "", _
          "Memo: " & data(6), "", ""))
      Else    'The entry is a deposit
        lstTransactions.Items.Add(String.Format(fmtStr, data(7), _
          "Deposit #: " & data(4), CDbl(data(5)), CDbl(data(2))))
        lstTransactions.Items.Add(String.Format(fmtStr, "", _
          "Source: " & data(1), "", ""))
        lstTransactions.Items.Add(String.Format(fmtStr, "", _
          "Memo: " & data(6), "", ""))
      End If
      balance = data(2)
    Loop
    'Display the ending balance
    lstTransactions.Items.Add("")
    lstTransactions.Items.Add(String.Format(fmtStr, "", _
                  "Ending Balance: " & FormatCurrency(balance), "", ""))
  Catch exc As IO.IOException
    'Any IO error reading the text file
    'Display an error message
    MsgBox("Could not read file " & fileName & ".", 0, "Error")
  Catch
    'Any non-IO error encountered. The two possibilities are:
    '1) The entry did not have 8 fields separated by the separator, or
    '2) The numeric data could not be displayed by FormatCurrency
    'Display an error message
    MsgBox("File " & fileName & " has invalid format.", 0, "Error")
  Finally
    'Close the reader no matter what happens above
    Try
      sr.Close()
    Catch
    End Try
  End Try
End Sub

Private Sub btnQuit_Click(...) Handles btnQuit.Click
  'Exit the program
  End
End Sub
```

CHAPTER 8   SUMMARY

1. When sequential files are opened, we must specify whether they will be read from with a StreamReader or written to with a StreamWriter. Output files can be created anew (File.CreateText) or just added to (File.AppendText). A line of data is written to a file with the WriteLine method and read from a file with the ReadLine method.

2. Structured exception handling can reduce the likelihood that a program will crash. If an exception occurs while the code in the Try block is running, execution branches to the code in a Catch block that alerts the user of a mishap. The Finally block does its best to clean up before the program moves on to other tasks.

3. When data are stored with CSV format, an entire record is placed in a single line with fields separated by commas.

4. A sequential file can be ordered by placing its data in an array of structures, sorting the array, and then writing the ordered data into a file.

CHAPTER 8   PROGRAMMING PROJECTS

1. Table 8.5 gives the leading seven soft drinks in 2003 and their percentage share of the market. Write a program whose form contains two buttons and a list box. When the first button is clicked, these data should be placed into a sequential file. When the second button is clicked, the sequential file should be used to

   (a) display the seven brands and their sales in millions of gallons. (The entire soft drink industry sold about 15.3 billion gallons in 2003.)

   (b) calculate the total percentage market share of the leading seven soft drinks.

TABLE 8.5	Leading soft drinks and percentages of 2003 market share.
Coke Classic	18.6
Pepsi-Cola	12.5
Diet Coke	9.4
Mountain Dew	6.4
Sprite	5.9
Dr. Pepper	5.6
Diet Pepsi	5.5

Source: Beverage World.

2. Suppose that the sequential file ALE.TXT contains the information shown in Table 8.6. Write a program to use the file to produce Table 8.7 in which the baseball teams are in descending order by the percentage of games won.

3. Write a rudimentary word-processing program. The program should do the following:

   (a) Use InputBox to request the name of the sequential file to hold the document being created.

   (b) Set the label for a text box to "Enter Line 1," and allow the user to enter the first line of the document into the text box.

TABLE 8.6	American League East games won and lost in 2004.		
Team	Won	Lost	
Baltimore	78	84	
Boston	98	64	
New York	101	61	
Tampa Bay	70	91	
Toronto	67	94	

TABLE 8.7	Final 2004 American League East standings.		
	W	L	Pct
New York	101	61	0.623
Boston	98	64	0.605
Baltimore	78	84	0.481
Tampa Bay	70	91	0.435
Toronto	67	94	0.416

(c) When the "Record Line" button is clicked, determine if the line is acceptable. Blank lines are acceptable input, but lines exceeding 60 characters in length should not be accepted. Advise the user of the problem with a message box, and then set the focus back to the text box so that the user can edit the line to an acceptable length. When an acceptable line is entered, write this line to the file and display it in a list box.

(d) Change the label to "Enter Line 2," clear the text box, allow the user to enter the second line of the document into the text box, and carry out (c) for this line using the same list box.

(e) Continue as in (d) with appropriate labels for subsequent lines until the user clicks on a Finished button.

(f) Clear the list box, and display the number of lines written and the name of the text file created.

4. Write a program that counts the number of times a word occurs in the sequential file created in Programming Project 3. The filename and word should be read from text boxes. The search should not be sensitive to the case of the letters. For instance, opening a file that contained the first three sentences of the directions to this problem and searching for "the" would produce the output: "the" occurs six times.

5. *Create and Maintain Telephone Directories.* Write a program to create and maintain telephone directories. Each directory will be a separate sequential file. The following buttons should be available:

(a) Select a directory to access. A list of directories that have been created should be stored in a separate sequential file. When a request is made to open a directory, the list of available directories should be displayed as part of an InputBox prompt requesting the name of the directory to be accessed. If the user responds with a directory name not listed, the desire to create a new directory should be confirmed and then the new directory created and added to the list of existing directories.

(b) Add name and phone number (as given in the text boxes) to the end of the current directory.

(c) Delete name (as given in the text box) from the current directory.

(d) Sort the current directory into name order.

(e) Display the names and phone numbers contained in the current directory.

(f) Terminate the program.

6. Table 8.8 contains the statistics for a stock portfolio. (The current prices are given for February 1, 2005.)

TABLE 8.8   **Stock portfolio.**

Stock	Number of Shares	Date Purchased	Purchase Price/Share	Current Price/Share
Amgen	200	8/19/97	12.625	61.30
Delta Airlines	100	12/3/97	55.875	5.03
Novell	500	8/27/97	10.375	5.57
PPG	100	12/18/97	28.375	67.87
Timken	300	3/13/98	34.625	25.21

(a) Compose a program to create the sequential file csvSTOCKS.TXT containing the information in Table 8.8.

(b) Compose a program to perform the following tasks. A possible form design is shown in Figure 8.10.

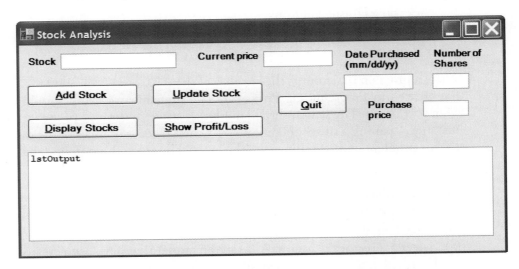

FIGURE 8.10   **Possible form design for Programming Project 6.**

(1) Display the information in the file csvSTOCKS.TXT as in Table 8.8 when the user clicks on a Display Stocks button.

(2) Add an additional stock onto the end of the file csvSTOCKS.TXT when the user clicks on an Add Stock button. The data for the new stock should be read from appropriately labeled text boxes.

(3) Update the Current Price/Share of a stock in the file csvSTOCKS.TXT when the user clicks on an Update Stock button. The name of the stock to be updated and the new price should be read from the appropriate text boxes. The file csvSTOCKS.TXT should then be copied to a temp file until the specified stock is found. The update record for this stock should then be written to the temp file, followed by all remaining records in csvSTOCKS.TXT. Finally, the original csvSTOCKS.TXT file should be erased and the temp file renamed to csvSTOCKS.TXT.

(4) Process the data in the file csvSTOCKS.TXT, and produce the display shown in Figure 8.11 when a "Show Profit/Loss" button is clicked.

(5) Quit.

Stock	Cost	Current Value	Profit (or Loss)
Amgen	$2,525.00	$12,260.00	$9,735.00
Delta Airlines	$5,587.50	$503.00	($5,084.50)
Novell	$5,187.50	$2,500.00	($2,687.50)
PPG	$2,837.50	$6,787.00	$3,949.50
Timken	$10,387.50	$7,563.00	($2,824.50)

FIGURE 8.11   Output of Programming Project 6.

7. A department store has a CSV file containing all sales transacted for a year. Each record contains a customer's name, zip code, and amount of the sale. The file is ordered first by zip code and then by name. Write a program to display the total sales for each customer, the total sales for each zip code, and the total sales for the store. For instance, if the first six records of the file are

```
Adams, John, 10023, 34.50
Adams, John, 10023, 60.00
Jones, Bob, 10023, 62.45
Green, Mary, 12345, 54.00
Howard, Sue, 12345, 79.25
Smith, George, 20001, 25.10
```

then the output in the list box will begin as shown in Figure 8.12 (on the next page).

8. *Savings Account.* The sequential file csvACCOUNTS.TXT contains the name, account number, and beginning-of-month balance for each depositor. The sequential file csvTRANS.TXT contains all the transactions (deposits and withdrawals) for the month. Use csvTRANS.TXT to update the file csvACCOUNTS.TXT. Both files are sorted by account number. For each customer, display a statement similar to the one received from banks that shows all transactions and the end-of-month balance. Also, record all overdrawn accounts in a file. (As an optional embellishment,

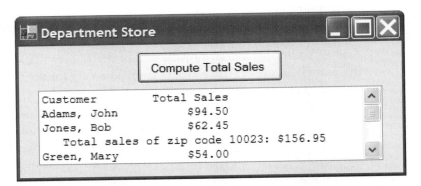

FIGURE 8.12   Sample output for Programming Project 7.

deduct a penalty if the balance fell below a certain level any time during the month. The penalty could include a fixed fee of $10, plus a charge of $1 for each check and deposit.)

9. A fuel economy study was carried out for five models of cars. Each car was driven for 100 miles of city driving, and then the model of the car and the number of gallons used were placed in a line of the sequential file csvMILEAGE.TXT. Table 8.9 shows the first entries of the file. Write a program to display the models and their average miles per gallon in decreasing order with respect to mileage. The program should utilize an array of structures with upper-bound 4, where each structure has three members. The first member should record the name of each model of car. This member is initially empty; each car model name is added when first encountered in reading the file. The second member should record the number of test vehicles for each model. The third member should record the total number of gallons used by that model. **Note:** The first members of the elements of the array should be searched each time a record is read to determine the appropriate index to use with the other two members.

TABLE 8.9   Gallons of gasoline used in 100 miles of city driving.

Model	Gal	Model	Gal	Model	Gal
LeBaron	4.9	Cutlass	4.5	Cutlass	4.6
Escort	4.1	Escort	3.8	LeBaron	5.1
Beretta	4.3	Escort	3.9	Escort	3.8
Skylark	4.5	Skylark	4.6	Cutlass	4.4

10. Each item in a supermarket is identified by its Universal Product Code (UPC), which consists of a sequence of 12 digits appearing below a rectangle of bars. See Figure 8.13. The bars have these digits encoded in them so that the UPC can be read by an optical scanner. Let's refer to the UPC as d_1-d_2 d_3 d_4 d_5 d_6-d_7 d_8 d_9 d_{10} d_{11}-d_{12}. The single digit on the left, d_1, identifies the type of product (for instance, 0 for general groceries, 2 for meat and produce, 3 for drug and health products, and 5 for coupons). The first set of

70734 00003

FIGURE 8.13   A Universal Product Code.

five digits, $d_2\ d_3\ d_4\ d_5\ d_6$, identifies the manufacturer, and the second set of five digits, $d_7\ d_8\ d_9\ d_{10}\ d_{11}$, identifies the product. The twelfth digit on the right, d_{12}, is a check digit. It is chosen so that

$$3 \cdot d_1 + d_2 + 3 \cdot d_3 + d_4 + 3 \cdot d_5 + d_6 + 3 \cdot d_7 + d_8$$
$$+\ 3 \cdot d_9 + d_{10} + 3 \cdot d_{11} + d_{12}. \qquad (*)$$

is a multiple of 10. For instance, for the UPC in Figure 8.11,

$$3 \cdot 0 + 7 + 3 \cdot 0 + 7 + 3 \cdot 3 + 4 + 3 \cdot 0 + 0 + 3 \cdot 9 + 0 \cdot 0 + 3 \cdot 3 + 4 = 40.$$

Since $40 = 4 \cdot 10$, 40 is a multiple of 10. In the event that the cashier has to enter the UPC manually and mistypes a digit, the above sum will usually not add up to a multiple of 10.

Write a program to simulate an automated check-out counter at a supermarket. A master sequential file, called UPC.TXT, should have a record for each item consisting of fields for the UPC, name of the item, and the price of the item. For instance, the file might contain the following record:

070734000034
Celestial Seasons Sleepytime Tea
2.59

The file should be ordered with respect to the UPCs. The program should allow the cashier to enter UPCs one at a time, should keep a running total of the number of items processed, and should place the UPCs in an array. Each UPC should be checked with the sum (*) as soon as it is entered and should be reentered if the sum is not a multiple of 10. After all items have been processed, the program should sort the array of UPCs and then produce a receipt similar to the one in Figure 8.14 after making just one pass through the master sequential file.

22-oz Jif Peanut Butter	2.29
Celestial Seasons Sleepytime Tea	2.59
365 Soda Root Beer	.55
Total = = = = = = = = = = = = >	$5.43

FIGURE 8.14   Sample output of Programming Project 10.

9

Additional Controls
and Objects

9.1 List Boxes, Combo Boxes, and the File-Opening Control 462

- The List Box Control ◆ The Combo Box Control
- The OpenFileDialog Control

9.2 Seven Elementary Controls 472

- The Group Box Control ◆ The Check Box Control
- The Radio Button Control ◆ The Timer Control
- The Picture Box Control
- The Horizontal and Vertical Scroll Bar Controls

9.3 Four Additional Objects 484

- The Clipboard Object ◆ The Random Class
- The MenuStrip Control ◆ Multiple Forms

9.4 Graphics 496

- Graphics Objects ◆ Lines, Rectangles, Circles, and Sectors
- Pie Charts ◆ Bar Charts ◆ Animation

Summary 509

Programming Projects 510

9.1 List Boxes, Combo Boxes, and the File-Opening Control

Throughout this book, we have used list boxes to display the output of a program. However, list boxes also provide a potent means for obtaining input by selecting an item from a list. Two other controls that allow us to choose an item from a list are the ComboBox and the OpenFileDialog controls.

■ The List Box Control

The list boxes discussed in this text display a single column of strings, referred to as **items**. The items to appear initially can either be specified at design time with the Items property or set with code in a procedure. Code is then used to access, add, or delete items from the list. We will first carry out all tasks with code and then show how the initial items can be specified at design time.

At any time, the value of

```
lstBox.Items.Count
```

is the number of items in the list box.

Each item in lstBox is identified by an index number ranging from 0 through lstBox.Items.Count − 1.

The Sorted property is perhaps the most interesting list box property. When it is set to True, the items will automatically be displayed in alphabetical (i.e., ANSI) order. The default value of the Sorted property is False. When the Sorted property is set to True, the statement

```
num = lstBox.Items.Add(str)
```

inserts *str* into the list at the proper sorted position and assigns to the Integer variable *num* the index number of that position.

During run time, you can highlight an item from a list by clicking on it with the mouse or by moving to it with the up- and down-arrow keys when the list box has the focus. (The second method triggers the SelectedIndexChanged event each time an arrow key causes the highlight to move.) The value of

```
lstBox.SelectedIndex
```

is the index number of the item currently highlighted in lstBox. If no item is highlighted, the value of SelectedIndex is −1. The statement

```
lstBox.ListIndex = -1
```

will unhighlight any highlighted item in the list.

The list of items stored in the list box are held in lstBox.Items(). In particular, the value of

```
lstBox.Items(n)
```

is the item of lstBox having index *n*. The elements of the list are of a data type called Object. A variable of any type may be assigned to an element of the list. However, type casting must take place whenever an element of the list is assigned to a numeric or string variable or concatenated with another variable or literal. For instance, the statement

```
txtBox.Text = CStr(lstBox.Items(0))
```

displays the first item of lstBox.

The value of

```
lstBox.Items(lstBox.SelectedIndex)
```

is the item currently highlighted in lstBox. Alternatively, the value of

```
lstBox.Text
```

is also the currently highlighted item. Setting this property to a string value will select the item in the list box that matches the value.

The statement

```
lstBox.Items.RemoveAt(n)
```

deletes the item of index *n* from lstBox. The statement

```
lstBox.Items.Remove(str)
```

deletes the first occurrence of the value of *str* in lstBox.

When the user selects an item in a list box, an event is triggered. A program can respond to three main types of events. If the user clicks on an item, the Click event is processed. If the user clicks on a different item or uses the arrow keys to select it, the SelectedIndexChanged event is processed. If the user double-clicks on an item, then the Click, DoubleClick, and SelectedIndexChanged events are triggered.

   Example 1   An oxymoron is a pairing of contradictory or incongruous words. The following program displays a list of oxymorons. When you select an item, it is displayed in a text box. A button allows you to add an additional item with an input dialog box. You can delete an item by double-clicking on it with the mouse. After running the program, click on different items, add an item or two (such as "same difference" or "liquid gas"), and delete an item.

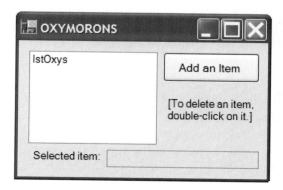

OBJECT	PROPERTY	SETTING
frmOxymoron	Text	OXYMORONS
lstOxys	Sorted	True
btnAdd	Text	Add an Item
lblDelete	AutoSize	False
	Text	[To delete an item, double-click on it.]
lblSelected	Text	Selected item:
txtSelected	ReadOnly	True

```
Private Sub lstOxys_SelectedIndexChanged(...) Handles _
            lstOxys.SelectedIndexChanged
  txtSelected.Text = CStr(lstOxys.Text)
End Sub

Private Sub btnAdd_Click(...) Handles btnAdd.Click
  Dim item As String
  item = InputBox("Item to Add:")
  lstOxys.Items.Add(item)
End Sub

Private Sub lstOxys_DoubleClick(...) Handles lstOxys.DoubleClick
  lstOxys.Items.RemoveAt(lstOxys.SelectedIndex)
  txtSelected.Clear()
End Sub
```

[Run, add some items and then click on an item of the list box.]

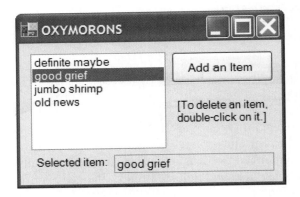

The following steps show how to fill a list box at design time. (This method is used in Example 2.)

1. Select the Items property of the list box.
2. Click on the ellipsis button on the right side of the Settings box. (A window titled String Collection Editor will be displayed.)
3. Type in the first item, and press Enter.
4. Repeat Step 3 for each of the other items.
5. When you are finished entering items, click on the OK button.

◼ The Combo Box Control

A combo box is best thought of as a text box with a helping list box attached. With an ordinary text box, the user must type information into the box. With a combo box, the user has the option of either typing in information or just selecting the appropriate piece of information from a list. The information is then displayed at the top of the combo box. The three types of combo box, called Simple, DropDown, and DropDownList, are specified by the DropDownStyle property. See Figure 9.1. DropDown combo boxes are used in Windows applications as text boxes with a "history list" (list of past entries) from which you can either type a new entry or select an old entry. The standard prefix for the name of a combo box is *cbo*.

Simple combo box

DropDown (and DropDownList) combo box

FIGURE 9.1   **Styles of combo boxes.**

With a Simple combo box, the list is always visible. With a DropDown combo box, the list drops down when the user clicks on the arrow and then disappears after a selection is made. In either case, when an item from the list is highlighted, the item automatically appears in the text box at the top and its value is assigned to the Text property of the combo box. The DropDownList combo box looks like the DropDown combo box; the difference is that the user can only select an item from the list and cannot type into the text box.

Combo boxes have essentially the same properties, events, and methods as list boxes. In particular, all the statements discussed for list boxes also hold for combo boxes. The Text property determines what appears at the top of the combo box before the user accesses the combo box. The DropDownStyle property of a combo box must be specified at design time.

 Example 2   The following program uses a Simple combo box to obtain a person's title for the first line of the address of a letter. **Note:** At design time, first set the combo box's DropDownStyle property to Simple, and then lengthen the height of the combo box.

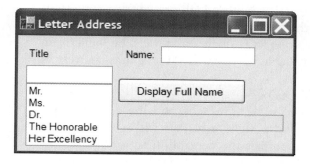

OBJECT	PROPERTY	SETTING
frmAddress	Text	Letter Address
lblTitle	Text	Title
cboTitle	Items	Mr.
		Ms.
		Dr.
		The Honorable
		Her Excellency
	DropDownStyle	Simple
	Text	(blank)
lblName	Text	Name:
txtName		
btnDisplay	Text	Display Full Name
txtDisplay	ReadOnly	True

```
Private Sub btnDisplay_Click(...) Handles btnDisplay.Click
  txtDisplay.Text = cboTitle.Text & " " & txtName.Text
End Sub
```

[Run, select an item from the combo box, type a name into the Name text box, and click the button.]

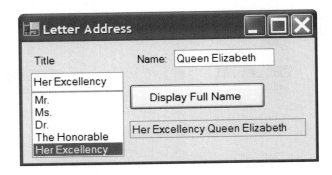

The same program with a style DropDown or DropDownList combo box produces the output shown below.

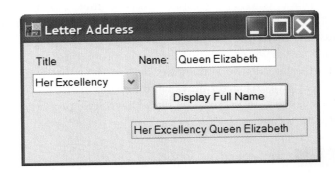

■ The OpenFileDialog Control

Windows applications, such as Word, Excel, and Notepad, all provide the same standard Open dialog box to help you specify the file you want to open. Figure 9.2 shows an Open dialog box that could be used with Notepad to open a text file. The same Open dialog box, with all its functionality, is available to Visual Basic programs courtesy of the OpenFileDialog control.

The OpenFileDialog control is in the Dialogs section of the Toolbox. When you place the control on a form it will not be visible. The icon and the default name, OpenFileDialog1, appear in the pane below the Main area. (We will not change the name since the default name completely describes the control's function.) The only property we will set for the control is the Filter property, which determines what text appears in the "Files of type:" combo box and what types of files will be displayed in the Main region of the dialog box. The simplest setting has the form

text for combo box | * *.ext*

where *ext* is a two- or three-letter extension describing the types of files to display. For our purposes, the most used setting for the Filter property will be

`Text Documents (*.TXT)|*.TXT`

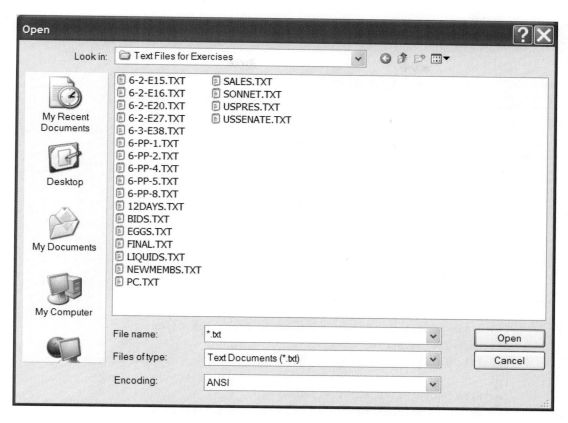

FIGURE 9.2   An Open dialog box.

The statement

OpenFileDialog1.ShowDialog()

brings the Open dialog box into play. After a file has been selected and the Open button pressed, the value of

OpenFileDialog1.*FileName*

will be the file's filespec; including drive, path, file name, and extension.

Example 3 The following program displays the contents of a text file selected by the user with an Open dialog box:

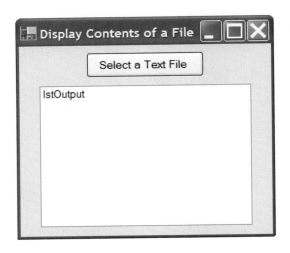

OBJECT	PROPERTY	SETTING
frmDisplayFile	Text	Display Contents of a File
btnSelect	Text	Select a Text File
lstOutput		
OpenFileDialog1	Filter	Text Files (*.TXT)|*.TXT

```
Private Sub btnSelect_Click(...) Handles btnSelect.Click
  Dim textFile As String
  OpenFileDialog1.ShowDialog()  'Open dialog box appears and program
                                'pauses until a selection is made
  textFile = OpenFileDialog1.FileName
  Dim sr As IO.StreamReader = IO.File.OpenText(textFile)
  lstOutput.Items.Clear()
  Do While sr.Peek <> -1
    lstOutput.Items.Add(sr.ReadLine)
  Loop
  sr.Close()
End Sub
```

[Run, and press the button. (Assume that the user makes choices leading to the situation in Figure 9.2.) Select the file USPRES.TXT, and click on the Open button in the dialog box.]

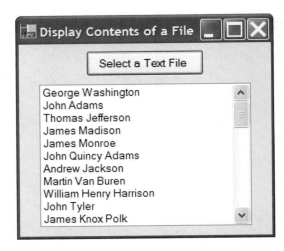

Practice Problems 9.1

1. Write code to copy the contents of a list box into a file.
2. Give a statement that will display the last item in the combo box cboBox.

EXERCISES 9.1

For Exercises 1 through 16, suppose that the list box lstBox is as shown and determine the effect of the code. (Assume that the Sorted property is set to True.)

```
Bach
Beethoven
Chopin
Mozart
Tchaikovsky
```

1. `txtOutput.Text = lstBox.Text`

2. `lstBox.Text = CStr(lstBox.Items(2))`

3. `txtOutput.Text = CStr(lstBox.Items(lstBox.Items.Count - 1))`

4. `txtOutput.Text = CStr(lstBox.Item(lstBox.SelectedIndex))`

5. `txtOutput.Text = CStr(lstBox.SelectedIndex)`

6. `lstBox.Items.Add(lstBox.Text)`

7. `lstBox.Items.Add("Haydn")`

8. `lstBox.Items.Remove("Chopin")`

9. `lstBox.Items.RemoveAt(0)`

10. `lstBox.Items.RemoveAt(lstBox.SelectedIndex)`

11. `lstBox.Items.RemoveAt(lstBox.Items.Count − 1)`

12. `lstBox.Items.Clear()`

13.
```
Dim total As Integer = 0
For n As Integer = 0 To lstBox.Items.Count - 1
  If CStr(lstBox.Items(n)).Length = 6 Then
    total += 1
  End If
Next
txtOutput.Text = CStr(total)
```

14.
```
Dim sw As IO.StreamWriter = IO.File.CreateText("COMPOSERS.TXT")
For n As Integer = 0 To lstBox.Items.Count - 1
  sw.WriteLine(lstBox.Items(n))
Next
sw.Close()
```

15.
```
Dim composer(10) As String
For n As Integer = 0 To lstBox.Items.Count - 1
  composer(n) = CStr(lstBox.Items(n)) 'Composer() is a string array
Next
```

```
lstBox.Items.Clear()
lstBox.Sorted = False
For n As Integer = lstBox.Items.Count - 1 To 0 Step -1
  lstBox.Items.Add(composer(n))
Next
```

16.
```
Dim composer(100) As String
Dim highestIndex As Integer = lstBox.Items.Count - 1
For n As Integer = 0 To highestIndex
  composer(n) = CStr(lstBox.Items(n)) 'Composer() is a string array
Next
lstBox.Items.Clear()
lstBox.Sorted = False
For n As Integer = highestIndex To 0 Step -1
  lstBox.Items.Add(composer(n))
Next
```

In Exercises 17 through 26, assume that the Simple combo box cboBox appears as shown and that the Sorted property is set to True. Give a statement or statements that will carry out the stated task.

17. Highlight the name Dante.

18. Highlight the third item of the list. (The statement should do the job even if additional items were added to the list.)

19. Delete the name Shakespeare.

20. Delete the name Goethe.

21. Delete the last name in the list. (The statement should do the job even if additional items were added to the list.)

22. Insert the name Cervantes. Where will it be inserted?

23. Display every other item of the list in another list box.

24. Delete every item beginning with the letter M. (The code should do the job even if additional items were added to the list.)

25. Determine if Cervantes is in the list. (The statement should do the job even if additional items were added to the list.)

26. Store the items in the file AUTHORS.TXT.

In Exercises 27 through 32, suppose that the form has a list box containing positive single-digit numbers, a button, and a text box. Write a Click event procedure for the button that displays the requested information in the text box or another list box.

27. The average of the numbers in the list box.

28. The largest number in the list box.

29. Every other number in the list box.

30. All numbers greater than the average.

31. The spread of the list, that is, the difference between the largest and smallest numbers in the list box.

32. The median of the numbers in the list. (The *median* of a set of n numbers is a number such that half the n numbers fall below the median, and half fall above. If the number of numbers n is odd, the median is the middle number when the numbers are arranged in ascending order. If the number of numbers n is even, the median is the average of the two middle numbers when the numbers are arranged in ascending order.)

33. The file POPULAR_NAMES.TXT contains the 20 most popular names given to newborns in the year 2000. Use a list box to sort the names into alphabetical order, and then place the alphabetized list into a new ordered file.

34. Write a program that contains a list box (with Sorted = False), a label, and two buttons captioned "Add an Item" and "Delete an Item". When the Add an Item button is clicked, the program should request an item with an input dialog box and then insert the item above the currently highlighted item. When the Delete an Item button is clicked, the program should remove the highlighted item from the list. At all times, the label should display the number of items in the list.

35. Consider the Length Converter in Figure 9.3. Write a program to place the items in the list and carry out the conversion. (See the first programming project in Chapter 7 for a table of equivalent lengths.)

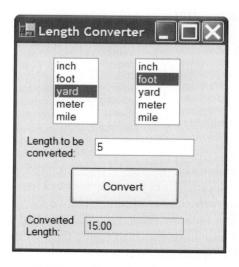

FIGURE 9.3   Form for Exercise 35.

36. Write a program to ask a person which Monopoly® space he or she has landed on and then display the result in a text box. The response should be obtained with a combo box listing the squares most commonly landed on: Park Place, Illinois Avenue, Go, B&O Railroad, and Free Parking. (One possible outcome to be displayed in the text box is "You have landed on Park Place.")

37. Write a program to question a person about his or her IBM-compatible computer and then display a descriptive sentence in a text box. The form should contain combo boxes for brand, amount of memory, and size of screen. The lists should contain the most common responses for each category. The most common PCs are Compaq, Dell, Hewlett Packard, IBM, and Gateway 2000. The most common amounts of memory are 128MB, 256MB, 512MB, and 1GB. The most common screen sizes are 15 inches, 17 inches, and 21 inches. (One possible outcome to be displayed in the text box is "You have a Gateway 2000 computer with 256MB of memory and a 17-inch monitor.")

Solutions to Practice Problems 9.1

```
1. Sub SaveListBox()
     Dim sw As IO.StreamWriter = IO.File.CreateText("LISTDATA.TXT")
     For i As Integer = 0 to lstBox.Items.Count - 1
       sw.WriteLine(lstBox.Items(i))
     Next
     sw.Close()
   End Sub

2. txtBox.Text = CStr(cboBox.Items(cboBox.Items.Count - 1))
```

9.2   Seven Elementary Controls

■ The Group Box Control

Group boxes are passive objects used to group related sets of controls for visual effect. You rarely write event procedures for group boxes. The preceding group box has a group of three text boxes attached to it. When you move the group box, the attached controls follow as a unit. If you hide the group box, the attached controls will be hidden as well. To attach a control to a group box, just create the control any way you like, and drag it inside the group box. As shown later in this section, the group box control is particularly important when working with groups of radio button controls. The standard prefix for the name of a group box is *grp*. The title sunk into the border can be set with the Text property. Although group boxes cannot receive the focus, they can have an access key that sends the focus to the first control inside the group box that can receive the focus.

The Check Box Control

A check box, which consists of a small square and a caption (set with the Text property), presents the user with a yes/no choice. The form in Example 1 uses four check box controls. The Checked property of a check box has the value False when the square is empty and True when the square is checked. At run time, the user clicks on the square (or its accompanying caption) to toggle between the unchecked and checked states. So doing also triggers the CheckedChanged event.

Example 1   The following program allows an employee to compute the monthly cost of various benefit packages:

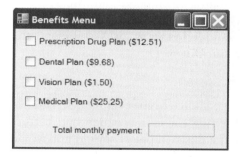

OBJECT	PROPERTY	SETTING
frmBenefits	Text	Benefits Menu
chkDrugs	Text	Prescription Drug Plan ($12.51)
chkDental	Text	Dental Plan ($9.68)
chkVision	Text	Vision Plan ($1.50)
chkMedical	Text	Medical Plan ($25.25)
lblTotal	Text	Total monthly payment:
txtTotal	ReadOnly	True

```
Private Sub Tally(...) Handles chkDrugs.CheckedChanged,_
                  chkDental.CheckedChanged,_
              chkVision.CheckedChanged, chkMedical.CheckChanged
  Dim sum As Double = 0
  If chkDrugs.Checked Then
    sum += 12.51
  End If
  If chkDental.Checked Then
    sum += 9.68
  End If
  If chkVision.Checked Then
    sum += 1.5
  End If
  If chkMedical.Checked Then
    sum += 25.25
  End If
  txtTotal.Text = FormatCurrency(sum)
End Sub
```

[Run, and then click on the desired options.]

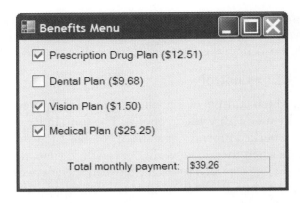

When a check box has the focus, the spacebar can be used to check (or uncheck) the box and invoke the CheckedChanged event. In addition, the state of a check box can be toggled from the keyboard without first setting the focus to the check box, if you create an access key for the check box by including an ampersand in the Text property. (At run time, access keys appear underlined after the Alt key is pressed.) For instance, if the Text property for the Dental Plan in Example 1 is set as "&Dental Plan", then the user can check (or uncheck) the box by pressing Alt + D.

■ The Radio Button Control

Radio buttons are used to give the user a single choice from several options. The name "radio button" comes from a reference to the first car radios, which had buttons that pressed in. Pressing one button would move the dial to a preset station and would raise any other button that was depressed.

Normally, a group of several radio buttons is attached to a group box. Each button consists of a small circle accompanied by a caption that is set with the Text property. (As with a button and a check box, an ampersand can be used to create an access key for a radio button.) When a circle or its accompanying caption is clicked, a solid dot appears in the circle and the button is said to be "on." At most, one radio button in a group can be on at the same time. Therefore, if one button is on and another button in the group is clicked, the first button will turn off. By convention, the names of radio buttons have the prefix *rad*. A single form can have several groups of radio buttons. However, each group must be attached to its own group box or to the form itself (with only one group on the form).

The Checked property of a radio button tells if the button is on or off. The property

radButton.Checked

is True when radButton is on and False when radButton is off. The statement

radButton.Checked = True

turns on radButton and turns off all other buttons in its group. The statement

radButton.Checked = False

turns off radButton and has no effect on the other buttons in its group.

The CheckedChanged event for a radio button is triggered when an off button is turned on or an on button is turned off. Therefore, CheckedChanged events are usually triggered in pairs, and provide limited value. In most programming situations, the best way to determine which button is selected is to employ a button control as in Example 2.

 Example 2   The following voting program allows undervotes (voting for neither), but prevents overvotes (voting for both):

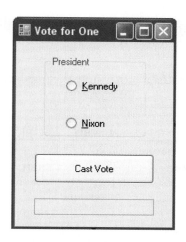

OBJECT	PROPERTY	SETTING
frmBallot	Text	Vote for One
grpCandidates	Text	President
radCandidate1	Text	&Kennedy
	Checked	False
radCandidate2	Text	&Nixon
	Checked	False
btnVote	Text	Cast Vote
txtVote	ReadOnly	True

```
Private Sub btnVote_Click(...) Handles btnVote.Click
  If radCandidate1.Checked Then
    txtVote.Text = "You voted for Kennedy."
  ElseIf radCandidate2.Checked Then
    txtVote.Text = "You voted for Nixon."
  Else
    txtVote.Text = "You voted for neither."
  End If
End Sub
```

[Run, click on one of the radio buttons, and then click the Cast Vote button.]

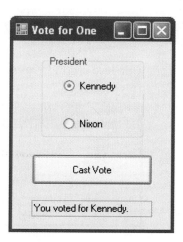

■ The Timer Control

The timer control, which is invisible during run time, triggers an event after a specified amount of time has passed. (When you double-click on the timer control in the Toolbox, it appears in a separate pane called the tray, at the bottom part of the Form designer.) The length of time, measured in milliseconds, is set with the Interval property to be any integer from 1 to 2,147,483,647 (about 596 hours). The event triggered each time Timer1.Interval milliseconds elapses is called Timer1.Tick. In order to begin timing, a timer must first be turned on by setting its Enabled property to True. A timer is turned off by setting its Enabled property to False. The standard prefix for the name of a timer control is *tmr*.

 Example 3 The following program creates a stopwatch that updates the time every tenth of a second.

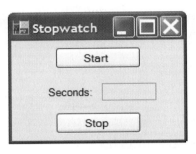

OBJECT	PROPERTY	SETTING
frmStopwatch	Text	Stopwatch
btnStart	Text	Start
lblSeconds	Text	Seconds:
txtSeconds	ReadOnly	True
btnStop	Text	Stop
tmrWatch	Interval	100
	Enabled	False

```
Private Sub btnStart_Click(...) Handles btnStart.Click
  txtSeconds.Text = "0"      'Reset watch
  tmrWatch.Enabled = True
End Sub

Private Sub btnStop_Click(...) Handles btnStop.Click
  tmrWatch.Enabled = False
End Sub

Private Sub tmrWatch_Tick(...) Handles tmrWatch.Tick
  'Next line displays the time rounded to one decimal place
  txtSeconds.Text = CStr((CDbl(txtSeconds.Text) + 0.1))
End Sub
```

[Run, click the Start button, wait 10.5 seconds, and click the Stop button.]

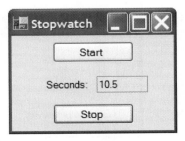

The Picture Box Control

The picture box control is designed to hold drawings created with graphics commands or pictures stored in graphics files such as .BMP files created with Windows Paint, ICO files of icons that come with Visual Basic, or GIF and JPEG images used on the World Wide Web.

A statement of the form

```
picBox.CreateGraphics.DrawRectangle(Pens.Blue, x, y, w, h)
```

where x, y, w, h are of type integer, draws a blue rectangle of width w pixels and height h pixels in the picture box. The upper-left corner of the rectangle will be x pixels from the left side and y pixels from the top side of the picture box. To get a feel for how big a pixel is, the initial size of the form when you create a new project is 300 pixels by 300 pixels.

The color Blue can be replaced by other colors. If DrawRectangle is replaced with DrawEllipse, the statement just displayed will draw the ellipse that would be inscribed in the rectangle just described. Also, if w and h have the same value, the ellipse will be a circle with a diameter of that value. In Figure 9.4, the picture box has a size of 140 by 140 pixels and a FixedSingle border style. The circle is drawn with the statement

```
picBox.CreateGraphics.DrawEllipse(Pens.Red, 35, 35, 70, 70)
```

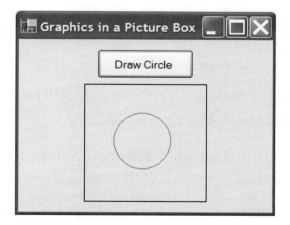

FIGURE 9.4   **Picture box containing red circle.**

A picture can be placed in a picture box control with the Image property. If you double-click on the Image property during design time, an Open dialog box appears and assists you in selecting an appropriate file. However, prior to setting the Image property, you should set the SizeMode property. If the SizeMode property is set to AutoSize, the picture box control will be resized to fit the picture. If the SizeMode property is set to StretchImage, the picture will be resized to fit the picture box control. Therefore, with the StretchImage setting, pictures can be reduced (by placing them into a small picture box control) or enlarged (by placing them into a picture box control bigger than the picture). Figure 9.5 shows a picture created with Paint and reduced by StretchImage to fit the picture box. By convention, names of picture box controls have the prefix *pic*.

FIGURE 9.5   Picture box with desert scene.

A picture also can be assigned to a picture box control at run time. However, a statement such as

```
picBox.Image = filespec
```

will not do the job. Instead, we must use the Image object with a statement such as

```
picBox.Image = Image.FromFile(filespec)
```

The SizeMode property can be altered at run time with a statement such as

```
picBox.SizeMode = PictureBoxSizeMode.AutoSize
```

■ The Horizontal and Vertical Scroll Bar Controls

Figure 9.6 shows the two types of scroll bars. When the user clicks on one of the arrow buttons, the scroll box moves a small amount toward that arrow. When the user clicks between the scroll box and one of the arrow buttons, the scroll box moves a large amount toward that arrow. The user can also move the scroll box by dragging it. The main properties of a scroll bar control are Minimum, Maximum, Value, SmallChange, and LargeChange, which are set to integers. At any time, hsbBar.Value is a number between hsbBar.Minimum and hsbBar.Maximum determined by the position of the left side of the scroll box. If the left side of the scroll box is halfway between the two arrows, then hsbBar.Value is a number halfway between hsbBar.Minimum and hsbBar.Maximum. If the scroll box is near the left arrow button, then hsbBar.Value is an appropriately pro-portioned value near hsbBar.Minimum. When an arrow button is clicked, hsbBar.Value changes by hsbBar.SmallChange and the scroll box moves accordingly. When the bar between the scroll box and one of the arrows is clicked, hsbBar.Value changes by hsbBar.LargeChange and the scroll box moves accordingly. When the scroll box is dragged, hsbBar.Value changes accordingly. The default values of Minimum, Maximum,

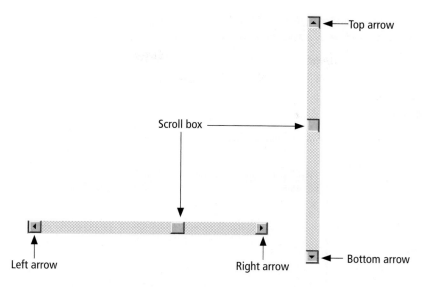

FIGURE 9.6   **Horizontal and vertical scroll bars.**

Value, SmallChange, and LargeChange are 0, 100, 0, 1, and 10, respectively. However, these values are usually set at design time. Vertical scroll bars behave similarly.

Note: The setting for the Minimum property must be less than the setting for the Maximum property. The Minimum property determines the values for the left and top arrows. The Maximum property determines the values for the right and bottom arrows.

The Scroll event is triggered whenever any part of the scroll bar is clicked.

✔ **Example 4**   The following program uses scroll bars to move a smiling face around the form. The face is a large Wingdings character J inside a label. The values lblFace.Left and lblFace.Top are the distances in pixels of the label from the left side and top of the form. (One inch is about 88 pixels.)

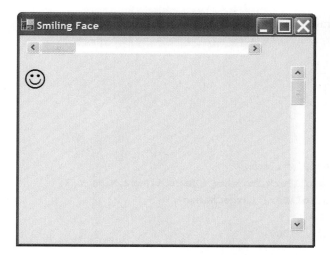

OBJECT	PROPERTY	SETTING
frmFace	Text	Smiling Face
hsbXPos	Minimum	0
	Maximum	300
	SmallChange	10
	LargeChange	50
	Value	0
vsbYPos	Minimum	30
	Maximum	300
	SmallChange	10
	LargeChange	50
	Value	30
lblFace	Text	J
	Font	Wingdings, 24pt

```
Private Sub hsbXpos_Scroll(...) Handles hsbXpos.Scroll
  lblFace.Left = hsbXpos.Value
End Sub

Private Sub vsbYpos_Scroll(...) Handles vsbYpos.Scroll
  lblFace.Top = vsbYpos.Value
End Sub
```

[Run, and move the scroll boxes on the scroll bars.]

Practice Problem 9.3

What is the difference between a set of check boxes attached to a group box and a set of radio buttons attached to a group box?

EXERCISES 9.2

In Exercises 1 through 16, determine the effect of setting the property to the value shown.

1. `GroupBox1.Text = "Income"`
2. `CheckBox1.Checked = True`
3. `CheckBox1.Checked = False`
4. `CheckBox1.Text = "&Vanilla"`
5. `RadioButton1.Checked = False`
6. `RadioButton1.Text = "Punt"`
7. `HScrollBar2.Value = HScrollBar2.Maximum`
8. `HScrollBar2.Value = CInt((HScrollBar2.Maximum + HScrollBar2.Min) / 2)`
9. `VScrollBar2.SmallChange = VScrollBar2.LargeChange`
10. `Timer1.Interval = 5000`
11. `Timer1.Interval = CInt(intVar * 1000)`
12. `Timer1.Enabled = False`

13. `PictureBox1.SizeMode = PictureBoxSizeMode.StretchImage`
14. `PictureBox1.CreateGraphics.DrawEllipse(Pens.Blue, 20, 30, 100, 100)`
15. `PictureBox1.CreateGraphics.DrawRectangle(Pens.Green, 25, 50, 200, 100)`
16. `PictureBox1.Image = Image.FromFile("AIRPLANE.BMP")`

In Exercises 17 through 24, write one or more lines of code to carry out the task.

17. Set the caption for RadioButton1 to "Yes".
18. Clear the small rectangular box of CheckBox1.
19. Turn off RadioButton2.
20. Move the scroll box of VScrollBar2 as high as possible.
21. Move the scroll box of HScrollBar2 one-third of the way from the left arrow to the right arrow.
22. Specify that Timer1 trigger an event every half second.
23. Draw a yellow circle of diameter 100 pixels in PictureBox1.
24. Specify that Timer1 cease to trigger the Tick event.

In Exercises 25 and 26, determine the state of the two radio buttons after the button is clicked.

25.
```
Private Sub Button1_Click(...) Handles Button1.Click
    RadioButton1.Checked = True
    RadioButton2.Checked = True
End Sub
```

26.
```
Private Sub Button1_Click(...) Handles Button1.Click
    RadioButton1.Checked = False
    RadioButton2.Checked = False
End Sub
```

27. Which of the controls presented in this section can receive the focus? Design a form containing all of the controls, and repeatedly press the Tab key to confirm your answer.

28. Create a form with two group boxes, each having two radio buttons attached to it. Run the program, and confirm that the two pairs of radio buttons operate independently of each other.

29. Suppose that a group box has two radio buttons attached to it. If the statement

    `GroupBox1.Visible = False`

    is executed, will the radio buttons also vanish? Test your answer.

30. Why are radio buttons also called "option buttons"?

A form contains a button and a group box with three check boxes named CheckBox1, CheckBox2, and CheckBox3 attached to it. In Exercises 31 and 32, write a Click event procedure for the button that displays the stated information in a text or list box when the button is clicked.

31. The number of boxes checked.
32. The captions of the checked boxes.

33. A computer dealer offers two basic computers, the Deluxe ($1500) and the Super ($1700). The customer can order any of the following additional options: multimedia kit ($300), internal modem ($100), or 256MB of added memory ($50). Write a program that computes the cost of the computer system selected.

34. Item 37a of Form 1040 for the U.S. Individual Income Tax Return reads as follows:

    37a. *Check if:* ☐ **You** *were 65 or older,* ☐ *Blind;* ☐ **Spouse** *was 65 or older,* ☐ *Blind Add the number of boxes checked above and enter the total here.* → *37a* ☐

    Write a program that looks at the four check boxes and displays the number of boxes checked in the text box.

35. The Programs\Ch09\Pictures folder contains files named MOON1.BMP, MOON2.BMP, ..., MOON8.BMP, which show eight phases of the moon. Create a form consisting of a picture box control and a timer control. Every two seconds assign another file to the Image property of the picture box control to see the moon cycle through its phases every 16 seconds. One phase is shown in Figure 9.7.

FIGURE 9.7 **Form for Exercise 35.**

36. Subscribers to the Matinee Series for a recent season at the Kennedy Center for the Performing Arts had to select four performances out of the six shown in the Matinee Series form in Figure 9.8 and had to indicate the method of payment. Write the Click event procedure for the button. The procedure should first determine whether exactly four performances have been checked. If not, the user should be so informed with a message dialog box. Then the method of payment should be examined. If no method has been indicated, the user must be reminded to select one. Depending on the method of payment, the user should be told with a message box to either mail in the check with the order form or give the credit card number with an input dialog box request. At the end of the process, the caption on the button should change to "Thank You".

37. Write a program to synchronize the two thermometers shown in the Temperatures form in Figure 9.9. When the scroll box of either thermometer is moved, the other thermometer moves to the corresponding temperature and each temperature is displayed above the thermometer. **Note**: C = (5/9)(F − 32), F = (9/5)C + 32.

38. Write a program to create a decorative digital clock. The clock in the Digital Clock form in Figure 9.10 is inserted in a picture box control containing the TREES.BMP picture. The values for hour, minute, and second can be obtained as Hour(Now), Minute(Now), and Second(Now).

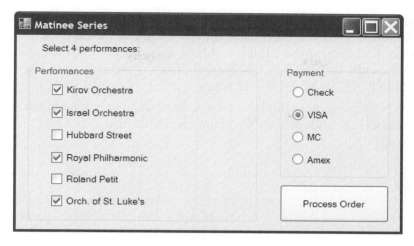

FIGURE 9.8   Form for Exercise 36.

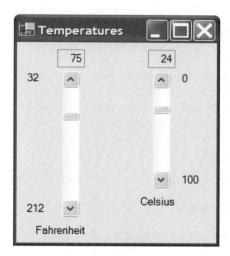

FIGURE 9.9   Form for Exercise 37.

FIGURE 9.10   Form for Exercise 38.

39. *Simulation of Times Square Ball.* Create a form with a vertical scroll bar and a timer control. When the program is run, the scroll box should be at the top of the scroll bar. Each second the scroll box should descend one-tenth of the way down. When the scroll box reaches the bottom after 10 seconds, a message box displaying HAPPY NEW YEAR should appear.

40. Write a program to display a picture (contained in a .bmp file in the Windows directory) in a picture box. The .bmp file should be selected with an OpenFileDialog control.

Solutions to Practice Problems 9.2

With radio buttons, at most one button can be on at any given time, whereas several check boxes can be checked simultaneously.

9.3 Four Additional Objects

■ The Clipboard Object

The Clipboard object is used to copy or move information from one location to another. It is maintained by Windows and therefore even can be used to transfer information from one Windows application to another. It is actually a portion of memory that holds information and has no properties or events.

If *str* is a string, then the statement

```
Clipboard.SetText(str)
```

replaces any text currently in the clipboard with the value of *str*. The statement

```
str = Clipboard.GetText
```

assigns the text in the clipboard to the string variable *str*. The statement

```
Clipboard.SetText("")
```

deletes the contents of the clipboard.

A portion of the text in a text box or combo box can be **selected** by dragging the mouse across it or by moving the cursor across it while holding down the Shift key. After you select text, you can place it into the clipboard by pressing Ctrl + C. Also, if the cursor is in a text box and you press Ctrl + V, the contents of the clipboard will be inserted at the cursor position. These tasks also can be carried out in code. The SelectedText property of a text box holds the selected string from the text box, and a statement such as

```
Clipboard.SetText(txtBox.SelectedText)
```

copies this selected string into the clipboard. The statement

```
txtBox.SelectedText = Clipboard.GetText
```

replaces the selected portion of txtBox with the contents of the clipboard. If nothing has been selected, the statement inserts the contents of the clipboard into txtBox at the cursor position. The clipboard can actually hold any type of data, including graphics. Any time you use the Copy menu item, you are putting information into the clipboard. The Paste menu item sends that data to your program.

The Random Class

VisualBasic has a useful object called a random number generator that is declared with a statement of the form

```
Dim randomNum As New Random
```

If m and n are whole numbers, with $m < n$, then the value of

```
randomNum.Next(m, n)
```

is a randomly selected whole number from m through n, including m but excluding n. The Next method of this built-in object allows us to produce some interesting applications.

✔   **Example 1**   The DC Lottery number is obtained by selecting a Ping-Pong ball from each of three separate bowls. Each ball is numbered with an integer from 0 through 9. The following program produces a lottery number. Such a program is said to **simulate** the selection of Ping-Pong balls.

```
Private Sub btnSelect_Click(...) Handles btnSelect.Click
  'Display the winning lottery numbers
  Dim randomNum As New Random
  Dim num1, num2, num3 As Integer
  num1 = randomNum.Next(0, 10)
  num2 = randomNum.Next(0, 10)
  num3 = randomNum.Next(0, 10)
  txtNumbers.Text = num1 & "   " & num2 & "   " & num3
End Sub
```

[Run, and then press the button.]

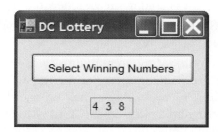

▣ The MenuStrip Control

Visual Basic forms can have menu bars similar to those in most Windows applications. Figure 9.11 shows a typical menu, with the Order menu revealed. Here, the menu bar contains two menu items (Order and Color), referred to as **top-level** menu items. When the Order menu item is clicked, a dropdown list containing two second-level menu items (Ascending and Descending) appears. Although not visible here, the dropdown list under Color contains the two second-level menu items Foreground and Background. Each menu item is treated as a distinct control that responds to a click event. The click event is triggered not only by the click of the mouse button, but also for top-level items by pressing Alt + accessKey and for second-level items by just pressing the access key. The event procedure for the Ascending or Descending menu item also can be triggered by pressing the shortcut key combination Ctrl + A or Ctrl + D.

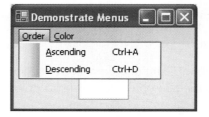

FIGURE 9.11   A simple menu.

Menus are created with the MenuStrip control, which is usually the third control in the Menus & Toolbars section of the Toolbox. Each menu item has a Text property (what the user sees) and a Name property (used to refer to the item in the code.) The following steps are used to create the Order-Color menu:

1. Start a new project.

2. Double-click on the MenuStrip control in the Toolbox. The control appears in a pane below the Main area, and a menu designer appears just below the title bar in the Form designer. See Figure 9.12.

3. Click on the rectangle that says "Type Here", type in the text &Order, and press the Enter key. (The ampersand specifies O as an access key for the menu item.)

   "Type Here" rectangles appear below and to the right of the Order menu item. The rectangle below is used to create a second-level item for the Order menu. The rectangle on the right is used to create a new first-level menu item.

4. Type the text "&Ascending" into the rectangle below the Order rectangle, and press the Enter key.

5. Click on the Ascending menu item to display its Property window. In the Property window, change the name property of the menu item from AscendingToolStrip-MenuItem to mnuOrderAsc. Also, click on the down-arrow at the right of the ShortcutKeys setting box, click on the "Ctrl" Modifier check box, select "A" from the Key drop-down combo box, and then press the Enter key. (When the program is run, "Ctrl + A" will appear to the right of the word "Ascending".)

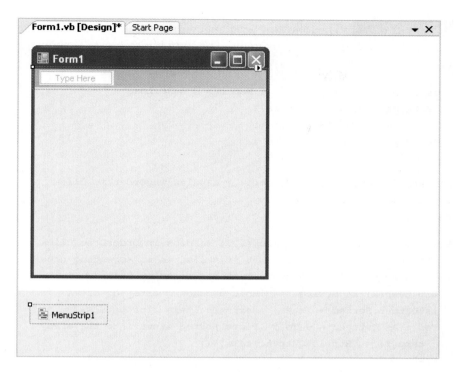

FIGURE 9.12 **The MenuStrip control added to a form.**

6. Type "&Descending" into the rectangle below the Ascending rectangle, set the Name property of the Descending menu item to mnuOrderDesc, and set the ShortcutKeys Property to Ctrl + D.

7. Click on the rectangle to the right of the Order rectangle and enter the text "&Color".

8. Type "&Foreground" into the rectangle below the Color rectangle, and set its Name property to mnuColorFore.

9. Type "&Background" into the rectangle below the Foreground rectangle, and set its Name property to mnuColorBack.

10. Click on the Foreground rectangle, and type "&Red" into the rectangle on its right. (We have just created a third-level menu item.) Set its Name property to mnuColorForeRed.

11. Type "&Blue" into the rectangle below the Red rectangle, and set its Name property to mnuColorForeBlue.

12. Click on the Background rectangle, type "&Yellow" into the rectangle on its right, and set its Name property to mnuColorBackYellow.

13. Type "&White" into the rectangle below the Yellow rectangle, and set its Name property to mnuColorBackWhite. Then set its Checked property to True. A check mark will appear to the left of the word "White."

14. Run the program; click on Order to see its menu items; click on Color and hover over the word Foreground to see its menu items. Each menu item has a Click event procedure. The menu items are only useful after we write code for the relevant event procedures.

Example 2 The following program uses the menu just created to alter the colors of a list box and the order of its items. The form has the text "Demonstrate Menus" in its title bar.

```
Private Sub frmDemo_Load(...) Handles MyBase.Load
  lstOutput.Items.Add("makes")
  lstOutput.Items.Add("haste")
  lstOutput.Items.Add("waste")
End Sub

Private Sub mnuOrderAsc_Click(...) Handles mnuOrderAsc.Click
  lstOutput.Sorted = True
End Sub

Private Sub mnuOrderDesc_Click(...) Handles mnuOrderDesc.Click
  'This code uses the fact that if a list is in ascending order,
  'then reading it backwards gives a descending list
  Dim temp(2) As String     'Hold ascending array of items
  lstOutput.Sorted = True    'Sort the items alphabetically
  For i As Integer = 0 To 2 'Place sorted items into the array
    temp(i) = CStr(lstOutput.Items(i))
  Next
  lstOutput.Sorted = False   'Turn off the Sorted property
  lstOutput.Items.Clear()
  For i As Integer = 2 To 0 Step -1
    lstOutput.Items.Add(temp(i))
  Next
End Sub

Private Sub mnuColorForeRed_Click(...) Handles mnuColorForeRed.Click
  lstOutput.ForeColor = Color.Red
End Sub

Private Sub mnuColorForeBlue_Click(...) Handles mnuColorForeBlue.Click
  lstOutput.ForeColor = Color.Blue
End Sub

Private Sub mnuColorBackYellow_Click(...) Handles_
          mnuColorBackYellow.Click
  'Make Yellow the background color of the list box, guarantee that a
  'check mark appears in front of the menu item Yellow and not in front
  'of the White menu item
  lstOutput.BackColor = Color.Yellow
  mnuColorBackYellow.Checked = True
  mnuColorBackWhite.Checked = False
End Sub
```

```
Private Sub mnuColorBackWhite_Click(...) Handles mnuColorBackWhite.Click
  lstOutput.BackColor = Color.White
  mnuColorBackYellow.Checked = False
  mnuColorBackWhite.Checked = True
End Sub
```

[Run, click on the Ascending item in the Order menu, click on the Color menu item, hover over the Foreground item, and click on Red.]

▨ Multiple Forms

A Visual Basic program can contain more than one form. Additional forms are created from the Project menu with Add Windows Form (Alt/P/F), which brings up an Add New Item dialog box. See Figure 9.13. To add the new form select Windows Form from the Installed Templates pane, optionally type in a name, and press the Add button. The second form has default name Form2.

![The Add New Item dialog box]

FIGURE 9.13   The Add New Item dialog box.

The name of each form appears in the Solution Explorer window (see Figure 9.14), and either form can be made the active form by double-clicking on its name. (When a form is active, its Form designer and Code window are displayed in the Main area.) Also, the names of both forms appear on tabs in the Main area.

FIGURE 9.14   **Solution Explorer after second form is added.**

The most common use of a second form is as a customized dialog box that is displayed to present a special message or request specific information. When a Message or Input dialog box appears, the user cannot shift the focus to another form without first closing the dialog box by clicking on OK or Cancel. If a form is displayed with the ShowDialog method, then the form will exhibit this same behavior. The user will not be allowed to shift the focus back to the first form until the second form disappears. Such a form is said to be **modal**. It is customary to set the FormBorderStyle property of modal forms to Fixed Dialog. When a program is run, the first form created is the only one visible. After that, the second form will appear when the ShowDialog method is executed and disappear when its Close method is invoked.

Form2 is actually a template for a form in the same manner that the TextBox class denoted by the TextBox icon on the ToolBar is a template for the actual text boxes appearing on a form. A text box on a form is said to be an **instance** of the TextBox class. An instance of Form2 is created with a statement such as

```
Dim secondForm As New Form2()
```

which also provides a variable, *secondForm*, that will be used to refer to the instance of the form.

Variables declared with Dim statements are either local (visible only to the procedure where they are declared) or class-level (visible to the entire form where they were declared). If a variable is declared in the Declarations section of Form2 with the word "Dim" replaced with "Public," then the value of the variable will be available to all forms in the program. However, when a Public variable is used in Form1, it is referred to by an expression such as secondForm.*variableName*. (As a personal analogy, at home you might be called John, but to strangers you might be introduced as "Fred's son John" to distinguish you from anyone else named John.)

Example 3 The following program uses a second form as a dialog box to total the different sources of income. Initially, only frmIncome is visible. The user types in his or her name and then either can type in the income or click on the button for assistance in totaling the different sources of income. Clicking on the button from frmIncome causes frmSources to appear and be active. The user fills in the three text boxes and then clicks on the button to have the amounts totaled and displayed in the Total Income text box of frmIncome.

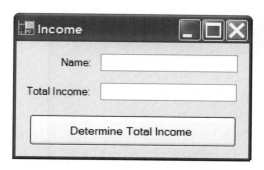

OBJECT	PROPERTY	SETTING
frmIncome	Text	Income
lblName	Text	Name:
txtName		
lblTotIncome	Text	Total Income:
txtTotIncome		
btnDetermine	Text	Determine Total Income

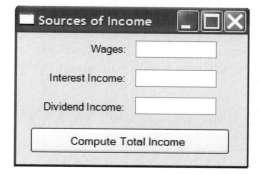

OBJECT	PROPERTY	SETTING
frmSources	Text	Sources of Income
	FormBorderStyle	FixedDialog
lblWages	Text	Wages:
txtWages		
lblIntIncome	Text	Interest Income:
txtIntIncome		
lblDivIncome	Text	Dividend Income:
txtDivIncome		
btnCompute	Text	Compute Total Income

```
'frmIncome's code
Private Sub btnDetermine_Click(...) Handles btnDetermine.Click
    Dim secondForm As New frmSources()      'Instantiate the second form
    secondForm.ShowDialog()  'Show second form and wait until it closes.
                      'Then execute rest of the code in this procedure.
    txtTotIncome.Text = FormatCurrency(secondForm.sum)
End Sub


'frmSources's code
Public sum As Double    'Holds the sum of the text boxes' values
'The keyword Public makes the variable sum available to frmIncome.

Private Sub btnCompute_Click(...) Handles btnCompute.Click
    'Store the total into the Public variable sum
    sum = CDbl(txtWages.Text) + CDbl(txtIntIncome.Text) _
        + CDbl(txtDivIncome.Text)
    Me.Close() 'Close the form as it is not needed anymore
End Sub
```

[Run, enter name, click the button, and fill in the sources of income.] **Note:** After the Compute Total Income button is pressed, frmSources will disappear and the sum of the three numbers will be displayed in the Total Income text box of frmIncome.

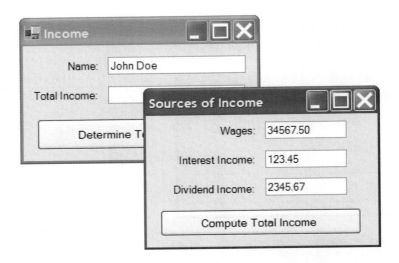

Note: If a Structure is defined in frmIncome, it can be used as a data type in frmSources. However, in frmSources it must be referred to as frmIncome. *structureName*.

Practice Problem 9.3

What is the effect of the following event procedure?

```
Private Sub btnDisplay_Click(...) Handles btnDisplay.Click
  Dim randomNum As New Random
  Dim contestant() As String = {"Mary", "Pat", "Linda", _
                                "Barbara", "Maria"}
  Dim number As Integer, temp As String
  For i As Integer = 0 To 4
    number = randomNum.Next(i, 5)
    temp = contestant(i)
    contestant(i) = contestant(number)
    contestant(number) = temp
  Next
  lstOutput.Items.Clear()
  For i As Integer = 0 To 4
    lstOutput.Items.Add(contestant(i))
  Next
End Sub
```

EXERCISES 9.3

In Exercises 1 through 18, describe the effect of executing the statement(s).

1. `Clipboard.SetText("")`

2. `Clipboard.SetText("Hello")`

3. `Clipboard.SetText(txtBox.SelectedText)`

4. `txtBox.SelectedText = Clipboard.GetText()`

5. `txtBox.Text = Clipboard.GetText`

6. `Dim strVar As String = "Happy"`
   `Clipboard.SetText(strVar)`

7. `Dim strVar As String`
   `strVar = Clipboard.GetText`

8. `Dim randomNum As New Random`
   `txtBox.Text = CStr(randomNum.Next(1, 10))`

9. `Dim randomNum As New Random`
   `Dim number As Integer`
   `'Assume the array Pres() contains the names of the 43 U.S. Presidents`
   `number = randomNum.Next(0, 43)`
   `txtBox.Text = Pres(number)`

10. `Dim randomNum As New Random`
    `'95 characters can be produced by the computer keyboard`
    `txtBox.Text = Chr(randomNum.Next(32, 127))`

11. `Dim randomNum As New Random`
    `Dim number As Integer, temp As String`
    `'Suppose the array states() contains the names of the 50 states`
    `number = randomNum.Next(0, 50)`
    `lstBox.Items.Add(states(number))`
    `temp = states(number)`
    `states(number) = states(49)`
    `states(49) = temp`
    `lstBox.Items.Add(states(randomNum.Next(0, 49)))`

12. `Dim randomNum As New Random`
    `Dim suit() As String = {"Hearts", "Clubs", "Diamonds", "Spades"}`
    `Dim denomination() As String = {"2", "3", "4", "5", "6", _`
    `        "7", "8", "9", "10", "Jack", "Queen", "King", "Ace"}`
    `txtBox.Text = denomination(randomNum.Next(0, 13)) & " of " & _`
    `            suit(randomNum.Next(0, 4))`

13. `mnuOrderAsc.Checked = True`

14. `mnuOrderAsc.Checked = False`

15. `mnuOrderAsc.Text = "Increasing Order"`

16. `Me.Close()`

17. `Public address As String    'In Declarations section of Form2`

18. `Dim secondForm As New Form2()`
    `secondForm.ShowDialog()`

In Exercises 19 through 34, write one or more lines of code to carry out the task.

19. Replace the selected portion of txtBox with the contents of the clipboard.

20. Clear out the contents of the clipboard.

21. Place the word "Rosebud" into the clipboard.

22. Copy the selected text in txtBox into the clipboard.

23. Delete the selected portion of txtBox.

24. Assign the contents of the clipboard to the Integer variable *amount*.

25. Display in txtBox a randomly selected number from 1 to 100.

26. Twenty names are contained in the array *Names*( ). Display a randomly selected name in txtBox.

27. Display in txtBox a letter randomly selected from the alphabet.

28. The file CITIES.TXT contains the names of fifty cities. Display a randomly selected city in txtBox.

29. Display in txtBox the sum of the faces after tossing a pair of dice.

30. Twenty names are contained in the array *Rivers*( ). Randomly select two different names from the array and display them in lstBox.

31. Remove the check mark in front of the menu item named mnuOrderDesc.

32. Change the text for mnuOrderDesc to "Decreasing Order".

33. Close the form containing the line of code.

34. Declare the Double variable *number* so that its value will be available to other forms.

Exercises 35 and 36 refer to Example 2.

35. Conjecture on the effect of the statement

    `mnuOrderAsc.Enabled = False`

    and test your conjecture.

36. Conjecture on the effect of the statement

    `mnuOrderAsc.Visible = False`

    and test your conjecture.

37. Write a program with a single text box and a menu with the single top-level item Edit and the four second-level items Copy, Paste, Cut, and Exit. Copy should place a copy of the selected portion of txtBox into the clipboard, Paste should duplicate the contents of the clipboard at the cursor position, Cut should delete a selected portion of the text box and place it in the clipboard, and Exit should terminate the program.

38. The file MEMBERS.TXT contains the names of the 100 members of a club. Write a program to randomly select people to serve as President, Treasurer, and Secretary. *Note:* A person cannot hold more than one office.

39. Place the names of the 52 playing cards into the array *deckOfCards*( ). Then display the names of five randomly chosen cards in lstPokerHand.

40. Write a program that repeatedly "throws" a pair of dice and tallies the number of tosses and the number of those tosses that total seven. The program should stop when 100 sevens have been tossed. The program should then report the approximate odds of tossing a seven. (The approximate odds will be "1 in " followed by the result of dividing the number of tosses by the number of tosses that came up seven.)

41. Write a program using the form in Figure 9.15. Each time the button is pressed, a Random object is used to simulate a coin toss and the values are updated. The figure shows the status after the button has been pressed 537 times.

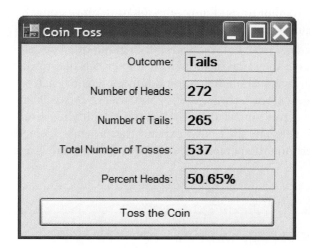

FIGURE 9.15   Sample run of Exercise 41.

Note: You can produce tosses quickly by just holding down the Enter key. Although the percentage of heads initially will fluctuate considerably, it should stay close to 50% after many (say, 1000) tosses.

42. Write a program containing the two forms shown in Figure 9.16. Initially, the Number to Dial form appears. When the Show Push Buttons button is clicked, the Push Button form appears. The user enters a number by clicking on successive push buttons and then clicks on Enter to have the number transferred to the read-only text box at the bottom of the first form.

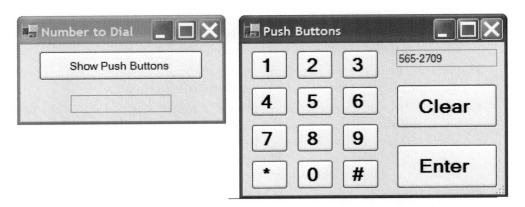

FIGURE 9.16   Sample run of Exercise 42.

43. Write a program to randomly select 40 different people from a group of 100 people whose names are contained in a text file.

44. *The Birthday Problem.* Given a random group of 23 people, how likely is it that two people have the same birthday? To answer this question, write a program that creates an array of 23 elements, randomly assigns to each subscripted variable one of the integers from 1 through 365, and checks to see if any of the subscripted variables have the same value. (Make the simplifying assumption that no birthdays occur on February 29.) Now expand the program to repeat the process 100 times and determine the percentage of the time that there is a match.

Solution to Practice Problem 9.3

The event procedure places the names of the contestants in a randomly ordered list.

9.4   Graphics

In this section, we draw bar charts and pie charts in a picture box, and illustrate one method for creating animation on a form.

◼ Graphics Objects

A statement of the form

```
Dim gr As Graphics = picBox.CreateGraphics
```

declares *gr* to be a Graphics object for the picture box picBox.

The unit of measurement used in graphics methods is the *pixel*. To get a feel for how big a pixel is, the title bar of a form is 30 pixels high, and the border of a form is four pixels thick. The setting for the Size property of a picture box is two numbers separated by a comma. The two numbers give the width and height of the picture box in pixels. You can alter these numbers to specify a precise size. Each point of a picture box is identified by a pair of coordinates

`(x, y)`

where *x* (between 0 and picBox.Width) is its distance in pixels from the left side of the picture box, and *y* (between 0 and picBox.Height) is its distance in pixels from the top of the picture box.

Text is placed in a picture box with a statement of the form

`gr.DrawString(string, Me.Font, Brushes.Color, x, y)`

where *string* is either a string variable or literal, Me.Font specifies that the Form's font be used to display the text, and the upper-left corner of the first character of the text has coordinates (*x*, *y*). The color of the text is determined by *Color*. IntelliSense will provide a list of about 140 possible colors after `"Brushes."` is typed. As an example, the statements

```
Dim gr As Graphics = picBox.CreateGraphics
Dim strVar As String = "Hello"
gr.DrawString(strVar, Me.Font, Brushes.Blue, 4, 30)
gr.DrawString("World", Me.Font, Brushes.Red, 35, 50)
```

produce the output shown in Figure 9.17.

FIGURE 9.17   DrawString method.

▪ Lines, Rectangles, Circles, and Sectors

Let *gr* be a graphics object for picBox. Then the statement

`gr.DrawLine(Pens.Color, x1, y1, x2, y2)`

draws a straight line segment from the point with coordinates (*x1*, *y1*) to the point with coordinates (*x2*, *y2*). The color of the line is determined by *Color*. IntelliSense will provide an extensive list of possible colors after `"Pens."` is typed. For instance, the statement

`gr.DrawLine(Pens.Blue, 50, 20, 120, 75)`

draws a blue line from the point with coordinates (50, 20) to the point with coordinates (120, 75). See Figure 9.18.

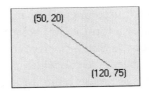

FIGURE 9.18   DrawLine method.

The statement

`gr.FillRectangle(Brushes.Color, x, y, w, h)`

draws a solid rectangle of width w and height h in the color specified and having the point with coordinates (x, y) as its upper-left vertex. For instance, the statement

`gr.FillRectangle(Brushes.Blue, 50, 20, 70, 55)`

draws the rectangle shown in Figure 9.19.

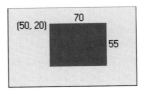

FIGURE 9.19   FillRectangle method.

The FillEllipse method draws a solid ellipse of a specified color, given the specifications of a circumscribed rectangle. The rectangle is specified by the coordinates of its upper-left point, its width, and its height. This method produces a circle when the width and height of the rectangle are the same. In particular, the statement

`gr.FillEllipse(Brushes.Color, x - r, y - r, 2 * r, 2 * r)`

draws a solid circle of the specified color with center (x, y) and radius r. For instance, the statement

`gr.FillEllipse(Brushes.Blue, 80 - 40, 50 - 40, 2 * 40, 2 * 40)`

draws a solid blue circle with center (80, 50) and radius 40. **Note:** If a rectangle were circumscribed about the circle, the rectangle would be a square with its upper-left vertex at (40, 10) and each side of length 80.

The FillPie method draws a solid sector of an ellipse in a color. The ellipse is specified by giving the coordinates, width, and height for the circumscribing rectangle, as in the FillEllipse method. The sector is determined by a radius line and the angle swept out by the radius line. We are interested solely in the case where the ellipse is a circle. The shaded region in Figure 9.20 is a typical sector (or pie shaped region) of a circle. The sector is determined by the two angles θ_1 and θ_2. The start angle, θ_1, is the angle through which the horizontal radius line must be rotated clockwise to reach the start-

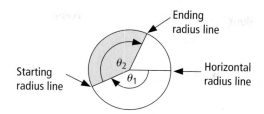

FIGURE 9.20   A typical sector of a circle.

ing radius line of the sector. Angle θ_2 is the number of degrees through which the starting radius line must sweep (clockwise) to reach the ending radius line of the sector. The angles θ_1 and θ_2 are referred to as the **start angle** and the **sweep angle**, respectively. Figure 9.21 shows the start and sweep angles for three sectors.

   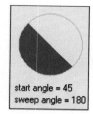   

FIGURE 9.21   FillPie method.

The Brushes, Pens, and Fonts appearing in the drawing statements so far are literals of objects. Variables also can be used to provide these values. For instance, the statement `gr.FillRectangle(Brushes.Blue, 50, 20, 70, 55)` can be replaced by the pair of statements

```
Dim br As Brush = Brushes.Blue
gr.FillRectangle(br, 50, 20, 70, 55)
```

The first statement declares *br* to be a variable of type Brush and assigns it the value Brushes.Blue.

Numeric variables used in the Draw and Fill statements discussed in this section must be of type Integer or Single. The **Single data type** is similar to the Double data type, but has a smaller range. A variable of type Single can hold whole numbers, fractional, or mixed number between about $-3.4 \cdot 10^{38}$ and $3.4 \cdot 10^{38}$. The **CSng** function converts other data types to the Single data type.

▨ Pie Charts

Consider the three pieces of data in Table 9.1. A pie chart can be used to graphically display the relative sizes of these numbers. The first step in creating a pie chart is to convert the numbers to percents. Since the total expenditures are $419 billion, the federal outlay is 33/419 ≈ .08 or 8%. Similarly, the state and local expenditures are 49% and 43%. See Table 9.2. Our goal is to write a program to display the information in the pie chart of Figure 9.22.

TABLE 9.1	Financing public schools (in billions).
Federal	$33
State	$206
Local	$180

TABLE 9.2	Financing public schools.
Federal	.08 or 8%
State	.49 or 49%
Local	.43 or 43%

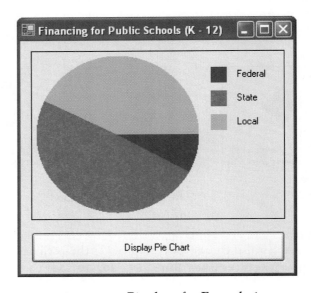

FIGURE 9.22   Pie chart for Example 1.

The blue sector in Figure 9.22 has start angle 0 and sweep angle .08 * 360. The red sector has start angle .08 * 360 and sweep angle .49 * 360. The tan sector has start angle .08 * 360 + .49 * 360 [or (.08 + .49) * 360] and sweep angle .43 * 360. Notice that each start angle is (sum of previous percentages) * 360. The sweep angle for each sector is the corresponding percentage times 360.

 Example 1   The following program creates the pie chart (see Figure 9.22) for the financing of public schools. The program is written so that it can be easily converted to handle a pie chart with up to six sectors. All that is required is to change the first two Dim statements and the Me.Text statement. The "Dim br() As Brush" line, which creates an array of brushes, has six brushes in order to accommodate additional sectors.

```
Private Sub btnDisplay_Click(...) Handles btnDisplay.Click
  Dim legend() As String = {"Federal", "State", "Local"}
  Dim quantity() As Single = {33, 206, 180}
  Dim percent(quantity.GetUpperBound(0)) As Single
```

```
  Dim sumOfQuantities As Single = 0
  Dim sumOfSweepAngles As Single = 0
  Dim br() As Brush = {Brushes.Blue, Brushes.Red, Brushes.Tan, _
           Brushes.Green, Brushes.Orange, Brushes.Gray}
  Dim gr As Graphics = picOutput.CreateGraphics
  'The picture box has width 312 and height 215
  Dim r As Integer = 100     'Radius of circle
  Dim c As Integer = 105       'Center of circle has coordinates (c, c)
  Me.Text = "Financing for Public Schools (K - 12)"
  'Sum the numbers for the quantities
  For i As Integer = 0 To quantity.GetUpperBound(0)
    sumOfQuantities += quantity(i)
  Next
  'Convert the quantities to percents
  For i As Integer = 0 To quantity.GetUpperBound(0)
    percent(i) = quantity(i) / sumOfQuantities
  Next
  'Display the pie chart and the legends
  For i As Integer = 0 To quantity.GetUpperBound(0)
    gr.FillPie(br(i), c - r, c - r, 2 * r, 2 * r, _
            sumOfSweepAngles, percent(i) * 360)
    sumOfSweepAngles += percent(i) * 360
    gr.FillRectangle(br(i), 220, 20 + 30 * i, 20, 20)
    gr.DrawString(legend(i), Me.Font, Brushes.Black, 250, 22 + 30 * i)
  Next
End Sub
```

■ Bar Charts

Our goal here is to produce the bar chart of Figure 9.23. The picture box for the chart has a width of 210 and height of 150 pixels. (Here, the BorderStyle property is set to FixedSingle for instructional reasons. In general, the bar chart will look better with the BorderStyle property left at its default setting: None.)

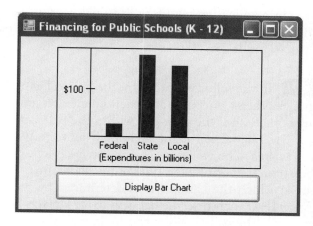

FIGURE 9.23   Bar chart for Example 2.

The three magnitudes for the graph are 33, 206, and 180. If we let a pixel correspond to one unit, then the largest rectangle will be 206 pixels high—a bit too large. With a pixel corresponding to 2 units, the largest rectangle will be 206 / 2 or 103 pixels high— a reasonable size. By setting the x-axis 110 pixels from the top of the picture box, the largest rectangle is accomodated comfortably. The top of the largest rectangle is 110 − 103 [that is, 110 − (206/2)] pixels from the top of the picture box. In general, a rectangle corresponding to the quantity q will be 110 − (q/2) pixels from the top of the picture box, and the height will be q / 2 pixels.

 Example 2   The following program produces the bar chart of Figure 9.23. Each rectangle is 20 pixels wide, and there are 20 pixels between rectangles.

```
Private Sub btnDisplay_Click(...) Handles btnDisplay.Click
  Dim quantity() As Single = {33, 206, 180}
  Dim gr As Graphics = picOutput.CreateGraphics
  'The picture box has width 210 and height 150
  gr.DrawLine(Pens.Black, 40, 110, picOutput.Width, 110) 'Draw x-axis
  gr.DrawLine(Pens.Black, 40, 110, 40, 0)                 'Draw y-axis
  gr.DrawLine(Pens.Black, 35, 100 / 2, 45, 100 / 2)    'Draw tick mark
  gr.DrawString("$100", Me.Font, Brushes.Black, 5, 45)
  Me.Text = "Financing for Public Schools (K - 12)"
  For i As Integer = 0 To quantity.GetUpperBound(0)
    gr.FillRectangle(Brushes.Blue, 60 + i * 40, _
                (110 - quantity(i) / 2), 20, quantity(i) / 2)
  Next
  gr.DrawString("Federal    State    Local", Me.Font, _
            Brushes.Black, 50, 115)
  gr.DrawString("(Expenditures in billions)", Me.Font, _
            Brushes.Black, 50, 130)
End Sub
```

▓ Animation

One way to produce animation on a form is to place an image into a picture box and then move the picture by steadily changing the location of the picture box. Figure 9.24 shows a ball placed inside a small picture box.

 Example 3   In the following program, the ball in Figure 9.24 will initially move diagonally in a Southeast direction and then bounce off any side of the form it hits. The **client area** of a form is the gray area within the title bar and borders of the form. The values of Me.ClientSize.Height and Me.ClientSize.Width are the height and width of the gray area. The values of picBox.Top and picBox.Left are the distances of the picture box from the top and left sides of the client area.

The speed at which the ball moves is determined by the setting for the Interval property of Timer1. At each tick, the ball will move x pixels horizontally, where $x = 1$ or −1. When $x = 1$ the ball moves to the right, and when $x = -1$ the ball moves to

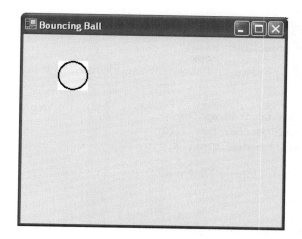

FIGURE 9.24 **The form for Example 3.**

OBJECT	PROPERTY	SETTING
frmBall	Text	Bouncing Ball
picBall	Image	MOON5.BMP
Timer1	Interval	10

the left. The value of *x* reverses when the ball strikes the right or left side of the form. The value of *y* determines the vertical motion of the ball in a similar manner,

```
Dim x As Integer = 1
Dim y As Integer = 1

Private Sub frmBall_Load(...) Handles MyBase.Load
  Timer1.Enabled = True
End Sub

Private Sub Timer1_Tick(...) Handles Timer1.Tick
  If picBall.Top <= 0 Or _
     picBall.Top >= (Me.ClientSize.Height - picBall.Height) Then
    x = -x
  End If
  picBall.Top += x
  If picBall.Left <= 0 Or _
     picBall.Left >= (Me.ClientSize.Width - picBall.Width) Then
    y = -y
  End If
  picBall.Left += y
End Sub
```

Comments

1. A statement of the form

```
Dim pn As Pen = Pens.Color
```

declares *pn* to be a variable of type Pen and assigns it the value Pens.*Color*.

2. A statement of the form

```
Dim fnt As Font = New Font(fontName, size)
```

declares *fnt* to be a variable of type Font and assigns it the specified font and size. For instance, the statements

```
Dim gr As Graphics = picBox.CreateGraphics
Dim fnt As Font = New Font("Courier New", 10)
gr.DrawString("Hello", fnt, Brushes.Blue, 4, 30)
```

display the word Hello in 10-point Courier New font.

3. The statement

```
picBox.Refresh()
```

clears all graphics and text from the picture box.

4. The client area of a picture box is the gray area within the borders of the picture box. When the BorderStyle property is set to None, the client area is the entire picture box. When the BorderStyle property is set to FixedSingle, the width and height of the client area are each two pixels less than the width and height of the entire picture box. For instance, if the BorderStyle setting of picBox is FixedSingle, if picBox.Width is 200 and picBox.Height is 100, then picBox.ClientSize.Width is 198 and picBox.ClientSize.Height is 98.

Practice Problems 9.4

1. (True or False) The Draw and Fill methods discussed in this section use colored Brushes.
2. Suppose the Size property of picBox is "200, 100." Give the lines of code that draw the uppermost and lowermost red horizontal lines possible in the picture box.

EXERCISES 9.4

In Exercises 1 through 4, write an event procedure to draw the given figures in a picture box.

1. Draw a circle whose center is located at the center of a picture box.
2. Draw a circle whose leftmost point is at the center of a picture box.
3. Use the FillEllipse method to create an unfilled red circle of radius 20.
4. Draw a triangle with two sides of the same length.

In Exercises 5 through 8, write a program to create the flag of the designated country. Refer to Figure 9.25. *Note:* The Swiss flag is square. For the other three flags, the width is 1.5 times the height.

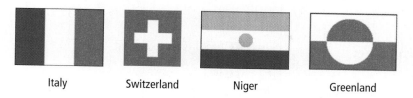

Italy   Switzerland   Niger   Greenland

FIGURE 9.25   **Flags of four countries.**

5. Italy   **6.** Switzerland   **7.** Niger   **8.** Greenland

9. Write a program to draw displays such at the one in Figure 9.26. Let the user specify the maximum number (in this display, 8).

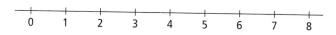

FIGURE 9.26   **Drawing for Exercise 9.**

10. Write a program to draw displays such at the one in Figure 9.27. Let the user specify the number of lines (in this display, 3).

——————————— Line 1
——————————— Line 2
——————————— Line 3

FIGURE 9.27   **Drawing for Exercise 10.**

11. Use the data in Table 9.3 to create a pie chart.

TABLE 9.3	United States recreational beverage consumption.
Soft Drinks	52.9%
Beer	14.7%
Bottled Water	11.1%
Other	21.3%

12. Use the data in Table 9.4 to create a bar chart.

TABLE 9.4	United States minimum wage.
1959	1.00
1968	1.15
1978	2.65
1988	3.35
1998	5.15

13. Write a program to create the line chart in Figure 9.28. Use the data in Table 9.5.

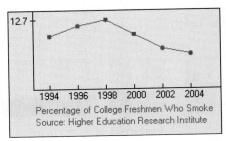

FIGURE 9.28 **Line chart for Exercise 13.**

TABLE 9.5	Percentage of college freshmen who smoke.					
	1994	1996	1998	2000	2002	2004
Percent	9.7	11.6	12.7	10.0	7.4	6.4

Source: Higher Education Research Institute

14. Write a program to create the line chart in Figure 9.29. Use the data in Table 9.6

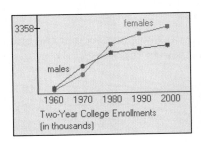

FIGURE 9.29 **Line chart for Exercise 14.**

TABLE 9.6	Two-year college enrollments (in thousands).				
	1960	1970	1980	1990	2000
Male	283	1375	2047	2233	2398
Female	170	945	2479	3007	3358

15. Write a program to create the bar chart in Figure 9.30.

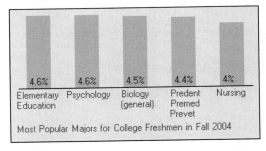

FIGURE 9.30 **Bar chart for Exercise 15.**

16. Write a program to create the bar chart in Figure 9.31. Use the data in Table 9.7

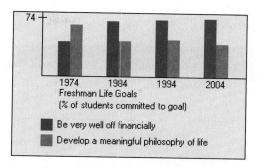

FIGURE 9.31   **Bar chart for Exercise 16.**

TABLE 9.7   **Freshman life goals (% of students committed to goal).**

	1974	1984	1994	2004
Be very well off financially	44	70	72	74
Develop a meaningful philosophy of life	65	45	47	42

Source: Higher Education Research Institute

17. Write a program to create the bar chart in Figure 9.32. Use the data in Table 9.8. **Note:** Mandarin and Wu are spoken primarily in China.

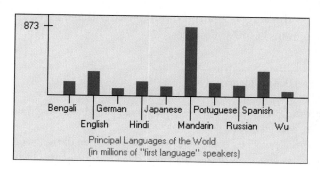

FIGURE 9.32   **Bar chart for Exercise 17.**

TABLE 9.8   **Principal languages of the world.**

Bengali	171
English	309
German	95
Hindi	180
Japanese	122
Mandarin	873
Portuguese	177
Russian	145
Spanish	322
Wu	77

18. Write a program that allows the user to display a budget as a pie chart. See Figure 9.33. After the user enters numbers into the four text boxes and presses the button, the pie chart should be displayed.

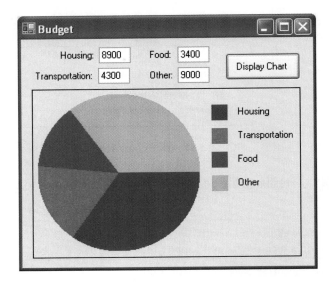

FIGURE 9.33 **Form for Exercise 18.**

19. Write a program in which an airplane flies horizontally to the right across a form. After it flies off the form, the airplane should reappear on the left and fly horizontally across the screen again. **Note:** Use the image AIRPLANE.BMP found in the folder Programs\Ch09\Pictures.

Solutions to Practice Problems 9.4

1. False. Only the Fill methods and the DrawString method use colored Brushes. The DrawLine method uses colored Pens.

2. If the BorderStyle property of picBox is set to "None," then the following code draws the lines. **Note:** There are 200 pixels across the top of picBox. They are represented by the numbers 0, 1, 2, . . . , 199.

```
Dim gr As Graphics = picBox.CreateGraphics
gr.DrawLine(Pens.Red, 0, 0, 199, 0)
gr.DrawLine(Pens.Red, 0, 99, 199, 99)
```

If the BorderStyle property of picBox is set to "FixedSingle," then the following code draws the lines.

```
Dim gr As Graphics = picBox.CreateGraphics
gr.DrawLine(Pens.Red, 0, 0, 197, 0)
gr.DrawLine(Pens.Red, 0, 97, 197, 97)
```

The following code will work with any setting of the BorderStyle property.

```
Dim gr As Graphics = picBox.CreateGraphics
gr.DrawLine(Pens.Red, 0, 0, picBox.ClientSize.Width - 1, 0)
gr.DrawLine(Pens.Red, 0, picBox.ClientSize.Height - 1, _
        picBox.ClientArea.Width - 1, picBox.ClientSize.Height - 1)
```

CHAPTER 9   SUMMARY

1. *List boxes* provide easy access to lists of strings. Items() holds the items stored in the list. Each item is identified by an index number (0, 1, 2, . . .). The lists can be automatically sorted (Sorted property = True) and altered (Items.AddItem, Items.RemoveAt, and Items.Remove methods), the currently highlighted item identified (Text property), and the number of items determined (Items.Count property).

2. *Combo boxes* are enhanced text boxes. They not only allow the user to enter information by typing it into a text box (read with the Text property), but also allow the user to select the information from a list of items.

3. The *OpenFileDialog control* provides a simple way to locate a file to be opened. The programmer can specify the types of files to display via the Filter property.

4. Selections are made with *check boxes* (allow several) and *radio buttons* (allow at most one). The state of the control (checked vs. unchecked or on vs. off) is stored in the Checked property. Clicking on a check box toggles its state. Clicking on a radio button gives it the on state and turns off the other radio buttons in its group.

5. *Group box controls* are used to band together other controls, especially radio buttons, as a unit.

6. The *timer control* triggers an event repeatedly after the duration of a specified time interval.

7. The *picture box control*, which displays pictures or geometric shapes, can expand to accommodate the size of the picture or have the picture alter its size to fit the control.

8. *Horizontal* and *vertical scroll bar controls* permit the user to select from among a range of integers by clicking or dragging with the mouse. The range is specified by the Minimum and Maximum properties, and changes trigger the Scroll event.

9. The *clipboard* is filled with the SetText method or by pressing Ctrl + C, and is copied with the GetText method or by pressing Ctrl + V.

10. An object of type *Random* can generate a randomly selected integer from a specified range.

11. Menus, similar to the menus of Visual Basic itself, can be created with the *MenuStrip control*.

12. Additional forms can serve as customized dialog boxes. They are revealed with the ShowDialog method and removed with the Close method.

13. After a graphics object is produced with a *CreateGraphics* method, the *DrawString*, *DrawLine*, *FillRectangle*, *FillEllipse*, and *FillPie* methods can be used to display strings, lines, solid rectangles, solid ellipses, and solid sectors with colors supplied by Pen and Brush objects.

14. Animation can be produced by steadily moving a picture box containing an image.

CHAPTER 9 PROGRAMMING PROJECTS

1. *Membership List.* Write a menu-driven program to manage a membership list. See Figure 9.34. Assume that the names and phone numbers of all members are stored in alphabetical order in the text file MEMBERPHONES.TXT. The names and phone numbers should be read into an array of structures, and the names should be displayed in a list box when the form is loaded. When a name is highlighted, both the name and phone number of the person should appear in the text boxes at the bottom of the screen. To delete a person, highlight his or her name and click on the Delete menu item. To change either the phone number or the spelling of the person's name, make the corrections in the text boxes, and click on the menu item Modify. To add a new member, type his or her name and phone number into the text boxes, and click on the menu item Add. When Exit is clicked, the new membership list should be written to the file, and the program should terminate.

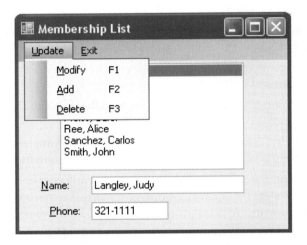

FIGURE 9.34 Form for Programming Project 1.

2. *Grade Book.* Write a comprehensive program that a professor could use to record student grades for several classes and save the records in sequential files. Each class has three hour exams and a final exam. The file for a single class should consist of the number of students in the class, call it n, and a record of five fields (name, grade1, grade2, grade3, and final) for each student, with the records ordered alphabetically by the student's name. (A typical name might appear as "Doe, John".) Initially, the four grade fields should contain zeros. The program should contain a top-level menu item, File, with second-level subitems for Open, Save, Add Student, and Remove Student. When a file is opened (via an OpenFileDialog control), the data for the students should be loaded into a list box. (The last two columns should remain blank.) The professor should be able to enter (or alter) exam data by double-clicking on a line of the list box to invoke a second form as a customized dialog box for inputting grades. See Figure 9.35. When a student is added, the student is inserted in proper alphabetical position. When the Calculate Semester Grades button is clicked, the last two columns should be filled in by the program. (Assume that the final exam counts as two hour exams.) If a grade is changed after the last

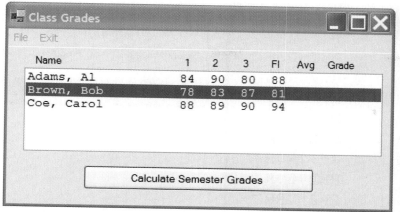
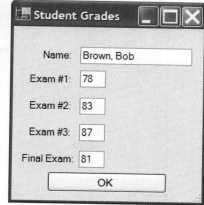

FIGURE 9.35   **Forms for Programming Project 2.**

two columns have been filled in, the corresponding average and grade should be recomputed.

3. *Inventory Control.* Write an inventory program for a book store, and save the information in a sequential file. Each record should consist of five fields—title, author, category, wholesale price, and number in stock. (The two categories are fiction and nonfiction.) At any time, the program should display the titles of the books in stock in a list box, for which the user should have the option of displaying either all titles or just those in one of the two categories. When a book is selected from the list, its title, author, category, wholesale price, and number in stock should be displayed in a list box. The user should be able to add a new book, delete a book, or change the inventory level of a book in stock. At any time, the user should be able to calculate the total value of all books, or the total value of the books in either category.

4. *Voting Machine.* The members of the local "Gilligan's Island" fan club bring a computer to their annual meeting to use in the election of a new president. Write a program to handle the election. The program should add each candidate to a list box as he or she is nominated. After the nomination process is complete, club members should be able to approach the computer one at a time and double-click on the candidate of their choice. When a "Tally Votes" button is clicked, a second list box, showing the number of votes received by each candidate, should appear alongside the first list box. Also, the name(s) of the candidate(s) with the highest number of votes should be displayed in a list box.

5. *Airplane Seating Chart.* An airplane has 15 rows (numbered 1 through 15), with six seats (labeled A, B, C, D, E, and F) in each row. Write a program to display the seating chart in a list box with a line for each row. When the ticket agent clicks on the desired row in the list box, the row number and the status of the seats in the row are displayed in seven read-only text boxes. When the agent clicks on one of the text boxes, a second form containing four option buttons labeled Unoccupied, Regular, Low Calorie, and Vegetarian appears. See Figure 9.36. Clicking on any radio button closes the second form and updates both the text box and the row for that seat in the list box. Unoccupied seats should be denoted with a period, while occupied seats are denoted with the first letter of their meal type. At any time, the

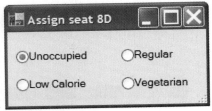

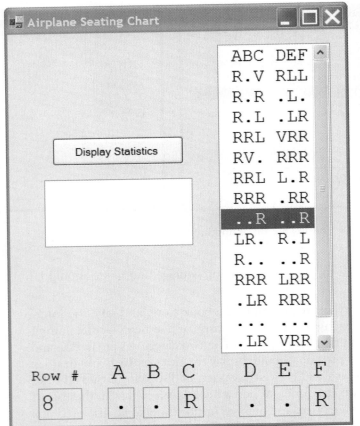

FIGURE 9.36   **Forms for Programming Project 5.**

agent can request the number of seats filled, the number of window seats vacant, and the numbers of each type of meal ordered.

6. *The Underdog and the World Series.* What is the probability that the underdog will win the World Series of Baseball? What is the average number of games for a World Series? Write an animated program to answer these questions. For instance, suppose that the underdog is expected to win 40% of the time. We say that the probability of the underdog winning a game is 40%. (**Note:** In order for a team to be the underdog, the probability that the team wins a game must be less than 50%.) Figure 9.37 shows that the probability that a 40% underdog wins the World Series is about 28.71% and that such a series should be expected to last an average of about 5.69 games. The program should simulate the playing of 10,000 World Series where the underdog has the probability of winning input in the text box. The values of the horizontal scroll bars should extend from 0 to 10,000 and should be calculated after each series so that the scroll boxes steadily move across the bars.

Note: In order for the text boxes to the right of the scroll bars to display data as the program progresses (and not just at the end of the program), execute a statement such as **txtUnderdog.Refresh** in about one-tenth of the 10,000 passes through the loop.

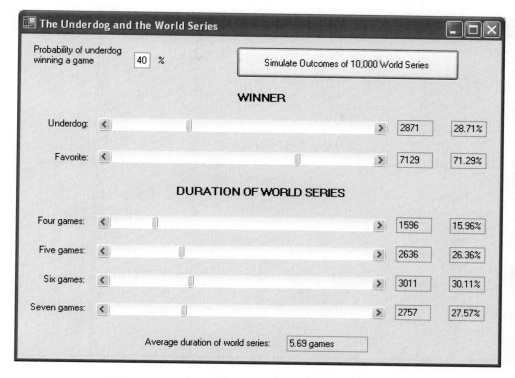

FIGURE 9.37   A sample run of Programming Project 6.

7. The admissions offices of large colleges often rely on a point system. A point system similar to the one in Figure 9.38 is used by a large state university. Write a program that displays the information in Figure 9.38 and allows an admissions officer to de-termine whether an applicant should be admitted. The numbers in brackets give the point count for each response. The GPA score displayed in the text box to the right of the horizontal scroll bar should change (from 2.0 to 4.0 in steps of .1) as the user clicks on the bar's right arrow. The point value in the brackets to the right of the text box is 20 times the GPA. A total of at most 40 points can be earned for the responses below the line. The program should calculate the total score and then admit every applicant whose score is at least 100.

8. Figure 9.39 is called a *range* chart. Using the data in Table 9.9, write a program to produce this chart.

TABLE 9.9	**Range of normal monthly rainfall for selected cities (in inches).**	
	Lowest NMR	Highest NMR
Mobile	2.6	7.7
Portland	.5	6.4
Phoenix	.1	1.0
Washington	2.6	4.4
Juneau	2.9	7.7
New York	3.1	4.2

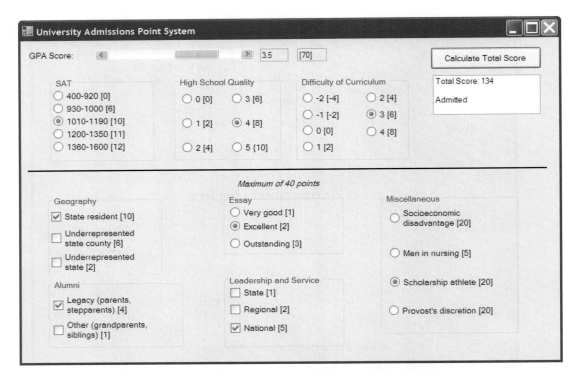

FIGURE 9.38   Sample run of Programming Project 7.

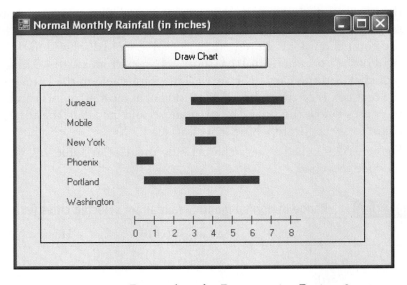

FIGURE 9.39   Range chart for Programming Project 8.

9. A community of 10,000 individuals is exposed to a flu epidemic in which infected individuals are sick for two days and then are immune from the illness. When we first start to observe the epidemic (that is, on day 0), 200 people have had the illness for one day, and 100 people have had the illness for two days. At any time, the rate at which the epidemic is spreading is proportional to the product of the number currently ill and the number susceptible. Specifically, each day

[# of individuals in the first day of the illness] =

  CInt(0.0001735 * [# sick the previous day] * [# susceptible the previous day])

Write a program that displays successive bar graphs illustrating the progress of the epidemic. When the "Show Day 0" button is pressed, the bar graph should show the distribution for day 0 (Figure 9.40). Each time the "Advance One Day" button is pressed, a bar graph showing the distribution for the next day should appear. Figure 9.41 shows the bar graph after this button has been pressed three times.

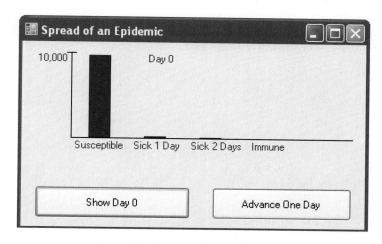

FIGURE 9.40   Initial distribution.

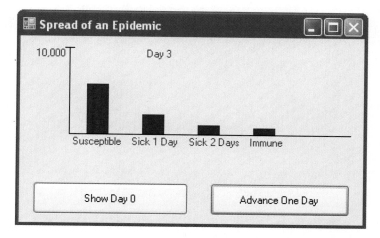

FIGURE 9.41   Distribution on day 3 of epidemic.

10

Database Management

10.1   An Introduction to Databases 518

◆ Database Explorer ◆ Accessing a Database with a Data Table

10.2   Relational Databases and SQL 531

◆ Primary and Foreign Keys ◆ SQL ◆ Four SQL Requests
◆ The DataGridView Control ◆ Changing the Contents of a
Database ◆ Calculated Columns with SQL

Summary 548

Programming Projects 549

10.1   An Introduction to Databases

The management of databases is the number one use of computers today. Airlines use databases to handle nearly 1.5 billion passenger reservations per year. The 6,500 hospitals in the United States utilize databases to document the care of over 30 million patients per year. Banks in the United States utilize databases to monitor the use of 350 million credit cards. Although databases vary considerably in size and complexity, most of them adhere to the fundamental principles of design discussed in this chapter. That is, they are composed of a collection of interrelated tables.

A **table** is a rectangular array of data. Table 10.1 provides information about large cities. Each column of the table is called a **field**. (The third column gives the 2005 population in millions and the fourth column gives the projected 2015 population in millions.) The names of the fields are *city*, *country*, *pop1995*, and *pop2015*. Each row, called a **record**, contains the same type of information as every other row. Also, the pieces of information in each row are related; they all apply to a specific city. Table 10.2, Countries, has three fields and nine records.

TABLE 10.1   **Cities.**

city	country	pop2005	pop2015
Bombay	India	18.2	22.6
Calcutta	India	14.3	16.8
Delhi	India	15.1	20.9
Dhaka	Bangladesh	12.4	17.9
Jakarta	Indonesia	13.0	17.5
Lagos	Nigeria	11.0	17.0
Mexico City	Mexico	19.0	20.6
New York	USA	18.5	19.7
Sao Paulo	Brazil	18.2	20.0
Tokyo	Japan	35.2	36.2

Note: The population figures are for "urban agglomerations"—that is, contiguous densely populated urban areas.

TABLE 10.2   **Countries.**

country	pop2005	monetaryUnit
Bangladesh	141.8	taka
Brazil	186.4	real
China	1316.8	yuan
India	1103.4	rupee
Indonesia	222.8	rupiah
Japan	128.1	yen
Mexico	107.0	peso
Nigeria	131.5	naira
Russia	143.2	ruble
USA	298.2	dollar

Source: United Nations, Dept. for Economic and Social Information and Policy Analysis.

A **database** (or **relational database**) is a collection of one or more (usually related) tables that has been created with **database-management software**. Microsoft Access is one of the best known database-management products. Some other prominent ones are Oracle, SQL Server, and DB2. VB.NET can manage, revise, and analyze a database that has been created with any of these products. VB.NET also has a powerful data viewer that can be used to browse through all portions of a database.

The database used in each example is found in the *Debug* subfolder for the program. The databases needed for the exercises are contained in the folder MajorDatabases located in the folder Programs\Ch10. The database files were created with Microsoft Access and have the extension .MDB. For instance, the file MEGACITIES.MDB is a database file containing the two tables presented on the preceding page. MDB files should be copied onto a hard drive and accessed from the hard drive. If the files originally resided on a CD, they might have the attribute "Read-only" set. If so, you should change this attribute for each file. To change the attribute setting, first use Windows Explorer to locate the file on the hard drive. Then right-click on the file, click Properties, and uncheck the "Read-only" box under Attributes.

■ Database Explorer

Visual Basic Express has a tool called Database Explorer that allows a developer to browse through the contents of a database. The other editions of Visual Basic have a tool called Server Explorer that can not only browse a database, but also view information on another computer. The following steps refer to Database Explorer, but are applicable to Server Explorer with slight modifications.

1. Press Alt/V/D to bring up Database Explorer from the View menu. It will appear on the left side of the screen. (Server Explorer can be invoked from the Standard and Professional editions of Visual Basic 2005 with Alt/V/V.)

2. Right-click on "Data Connections", and select "Add Connection".

3. In the Add Connection dialog box that appears, the Data Source should be "Microsoft Access Database File (OLE DB)." If not, click on the Change button, select "Microsoft Access Database File" as the data source, and click on OK to return to the Add Connection dialog box.

4. Click on the "Browse. . ." button to the right of the "Database file name" text box. This will open up a file browser that allows you to locate any file. Select the file MEGACITIES.MDB from the folder Programs\Ch10\MajorDatabases, and press Open.

5. Clear the contents of the "User name" text box.

6. Press the Test Connection button at the bottom of the window. The message box stating "Test Connection Succeeded" will appear. Press the OK button on that message box, and then press the OK button on the Add Connection box.

7. An icon titled something like "ACCESS.D:\PROGRAMS\CH10\MEGA-CITIES.MDB" should appear in Database Explorer. Click on the + sign to the left of the icon to expand this entry. Four subentries will appear: Tables, Views, and Stored Procedures, and Functions.

8. Expand the Tables entry to reveal the two subentries, the tables Cities and Countries.

9. Expand the Cities entry to reveal the fields of the Cities table. See Figure 10.1.

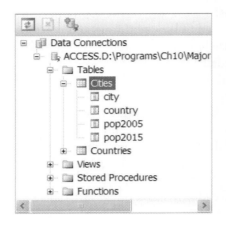

FIGURE 10.1   Server Explorer.

10. Right-click on Cities and select "Show Table Data." A grid similar to Figure 10.2 will appear. The grid not only displays all of the data in the Cities table, but also gives the names of the fields. **Note:** To remove the entry for the database in Database Explorer, right-click on the entry, and select Delete.

city	country	pop2005	pop2015
Bombay	India	18.2	22.6
Calcutta	India	14.3	16.8
Delhi	India	15.1	20.9
Dhaka	Bangladesh	12.4	17.9
Jakarta	Indonesia	13	17.5
Lagos	Nigeria	11	17
Mexico City	Mexico	19	20.6
New York	USA	18.5	19.7
Sao Paulo	Brazil	18.2	20
Tokyo	Japan	35.2	36.2

FIGURE 10.2   The Cities table of MEGACITIES.MDB.

The remainder of this section is devoted to creating programs that display information obtained from a database. A **DataTable** object is the representation of a table (with rows and columns) in ADO.NET. The ActiveX Data Objects .NET (ADO.NET) technology allows programs to access data seamlessly from multiple, varied, and distant servers.

Each time we begin a new program, there are two steps you must take in order to gain access to the Data Table object.

1. Add references to System.Data.dll and System.Xml.dll.
   To accomplish this step:
   (a) Click on Project in the Menu bar.
   (b) Click on Add Reference in the drop-down menu to invoke the "Add Reference" dialog box.
   (c) Make sure the .NET tab is selected.
   (d) Click on System.Data, and then hold down the Ctrl key and click on System.Xml This way both items will be selected.
   (e) Press the OK button.

2. At the top of the code window (before the line **Public Class Form1**), type the statement

   ```
   Imports System.Data
   ```

   Important Note: We will assume these two steps have been carried out for every program in this chapter.

Accessing a Database with a Data Table

A DataTable object holds the contents of a table as a rectangular array. (A data table is similar to a two-dimensional array; it has rows and columns.) The following six lines of code create a DataTable variable named "dt" and fill it with the contents of the Cities table from the database MEGACITIES.MDB:

```
Dim dt As New DataTable()
Dim connStr As String = "Provider=Microsoft.Jet.OLEDB.4.0;" & _
                    "Data Source=MEGACITIES.MDB"
Dim sqlStr As String = "SELECT * FROM Cities"
Dim dataAdapter As New OleDb.OleDbDataAdapter(sqlStr, connStr)
dataAdapter.Fill(dt)
dataAdapter.Dispose()
```

Treat these six lines of code as a boiler plate to be inserted into a program.

Note: You can save yourself time by storing this code fragment in the Toolbox and dragging it into the Code window when needed.

A database resides on a disk, and a data table resides in memory. A **data adapter** is an intermediary object that serves as a conduit to allow bidirectional data transfers between the two. The first statement in the boiler plate, which declares *dt* to be a variable of type DataTable, is often placed in the Declaration section of the Code window. The fifth statement of the boiler plate uses the data adapter to fill the data table with data from the database. The sixth statement of the boiler plate releases all resources of the data adapter.

The variable connString is called a **connection string**. A connection string has two parameters. The Provider parameter specifies the driver that is used to communicate with the database. The Data Source parameter gives the filespec of the database. When the database is in the *bin/Debug* folder of the current program, the filename can be used instead of the filespec.

The variable sqlStr is called an **SQL string**. SQL strings tell the data adapter which table to retrieve. SQL strings are discussed extensively in Section 10.2.

The second and third statements of the boiler plate have the following general form:

```
Dim connStr As String = "Provider=Microsoft.Jet.OLEDB.4.0;" & _
                         "Data Source=" & DataBaseName
Dim sqlStr As String = "SELECT * FROM " & TableName
```

where the database is assumed to be in the *Debug* subfolder of the *bin* subfolder of the program folder.

After the six lines of code are executed, the value of

```
dt.Rows.Count
```

is the number of records in the table, and the value of

```
dt.Columns.Count
```

is the number of fields in the table. The records are numbered 0 through **dt.Rows.Count - 1**, and the fields are numbered 0 through **dt.Columns.Count - 1**. The value of

```
dt.Columns(j)
```

is the name of the *j*th field. The value of

```
dt.Rows(i)(j)
```

is the entry in the *j*th field of the *i*th record. The value of

```
dt.Rows(i)(fieldName)
```

is the entry in the specified field of the *i*th record. In Table 10.3, *dt* holds the Cities table of MEGACITIES.MDB.

TABLE 10.3   Some values from cities table of MEGACITIES.MDB.

Expression	Value
`dt.Rows.Count`	10
`dt.Columns.Count`	4
`dt.Rows(7)(1)`	USA
`dt.Rows(1)("city")`	Calcutta

Note: The values of dt.Columns(j), dt.Row(i)(j), and dt.Row(i)(fieldName) must be converted to strings with CStr before being placed in a text box or assigned to a String variable. However, they need not be converted when placed in a list box.

Example 1 The following program displays one record at a time from Table 10.1 of the MEGACITIES.MDB database. The user can move forward or backward through the records, or specify the city to be displayed.

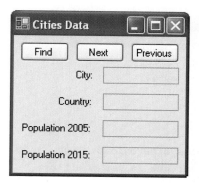

OBJECT	PROPERTY	SETTING
frmCities	Text	Cities Data
btnFind	Text	Find
btnNext	Text	Next
btnPrevious	Text	Previous
lblCity	Text	City:
txtCity	ReadOnly	True
lblCountry	Text	Country:
txtCountry	ReadOnly	True
lblPop2005	Text	Population 2005:
txtPop2005	ReadOnly	True
lblPop2015	Text	Population 2015:
txtPop2015	ReadOnly	True

```
Dim dt As New DataTable()
Dim rowIndex As Integer = 0

Private Sub frmCities_Load(...) Handles MyBase.Load
  'Get data from the database, put it into the DataTable object dt,
  'and display the initial record's data in text boxes.
  Dim connStr As String = "Provider=Microsoft.Jet.OLEDB.4.0;" & _
                    "Data Source=MEGACITIES.MDB"
  Dim sqlStr As String = "SELECT * FROM Cities"
  Dim dataAdapter As New OleDb.OleDbDataAdapter(sqlStr, connStr)
  dataAdapter.Fill(dt)
  dataAdapter.Dispose()
  UpdateTextBoxes()
End Sub


Private Sub btnFind_Click(...) Handles btnFind.Click
  'Search through each row looking for the requested city.
  'Update the fields if that city is found.
  'Otherwise display a message box.
  Dim cityName As String
  Dim cityFound As Boolean = False
  cityName = InputBox("Enter the name of the city to search for.")
  For i As Integer = 0 To (dt.Rows.Count - 1)
    If CStr(dt.Rows(i)("city")) = cityName Then
      cityFound = True
      rowIndex = i
      UpdateTextBoxes()
    End If
```

```
        Next
      If (Not cityFound) Then
        MsgBox("Cannot find the requested city", 0, "Not in Table")
      End If
    End Sub

    Private Sub btnNext_Click(...) Handles btnNext.Click
      'Show the next record if the current one is not the last.
      If (rowIndex < dt.Rows.Count - 1) Then
        rowIndex += 1   'Increase the rowIndex by 1.
        UpdateTextBoxes()
      End If
    End Sub

    Private Sub btnPrevious_Click(...) Handles btnPrevious.Click
      'Show the previous record if the current one is not the first.
      If (rowIndex > 0) Then
        rowIndex = rowIndex - 1
        UpdateTextBoxes()
      End If
    End Sub

    Sub UpdateTextBoxes()
      'Display the contents of the row specified by the rowIndex variable.
      txtCity.Text = CStr(dt.Rows(rowIndex)("city"))
      txtCountry.Text = CStr(dt.Rows(rowIndex)("country"))
      txtPop2005.Text = CStr(dt.Rows(rowIndex)("pop2005"))
      txtPop2015.Text = CStr(dt.Rows(rowIndex)("pop2015"))
    End Sub
```

[Run, and then click the Next button seven times.]

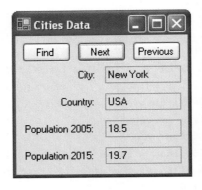

Example 2   The following program displays the contents of the Table 10.1 of MEGACITIES.MDB in a list box, along with the percentage increases for the populations:

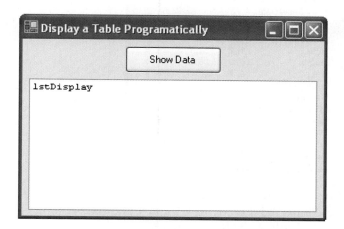

OBJECT	PROPERTY	SETTING
frmCities	Text	Display a Table Programatically
btnShow	Text	Show Data
lstDisplay		

```
Private Sub btnShow_Click(...) Handles btnShow.Click
  Dim fmtStr As String = "{0,-15}{1,-10}{2,7:N1}{3,7:N1}{4,7:P0}"
  Dim percentIncrease As Double
  'Place contents of Cities table into a DataTable.
  Dim dt As New DataTable()
  Dim connStr As String = "Provider=Microsoft.Jet.OLEDB.4.0;" & _
                   "Data Source=MEGACITIES.MDB"
  Dim sqlStr As String = "SELECT * FROM Cities"
  Dim dataAdapter As New OleDb.OleDbDataAdapter(sqlStr, connStr)
  dataAdapter.Fill(dt)
  dataAdapter.Dispose()
  'Fill the list box.
  lstDisplay.Items.Add(String.Format(fmtStr, "CITY", "COUNTRY", _
                             "2005", "2015", "INCR."))
  For i As Integer = 0 To dt.Rows.Count - 1
    percentIncrease = (CDbl(dt.Rows(i)("pop2015")) - _
        CDbl(dt.Rows(i)("pop2005"))) / CDbl(dt.Rows(i)("pop2005"))
    lstDisplay.Items.Add(String.Format(fmtStr, dt.Rows(i)(0), _
        dt.Rows(i)(1), dt.Rows(i)(2), dt.Rows(i)(3), percentIncrease))
  Next
End Sub
```

[Run, and click the button.]

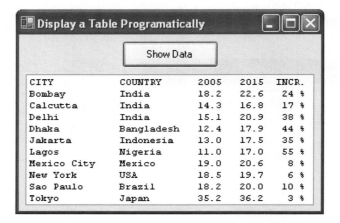

In Example 2, we placed information from a data table into a list box one line at a time. However, a data table can be connected directly to a list box and have information transferred automatically into the list box. In such a situation, the list box is said to be **bound** to the data table. The statement

```
lstBox.DataSource = dt
```

binds the list box to the data table, and the statement

```
lstBox.DisplayMember = "country"
```

displays the contents of the specified field in the list box.

 Example 3   The following program uses a list box to display a column of data named "country" from a data table. When a particular country is selected, the event procedure retrieves the country's monetary unit from the corresponding record and displays it in a text box.

OBJECT	PROPERTY	SETTING
frmCountries	Text	Currency
lstCountries		
lblMonetaryUnit	Text	Monetary unit:
txtMonetaryUnit	ReadOnly	True

```
Dim dt As New DataTable()

Private Sub frmCountries_Load(...) Handles MyBase.Load
  Dim connStr As String = "Provider=Microsoft.Jet.OLEDB.4.0;" & _
                    "Data Source=MEGACITIES.MDB"
  Dim sqlStr As String = "SELECT * FROM Countries"
```

```
   Dim dataAdapter As New OleDb.OleDbDataAdapter(sqlStr, connStr)
   dataAdapter.Fill(dt)
   dataAdapter.Dispose()
   lstCountries.DataSource = dt   'Bind the list box to the data table.
   lstCountries.DisplayMember = "country"   'Display the specified field.
End Sub

Private Sub lstCountries_SelectedIndexChanged(...) _
          Handles lstCountries.SelectedIndexChanged
   txtMonetaryUnit.Text = _
      CStr(dt.Rows(lstCountries.SelectedIndex)("monetaryUnit"))
End Sub
```

[Run, and click on one of the countries.]

Practice Problem 10.1

Determine the output displayed when the button is clicked.

```
Private Sub btnDisplay_Click(...) Handles btnDisplay.Click
  Dim dt As New DataTable()
  Dim connStr As String = "Provider=Microsoft.Jet.OLEDB.4.0;" & _
                     "Data Source=MEGACITIES.MDB"
  Dim sqlStr As String = "SELECT * FROM Countries"
  Dim dataAdapter As New OleDb.OleDbDataAdapter(sqlStr, connStr)
  dataAdapter.Fill(dt)
  dataAdapter.Dispose()
  lstOutput.Items.Add(dt.Columns(2))
  lstOutput.Items.Add(dt.Rows(5)(0))
  lstOutput.Items.Add(dt.Rows(8)(dt.Columns.Count - 2))
  lstOutput.Items.Add(dt.Rows(0)("monetaryUnit"))
  lstOutput.Items.Add(dt.Rows(dt.Rows.Count - 1)(2))
End Sub
```

Exercises 1 through 16 refer to the database MEGACITIES.MDB. In Exercises 1 through 4, determine the output displayed when the button is clicked.

1.
```
Private Sub btnDisplay_Click(...) Handles btnDisplay.Click
    Dim dt As New DataTable()
    Dim sum As Double
    Dim connStr As String = "Provider=Microsoft.Jet.OLEDB.4.0;" & _
                            "Data Source=MEGACITIES.MDB"
    Dim sqlStr As String = "SELECT * FROM Cities"
    Dim dataAdapter As New OleDb.OleDbDataAdapter(sqlStr, connStr)
    dataAdapter.Fill(dt)
    dataAdapter.Dispose()
    sum = 0
    For i As Integer = 0 To dt.Rows.Count - 1
      sum += CDbl(dt.Rows(i)("pop2015"))
    Next
    txtOutput.Text = sum & " million"
End Sub
```

2.
```
Private Sub btnDisplay_Click(...) Handles btnDisplay.Click
    Dim dt As New DataTable()
    Dim connStr As String = "Provider=Microsoft.Jet.OLEDB.4.0;" & _
                            "Data Source=MEGACITIES.MDB"
    Dim sqlStr As String = "SELECT * FROM Cities"
    Dim dataAdapter As New OleDb.OleDbDataAdapter(sqlStr, connStr)
    dataAdapter.Fill(dt)
    dataAdapter.Dispose()
    For i As Integer = 0 To dt.Rows.Count - 1
      If CDbl(dt.Rows(i)("pop2015")) > 22 Then
        lstOutput.Items.Add(dt.Rows(i)(0))
      End If
    Next
End Sub
```

3.
```
Private Sub btnDisplay_Click(...) Handles btnDisplay.Click
    Dim dt As New DataTable()
    Dim connStr As String = "Provider=Microsoft.Jet.OLEDB.4.0;" & _
                            "Data Source=MEGACITIES.MDB"
    Dim sqlStr As String = "SELECT * FROM Countries"
    Dim dataAdapter As New OleDb.OleDbDataAdapter(sqlStr, connStr)
    dataAdapter.Fill(dt)
    dataAdapter.Dispose()
    For i As Integer = 0 To dt.Rows.Count - 1
      If CStr(dt.Rows(i)("country")).Length = 5 Then
        lstOutput.Items.Add(dt.Rows(i)(0))
      End If
    Next
End Sub
```

4.
```
Private Sub btnDisplay_Click(...) Handles btnDisplay.Click
    Dim dt As New DataTable()
    Dim connStr As String = "Provider=Microsoft.Jet.OLEDB.4.0;" & _
                            "Data Source=MEGACITIES.MDB"
    Dim sqlStr As String = "SELECT * FROM Countries"
    Dim dataAdapter As New OleDb.OleDbDataAdapter(sqlStr, connStr)
    dataAdapter.Fill(dt)
    dataAdapter.Dispose()
    For j As Integer = 0 To dt.Columns.Count - 1
        lstOutput.Items.Add(dt.Columns(j))
    Next
End Sub
```

5. Write a program to place in a list box the names of the countries in the Countries table in the order that they appear in the table.

6. Write a program to place in a list box the names of the countries in the Countries table in the reverse order that they appear in the table.

7. Write a program to place in a list box the names of the cities in the Cities table whose populations are projected to exceed 20 million in the year 2015.

8. Write a program to place in a list box the names of the cities in the Cities table whose 2005 populations are between 12 and 16 million.

9. Write a program to place in a list box the names of the countries in the Countries table, where each name is followed by a hyphen and the name of its monetary unit.

10. Write a program to find and display the city in the Cities table that will experience the greatest percentage growth from 2005 to 2015. **Note:** The percentage growth is (pop2015 − pop2005) / pop2005.

11. Write a program to place the countries from the Countries table in a list box in descending order of their 2005 populations. **Hint:** Place the countries and their 2005 populations in an array of structures, and sort the array in descending order based on the populations.

12. Write a program to place the cities from the Cities table in a list box in descending order of their percentage population growth from 2005 to 2015.

13. Write a program to display the name and currency of each city in the table Cities.

14. Write a program to display in a list box the names of each country in Table 10.1 followed by the cities in that country that are listed in the Cities table.

15. Write a program to back up the contents of the Cities table in one sequential file and the Countries table in another sequential file. Run the program, and compare the sizes of these two sequential files with the size of the file MEGACITIES.MDB.

16. Write a program that allows the user to specify a city and then displays the percentage of its country's 2005 population that lives in that city. **Hint:** Use two Data-Tables.

Exercises 17 through 20 refer to the BIBLIO.MDB database from the folder Programs\Ch10\MajorDatabases.

17. How many tables are in the database? What are their names?

18. Give the names of the fields in the table Publishers.

19. How many records are in the table Publishers?

20. Write a program that requests the name of a publisher (such as Prentice Hall or Microsoft Press) and gives the publisher's address.

21. The folder Programs\Ch10\MajorDatabases contains the database STATE_ABBR .MDB consisting of one table, States, having two fields, abbreviation and state. Each record consists of a two-letter abbreviation and the name of a state. Some records are (AZ, Arizona) and (MD, Maryland). Write a program that allows the user to enter a two-letter abbreviation and obtain the name of the state. Of course, if the two-letter abbreviation does not correspond to any state, the user should be so informed.

The folder Programs\Ch10\MajorDatabases contains the database BASEBALL.MDB that has the two tables Players and Teams. The fields for the Players table are *player, team, atBats,* and *hits.* The fields for the Teams table are *team, location, league, stadium, atBats,* and *hits.* The database has been filled with information from the 2004 baseball season for the major leagues. Three sample records from each table are as follows.

PLAYERS

Barry Bonds, Giants, 373, 135
Ichiro Suzuki, Mariners, 704, 262
Manny Ramirez, Red Sox, 568, 175

TEAMS

Giants, San Francisco, National, SBC Park, 5546, 1500
Diamondbacks, Arizona, National, Bank One Ballpark, 5544, 1401
Red Sox, Boston, American, Fenway Park, 5720, 1613

The database BASEBALL.MDB should be used in Exercises 22 through 26.

22. Write a program to determine the player in the Players table with the most hits. In the case of a tie, the program should list all players having the most hits.

23. Write a program to determine the player (or players) in the Players table with the highest batting average.

24. Write a program that displays all the teams in the Teams table in a list box. When the user clicks on one of the teams, the program should display the team's home stadium in a text box.

25. Write a program that displays all the teams in the Teams table in a list box. When the user clicks on one of the teams, the program should display the names of all the players in the Players table from that team. *Hint:* Use two DataTables.

26. Write a program to count the number of players in the Players table who play for a National League team. *Hint:* Use two DataTables.

Solution to Practice Problem 10.1

```
monetaryUnit
Japan
143.2
taka
dollar
```

10.2 Relational Databases and SQL

▧ Primary and Foreign Keys

A well-designed table should have a field (or set of fields) that can be used to uniquely identify each record. Such a field (or set of fields) is called a **primary key**. For instance, in the Countries table of Section 10.1 (Table 10.2), the country field is a primary key. In the Cities table (Table 10.1), because we are only considering very large cities (of over 1 million population), the city field is a primary key. Databases of student enrollments in a college usually use a field of Social Security numbers as the primary key. Names would not be a good choice because there could easily be two students having the same name.

When a database is created, a field can be specified as a primary key. If so, Visual Basic will insist that every record have an entry in the primary-key field and that the same entry does not appear in two different records. If the user tries to add a record with no data in the primary key, the error message "Index or primary key cannot contain a Null Value." will be generated. If the user tries to add a record with the same primary key data as another record, the error message "The changes you requested to the table were not successful because they would create duplicate values in the index, primary key, or relationship. Change the data in the field or fields that contain duplicate data, remove the index, or redefine the index to permit duplicate entries and try again." will be displayed.

When a database contains two or more tables, the tables are usually related. For instance, the two tables Cities and Countries are related by their country field. Let's refer to these two fields as Cities.country and that Countries.country. Notice that every entry in Cities.country appears uniquely in Countries.country and that Countries.country is a primary key. We say that Cities.country is a **foreign key** of Countries.country. Foreign keys are usually specified when a table is first created. If so, Visual Basic will insist on the **Rule of Referential Integrity**, namely, that each value in the foreign key must also appear in the primary key of the other table.

In the database MEGACITIES.MDB, Cities.city and Countries.country have been specified as primary keys for their respective tables, and Cities.country has been specified as a foreign key of Countries.country. If the user tries to add a city to the Cities table whose country does not appear in the Countries table, then the error message "You cannot add or change a record because a related record is required in table 'Countries'." will be displayed. The message will also be generated if the user tries to delete a country from the Countries.country field that appears in the Cities.country field. Due to the interdependence of the two tables in MEGACITIES.MDB, this database is called a **relational database**.

A foreign key allows Visual Basic to link (or **join**) together two tables from a relational database in a meaningful way. For instance, when the two tables Cities and Countries

TABLE 10.4	A join of two tables.					
Cities. city	Cities. country	Cities. pop2005	Cities. pop2015	Countries. country	Countries. pop2005	Countries. monetaryUnit
Bombay	India	18.2	22.6	India	1103.4	rupee
Calcutta	India	14.3	16.8	India	1103.4	rupee
Delhi	India	15.1	20.9	India	1103.4	rupee
Dhaka	Bangladesh	12.4	17.9	Bangladesh	141.8	taka
Jakarta	Indonesia	13.0	17.5	Indonesia	222.8	rupiah
Lagos	Nigeria	11.0	17.0	Nigeria	131.5	naira
Mexico City	Mexico	19.0	20.6	Mexico	107	peso
New York	USA	18.5	19.7	USA	298.2	dollar
Sao Paulo	Brazil	18.2	20.0	Brazil	186.4	real
Tokyo	Japan	35.2	36.2	Japan	128.1	yen

from MEGACITIES.MDB are joined based on the foreign key Cities.country, the result is Table 10.4. The record for each city is expanded to show its country's population and its monetary unit. This joined table is very handy if, say, we want to navigate through a table with buttons as in Example 1 of Section 10.1, but display a city's name and monetary unit. We only have to create the original two tables; Visual Basic creates the joined table as needed. The request for a joined table is made in a language called SQL.

▦ SQL

Structured Query Language (SQL) was developed in the early 1970s at IBM for use with relational databases. The language was standardized in 1986 by ANSI (American National Standards Institute). Visual Basic uses a version of SQL that is compliant with ANSI-92 SQL. There are some minor variations that are of no concern in this book.

SQL is a very powerful language. One use of SQL is to request specialized information from an existing database or to have the information presented in a specified order.

▦ Four SQL Requests (Queries)

We will focus on four basic types of requests that can be made with SQL.

Request I: Show the records of a table in a specified order.
Some variations of ordering with Cities are

- (a) alphabetical order based on the name of the city,
- (b) alphabetical order based on the name of the country, and within each country group, the name of the city,
- (c) descending order based on the projected 2015 population.

Request II: Show just the records that meet certain criteria.
Some examples of criteria with Cities are

- (a) cities that are in India,
- (b) cities whose 2015 population is projected to be at least 20 million,
- (c) cities whose name begins with the letter "D".

Request III: Join the tables together, connected by a foreign key, and present the records as in Requests I and II.
Some examples with MEGACITIES.MDB are

   (a) show the cities in descending order of the populations of their countries,
   (b) show the cities whose monetary unit has "u" as its second letter.

Request IV: Make available just some of the fields of either the basic tables or the joined table.
Some examples with MEGACITIES.MDB are

   (a) make available just the city and country fields of the Cities table,
   (b) make available just the city and monetary unit fields of the joined table.

Normally, we set the SQL statement of a data adapter to an entire table. Also, the records of the table are normally presented in the order they are physically stored in the table. We make the requests just discussed by specifying the SQL statement as one of the following types:

Request I: SELECT * FROM *Table1* ORDER BY *field1* ASC or SELECT * FROM *Table1* ORDER BY *field1* DESC

Request II: SELECT * FROM *Table1* WHERE *criteria*

Request III: SELECT * FROM *Table1* INNER JOIN Table2 ON *foreign field* = *primary field* WHERE *criteria*

Request IV: SELECT *field1*, *field2*, ..., *fieldN* FROM *Table1* WHERE *criteria*

"ASC" and "DESC" specify ASCending and DESCending orders, respectively. A *criteria* clause is a string containing a condition of the type used with If blocks. In addition to the standard operators $<$, $>$, and $=$, *criteria* strings frequently contain the operator Like. Essentially, Like uses the wildcard characters "_" and "%" to compare a string to a pattern. An underscore character stands for a single character in the same position as the underscore character. For instance, the pattern "B_d" is matched by "Bid", "Bud", and "Bad". A percent sign stands for any number of characters in the same position as the percent sign. For instance, the pattern "C%r" is matched by "Computer", "Chair", and "Car". See Comments 3 through 5 for further information about Like.

In the sentence

SELECT *fields* FROM *clause*

fields is either * (to indicate all fields) or a sequence of the fields to be available (separated by commas), and *clause* is either a single table or a join of two tables. A join of two tables is indicated by a clause of the form

tblA INNER JOIN _tblB_ ON _foreign key of tblA=primary key of tblB_

Appending

WHERE *criteria*

to the end of the sentence restricts the records to those satisfying *criteria*. Appending

ORDER BY *field(s)* ASC (or DESC)

presents the records ordered by the specified field or fields.

In general, the SQL statements we consider will look like

SELECT *www* **FROM** *xxx* **WHERE** *yyy* **ORDER BY** *zzz*

where SELECT *www* FROM *xxx* is always present and accompanied by one or both of WHERE *yyy* and ORDER BY *zzz*. In addition, the *xxx* portion might contain an INNER JOIN phrase.

The settings for the examples mentioned earlier are as follows:

I (a) Show the records from Cities in alphabetical order based on the name of the city with

SELECT * FROM Cities ORDER BY city ASC

I (b) Show the records from Cities in alphabetical order based first on the name of the country and, within each country group, the name of the city with

SELECT * FROM Cities ORDER BY country, city ASC

I (c) Show the records from Cities in descending order based on the projected 2015 population, using

SELECT * FROM Cities ORDER BY pop2015 DESC

II (a) Show the records for the Cities in India with

SELECT * FROM Cities WHERE country = 'India'

II (b) Show the records from Cities whose 2015 population is projected to be at least 20 million, as in

SELECT * FROM Cities WHERE pop2015 >= 20

II (c) Show the records from Cities whose name begins with the letter "D", with

SELECT * FROM Cities WHERE city Like 'D%'

III (a) Show the records from the joined table in descending order of the populations of their countries, using

SELECT * FROM Cities INNER JOIN Countries ON Cities.country = Countries.country ORDER BY Countries.pop2005 DESC

III (b) Show the records from the joined table whose monetary unit has "u" as its second letter with

SELECT * FROM Cities INNER JOIN Countries ON Cities.country = Countries.country WHERE monetaryUnit Like '_u%'

IV (a) Make available just the city and country fields of the table Cities, using

SELECT city, country FROM Cities

IV (b) Make available just the city and monetaryUnit fields of the joined table, as in

SELECT city, monetaryUnit FROM Cities INNER JOIN Countries ON Cities.country = Countries.country

Note: In several of the statements the single quote, rather than the normal double quote, was used to surround strings. This is standard practice with SQL statements.

We can think of an SQL statement as creating in essence a new "virtual" table from existing tables. For instance, we might regard the statement

```
SELECT city, pop2015 FROM Cities WHERE pop2015>=20
```

as creating the "virtual" table

city	pop2015
Bombay	22.6
Delhi	20.9
Mexico City	20.6
Sao Paulo	20.0
Tokyo	36.2

This table is a subtable of the original table Cities—that is, it consists of what is left after certain columns and rows are omitted.

As another example, the statement

```
SELECT Cities.city, Cities.Country, Countries.monetaryUnit FROM Cities
INNER JOIN Countries ON Cities.country = Countries.country
WHERE Countries.country>'K'
```

creates in essence the "virtual" table

Cities.city	Cities.country	Countries.monetaryUnit
Lagos	Nigeria	naira
Mexico City	Mexico	peso
New York	USA	dollar

which is a subtable of a join of the two tables Cities and Countries.

These "virtual" tables don't exist physically. However, for all practical purposes, Visual Basic acts as if they did. In standard relational database books, a "virtual" table is called a **view**.

The programs in Section 10.1 all contain a statement of the form

```
Dim sqlStr As String = "SELECT * FROM tableName"
```

that creates an entire existing table as a view. Replacing this string with a different SQL statement will result in a different "virtual" table for the data table when it is filled by the data adapter.

■ **The DataGridView Control**

In Section 10.1, information from databases is displayed in text boxes and list boxes. Another control, called the DataGridView, displays the values for an entire view in a table format identical to the table displayed by Database Explorer. The standard prefix for the name of a DataGridView control is *dgv*.

After a data table has been filled, the statement

```
dgvDisplay.DataSource = dt
```

displays the contents of the data table *dt* in the data grid view.

 Example 1 The following program allows the user to alter the order and kinds of information displayed from a database. When the first button is pressed, the cities are presented in ascending order based on their 2005 populations. When the second button is pressed, the cities are presented in alphabetical order along with their monetary units.

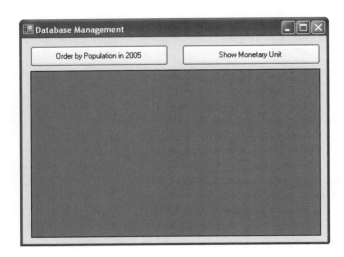

OBJECT	PROPERTY	SETTING
frmCities	Text	Database Management
btnOrderByPop	Text	Order by Population in 2005
btnShowMonUnit	Text	Show Monetary Unit
dgvDisplay		

```
Private Sub frmCities_Load(...) Handles MyBase.Load
  UpdateGrid("Select * From Cities")
End Sub

Private Sub btnOrderbyPop_Click(...) Handles btnOrderbyPop.Click
  'Display the data from the data table in the data grid.
  UpdateGrid("Select * From Cities Order By pop2005 ASC")
End Sub

Private Sub btnShowMonUnit_Click(...) Handles btnShowMonUnit.Click
  UpdateGrid("SELECT city, Cities.country, " & _
             "Cities.pop2005, monetaryUnit " & _
             "FROM Cities INNER JOIN Countries " & _
             "ON Cities.country=Countries.country " & _
             "ORDER BY city ASC")
End Sub

Sub UpdateGrid(ByVal sqlStr As String)
  Dim dt As New DataTable()
  Dim connStr As String = "Provider=Microsoft.Jet.OLEDB.4.0;" & _
                          "Data Source=MEGACITIES.MDB"
```

```
Dim dataAdapter As New OleDb.OleDbDataAdapter(sqlStr, connStr)
dataAdapter.Fill(dt)
dataAdapter.Dispose()
dgvDisplay.DataSource = dt
End Sub
```

[Run, and click on the Show Monetary Unit button.]

	city	country	pop2005	monetaryUnit
▶	Bombay	India	18.2	rupee
	Calcutta	India	14.3	rupee
	Delhi	India	15.1	rupee
	Dhaka	Bangladesh	12.4	taka
	Jakarta	Indonesia	13	rupiah
	Lagos	Nigeria	11	naira
	Mexico City	Mexico	19	peso
	New York	USA	18.5	dollar
	Sao Paulo	Brazil	18.2	real
	Tokyo	Japan	35.2	yen
✳				

The program in Example 3 of Section 10.1 searched a table for a specific record by looping through all the records. Whereas this technique is fine for small tables, it is not efficient for searches of large tables. A better way to find data that match a criteria is to include the criteria in the SQL string.

 Example 2   The following program displays the large cities in a country specified by the user. Notice the single quotes surrounding the criteria in the SQL string.

OBJECT	PROPERTY	SETTING
frmCities	Text	Search with SQL
lblCountry	Text	Country:
txtCountry		
btnFindCities	Text	Find Cities
dgvDisplay		

```
Private Sub btnFindCities_Click(...) Handles btnFindCities.Click
  UpdateGrid("SELECT city FROM Cities WHERE country = '" & _
               txtCountry.Text & "' ORDER BY city ASC")
End Sub

Sub UpdateGrid(ByVal sqlStr As String)
  'Declare and populate the data table.
  Dim dt As New DataTable()
  Dim connStr As String = "Provider=Microsoft.Jet.OLEDB.4.0;" & _
                    "Data Source=MEGACITIES.MDB"
  Dim dataAdapter As New OleDb.OleDbDataAdapter(sqlStr, connStr)
  dataAdapter.Fill(dt)
  dataAdapter.Dispose()
  'Display the names of the cities in the specified country.
  If dt.Rows.Count = 0 Then
    MsgBox("No cities from that country in the database")
  Else
    dgvDisplay.DataSource = dt
  End If
End Sub
```

[Run, type "India" into the text box, and press the button.]

▨ Changing the Contents of a Database

The programs presented so far only read data from a database. Data grid views can be used to add, modify, and delete records from a database. After a DataAdapter has been created, the statement

Dim commandBuilder As New OleDb.OleDbCommandBuilder(dataAdapter)

will automatically enable any modifications to be stored. If *changes* is an Integer variable, then the statement

changes = dataAdapter.Update(dt)

will store all of the insertions, updates, and deletions made in the data table to the database and assign the number of records changed to the variable *changes*.

Example 3   The following program demonstrates loading data from a database to a data grid via a data adapter, allowing the user to make edits within the data grid, and saving the changes back to the database. To update a record, highlight the field, and make the change. To insert a new record, click on the bottom row that begins with an asterisk and has blank fields. (The values in the fields are initially filled with "(null)" and should be changed.) To delete a row, click on the box to the left of the row so that the entire row is highlighted, then click the Delete key. If you click the "Load Table From Database" button before clicking the "Save Changes To Database" button, any changes are lost. Run the program, and test it by clicking on the Load button, making some changes, and then clicking on the Save button.

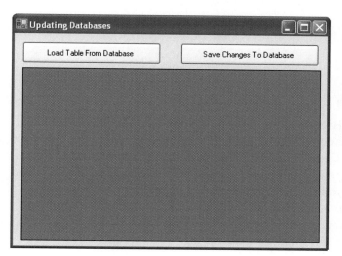

OBJECT	PROPERTY	SETTING
frmCities	Text	Updating Databases
btnLoad	Text	Load Table From Database
btnSave	Text	Save Changes To Database
dgvDisplay		

```
'Class-level variables
Dim connStr As String = "Provider=Microsoft.Jet.OLEDB.4.0;" & _
                        "Data Source=MEGACITIES.MDB"
Dim sqlStr As String = "SELECT * FROM Cities"
Dim dt As New DataTable()

Private Sub btnLoad_Click(...) Handles btnLoad.Click
  'Displays the table's data in the data grid
  'Clear the current contents of the table.
  dt.Clear()
  'Fill the data table with data from the database.
  Dim dataAdapter As New OleDb.OleDbDataAdapter(sqlStr, connStr)
  dataAdapter.Fill(dt)
  dataAdapter.Dispose()
  'Display the table in the data grid.
  dgvDisplay.DataSource = dt
End Sub
```

```
Private Sub btnSave_Click(...) Handles btnSave.Click
  'Save the tables's changes back to the database.
  Dim changes As Integer
  'Open a connection to the database for updating.
  Dim dataAdapter As New OleDb.OleDbDataAdapter(sqlStr, connStr)
  Dim commandBuilder As New OleDb.OleDbCommandBuilder(dataAdapter)
  'Update the database with changes from the data table.
  changes = dataAdapter.Update(dt)
  dataAdapter.Dispose()
  'Display the number of changes made.
  If changes > 0 Then
    MsgBox(changes & " changed rows were stored in the database.")
  Else
    MsgBox("No changes made.")
  End If
End Sub
```

■ Calculated Columns with SQL

Suppose we want to display in a data grid the cities in the database MEGACITIES.MDB database along with their expected population growth from 2005 to 2015. We could use Access to add a fifth field to the Cities table and fill it with the population growth. That is, for each record the entry in the new field would be the difference between its pop2015 and pop2005 fields. However, this would violate a fundamental principle of database design—*avoid fields whose values can be calculated from existing fields.* SQL provides a way to display a population growth column without creating a new field for the Cities table.

After the data table *dt* has been filled using the string

```
sqlStr = "SELECT city, (pop2015-pop2005) FROM Cities"
```

then the statement

```
dgvDisplay.DataSource = dt
```

causes the data grid view to display two columns, as shown in Figure 10.3, where the second column shows the population growth for each city. This column is called a **calculated column**.

city	Expr1001
Bombay	4.4000000000000021
Calcutta	2.5
Delhi	5.7999999999999989
Dhaka	5.4999999999999982
Jakarta	4.5
Lagos	6
Mexico City	1.6000000000000014
New York	1.1999999999999993
Sao Paulo	1.8000000000000007
Tokyo	1

FIGURE 10.3

The display in Figure 10.3 has two flaws—the second column does not have a meaningful name, and the numbers in the second column are not rounded to one decimal place. The first flaw can be corrected by adding the clause **AS popGrowth** after **(pop2015–pop2005).** This will give the column the heading *popGrowth*. The second flaw can be corrected by replacing **(pop2015–pop2005)** with **Round(pop2015–pop2005, 1).** Therefore, using the string

```
sqlStr = "SELECT city, Round(pop2015-pop2005, 1) AS popGrowth " & _
         "FROM Cities"
```

to fill the table produces the output shown in Figure 10.4.

city	popGrowth
Bombay	4.4
Calcutta	2.5
Delhi	5.8
Dhaka	5.5
Jakarta	4.5
Lagos	6
Mexico City	1.6
New York	1.2
Sao Paulo	1.8
Tokyo	1

FIGURE 10.4

Note: The column title following the AS keyword can contain spaces. If so, the title should be surrounded by brackets. For instance, if the clause is AS [Population Growth], then the column title will be Population Growth.

Calculated values can be used in an ORDER clause to sort the displayed data. For instance, if the SQL string above is changed to

```
sqlStr = "SELECT city, Round(pop2015-pop2005, 1) AS popGrowth " & _
         "FROM Cities ORDER by (pop2015-pop2005) DESC"
```

then the cities will be sorted by their population growth.

▨ Comments

1. Each record of the Countries table is related to one or more records of the Cities table, but each record of the Cities table is related to only one record of the Countries table. Therefore, we say that there is a **one-to-many relationship** from the Countries table to the Cities table.

2. SQL statements are insensitive to case. For instance, the following choices for criteria have the same effect: City = 'Tokyo', city = 'tokyo', CITY = 'tokyo', CiTy = 'TOKYO'.

3. When the Like operator is used, the "pattern" must appear on the right of the operator. For instance, the SQL statement

   ```
   SELECT * FROM Cities WHERE city Like 'S%'
   ```

   cannot be replaced by

   ```
   SELECT * FROM Cities WHERE 'S%' Like city
   ```

4. The operator Like permits a refinement of the wildcard character "_". Whereas "_" is a placeholder for any letter, an expression such as "[letter1-letter2]" is a placeholder for any letter from letter1 to letter2. For instance, the pattern "[A-F]ad" is matched by Bad and Dad, but not Sad.

5. The Like operator can be used in If blocks in much the same way as the operators $>$, $=$, and $<$. In this situation, the operator is case sensitive. For instance, the condition ("bad" Like "[A-F]ad") is False. However, when Like is used in SQL statements, it is case insensitive. That is, ('bad' Like '[A-F]ad') is True. Furthermore, when Like is used in an If block, the asterisk is used instead of the percent sign to denote any number of characters, and the question mark stands for any one character.

6. The requirement that no record may have a null primary key and that entries for primary keys be unique is called the **Rule of Entity Integrity**.

Practice Problems 10.2

For each of the following grids, give an SQL statement that can be used to create the grid from the MEGACITIES.MDB database:

1.

country	pop2005	monetaryUnit
Indonesia	222.8	rupiah
India	1103.4	rupee

2.

country
Mexico
Brazil

EXERCISES 10.2

Exercises 1 and 4 refer to the database MEGACITIES.MDB, where the primary keys of Cities and Countries are city and country, respectively, and Cities.country is a foreign key to Countries.country. Determine whether the stated action could ever cause a problem. Explain.

1. Add a new record to the Cities table.

2. Delete a record from the Countries table.

3. Delete a record from the Cities table.

4. Add a new record to the Countries table.

The following tables are "virtual" tables derived from the MEGACITIES.MDB database. In Exercises 5 through 8, identify the "virtual" table associated with the SQL statement.

(A)

country	pop2005	monetary-Unit
Russia	143.2	ruble
Indonesia	222.8	rupiah
India	1103.4	rupee
Brazil	186.4	real

(B)

country	pop2005	monetary-Unit
China	1316.8	yuan

(C)

country	pop2005	monetary-Unit
China	1316.8	yuan
India	1103.4	rupee

(D)

country	pop2005	monetary-Unit
China	1316.8	yuan
Brazil	186.4	real
Bangladesh	141.8	taka

5. `SELECT * FROM Countries WHERE pop2005>1200 ORDER BY pop2005 ASC`

6. `SELECT * FROM Countries WHERE country<'E' ORDER BY pop2005 DESC`

7. `SELECT * FROM Countries WHERE monetaryUnit Like 'r%' ORDER BY country DESC`

8. `SELECT * FROM Countries WHERE pop2005>700 ORDER BY country ASC`

The following tables are "virtual" tables derived from the MEGACITIES.MDB database. In Exercises 9 through 12, identify the "virtual" table associated with the SQL statement.

(A)

city	monetaryUnit
Sao Paulo	real

(B)

city	monetaryUnit
Tokyo	yen
Bombay	rupee

(C)

city	monetaryUnit
Bombay	rupee
Delhi	rupee
Calcutta	rupee

(D)

city	monetaryUnit
Tokyo	yen

9. `SELECT city, monetaryUnit FROM Cities INNER JOIN Countries ON Cities.country = Countries.country WHERE city='Tokyo'`

10. `SELECT city, monetaryUnit FROM Cities INNER JOIN Countries ON Cities.country = Countries.country WHERE pop2015>22 ORDER BY pop2015 DESC`

11. `SELECT city, monetaryUnit FROM Cities INNER JOIN Countries ON Cities.country = Countries.country WHERE Cities.country = 'India' ORDER BY Cities.pop2005 DESC`

12. ```
SELECT city, monetaryUnit FROM Cities INNER JOIN Countries
    ON Cities.country = Countries.country
    WHERE city Like 'S%' ORDER BY Countries.pop1995 ASC
```

For each grid in Exercises 13 through 20, give an SQL statement that can be used to create the grid from the MEGACITIES.MDB database. Then test your answer with a DataGridView filled from a table whose DataAdapter uses the SQL statement. *Note:* Several of the exercises here have more than one correct answer.

13.

| country | monetaryUnit |
| --- | --- |
| Nigeria | naira |
| Bangladesh | taka |
| Russia | ruble |
| Brazil | real |

14.

| country | pop2005 | monetaryUnit |
| --- | --- | --- |
| India | 1103.4 | rupee |
| Indonesia | 222.8 | rupiah |
| Brazil | 186.4 | real |
| Russia | 143.2 | ruble |

15.

| city | country | pop2005 | pop2015 |
| --- | --- | --- | --- |
| Bombay | India | 18.2 | 22.6 |
| Delhi | India | 15.1 | 20.9 |
| Calcutta | India | 14.3 | 16.8 |

16.

| city | country | pop2005 | pop2015 |
| --- | --- | --- | --- |
| Sao Paulo | Brazil | 18.2 | 20 |
| Mexico City | Mexico | 19 | 20.6 |
| Delhi | India | 15.1 | 20.9 |
| Bombay | India | 18.2 | 22.6 |
| Tokyo | Japan | 35.2 | 36.2 |

17.

| city | country | pop2005 | pop2015 |
| --- | --- | --- | --- |
| Sao Paulo | Brazil | 18.2 | 20 |
| Bombay | India | 18.2 | 22.6 |
| New York | USA | 18.5 | 19.7 |

18.

| city | country | pop2005 | pop2015 |
| --- | --- | --- | --- |
| Sao Paulo | Brazil | 18.2 | 20 |
| Mexico City | Mexico | 19 | 20.6 |
```

19.

city	pop2015	monetaryUnit
Bombay	22.6	rupee
Delhi	20.9	rupee
Calcutta	16.8	rupee

20.

city	Cities.pop2005	Countries.pop2005
Tokyo	35.2	128.1
Mexico City	19	107
New York	18.5	298.2

Exercises 21 through 23 use the database EXCHRATE.MDB from the folder Programs\Ch10\MajorDatabases. It gives the exchange rates (in terms of American dollars) for 45 currencies of major countries on January 14, 2005. Figure 10.5 shows the first eight records in the database in a DataGrid control. The dollarRate column gives the number of units of the currency that can be purchased for one American dollar. For instance, one American dollar purchases 1.20809 Canadian dollars.

country	monetaryUnit	dollarRate
America	Dollar	1
Argentina	Peso	2.918
Australia	Dollar	1.27099
Brazil	Real	2.76443
Canada	Dollar	1.20809
Chile	Peso	589.55
China	Yuan	8.2762
Colombia	Peso	2348

FIGURE 10.5   Exchange rates.

21. Write a program that displays the names of the countries in a data-bound list box. When the user clicks on one of the names, the monetary unit and the exchange rate should be displayed.

22. Write a program that displays the names of the countries in a data-bound list box in ascending order determined by the number of units that can be purchased by one American dollar. When the user clicks on one of the names, the monetary unit and exchange rate should be displayed.

23. Write a program containing two data-bound list boxes as shown in Figure 10.6. When the user selects two countries and an amount of money, and clicks on the button, the program should convert the amount from one currency to the other. *Hint*: Use two DataTables.

FIGURE 10.6 **A possible output for Exercise 23.**

24. The database MOVIES.MDB has the following two tables, named Lines and Actors. The left table contains famous lines from films that were spoken by the leading male actor. Use this database in a program that displays a grid of two columns, where the first column contains a famous line and the second column contains the name of the actor who spoke the line.

famousLine	film	film	maleLead
Rosebud.	Citizen Kane	Citizen Kane	Orson Wells
We'll always have Paris.	Casablanca	Casablanca	Humphrey Bogart
You're going to need a bigger boat.	Jaws	Jaws	Roy Scheider
The name is Bond. James Bond.	Goldfinger	Goldfinger	Sean Connery
I stick my neck out for nobody.	Casablanca		

25. Suppose the database USSTATES.MDB contains the table States consisting of the three fields *name*, *population*, and *area* with one record for each of the 50 U.S. states. Give an SQL string that can be used to display a data grid view having two columns with the first column containing the names of the states and the second column containing their population densities. The states should appear in decreasing order of their population densities.

26. Suppose the database EMPLOYEES.MDB contains the table Payroll consisting of the four fields *name*, *phoneNumber*, *hoursWorked*, and *hourlyPayRate*. Assume that each entry *phoneNumber* field has the form xxx-xxx-xxxx, and the *hoursWorked* field is filled with the number of hours the person worked during a week. Give an

SQL string that can be used to display a data grid view having two columns, with the first column containing the names of the people whose area code is 301 and the second column containing their wages for the week. The names should appear in increasing order of their earnings for the week. **Note:** In SQL, the left 3 characters of strVar are computed as Left(strVar, 3).

Exercises 27 through 35 use the database BASEBALL.MDB discussed in the exercises in Section 10.1. In Exercises 27 through 33, write a program to display the stated information in a DataGridView control.

27. The names of the players who play for a team based in New York.

28. The name(s) of the player(s) in the American League having the most hits.

29. The name(s) of the National League player(s) with the highest batting average for that league.

30. The names of all the players and their batting averages. The records should be sorted in descending order by batting average.

31. The names of all the teams, their home stadiums, and the team batting averages. Records should be sorted in ascending order by team batting average.

32. The names of all the players, their leagues, and their team's batting averages.

33. The names of players and their batting averages. The records should be sorted in descending order by batting average and should only show the players whose batting average exceeded their team's batting average.

34. Write a program that requests a batting average and a league (American or National) and then displays the names of all the players in the league whose batting average is above the given batting average. The program should not permit the given batting average to be greater than 1 or less than 0.

Exercises 35 and 36 refer to the database PHONEBOOK.MDB, which holds all the information for the residence listings of a telephone book for a city. Assume the database consists of one table, Entries, with the six fields: lastName, firstName, middleInitial, streetNumber, street, and phoneNumber.

35. Write a program that will display the contents of the phone book in the standard form shown in Figure 10.7(a).

36. Write a program that will display a "criss-cross" directory that gives phone numbers with the entries organized by street as in Figure 10.7(b).

AAKER Larry 3 Main St	874-2345	APPLE ST 3 Carl Aaron	405-2345
AARON Alex 23 Park Ave	924-3456	5 John Smith	862-1934
Bob R 17 Elm St	347-3456	7 Ted T Jones	405-1843
Carl 3 Apple St	405-2345	ARROW RD 1 Ben Rob	865-2345
(a)		(b)	

FIGURE 10.7   (a) Standard phone directory and (b) criss-cross directory.

Solutions to Practice Problems 10.2
---

1. `SELECT * FROM Countries WHERE country Like 'I%'`
   `ORDER BY pop2005 ASC`

2. `SELECT country FROM Countries WHERE country='Mexico'`
   `OR country='Brazil' ORDER BY pop2005 ASC`

CHAPTER 10 **SUMMARY**

1. A *table* is a group of data items arranged in a rectangular array, each row containing the same categories of information. Each data item (row) is called a *record*. Each category (column) is called a *field*. Two tables with a common field are said to be *related*. A *database* is a collection of one or more tables that are usually related.

2. Visual Basic's Database Explorer can be used to identify and view the tables of a database.

3. The *DataTable* object is used to access the information in a table. This information is supplied via a *data adapter*. The data adapter must be provided three pieces of information—the software serving as the database provider, the location of the database, and a statement telling it what part of the database to access. The first two pieces of information are combined into a string called a *connection string*.

4. When a list box is *bound* to a data table, information from the database can be inserted automatically into the list box.

5. A *primary key* is a field or set of fields that uniquely identifies each row of a table. The *Rule of Entity Integrity* states that no record can have a null entry in a primary key. A foreign key is a field or set of fields in one table that refers to a primary key in another table. The *rule of referential integrity* states that each value in the foreign key must also appear in the primary key.

6. Structured Query Language (SQL) is used to create a "virtual" table, or *view*, consisting of a subtable of a table or of a join of two tables and imposes an order on the records. The subtable or join is specified with the reserved words SELECT, FROM, WHERE, ORDER BY, and INNER JOIN ... ON. The WHERE clause of an SQL statement commonly uses the Like operator in addition to the standard operators. Data adapters use SQL statements to specify the views they will use to fill a data tables.

7. The DataGridView control can show an entire "virtual" table in a spreadsheetlike display. It can also be used to make changes in a database.

8. A *computed column* of a data grid does not contain values from a field in a database table, but rather, it contains values that are computed from one or more fields.

CHAPTER 10 PROGRAMMING PROJECTS

1. The database MICROLAND.MDB is maintained by the Microland Computer Warehouse, a mail-order computer-supply company. Tables 10.5 through 10.7 show parts of three tables in the database. The table Customers identifies each customer by an ID number and gives, in addition to the name and address, the total amount of purchases during the current year prior to today. The table Inventory identifies each product in stock by an ID number and gives, in addition to its description and price (per unit), the quantity in stock at the beginning of the day. The table Orders gives the orders received today. Suppose that it is now the end of the day. Write a program that uses the three tables to do the following:

(a) Display in a list box the items that are out of stock and therefore must be reordered.

(b) Display in a list box bills for all customers who ordered during the day. The bill should indicate if an item is currently out of stock.

TABLE 10.5   **First three records of the Customers table.**

custID	name	street	city	amtPurchases
1	Michael Smith	2 Park St.	Dallas, TX 75201	234.50
2	Brittany Jones	5 Second Ave	Tampa, FL 33602	121.90
3	Warren Pease	7 Maple St.	Boston, MA 02101	387.20

TABLE 10.6   **First three records of the Inventory table.**

itemID	description	price	quantity
PL208	Visual Basic	89.50	12
SW109	MS Office Upgrade	195.95	2
HW913	Scanner	49.95	8

TABLE 10.7   **First four records of the Orders table.**

custID	itemID	quantity
3	SW109	1
1	PL208	3
1	HW913	2
2	PL208	1

2. *Grade Book.* A teacher maintains a database containing two tables—Students and Grades. The Students table has six fields: *socSecNumber*, *lastName*, *firstName*, *streetAddress*, *cityAndState*, and *zipCode*. The Grades table has four fields: *socSecNumber*, *firstExam*, *secondExam*, and *finalExam*. At the beginning of the semester, the Students table is filled in completely with a record for each student in a class, and the Grades table has a record for each student that contains only the student's social security number. (**Note:** The database is contained in the file GRADEBOOK.MDB from the folder Programs\Ch10\MajorDatabases.) Write a program that allows the instructor to record and process the grades for the semester. The program should do the following.

(a) Create a data grid view that can be used to fill in the grades for each student after each exam.

(b) At the end of the semester, display a data grid view showing the name of each student and his or her semester average. The semester average should be calculated as (firstExam + secondExam + 2 * finalExam)/4.

(c) Print a list of semester grades that the instructor can post on his or her office door. The list should contain the last four digits of each student's social security number and the student's semester grade. The semester grade should be determined by the semester average with an A for 90–100, a B for 80–89, and so on. The list should be ordered by semester average. Note: You can just display the list in a list box instead of actually printing it.

(d) Print a letter for a student (identified by his or her social security number) similar to the one shown below. **Note:** You can just display the letter in a list box instead of actually printing it.

George Jackson
123 Main Street
Washington, DC 20015

Dear George,

Your grades for CMSC 100 are as follows:
    Final Exam: 87
    Semester Grade: B

Best wishes for a good summer,
Professor Jones

11

Object-Oriented

Programming

11.1 Classes and Objects 552

  ◆ Object Constructors

11.2 Arrays of Objects; Events; Containment 569

  ◆ Arrays of Objects ◆ Events ◆ Containment

11.3 Inheritance 582

  ◆ Polymorphism and Overriding
  ◆ Abstract Properties, Methods, and Classes

Summary 601

Programming Projects 602

11.1 Classes and Objects

noun A word used to denote or name a person, place, thing, quality, or act.

verb That part of speech that expresses existence, action, or occurrence.

adjective Any of a class of words used to modify a noun or other substantive by limiting, qualifying, or specifying.

The American Heritage Dictionary of the English Language

"A good rule of thumb for object-oriented programming is that classes are the nouns in your analysis of the problem. The methods in your object correspond to verbs that the noun does. The properties are the adjectives that describe the noun."

Gary Cornell & David Jezak

Practical experience in the financial, scientific, engineering, and software design industries has revealed some difficulties with traditional program design methodologies. As programs grow in size and become more complex, and as the number of programmers working on the same project increases, the number of dependencies and interrelationships throughout the code increases exponentially. A small change made by one programmer in one place may have many effects, both intended and unintended, in many other places. The effects of this change may ripple throughout the entire program, requiring the rewriting of a great deal of code along the way.

A partial solution to this problem is "data hiding" where, within a unit, as much implementation detail as possible is hidden. Data hiding is an important principle underlying object-oriented programming. An object is an encapsulation of data and procedures that act on the data. The only things of concern to a programmer using an object are the tasks that the object can perform and the parameters used by these tasks. The details of the data structures and procedures are hidden within the object.

Two types of objects will be of concern to us: **control objects** and **code objects**. Examples of control objects are text boxes, list boxes, buttons, and all the other controls that can be created from the Toolbox. So far, most of our programs have contained a single class block beginning with a line, such as "Public Class frmName" and ending with the line "End Class." A code object is a specific instance of a user-defined type, called a **class**, which is defined similarly to a structure, but in a separate class block of the form

```
Class ClassName
    statements
End Class
```

Each class block is delineated in the Code window by an elongated left bracket appearing to the left of the block. Both control objects and class objects have properties and respond to methods. The main differences are that control objects are predefined and have physical manifestations, whereas the programmer must create the class blocks for code objects. In this section, when we use the word "object" without a qualifier, we mean "code object."

Whenever you double-click on the TextBox icon in the Toolbox, a new text box is created. Although each text box is a separate entity, they all have the same properties and methods. Each text box is said to be an **instance** of the class TextBox. In some sense, the TextBox icon in the Toolbox is a template or blueprint for creating text boxes.

When you look at the Properties window for a text box, the dropdown list box at the top of the window reads something like "TextBox1 System.Windows.Forms.TextBox." TextBox1 is the name of the control object and it is said to be an instance of the class "TextBox." You can't set properties or invoke methods of the TextBox class; you can only set properties or invoke methods of the specific text boxes that are instances of the class. The analogy is often made between a class and a cookie cutter. The cookie cutter is used to create cookies that you can eat, but you can't eat the cookie cutter.

Object-oriented programs are populated with objects that hold data, have properties, respond to methods, and raise events. (The generation of events will be discussed in the next section.) Six examples are as follows:

1. In a professor's program to assign and display semester grades, a student object might hold a single student's name, social security number, midterm grade, and final exam grade. A CalcSemGrade method might calculate the student's semester grade. Events might be raised when improper data are passed to the object.

2. In a payroll program, an employee object might hold an employee's name, hourly wage, and hours worked. A CalculatePay method would tell the object to calculate the wages for the current pay period.

3. In a checking account program, a check register object might have methods that record and total the checks written during a certain month, a deposit slip object might record and total the deposits made during a certain month, and an account object might keep a running total of the balance in the account. The account object would raise an event to alert the bank when the balance gets too low.

4. In a bookstore inventory program, a textbook object might hold the name, author, quantity in stock, and wholesale price of an individual textbook. A CalculateRetailPrice method might instruct the textbook object to calculate the selling price of the textbook. An event could be triggered when the book goes out of stock.

5. In a game program, an airplane object might hold the location of an airplane. At any time, the program could tell the object to display the airplane at its current location or to drop a bomb. An event can be triggered each time a bomb is released so that the program can determine if anything was hit.

6. In a card game program, a card object might hold the denomination and suit of a specific card. An IdentifyCard method might return a string such as "Ace of Spades." A deck of cards object might consist of an array of card objects and a ShuffleDeck method that thoroughly shuffles the deck. A Shuffling event might indicate the progress of the shuffle.

The most important object-oriented term is **class**. A class is a template from which objects are created. The class specifies the properties and methods that will be common to all objects that are instances of that class. Classes are formulated in class blocks. An object, which is an instance of a class, can be created in a program with a pair of statements of the form

```
Dim objectName As className
objectName = New className(arg1, arg2, ...)
```

The first of these two lines of code declares what type of object the variable will refer to. The actual object does not exist until it is created with the New keyword, as done in the second line. This is known as creating an **instance** of an object and is where an object is actually created from its corresponding class. After this second line of code executes, the object is then ready for use. The first line can appear either in the Declarations section of a program (to declare a class-level variable) or inside a procedure (to declare a local variable). The instantiation line can only appear in a procedure; however, any object variable can be instantiated when declared (as either class-level or local) by using the single line

```
Dim objectName As New className(arg1, arg2, ...)
```

In a program, properties, methods, and events of the object are accessed with statements of the form shown in the following table:

TASK	STATEMENT
Assign a value to a property	`objectName.propertyName = value`
Assign the value of a property to a variable	`varName = objectName.propertyName`
Carry out a method	`objectName.methodName(arg1, ...)`
Raise an event	`RaiseEvent eventName`

The program in Example 1 uses a class named Student to calculate and display a student's semester grade. The information stored by an object of the type Student consists of a student's name, Social Security number, and grades on two exams (midterm and final). This data is stored in variables declared with the statements

```
Private m_name As String        'Name
Private m_ssn As String         'Social security number
Private m_midterm As Double     'Numerical grade on midterm exam
Private m_final As Double        'Numerical grade on final exam
```

The word Private guarantees that the variables cannot be accessed directly from outside the object. In object-oriented programming terminology, these variables are called **member variables** (or **instance variables**). We will follow the common convention of beginning the name of each member variable with the prefix "m_". Each of these variables is used to hold the value of a property. However, instead of being accessed directly, each member variable is accessed indirectly by a **property block**. For instance, the following property block consists of a Get property procedure to retrieve (or *read*) the value of the Name property and a Set property procedure to assign (or *write*) the value of the Name property:

```
Public Property Name() As String
  Get
    Return m_name
  End Get
  Set(ByVal value As String)
    m_name = value
  End Set
End Property
```

In a property block, additional code can be added after the Get and Set statements to validate the data before they are returned or stored. The word Public allows the property to be accessed from outside the code for the Student class block. For instance, the Name property can be accessed by code in the form's class block. On the other hand, since the member variables were declared as Private, they cannot be accessed directly from code in the form's block. They can only be accessed through Property procedures that allow values to be checked and perhaps modified. Also, a Property procedure is able to take other steps necessitated by a change in the value of a member variable.

A property block needn't contain both Get and Set property procedures. For instance, the block

```
Public WriteOnly Property MidGrade() As Double
    Set(ByVal value As double)
      m_midterm = value
    End Set
End Property
```

specifies the MidGrade property as "write only." This property could be specified to be "read only" with the block

```
Public ReadOnly Property MidGrade() As Double
    Get
        Return m_midterm
    End Get
End Property
```

Methods are constructed with Sub or Function procedures. A Function procedure is used when the method returns a value; otherwise a Sub procedure will suffice. For instance, the method CalcSemGrade, which is used to calculate a student's semester grade, is created as follows:

```
Function CalcSemGrade() As String
    Dim grade As Double
    grade = (m_midterm + m_final) / 2
    grade = Math.Round(grade)   'Round the grade.
    Select Case grade
      Case Is >= 90
        Return "A"
      Case Is >= 80
        Return "B"
      Case Is >= 70
        Return "C"
      Case Is >= 60
        Return "D"
      Case Else
        Return "F"
    End Select
End Function
```

An object of the type Student is declared in the code for the form with a pair of statements such as

```
Dim pupil As Student    'Declare pupil as object of type Student
pupil = New Student()   'Create an instance of Student
```

After these two statements are executed, properties and methods can be utilized with statements such as

```
pupil.Name = "Adams, Al"              'Assign a value to m_name
txtBox.Text = pupil.Name              'Display the student's name
lstBox.Items.Add(pupil.CalcSemGrade)  'Display semester grade.
```

The first statement calls the Set property procedure for the Name property, the second statement calls the Get property procedure for the Name property, and the third statement calls the method CalcSemGrade.

   Example 1   The following program uses the class Student to calculate and display a student's semester grade:

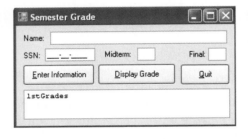

OBJECT	PROPERTY	SETTING
frmGrades	Text	Semester Grade
lblName	Text	Name:
txtName		
lblSSN	Text	SSN:
mtxtSSN	Mask	000-00-000
lblMidterm	Text	Midterm:
txtMidterm		
lblFinal	Text	Final:
txtFinal		
btnEnter	Text	&Enter Information
btnDisplay	Text	&Display Grade
btnQuit	Text	&Quit
lstGrades		

```
Public Class frmGrades
  Dim pupil As Student   'pupil is an object of class Student

  Private Sub btnEnter_Click(...) Handles btnEnter.Click
    pupil = New Student()     'Create an instance of Student.
    'Read the values stored in the text boxes.
    pupil.Name = txtName.Text
    pupil.SocSecNum = mtxtSSN.Text
    pupil.MidGrade = CDbl(txtMidterm.Text)
    pupil.Final = CDbl(txtFinal.Text)
    'Clear text boxes and list box
    txtName.Clear()
    mtxtSSN.Clear()
    txtMidterm.Clear()
    txtFinal.Clear()
```

```
        lstGrades.Items.Clear()
        'Notify user that grades for the student have been recorded.
        lstGrades.Items.Add("Student Recorded.")
    End Sub

    Private Sub btnDisplay_Click(...) Handles btnDisplay.Click
        Dim fmtStr As String = "{0,-20}{1,-15}{2,-4}"
        lstGrades.Items.Clear()
        lstGrades.Items.Add(String.Format(fmtStr, pupil.Name, _
                        pupil.SocSecNum, pupil.CalcSemGrade))
    End Sub

    Private Sub btnQuit_Click(...) Handles btnQuit.Click
        End
    End Sub
End Class

Class Student
    Private m_name As String        'Name
    Private m_ssn As String         'Social security number
    Private m_midterm As Double     'Numerical grade on midterm exam
    Private m_final As Double        'Numerical grade on final exam

    Public Property Name() As String
        Get
            Return m_name
        End Get
        Set(ByVal value As String)
            m_name = value
        End Set
    End Property

    Public Property SocSecNum() As String
        Get
            Return m_ssn
        End Get
        Set(ByVal value As String)
            m_ssn = value
        End Set
    End Property

    Public WriteOnly Property MidGrade() As Double
        Set(ByVal value As Double)
            m_midterm = value
        End Set
    End Property

    Public WriteOnly Property Final() As Double
        Set(ByVal value As Double)
            m_final = value
        End Set
    End Property
```

```
Function CalcSemGrade() As String
  Dim grade As Double
  grade = (m_midterm + m_final) / 2
  grade = Math.Round(grade)    'Round the grade.
  Select Case grade
    Case Is >= 90
      Return "A"
    Case Is >= 80
      Return "B"
    Case Is >= 70
      Return "C"
    Case Is >= 60
      Return "D"
    Case Else
      Return "F"
  End Select
End Function
End Class
```

[Run, enter the data for a student (such as "Adams, Al", "123-45-6789", "82", "87"), press the Enter Information button to send the data to the object, and press the Display Grade button to display the student's name, Social Security number, and semester grade.]

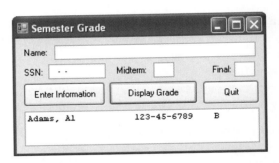

In summary, the following six steps are used to create a class:

1. Identify a *thing* in your program that is to become an object.

2. Determine the properties and methods that you would like the object to have. (As a rule of thumb, properties should access data, and methods should perform operations.)

3. A class will serve as a template for the object. The code for the class is placed in a class block of the form

```
Class ClassName
   statements
End Class
```

4. For each of the properties in Step 2, declare a private member variable with a statement of the form

```
Private m_variableName As DataType
```

Member variables can be preceded with the keyword Public, which allows direct access to the member variables from the code in the form. However, this is considered poor programming practice. By using Set property procedures to update the data, we can enforce constraints and carry out validation.

5. For each of the member variables in Step 4, create a Property block with Get and/or Set procedures to retrieve and assign values of the variable. The general forms of the procedures are

```
Public Property PropertyName() As DataType
  Get
    (Possibly additional code.)
    Return m_variableName
  End Get
  Set(ByVal value As DataType)
    (Possibly additional code.)
    m_variableName = value
  End Set
End Property
```

In the Get or Set code, additional code can be added to prevent the object from storing or returning invalid or corrupted data. For example, an If... Then block could be added to only allow valid Social Security numbers, alerting the user in the event of an invalid number.

6. For each method in Step 2, create a Sub procedure or Function procedure to carry out the task.

Example 2   The following modification of the program in Example 1 calculates semester grades for students who have registered on a "Pass/Fail" basis. We create a new class, named PFStudent, with the same member variables and property procedures as the class Student. The only change needed in the class block occurs in the CalcSemGrade method. The new code for this method is

```
Function CalcSemGrade() As String
  Dim grade As Double
  grade = (m_midterm + m_final) / 2
  grade = Math.Round(grade)   'Round the grade.
  If grade >= 60 Then
    Return "Pass"
  Else
    Return "Fail"
  End If
End Function
```

The only change needed in the form's code is to replace the two occurrences of *Student* with *PFStudent*. When the program is run with the same input as in Example 1, the output will be

```
Adams, Al     123-45-6789   Pass
```

■ Object Constructors

Each class has a special method called a **constructor** that is always invoked as an object is instantiated. The constructor takes zero or more arguments, and the code inside the procedure block performs any tasks needed for initializing an object. It is often used to set default values for member variables and to create other objects associated with this object. The first line of the constructor for a class has the form

```
Public Sub New(ByVal par1 As dataType1, ByVal par2 As dataType2, ...)
```

The graphical program in Example 3 illustrates the use of a constructor to specify the size and placement of a circle. This task involves "pixels," which are a unit of screen measurement. (The width of the screen is about 1000 pixels.) The settings for the Top, Left, Height, and Width properties of a control are given in pixels. For instance, the statements

```
picBox.Width = 85      'About 1 inch
picBox.Height = 128    'About 1.5 inch
picBox.Top = 170       'About 2 inches
picBox.Left = 425      'About 5 inches
```

set the size of the picture box control as 1" by 1.5" and place the control 2 inches from the top of the form and 5 inches from the left side of the form. Refer to Section 9.2 for a discussion of drawing graphics in a picture box.

 Example 3   The following program contains a circle object. The object keeps track of the location and diameter of the circle. (The location is specified by two numbers, called the coordinates, giving the distance from the left side and top of the picture box. Distances and the diameter are measured in pixels.) A Show method displays the circle and a Move method adds 20 pixels to each coordinate of the circle. Initially, the (unseen) circle is located at the upper-left corner of the picture box and has a diameter of 40. The form has a button captioned "Move and Show Circle" that invokes both methods. Notice that the Xcoord, Ycoord, and Diameter properties, rather than the member variables, appear in the methods.

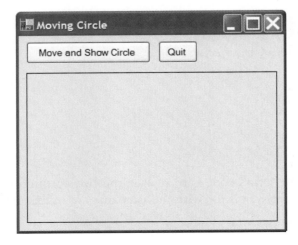

OBJECT	PROPERTY	SETTING
frmCircle	Text	Moving Circle
btnMove	Text	Move and Show Circle
btnQuit	Text	Quit
picCircle		

```
Public Class frmCircle
  Dim round As New Circle()

  Private Sub btnMove_Click(...) Handles btnMove.Click
    round.Move(20)
      round.Show(picCircle.CreateGraphics)
  End Sub

  Private Sub btnQuit_Click(...) Handles btnQuit.Click
    End
  End Sub
End Class

Class Circle
  Private m_x As Integer   'Dist from left side of picture box to circle
  Private m_y As Integer   'Distance from top of picture box to the circle
  Private m_d As Integer   'Diameter of circle

  Public Sub New()
    'Set the initial location of the circle to the upper left
    'corner of the picture box, and set its diameter to 40.
    Xcoord = 0
    Ycoord = 0
    Diameter = 40
  End Sub

  Public Property Xcoord() As Integer
    Get
      Return m_x
    End Get
    Set(ByVal value As Integer)
      m_x = value
    End Set
  End Property

  Public Property Ycoord() As Integer
    Get
      Return m_y
    End Get
    Set(ByVal value As Integer)
      m_y = value
    End Set
  End Property

  Public Property Diameter() As Integer
    Get
      Return m_d
    End Get
    Set(ByVal value As Integer)
      m_d = value
    End Set
  End Property
```

```
Sub Show(ByRef g As Graphics)
  'Draw a circle with the given graphics context.
   g.DrawEllipse(Pens.Black, Xcoord, Ycoord, Diameter, Diameter)
End Sub

Sub Move(ByVal distance As Integer)
  Xcoord += distance
  Ycoord += distance
End Sub
End Class
```

[Run, and press the button ten times.]

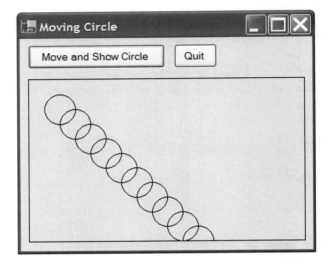

When the line that instantiates an object contains arguments, the values of these arguments are passed to the object's New procedure. For instance, in Example 3, the first line typed in the form's code can be changed to

```
Dim round As New Circle(0, 0, 40)
```

and the New procedure for the Circle class can be changed to

```
Public Sub New(ByVal x As Integer, ByVal y As Integer, ByVal d As
             Integer)
  'Set the initial location of the circle to x pixels from
  'the left side and y pixels from the top of the picture box.
  'Set the diameter to d pixels.
  Xcoord = x
  Ycoord = y
  Diameter = d
End Sub
```

1. Which of the following analogies is out of place?

   (a) class : object

   (b) sewing pattern : garment

   (c) blueprint : house

   (d) programmer : program

   (e) cookie cutter : cookie

2. In Example 1, suppose that the first four lines of the event procedure btnEnter_Click are replaced with

```
Private Sub btnEnter_Click(...) Handles btnEnter.Click
  'Create an instance of Student.
  Dim ssn As String = "123-45-6789"     'Social Security Number
  pupil = New Student(ssn)
```

Create a New procedure and revise the SocSecNum property block for the Student class to be consistent with the last line in the preceding code.

Exercises 1 through 14 refer to the class Student. When applicable, assume that *pupil* is an instance of the class.

1. What will be the effect if the *MidGrade* property block is changed to the following?

```
Public WriteOnly Property MidGrade() As Double
  Set(ByVal value As Double)
    Select Case midterm
      Case Is < 0
        m_midterm = 0
      Case Is > 100
        m_midterm = 100
      Case Else
        m_midterm = value
    End Select
  End Set
End Property
```

2. What will be the effect if the *MidGrade* property block is changed to the following?

```
Public WriteOnly Property MidGrade() As Double
  Set(ByVal value As Double)
    m_midterm = value + 10
  End Set
End Property
```

3. Modify the class block for *Student* so that the following statement will display the student's midterm grade:

```
lstGrades.Items.Add(pupil.MidGrade)
```

4. Modify the class block for *Student* so that the student's semester average can be displayed with a statement of the form

```
lstGrades.Items.Add(pupil.Average)
```

5. In the class block for Student, why can't the third line of the CalcSemGrade method be written

```
grade = (MidGrade + Final) / 2
```

6. Write code for the class block that sets the two grades to 10 whenever an instance of the class is created.

7. What is the effect of adding the following code to the class block:

```
Public Sub New()
    m_ssn = "999-99-9999"
End Sub
```

In Exercises 8 through 14, determine the error in the given form code.

8.
```
Dim scholar As Student

Private Sub btnGo_Click(...) Handles btnGo.Click
    Dim firstName as String
    scholar.Name = "Warren"
    firstName = scholar.Name
End Sub
```

9.
```
Dim scholar As Student

Private Sub btnGo_Click(...) Handles btnGo.Click
    Dim nom as String
    scholar = Student()
    scholar.Name = "Peace, Warren"
    nom = scholar.Name
End Sub
```

10.
```
Dim scholar As Student

Private Sub btnGo_Click(...) Handles btnGo.Click
    Dim nom as String
    scholar = New Student()
    m_name = "Peace, Warren"
    nom = scholar.Name

End Sub
```

11.
```
Dim scholar As Student

Private Sub btnGo_Click(...) Handles btnGo.Click
    Dim nom As String
    scholar = New Student()
```

```
        scholar.Name = "Peace, Warren"
        nom = m_name
    End Sub
```

12. ```
    Dim scholar As Student

    Private Sub btnGo_Click(...) Handles btnGo.Click
      Dim grade As String
      scholar = New Student()
      scholar.CalcSemGrade = "A"
      grade = scholar.CalcSemGrade()
    End Sub
    ```

13. ```
    Dim pupil, scholar As Student

    Private Sub btnGo_Click(...) Handles btnGo.Click
      scholar = New Student()
      pupil = New Student()
      scholar.MidGrade = 89
      pupil.MidGrade = scholar.MidGrade
      lstGrades.Items.Add(pupil.MidGrade)
    End Sub
    ```

14. ```
    Dim scholar As Student
    scholar = New Student()

    Private Sub btnGo_Click(...) Handles btnGo.Click
      scholar.Name = "Transmission, Manuel"
    End Sub
    ```

15. In the following program, determine the output displayed in the list box when the button is pressed:

    ```
    Public Class frmCountry
      Dim nation As New Country("Canada", "Ottawa")

      Private Sub btndisplay_Click(...) Handles btnDisplay.Click
        nation.Population = 31
        lstBox.Items.Add("Country: " & nation.Name)
        lstBox.Items.Add("Capital: " & nation.Capital)
        lstBox.Items.Add("Pop: " & nation.Population & " million")
      End Sub
    End Class

    Class Country
      Private m_name As String
      Private m_capital As String
      Private m_population As Double

      Sub New(ByVal name As String, ByVal capital As String)
        m_name = name
        m_capital = capital
      End Sub
    ```
    ```

```
    Public ReadOnly Property Name() As String
      Get
        Return m_name
      End Get
    End Property

    Public ReadOnly Property Capital() As String
      Get
        Return m_capital
      End Get
    End Property

    Public Property Population() As Double
      Get
        Return m_population
      End Get
      Set(ByVal value As Double)
        m_population = value
      End Set
    End Property
  End Class
```

Exercises 16 through 18 refer to the class *Circle*.

16. Enhance the program in Example 3 so that the Get property procedures and the Set property procedures of the Xcoord and Ycoord properties are used by the form code.

17. Modify Example 3 so that the circle originally has its location at the lower-right corner of the picture box and moves diagonally upward each time *btnMove* is pressed.

18. Modify the form code of Example 3 so that each time *btnMove* is pressed, the distance moved (in pixels) is a randomly selected number from 0 to 40.

19. Write the class block for a class called *Square*. The class should have three properties, Length, Perimeter, and Area, with their obvious meanings. When a value is assigned to one of the properties, the values of the other two should be recalculated automatically. When the following form code is executed, the numbers 5 and 20 should be displayed in the text boxes:

```
Dim poly As Square

Private Sub btnGo_Click(...) Handles btnGo.Click
  poly = New Square()
  poly.Area = 25
  txtLength.Text = CStr(poly.Length)
  txtPerimeter.Text = CStr(poly.Perimeter)
End Sub
```

20. Modify the class *Square* in the previous exercise so that all squares will have lengths between 1 and 10. For instance, the statement `poly.Area = .5` should result in a square of length 1, and the statement `poly.Area = 200` should result in a square of length 10.

21. Write the class block for a class called PairOfDice. A Random object should be used to obtain the value for each die. When the following form code is executed, three numbers (such as 3, 4, and 7) should be displayed in the text boxes.

```
Dim cubes As PairOfDice

Private Sub btnGo_Click(...) Handles btnGo.Click
  cubes = New PairOfDice()
  cubes.Roll()
  txtOne.Text = CStr(cubes.Die1)
  txtTwo.Text = CStr(cubes.Die2)
  txtSum.Text = CStr(cubes.SumOfFaces)
End Sub
```

22. Write a program to toss a pair of dice 1000 times, and display the number of times that the sum of the two faces is 7. The program should use an instance of the class PairOfDice discussed in the previous exercise.

23. Write the code for a class called College. The class should have properties Name, NumStudents, and NumFaculty. The method SFRatio should compute the student–faculty ratio. When the following form code is executed, the number 18.7 should be displayed in the text box:

```
Dim school As College

Private Sub btnGo_Click(...) Handles btnGo.Click
  school = New College()
  school.Name = "University of Maryland, College Park"
  school.NumStudents = 30648
  school.NumFaculty = 1638
  txtBox.Text = FormatNumber(school.SFRatio, 1)
End Sub
```

24. Write a program that calculates an employee's pay for a week based on the hourly wage and the number of hours worked. All computations should be performed by an instance of the class Wages.

25. Write a program to implement the cash register in Figure 11.1. The program should have a class called CashRegister that keeps track of the balance and allows deposits and withdrawals. The class should not permit a negative balance.

FIGURE 11.1   Form for Exercise 25.

26. Write a program that calculates the average of up to 50 numbers input by the user and stored in an array. See Figure 11.2. The program should use a class named Statistics and have an AddNumber method that stores numbers into an array one at a time. The class should have a Count property that keeps track of the number of numbers stored and a method called Average that returns the average of the numbers.

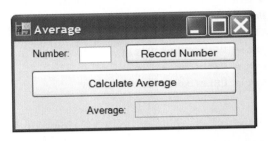

FIGURE 11.2   **Form for Exercise 26.**

27. Write a program that a college bookstore can use to keep track of and determine the retail prices of textbooks. All computations should be performed by an instance of the class Textbook. The class should have properties Title, Author, Cost (wholesale cost), Quantity (number of copies in stock), and the method Price, that is, the retail price. Assuming that the bookstore marks up books by 25%, the Price should be 1.25 times the Cost.

28. Write a program that calculates an employee's FICA tax, with all computations performed by an instance of a class FICA. The FICA tax has two components: the Social Security benefits tax, which in 2005 is 6.2 percent of the first $90,000 of earnings for the year, and the Medicare tax, which is 1.45 percent of earnings.

29. Write a program that adds two fractions and displays their sum in reduced form. The program should use a Fraction class that stores the numerator and denominator of a fraction and has a Reduce method that divides each of the numerator and denominator by their greatest common divisor. Exercise 39 of Section 6.1 contains an algorithm for calculating the greatest common divisor of two numbers.

Solutions to Practice Problems 11.1

1. (d) A programmer is not a template for creating a program.

2.
```
Public Sub New(ByVal ssn As String)
    'Assign the value of ssn to the member variable m_ssn.
   m_ssn = ssn
End Sub

Public ReadOnly Property SocSecNum() As String
  Get
    Return m_ssn
  End Get
End Property
```

Note: Since a student's Social Security number never changes, there is no need to have a Set property procedure for SocSecNum.

11.2   Arrays of Objects; Events; Containment

"An object without an event is like a telephone without a ringer."

Anonymous

■ Arrays of Objects

The elements of an array can have any data type—including a user-defined object. The program in Example 1 uses an array of type Student.

  Example 1   In the following program, which uses the same form design as Example 1 of the previous section, the user enters four pieces of data about a student into text boxes. When the Enter Information button is pressed, the data are used to create and initialize an appropriate object and the object is added to an array. When the Display Grades button is pressed, the name, Social Security number, and semester grade for each student in the array are displayed in the list box.

```
Public Class frmGrades
  Dim students(50) As Student
  Dim lastStudentAdded As Integer = -1      'Position in array of student
                                            'most recently added
  Private Sub btnEnter_Click(...) Handles btnEnter.Click
    'Create an instance of student.
    'Read the values stored in the text boxes.
    Dim pupil As New Student()
    pupil.Name = txtName.Text
    pupil.SocSecNum = mtxtSSN.Text
    pupil.MidGrade = CDbl(txtMidterm.Text)
    pupil.Final = CDbl(txtFinal.Text)
    'Add the student to the array
    lastStudentAdded += 1
    students(lastStudentAdded) = pupil
    'Clear text boxes
    txtName.Clear()
    mtxtSSN.Clear()
    txtMidterm.Clear()
    txtFinal.Clear()
    lstGrades.Items.Add("Student Recorded.")
  End Sub

  Private Sub btnDisplay_Click(...) Handles btnDisplay.Click
    Dim fmtStr As String = "{0,-20}{1,-15}{2,-1}"
    lstGrades.Items.Clear()
    lstGrades.Items.Add(String.Format(fmtStr, "Student Name", _
                                "SSN", "Grade"))
```

```vb
              For i As Integer = 0 To lastStudentAdded
                lstGrades.Items.Add(String.Format(fmtStr, students(i).Name, _
                              students(i).SocSecNum, students(i).CalcSemGrade))
          Next
        End Sub

        Private Sub btnQuit_Click(...) Handles btnQuit.Click
          End
        End Sub
    End Class

    Class Student
      Private m_name As String
      Private m_ssn As String
      Private m_midterm As Double
      Private m_final As Double

      Public Property Name() As String
        Get
          Return m_name
        End Get
        Set(ByVal value As String)
          m_name = value
        End Set
      End Property

      Public Property SocSecNum() As String
        Get
          Return m_ssn
        End Get
        Set(ByVal value As String)
          m_ssn = value
        End Set
      End Property

      Public WriteOnly Property MidGrade() As Double
        Set(ByVal value As Double)
          m_midterm = value
        End Set
      End Property

      Public WriteOnly Property Final() As Double
        Set(ByVal value As Double)
          m_final = value
        End Set
      End Property

      Function CalcSemGrade() As String
        Dim grade As Double
        grade = (m_midterm + m_final) / 2
        grade = Math.Round(grade)    'Round the grade.
```

```
        Select Case grade
          Case Is >= 90
            Return "A"
          Case Is >= 80
            Return "B"
          Case Is >= 70
            Return "C"
          Case Is >= 60
            Return "D"
          Case Else
            Return "F"
        End Select
      End Function
    End Class
```

[Run, type in data for Al Adams, press the Enter Information button, repeat the process for Brittany Brown and Carol Cole, press the Display Grades button, and then enter data for Daniel Doyle.]

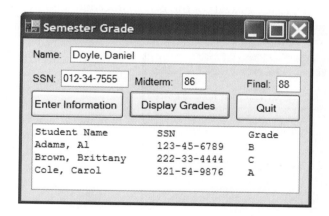

■ Events

In the previous section, we drew a parallel between objects and controls and showed how to define properties and methods for classes. In addition to the predefined event New for classes, other events can be defined by the programmer to communicate changes of properties, errors, and the progress of lengthy operations. Such events are called **user-defined events**. The statement for triggering an event is located in the class block, and the event is dealt with in the form's code. Suppose that the event is named UserDefinedEvent and has the parameters *par1*, *par2*, and so on. In the class block, the statement

```
Public Event UserDefinedEvent(ByVal par1 As DataType1, _
                              ByVal par2 As DataType2, ...)
```

should be placed in the Declarations section, and the statement

```
RaiseEvent UserDefinedEvent(arg1, arg2, ...)
```

should be placed at the locations in the class block code at which the event should be triggered. In the form's code, an instance of the class, call it *object1*, must be declared with a statement of the type

```
Dim WithEvents object1 As ClassName
```

or the type

```
Dim WithEvents object1 As New ClassName
```

in order to be able to respond to the event. That is, the keyword WithEvents must be inserted into the declaration. The header of an event procedure for *object1* will be

```
Private Sub object1_UserDefinedEvent(par1, par2, ...) _
        Handles object1.UserDefinedEvent
```

Example 2   Consider the circle class defined in Example 3 of Section 11.1. In the following program, we add a user-defined event that is triggered whenever the location of a circle changes. The event has parameters to pass the location and diameter of the circle. The form's code uses the event to determine if part (or all) of the drawn circle will fall outside the picture box. If so, the event procedure displays the message "Circle Off Screen" in a text box. Let's call the event PositionChanged.

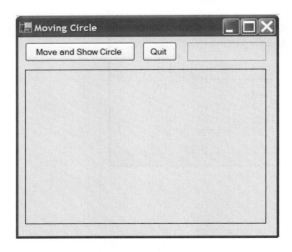

OBJECT	PROPERTY	SETTING
frmCircle	Text	Moving Circle
btnMove	Text	Move and Show Circle
btnQuit	Text	Quit
txtCaution	ReadOnly	True
picCircle		

```
Public Class frmCircle
  Dim WithEvents round As New Circle()

  Private Sub btnMove_Click(...) Handles btnMove.Click
    round.Move(20)
  End Sub

  Private Sub btnQuit_Click(...) Handles btnQuit.Click
    End
  End Sub
```

```
    Private Sub round_PositionChanged(ByVal x As Integer, _
       ByVal y As Integer, ByVal d As Integer) Handles round.PositionChanged
       'This event is triggered when the location of the circle changes.
       'The code determines if part of the circle is off the screen.
       If (x + d > picCircle.Width) Or _
          (y + d > picCircle.Height) Then
          txtCaution.Text = "Circle Off Screen"
       End If
       round.Show(picCircle.CreateGraphics)
    End Sub
End Class

Class Circle
    Private m_x As Integer 'Dist from left side of picture box to circle
    Private m_y As Integer 'Distance from top of picture box to circle
    Private m_d As Integer 'Diameter of circle

    Public Event PositionChanged(ByVal x As Integer, _
                                 ByVal y As Integer, ByVal d As Integer)
    'Event is triggered when the circle moves.

    Public Sub New()
       'Set the initial location of the circle to the upper-left
       'corner of the picture box, and set its diameter to 40.
       Xcoord = 0
       Ycoord = 0
       Diameter = 40
    End Sub

    Public Property Xcoord() As Integer
       Get
          Return m_x
       End Get
       Set(ByVal value As Integer)
          m_x = value
       End Set
    End Property

    Public Property Ycoord() As Integer
       Get
          Return m_y
       End Get
       Set(ByVal value As Integer)
          m_y = value
       End Set
    End Property
```

```
Public Property Diameter() As Integer
  Get
    Return m_d
  End Get
  Set(ByVal value As Integer)
    m_d = value
  End Set
End Property

Sub Show(ByRef g As Graphics)
  'Draw a circle with the given graphics context.
  g.DrawEllipse(Pens.Black, Xcoord, Ycoord, Diameter, Diameter)
End Sub

Sub Move(ByVal distance As Integer)
  Xcoord += distance
  Ycoord += distance
  RaiseEvent PositionChanged(Xcoord, Ycoord, Diameter)
End Sub
End Class
```

[Run, and press the "Move and Show Circle" button eleven times.]

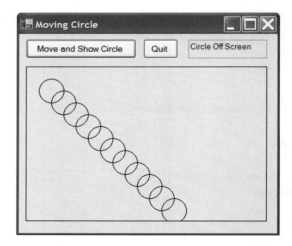

Note: As the last circle appears, the words "Circle Off Screen" are displayed in the text box.

▓ Containment

We say that class A **contains** class B when a member variable of class A makes use of an object of type class B. In Example 3, the class DeckOfCards contains the class Card.

Example 3   The following program deals a five-card poker hand. The program has a deck-of-cards object containing an array of 52 card objects. The card object has two properties, Denomination and Suit, and one method, IdentifyCard. The IdentifyCard method returns a string such as "Ace of Spades." In the DeckOfCards object, the New event

procedure assigns denominations and suits to the 52 cards. The method ReadCard(n) returns the string identifying the *n*th card of the deck. The method ShuffleDeck uses the Random class to mix up the cards while making 2000 passes through the deck. The event

```
Shuffling(n As Integer, nMax As Integer)
```

is triggered during each shuffling pass through the deck, and its parameters communicate the number of the pass and the total number of passes, so that the program that uses it can keep track of the progress.

OBJECT	PROPERTY	SETTING
frmPoker	Text	Poker Hand
lstHand		
btnShuffle	Text	&Shuffle
btnDeal	Text	&Deal
btnQuit	Text	&Quit

```
Public Class frmPoker
  Dim WithEvents cards As New DeckOfCards()

  Private Sub btnShuffle_Click(...) Handles btnShuffle.Click
    cards.ShuffleDeck
  End Sub

  Private Sub btnDeal_Click(...) Handles btnDeal.Click
    Dim str As String
    lstHand.Items.Clear()
    For i As Integer = 0 To 4
      str = cards.ReadCard(i)
      lstHand.Items.Add(str)
    Next
  End Sub

  Private Sub Quit_Click(...) Handles Quit.Click
    End
  End Sub

  Private Sub cards_Shuffling(ByVal n As Integer, _
                    ByVal nMax As Integer) Handles cards.Shuffling
    'n is the number of the specific pass through the deck (1, 2, 3...).
    'nMax is the total number of passes when the deck is shuffled.
    lstHand.Items.Clear()
    lstHand.Items.Add("Shuffling Pass: " & n & " out of " & nMax)
    For i As Integer = 1 To 1000000      'Slow down the shuffle.
    Next
    lstHand.Update()   'Refresh contents of list box
  End Sub
End Class
```

```
Class Card
  Private m_denomination As Integer   'A number from 0 through 12
  Private m_suit As String            'Hearts, Clubs, Diamonds, Spades

  Public Property Denomination() As Integer
    Get
      Return m_denomination
    End Get
    Set(ByVal value As Integer)
      'Only store valid values.
      If (value >= 0) And (value <= 12) Then
        m_denomination = value
      End If
    End Set
  End Property

  Public Property Suit() As String
    Get
      Return m_suit
    End Get
    Set(ByVal value As String)
      'Only store valid values.
      If (value = "Hearts") Or (value = "Clubs") Or _
         (value = "Diamonds") Or (value = "Spades") Then
        m_suit = value
      End If
    End Set
  End Property

  Function IdentifyCard() As String
    Dim denom As String = ""
    Select Case m_denomination + 1
      Case 1
        denom = "Ace"
      Case Is <= 10
        denom = CStr(m_denomination + 1)
      Case 11
        denom = "Jack"
      Case 12
        denom = "Queen"
      Case 13
        denom = "King"
    End Select
    Return denom & " of " & m_suit
  End Function
End Class
```

```
Class DeckOfCards
  Private m_deck(51) As Card 'Class DeckOfCards contains class Card
  Public Event Shuffling(ByVal n As Integer, ByVal nMax As Integer)

  Public Sub New()
    'Make the first thirteen cards hearts, the
    'next thirteen cards diamonds, and so on.
    Dim suits() As String = {"Hearts", "Clubs", "Diamonds", "Spades"}
    For i As Integer = 0 To 3
      'Each pass corresponds to one of the four suits.
      For j As Integer = 0 To 12
        'Assign numbers from 0 through 12 to the
        'cards of each suit.
        m_deck(i * 13 + j) = New Card()
        m_deck(i * 13 + j).Suit = suits(i)
        m_deck(i * 13 + j).Denomination = j
      Next
    Next
  End Sub

  Function ReadCard(ByVal cardNum As Integer) As String
    Return m_deck(cardNum).IdentifyCard()
  End Function

  Sub Swap(ByVal i As Integer, ByVal j As Integer)
    'Swap the ith and jth card in the deck.
    Dim tempCard As Card
    tempCard = m_deck(i)
    m_deck(i) = m_deck(j)
    m_deck(j) = tempCard
  End Sub

  Sub ShuffleDeck()
    'Do 2000 passes through the deck.  On each pass,
    'swap each card with a randomly selected card.
    Dim index As Integer
    Dim randomNum As New Random()
    For i As Integer = 1 To 2000
      For k As Integer = 0 To 51
        index = randomNum.Next(0, 52)  'Randomly select a number
                                        'from 0 through 51 inclusive.
        Swap(k, index)
      Next
      RaiseEvent Shuffling(i, 2000)
    Next
  End Sub
End Class
```

[Run, click on the Shuffle button, and click on the Deal button after the shuffling is complete.]

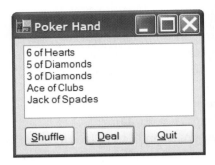

Consider the program in Example 1, and suppose that mtxtSSN is an ordinary text box.

1. Alter the Set SocSecNum property procedure to raise the event ImproperSSN when the Social Security number does not have 11 characters. The event should pass the length of the Social Security number and the student's name to the form's code.
2. What statement must be placed in the Declarations section of the class block?
3. Write an event procedure for the event ImproperSSN.
4. What statement in the form's code must be altered?

EXERCISES 11.2

1. In Example 1, modify the event procedure btnDisplay_Click so that only the students who receive a grade of A are displayed.

   The file STATES.TXT provides data on the 50 states. (This file is used in Exercises 2 through 5.) Each record contains five pieces of information about a single state: name, abbreviation, date it entered the union, land area (in square miles), and population in the year 2000. The records are ordered by the date of entry into the union. The first five lines of the file are

   ```
   Delaware
   DE
   Dec. 1787
   1954
   759000
   ```

2. Create (a) a class State with five properties to hold the information about a single state and (b) a method that calculates the density (people per square mile) of the state.
3. Write a program that requests a state's name in an input dialog box and displays the state's abbreviation, density, and date of entrance into the union. The program should use an array of State objects.

4. Write a program that displays the names of the states and their densities in a list box ordered by density. The program should use an array of State objects.

5. Write a program that reads the data from the file into an array of State objects and raises an event whenever the population of a state exceeds ten million. States with a large population should have their names and populations displayed in a list box by the corresponding event procedure. *Hint*: Create a class called UnitedStates that contains the array and defines a method Add that adds a new state to the array. The Add method should raise the event.

6. Consider the class Square from Exercise 19 of Section 11.1 Add the event IllegalNumber that is raised when any of the properties is set to a negative number. Show the new class block and write an event procedure for the event that displays an error message.

7. Consider the CashRegister class in Exercise 25 of Section 11.1. Add the event AttemptToOverdraw that is raised when the user tries to subtract more money than is in the cash register.

8. Consider the class PairOfDice discussed in Exercise 21 of Section 11.1. Add the event SnakeEyes that is raised whenever two ones appear during a roll of the dice. Write a program that uses the event.

9. Consider the Fraction class in Exercise 29 of Section 11.1. Add the event ZeroDenominator, that is triggered whenever a denominator is set to 0. Write a program that uses the event.

10. Write a program for the fraction calculator shown in Figure 11.3. After the numerators and denominators of the two fractions to the left of the equals sign are placed in the four text boxes, one of four operations buttons should be pressed. The result appears to the right of the equals sign. The program should use a Calculator class, which contains three members of the type Fraction discussed in Exercise 29 of Section 11.1. **Note:** In Figure 11.3, the fraction bars are very short list boxes.

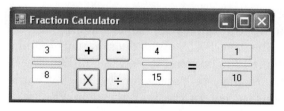

FIGURE 11.3   Sample Output for Exercise 10.

11. Write a program that takes orders at a fast food restaurant. See Figure 11.4. The restaurant has two menus, a regular menu and a kids menu. An item is ordered by highlighting it in one of the list boxes and then pushing the ≫ or ≪ button to place it in the order list box in the center of the form. As each item is ordered, a running total is displayed in the text box at the lower right part of the form. The program should use a Choices class, which contains a Food class. (The contents of each of the three list boxes should be treated as Choices objects.) Each Food object should hold the name and price of a single food item. Each Choices object should have a ChoiceChanged event that can be used by the form code to update the cost of the order.

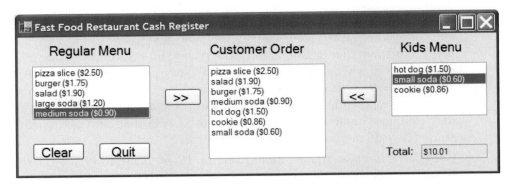

FIGURE 11.4 **Sample Output for Exercise 11.**

12. Write a program for a simple game in which each of two players rolls a pair of dice. The person with the highest tally wins. See Figure 11.5. The program should use a Game class (HighRoller) having two member variables of the type PairOfDice discussed in Exercise 21 of Section 11.1.

FIGURE 11.5 **Sample output for Exercise 12.**

13. Write a program to produce an employee's weekly paycheck receipt. The receipt should contain the employee's name, amount earned for the week, total amount earned for the year, FICA tax deduction, withholding tax deduction, and take-home amount. The program should use an Employee class and a Tax class. The Tax class must have properties for the amount earned for the week, the prior total amount earned for the year, the number of withholding exemptions, and marital status. It should have methods for computing FICA and withholding taxes. The Employee class should store the employee's name, number of withholding allowances, marital status, hours worked this week, hourly salary, and previous amount earned for the year. The Employee class should use the Tax class to calculate the taxes to be deducted. The formula for calculating the FICA tax is given in Exercise 28 of Section 11.1. To compute the withholding tax, multiply the number of withholding allowances by $61.54, subtract the product from the amount earned, and use Table 11.1 or Table 11.2.

TABLE 11.1	2005 Federal income tax withheld for a single person paid weekly.
Adjusted Weekly Income	Income Tax Withheld
$0 to $51	$0
Over $51 to $188	10% of amount over $51
Over $188 to $606	$13.70 + 15% of amount over $188
Over $606 to $1,341	$76.40 + 25% of amount over $606
Over $1,341 to $2,922	$260.15 + 28% of amount over $1,341
Over $2,922 to $6,313	$702.83 + 33% of amount over $2,922
Over $6,313	$1,821.86 + 35% of amount over $6,313

TABLE 11.2	2005 Federal income tax withheld for a married person paid weekly.
Adjusted Weekly Income	Income Tax Withheld
$0 to $154	$0
Over $154 to $435	10% of amount over $154
Over $435 to $1,273	$28.10 + 15% of amount over $435
Over $1,273 to $2,322	$153.80 + 25% of amount over $1,273
Over $2,322 to $3,646	$416.05 + 28% of amount over $2,322
Over $3,646 to $6,409	$786.77 + 33% of amount over $3,646
Over $6,409	$1,698.56 + 35% of amount over $6,409

Solutions to Practice Problems 11.2

```
1. Public Property SocSecNum() As String
     Get
       Return m_ssn
     End Get
     Set(ByVal value As String)
       If value.Length = 11 Then
         m_ssn = value
       Else
         RaiseEvent ImproperSSN(value.Length, m_name)
       End If
     End Set
   End Property

2. Public Event ImproperSSN(ByVal length As Integer, _
                            ByVal studentName As String)

3. Private Sub pupil_ImproperSSN(ByVal length As Integer, _
            ByVal studentName As string) Handles pupil.ImproperSSN
     MsgBox("The social security number entered for " & _
         studentName & " consisted of " & length & _
         " characters. Reenter the data for " & studentName & ".")
   End Sub
```

4. The statement

`Dim pupil As New Student()`

must be changed to

`Dim WithEvents pupil As New Student()`

and moved to the Declaration section.

11.3 Inheritance

The three relationships between classes are "use," "containment," and "inheritance." One class **uses** another class if it manipulates objects of that class. We say that class A **contains** class B when a member variable of class A makes use of an object of type class B. Sections 11.1 and 11.2 present examples of use and containment.

Inheritance is a process by which one class (the **child** or **derived** class) inherits the properties, methods, and events of another class (the **parent** or **base** class). The child has access to all of its parent's properties, methods and events as well as to all of its own. If the parent is itself a child, then it and its children have access to all of its parent's properties, methods and events. Consider the classes shown in Figure 11.6. All three children inherit Property A and Sub B from their parent. Child2 and Child3 have an additional event and a property, respectively. GrandChild1 has access to Property A, Sub B, and Event C from its parent and adds Function E and Sub F. The collection of a parent class along with its descendants is called a **hierarchy**.

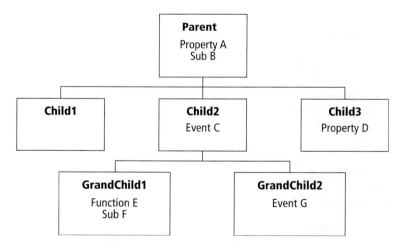

FIGURE 11.6   **Example of inheritance hierarchy.**

There are two main benefits gained by using inheritance: First, it allows two or more classes to share some common features yet differentiate themselves on others. Second, it supports code reusability by avoiding the extra effort required to maintain duplicate code in multiple classes. For these reasons, inheritance is one of the most powerful tools of object-oriented programming. Considerable work goes into planning and defining the member variables and methods of the parent class. The child classes are beneficiaries of this effort.

Just as structured programming requires the ability to break complex problems into simpler subproblems, object-oriented programming requires the skill to identify useful hierarchies of classes and derived classes. Software engineers are still working on the guidelines for when and how to establish hierarchies. One useful criterion is the **ISA test**: If one class *is a* more specific case of another class, the first class should be derived from the second class.

The Visual Basic keyword Inherits identifies the parent of a class. The code used to define the class Parent and its child class Child2 as illustrated in Figure 11.6 is

```
Class Parent
  Public Property A
    'Property Get and Set blocks
  End Property

  Sub B()
    'Code for Sub procedure B
  End Sub
End Class

Class Child2
  Inherits Parent
  Event C()
End Class
```

As Child2 is itself a parent, its child GrandChild1 can be declared using a similar statement:

```
Class GrandChild1
  Inherits Child2

  Function E()
    'Code for function E
  End Sub

  Sub F()
    'Code for Sub procedure F
  End Sub
End Class
```

 Example 1   In the following program, the user is presented with a basic adding machine. The Calculator class implements the Multiply and Divide methods and inherits the FirstNumber and SecondNumber properties and the Add and Subtract methods from its AddingMachine parent. When the Adding Machine radio button is selected, the user may add or subtract two numbers using an AddingMachine object. When the Calculator radio button is selected, the user may add, subtract, multiply, or divide two numbers using a Calculator object. Notice that the multiply and divide buttons are hidden when the Adding Machine is selected, and how the Click event procedures for the btnAdd and btnSubtract buttons examine the state of the radio button to determine which machine to use.

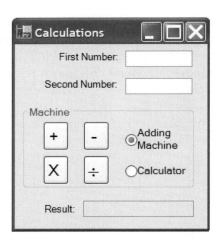

OBJECT	PROPERTY	SETTING
frmCalculate	Text	Calculations
lblNumber1	Text	First Number:
txtNumber1		
lblNumber2	Text	Second Number:
txtNumber2		
lblResult	Text	Result:
txtResult	ReadOnly	True
grpMachine	Text	Machine
rdoAddingMachine	Text	Adding Machine
	Checked	True
rdoCalculator	Text	Calculator
btnAdd	Text	+
btnSubtract	Text	−
btnMultiply	Text	×
btnDivide	Font	Symbol
	Text	¸ (Cedilla)

```vb
Public Class frmCalculate
  'Create both machines.
  Dim adder As New AddingMachine()
  Dim calc As New Calculator()

  Private Sub rdoAddingMachine_CheckedChanged(...) _
                    Handles rdoAddingMachine.CheckedChanged
    'Hide the multiply and divide functionality.
    btnMultiply.Visible = False
    btnDivide.Visible = False
  End Sub

  Private Sub rdoCalculator_CheckedChanged(...) _
                    Handles rdoCalculator.CheckedChanged
    'Show the multiply and divide functionality.
    btnMultiply.Visible = True
    btnDivide.Visible = True
  End Sub

  Private Sub btnAdd_Click(...) Handles btnAdd.Click
    'Add two numbers.
    If rdoAddingMachine.Checked Then
      'If adding machine selected, use it to get the result.
      adder.FirstNumber = CDbl(txtNumber1.Text)
      adder.SecondNumber = CDbl(txtNumber2.Text)
      txtResult.Text = CStr(adder.Add)
    Else
      'If calculator selected, use it to get the result.
      calc.FirstNumber = CDbl(txtNumber1.Text)
      calc.SecondNumber = CDbl(txtNumber2.Text)
      txtResult.Text = CStr(calc.Add)
    End If
  End Sub
```

```vb
    Private Sub btnSubtract_Click(...) Handles btnSubtract.Click
        'Subtract two numbers.
      If rdoAddingMachine.Checked Then
          'If adding machine selected, use it to get the result.
        adder.FirstNumber = CDbl(txtNumber1.Text)
        adder.SecondNumber = CDbl(txtNumber2.Text)
        txtResult.Text = CStr(adder.Subtract)
      Else
          'If calculator selected, use it to get the result.
        calc.FirstNumber = CDbl(txtNumber1.Text)
        calc.SecondNumber = CDbl(txtNumber2.Text)
        txtResult.Text = CStr(calc.Subtract)
      End If
    End Sub

    Private Sub btnMultiply_Click(...) Handles btnMultiply.Click
        'Multiply two numbers.
      calc.FirstNumber = CDbl(txtNumber1.Text)
      calc.SecondNumber = CDbl(txtNumber2.Text)
      txtResult.Text = CStr(calc.Multiply)
    End Sub

    Private Sub btnDivide_Click(...) Handles btnDivide.Click
        'Divide two numbers.
      calc.FirstNumber = CDbl(txtNumber1.Text)
      calc.SecondNumber = CDbl(txtNumber2.Text)
      txtResult.Text = CStr(calc.Divide)
    End Sub
End Class

Class AddingMachine
  Private m_num1, m_num2 As Double

  Public Property FirstNumber() As Double
    Get
      Return m_num1
    End Get
    Set(ByVal value As Double)
      m_num1 = value
    End Set
  End Property

  Public Property SecondNumber() As Double
    Get
      Return m_num2
    End Get
    Set(ByVal value As Double)
      m_num2 = value
    End Set
  End Property
```

```
Function Add() As Double
   Return FirstNumber + SecondNumber
End Function

Function Subtract() As Double
   Return FirstNumber - SecondNumber
End Function
End Class

Class Calculator
  Inherits AddingMachine
  'Calculator inherits properties FirstNumber and SecondNumber
  'and functions Add() and Subtract().

  Function Multiply() As Double
     Return FirstNumber * SecondNumber
  End Function

  Function Divide() As Double
     Return FirstNumber / SecondNumber
  End Function
End Class
```

[Run, type in 12 and 3, and press the + and − buttons. Click the Calculator radio button, and press the +, −, ×, and ÷ buttons.]

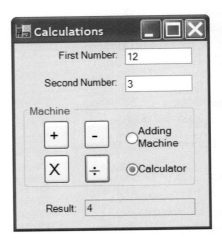

Polymorphism and Overriding

The set of properties, methods, and events for a class is called the class **interface**. In essence, the interface of a class defines how it should behave. The interfaces of the classes AddingMachine and Calculator used in Example 1 are shown in Table 11.3.

Consider the classes used in Examples 1 and 2 of Section 11.1. Both Student and PFStudent have the same interface even though they carry out the task of computing a semester grade differently. See Table 11.4.

TABLE 11.3   Interfaces used in Example 1.

	AddingMachine	Calculator
Properties	FirstNumber	FirstNumber
	SecondNumber	SecondNumber
Methods	Add	Add
	Subtract	Subtract
		Multiply
		Divide
Events	(none)	(none)

TABLE 11.4   Interfaces used in Examples 1 and 2 in Section 11.1.

	Student	PFStudent
Properties	Name	Name
	SocSecNum	SocSecNum
	midGrade	midGrade
	Final	Final
Methods	CalcSemGrade	CalcSemGrade
Events	(none)	(none)

If a programmer wants to write a program that manipulates objects from these two classes, he or she need only know how to use the interface. The programmer need not be concerned with what specific implementation of that interface is being used. The object will then behave according to its specific implementation.

The programmer need only be aware of the CalcSemGrade method and needn't be concerned about its implementation. The feature that two classes can have methods that are named the same and have essentially the same purpose, but different implementations, is called **polymorphism**.

A programmer may employ polymorphism in three easy steps. First, the properties, methods, and events that make up an interface are defined. Second, a parent class is created that performs the functionality dictated by the interface. Finally, a child class inherits the parent and overrides the methods that require different implementation than the parent. The keyword Overridable is used to designate the parent's methods that can be overridden, and the keyword Overrides is used to designate the child's methods that are doing the overriding.

There are situations where a child class needs to access the parent class's implementation of a method that the child is overriding. Visual Basic provides the keyword MyBase to support this functionality.

Consider the code from Example 1 of Section 11.1. To employ polymorphism, the keyword Overridable is inserted into the header of the CalcSemGrade method in the Student class:

```
Overridable Function CalcSemGrade() As String
```

The PFStudent class inherits all of the properties and methods from its parent, overriding the CalcSemGrade method as follows:

```
Class PFStudent
  Inherits Student

  Overrides Function CalcSemGrade() As String
    'The student's grade for the semester
    If MyBase.CalcSemGrade = "F" Then
      Return "Fail"
    Else
      Return "Pass"
    End If
  End Function
End Class
```

   Example 2   In the following program, the user can enter student information and display the semester grades for the class. The PFStudent class inherits all of the properties from its parent Student, but overrides the CalcSemGrade method with its own implementation. The btnEnter_Click event procedure stores an element created by either class into the *students* array. However, the btnDisplay_Click event procedure does not need to know which elements are from which class, thus demonstrating polymorphism.

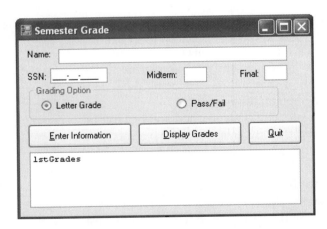

OBJECT	PROPERTY	SETTING
frmGrades	Text	Semester Grade
lblName	Text	Name:
txtName		
lblSSN	Text	SSN:
mtxtSSN	Mask	000-00-0000
lblMidterm	Text	Midterm:
txtMidterm		
lblFinal	Text	Final:
txtFinal		
btnEnter	Text	&Enter Information
btnDisplay	Text	&Display Grades
btnQuit	Text	&Quit
grpGradingOption	Text	Grading Option
rdoLetterGrade	Text	Letter Grade
	Checked	True
rdoPassFail	Text	Pass/Fail
lstGrades		

```
Public Class frmGrades
  Dim students(49) As Student        'Stores the class
  Dim lastStudentAdded As Integer = -1   'Last student added to students

  Private Sub btnEnter_Click(...) Handles btnEnter.Click
    'Stores a student into the array.
    Dim pupil As Student
    'Create the appropriate object depending upon the radio button.
    If rdoPassFail.Checked Then
      pupil = New PFStudent()
```

```vbnet
      Else
         pupil = New Student()
      End If
      'Store the values in the text boxes into the object.
      pupil.Name = txtName.Text
      pupil.SocSecNum = mtxtSSN.Text
      pupil.Midterm = CDbl(txtMidterm.Text)
      pupil.Final = CDbl(txtFinal.Text)
      'Add the student to the array.
      lastStudentAdded += 1
      students(lastStudentAdded) = pupil
      'Clear text boxes and list box.
      txtName.Clear()
      mtxtSSN.Clear()
      txtMidterm.Clear()
      txtFinal.Clear()
      lstGrades.Items.Add("Student #" & lastStudentAdded + 1 _
                     & " recorded.")
   End Sub

   Private Sub btnDisplay_Click(...) Handles btnDisplay.Click
      'Display the students' information and semester grade.
      Dim fmtStr As String = "{0,-20}{1,-15}{2,-4}"
      lstGrades.Items.Clear()
      'Loop over all available elements of the Student array.
      For i As Integer = 0 To lastStudentAdded
         lstGrades.Items.Add(String.Format(fmtStr, students(i).Name, _
                        students(i).SocSecNum, students(i).CalcSemGrade))
      Next
   End Sub

   Private Sub btnQuit_Click(...) Handles btnQuit.Click
      'Quit the program
      End
   End Sub
End Class

Class Student
   'Member variables to hold the property values
   Private m_name As String
   Private m_ssn As String
   Private m_midterm As Double
   Private m_final As Double

   Public Property Name() As String
      'The student's name
      Get
         Return m_name
      End Get
```

```
      Set(ByVal value As String)
        m_name = value
      End Set
    End Property

    Public Property SocSecNum() As String
      'The student's Social Security Number
      Get
        Return m_ssn
      End Get
      Set(ByVal value As String)
        m_ssn = value
      End Set
    End Property

    Public WriteOnly Property Midterm() As Double
      'The student's score on the midterm exam
      Set(ByVal value As Double)
        m_midterm = value
      End Set
    End Property

    Public WriteOnly Property Final() As Double
      'The student's score on the final exam
      Set(ByVal value As Double)
        m_final = value
      End Set
    End Property

    Overridable Function CalcSemGrade() As String
      'The student's grade for the semester
      Dim grade As Double
      'The grade is based upon average of the midterm and final exams.
      grade = (m_midterm + m_final) / 2
      grade = Math.Round(grade)   'Round the grade.
      Select Case grade
        Case Is >= 90
          Return "A"
        Case Is >= 80
          Return "B"
        Case Is >= 70
          Return "C"
        Case Is >= 60
          Return "D"
        Case Else
          Return "F"
      End Select
    End Function
  End Class
```

```
Class PFStudent
  Inherits Student

  Overrides Function CalcSemGrade() As String
    'The student's grade for the semester
    If MyBase.CalcSemGrade = "F" Then
      Return "Fail"
    Else
      Return "Pass"
    End If
  End Function
End Class
```

[Enter the data, press the Enter Information button for three student, press the Display Grades button, and then enter the data for another student.]

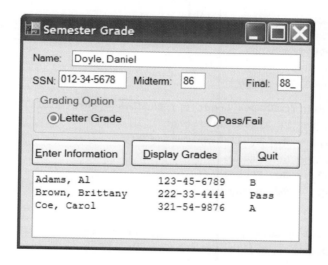

Example 2 employs inheritance and overriding to provide functionality to one child class. If a program contains two or more children of a class, however, the technique of overriding can lead to confusing programs. Visual Basic provides a cleaner design through the use of abstract classes.

■ Abstract Properties, Methods, and Classes

Sometimes you want to insist that each child of a class have a certain property or method that it must implement for its own use. Such a property or method is said to be **abstract** and is declared with the keyword MustOverride. An **abstract** property or method consists of just a header with no code following it. It has no corresponding **End Property**, **End Sub**, or **End Function** statement. Its class is called an **abstract base class** and must be declared with the keyword MustInherit. Abstract classes cannot be instantiated, only their children can be instantiated.

Example 3 The following program calculates the area of several regular two-dimensional shapes given the length of one side. (A regular shape is a shape whose sides have identical length and whose interior angles are identical.) The abstract parent class Shape implements the Length property and declares the Name and Area functions as MustOverride. Notice that methods declared with MustOverride do not have any implementation code. Each child class inherits the property from the parent and implements the two functions. The btnDisplay_Click event procedure uses polymorphism to set the shapes' length and display the shapes' names and areas.

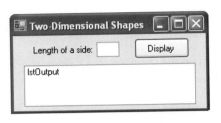

OBJECT	PROPERTY	SETTING
frmShapes	Text	Two-Dimensional Shapes
lblLength	Text	Length of a side:
txtLength		
btnDisplay	Text	Display
lstOutput		

```
Public Class frmShapes
  'Declare shape array.
  Dim shape(3) As Shape

  Private Sub frmShapes_Load(...) Handles MyBase.Load
    'Populate the array with shapes.
    shape(0) = New EquilateralTriangle()
    shape(1) = New Square()
    shape(2) = New Pentagon()
    shape(3) = New Hexagon()
  End Sub

  Private Sub btnDisplay_Click(...) Handles btnDisplay.Click
    Dim length As Double
    'Set lengths of all shapes.
    length = CDbl(txtLength.Text)
    For i As Integer = 0 To 3
      shape(i).Length = length
    Next
    'Display results.
    lstOutput.Items.Clear()
    For i As Integer = 0 To 3
      lstOutput.Items.Add("The " & shape(i).Name & " has area " _
                    & FormatNumber(shape(i).Area))
    Next
  End Sub
End Class

MustInherit Class Shape
  Private m_length As Double      'Stores the value of Length property
```

```
    Public Property Length() As Double
        'Length of a side
        Get
            Return m_length
        End Get
        Set(ByVal value As Double)
            m_length = value
        End Set
    End Property

    MustOverride Function Name() As String
    'Returns the name of the shape.

    MustOverride Function Area() As Double
    'Returns the area of the shape.
End Class

Class EquilateralTriangle
    Inherits Shape

    Overrides Function Name() As String
        'The name of this shape
        Return "Equilateral Triangle"
    End Function

    Overrides Function Area() As Double
        'Formula for the area of an equilateral triangle
        Return Length * Length * Math.Sqrt(3) / 4
    End Function
End Class

Class Square
    Inherits Shape

    Overrides Function Name() As String
        'The name of this shape
        Return "Square"
    End Function

    Overrides Function Area() As Double
        'Formula for the area of a square
        Return Length * Length
    End Function
End Class

Class Pentagon
    Inherits Shape

    Overrides Function Name() As String
        'The name of this shape
        Return "Pentagon"
    End Function
```

```
   Overrides Function Area() As Double
     'Formula for the area of a pentagon
     Return Length * Length * Math.Sqrt(25 + (10 * Math.Sqrt(5))) / 4
   End Function
End Class

Class Hexagon
   Inherits Shape

   Overrides Function Name() As String
     'The name of this shape
     Return "Hexagon"
   End Function

   Overrides Function Area() As Double
     'Formula for the area of a hexagon
     Return Length * Length * 3 * Math.Sqrt(3) / 2
   End Function
End Class
```

[Run the program, enter 5, and press the Display button.]

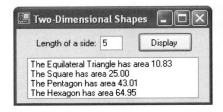

■ **Comments**

1. Visual Basic uses inheritance in every Windows application that is written. Examination of any program's code reveals that the form's class inherits from the class System.Windows.Forms.Form.

2. In Example 2, the btnDisplay_Click event procedure does not need to know which elements of the Student array are instances of the Student class and which are instances of the PFStudent class. In some situations, however, the program may want to know this. Visual Basic provides the expression **TypeOf...Is** to test if an instance was created from a particular class (or from the class' parents, grandparents, etc.) For example, the following procedure counts the number of pass/fail students in the *students* array:

```
Sub CountPassFail()
  Dim count As Integer = 0
  For i As Integer = 0 To lastStudentAdded
    If TypeOf students(i) Is PFStudent Then
      count += 1
    End If
  Next
  MsgBox("There are " & count & " pass/fail students out of " _
    & lastStudentAdded & " students in the class.")
End Sub
```

3. Child classes do not inherit or have access to the parent's Private member variables.

1. In the class AddingMachine of Example 1, the Add function could have been defined with

```
Function Add() As Double
   Return m_num1 + m_num2
End Function
```

Explain why the Multiply function of the class Calculator cannot be defined with

```
Function Multiply() As Double
   Return m_num1 * m_num2ß
End Function
```

2. Consider the hierarchy of classes shown below. What value is assigned to the variable *phrase* by the following two lines of code?

```
Dim mammal As New Mammals()
Dim phrase As String = mammal.Msg

Class Animals

  Overridable Function Msg() As String
    Return "Can move"
  End Function
End Class

Class Vertebrates
  Inherits Animals

  Overrides Function Msg() As String
    Return MyBase.Msg & " " & "Has a backbone"
  End Function
End Class

Class Mammals
  Inherits Vertebrates

  Overrides Function Msg() As String
    Return MyBase.Msg & " " & "Nurtures young with mother's milk"
  End Function
End Class

Class Anthropods
  Inherits Animals

  Overrides Function Msg() As String
    Return MyBase.Msg & " " & "Has jointed limbs and no backbone"
  End Function
End Class
```

EXERCISES 11.3

In Exercises 1 through 4, identify the output of the code that uses the following two classes:

```
Class Square
  Overridable Function Result(ByVal num As Double) As Double
    Return num * num
  End Function
End Class

Class Cube
  Inherits Square
  Overrides Function Result(ByVal num As Double) As Double
    Return num * num * num
  End Function
End Class
```

1. ```
Dim sq As Square = New Square()
txtOutput.Text = CStr(sq.Result(2))
```

2. ```
Dim cb As Cube = New Cube()
txtOutput.Text = CStr(cb.Result(2))
```

3. ```
Dim m As Square = New Square()
Dim n As Cube = New Cube()
txtOutput.Text = CStr(m.Result(n.Result(2)))
```

4. ```
Dim m As Square = New Cube()
txtOutput.Text = CStr(m.Result(2))
```

5. Consider the class hierarchy in the second practice problem. What value is assigned to the variable *phrase* by the following two lines of code?

```
Dim anthropod As New Anthropods()
Dim phrase As String = anthropod.Msg
```

6. Consider the class hierarchy in the second practice problem. What value is assigned to the variable *phrase* by the following two lines of code?

```
Dim vertebrate As New Vertebrates()
Dim phrase As String = vertebrate.Msg
```

In Exercises 7 through 16, identify the error in the code.

7. ```
Class Hello
  Function Hi() As String
    Return "hi!"
  End Function
End Class
```
```

```
   Class Greetings
     Overrides Hello
     Function GoodBye() As String
       Return "goodbye"
     End Function
   End Class
```

8.
```
Class Hello
   Function Hi() As String
     Return "hi!"
   End Function
End Class

Class Greetings
  Inherits Hi()
  Function GoodBye() As String
    Return "goodbye"
  End Function
End Class
```

9.
```
Class Hello
   Function Hi() As String
     Return "hi!"
   End Function
End Class

Class Aussie
  Inherits Hello
  Function Hi() As String
    Return "G'day mate!"
  End Function
End Class
```

10.
```
Class Hello
   Function Hi() As String
     Return "hi!"
   End Function
End Class

Class WithIt
  Inherits Hello
  Overrides Function Hi() As String
    Return "Hey"
  End Function
End Class
```

11.
```
Class Hello
   Overridable Function Hi() As String
     Return "hi!"
   End Function
End Class
```

```
Class Cowboy
   Inherits Hello
   Function Hi() As String
     Return "howdy!"
   End Function
End Class
```

12.
```
Class Hello
   MustOverride Function Hi() As String
     Return "hi!"
   End Function
End Class

Class DragRacer
   Inherits Hello
   Overrides Function Hi() As String
     Return "Start your engines!"
   End Function
End Class
```

13.
```
Class Hello
   MustInherit Function Hi() As String
End Class

Class Gentleman
   Inherits Hello
   Overrides Function Hi() As String
     Return "Good day"
   End Function
End Class
```

14.
```
Class Hello
   MustOverride Function Hi() As String
End Class

Class Euro
   Inherits Hello
   Overrides Function Hi() As String
     Return "Caio"
   End Function
End Class
```

15.
```
MustOverride Class Hello
   MustOverride Function Hi() As String
End Class

Class Southerner
   Inherits Hello
   Overrides Function Hi() As String
     Return "Hi y'all"
   End Function
End Class
```

16.
```
MustInherit Class Hello
    MustOverride Function Hi() As String
End Class

Class NorthEasterner
    Inherits Hello
    Overrides Function Hi(ByVal name As String) As String
        Return "How ya doin', " & name
    End Function
End Class
```

17. Expand Example 1 to use a class ScientificCalculator that is derived from the class Calculator and has an exponentiation button in addition to the four arithmetic buttons.

18. Rewrite Example 2 so that the class Student has an abstract method CalcSemGrade and two derived classes called LGStudent (LG stands for "Letter Grade") and PFStudent.

19. Consider the class CashRegister from Exercise 25 of Section 11.1. Create a derived class called FastTrackRegister that could be used by at a toll booth to collect money from vehicles and keep track of the number of vehicles processed. Write a program using the class and having the form in Figure 11.7. One dollar should be collected from each car and two dollars from each truck.

FIGURE 11.7   Form for Exercise 19.

20. Write a program that keeps track of a bookstore's inventory. The store orders both trade books and textbooks from publishers. The program should define an abstract class Book that contains the MustOverride property Price, and the ordinary properties Quantity, Name, and Cost. The Textbook and Tradebook classes should be derived from the class Book and should override property Price by adding a markup. (Assume that the markup is 40% for a trade book and 20% for a textbook.) The program should accept input from the user on book orders and display the following statistics: total number of books, number of textbooks, total cost of the orders, and total value of the inventory. (The value of the inventory is the amount of money that the bookstore can make if it sells all of the books in stock.) A sample output is shown in Figure 11.8.

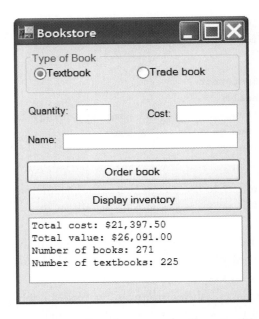

FIGURE 11.8   Sample output for Exercise 20.

21. Write a program that records the weekly payroll of a department that hires both salaried and hourly employees. The program should accept user input and display the number of employees, the number of salaried employees, the total payroll, and the average number of hours worked. The abstract class Employee should contain Name and Rate properties. (The Rate text box should be filled in with the weekly salary for salaried workers and the hourly wage for hourly workers.) The Salaried and Hourly classes should inherit the Employee class and override the method GrossPay that accepts the number of hours worked as a parameter. A sample output is shown in Figure 11.9. **Hint:** Use an array of a structure that holds the employee object and the number of hours worked during the week.

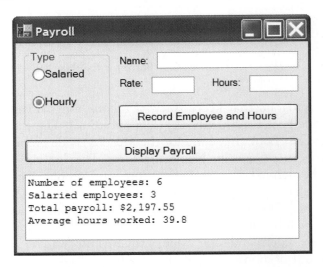

FIGURE 11.9   Sample output for Exercise 21.

22. Consider the class Statistics from Exercise 26 of Section 11.1. Create a derived class called CompleteStats that also provides a Spread function and an event called NewSpread. This event should be raised whenever the spread changes. Write a program that uses the classes to analyze up to 50 exam grades input by the user. The program should display the number of grades and the current spread at all times. When the Calculate Average button is pressed, the program should display the average of the grades. A sample output is shown in Figure 11.10.

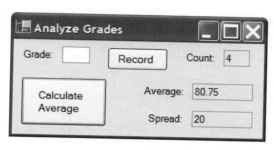

FIGURE 11.10   **Sample output for Exercise 22.**

Solutions to Practice Problems 11.3

---

1. While the derived class Calculator has access to the Properties and Methods of the base class AddingMachine, it does not have access to its Private member variables.

2. The string "Can move Has a backbone Nurtures young with mother's milk"

CHAPTER 11 SUMMARY

1. An *object* is an entity that stores data, has methods that manipulate the data, and can trigger events. A *class* is a template from which objects are created. A *method* specifies the way in which an object's data are manipulated. An *event* is a message sent by an object to signal the occurrence of a condition.

2. Each class is defined in a separate block of code starting with Class *className* and ending with End Class. Data are stored in member variables and accessed by procedures called properties.

3. A property routine contains a Get block to retrieve the value of a member variable or a Set block to assign a value to a member variable. These procedures can also be used to enforce constraints and carry out validation.

4. Visual Basic automatically invokes a New procedure when an object is created.

5. An object variable is declared with a statement of the form `Dim objectName As className`, and the object is created with a statement of the form `objectName = New className(arg1, arg2, ...)`. These two statements are often combined into the single statement `Dim objectName As New className(arg1, arg2, ...)`.

6. Events are declared in the Declarations section of a class with a statement of the form `Public Event UserDefinedEvent(arg1, arg2, ...)` and triggered with a `RaiseEvent` statement. The declaration statement for the object must include the keyword `WithEvents` in order for the events coming from the object to be processed. The header of an event-handling procedure has the form `Private Sub procedureName(par1, par2, ...) Handles objectName.UserDefinedEvent`.

7. The properties, methods, and events of a class are referred to as its *interface*.

8. Inheritance, which is implemented with the keyword Inherits, allows a new class (called the *derived* or *child* class) to be created from an existing class (called the *base* or *parent* class) and to gain its interface.

9. Polymorphism is the feature that two classes can have methods that are named the same and have essentially the same purpose, but different implementations.

10. The keywords, Overridable, Overrides, MustInherit, and MustOverride allow derived classes to customize inherited properties and methods.

CHAPTER 11 PROGRAMMING PROJECTS

1. *Son of Deep Blue.* Write a program that plays a game of tic-tac-toe in which a person competes with the computer. The game should be played in a control array of nine text boxes. See Figure 11.11. After the user moves by placing an X in a text box, the program should determine the location for the O. The program should use a tic-tac-toe object that raises events when a player moves and when the game is over. The outcome of the game should be announced in a message dialog box.

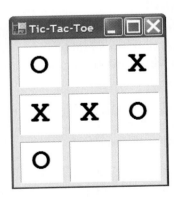

FIGURE 11.11 Tic-Tac-Toe.

2. *Bank Account.* Write a program to maintain a person's Savings and Checking accounts. The program should keep track of and display the balances in both accounts, and maintain a list of transactions (deposits, withdrawals, fund transfers, and check clearings) separately for each account. The two lists of transactions should be stored in sequential files so that they will persist between program sessions.

Consider the form in Figure 11.12. The two dropdown combo boxes should each contain the items Checking and Savings. Each of the four group boxes corresponds to a type of transaction. (When Savings is selected in the Account combo box, the Check group box should disappear.) The user makes a transaction by typing data into the text boxes of a group box and pressing the button. The items appearing in the Transactions list box should correspond to the type of account that has been selected. The caption of the second label in the Transfer group box should toggle between "to Checking" and "to Savings" depending on the item selected in the "Transfer from" combo box. If a transaction cannot be carried out, a message (such as "Insufficient funds") should be displayed.

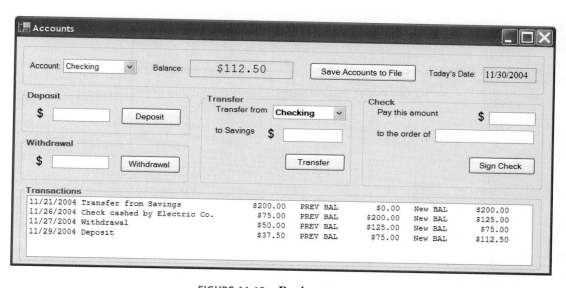

FIGURE 11.12   Bank accounts.

The program should use two classes, Transaction and Account. The class Transaction should have properties for transaction name, amount, date, and whether it is a credit (deposit) or debit (withdrawal/check).

The class Account, which will have both a checking account and a savings account as instances, should use an array of Transaction objects. In addition, it should have properties for name (Checking or Savings) and balance. It should have methods to carry out a transaction (if possible), to display the list of transactions, and to load and retrieve the set of transactions into or from a sequential file. The events InsufficientFunds and TransactionCommitted should be triggered at appropriate times. A technique for obtaining a string containing today's date can be found in the frmAccount_Load procedure of the case study "Recording Checks and Deposits" in Section 8.3.

Hint: In order for an Account object to display a list of transactions, a list box should be passed to a method as an argument. The method might be declared with

```
Sub EnumerateTransactions(ByVal lb As ListBox).
```

3. Write a program for the game BlackJack. See Figure 11.13. The program should use a Blackjack class (Blackjack) that contains a member variable of the type DeckOfCards presented in Example 3 of Section 11.2.

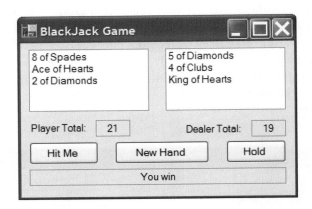

FIGURE 11.13   Sample output for Programming Project 3.

APPENDIX A

ANSI VALUES

ANSI Value	Character	ANSI Value	Character	ANSI Value	Character
000	(null)	041	)	082	R
001	☐	042	*	083	S
002	☐	043	+	084	T
003	☐	044	,	085	U
004	☐	045	−	086	V
005	☐	046	.	087	W
006	☐	047	/	088	X
007	☐	048	0	089	Y
008	☐	049	1	090	Z
009	(tab)	050	2	091	[
010	(line feed)	051	3	092	\
011	☐	052	4	093	]
012	☐	053	5	094	^
013	(carriage return)	054	6	095	_
014	☐	055	7	096	`
015	☐	056	8	097	a
016	☐	057	9	098	b
017	☐	058	:	099	c
018	☐	059	;	100	d
019	☐	060	<	101	e
020	☐	061	=	102	f
021	☐	062	>	103	g
022	☐	063	?	104	h
023	☐	064	@	105	i
024	☐	065	A	106	j
025	☐	066	B	107	k
026	☐	067	C	108	l
027	☐	068	D	109	m
028	☐	069	E	110	n
029	☐	070	F	111	o
030	☐	071	G	112	p
031	☐	072	H	113	q
032		073	I	114	r
033	!	074	J	115	s
034	"	075	K	116	t
035	#	076	L	117	u
036	$	077	M	118	v
037	%	078	N	119	w
038	&	079	O	120	x
039	'	080	P	121	y
040	(	081	Q	122	z

ANSI Value	Character	ANSI Value	Character	ANSI Value	Character
123	{	170	ª	217	Ù
124	|	171	«	218	Ú
125	}	172	¬	219	Û
126	~	173		220	Ü
127	□	174	®	221	ý
128	□	175	¯	222	þ
129	□	176	°	223	ß
130	‚	177	±	224	à
131	ƒ	178	²	225	á
132	„	179	³	226	â
133	…	180	´	227	ã
134	†	181	µ	228	ä
135	‡	182	¶	229	å
136	ˇ	183	·	230	æ
137	‰	184	¸	231	ç
138	Š	185	¹	232	è
139	‹	186	º	233	é
140	Œ	187	»	234	ê
141	□	188	1/4	235	ë
142	□	189	1/2	236	ì
143	□	190	3/4	237	í
144	□	191	¿	238	î
145	'	192	À	239	ï
146	'	193	Á	240	ð
147	"	194	Â	241	ñ
148	"	195	Ã	242	ò
149	•	196	Ä	243	ó
150	–	197	Å	244	ô
151	—	198	Æ	245	õ
152	~	199	Ç	246	ö
153	™	200	È	247	÷
154	š	201	É	248	ø
155	›	202	Ê	249	ù
156	œ	203	Ë	250	ú
157	□	204	Ì	251	û
158	□	205	Í	252	ü
159	Ÿ	206	Î	253	ý
160		207	Ï	254	þ
161	¡	208	Ð	255	ÿ
162	¢	209	Ñ		
163	£	210	Ò		
164	¤	211	Ó		
165	¥	212	Ô		
166	¦	213	Õ		
167	§	214	Ö		
168	¨	215	×		
169	©	216	Ø		

APPENDIX B
HOW TO

Invoke and Exit Visual Basic

Note: Visual Basic is part of a suite of programs called Visual Studio, which also contains the C# (pronounced "C-sharp") and C++ ("C-plus-plus") programming languages.

A. Invoke Visual Basic Express Edition

1. Click the Start button.
2. Hover over All Programs.
3. Click on Microsoft Visual Basic 2005 Express Edition.

B. Invoke Standard or Professional Editions of Visual Basic.

1. Click the Start button.
2. Point to All Programs. (A new panel will open on the right.)
3. Point to Microsoft Visual Studio 2005. (A new panel will open on the right.)
4. In the new panel, click on Microsoft Visual Studio 2005.

C. Exit Visual Basic

1. Press Alt/F/X.

or

1. Click on the Close button; that is, the small square button containing an "X" located at the upper-right corner of the window.

Note: If an unsaved program is present, Visual Studio will prompt you about saving it.

Manage Programs

A. Run a program from Visual Basic

1. Click on the Start Debugging icon (right arrowhead) in the Toolbar.

or

1. Press F5.

or

1. Press Alt/D/S.

B. Save the current program.

   1. Press Alt/F/L, or click the Save All icon (shows three diskettes) on the Toolbar.

C. Begin a new program.

   1. Press Ctrl + N. (If the previous program has not been saved, Visual Basic will prompt you about saving it.)

   2. Check that Windows Application is highlighted.

   3. Optionally type a name for the program into the Name box.

   4. Press the OK button.

D. Open a recent project.

   1. Press Alt/F/J.

   2. Click on a recent project, or press the corresponding number.

E. Open a program stored on a disk.

   1. Press Ctrl + O.

   2. Navigate to the directory containing the program.

   3. Highlight the program.

   4. Click the Open button.

   5. Double-click on the file with extension *vbprog*.

Note 1: In Step 1, if an unsaved program is present, Visual Basic will prompt you about saving it.

Note 2: If neither the Form designer nor the Code window for the program appears, double-click on *formName*.vb in the Solution Explorer window.

F. Change the name of a program. (Method I.)

   1. Click on Close Project in the File menu to close the program.

   2. Use Windows Explorer or My Computer to locate the program's folder and rename it with the new name.

   3. Open the program in Visual Basic.

   4. In the second Open Project dialog box, replace every occurrence of the old name with the new name.

   5. Double-click on the file with extension *vbprog*.

   6. Double-click on My project in the Solution Explorer.

   7. Type the new name into both the "Assembly name" box and the "Root namespace" box.

G. Change the name of a program. (Method II.)

   1. Create a new program with the new name.

   2. Give the form the same name as the form in the program to be renamed.

   3. Without writing any code or placing any controls on the form, save the program with the new name.

   4. Close the program.

5. Use Windows Explorer to locate the program with the old name, and Copy the two files having the extension .vb; that is *formName*.Designer.vb and *formName*.vb.
6. Paste the two .vb files into the folder for the program having the new name.
7. Delete the folder for the program having the old name.

H. Use the Solution Explorer.

Note: Just below the Solution Explorer title bar are five or six icons. The fourth and fifth icons are View Code and View Designer. If there are less than five icons present, click on the *formName*.vb item to make it active and all five or six icons will appear.

1. Click on the View Code icon to see the Code window for the current program.
2. Click on the View Designer icon to see the form for the current program.
3. If the program has more than one form, click on the name of a form to make that form the active form.

Use the Editor

A. Select (or highlight) text as a block.

1. Move the cursor to the beginning or end of the text.
2. Hold down a Shift key and use the direction keys to highlight a block of text.
3. Release the Shift key.

or

1. Move the mouse to the beginning or end of the text.
2. Hold down the left mouse button and move the mouse to the other end of the text.
3. Release the left mouse button.

Note 1: To de-select text, press the Esc key or click outside the text.

Note 2: To select a word, double-click on it. To select a line, move the mouse pointer just far enough into the left margin so that the pointer changes to an arrow, and then single-click there.

B. Delete a line of a program.

1. Mark the line as a block. (See item A of this section.)
2. Press Alt/E/T, or press Ctrl + X.

Note: In the preceding maneuver, the line is placed in the clipboard and can be retrieved by pressing Ctrl + V. To delete the line without placing it in the clipboard, mark it as a block, and press the Delete key.

C. Move a line within the Code window.

1. Mark the line as a block, and drag it to the new location with the mouse.

D. Use the Clipboard to move or duplicate statements.

1. Mark the statements as a block.
2. Press Ctrl + X to delete the block and place it into the clipboard, or press Ctrl + C to place a copy of the block into the clipboard.
3. Move the cursor to the location where you desire to place the block.
4. Press Ctrl + V to place a copy of the text from the clipboard at the cursor position.

E. Search for specific text in the program.

1. Press Alt/E/F or Ctrl + F.
2. Type the sought-after text into the "Find what:" rectangle. (Alternatively, press the down-arrow button on the right side of the rectangle to select from a list of the text items most recently searched for.)
3. If you would like to specify certain search options, such as "Match case," click on the plus button to the left of "Find Options."
4. Press the Find Next button.
5. To repeat the search, press F3.

F. Find and Replace.

1. Press Alt/E/R or Ctrl + H.
2. Type the text to be replaced into the "Find what:" rectangle. (Alternatively, press the down-arrow button on the right side of the rectangle to select from a list of the text items most recently searched for.)
3. Type the replacement text into the "Replace with:" rectangle. (Alternatively, press the down-arrow button on the right side of the rectangle to select from a list of the text items most recently used as replacements.)
4. If you would like to specify certain search options, such as "Match case," click on the plus button to the left of "Find Options."
5. Press either the "Replace All" button to replace all occurrences of the text to be replaced, or press "Find Next" to highlight the first occurrence of the text to be replaced. With the second option, either click "Replace" to replace the highlighted text, or press "Find Next" to highlight (and possibly replace) the next occurrence of the sought-after text.

G. Undo a change to the code.

1. Press Alt/E/U or Ctrl + Z to undo the last change made.

Note: If desired, an undone change can be redone by pressing Ctrl + Y

H. Turn off the IntelliSense feature.

1. Press Alt/T/O.
2. If the check box to the left of "Show all settings" is unchecked, check it.
3. In the left pane, expand "Text Editor."
4. Expand the subheading "Basic."
5. Click on the subtopic "General."
6. Ensure that all the check boxes under the "Statement Completion" heading are unchecked.

I. Wrap words to the next line in the Code editor rather than having a horizontal scrollbar.

1. Follow steps 1 through 5 of part H above.
2. In the right pane, place a check mark in the check box labeled "Word Wrap."

J. Hide a long procedure.

1. Scroll to the top of the procedure.
2. Click on the box with a minus sign in it that is to the left of the header of the procedure. (Notice that the box now contains a plus sign and that the entire procedure is hidden on the one line. Click on the box again to show the procedure.)

K. Add a collapsible region.

1. Type #Region "regionName" on the line before the code to be included in the region.
2. Type #End Region on the line after the last line of code in the region.
3. The region of code can then be collapsed by clicking on the minus box and restored by clicking on the plus box.

Note: A region cannot be defined within a Function or Sub procedure.

L. Instruct the editor to indent by two spaces.

1. Follow steps 1 through 4 of part H.
2. Click on the subtopic "Tabs."
3. In the right pane, change the number in the "Indent Size:" text box to 2.

Get Help

A. Obtain information about a Visual Basic topic.

1. Press Alt/H/I to invoke the index.
2. Type the topic into the "Look for:" box.
3. Click on the topic or a subheading under the topic.
4. If a second list pops up on the screen, double-click on an item from it.

B. View the syntax and purpose of a Visual Basic keyword.

1. Type the word into a Code window.
2. Place the cursor on, or just following, the keyword.
3. Press F1.

C. Display an ASCII (similar to ANSI) table.

1. Press Alt/H/I to invoke the index.
2. Type the topic "ASCII" into the "Look for:" box.
3. Click on the "ASCII characters" topic.
4. In the page that appears, click either the Chart 1 or Chart 2 link.

   D. Obtain a list of Visual Basic's reserved words.

       1. Press Alt/H/I to invoke the index.
       2. Type "reserved words" into the "Look for:" box.
       3. Click on the subheading Visual Basic keywords.
       4. Double-click on the entry titled "Visual Basic Language Keywords" in the second list.

   E. Obtain a list of shortcut keys.

       1. Press Alt/H/I to invoke the index.
       2. Type "keyboard shortcuts" into the "Look for:" box.
       3. Click on the topic "keyboard shortcuts."
       4. Click on "Shortcut Keys" in the small window that pops up.

   F. Obtain information about a control.

       1. Click on the control in the Form Designer.
       2. Press F1.

Manipulate a Dialog Box

   A. Use a dialog box.

   Note: A dialog box contains three types of items: rectangles (text or list boxes), option lists, and buttons. An option list is a sequence of radio buttons or check boxes.

       1. Move from item to item with the Tab key. (The movement is from left to right and top to bottom. Use Shift + Tab to reverse the direction.)
       2. Inside a rectangle, either type in the requested information, or use the direction keys to make a selection.
       3. In an option list, a radio button can be selected with the direction keys. A dot inside the circle indicates that the button has been selected.
       4. In an option list, a check box can be checked or unchecked by pressing the spacebar. An X or "✓" inside the square indicates that the option has been checked.
       5. A highlighted button is invoked by pressing the Enter key.

   B. Cancel a dialog box.

       1. Press the Esc key.

   or

       1. Press the Tab key until the button captioned "Cancel" is highlighted, and then press the Enter key.

Use Menus

A. Open a dropdown menu.

    1. Click on the menu name.

    or

    1. Press Alt.

    2. Press the underlined letter in the name of the menu. Alternatively, use the right-arrow key to move the highlighted cursor bar to the menu name, and then press the down-arrow key.

B. Make a selection from a dropdown menu.

    1. Click on the dropdown menu.

    2. Click on the desired item.

    or

    1. Press the Alt key and then click on the dropdown menu. One letter in each item that is eligible to be used will be underlined.

    2. Press the underlined letter. Alternatively, use the down-arrow key to move the cursor bar to the desired item, and then press the Enter key.

C. Look at all the menus in the menu bar.

    1. Press Alt/F.

    2. Press the right-arrow key to cycle through available menus.

D. Close a dropdown menu.

    1. Press the Esc key, or click anywhere outside the menu.

Utilize the Windows Environment

A. Place text in the Windows clipboard.

    1. Mark the text as a block as described in the How to Use the Editor section.

    2. Press Ctrl + C.

B. Access Windows Notepad.

    1. Click the Start button.

    2. Point to All Programs.

    3. Point to Accessories.

    4. Click Notepad.

C. Display all characters in a font.

    1. Click the Start button.

    2. Point to All Programs.

    3. Point to Accessories.

    4. Point to System Tools.

5. Click Character Map.
6. Click on the down-arrow at the right end of the Font box.
7. Highlight the desired font, and press the Enter key, or click on the desired font.

D. Configure Windows to display filename extensions.

1. Double-click on the My Computer icon residing on the Windows desktop.
2. Press Alt/T/O.
3. Click on the View tab.
4. Ensure that the box next to the option "Hide extensions for known file types" is unchecked.
5. Click the OK button.

Design a Form

A. Display the Toolbox containing the available controls.

1. Press Alt/V/X.

B. Place a new control on the form.

Option I: (new control with default size)

1. Drag the control onto the form and release the mouse button.

Option II: (new control with default size and position)

1. Double-click on the control's icon in the Toolbox. The new control will be placed on top of the last-drawn control.
2. Size and position the control as described in items G and H, which follow.

Option III: (a single new control sized and positioned as it is created)

1. Click on the control's icon in the Toolbox.
2. Move the mouse to the approximate position on the form desired for the upper-left corner of the control.
3. Press and hold the left mouse button.
4. Move the mouse to the position on the form desired for the lower-right corner of the control. A rectangle will indicate the overall shape of the new control.
5. Release the left mouse button.
6. The control can be resized and repositioned as described in items G and H.

C. Create a related group of controls.

1. Place a group box on the form to hold the related group of controls.
2. Use the options in item B of this section to place controls in the group box.

D. Select a particular control.

1. Click on the control.

or

1. Press the Tab key until the control is selected.

E. Delete a control.

    1. Select the control to be deleted.

    2. Press the Delete key.

F. Delete a related group of controls.

    1. Select the group box holding the related group of controls.

    2. Press the Delete key.

G. Move a control or related group of controls to a new location.

    1. Move the mouse onto the control or the group box containing the related group of controls.

    2. Drag the object to the new location.

H. Change the size of a control.

    1. Select the desired control.

    2. Move the mouse to one of the sizing handles located around the edge of the control. The mouse pointer will change to a double-arrow, which points in the directions that resizing can occur.

    3. Drag to the desired size.

I. Change the size of a form.

    1. Move the mouse to the edge or corner of the selected form that is to be stretched or shrunk. The mouse pointer will change to a double-arrow, which points in the directions that resizing can occur.

    2. Drag to the desired size.

Work with the Properties of a Form or Control

A. Activate the Properties window.

    1. Press Alt/V/W.

or

    1. Press F4.

or

    1. Click on an object on the form with the right mouse button.

    2. In the context menu, click on Properties.

B. Highlight a property in the Properties window.

    1. Activate the Properties window.

    2. Use the up- or down-arrow keys to move the highlight bar to the desired property.

or

    1. Activate the Properties window.

    2. Click on the up-or-down arrow located at the ends of the vertical scrollbar at the right side of the Properties window until the desired property is visible.

    3. Click on the desired property.

C. Select or specify a setting for a property.

    1. Highlight the property whose setting is to be changed.

    2. Click on the settings box or press Tab to place the cursor in the settings box.

        a. If a down-arrow button appears at the right end of the settings box, click on the down arrow to display a list of all allowed settings, and then click on the desired setting.

        b. If an ellipsis (three periods: . . .) appears at the right end of the settings box, press F4, or click on the ellipsis to display a dialog box. Answer the questions in the dialog box, and click on OK or Open, as appropriate.

        c. If the cursor moves to the settings box, type in the new setting for the property.

D. Use the Color palette to set foreground and background colors.

    1. Select the desired control or the form.

    2. Press Alt/V/W or F4 to activate the Properties window.

    3. To set the foreground color, click on the down-arrow to the right of the ForeColor settings box, click on the Custom tab, and click on the desired color.

    4. To set the background color, click on the down-arrow to the right of the BackColor settings box, click on the Custom tab, and click on the desired color.

E. Let a label change size to accommodate its caption (that is, the setting of its Text property.)

    1. Keep the label's AutoSize property set to True. (The label will shrink to the smallest size needed to hold the current caption. If the caption is changed, the label automatically will grow or shrink horizontally to accommodate the new caption.)

F. Let a label caption use more than one line.

    1. Change the label's AutoSize property setting to False and increase its height. (If the label is not wide enough to accommodate the entire caption on one line, part of the caption will wrap to additional lines. If the label height is too small, then part or all of these additional lines will not be visible.)

G. Let a text box display more than one line.

    1. Set the text box's MultiLine property to True. (If the text box is not wide enough to accommodate the text entered by the user, the text will wrap down to new lines. If the text box is not tall enough, lines will scroll out of view, but can be displayed with the cursor up or down keys.)

H. Assign an access key to a button, check box, or radio button.

    1. When assigning a value to the Text property, precede the desired access-key character with an ampersand (&).

I. Allow a particular button to be activated by a press of the Enter key.

    1. Set the form's AcceptButton property to the particular button.

J. Allow the pressing of Esc to activate a particular button.

    1. Set the form's CancelButton property to the particular button.

K. Adjust the order in which the Tab key moves the focus.

    1. Select the first control in the tabbing sequence.
    2. Change the setting of the TabIndex property for this control to 0.
    3. Select the next control in the tabbing sequence.
    4. Change the setting of the TabIndex property for this control to 1.
    5. Repeat Steps 3 and 4 (adding 1 to the Tab Index property) until all controls on the form that belong in the tabbing sequence have been assigned a new TabIndex setting with the desired order.

    or

    1. Press Alt/V/B to show the current tab order. (Each control on the form has a small box in its upper-left corner with a number in it. This number is the TabIndex property setting.)
    2. Hover over the first control in the new tabbing sequence. (Notice that the cursor becomes a cross.) Click on the control to change its TabIndex property to 0.
    3. Hover over the second control in the new tabbing sequence. Click on the control to change its TabIndex property to 1.
    4. Repeat Steps 2 and 3 until all controls on the form that belong in the tabbing sequence have been assigned a new TabIndex setting in the desired order.
    5. Press Alt/V/B to hide the tab order numbers.

L. Change a common property in more than one control.

    1. Click on the first control.
    2. While holding the Ctrl key down, click on the second control.
    3. Repeat Step 2 for each additional control.
    4. Press F4. (The Properties window is shown.)
    5. Click on a property and change its setting.

Note: Only properties that are available in all of the selected controls (such as background color) may be changed in this manner.

M. Automatically center the window in the screen when a program executes.

    1. Click on the form.
    2. Press F4. (The properties window is shown.)
    3. Click on the StartPosition property.
    4. Set the property to CenterScreen.

N. Change the Name property of Form1 to frmElse.

    1. In the Solution Explorer, right click on the file Form1.vb.
    2. Click on Rename in the context menu that appears.
    3. Change the name of the file Form1.vb to frmElse.vb.

How To: Manage Procedures

A. Access the Code window.

   1. Press Alt/V/C or F7.

or

   1. Press Alt/V/P to activate the Solution Explorer window.
   2. Select the file *formName*.vb.
   3. Click on the View Code button.

B. Create a general procedure.

   1. Access the Code window.
   2. Move to a blank line that is not inside a procedure.
   3. Type "Sub" (for a Sub procedure) or "Function" (for a Function procedure) followed by the name of the procedure and any parameters.
   4. Press the Enter key. (The Code window will now display the new procedure heading and an End Sub or End Function statement.)
   5. Type the body of the procedure into the Code window.

C. Create an event procedure.

   1. Access the Code window.
   2. Click on the down-arrow at the right of the Class Name box, and then select an object.
   3. Click on the down-arrow at the right of the Method Name box, and then select an event. (An empty event procedure that handles the event is created.)

D. Alter a procedure.

   1. View the procedure in the Code window.
   2. Make changes as needed.

E. Remove a procedure.

   1. Bring the procedure into the Code window.
   2. Mark the entire procedure as a block.
   3. Press the Delete key.

F. Insert an existing procedure into a program.

   1. Open the program containing the procedure.
   2. View the procedure in the Code window.
   3. Mark the entire procedure as a block.
   4. Press Ctrl + C to place the procedure into the clipboard.
   5. Open the program in which the procedure is to be inserted, and access the Code window.
   6. Move the cursor to a blank line.
   7. Press Ctrl + V to place the contents of the clipboard into the program.

Manage Windows

A. Enlarge the active window to fill the entire screen.

    1. Click on the Maximize button (page icon; second icon from the right) on the title bar of the window.

    2. To return the window to its original size, click on the Restore (double-page) button that has replaced the Maximize button.

B. Move a window.

    1. Move the mouse to the title bar of the window.

    2. Drag the window to the desired location.

C. Change the size of a window.

    1. Move the mouse to the edge of the window that is to be adjusted or to the corner joining the two edges to be adjusted.

    2. When the mouse becomes a double arrow, drag the edge or corner until the window has the desired size.

D. Close a window.

    1. Click on the X button on the far right corner of the title bar.

Use the Printer

A. Obtain a printout of a program.

    1. Press Ctrl + P from the Code window.

    2. Press the Enter key.

Use the Debugger

(See Appendix D for more details.)

A. Break a program at a specified line.

    1. Place the cursor on the desired line.

    2. Press F9. A red dot will appear to the left of the line on the gray bar to indicate that the line has been set as a *breakpoint*. Whenever the running program reaches the breakpoint, it will go into debug mode.

Note: To remove this breakpoint, repeat Steps 1 and 2.

or

    1. Click on the thick gray bar at a point to the left of the line. Click again to remove the breakpoint.

or

    1. Place the cursor on the line, press the right mouse button, and click on "Run to Cursor." In this case, the line is not set as a breakpoint; however, execution will stop the first time the line is reached.

B. Remove all breakpoints.

  1. Press Alt/D/D or Ctrl + Shift + F9.

C. Run a program one statement at a time.

  1. Break the program at a specific line using a technique described in Item A of this section.
  2. Press the F8 key to execute each statement.

D. Run the program one statement at a time, but execute each general procedure call without stepping through the statements in the procedure one at a time.

  1. Break the program at a specific line using a technique described in Item A of this section.
  2. Repeatedly press the Shift + F8 key to execute successive liines and each general procedure without stepping through each statement in the procedure.

E. Continue execution of a program that has been suspended.

  1. Press F5.

F. Set the next statement to be executed in the current procedure.

  1. Place the cursor anywhere in the desired statement.
  2. Right-click on the line, and select "Set next statement."

G. Determine the value of an expression during debug mode.

  1. Press Ctrl + Alt + W, followed by 1.

  2. Type the expression into the Name list, and press Enter.

  or

  1. In debug mode, hover the cursor over the variable to have its value displayed.

APPENDIX C

CONVERTING FROM VISUAL BASIC 6.0 TO VISUAL BASIC 2005

This appendix, which shows how the language has changed from VB6 to VB2005, is intended for people who have used Visual Basic 6.0. The language changes from VB6 to VB2005 are vast, much greater than in any previous upgrade of Visual Basic. The topics covered in this appendix are restricted to material discussed in this textbook.

Section 3.1

In VB2005, programs can be given a name as soon as they are started.

The Command Button of VB6 is called a Button in VB2005, and its naming convention calls for the use of the prefix *btn*. The default name has changed from Command1 to Button1.

In VB2005, the default name for a text box has been changed from VB6's Text1 to TextBox1.

The Caption property for a button, form, or label in VB6 is called the Text property in VB2005

The Alignment property for a label or text box in VB6 is called the TextAlign property in VB2005.

In VB2005, Shift + Ctrl + *letter* cannot be used to navigate the Properties window as was possible in VB6.

In VB2005, the Name property of a form cannot be altered by just changing the contents of the settings box in the Properties window. (See Appendix B for details.)

Section 3.2

In a VB2005 event procedure header line, the event(s) is specified following the Handles keyword. The default procedure name for the event can be altered.

In VB2005, controls do not have default properties. For instance, the VB6 statement `txtBox = "Hello, World"` must be replaced with `txtBox.Text = "Hello, World"`.

In VB2005, the form object is referred to inside the form's code as Me, not Form1. For instance, the phrase in the form's title bar is specified with a statement such as `Me.Text = "New Caption"`.

The events LostFocus and GotFocus can still be used in VB2005. However, the preferred names for these events are Leave and Enter.

The DblClick event procedure of VB6 is called DoubleClick in VB2005.

In VB2005, font properties can be altered during run time; however, not with statements such as `txtBox.Font.Bold = True`.

In VB2005, all of the code required for creating a form is contained in the file *formName*.Designer.vb. Whenever the form is modified with the Form Designer, those changes are reflected by changes to the code in this file.

Section 3.3

In VB2005, you can declare multiple variables of the same data type on a single line without having to repeat the type keyword. For instance, a statement such as `Dim m, n As Double` specifies that both variables have data type Double. (In VB6, only *n* would have type Double.)

In VB2005, all variables must be declared as being of a specific type.

In VB2005 variables can be given an initial value when they are declared.

VB2005 does not allow the use of the Print method to display text in a picture box or on a form.

In VB2005, Option Explicit defaults to On.

The built-in functions Sqr and Round from VB6 are replaced in VB2005 by the functions Math.Sqrt and Math.Round.

In VB2005, the $+=$, $-=$, $*=$, $/=$ and $^=$ operators are available as shortcuts for certain types of assignment statements.

Section 3.4

In VB2005, the positions of the characters in a string are now numbered beginning with 0.

Option Strict, which enforces the proper use of variable types, has been added in VB2005 and defaults to Off.

TABLE C.1   Replacements for Functions.

VB6	VB2005
`UCase(str)`	`str.ToUpper`
`Len(str)`	`str.Length`
`Left(str, n)`	`str.Substring(0, n)`
`Mid(str, m, n)`	`str.Substring(m - 1, n)`
`Right(str, n)`	`str.Substring(str.Length - n)`
`Instr(str1, str2)`	`str1.IndexOf(str2)`
`Trim(str)`	`str.Trim`

Section 3.5

In VB2005, strings can be formatted and tables organized with the String.Format method.

In VB2005, files are not accessed with Open statements. Instead they are read with an IO.StreamReader object.

Section 4.1

In VB2005, every parameter in the header of a Sub or Function procedure must explicitly be declared as ByVal or ByRef. If neither is stated, VB2005 will automatically insert ByVal before the parameter name.

In a VB2005 call statement, the name of the Sub procedure must be followed with parentheses even if there are no arguments.

Section 4.2

In VB2005, the default way of passing a variable to a procedure is ByVal instead of ByRef.

Section 4.3

In VB2005, the Return statement is the preferred way to set the value returned by a Function.

Section 6.3

In VB2005, the control variable of a For...Next loop can be declared in the For statement. Also, the **Continue For** statement allows an iteration of the loop to be skipped.

Section 7.1

In VB2005, there are no fixed-sized arrays; all arrays are dynamic. That is, no matter how an array is declared, it can always be resized.

In VB2005, arrays must have a lower bound 0. A range cannot be specified using the To keyword.

In VB2005, statements of the form **Dim *arrayName*(*intVar*) As *varType*** are valid.

In VB2005, you cannot use ReDim in the initial declaration of an array. You can use it only to change the size of an array that has been declared.

In VB2005, ReDim no longer accepts an As clause to change the type of an array.

In VB2005, when an array is an argument of a procedure call, the name of the array is not followed by parentheses.

In VB2005, statements of the form **array1 = array2** can be used to assign all of array2's values to array1.

Section 7.3

The control arrays discussed in this section are not the same as those available in VB6; they are really just arrays of controls. Lost is the ease of creating the controls in code and the ease of handling event procedures.

The Type blocks from VB6 are replaced by Structure blocks in VB2005.

VB2005 does not support fixed-length strings

Section 8.1

The **Name** method of VB6 is replaced in VB2005 by **File.Move.** For instance, **Name** *oldfilespec* **As** *newfilespec* becomes **File.Move(***oldfilespec, newfilespec).*

Although GoSub is not supported by VB2005, On Error GoTo is supported. However, structured exception handling with Try-Catch-Finally blocks is preferable to the unstructured error handling available with VB6.

Section 9.1

TABLE C.2	List Box or Combo Box Name Changes.	
	VB6	VB2005
	List property	Items
	AddItem method	Items.Add
	RemoveItem method	Items.RemoveAt
	Clear method	Items.Clear
	Style property	DropDownStyle
	ListIndex property	SelectedIndex

The default event procedure for list boxes and combo boxes has changed from Click in VB6 to SelectedItemChanged in VB2005.

In VB2005, list boxes no longer have an ItemData property.

The common dialog control from VB6, which was an amalgam of five controls, has been replaced in VB2005 by five individual controls.

Section 9.2

For the check box and radio button controls, the Value property of VB6 has been replaced in VB2005 with the Checked property.

The Frame control of VB6 has been replaced in VB2005 by the GroupBox control.

VB2005 does not have a Line, Shape, or Image control. As alternatives, VB2005's Label control can be used to draw lines and rectangular shapes, and VB2005's PictureBox control has most of the capabilities of VB6's Image control.

For the picture box control, the Picture property of VB6 has been replaced in VB2005 by the Image property.

In VB2005, the picture box control has a StretchImage property that is analogous to the Stretch property for the image control in VB6.

With VB2005, a Timer is turned off with the statement Timer1.Enabled = False instead of with the statement Timer1.Interval = 0.

The Max and Min properties for scrollbars of VB6 have been changed to Maximum and Minimum. The default value for Maximum is 100. (The Max property had a default value of 32,767.) In VB6, Min could be set to a value greater than Max; in VB2005, this is not allowed.

In VB2005, the unit of measure for graphics is pixels. (Twips was the unit in VB6.)

The graphics Scale method of VB6 is not supported in VB2005.

For the timer control, the Timer event of VB6 has been replaced with the Tick event in VB2005.

In VB2005, the Timer control is not visible on the form in the Form Designer.

Section 9.3

In VB2005, a primary Form (usually called Form1) is displayed when the program is executed. Secondary forms may be defined and displayed using the form's ShowDialog method.

The SelText property of a text box in VB6 is called SelectedText in VB2005.

In VB2005, menus are created with the MenuStrip control found in the Toolbox instead of VB6's Menu Editor that was invoked from the Tools menu.

The Random object, new to VB2005, is much easier to use than the Rnd function of VB6.

Section 9.4

The PSet, Line, and Circle methods of picture boxes from VB6 are not supported in VB2005. Instead, points, lines, and circles are drawn with the SetPixel, DrawLine, and DrawEllipse methods of a Graphics object.

The FillColor property of VB6 is replaced by colors passed via a Brushes object to either the FillRectangle, FillEllipse, or FillPie methods of a Graphics object.

Section 10.1

VB2005's Database Explorer displays a database's tables and data.

In VB6, data are accessed through a data control. In VB2005, database data are loaded with a database adapter into a data table. The rows and columns of the data table may be accessed similarly to a two-dimensional array.

Section 10.2

VB6 uses Find methods and bookmarks to locate records within a data table. VB2005 uses the WHERE clause in the SQL statement to establish search criteria.

In VB2005, a data table can be bound to a DataGridView control that displays the entire table or a ListBox control that displays an entire column.

In VB2005, changes to data are saved in the database using the database adapter.

Section 11.1

VB6 has separate Property Let and Property Get procedures. VB2005 has a Property block that contains Set and Get procedures.

In VB2005, classes can be written in the form's Code window using Class blocks.

VB6's Initialize event is called New in VB2005 and takes optional parameters.

Section 11.3

VB2005's classes have full object-oriented capability, including inheritance, polymorphism, and abstraction.

APPENDIX D
VISUAL BASIC DEBUGGING TOOLS

Errors in programs are called bugs, and the process of finding and correcting them is called **debugging**. Since the Visual Basic editor does not discover errors due to faulty logic, these errors present the most difficulties in debugging. One method of discovering a logical error is by **desk-checking**, that is, tracing the values of variables on paper by writing down their expected value after "mentally executing" each line in the program. Desk checking is rudimentary and highly impractical except for small programs.

Another method of debugging involves placing MsgBox statements at strategic points in the program and displaying the values of selected variables or expressions until the error is detected. After correcting the error, the MsgBox statements are removed. For many programming environments, desk checking and MsgBox statements are the only debugging methods available to the programmer.

The Visual Basic debugger offers an alternative to desk checking and MsgBox statements. It allows you to pause during the execution of your program in order to view and alter values of variables. These values can be accessed through the Immediate, Watch, and Locals windows, known as debugging windows.

The Three Program Modes

At any time, a program is in one of three modes—**design mode**, **run mode**, or **debug mode**. (Debug mode is also known as **break mode**.) When the current

Title bar and toolbars during design mode.

Title bar and toolbars during run mode.

Title bar and toolbars during debug mode.

mode is "run" or "debug," the words "Running" or "Debugging" are displayed (in parentheses) in the Visual Basic title bar. The absence of these words indicates that the current mode is "design."

With the program in design mode, you place controls on a form, set their initial properties, and write code. Run mode is initiated by pressing F5 or the Start button. Debug mode is invoked automatically when a run-time error occurs. You can use Debug options to break the program at specified places. While the program is in debug mode, you can hover the cursor over any variable to obtain its current value. Also, you can use the debugging windows, such as the Immediate, Watch, and Locals windows, to examine values of expressions. When you enter debug mode, the Toolbar contains a Continue button. You can click on it to continue with the execution of the program.

Stepping through a Program

The program can be executed one statement at a time, with each press of an appropriate function key executing a statement. This process is called **stepping**. After each step, values of variables, expressions, and conditions can be displayed in the debugging windows, and the values of variables can be changed.

When a procedure is called, the lines of the procedure can be executed one at a time, referred to as **stepping into** the procedure, or the entire procedure can be executed at once, referred to as **stepping over** a procedure. A step over a procedure is called a **procedure step**. In addition, you can execute the remainder of the current procedure at once, referred to as **stepping out** of the procedure. The three toolbar buttons shown in Figure D.1 can be used for stepping.

FIGURE D.1 **The toolbar buttons used to Step Into, Step Over, and Step Out.**

As another debugging tool, Visual Basic allows the programmer to specify certain lines as **breakpoints**. Then, when the program is run, execution will stop at the first breakpoint reached. The programmer can then either step through the program or continue execution to the next breakpoint. Also, the programmer can place the cursor on any line in the program and have execution stop at that line with a "Run to Cursor" command. Program execution normally proceeds in order through the statements in the procedure. However, at any time the programmer can specify the next statement to be executed.

The tasks discussed previously are summarized next, along with a means to carry out each task. The tasks invoked with function keys also can be produced from the menu bar, the context menu (produced by clicking the right mouse button), or the toolbar.

Run to cursor	Press Ctrl + F8
Step Into	Press F8
Step Over	Press Shift + F8
Step Out	Press Ctrl + Shift + F8
Set a breakpoint	Move cursor to line, press F9

Remove a breakpoint	Move cursor to line containing breakpoint, press F9
Clear all breakpoints	Press Ctrl + Shift + F9
Continue execution to next breakpoint or the end of the program	Press F5
Stop debugging	Ctrl + Alt + Break

The Immediate Window

While in Break mode, you can set the focus to the **Immediate window** by clicking on it (if visible), by pressing Ctrl + Alt + I, or by hovering the cursor over "Windows" in the Debug menu and clicking on Immediate. When you type a statement into the Immediate window and press the Enter key, the statement is executed at once. A statement of the form

? expression

displays the value of the expression on the next line of the Immediate window. (The question mark is shorthand for Debug.Print.) A statement of the form

var = value

assigns a value to a variable. In Figure D.2, the variable *numVar* had the value 10 when the program was interrupted.

FIGURE D.2   Three statements executed in the Immediate window.

The Watch Window

The **Watch window**, which only can be viewed in Break mode, permits you to view the values of variables and expressions. The Watch window in Figure D.3 shows the values of one variable and two expressions. If you don't see a Watch window when you enter Break mode, hover the cursor over Windows in the Debug menu, and then click on Watch.

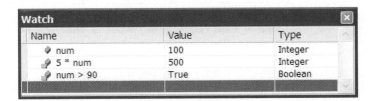

FIGURE D.3   A typical Watch window.

Although you can type directly into the Watch window, the easiest way to add an expression to the window is to right-click on a variable in the Code window and then click on "Add Watch" in the context menu. You can then alter the expression in the Name column of the Watch window. To delete an expression from the Watch window, right-click on the expression and then click on "Delete Watch." Also, you can directly alter the value of any variable in the Watch window and have the values of the other expressions change accordingly.

The Locals Window

While in Break mode, you can invoke the Locals window from the Debug menu by positioning the cursor over Windows and then clicking on Locals. This window automatically displays the names, values, and types of all variables in the current procedure. See Figure D.4. You can alter the values of variables at any time. In addition, you can examine and change properties of controls through the Locals window.

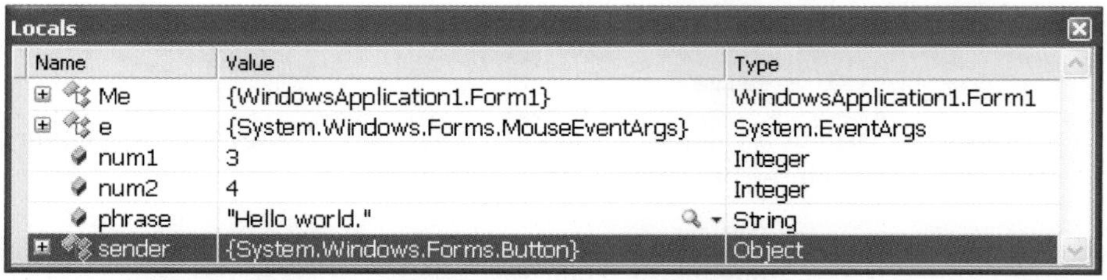

Name	Value	Type
⊞ Me	{WindowsApplication1.Form1}	WindowsApplication1.Form1
⊞ e	{System.Windows.Forms.MouseEventArgs}	System.EventArgs
num1	3	Integer
num2	4	Integer
phrase	"Hello world."	String
⊞ sender	{System.Windows.Forms.Button}	Object

FIGURE D.4   A typical Locals window.

Six Walkthroughs

The following walkthroughs use the debugging tools with the programming structures covered in Chapters 3, 4, 5, and 6.

Stepping through an Elementary Program: Chapter 3

The following walkthrough demonstrates several capabilities of the debugger:

1. Create a form with a button (btnPush) and a text box (txtBox).

2. Double-click on the button and enter the following event procedure:

```
Private Sub btnPush_Click(...) Handles btnPush.Click
  Dim num As Integer
  num = CInt(InputBox("Enter a number:"))
  num += 1
  num += 2
  txtBox.Text = CStr(num)
End Sub
```

3. Place the cursor on the line beginning Private Sub, press the right mouse button, and click on "Run to Cursor." The program will execute, and the form will appear.

4. Click on the button. In the Code window, a yellow arrow points to the Private Sub statement.

5. Press F8. The yellow arrow now points to the statement containing InputBox to indicate that it is the next statement to be executed. (Pressing F8 is referred to as *stepping into*. You can also step to the next statement of a program with the Step Into option from the Debug menu or with the Step Into icon.)

6. Press F8. The statement containing InputBox is executed, and an Input dialog box requesting a number appears. Respond to the request by typing 5 and clicking the OK button.

7. Press F8 again to execute the statement **num += 1.**

8. Let the mouse hover over any occurrence of the variable *num* for a second or so. The current value of the variable will be displayed in a small box.

9. Press Ctrl + Alt + Break to stop debugging. (You also can stop debugging by clicking on "Stop Debugging" in the Debug menu.)

10. Move the cursor to the line

    num += 2

    and then press F9. A red dot appears on the gray border to the left of the line. This indicates that the line is a breakpoint. Pressing F9 is referred to as *toggling a breakpoint.*

11. Press F5 and click on the button. Respond to the request by entering 5 and pressing OK. The program executes the first three lines and stops at the breakpoint. The breakpoint line is not executed.

12. Open the Immediate window by pressing Ctrl + Alt + I. If necessary, clear the contents of the window by pressing the right mouse button and selecting "Clear All." Type the statement

    ? num

    into the Immediate window, and then press Enter to execute the statement. The appearance of "6" on the next line of the Immediate window confirms that the breakpoint line was not executed.

13. Click on the Code window.

14. Move the cursor to the line "num += 1," click the right mouse button, and then click on "Set next Statement."

15. Press F8 to execute the selected line.

16. Return to the Immediate window by clicking on it. Type the statement "? num," and press Enter to confirm that the value of *num* is now 7. Then return to the Code window.

17. Move the cursor to the breakpoint line, and press F9 to deselect the line as a breakpoint.

18. Press F5 to execute the remaining lines of the program. Observe that the value displayed in the text box is 9.

Stepping through a Program Containing a General Procedure: Chapter 4

The following walkthrough uses the single-stepping feature of the debugger to trace the flow through a Sub procedure:

1. Create a form with a button (btnPush) and a text box (txtBox). Then enter the following two procedures:

```
Private Sub btnPush_Click(...) Handles btnPush.Click
  Dim p, b As Double
  p = 1000          'Principal
  GetBalance(p, b)
  txtBox.Text = "The balance is " & FormatCurrency(b)
End Sub

Sub GetBalance(ByVal prin As Double, ByRef bal As Double)
  'Calculate the balance at 5% interest rate
  Dim interest As Double
  interest = 0.05 * prin
  bal = prin + interest
End Sub
```

2. Place the cursor on the line beginning "Private Sub," press the right mouse button, and click on "Run to Cursor." The program will execute, and the form will appear.

3. Click on the button. In the Code window, a yellow arrow points to the Private Sub statement.

4. Press F8 once, and observe that the yellow arrow now points to the statement "p = 1000." This statement will be executed when F8 is next pressed.

5. Press F8 again. The statement "p = 1000" was executed, and the yellow arrow now points to the statement calling the Sub procedure GetBalance.

6. Press F8, and observe that the yellow arrow is now pointing to the header of the Sub procedure.

7. Press F8 three times to execute the assignment statements. The yellow arrow now points to the End Sub statement. (Notice that the Dim and comment statements were skipped.)

8. Press F8, and notice that the yellow arrow has moved back to the btnPush_Click event procedure and is pointing to the calling statement. By hovering the cursor over the variable *b*, you can verify that the Sub procedure was executed.

9. Press Ctrl + Alt + Break to terminate debugging.

10. Repeat Steps 2 through 5, and then press Shift + F8 to *step over* the Sub procedure GetBalance. The Sub procedure has been executed in its entirety.

11. Press Ctrl + Alt + Break to terminate debugging.

Communicating between Arguments and Parameters

The following walkthrough uses the Locals window to monitor the values of arguments and parameters during the execution of a program.

1. If you have not already done so, type the preceding program into the Code window.

2. Place the cursor on the line beginning "Private Sub," press the right mouse button, and click on "Run to Cursor." The program will execute, and the form will appear.

3. Click on the button.

4. Select the Debug menu, hover the cursor over "Windows," and then click on "Locals." Notice that the variables *b* and *p* from the btnPush_Click event procedure appear in the Locals window. The other variables in the list (Me, sender, and e) needn't concern us.

5. Press F8 twice to point to the calling statement. Notice that the value of the variable *p* has changed.

6. Press F8 to call the Sub procedure. Notice that the variables displayed in the Locals window are now those of the procedure GetBalance.

7. Press F8 three times to execute the procedure.

8. Press F8 to return to the btnPush_Click event procedure. Notice that the value of the variable *b* has inherited the value of the variable *bal*.

9. Press Ctrl + Alt + Break to terminate debugging.

Stepping through Programs Containing Selection Structures: Chapter 5

If Blocks

The following walkthrough demonstrates how an If statement evaluates a condition to determine whether to take an action:

1. Create a form with a button (btnPush), a text box (txtBox), and the following code:

```
Private Sub btnPush_Click(...) Handles btnPush.Click
  Dim wage As Double
  wage = CDbl(InputBox("Wage:"))
  If wage < 5.15 Then
    txtBox.Text = "Below minimum wage."
  Else
    txtBox.Text = "Wage Ok."
  End If
End Sub
```

2. Place the cursor on the line beginning "Private Sub," press the right mouse button, and click on "Run to Cursor." The program will execute and the form will appear.

3. Click on the button, and then press F8. The yellow arrow points to the statement containing InputBox.

4. Press F8 once to execute the statement containing InputBox. Type a wage of 3.25, and press the Enter key. The If statement is highlighted, but has not been executed.

5. Press F8 once, and notice that the yellow arrow has jumped to the statement **txtBox.Text = "Below minimum wage."** Because the condition "wage < 5.15" is true, the action associated with Then was chosen.

6. Press F8 to execute the txtBox.Text statement. Notice that Else is skipped and the yellow arrow points to End If.

7. Press F8 again. We are through with the If block, and the statement following the If block, End Sub, is highlighted.

8. Press Ctrl + Alt + Break to terminate debugging.

9. If desired, try stepping through the program again with 5.75 entered as the wage. Since the condition "wage < 5.15" will be false, the Else action will be executed instead of the Then action.

Select Case Blocks

The following walkthrough illustrates how a Select Case block uses the selector to choose from among several actions:

1. Create a form with a button (btnPush) and a text box (txtBox). Double-click on the button and enter the following procedure:

```
Private Sub btnPush_Click(...) Handles btnPush.Click
  Dim age, price As Double
  age = CDbl(InputBox("Age:"))
  Select Case age
    Case Is < 12
      price = 0
    Case Is < 18
      price = 3.5
    Case Is >= 65
      price = 4
    Case Else
      price = 5.5
  End Select
  txtBox.Text = "Your ticket price is " & FormatCurrency(price)
End Sub
```

2. Place the cursor on the line beginning "age =", press the right mouse button, and click on "Run to Cursor." The program will execute, and the form will appear.

3. Click on the button. The arrow will point to the statement beginning "age =".

4. Press F8 once to execute the statement beginning "age ='. Type an age of 8, and press the Enter key. The arrow points to the Select Case statement, but the statement has not been executed.

5. Press F8 twice, and observe that the arrow points to the action associated with "Case Is < 12".

6. Press F8 once to execute the assignment statement. Notice that the arrow now points to End Select. This demonstrates that when more than one Case clause is true, only the first is acted upon.

7. Press Ctrl + Alt + Break to terminate debugging.

8. If desired, step through the program again, entering a different age and predicting which Case clause will be acted upon. (Some possible ages to try are 12, 14, 18, 33, and 67.)

Stepping through a Program Containing a Do Loop: Chapter 6

Do Loops

The following walkthrough demonstrates use of the Watch window to monitor the value of a condition in a Do loop that searches for a name:

1. Create a form with a button (btnPush) and a text box (txtBox). Then double-click on the button, and enter the following event procedure:

```
Private Sub btnPush_Click(...) Handles btnPush.Click
  'Look for a specific name.
  Dim searchName As String, name As String = ""
  Dim sr As IO.StreamReader = IO.File.OpenText("DATA.TXT")
  searchName = InputBox("Name:") 'Name to search for in list
  Do While (name <> searchName) And (sr.Peek <> -1)
    name = sr.ReadLine
  Loop
  sr.Close()
  If name = searchName Then
    txtBox.Text = name
  Else
    txtBox.Text = "Name not found"
  End If
End Sub
```

2. Access Windows Notepad, enter the following lines of data, and save the file in the program's *Debug* subfolder inside the *bin* folder with the name DATA.TXT:

Bert
Ernie
Grover
Oscar

3. Place the cursor on the line beginning "Private Sub," press the right mouse button, and click on "Run to Cursor." The program will execute, and the form will appear.

4. Click on the button. The yellow arrow points to the header of the event procedure.

5. Click on the variable *searchName*, click the right mouse button, and click on "Add Watch." The variable *searchName* has been added to a window titled Watch.

6. Repeat Step 5 for the variable *name*.

7. Press F8 four times to execute the File.OpenText statement and the statement containing InputBox. Enter the name "Ernie" in the input dialog box, and then click OK.

8. Press F8 repeatedly until the entire event procedure has been executed. Pause after each keypress, and notice how the values of the expressions in the Watch window change.

9. Press Ctrl + Alt + Break to terminate debugging.

ANSWERS

To Selected Odd-Numbered Exercises

CHAPTER 1

EXERCISES 1.2

1. The program is busy carrying out a task, please wait.

3. Double-clicking means clicking the left mouse button twice in quick succession.

5. The blinking vertical line is called the cursor. Each character that you type appears at the cursor's location.

7. Starting with an uppercase W, Windows refers to Microsoft's Windows operating system. Starting with a lowercase w, windows refers to the rectangular regions of the screen in which different programs are displayed.

9. Untitled

11. Backspace

13. Del

15. End

17. Ctrl + Home

19. Alt

21. Esc

23. Alt/F/S or Alt/F/A

EXERCISES 1.3

1. A filename cannot contain a question mark.

3. Forward slashes (/) are not allowed in filespecs. To separate folders and files in a filespec, use a backslash (\ ).

5. C:\Revenue\Chicago

7. No

9. Files are sorted by size.

11. Files are sorted by the date they were last modified.

13. Smaller versions of the pictures (called "thumbnails") that are stored in the files are shown.

CHAPTER 3

EXERCISES 3.1

1. After a button is clicked, it has a blue border.

(In Exercises 3 through 24, begin by pressing Alt/F/N/P to begin a new project.)

3. Click on the form to make it the selected object.
   Click on the Properties window or Press F4 to activate the Properties window.
   Move around with the up- and down-arrow keys until the Text property is highlighted.
   Type "CHECKING ACCOUNT".

5. Double-click the TextBox icon in the Toolbox.
   Activate the Properties window, and highlight the BackColor property.
   Click on the down-arrow button to the right of the Settings box.
   Click on the Custom tab.
   Click on the desired yellow in the palette.
   Click on the form to see the empty, yellow text box.

7. Double-click on the Label icon in the Toolbox.
   Activate the Properties window, and highlight the AutoSize property.
   Set the AutoSize property to False.
   Highlight the Text property.
   Type the requested sentence.
   Highlight the TextAlign property.
   Click on the down-arrow button to the right of the Settings box, and click on one of the center rectangles.
   Click on the form.
   Use the mouse to resize the label so that the sentence occupies three lines.

9. Double-click on the TextBox icon in the Toolbox.
   Activate the Properties window, and highlight the Text property.
   Type "Visual Basic 2005".
   Set the Name property to txtLanguage.
   Highlight the Font property.
   Click on the ellipsis to the right of the Settings box.
   Scroll up the font list box, and click on Courier New in the Font box.
   Click OK.
   Resize the text box to accommodate its text.
   Click on the form to see the resulting text box.

11. Double-click on the Button icon in the Toolbox.
    Activate the Properties window, and highlight the BackColor property.
    Click on the down-arrow button to the right of the Settings box.
    Click on the Custom tab, and then click on the white square in the palette.
    Highlight the Text property.
    Type "PUSH".
    Highlight the Font property, and click on the ellipsis.

Click on Italic in the Font style box.
Click on 24 in the Size box.
Click OK.
Click on the form to see the resulting button.

13. Double-click on the Button icon in the Toolbox.
Activate the Properties window, and highlight the Text property.
Type "PUS&H".
Click on the form to see the resulting button.

15. Double-click on the Label icon in the Toolbox.
Activate the Properties window, and highlight the Name property.
Type "lblAKA". (The name will appear in the Settings box.)
Highlight the Text property.
Type "ALIAS".
Highlight the AutoSize property.
Set the AutoSize property to False.
Highlight the Font property, and click on the ellipsis.
Click on Italic in the Font style box.
Click OK.
Highlight the TextAlign property.
Click on the down-arrow box to the right of the Settings box, and click on one of the center rectangles.

17. Double-click on the Label icon in the Toolbox.
Highlight the AutoSize property.
Set the AutoSize property to False.
Activate the Properties window, and highlight the TextAlign property.
Click on the down-arrow box to the right of the Settings box, and click on one of the rectangles on the right.
Highlight the Text property.
Type "VISUAL BASIC" and press Enter.
If the words "VISUAL BASIC" are on one line, make the label narrower and longer, until the words appear on two lines.

19. Double-click on the Label icon in the Toolbox.
Activate the Properties window, and highlight the Font property.
Click on the ellipsis to the right of the Settings box.
Click on Wingdings in the Font box.
Click on the largest size available (72) in the Size box.
Click OK.
Highlight the Text property.
Change the setting to a less than sign (<).
Click on the label.

Note: If you didn't know that the less than symbol corresponded to a diskette in the Wingdings font, you could double-click on the diskette character in the Character Map, click the Copy button, highlight the Text property, and press Ctrl + V. The less than character would appear in the Text settings box.

21. Double-click on the ListBox icon in the Toolbox.
Activate the Properties window, and highlight the BackColor property.
Click on the down-arrow button to the right of the Settings box.
Click on the Custom tab.
Click on the desired yellow square in the palette.
Click on the form to see the yellow list box.

23. In the Solution Explorer window, right click on "Form1.vb" and select Rename from the Context menu.
Type "frmYellow.vb".
Right-click on the form in the Form Designer, and select Properties from the Context menu.
Click on the BackColor property in the Properties Window.
Click on the down-arrow button in the right part of the Settings box, and then click on the Custom tab.
Click on a square colored yellow.

25. Begin a new project.
Change the text in the form's title bar to "Dynamic Duo".
Place two buttons on the form.
Enter as the text on the first Batman and on the second Robin.
Increase the font size for both buttons to 14.

27. Begin a new project.
Change the text in the form's title bar to "Fill in the Blank".
Place a label, a text box, and another label on the form at appropriate locations.
Change the Text setting of the first label to "Toto, I don't think we're in" and of the second label to "A Quote from the Wizard of Oz".
Position the labels and text box as needed.

29. Begin a new project.
Change the text in the form's title bar to "An Uncle's Advice".
Place on the form five labels and three buttons.
Set the AutoSize properties of the first and last labels to False.
Set the BackColor property of the last label to Blue, and set its ForeColor property to Yellow.
Change the Text property of each label as indicated.
Change the settings of the buttons' Text properties to "1", "2", and "3". Resize and position the labels and buttons as is appropriate.

33. Each arrow key moves the text box in the indicated direction.

35. "Center" refers to the midpoint horizontally, whereas "middle" refers to the midpoint vertically

37. (a) All three buttons move left. (b) All three buttons become narrower. (c) The color of the text on all three buttons changes to blue at the same time. (d) The button with white sizing handles does not move or change size. The buttons with black sizing handles align with, and assume the size of, the button with white sizing handles.

39. The setting toggles between True and False.

EXERCISES 3.2

1. The word "Hello"

3. The word "Hello" on an orange-colored background

5. The text box vanishes; nothing is visible.

7. The word "Hello" in green letters

9. The word "Hello" on a gold background

11. Form1.Text should be Me.Text.

13. Red should be replaced with Color.Red.

15. Font.Size is a read-only property. The statement `txtOutput.Text = txtBox.Font.Size` is valid since it is reading the value of txtBox.Font.Size. However, `txtBox.Font.Size = 20` is not valid since it is setting the value of txtBox.Font.Size.

17. `lblTwo.Text = "E.T. phone home."`

19. `txtBox.ForeColor = Color.Red`
    `txtBox.Text = "The stuff that dreams are made of."`

21. `txtBox.Enabled = False`

23. `lblTwo.Visible = False`

25. `btnOutcome.Enabled = True`

27. `Me.BackColor = Color.White`

29. The Enter event occurs when the object gets the focus.

33.
```
Private Sub btnLeft_Click(...) Handles btnLeft.Click
    txtBox.Text = "Left Justify"
    txtBox.TextAlign = HorizontalAlignment.Left
End Sub

Private Sub btnCenter_Click(...) Handles btnCenter.Click
    txtBox.Text = "Center"
    txtBox.TextAlign = HorizontalAlignment.Center
End Sub

Private Sub btnRight_Click(...) Handles btnRight.Click
    txtBox.Text = "Right Justify"
    txtBox.TextAlign = HorizontalAlignment.Right
End Sub
```

35.
```
Private Sub btnRed_Click(...) Handles btnRed.Click
    txtBox.BackColor = Color.Red
End Sub

Private Sub btnBlue_Click(...) Handles btnBlue.Click
    txtBox.BackColor = Color.Blue
End Sub

Private Sub btnWhite_Click(...) Handles btnWhite.Click
    txtBox.ForeColor = Color.White
End Sub
```

```
    Private Sub btnYellow_Click(...) Handles btnYellow.Click
      txtBox.ForeColor = Color.Yellow
    End Sub
```

37.
```
    Private Sub txtLife_Enter(...) Handles txtLife.Enter
      txtQuote.Text = "I like life, it's something to do."
    End Sub

    Private Sub txtFuture_Enter(...) Handles txtFuture.Enter
      txtQuote.Text = "The future isn't what it used to be."
    End Sub

    Private Sub txtTruth_Enter(...) Handles txtTruth.Enter
      txtQuote.Text = "Tell the truth and run."
    End Sub
```

39.
```
    Private Sub btnOne_Click(...) Handles btnOne.Click
      btnOne.Visible = False
      btnTwo.Visible = True
      btnThree.Visible = True
      btnFour.Visible = True
    End Sub

    Private Sub btnTwo_Click(...) Handles btnTwo.Click
      btnOne.Visible = True
      btnTwo.Visible = False
      btnThree.Visible = True
      btnFour.Visible = True
    End Sub

    Private Sub btnThree_Click(...) Handles btnThree.Click
      btnOne.Visible = True
      btnTwo.Visible = True
      btnThree.Visible = False
      btnFour.Visible = True
    End Sub

    Private Sub btnFour_Click(...) Handles btnFour.Click
      btnOne.Visible = True
      btnTwo.Visible = True
      btnThree.Visible = True
      btnFour.Visible = False
    End Sub
```

41.
```
    Private Sub btnVanish_Click(...) Handles btnVanish.Click
      lblFace.Visible = False
    End Sub

    Private Sub btnReappear_Click(...) Handles btnReappear.Click
      lblFace.Visible = True
    End Sub
```

43.
```
    Private Sub btnAny_Click(...) Handles btnOne.Click, btnTwo.Click
      txtOutput.Text = "You just clicked on a button."
    End Sub
```

EXERCISES 3.3

1. 12

3. .125

5. 8

7. 0

9. 1

11. Not valid

13. Valid

15. Not valid

17. 10

19. 16

21. 9

23.
```
Private Sub btnCompute_Click(...) Handles btnCompute.Click
    lstOutput.Items.Add((7 * 8) + 5)
End Sub
```

25.
```
Private Sub btnCompute_Click(...) Handles btnCompute.Click
    lstOutput.Items.Add(0.055 * 20)
End Sub
```

27.
```
Private Sub btnCompute_Click(...) Handles btnCompute.Click
    lstOutput.Items.Add(17 * (3 + 162))
End Sub
```

29.

	x	y
`Private Sub btnEvaluate_Click(...) Handles btnEvaluate.Click`		
`Dim x, y As Double`	0	0
`x = 2`	2	0
`y = 3 * x`	2	6
`x = y + 5`	11	6
`lstResults.Items.Clear()`	11	6
`lstResults.Items.Add(x + 4)`	11	6
`y = y + 1`	11	7
`End Sub`		

31. 6

33. 1
    8
    9

35. 1
    64

37. 25
    20

39. The third line should read `c = a + b`

41. The first assignment statement should not contain a comma. The second assignment statement should not contain a dollar sign.

43. 9W is not a valid variable name.

45. `Dim quantity As Integer = 12`

47. `10`

49. `6`

51. `3.128`

53. `−3`

55. `0`

57. `6`

59.
```
Private Sub btnCompute_Click(...) Handles btnCompute.Click
    Dim revenue, costs, profit As Double
    revenue = 98456
    costs = 45000
    profit = revenue - costs
    lstOutput.Items.Add(profit)
End Sub
```

61.
```
Private Sub btnCompute_Click(...) Handles btnCompute.Click
    Dim price, discountPercent, markdown As Double
    price = 19.95
    discountPercent = 30
    markdown = (discountPercent / 100) * price
    price = price - markdown
    lstOutput.Items.Add(price)
End Sub
```

63.
```
Private Sub btnCompute_Click(...) Handles btnCompute.Click
    Dim balance As Double
    balance = 100
    balance += 0.05 * balance
    balance += 0.05 * balance
    balance += 0.05 * balance
    lstOutput.Items.Add(balance)
End Sub
```

65.
```
Private Sub btnCompute_Click(...) Handles btnCompute.Click
    Dim balance As Double
    balance = 100
    balance = balance * (1.05 ^ 10)
    lstOutput.Items.Add(balance)
End Sub
```

67.
```
Private Sub btnCompute_Click(...) Handles btnCompute.Click
    Dim acres, yieldPerAcre, corn As Double
    acres = 30
    yieldPerAcre = 18
    corn = yieldPerAcre * acres
    lstOutput.Items.Add(corn)
End Sub
```

69.
```
Private Sub btnCompute_Click(...) Handles btnCompute.Click
    Dim distance, elapsedTime, averageSpeed As Double
    distance = 233
    elapsedTime = 7 - 2
    averageSpeed = distance / elapsedTime
    lstOutput.Items.Add(averageSpeed)
End Sub
```

71.
```
Private Sub btnCompute_Click(...) Handles btnCompute.Click
    Dim waterPerPersonPerDay, people, days, waterUsed As Double
    waterPerPersonPerDay = 1600
    people = 300000000
    days = 365
    waterUsed = waterPerPersonPerDay * people * days
    lstOutput.Items.Add(waterUsed)
End Sub
```

EXERCISES 3.4

1. Visual Basic

3. Ernie

5. flute

7. 123

9. Your age is 21.

11. A ROSE IS A ROSE IS A ROSE

13. 5.5

15. goodbye

17. WALLAWALLA

19. ABC
    2
    4
    55 mph
    STU

21. 12
    MUNICIPALITY
    city
    6

23. 8 (0 through 7)

25. True

27. The variable *phoneNumber* should be declared as type String, not Double.

29. *End* is a keyword and cannot be used as a variable name.

31. The IndexOf method cannot be applied to a number, only a String.

33.
```
Private Sub btnDisplay_Click(...) Handles btnDisplay.Click
    Dim firstName, middleName, lastName As String
    Dim yearOfBirth As Integer
    firstName = "Thomas"
```

```
        middleName = "Alva"
        lastName = "Edison"
        yearOfBirth = 1847
        txtOutput.Text = firstName & " " & middleName & " " & lastName & _
                         ", " & yearOfBirth
     End Sub
```

35.
```
Private Sub btnDisplay_Click(...) Handles btnDisplay.Click
   Dim publisher As String
   publisher = "Prentice-Hall, Inc."
   txtOutput.Text = "(c)" & " " & publisher
End Sub
```

37.
```
Private Sub btnCompute_Click(...) Handles btnCompute.Click
   Dim distance As Double
   distance = CDbl(txtNumSec.Text) / 5
   distance = Math.Round(distance, 2)
   txtOutput.Text = "The distance of the storm is " & distance & _
                    " miles."
End Sub
```

39.
```
Private Sub btnCompute_Click(...) Handles btnCompute.Click
   Dim cycling, running, swimming, pounds As Double
   cycling = CDbl(txtCycle.Text)
   running = CDbl(txtRun.Text)
   swimming = CDbl(txtSwim.Text)
   pounds = (200 * cycling + 475 * running + 275 * swimming) / 3500
   pounds = Math.Round(pounds, 1)
   txtWtLoss.Text = pounds & " pounds were lost."
End Sub
```

41.
```
Private Sub btnCompute_Click(...) Handles btnCompute.Click
   Dim income As Double
   income = CDbl(txtRevenue.Text) - CDbl(txtExpenses.Text)
   txtNetIncome.Text = CStr(income)
End Sub
```

43.
```
Private Sub btnCompute_Click(...) Handles btnCompute.Click
   Dim tip As Double
   tip = CDbl(txtAmount.Text) * CDbl(txtPercentage.Text) / 100
   txtTip.Text = CStr(Math.Round(tip, 2))
End Sub
```

45.
```
Private Sub btnPressMe_Click(...) Handles btnPressMe.Click
   txtOutput.Text = CStr(CInt(txtOutput.Text) + 1)
End Sub
```

47.
```
Private Sub btnModifySentence_Click(...) Handles _
            btnModifySentence.Click
   'Replace the first occurrence of a word
   'in a given sentence with another word.
   Dim sentence, oldWord, newWord As String
   Dim position As Integer
   sentence = txtSentence.Text
   oldWord = txtOriginalWord.Text
   newWord = txtReplacementWord.Text
   position = sentence.IndexOf(oldWord)
   txtOutput.Text = sentence.Substring(0, position) & newWord & _
                    sentence.Substring(position + oldWord.Length)
End Sub
```

49.
```
Private Sub btnDisplay_Click(...) Handles btnDisplay.Click
    'Estimate the speed of a car given the stopping distance.
    Dim speed, distance As Double
    distance = CDbl(txtDistanceSkidded.Text)
    speed = Math.Sqrt(24 * distance)
    txtEstimatedSpeed.Text = CStr(speed) & "mph"
End Sub
```

EXERCISES 3.5

1. 1,235

3. 1,234.0

5. 0.0

7. –0.67

9. 12,346.000

11. 12

13. $12,346

15. ($0.23)

17. $0.80

19. 7.50%

21. 100.00%

23. 66.67%

25. Pay to France $27,267,622.00

27. 25.6% of the U.S. population 25+ years old are college graduates.

29. The likelihood of Heads is 50%

31.
```
12345678901234567890
   1         2
```

33.
```
12345678901234567890
     12
```

35.
```
12345678901234567890

    A      Alice
```

37.
```
12345678901234567890
       College   Mascot
   Univ. of MD   Terrapins
          Duke   Blue Devils
```

39.
```
12345678901234567890
 Element  Weight   Percent
 Oxygen    97.5     65.0 %
 Carbon    27.0     18.0 %
```

41. 16

43. baseball

45. Age: 20

47. The White House has 132 rooms.

49. `Sum: 444`

51. `Harvard`
    `Harvard`

53. `You might win 360 dollars.`

55. `Hello John Jones`

57. `MsgBox("Keep cool, but don't freeze.", 0, "Good Advice")`

59. In the text file, an expression was used where a numerical literal was expected.

61. The second line should use CDbl to convert the right-hand side to Double.

63. FormatNumber(123456) is a string and therefore cannot be assigned to a Double variable.

65. You must insert **String.Format(** after the left parenthesis.

67.
```
Private Sub btnDisplay_Click(...) Handles btnDisplay.Click
    'Displays information about Americans' eating habits
    Dim food, units As String, quantityPerDay As Double
    Dim sr As IO.StreamReader = IO.File.OpenText("SODA.TXT")
    food = sr.ReadLine
    units = sr.ReadLine
    quantityPerDay = CDbl(sr.ReadLine)
    lstOutput.Items.Add("Americans consume " & quantityPerDay & _
                        " " & units)
    lstOutput.Items.Add("of " & food & " per day.")
    sr.Close()
End Sub
```

69.
```
Private Sub btnDisplay_Click(...) Handles btnDisplay.Click
    'Report percent increase for a basket of goods.
    Dim begOfYearPrice, endOfYearPrice As Double
    Dim percentIncrease As Double
    begOfYearPrice = 200
    endOfYearPrice = CDbl(InputBox("Enter price at the end of year:"))
    percentIncrease = 100 * (endOfYearPrice - _
                      begOfYearPrice) / begOfYearPrice
    txtOutput.Text = "The percent increase for the year is " & _
                     percentIncrease & "."
End Sub
```

71. 000

73. LLL000

75. 0-00-000000-&

77.
```
Private Sub btnDisplay_Click(...) Handles btnDisplay.Click
    'Report checking account balances.
    Dim account As String
    Dim beginningBalance, deposits, withdrawals As Double
    Dim endOfMonthBalance, total As Double
    Dim sr As IO.StreamReader = IO.File.OpenText("3-5-E77.TXT")
    Dim fmtStr As String = "{0,-10}{1,10:C}"
    lstOutput.Items.Clear()
    lstOutput.Items.Add(String.Format(fmtStr, "Account", "Balance"))
    '1st account
    account = sr.ReadLine
```

```vb
      beginningBalance = CDbl(sr.ReadLine)
      deposits = CDbl(sr.ReadLine)
      withdrawals = CDbl(sr.ReadLine)
      endOfMonthBalance = beginningBalance + deposits - withdrawals
      lstOutput.Items.Add(String.Format(fmtStr, account, _
                      endOfMonthBalance))
      total = endOfMonthBalance
      '2nd account
      account = sr.ReadLine
      beginningBalance = CDbl(sr.ReadLine)
      deposits = CDbl(sr.ReadLine)
      withdrawals = CDbl(sr.ReadLine)
      endOfMonthBalance = beginningBalance + deposits - withdrawals
      lstOutput.Items.Add(String.Format(fmtStr, account, _
                      endOfMonthBalance))
      total += endOfMonthBalance    'Increase total by endOfMonthBalance.
      '3rd account
      account = sr.ReadLine
      beginningBalance = CDbl(sr.ReadLine)
      deposits = CDbl(sr.ReadLine)
      withdrawals = CDbl(sr.ReadLine)
      endOfMonthBalance = beginningBalance + deposits - withdrawals
      lstOutput.Items.Add(String.Format(fmtStr, account, _
                      endOfMonthBalance))
      total += endOfMonthBalance    'Increase total by endOfMonthBalance.
      lstOutput.Items.Add(String.Format(fmtStr, "Total", total))
      sr.Close()
    End Sub

79. Private Sub btnDisplay_Click(...) Handles btnDisplay.Click
      'Compute semester averages.
      Dim socNmb As String
      Dim exam1, exam2, exam3, final, average, total As Double
      Dim fmtStr As String = "{0,-15}{1,8:N0}"
      Dim sr As IO.StreamReader = IO.File.OpenText("3-5-E79.TXT")
      lstOutput.Items.Clear()
      lstOutput.Items.Add(String.Format(fmtStr, "Soc. Sec. No.", _
                      "Average"))
      '1st student
      socNmb = sr.ReadLine
      exam1 = CDbl(sr.ReadLine)
      exam2 = CDbl(sr.ReadLine)
      exam3 = CDbl(sr.ReadLine)
      final = CDbl(sr.ReadLine)
      average = (exam1 + exam2 + exam3 + final * 2) / 5
      lstOutput.Items.Add(String.Format(fmtStr, socNmb, average))
      total = average
      '2nd student
      socNmb = sr.ReadLine
      exam1 = CDbl(sr.ReadLine)
      exam2 = CDbl(sr.ReadLine)
      exam3 = CDbl(sr.ReadLine)
      final = CDbl(sr.ReadLine)
      average = (exam1 + exam2 + exam3 + final * 2) / 5
      lstOutput.Items.Add(String.Format(fmtStr, socNmb, average))
      total += average    'Increase value of total by value of average.
```

```
    '3rd student
    socNmb = sr.ReadLine
    exam1 = CDbl(sr.ReadLine)
    exam2 = CDbl(sr.ReadLine)
    exam3 = CDbl(sr.ReadLine)
    final = CDbl(sr.ReadLine)
    average = (exam1 + exam2 + exam3 + final * 2) / 5
    lstOutput.Items.Add(String.Format(fmtStr, socNmb, average))
    total += average   'Increase value of total by value of average.
    lstOutput.Items.Add(String.Format(fmtStr, "Class Average", _
                        total / 3))
    sr.Close()
  End Sub
```

81.
```
Private Sub txtPhoneNumber_Enter(...) Handles txtPhoneNumber.Enter
    MsgBox("Be sure to include the area code!", 0, "Reminder")
  End Sub
```

83.
```
Private Sub btnCompute_Click(...) Handles btnCompute.Click
    'Show growth of money in a savings account.
    Dim principal, intRate, yrs, amt As Double
    lstOutput.Items.Clear()
    principal = CDbl(txtPrincipal.Text)
    intRate = CDbl(txtIntRate.Text)
    yrs = 10
    amt = principal * (1 + intRate) ^ yrs
    lstOutput.Items.Add("When " & FormatCurrency(principal))
    lstOutput.Items.Add("is invested at " & FormatPercent(intRate))
    lstOutput.Items.Add("interest for " & yrs & " years,")
    lstOutput.Items.Add("the balance is " & FormatCurrency(amt))
  End Sub
```

85.
```
Private Sub btnCompute_Click(...) Handles btnCompute.Click
    Dim price, quantity, revenue As Double
    Dim sr As IO.StreamReader = IO.File.OpenText("3-5-E85.TXT")
    price = CDbl(sr.ReadLine)
    quantity = CDbl(sr.ReadLine)
    revenue = price * quantity
    txtOutput.Text = "Revenue: " & FormatCurrency(revenue)
    sr.Close()
  End Sub
```

CHAPTER 4

EXERCISES 4.1

1.
```
Time's fun when you're having flies.
Kermit the frog
```

3.
```
Why do clocks run clockwise?
```

```
Since they were invented in the northern
hemisphere where sundials go clockwise.
```

5. `divorced`
   `beheaded`
   `died,`
   `divorced`
   `beheaded`
   `survived`

7. `Keep cool, but don't freeze.`
   `Source: A jar of mayonnaise.`

9. `88 keys on a piano`

11. `It was the best of times.`
    `It was the worst of times.`

13. `Your name has 7 letters.`
    `The first letter is G`

15. `abcde`

17. `144 items in a gross`

19. `30% of M&M's Plain Chocolate Candies are brown.`

21. `1440 minutes in a day`

23. `t is the 6th letter of the word.`

25. `A recent salary survey of readers of`
    `Visual Basic Programmer's Journal gave`
    `average salaries of database developers`
    `according to the database used.`

    `Sybase SQL Server programmers earned $75,633.`
    `Oracle programmers earned $73,607.`
    `Windows CE programmers earned $73,375.`
    `Microsoft SQL Server programmers earned $68,295.`

27. `President Clinton is a graduate of Georgetown University.`
    `President Bush is a graduate of Yale University.`

29. `The first 6 letters are Visual.`

31. `The negative of worldly is unworldly`

33. `24 blackbirds`
    `baked in`
    `a pie.`

35. There is a parameter in the Sub procedure, but no argument in the statement calling the Sub procedure.

37. Since Handles is a keyword, it cannot be used as the name of a Sub procedure.

39.
```
Private Sub btnDisplay_Click(...) Handles btnDisplay.Click
    'Display a lucky number.
    Dim num As Integer = 7
    Lucky(num)
End Sub

Sub Lucky(ByVal num As Integer)
  'Display message.
  txtOutput.Text = num & " is a lucky number."
End Sub
```

41.
```
Private Sub btnDisplay_Click(...) Handles btnDisplay.Click
    'Information about trees
    Dim tree As String, ht As Double
    Dim sr As IO.StreamReader = IO.File.OpenText("TREES.TXT")
    lstBox.Items.Clear()
    tree = sr.ReadLine
    ht = CDbl(sr.ReadLine)
    Tallest(tree, ht)
    tree = sr.ReadLine
    ht = CDbl(sr.ReadLine)
    Tallest(tree, ht)
    sr.Close()
End Sub

Sub Tallest(ByVal tree As String, ByVal ht As Double)
    'Display information about tree.
    lstBox.Items.Add("The tallest " & tree & " in the U.S. is " _
                    & ht & " feet.")
End Sub
```

43.
```
Private Sub btnTriple_Click(...) Handles btnTriple.Click
    'Given a number, display its triple.
    Dim num As Double
    num = CDbl(InputBox("Enter a number:"))
    Triple(num)
End Sub

Sub Triple(ByVal num As Double)
    'Multiply the value of the number by 3.
    txtResult.Text = "The triple of " & num & " is " & 3 * num & "."
End Sub
```

45.
```
Private Sub btnDisplay_Click(...) Handles btnDisplay.Click
    Dim word As String, widthOfZone As Integer
    'Enter a word and column number to display.
    word = InputBox("Enter a word of at most ten letters.")
    widthOfZone = CInt(InputBox("Enter a number between 10 and 20."))
    PlaceNShow(word, widthOfZone)
End Sub

Sub PlaceNShow(ByVal word As String, _
              ByVal widthOfZone As Integer)
    'Display the word at the given column number.
    Dim fmtStr As String = "{0," & widthOfZone & "}"
    lstOutput.Items.Add("12345678901234567890")
    lstOutput.Items.Add(String.Format(fmtStr, word))
End Sub
```

47.
```
Private Sub btnDisplay_Click(...) Handles btnDisplay.Click
    'Intended college majors
    lstOutput.Items.Clear()
    DisplaySource()
    Majors(16, "business")
    Majors(1.4, "computer science")
End Sub

Sub DisplaySource()
    'Display the source of the information.
    Dim phrase As String
    phrase = "According to a 2004 survey of college freshmen"
```

```
  lstOutput.Items.Add(phrase)
  phrase = "taken by the Higher Educational Research Institute:"
  lstOutput.Items.Add(phrase)
  lstOutput.Items.Add("")
End Sub

Sub Majors(ByVal students As Double, ByVal field As String)
  lstOutput.Items.Add(students & _
              " percent said they intend to major in " & field & ".")
End Sub
```

49.
```
Private Sub btnDisplay_Click(...) Handles btnDisplay.Click
  'Favorite number
  Dim num As Double
  lstOutput.Items.Clear()
  num = CDbl(txtBox.Text)
  Sum(num)
  Product(num)
End Sub

Sub Sum(ByVal num As Double)
  Dim phrase As String
  phrase = "The sum of your favorite number with itself is "
  lstOutput.Items.Add(phrase & (num + num) & ".")
End Sub

Sub Product(ByVal num As Double)
  Dim phrase As String
  phrase = "The product of your favorite number with itself is "
  lstOutput.Items.Add(phrase & (num * num) & ".")
End Sub
```

51.
```
Private Sub btnDisplay_Click(...) Handles btnDisplay.Click
  'Old McDonald Had a Farm.
  Dim animal, sound As String
  Dim sr As IO.StreamReader = IO.File.OpenText("FARM.TXT")
  animal = sr.ReadLine
  sound = sr.ReadLine
  ShowVerse(animal, sound)
  animal = sr.ReadLine
  sound = sr.ReadLine
  ShowVerse(animal, sound)
  animal = sr.ReadLine
  sound = sr.ReadLine
  ShowVerse(animal, sound)
  sr.Close()
End Sub

Sub ShowVerse(ByVal animal As String, ByVal sound As String)
  lstOutput.Items.Add("Old McDonald had a farm. Eyi eyi oh.")
  lstOutput.Items.Add("And on his farm he had a " & animal & _
                  ". Eyi eyi oh.")
  lstOutput.Items.Add("With a " & sound & " " & sound & _
                  " here, and a " & sound & " " & sound & " there.")
  lstOutput.Items.Add("Here a " & sound & ", there a " & sound & _
                  ", everywhere a " & sound & " " & sound & ".")
  lstOutput.Items.Add("Old McDonald had a farm. Eyi eyi oh.")
  lstOutput.Items.Add("")
End Sub
```

53.
```
Private Sub btnDisplay_Click(...) Handles btnDisplay.Click
    Dim occupation As String, num00, num12 As Double
    Dim sr As IO.StreamReader = IO.File.OpenText("GROWTH.TXT")
    Dim fmtStr As String = "{0,-30}  {1,4}        {2,4}       {3,8}"
    lstOutput.Items.Clear()
    lstOutput.Items.Add(String.Format(fmtStr, "Occupation", 2000, _
                        2012, "Increase"))
    occupation = sr.ReadLine
    num00 = CDbl(sr.ReadLine)
    num12 = CDbl(sr.ReadLine)
    CalculateAndDisplay(occupation, num00, num12)
    occupation = sr.ReadLine
    num00 = CDbl(sr.ReadLine)
    num12 = CDbl(sr.ReadLine)
    CalculateAndDisplay(occupation, num00, num12)
    occupation = sr.ReadLine
    num00 = CDbl(sr.ReadLine)
    num12 = CDbl(sr.ReadLine)
    CalculateAndDisplay(occupation, num00, num12)
    occupation = sr.ReadLine
    num00 = CDbl(sr.ReadLine)
    num12 = CDbl(sr.ReadLine)
    CalculateAndDisplay(occupation, num00, num12)
    sr.Close()
End Sub

Sub CalculateAndDisplay(ByVal occupation As String, _
                        ByVal num00 As Double, ByVal num12 As Double)
    Dim perIncrease As Double
    Dim fmtStr As String = "{0,-30}  {1,4}         {2,4}        {3,8:P0}"
    perIncrease = (num12 - num00) / num00
    lstOutput.Items.Add(String.Format(fmtStr, occupation, num00, _
                        num12, perIncrease))
End Sub
```

EXERCISES 4.2

1. 9

3. Can Can

5. 25

7. Less is more.

9. Gabriel was born in the year 1980

11. Buckeyes

13. 0

15. 1
    1

17. 4 overwhelming
    8 whelming
    4 whelming
    4 ming
    4 whelming

19. The variable c should be a parameter in the Sub procedure. That is, the header for the Sub procedure should be

```
Sub Sum(ByVal x As Double, ByVal y As Double, ByRef c As Double)
```

Also, the Dim statement in the Sub procedure should be deleted.

21.
```
Private Sub btnCompute_Click(...) Handles btnCompute.Click
    'Calculate sales tax
    Dim price, tax, cost As Double
    lstOutput.Items.Clear()
    InputPrice(price)
    Compute(price, tax, cost)
    ShowData(price, tax, cost)
End Sub

Sub InputPrice(ByRef price As Double)
    'Get the price of the item
    price = CDbl(InputBox("Enter the price of the item:"))
End Sub

Sub Compute(ByVal price As Double, ByRef tax As Double, _
            ByRef cost As Double)
    'Calculate the cost
    tax = 0.05 * price
    cost = price + tax
End Sub

Sub ShowData(ByVal price As Double, ByVal tax As Double, _
             ByVal cost As Double)
    'Display bill
    lstOutput.Items.Add("Price: " & price)
    lstOutput.Items.Add("Tax:   " & tax)
    lstOutput.Items.Add("-------")
    lstOutput.Items.Add("Cost:  " & cost)
End Sub
```

23.
```
Private Sub btnDisplay_Click(...) Handles btnDisplay.Click
    'Determine the area of a rectangle.
    Dim length, width, area As Double
    InputSize(length, width)
    ComputeArea(length, width, area)
    ShowArea(area)
End Sub

Sub ComputeArea(ByVal length As Double, ByVal width As Double, _
                ByRef area As Double)
    'Calculate the area.
    area = length * width
End Sub

Sub InputSize(ByRef length As Double, ByRef width As Double)
    'Get the dimensions of the rectangle.
    length = CDbl(txtLength.Text)
    width = CDbl(txtWidth.Text)
End Sub

Sub ShowArea(ByVal area As Double)
    'Display the area of the rectangle.
    txtOutput.Text = "The area of the rectangle is " & area
End Sub
```

25. ```
Dim str As String   'Place in the Declarations section
```

27. ```
Private Sub btnDetermine_Click(...) Handles btnDetermine.Click
    'Get names, and display initials.
    Dim firstName As String = "", lastName As String = ""
    Dim firstInitial As String = "", lastInitial As String = ""
    InputNames(firstName, lastName)
    ExtractInitials(firstName, lastName, firstInitial, lastInitial)
    DisplayInitials(firstInitial, lastInitial)
End Sub

Sub InputNames(ByRef first As String, ByRef last As String)
    'Get the user's first and last name.
    first = InputBox("Enter your first name:")
    last = InputBox("Enter your last name:")
End Sub

Sub ExtractInitials(ByVal first As String, ByVal last As String, _
                    ByRef fInit As String, ByRef lInit As String)
    'Determine the initials of the first and last names.
    fInit = first.Substring(0, 1)
    lInit = last.Substring(0, 1)
End Sub

Sub DisplayInitials(ByVal fInit As String, _
                    ByVal lInit As String)
    'Display the initials.
    txtInitials.Text = fInit & "." & lInit & "."
End Sub
```

29. ```
Private Sub btnDetermine_Click(...) Handles btnDetermine.Click
    'Get input and display percentage markup.
    Dim cost, price, markup As Double
    InputAmounts(cost, price)
    ComputeMarkup(cost, price, markup)
    DisplayMarkup(markup)
End Sub

Sub InputAmounts(ByRef cost As Double, ByRef price As Double)
    cost = CDbl(InputBox("Enter the cost:"))
    price = CDbl(InputBox("Enter the selling price:"))
End Sub

Sub ComputeMarkup(ByVal cost As Double, ByVal price As Double, _
                  ByRef markup As Double)
    markup = (price - cost) / cost
End Sub

Sub DisplayMarkup(ByVal markup As Double)
    txtMarkup.Text = FormatPercent(markup)
End Sub
```

31. ```
Private Sub btnDetermine_Click(...) Handles btnDetermine.Click
    'Calculate batting average.
    Dim name As String = ""
    Dim atBats, hits As Integer
    Dim ave As Double
    ReadStats(name, atBats, hits)
    ComputeAverage(atBats, hits, ave)
    DisplayInfo(name, ave)
End Sub
```

```
     Sub ReadStats(ByRef name As String, ByRef atBats As Integer, _
                ByRef hits As Integer)
       Dim sr As IO.StreamReader = IO.File.OpenText("4-2-E31.TXT")
       name = sr.ReadLine
       atBats = CInt(sr.ReadLine)
       hits = CInt(sr.ReadLine)
       sr.Close()
     End Sub


     Sub ComputeAverage(ByVal atBats As Integer, _
                       ByVal hits As Integer, ByRef ave As Double)
       ave = hits / atBats
     End Sub

     Sub DisplayInfo(ByVal name As String, ByVal ave As Double)
       Dim fmtStr As String = "{0,-15}{1,-10:N3}"
       lstOutput.Items.Add(String.Format(fmtStr, "Name", _
                                         "Batting Average"))
       lstOutput.Items.Add(String.Format(fmtStr, name, ave))
     End Sub
```

33.
```
   Dim fmtStr As String = "{0,-14}{1,-10:C}{2,-10}{3,-10:C}"
   Dim sr As IO.StreamReader = IO.File.OpenText("MALLS.TXT")

   Private Sub btnDisplay_Click(...) Handles btnDisplay.Click
     'Display Hat Rack mall comparison table.
     lstOutput.Items.Clear()
     lstOutput.Items.Add(String.Format(fmtStr, "", "Rent per", "", ""))
     lstOutput.Items.Add(String.Format(fmtStr, "", "Square", "Total", _
                                       "Monthly"))
     lstOutput.Items.Add(String.Format(fmtStr, "Mall Name", "Foot", _
                                       "Feet", "Rent"))
     lstOutput.Items.Add("")
     DisplayInfo()
     DisplayInfo()
     DisplayInfo()
     sr.Close()
   End Sub

   Sub ComputeRent(ByVal rentPerSqFoot As Double, _
                ByVal squareFeet As Double, ByRef total As Double)
     'Compute monthly rent given rent/sq. foot and number of square feet.
     total = rentPerSqFoot * squareFeet
   End Sub

   Sub DisplayInfo()
     'Display the information for a single mall.
     Dim mall As String
     Dim rentPerSqFoot, squareFeet, rent As Double
     mall = sr.ReadLine
     rentPerSqFoot = CDbl(sr.ReadLine)
     squareFeet = CDbl(sr.ReadLine)
     ComputeRent(rentPerSqFoot, squareFeet, rent)
     lstOutput.Items.Add(String.Format(fmtStr, mall, rentPerSqFoot, _
                         squareFeet, rent))
   End Sub
```

35.
```
Dim total As Double    'In Declarations section of Code window

Private Sub btnProcessItem_Click(...) Handles btnProcessItem.Click
  'Process item; display part of sales receipt.
  Dim item As String = "", price As Double
  InputData(item, price)
  total = total + price
  ShowData(item, price)
  txtItem.Clear()
  txtPrice.Clear()
  txtItem.Focus()
End Sub

Private Sub btnDisplay_Click(...) Handles btnDisplay.Click
  'Display sum, tax, and total.
  Dim tax As Double
  tax = total * 0.05
  tax = Math.Round(tax, 2)
  lstReceipt.Items.Add("                  -------")
  ShowData("Sum", total)
  ShowData("Tax", tax)
  ShowData("Total", total + tax)
End Sub

Sub InputData(ByRef item As String, ByRef price As Double)
  'Input item name and price.
  item = txtItem.Text
  price = CDbl(txtPrice.Text)
End Sub

Sub ShowData(ByVal item As String, ByVal price As Double)
  'Display data on specified line.
  Dim fmtStr As String = "{0,-15}{1,8:C}"
  lstReceipt.Items.Add(String.Format(fmtStr, item, price))
End Sub
```

EXERCISES 4.3

1. 203

3. The population will double in 24 years.

5.
```
Volume of cylinder having base area 3.14159 and height 2 is 6.28318
Volume of cylinder having base area 28.27431 and height 4 is 113.09724
```

7. train

9.
```
moral has the negative amoral
political has the negative apolitical
```

11. The function header should end with "As String", not "As Integer".

13.
```
Dim total As Double    'In Declarations section of Code window

Private Sub btnDetermine_Click(...) Handles btnDetermine.Click
  'Tin Needed for a Tin Can
  Dim radius, height As Double
  lstOutput.Items.Clear()
  InputDims(radius, height)
  ShowAmount(radius, height)
End Sub
```

```
      Sub InputDims(ByRef radius As Double, ByRef height As Double)
        radius = CDbl(InputBox("Enter radius of can:"))
        height = CDbl(InputBox("Enter height of can:"))
      End Sub

      Sub ShowAmount(ByVal radius As Double, ByVal height As Double)
        lstOutput.Items.Add("A can of radius " & radius & " and height " & _
                          height)
        lstOutput.Items.Add("requires " & CanArea(radius, height) & _
                          " square centimeters to make.")
      End Sub

      Function CanArea(ByVal radius As Double, ByVal height As Double) _
                     As Double
        'Calculate surface area of a cylindrical can.
        Return 6.283 * (radius ^ 2 + radius * height)
      End Function
```

15.
```
   Private Sub btnCalculate_Click(...) Handles btnCalculate.Click
       txtBMI.Text = CStr(BMI(CDbl(txtWeight.Text), CDbl(txtHeight.Text)))
   End Sub

   Function BMI(ByVal w As Double, ByVal h As Double) As Double
       'Calculate body mass index.
       Return Math.Round((703 * w) / (h ^ 2))
   End Function
```

17.
```
   Private Sub btnDetermine_Click(...) Handles btnDetermine.Click
       'Popcorn profits
       Dim popcorn, butter, bucket, price As Double
       InputAmounts(popcorn, butter, bucket, price)
       ShowProfit(popcorn, butter, bucket, price)
   End Sub

   Sub InputAmounts(ByRef popcorn As Double, ByRef butter As Double, _
                   ByRef bucket As Double, ByRef price As Double)
       Dim phrase As String = "What is the cost (in dollars) of the "
       popcorn = CDbl(InputBox(phrase & "popcorn kernels?"))
       butter = CDbl(InputBox(phrase & "butter?"))
       bucket = CDbl(InputBox(phrase & "bucket?"))
       price = CDbl(InputBox("What is the sale price?"))
   End Sub

   Function Profit(ByVal popcorn As Double, ByVal butter As Double, _
                   ByVal bucket As Double, ByVal price As Double) As Double
       'Calculate the profit on a bucket of popcorn.
       Return price - (popcorn + butter + bucket)
   End Function

   Sub ShowProfit(ByVal popcorn As Double, ByVal butter As Double, _
                   ByVal bucket As Double, ByVal price As Double)
       txtProfit.Text = FormatCurrency(Profit(popcorn, butter, bucket, _
                          price))
   End Sub
```

19.
```
   Private Sub btnCompute_Click(...) Handles btnCompute.Click
       'Original Cost of Airmail
       Dim weight As Double
       InputWeight(weight)
       ShowCost(weight)
   End Sub
```

```
Function Ceil(ByVal x As Double) As Double
  Ceil = -Int(-x)
End Function

Function Cost(ByVal weight As Double) As Double
  'Calculate the cost of an airmail letter.
  Return 0.05 + 0.1 * Ceil(weight - 1)
End Function

Sub InputWeight(ByRef weight As Double)
  weight = CDbl(txtWeight.Text)
End Sub

Sub ShowCost(ByVal weight As Double)
  txtOutput.Text = "The cost of mailing the letter was " & _
                   FormatCurrency(Cost(weight)) & "."

End Sub
```

21.
```
Private Sub btnAddressNGreet_Click(...) Handles btnAddressNGreet.Click
  'Display a greeting for a senator.
  Dim name As String
  name = InputBox("Enter the senator's name:")
  lstOutput.Items.Clear()
  lstOutput.Items.Add("The Honorable " & name)
  lstOutput.Items.Add("United States Senate")
  lstOutput.Items.Add("Washington, DC 20001")
  lstOutput.Items.Add("")
  lstOutput.Items.Add("Dear Senator " & LastName(name) & ",")
End Sub

Function LastName(ByVal name As String) As String
  'Determine the last name of a two part name.
  Dim spaceNmb As Integer
  spaceNmb = name.IndexOf(" ")
  Return name.Substring(spaceNmb + 1)
End Function
```

CHAPTER 5

Exercises 5.1

1. `hi`

3. `The letter before G is F`

5. `"We're all in this alone." — Lily Tomlin`

7. True

9. True

11. True

13. True

15. False

17. False

19. True

21. True

23. False

25. False

27. False

29. True

31. Equivalent

33. Not Equivalent

35. Equivalent

37. Not Equivalent

39. Equivalent

41. `a <= b`

43. `(a >= b) Or (c = d)`

45. `(a = "") Or (a >= b) Or (a.Length >= 5)`

47. True

49. False

EXERCISES 5.2

1. `Less than ten.`

3. `tomorrow is another day.`

5. `10`

7. `Cost of call: $11.26`

9. `The number of vowels is 2`

11. `positive`

13. Incorrect condition. Should be `If ((1 < num) And (num < 3)) Then`

15. No `Then` in second line

17. Comparing numeric and string values in line 5

19. Incorrect condition. Should be `If ((j = 4) Or (k = 4)) Then`

21. `a = 5`

23.
```
If j = 7 Then
    b = 1
  Else
    b = 2
  End If
```

25.
```
message = "Is Alaska bigger than Texas and California combined?"
answer = InputBox(message)
If (answer.Substring(0, 1) = "Y") Then
  txtOutput.Text ="Correct"
Else
  txtOutput.Text ="Wrong"
End If
```

27.
```
Private Sub btnCompute_Click(...) Handles btnCompute.Click
    'Give server a tip.
    Dim cost, tip As Double
    cost = CDbl(InputBox("Enter cost of meal:"))
    tip = cost * 0.15
    If tip < 1 Then
      tip = 1
    End If
    txtOutput.Text = "Leave " & FormatCurrency(tip) & " for the tip."
  End Sub
```

29.
```
Private Sub btnCompute_Click(...) Handles btnCompute.Click
    'Order diskettes.
    Dim num, cost As Double
    num = CDbl(InputBox("Number of diskettes:"))
    If num < 100 Then
      cost = 0.25 * num    '25 cents each
    Else
      cost = 0.2 * num     '20 cents each
    End If
    txtOutput.Text = "The cost is " & FormatCurrency(cost) & "."
  End Sub
```

31.
```
Private Sub btnAskQuestion_Click(...) Handles btnAskQuestion.Click
    'Ask for first Ronald McDonald.
    Dim name As String
    name = (InputBox("Who was the first Ronald McDonald?")).ToUpper
    If name = "WILLARD SCOTT" Then
      txtOutput.Text = "Correct."
    Else
      txtOutput.Text = "Nice try."
    End If
  End Sub
```

33.
```
Private Sub btnCompute_Click(...) Handles btnCompute.Click
    'Savings account withdrawal
    Dim balance, amountOfWithdrawal As Double
    balance = CDbl(InputBox("Current balance:"))
    amountOfWithdrawal = CDbl(InputBox("Amount of withdrawal:"))
    If (balance >= amountOfWithdrawal) Then
      balance = balance - amountOfWithdrawal
      txtOutput.Text = "New balance is " & FormatCurrency(balance) & "."
      If balance < 150 Then
        MsgBox("Balance below $150", 0, "Warning")
      End If
    Else
      txtOutput.Text = "Withdrawal denied."
    End If
  End Sub
```

```
35. Private Sub btnCompute_Click(...) Handles btnCompute.Click
      'Display change from a transaction.
      Dim weight, cost, amount, change As Double
      weight = CDbl(txtWeight.Text)
      amount = CDbl(txtAmount.Text)
      cost = weight * 0.79
      If (amount >= cost) Then
        change = amount - cost
        txtOutput.Text = "Your change is " & FormatCurrency(change) & "."
      Else
        txtOutput.Text = "I need " & FormatCurrency(cost - amount) & _
                         " more."
      End If
    End Sub

37. Private Sub btnCompute_Click(...) Handles btnTranslate.Click
      'Convert to Pig Latin.
      Dim word, first As String
      word = InputBox("Enter a word (use all lowercase):")
      first = word.Substring(0, 1)
      If "aeiou".IndexOf(first) <> -1 Then
        word &= "way"
      Else
        word = word.Substring(1) & first & "ay"
      End If
      txtOutput.Text = "The word in pig latin is " & word & "."
    End Sub

39. Dim numLines As Integer = 0   'In Declarations section
    'numLines tells the number of lines displayed.

    Private Sub btnBogart_Click(...) Handles btnBogart.Click
      If numLines = 0 Then
        lstOutput.Items.Add("I came to Casablanca for the waters.")
        numLines += 1
      ElseIf numLines = 2 Then
        lstOutput.Items.Add("I was misinformed.")
        numLines += 1
      End If
    End Sub

    Private Sub btnRaines_Click(...) Handles btnRaines.Click
      If numLines = 1 Then
        lstOutput.Items.Add("But we're in the middle of the desert.")
        numLines += 1
      End If
    End Sub

41. Private Sub btnEvaluate_Click(...) Handles btnEvaluate.Click
      'Assume that the Text property of txtNumberOfGuesses
      'was set to 0 in the Form Designer
      Dim msg As String
      txtNumberOfGuesses.Text = CStr(CInt(txtNumberOfGuesses.Text) + 1)
      If txtAnswer.Text.ToUpper.IndexOf("COOLIDGE") <> -1 Then
        MsgBox("Calvin Coolidge was born on July 4, 1872.", 0, "Correct")
      End
      ElseIf CInt(txtNumberOfGuesses.Text) = 3 Then
        msg = "He once said, 'If you don't say anything," & _
              " you won't be called upon to repeat it.'"
```

```
      MsgBox(msg, 0, "Hint")
   ElseIf CInt(txtNumberOfGuesses.Text) = 7 Then
      MsgBox("His nickname was 'Silent Cal.'", 0, "Hint")
   ElseIf CInt(txtNumberOfGuesses.Text) = 10 Then
      msg = "Calvin Coolidge was born on July 4, 1872."
      MsgBox(msg, 0, "You've run out of guesses")
      End
   End If
   txtAnswer.Clear()
   txtAnswer.Focus()
End Sub
```

43.
```
Private Sub btnCalculateTax_Click(...) Handles btnCalculateTax.Click
   'Calculate New Jersey state income tax.
   Dim income, tax As Double
   income = CDbl(InputBox("Taxable income:"))
   If income <= 20000 Then
      tax = 0.02 * income
   Else
      If income <= 50000 Then
         tax = 400 + 0.025 * (income - 20000)
      Else
         tax = 1150 + 0.035 * (income - 50000)
      End If
   End If
   txtOutput.Text = "Tax is " & FormatCurrency(tax)
End Sub
```

EXERCISES 5.3

1. `The price is $3.75`
   `The price is $3.75`

3. `Mesozoic Era`
   `Paleozoic Era`
   `?`

5. `Nope.`
   `He worked with the developer, von Neumann, on the ENIAC.`
   `Correct.`

7. `The more things change, the less they remain the same.`
   `Less is more.`
   `Time keeps everything from happening at once.`

9. Should have a Case clause before the 4th line

11. `Case a = "Bob"` should be `Case "Bob"`

13. Error in second Case clause

15. Logical error: `>= "Peach"` should be `>= "PEACH"`.

    Syntax error: `"ORANGE TO PEACH"` should be `"ORANGE" To "PEACH"`.

17. Valid

19. Invalid

21. Valid

23.
```
Select Case a
  Case 1
    txtOutput.Text = "one"
  Case Is > 5
    txtOutput.Text = "two"
End Select
```

25.
```
Select Case a
  Case 2
    txtOutput.Text = "yes"
  Case Is < 5
    txtOutput.Text = "no"
End Select
```

27.
```
Private Sub btnDescribe_Click(...) Handles btnDescribe.Click
    'Determine degree of cloudiness.
    Dim percent As Double
    percent = CDbl(InputBox("Percentage of cloud cover:"))
    Select Case percent
      Case 0 To 30
        txtOutput.Text = "Clear"
      Case 31 To 70
        txtOutput.Text = "Partly cloudy"
      Case 71 To 99
        txtOutput.Text = "Cloudy"
      Case 100
        txtOutput.Text = "Overcast"
      Case Else
        txtOutput.Text = "Percentage must be between 0 and 100."
    End Select
End Sub
```

29.
```
Private Sub btnFindNumDays_Click(...) Handles btnFindNumDays.Click
    Dim monthName As String
    monthName = InputBox("Enter a month (do not abbreviate):")
    txtOutput.Text = monthName & " has " & GetDays(monthName) & " days."
End Sub

Function GetDays(ByVal monthName As String) As Integer
    'Compute number of days in the month.
    Dim answer As String, numberOfDays As Integer
    Select Case monthName.ToUpper
      Case "FEBRUARY"
        answer = InputBox("Is it a leap year?")
        If answer.ToUpper.Substring(0, 1) = "Y" Then
          numberOfDays = 29
        Else
          numberOfDays = 28
        End If
      Case "APRIL", "JUNE", "SEPTEMBER", "NOVEMBER"
        numberOfDays = 30
      Case "JANUARY", "MARCH", "MAY", "JULY", "AUGUST", _
          "OCTOBER", "DECEMBER"
        numberOfDays = 31
    End Select
    Return numberOfDays
End Function
```

31.
```
Private Sub btnAssign_Click(...) Handles btnAssign.Click
    'Give letter grade for number score.
    Dim score As Integer
    score = CInt(InputBox("What is the score?"))
    txtOutput.Text = "The letter grade is " & Grade(score) & "."
End Sub

Function Grade(ByVal score As Integer) As String
    'Return letter grade for score.
    Dim letterGrade As String
    Select Case score
      Case 90 To 100
        letterGrade = "A"
      Case 80 To 89
        letterGrade = "B"
      Case 70 To 79
        letterGrade = "C"
      Case 60 To 69
        letterGrade = "D"
      Case 0 To 59
        letterGrade = "F"
      Case Else
        letterGrade = "Invalid"
    End Select
    Return letterGrade
End Function
```

33.
```
Private Sub btnDescribe_Click(...) Handles btnDetermine.Click
    'Determine cash reward.
    Dim amountRecovered As Double
    amountRecovered = CDbl(InputBox("How much was recovered?"))
    txtOutput.Text = "The amount given as reward is " & _
                     FormatCurrency(Reward(amountRecovered)) & "."
End Sub

Function Reward(ByVal amountRecovered As Double) As Double
    Dim payment As Double
    Select Case amountRecovered
      Case Is <= 75000
        payment = 0.1 * amountRecovered
      Case Is <= 100000
        payment = 7500 + 0.05 * (amountRecovered - 75000)
      Case Is > 100000
        payment = 8750 + 0.01 * (amountRecovered - 100000)
        If payment > 50000 Then
          payment = 50000
        End If
    End Select
    Return payment
End Function
```

35.
```
Private Sub btnDisplay_Click(...) Handles btnDisplay.Click
    Dim pres, state, trivia, whichBush As String
    pres = txtLastName.Text
    Select Case pres.ToUpper
      Case "CARTER"
        state = "Georgia"
```

```
            trivia = "The only soft drink served in the Carter " & _
                     "White House was Coca-Cola."
          Case "REAGAN"
            state = "California"
            trivia = "His secret service code name was Rawhide."
          Case "BUSH"
            state = "Texas"
            whichBush = InputBox("Are his middle initials HW or W?")
            Select Case whichBush
              Case "HW"
                trivia = "He was the third left-handed president."
              Case "W"
                trivia = "He once owned the Texas Rangers baseball team."
            End Select
            state = "Texas"
          Case "CLINTON"
            state = "Arkansas"
            trivia = "In college he did a good imitation of Elvis Presley."
          Case Else
            state = ""
            trivia = ""
        End Select
        If state <> "" Then
          lstOutput.Items.Clear()
          lstOutput.Items.Add("President " & pres & "'s " & _
                           " home state was " & state & ".")
          lstOutput.Items.Add(trivia)
        End If
        txtLastName.Clear()
        txtLastName.Focus()
      End Sub
```

37.
```
    Private Sub btnHumor_Click(...) Handles btnHumor.Click
        If (CInt(mtxtNumber.Text) >= 1) And (CInt(mtxtNumber.Text) <= 3) Then
          txtOutput.Text = HumorMsg(CInt(mtxtNumber.Text))
        End If
        txtNumber.Clear()
        txtNumber.Focus()
      End Sub

    Private Sub btnInsult_Click(...) Handles btnInsult.Click
        If (CInt(mtxtNumber.Text) >= 1) And (CInt(mtxtNumber.Text) <= 3) Then
          txtOutput.Text = InsultMsg(CInt(mtxtNumber.Text))
        End If
        txtNumber.Clear()
        txtNumber.Focus()
      End Sub

    Function HumorMsg(ByVal num As Integer) As String
        Dim sentence As String
        Select Case num
          Case 1
            sentence = "I can resist everything except temptation."
          Case 2
            sentence = "I just heard from Bill Bailey." & _
                       " He's not coming home."
```

```
    Case 3
      sentence = "I have enough money to last the rest of my life," _
                  & " unless I buy something."
  End Select
  Return sentence
End Function

Function InsultMsg(ByVal num As Integer) As String
  Dim sentence As String
  Select Case num
    Case 1
      sentence = "How much would you charge to haunt a house?"
    Case 2
      sentence = "I bet you have no more friends than an alarm clock."
    Case 3
      sentence = "When your IQ rises to 30, sell."
  End Select
  Return sentence
End Function
```

CHAPTER 6

EXERCISES 6.1

1. `17`

3. `You are a super programmer!`

5. `2`

7. The value of *q* keeps growing until the program crashes when the value reaches the upper limit for a variable of type Double.

9. Do and Loop interchanged

11. `While num >= 7`

13. `Until response <> "Y"`

15. `Until name = ""`

17. `Until (a <= 1) Or (a >= 3)`

19. `While n = 0`

21.
```
Private Sub btnDisplay_Click(...) Handles btnDisplay.Click
    'Request and display three names.
    Dim name As String, num As Integer = 0
    Do While num < 3
      name = InputBox("Enter a name:")
      lstOutput.Items.Add(name)
      num += 1     'Add 1 to value of num.
    Loop
  End Sub
```

23.
```
Private Sub btnDisplay_Click(...) Handles btnDisplay.Click
    'Convert Celsius to Fahrenheit.
    Dim fmtStr As String = "{0,7}  {1,10}"
```

```
    Dim celsius As Double = -40
    lstOutput.Items.Add(String.Format(fmtStr, "Celsius", "Fahrenheit"))
    Do While celsius <= 40
      lstOutput.Items.Add(String.Format(fmtStr, celsius, _
                          Fahrenheit(celsius)))
      celsius += 5
  Loop
End Sub

Function Fahrenheit(ByVal celsius As Double) As Double
  'Convert Celsius to Fahrenheit.
  Return (9 / 5) * celsius + 32
End Function
```

25.
```
Private Sub btnDetermine_Click(...) Handles btnDetermine.Click
  'Determine the year that the world population will exceed
  '10 billion, assuming a 1.2% rate of increase.
  Dim yr As Integer, pop As Double
  yr = 2006          'Start at 2006.
  pop = 6.5          'Population of 6.5 billion
  Do While pop <= 10
    pop = (1 + 0.012) * pop
    yr += 1
  Loop
  txtOutput.Text = "The world population will reach 10 billion in " _
                  & yr & "."
End Sub
```

27.
```
Private Sub btnDetermine_Click (. . .) Handles btnDetermine.Click
  'Display first terms in the Fibonacci sequence
  Dim x As Integer = 1
  Dim y As Integer = 1
  Dim z As Integer = x + y
  lstOutput.Items.Clear()
  lstOutput.Items.Add(x)
  lstOutput.Items.Add(y)
  Do While z <= 100
    lstOutput.Items.Add(z)
    x = y
    y = z
    z = x + y
  Loop
End Sub
```

29.
```
Private Sub btnDetermine_Click(...) Handles btnDetermine.Click
  'When after 6:30, do clock hands exactly overlap?
  Dim minuteHandPos, hourHandPos, difference As Double
  minuteHandPos = 0
  hourHandPos = 30
  Do While hourHandPos - minuteHandPos >= 0.0001
    difference = hourHandPos - minuteHandPos
    minuteHandPos = minuteHandPos + difference
    hourHandPos += difference / 12
  Loop
  txtOutput.Text = "The hands overlap at " & _
                  FormatNumber(minuteHandPos, 2) & " minutes after six."
End Sub
```

31.
```
Private Sub btnBounceBall_Click(...) Handles btnBounceBall.Click
    'Drop a ball, and find number of bounces and total distance traveled.
    Dim height, bounceFactor, distance As Double
    Dim bounces As Integer
    InputData(height, bounceFactor)
    BounceBall(height, bounceFactor, bounces, distance)
    ShowData(bounces, distance)
End Sub

Sub InputData(ByRef height As Double, _
              ByRef bounceFactor As Double)
    'Input height and coefficient of restitution.
    Dim prompt As String
    prompt = "What is the coefficient of restitution of the " & _
             "ball (0 to 1)? Examples are .7 for a tennis ball, " & _
             ".75 for a basketball, .9 for a super ball, and " & _
             ".3 for a softball."
    bounceFactor = CDbl(InputBox(prompt))
    prompt = "From how many meters will the ball be dropped?"
    height = CDbl(InputBox(prompt))
    height = 100 * height    'Convert to centimeters.
End Sub

Sub BounceBall(ByVal hght As Double, ByVal bFactor As Double, _
               ByRef bounces As Integer, ByRef dist As Double)
    bounces = 1              'First bounce
    dist = hght
    Do While hght * bFactor >= 10
        bounces += 1
        hght = bFactor * hght
        dist += 2 * hght     'Up then down again
    Loop
End Sub

Sub ShowData(ByVal bounces As Integer, _
             ByVal distance As Double)
    txtOutput.Text = "The ball bounced " & bounces _
                     & " times and traveled about " & _
                     FormatNumber(distance / 100) & " meters."
End Sub
```

33.
```
Private Sub btnCompute_Click(...) Handles btnCompute.Click
    'Calculate number of years to deplete savings account.
    Dim amt As Double, yrs As Integer
    amt = CDbl(InputBox("Enter initial amount in account:"))
    yrs = 0
    If amt * 1.05 - 1000 >= amt Then
        txtOutput.Text = "Account will never be depleted."
    Else
        Do
            amt = amt * 1.05 - 1000
            yrs += 1
        Loop Until amt <= 0
        txtOutput.Text = "It takes " & yrs & _
                         " years to deplete the account."
    End If
End Sub
```

```
35. Private Sub btnCompute_Click(...) Handles btnCompute.Click
      'Compute age when year is the square of age.
      Dim age As Integer = 1
      Do While (1980 + age) <> (age * age)
        age += 1
      Loop
      txtOutput.Text = age & " years old"
    End Sub

37. Private Sub btnCapitalizeAll_Click(...) Handles btnCapitalizeAll.Click
      txtOutput.Text = txtSentence.Text.ToUpper
    End Sub

    Private Sub btnCapitalizeFirstLetters_Click(...) Handles _
              btnCapitalizeFirstLetters.Click
      'Capitalize first letter of each word.
      Dim info As String = txtSentence.Text.Trim
      Dim word As String
      Dim newSentence As String = ""
      Dim positionOfSpace As Integer = info.indexOf(" ")
      info = txtSentence.Text.Trim
      Do While info <> ""
        positionOfSpace = info.IndexOf(" ")
        If positionOfSpace <> -1 Then
          word = info.Substring(0, positionOfSpace + 1)
          info = info.Substring(positionOfSpace + 1)
          newSentence &= word.Substring(0, 1).ToUpper & word.Substring(1)
        Else
          newSentence &= info.Substring(0, 1).ToUpper & info.Substring(1)
          info = ""
        End If
      Loop
      txtOutput.Text = newSentence
    End Sub

39. Private Sub btnFind_Click(...) Handles btnFind.Click
      'Compute the greatest common divisor of two numbers.
      Dim m, n, t As Integer
      InputIntegers(m, n)
      Do While n <> 0
        t = n
        n = m Mod n        'Remainder after m is divided by n.
        m = t
      Loop
      txtOutput.Text = "The greatest common divisor is " & m & "."
    End Sub

    Sub InputIntegers(ByRef m As Integer, ByRef n As Integer)
      'Input two integers.
      m = CInt(InputBox("Enter first integer:", "GCD"))
      n = CInt(InputBox("Enter second integer:", "GCD"))
    End Sub
```

EXERCISES 6.2

1. `At least one word contains the letter A.`

3. `pie`
   `cake`
   `melon`

5.   `A`
   `Apple`
   `Apricot`
   `Avocado`

       `B`
   `Banana`
   `Blueberry`

       `G`
   `Grape`

       `L`
   `Lemon`
   `Lime`

7. `A brace of ducks.`

9. `counters`

11. Loop statement missing. Also, loop cannot be entered because the (default) value of *num* is 0.

13. Last president in file will not be displayed.

15.
```
Private Sub btnFind_Click(...) Handles btnFind.Click
    'Find largest of a collection of numbers.
    Dim largest, num As Double
    largest = 0
    Dim sr As IO.StreamReader = IO.File.OpenText("POSNUMS.TXT")
    Do While sr.Peek <> -1
      num = CDbl(sr.ReadLine)
      If num > largest Then
        largest = num
      End If
    Loop
    txtOutput.Text = "The largest number is " & largest & "."
    sr.Close()
End Sub
```

17.
```
Private Sub btnDisplay_Click(...) Handles btnDisplay.Click
    'Display percentage of grades that are above average.
    Dim total, grade, average As Double
    Dim numGrades, aaCount As Integer
    Dim sr As IO.StreamReader = IO.File.OpenText("FINAL.TXT")
    total = 0
    numGrades = 0
    Do While sr.Peek <> -1
      grade = CDbl(sr.ReadLine)
      total += grade
      numGrades += 1
    Loop
    sr.Close()
```

```
    If numGrades > 0 Then
      average = total / numGrades
      aaCount = 0
      sr = IO.File.OpenText("FINAL.TXT")
      Do While sr.Peek <> -1
        grade = CDbl(sr.ReadLine)
        If grade > average Then
          aaCount += 1
        End If
      Loop
      sr.Close()
      txtOutput.Text = FormatPercent(aaCount / numGrades) & _
                      " of grades are above the average of " & _
                      FormatNumber(average) & "."
    End If
  End Sub
```

19.
```
Private Sub btnDisplay_Click(...) Handles btnDisplay.Click
    'Display the name of the requested president.
    Dim n, num As Integer
    Dim name As String
    Dim sr As IO.StreamReader = IO.File.OpenText("USPRES.TXT")
    n = CInt(txtPresNum.Text)
    If (1 <= n) And (n <= 43) Then
      num = 0
      Do
        name = sr.ReadLine
        num += 1
      Loop Until num = n
      lstOutput.Items.Add(name & " was President number " & n & ".")
      sr.Close()
    End If
    txtPresNum.Clear()
    txtPresNum.Focus()
  End Sub
```

21.
```
Private Sub btnCompute_Click(...) Handles btnCompute.Click
    'Generate sequence with algorithm
    Dim n, numSteps As Double
    lstOutput.Items.Clear()
    n = CDbl(txtInitialNumber.Text)
    numSteps = 0
    Do While n <> 1
      numSteps += 1
      If (n / 2) = Int(n / 2) Then
        n = n / 2
        lstOutput.Items.Add(n)
      Else
        n = (3 * n) + 1
        lstOutput.Items.Add(n)
      End If
    Loop
    txtOutput.Text = "It took " & numSteps & " steps to reach 1."
  End Sub
```

23.
```
Private Sub btnFind_Click(...) Handles btnFind.Click
    'Analyze a Shakespearean sonnet.
    Dim totalWords, lineCount As Double
```

```
    Dim wordCount, positionOfSpace As Integer
    Dim sonnetLine, word As String
    Dim sr As IO.StreamReader = IO.File.OpenText("SONNET.TXT")
    totalWords = 0
    lineCount = 0
    Do While sr.Peek <> -1
      sonnetLine = sr.ReadLine
      lineCount += 1
      wordCount = 0
      Do While sonnetLine <> ""
        positionOfSpace = sonnetLine.IndexOf(" ")
        If positionOfSpace <> -1 Then
          word = sonnetLine.Substring(0, positionOfSpace + 1)
          sonnetLine = sonnetLine.Substring(positionOfSpace + 1)
        Else
          sonnetLine = ""
        End If
        wordCount += 1
      Loop
      totalWords += wordCount
    Loop
    sr.Close()
    txtOutput.Text = "The sonnet contains an average of " & _
                    FormatNumber(totalWords / lineCount) & _
                    " words per line and a total of " _
                    & totalWords & " words."
  End Sub

25. Private Sub btnRemoveParens_Click(...) Handles btnRemoveParens.Click
    'Remove parentheses and their contents from a sentence.
    Dim sentence, letter, newSentence As String
    Dim parensFlag As Boolean, position As Integer
    sentence = txtSentence.Text
    newSentence = ""
    parensFlag = False
    position = 0
    Do Until position > sentence.Length - 1
      letter = sentence.Substring(position, 1)
      Select Case letter
        Case "("
          parensFlag = True
        Case ")"
          parensFlag = False
          position = position + 1
        Case Else
          If parensFlag = False Then
            newSentence &= letter
          End If
      End Select
      position += 1
    Loop
    txtOutput.Text = newSentence
  End Sub

27. Private Sub btnDisplay_Click(...) Handles btnDisplay.Click
    'Display liquids available, given an amount of money.
    Dim money, price As Double
```

```
      Dim liquid, top As String
      lstOutput.Items.Clear()
      money = CDbl(txtAmount.Text)
      top = "You can purchase one gallon of any of the following liquids:"
      lstOutput.Items.Add(top)
      Dim sr As IO.StreamReader = IO.File.OpenText("LIQUIDS.TXT")
      Do While sr.Peek <> -1
        liquid = sr.ReadLine
        price = CDbl(sr.ReadLine)
        If price <= money Then
          lstOutput.Items.Add(liquid)
        End If
      Loop
      sr.Close()
    End Sub
```

EXERCISES 6.3

1. ```
Pass #1
Pass #2
Pass #3
Pass #4
```

3. ```
2
4
6
8
Who do we appreciate?
```

5. ```
5
6
7
```

7. ```
Steve Cram    3:46.31
Steve Scott   3:51.6
Mary Slaney   4:20.5
```

9. ```
1   4   7   10
2   5   8   11
3   6   9   12
```

11. `*******Hooray*******`

13. Loop is never executed since 1 is less than 25.5, and the step is negative.

15. For...Next loop will not execute since 20 is greater than 0. You must add **Step -1** to end of For statement.

17. ```
Private Sub btnDisplay_Click(...) Handles btnDisplay.Click
  For num As Integer = 1 To 9 Step 2
    lstBox.Items.Add(num)
  Next
End Sub
```

19. ```
Private Sub btnDisplay_Click(...) Handles btnDisplay.Click
  Dim row As String = ""
  For i As Integer = 1 To 9
    row &= "*"
  Next
  txtOutput.Text = row
End Sub
```
```

21.
```
Private Sub btnDisplay_Click(...) Handles btnDisplay.Click
  'Display 10 x 10 array of stars.
  Dim row As String
  For i As Integer = 1 To 10
    row = ""
    For j As Integer = 1 To 10
      row &= "*"
    Next
    lstOutput.Items.Add(row)
  Next
End Sub
```

23.
```
Private Sub btnCompute_Click(...) Handles btnCompute.Click
  'Compute the sum 1 + 1/2 + 1/3 + 1/4 + ... + 1/100.
  Dim sum As Double
  sum = 0
  For denominator As Double = 1 To 100
    sum += 1 / denominator
  Next
  txtOutput.Text = "The sum is " & FormatNumber(sum, 5) & "."
End Sub
```

25.
```
Private Sub btnAnalyzeOptions_Click(...) Handles _
            btnAnalyzeOptions.Click
  'Compare salaries.
  Dim opt1, opt2 As Double
  opt1 = Option1()
  opt2 = Option2()
  lstOutput.Items.Add("Option 1 = " & FormatCurrency(opt1))
  lstOutput.Items.Add("Option 2 = " & FormatCurrency(opt2))
  If opt1 > opt2 Then
    lstOutput.Items.Add("Option 1 pays better.")
  Else
    lstOutput.Items.Add("Option 2 pays better.")
  End If
End Sub

Function Option1() As Double
  'Compute total salary for 10 days,
  'with a flat salary of $100/day.
  Dim sum As Integer
  sum = 0
  For i As Integer = 1 To 10
    sum += 100
  Next
  Return sum
End Function

Function Option2() As Double
  'Compute the total salary for 10 days,
  'starting at $1 and doubling each day.
  Dim sum, daySalary As Integer
  sum = 0
  daySalary = 1
  For i As Integer = 1 To 10
    sum += daySalary
    daySalary = 2 * daySalary
  Next
```

```vb
      Return sum
   End Function
```

27.
```vb
   Private Sub btnComputeIdealWeights_Click(...) Handles _
               btnComputeIdealWeights.Click
      'Ideal weights for men and women
      Dim lower, upper As Integer
      lstWeightTable.Items.Clear()
      InputBounds(lower, upper)
      ShowWeights(lower, upper)
   End Sub

   Function IdealMan(ByVal height As Integer) As Double
      'Compute the ideal weight of a man given the height.
      Return 4 * height - 128
   End Function

   Function IdealWoman(ByVal height As Integer) As Double
      'Compute the ideal weight of a woman given the height.
      Return 3.5 * height - 108
   End Function

   Sub InputBounds(ByRef lower As Integer, ByRef upper As Integer)
      'Input the lower and upper bounds on height.
      lower = CInt(InputBox("Enter lower bound on height in inches:"))
      upper = CInt(InputBox("Enter upper bound on height in inches:"))
   End Sub

   Sub ShowWeights(ByVal lower As Integer, ByVal upper As Integer)
      'Display table of weights.
      Dim fmtStr As String = "{0,-11}{1,-13}{2,-11}"
      lstWeightTable.Items.Add(String.Format(fmtStr, "Height", _
                       "Wt-Women", "Wt-Men"))
      lstWeightTable.Items.Add("")
      For height As Integer = lower To upper
        lstWeightTable.Items.Add(String.Format(fmtStr, height, _
                         IdealWoman(height), IdealMan(height)))
      Next
   End Sub
```

29.
```vb
   Private Sub btnAnalyze_Click(...) Handles btnAnalyze.Click
      'Determine number of sibilants in sentence.
      txtOutput.Text = "There are " & Sibilants(txtSentence.Text) & _
                    " sibilants in the sentence."
   End Sub

   Function Sibilants(ByVal sentence As String) As Integer
      'Count the number of sibilants (i.e., the letters S and Z).
      Dim numSibs As Integer
      Dim letter As String
      numSibs = 0
      For i As Integer = 0 To sentence.Length - 1
        letter = sentence.Substring(i, 1).ToUpper
        If (letter = "S") Or (letter = "Z") Then
          numSibs += 1
        End If
      Next
      Return numSibs
   End Function
```

31.
```vb
Private Sub btnCalculate_Click(...) Handles btnCalculate.Click
    'Savings account balance after 10 years
    Dim amt As Double = 800
    For yearNum As Integer = 1 To 10
      amt = (1.04 * amt) + 100 '(Growth due to interest) + deposit
    Next
    txtOutput.Text = "The final amount is " & FormatCurrency(amt) & "."
End Sub
```

33.
```vb
Private Sub btnAnalyze_Click(...) Handles btnAnalyze.Click
    'Radioactive decay; cobalt-60 decays at a rate of about 12% per year
    Dim grams As Double = 10
    For yearNum As Integer = 1 To 5
      grams = 0.88 * grams
    Next
    lstOutput.Items.Add("Of 10 grams of cobalt-60,")
    lstOutput.Items.Add(FormatNumber(grams) & _
                        " grams remain after 5 years.")

End Sub
```

35.
```vb
Private Sub btnDisplay_Click(...) Handles btnDisplay.Click
    'Draw a hollow box.
    Dim stars As Integer
    lstOutput.Items.Clear()
    stars = CInt(InputBox("Number of stars?"))
    DrawSide(stars)
    For i As Integer = 1 To stars - 2
      DrawRow(stars)
    Next
    DrawSide(stars)
End Sub

Sub DrawSide(ByVal stars As Integer)
  'Draw a solid side of stars for top and bottom.
  Dim row As String = ""
  For i As Integer = 1 To stars
    row &= "*"
  Next
  lstOutput.Items.Add(row)
End Sub

Sub DrawRow(ByVal stars As Integer)
  'Draw a row (put spaces between the two stars).
  Dim row As String = "*"
  For i As Integer = 1 To stars - 2
    row &= " "
  Next
  row &= "*"
  lstOutput.Items.Add(row)
End Sub
```

37.
```vb
Private Sub btnDetermine_Click(...) Handles btnDetermine.Click
    'Gambling casino problem
    Dim testValue, amount As Double
    testValue = 4
    Do
      testValue += 1     'Start test with $5.
      amount = testValue
```

```
            For i As Integer = 1 To 3        'One iteration for each casino
               amount = amount - 1      'Entrance fee
               amount = amount / 2      'Funds lost
               amount = amount - 1      'Exit fee
            Next
         Loop Until amount = 0
         txtOutput.Text = "Beginning amount = " & FormatCurrency(testValue)
      End Sub
```

39.
```
   Private Sub btnCompute_Click(...) Handles btnCompute.Click
      'Compute total earnings at retirement
      'get 5% raise per year, retire at age 65
      Dim name As String, age As Integer, salary As Double
      Dim earnings As Double = 0
      name = InputBox("Enter the person's name: ")
      age = CInt(InputBox("Enter the person's age: "))
      salary = CDbl(InputBox("Enter the person's starting salary: "))
      For i As Integer = age To 64
        earnings += salary
        salary = (1.05) * salary
      Next
      txtOutput.Text = name & " will earn about " & _
                    FormatCurrency(earnings, 0)
   End Sub
```

CHAPTER 7

EXERCISES 7.1

1. 101

3. `Have a dessert spoon.`

5. `9`
`4`

7. `11`

9. `A rook is worth more than a bishop`

11. `Your total is 280.`

13. The ReDim statement should not end with an "As String" clause.

15. When $k > 5$, the array subscript will be a negative number.

17. The number 2 in the second statement should be deleted.

19.

river(0)	river(1)	river(2)	river(3)	river(4)
Thames	Ohio	Amazon	Volga	Nile

river(0)	river(1)	river(2)	river(3)	river(4)
Ohio	Amazon	Volga	Nile	Thames

21. (a) 2 (b) 7 (c) 10 (d) 9

23. Replace the *btnDisplay_Click* event with the following:

```
Private Sub btnDisplay_Click(...) Handles btnDisplay.Click
  'Display the numbers of the games won by the team in the text box.
  Dim foundFlag As Boolean = False
  lstGamesWon.Items.Clear()
  For i As Integer = 0 To upperBound
    If teamName(i) = txtName.Text Then
      lstGamesWon.Items.Add(i + 1)
      foundFlag = True
    End If
  Next
  If Not foundFlag Then
    lstGamesWon.Items.Add("Never won a Super Bowl.")
  End If
End Sub
```

25. ReDim quantities(100)

27.
```
Dim marx(3) As String   'In Declarations section of Code window
Private Sub frmMarx_Load(...) Handles MyBase.Load
  marx(0) = "Chico"
  marx(1) = "Harpo"
  marx(2) = "Groucho"
  marx(3) = "Zeppo"
End Sub
```

29.
```
'Store in b() the reverse of the values in a().
For i As Integer = 0 To 4
  b(i) = a(4 - i)
Next
```

31.
```
'Display the elements of the array a() in columns.
Dim fmtStr As String = "{0,15}{1,15}{2,15}{3,15}{4,15}"
For i As Integer = 0 To 25 Step 5
  lstOutput.Items.Add(String.Format(fmtStr, a(i), a(i + 1), _
                                    a(i + 2), a(i + 3), a(i + 4)))
Next
```

33.
```
'Compare arrays a() and b() for same values.
Dim differFlag As Boolean = False
For i As Integer = 0 To 9
  If a(i) <> b(i) Then
    differFlag = True
  End If
Next
If differFlag Then
  txtOutput.Text = "The arrays are not identical."
Else
  txtOutput.Text = "The arrays have identical values."
End If
```

35.
```
'Curve grades by adding 7.
For i As Integer = 0 To 11
  grades(i) += 7
Next
```

37.
```
Private Sub btnScores_Click(...) Handles btnScores.Click
  'Read data from a file, and display their frequencies.
  Dim frequency(4) As Integer     'Stores the results
  Dim num As Integer
  Dim fmtStr As String = "{0,-12} {1,-9:N0}"
  'Open the data file for input.
  Dim sr As IO.StreamReader = IO.File.OpenText("SCORES.TXT")
  'Loop over the 30 lines in the file.
  For i As Integer = 1 To 30
    num = CInt(sr.ReadLine)
    'Increment the frequency element that belongs to the number.
    'Divide by 10, and get the integer part.
    frequency(CInt(Int(num / 10))) += 1
  Next
  sr.Close()        'Always close the reader when finished with it.
  'Display the results.
  lstOutput.Items.Add(String.Format(fmtStr, "Interval", "Frequency"))
  For i As Integer = 0 To 4
    lstOutput.Items.Add(String.Format(fmtStr, _
        CStr(i * 10) & " to " & CStr((i + 1) * 10 - 1), _
        frequency(i)))
  Next
End Sub
```

39.
```
Dim pres(42) As String      'Holds the Presidents' names
Private Sub frmPres_Load(...) Handles MyBase.Load
  'Loads the data from the file into the array
  Dim sr As IO.StreamReader = IO.File.OpenText("USPRES.TXT")
  For i As Integer = 0 To 42
    pres(i) = sr.ReadLine
  Next
  sr.Close()
End Sub

Private Sub btnDisplayFullNames_Click(...) _
          Handles btnDisplayFullNames.Click
  'Display the presidents who have the requested first name.
  Dim space As Integer
  Dim firstName As String
  Dim foundFlag As Boolean = False
  lstFullNames.Items.Clear()
  'Loop over all presidents.
  For i As Integer = 0 To 42
    'The first name is the string before the first space.
    space = pres(i).IndexOf(" ")
    firstName = pres(i).Substring(0, space)
    'If the first name matches, then display the president.
    If firstName = txtFirstName.Text Then
      lstFullNames.Items.Add(pres(i))
      foundFlag = True
    End If
  Next
  'If not found, display message.
  If Not foundFlag Then
  lstFullNames.Items.Add("Name not found.")
  End If
End Sub
```

```
        Private Sub lstDisplayPres_Click(...) Handles lstDisplayPres.Click
          'Display the presidents between two numbers, inclusive.
          lstPres.Items.Clear()
          'Loop from the lower number to the upper number.
          For i As Integer = CInt(txtLowerNum.Text) To CInt(txtUpperNum.Text)
            lstPres.Items.Add(i & ". " & pres(i - 1))
          Next
        End Sub
```

41.
```
    Private Sub btnShow_Click(...) Handles btnShow.Click
      'Test two phrases to see if they are anagrams.
      Dim first(25), second(25) As Integer    'Holds frequencies
      Dim letter As String
      Dim result As Boolean = True
      'Convert both phrases to uppercase.
      txtFirst.Text = txtFirst.Text.ToUpper
      txtSecond.Text = txtSecond.Text.ToUpper
      'Count the frequencies of the first phrase.
      For i As Integer = 0 To txtFirst.Text.Length - 1
        letter = txtFirst.Text.Substring(i, 1)
        'Increment the frequency element belonging to the letter.
        If (letter >= "A") And (letter <= "Z") Then
          first(Asc(letter) - Asc("A")) += 1
        End If
      Next
      'Count the frequencies of the second phrase.
      For i As Integer = 0 To txtSecond.Text.Length - 1
        letter = txtSecond.Text.Substring(i, 1)
        'Increment the frequency element belonging to the letter.
        If (letter >= "A") And (letter <= "Z") Then
          second(Asc(letter) - Asc("A")) += 1
        End If
      Next
      'Compare the two frequencies.
      For i As Integer = 0 To 25
        'If the frequencies differ, set the result flag to False.
        If first(i) <> second(i) Then
          result = False
        End If
      Next
      'Display the result.
      If result Then
        txtOutput.Text = "The two phrases are anagrams."
      Else
        txtOutput.Text = "The two phrases are not anagrams."
      End If
    End Sub
```

EXERCISES 7.2

1. No

3. Michigan

5. less than
   greater than
   equals
   less than

7. `total rainfall for first quarter: 10 inches`

9. Change `txtOutput.Text = city` to `txtOutput.Text = city(1)`. You can't display an entire array with one statement.

11. *n* is incremented by 1 even if the user enters a negative number to stop and see the product. Move the incrementing inside the If block just before the statement *num(n) = number*.

13. In the Sub procedure *CopyArray*, the parentheses should be removed in the line `b() = a()`

15.
```
Sub Ascending()
    'Determine if array is ascending.
    Dim i As Integer = 0
    Dim orderFlag As Boolean = True
    Do While (i < scores.GetUpperBound(0)) And (orderFlag)
      If scores(i) > scores(i + 1) Then
        orderFlag = False
      End If
      i += 1
    Loop
    If orderFlag Then
      txtOutput.Text = "Array is ascending."
    Else
      txtOutput.Text = "Array is not ascending."
    End If
End Sub
```

17.
```
Sub WhatOrder()
    'Determine if order is ascending, descending, both, or neither.
    Dim ascFlag As Boolean = True
    Dim descFlag As Boolean = True
    Dim i as Integer = 0
    Do While (i < scores.GetUpperBound(0)) And (ascFlag Or descFlag)
      If scores(i) > scores(i + 1) Then
        ascFlag = False
      End If
      If scores(i) < scores(i + 1) Then
        descFlag = False
      End If
      i += 1
    Loop
    If ascendFlag And descendFlag Then
      txtOutput.Text = "Array is both ascending and descending."
    ElseIf (Not ascendFlag) And (Not descendFlag) Then
      txtOutput.Text = "Array is neither ascending nor descending."
    ElseIf ascendFlag Then
      txtOutput.Text = "Array is ascending."
    Else
      txtOutput.Text = "Array is descending."
    End If
End Sub
```

19.
```
Sub MergeOrderedWithDups()
    Dim indexA, indexB As Integer
    Dim doneA, doneB As Boolean
    'Merge ascending arrays, with duplications.
```

```
      ReDim c(39)
      indexA = 0
      indexB = 0
      doneA = False
      doneB = False
      'Loop over each element of the resulting array.
      For indexC As Integer = 0 To 39
        'If a's element is less than b's, add a's to c.
        If ((a(indexA) <= b(indexB)) And Not doneA) Or (doneB) Then
          c(indexC) = a(indexA)
          'Get next element from a.
          If indexA < 19 Then
            indexA = indexA + 1
          Else
            doneA = True
          End If
        Else
          'Otherwise, add b's element to c.
          c(indexC) = b(indexB)
          'Get next element from b
          If indexB < 19 Then
            indexB = indexB + 1
          Else
            doneB = True
          End If
        End If
      Next
    End Sub

21. Dim states(49) As String      'Holds state data
    Dim count As Integer          'Number of states stored

    Private Sub btnInsert_Click(...) Handles btnInsert.Click
      'Insert a state into the array.
      Dim position As Integer
      'If there is no more room in the array, display a message.
      If count >= 50 Then
        MsgBox("Fifty states have already been entered.", 0, _
               "No more room.")
      Else
        'Store the new state as the next element.
        states(count) = txtState.Text
        'Find the place to insert the state.
        position = 0
        Do While states(position) < txtState.Text
          position += 1
        Loop
        'If the position already holds the state, then display message.
        If (states(position) = txtState.Text) And (position < count) Then
          MsgBox("State already exists in the list.", 0, "Exists")
        Else
          'Shift the states above the position.
          For i As Integer = count - 1 To position Step -1
            states(i + 1) = states(i)
          Next
```

```
        'Insert the new state in the position, and increment counter.
        states(position) = txtState.Text
        count += 1
      End If
      'Clear input and output, and reset focus for next input.
      lstOutput.Items.Clear()
      txtState.Clear()
      txtState.Focus()
    End If
  End Sub

  Private Sub btnDelete_Click(...) Handles btnDelete.Click
    'Remove a state from the list.
    Dim position As Integer = 0
    'Find the state within the array.
    Do While (position < count - 1) And (txtState.Text > states(position))
      position += 1
    Loop
    'If the state is not found or no states stored, then display message.
    If (count = 0) Or (txtState.Text <> states(position)) Then
      MsgBox("The state is not in the list.", 0, "Not found")
    Else
      count = count − 1      'Decrement counter.
      'Shift array above position down by one.
      For i As Integer = position To count - 1
        states(i) = states(i + 1)
      Next
      lstOutput.Items.Clear()
      txtState.Clear()
      txtState.Focus()
    End If
  End Sub

  Private Sub btnDisplay_Click(...) Handles btnDisplay.Click
    'Display the array in the list box.
    lstOutput.Items.Clear()
    For i As Integer = 0 To count - 1
      lstOutput.Items.Add(states(i))
    Next
    txtState.Clear()
    txtState.Focus()
  End Sub
```

23.
```
Dim grades(99) As Integer     'Stores grade data
Dim count As Integer          'Number of grades stored

Private Sub btnRecord_Click(...) Handles btnRecord.Click
  'Add a score to the array.
  'If no more room, then display error message.
  If count >= 100 Then
    MsgBox("100 scores have been entered.", 0, "No more room.")
  Else
    'Store the input into the array.
    grades(count) = CInt(txtScore.Text)
    count += 1
    'Reset input.
    lstOutput.Items.Clear()
```

```
    txtScore.Clear()
    txtScore.Focus()
  End If
End Sub

Private Sub btnDisplay_Click(...) Handles btnDisplay.Click
  'Display average of grades and the number above average.
  Dim avg As Double, aboveAvg As Integer
  avg = Average(grades, count)
  aboveAvg = AboveAverage(grades, count, avg)
  lstOutput.Items.Clear()
  lstOutput.Items.Add("The average is " & FormatNumber(avg, 2)".")
  lstOutput.Items.Add(FormatNumber(aboveAvg, 0) & _
                    " students scored above the average.")
End Sub

Function Average(ByVal scores() As Integer, ByVal cnt As Integer) _
         As Double
  'Calculate the average score.
  Dim sum As Double = 0
  For i As Integer = 0 To cnt - 1
    sum += scores(i)
  Next
  'The average is the sum divided by the count; account for 0 count.
  If cnt = 0 Then
    Return 0
  Else
    Return sum / cnt
  End If
End Function

Function AboveAverage(ByVal scores() As Integer, _
                    ByVal cnt As Integer, _
                    ByVal average As Double) As Integer
  'Count the number of scores above the average score.
  Dim num As Integer = 0
  For i As Integer = 0 To cnt - 1
    If scores(i) > average Then
      num += 1
    End If
  Next
  Return num
End Function
```

25.
```
Private Sub btnUpdate_Click(...) Handles btnUpdate.Click
  'Merge two sets of data into a master set.
  Dim colors(71), retired(7), added(55) As String
  Dim i, j As Integer
  LoadArray(colors, "PRE1990COLORS.TXT")
  LoadArray(retired, "RETIREDCOLORS.TXT")
  LoadArray(added, "ADDEDCOLORS.TXT")
  'Remove the retired colors from the array.
  ReDim Preserve colors(120)
  i = 0
  j = 0        'Shift the array by the amount in j.
  Do While i <= 71 - 7
    If colors(i) = retired(j) Then
      j += 1
    End If
```

```
      colors(i) = colors(i + j)
       i += 1
    Loop
    'Insert the added colors into the master set.
    i = 0
    j = 0
    Do While j <= 55
      If added(j) < colors(i) Then     'Insert new color.
        For k As Integer = 63 + j To i Step -1
          colors(k + 1) = colors(k)    'Shift array.
        Next
        colors(i) = added(j)
        j += 1
      End If
      lstOutput.Items.Add(colors(i))
      i += 1
    Loop
    'Display the rest of the colors.
    For k As Integer = i To 119
      lstOutput.Items.Add(colors(k))
    Next
  End Sub

  Sub LoadArray(ByRef data() As String, ByVal fileName As String)
    'Load string data from a file.
    Dim sr As IO.StreamReader = IO.File.OpenText(fileName)
    'Fill the array, and close the reader.
    For i As Ineger = 0 To data.GetUpperBound(0)
      data(i) = sr.ReadLine()
    Next
    sr.Close()
  End Sub
```

EXERCISES 7.3

1. `Expenses for winter: $4,271.66`

3. `Summer bills top winter bills by $67.09`

5. `heights are same`
   `170`

7. `Mr. President lives in Washington, DC`

9. *peace* should be *prize.peace*, and *year* should be *prize.year*.

11. The condition `(game1 > game2)` is not valid. Structures can only be compared one member at a time.

13.
```
Private Sub btnDisplay_Click(...) Handles btnDisplay.Click
  lstOutput.Items.Clear()
  For i As Integer = 0 To club.GetUpperBound(0)
    lstOutput.Items.Add(club(i).name)
  Next
End Sub
```

15.
```
Private Sub btnDisplay_Click(...) Handles btnDisplay.Click
  'Displays the students who are enrolled in a course
  Dim subject As String = "CMSC 100"
```

```
    lstOutput.Items.Clear()
      'Loop over all students in the club.
    For i As Integer = 0 To club.GetUpperBound(0)
      'Loop over all courses for that student.
      For j As Integer = 0 To club(i).courses.GetUpperBound(0)
        'If a course matches, display the student's name.
        If club(i).courses(j) = subject Then
          lstOutput.Items.Add(club(i).name)
        End If
      Next
    Next
  End Sub
```

17.
```
Dim grades(5) As TextBox        'Refers to grade textboxes
Dim hours(5) As TextBox         'Refers to hours textboxes

Structure Course
  Dim grade As String           'Grade in the course
  Dim hours As Double           'Number of credit-hours
End Structure

Private Sub frmGrades_Load(...) Handles MyBase.Load
  'Associate the textbox arrays with the textboxes
  grades(0) = txtGrade1
  grades(1) = txtGrade2
  grades(2) = txtGrade3
  grades(3) = txtGrade4
  grades(4) = txtGrade5
  grades(5) = txtGrade6
  hours(0) = txtHours1
  hours(1) = txtHours2
  hours(2) = txtHours3
  hours(3) = txtHours4
  hours(4) = txtHours5
  hours(5) = txtHours6
End Sub

Private Sub btnDisplay_Click(...) Handles btnDisplay.Click
  'Calculate and display the grade point average.
  Dim courses(5) As Course      'Holds the courses
  Dim numGrades As Integer
  'Read the data into the courses array until there is no more data.
  numGrades = 0
  For count As Integer = 0 To 5
    If (grades(count).Text <> "") Then
      numGrades += 1
      courses(count).grade = grades(count).Text
      courses(count).hours = CDbl(hours(count).Text)
    End If
  Next
  If numGrades > 0 Then
    'Redimension the array for the final count.
    ReDim Preserve courses(count)
    'Compute the GPA, and display the result.
    DisplayGPA(GPA(courses))
  Else
    'Display the error message.
```

```
      txtOutput.Text = "No grade(s) entered."
    End If
  End Sub

  Function GPA(ByVal c() As Course) As Double
    'Compute the GPA of a set of courses.
    Dim credits, hours As Double
    'Add up the credits and hours based upon the grade.
    For i As Integer = 0 To c.GetUpperBound(0)
      'Ignore invalid grades.
      Select Case c(i).grade.ToUpper
        Case "A"
          credits += 4 * c(i).hours
          hours += c(i).hours
        Case "B"
          credits += 3 * c(i).hours
          hours += c(i).hours
        Case "C"
          credits += 2 * c(i).hours
          hours += c(i).hours
        Case "D"
          credits += 1 * c(i).hours
          hours += c(i).hours
        Case "F"
          hours += c(i).hours
      End Select
    Next
    'The GPA is the points divided by the total credit hours.
    If hours = 0 Then
      Return 0
    Else
      Return credits / hours
    End If
  End Function

  Sub DisplayGPA(ByVal gpa As Double)
    'Display the GPA and a congratulatory message.
    txtGPA.Text = FormatNumber(gpa, 2)
    If gpa >= 3 Then
      txtOutput.Text = "Congratulations, you made the Honor Roll."
    Else
      txtOutput.Text = "Congratulations on completing the semester."
    End If
  End Sub
```

19. ```
Structure Building
    Dim name As String   'Name
    Dim city As String   'City
    Dim height As Double   'Height in feet
    Dim stories As Integer   'Number of stories
End Structure

Dim buildings(4) As Building   'Holds data

Private Sub frmBuildings_Load(...) Handles MyBase.Load
  'Load data from file into structure array.
  Dim count As Integer = 0
  Dim sr As IO.StreamReader = IO.File.OpenText("BUILDINGS.TXT")
```
```

```
          'Loop until the end of file is reached.
          Do While sr.Peek <> -1
            'Make sure there is enough room to store data.
            If count > buildings.GetUpperBound(0) + 1 Then
              ReDim Preserve buildings(count + 5)
            End If
            'Store data from file into structure members.
            buildings(count - 1).name = sr.ReadLine()
            buildings(count - 1).city = sr.ReadLine()
            buildings(count - 1).height = CDbl(sr.ReadLine())
            buildings(count - 1).stories = CInt(sr.ReadLine())
            count += 1
          Loop
          sr.Close()
          'Resize array to exact number stored.
          ReDim Preserve buildings(count - 1)
        End Sub

        Private Sub btnDisplay_Click(...) Handles btnDisplay.Click
          'Look up building name, and display information.
          'Clear output.
          txtCity.Clear()
          txtHeight.Clear()
          txtStories.Clear()
          'Loop over all buildings in the array.
          For i As Integer = 0 To buildings.GetUpperBound(0)
            'If the name matches, display the information.
            If txtName.Text.ToUpper = buildings(i).name.ToUpper Then
              txtCity.Text = buildings(i).city
              txtHeight.Text = CStr(buildings(i).height)
              txtStories.Text = CStr(buildings(i).stories)
            End If
          Next
          'If no building matched, then display a message.
          If txtCity.Text = "" Then
            MsgBox("Building not found.", 0, "Not found.")
          End If
        End Sub

21.  Structure Franchise
        Dim name As String      'Franchise Name
        Dim stores As Integer   'Number of stores
      End Structure

      Private Sub btnDisplay_Click(...) Handles btnDisplay.Click
        'Loads data and displays a report on percentage of stores
        Dim pizza(9) As Franchise
        Dim count As Integer
        Dim fmtStr As String = "{0,-20} {1,7:P}"
        'Load data into array.
        pizza(0).name = "Pizza Hut"
        pizza(0).stores = 7523
        pizza(1).name = "Domino's"
        pizza(1).stores = 4904
        pizza(2).name = "Little Caesar's"
        pizza(2).stores = 2850
        pizza(3).name = "Papa John's"
```

```
         pizza(3).stores = 2574
         pizza(4).name = "Sbarro"
         pizza(4).stores = 790
         pizza(5).name = "Papa Murphy's"
         pizza(5).stores = 750
         pizza(6).name = "Godfather's"
         pizza(6).stores = 566
         pizza(7).name = "Round Table"
         pizza(7).stores = 485
         pizza(8).name = "CiCi's Pizza
         pizza(8).stores = 465
         pizza(9).name = "Chuck E. Cheese's"
         pizza(9).stores = 460
         'Calculate total number of stores.
         count = 0
         For i As Integer = 0 To 9
           count += pizza(i).stores
         Next
         'Display report.
         lstOutput.Items.Add(String.Format(fmtStr, "NAME", "PERCENT"))
         For i As Integer = 0 To 9
           lstOutput.Items.Add(String.Format(fmtStr, pizza(i).name, _
                                  pizza(i).stores / count))
       Next
       End Sub
```

EXERCISES 7.4

1. **200**
   100

3. **11**
   7
   Numbers interchanged.

5. Items are not properly swapped.

7. Sequential, since the array in not ordered

9. Four swaps

11. $(n{-}1) + (n{-}2) + \cdots + 1$. A shorter version of this formula is $n*(n{-}1)/2$.

13. 4 swaps

15. 8 comparisons

17. 16; 8 1/2; 5

19.
```
Sub SwapThree(ByRef x As String, ByRef y As String, _
           ByRef z As String)
   Dim temp As String
   temp = x
   x = y
   y = z
   z = temp
End Sub
```

21.
```
Structure CapitalEvent
    Dim name As String
    Dim crowd As Integer              'Estimate in thousands.
End Structure

Private Sub btnDisplay_Click(...) Handles btnDisplay.Click
    'Read and sort the event data.
    Dim sr As IO.StreamReader = IO.File.OpenText("7-4-E21.TXT")
    Dim temp, evt(8) As CapitalEvent      'Nine events total
    Dim fmtStr As String = "{0,-50} {1,5}"
    For i As Integer = 0 To 8
      evt(i).name = sr.ReadLine()
      evt(i).crowd = CInt(sr.ReadLine())
    Next
    sr.Close()
    'Use bubble sort to order.
    For i As Integer = 1 To 8
      For j As Integer = 1 To 9 - i
        If evt(j - 1).name > evt(j).name Then
          'Swap.
          temp = evt(j - 1)
          evt(j - 1) = evt(j)
          evt(j) = temp
        End If
      Next
    Next
    'Display the events.
    lstOutput.Items.Clear()
    lstOutput.Items.Add(String.Format(fmtStr, "EVENT", "CROWD"))
    For i As Integer = 0 To 8
      lstOutput.Items.Add(String.Format(fmtStr, evt(i).name, _
                                        evt(i).crowd))
    Next
End Sub
```

23.
```
Private Sub btnStore_Click(...) Handles btnStore.Click
    'Read 10 sorted words, then add one more.
    Dim i Integer
    Dim temp, words(10) As String      'Eleven words to store
    'Get all eleven words from the user.
    For j As Integer = 0 To 10
      words(j) = InputBox("Enter word #" & "Enter word #" & j + 1, "")
    Next
    'Find correct position of eleventh word.
    i = 0
    Do While words(i) < words(10)
      i += 1
    Loop
    'Shift the array, and insert the new word.
    temp = words(10)
    For j As Integer = 9 To i Step -1
      words(j + 1) = words(j)
    Next
    words(i) = temp
End Sub
```

25.
```
Private Sub btnSort_Click(...) Handles btnSort.Click
    'Read and sort a list of numbers
    Dim n As Integer = CInt(txtN.Text)
    Dim temp, nums(n - 1) As Double
    For i As Integer = 0 To n - 1 'Get numbers from the user
      nums(i) = CDbl(InputBox("Enter number #" & i + 1))
    Next
    'Use bubble sort to swap
    For i As Integer = 1 To n - 1
      For j As Integer = 1 To n - i
        If nums(j - 1) > nums(j) Then
          'Swap
          temp = nums(j - 1)
          nums(j - 1) = nums(j)
          nums(j) = temp
        End If
      Next
    Next
    'Display the ordered list of numbers
    For i As Integer = 0 To n - 1
      lstOutput.Items.Add(nums(i))
    Next
  End Sub
```

27.
```
Dim codes(25) As String

Private Sub frmCode_Load(...) Handles MyBase.Load
    'Read in the code for the 26 letters of the alphabet.
    Dim sr As IO.StreamReader = IO.File.OpenText("7-4-E27.TXT")
    For i As Integer = 0 To 25
      codes(i) = sr.ReadLine()
    Next
    sr.Close()
  End Sub

Private Sub btnDisplay_Click(...) Handles btnDisplay.Click
    'Display a word in morse code.
    Dim word, result As String
    'Convert input to uppercase.
    word = txtWord.Text.ToUpper
    result = ""
    'Loop over each character of the string. Note that the index starts at 0.
    For i As Integer = 0 To word.Length - 1
      If (word.Substring(i, 1) >= "A") And _
         (word.Substring(i, 1) <= "Z") Then
        result = result & codes(Asc(word.Substring(i, 1))_
                               - Asc("A")) & " "
      End If
    Next
    txtOutput.Text = result
  End Sub
```

29.
```
Private Sub btnDisplay_Click(...) Handles btnDisplay.Click
    'Get seven scores from the user, and display the average.
    Dim scores(6), temp As Integer
    Dim sum As Integer
    'Read the seven scores into the array.
```

```
    For i As Integer = 0 To 6
      scores(i) = CInt(InputBox("Enter score #" & i + 1, ""))
    Next
    'Bubble sort the scores.
    For i As Integer = 1 To 6
      For j As Integer = 1 To 7 - i
        If scores(j - 1) > scores(j) Then
          'Swap scores.
          temp = scores(j - 1)
          scores(j - 1) = scores(j)
          scores(j) = temp
        End If
      Next
    Next
    'Calculate and display the average.
    sum = 0
    For i As Integer = 2 To 6      'Throw out the two lowest scores.
      sum += scores(i)
    Next
    txtOutput.Text = FormatNumber(sum / 5)
  End Sub
```

31.
```
  Private Sub btnDisplay_Click(...) Handles btnDisplay.Click
    'Get data from the user, and display the median.
    Dim data(), temp, median As Double
    Dim n, p, q As Integer
    'Read the number of elements.
    n = CInt(InputBox("Enter number of data elements:"))
    ReDim data(n - 1)
    'Read the data into the array.
    For i As Integer = 0 To data.GetUpperBound(0)
      data(i) = CDbl(InputBox("Enter element #" & (i + 1)))
    Next
    'Bubble sort the data.
    For i As Integer = 1 To data.GetUpperBound(0)
      For j As Integer = 1 To data.GetUpperBound(0) + 1 - i
        If data(j - 1) > data(j) Then
          'Swap scores.
          temp = data(j - 1)
          data(j - 1) = data(j)
          data(j) = temp
        End If
      Next
    Next
    'Determine median based upon even or odd number of numbers
    q = data.GetUpperBound(0) + 1        'number of numbers
    p = CInt(Int((q - 1) / 2))
    If Math.Round(q / 2) = q / 2 Then
      'If q even, median is average of two middle elements
      median = (data(p) + data(p + 1)) / 2
    Else
      'If q odd, median is the middle element
      median = data(p)
    End If
    txtOutput.Text = CStr(median)
  End Sub
```

EXERCISES 7.5

1. `12`

3. `Dorothy`

5. `11`
   `15`

7. `1`
   `3`
   `5`

9. The declaration statement should read **Dim a(3, 2) As Integer.** (Once *j* gets to 3, there will be an "Index Out of Range" error.)

11.
```
Sub FillArray(ByRef a() As Double)
    'Fill an array.
  For row As Integer = 0 To 10
    For col As Integer = 0 To 10
      a(row, col) = col
    Next
  Next
End Sub
```

13.
```
Sub Exchange(ByRef a() As Double)
    'Interchange values of 2nd and 3rd rows.
  Dim temp As Double
  For col As Integer = 0 To 10
    temp = a(2, col)
    a(2, col) = a(3, col)
    a(3, col) = temp
  Next
End Sub
```

15.
```
Private Sub btnDisplay_Click(...) Handles btnDisplay.Click
    'Display a company's inventory from its two stores
    'Declare the inventory and sales arrays
  Dim inventory(,) As Integer = {{25, 64, 23}, {12, 82, 19}}
  Dim sales(,) As Integer = {{7, 45, 11}, {4, 24, 8}}
  Dim total(2) As Integer
  Dim fmtStr As String = "{0,1} {1,2} {2,2} {3,2} {4,3}"
    'Adjust the inventory values to reflect todays sales
  For store As Integer = 1 To 2
    For item As Integer = 1 To 3
      inventory(store − 1, item − 1) = _
            inventory(store − 1, item − 1) − sales(store − 1, item − 1)
      'Accumulate the total inventory per store
      total(store) += inventory(store - 1, item - 1)
    Next
  Next
    'Display the store's inventory and totals
  lstOutput.Items.Add(String.Format(fmtStr, "", "1", "2", "3", "TOT"))
  For store As Integer = 1 To 2
    lstOutput.Items.Add(String.Format(fmtStr, store, _
                    inventory(store - 1, 0), _
                    inventory(store - 1, 1), _
                    inventory(store - 1, 2), total(store)))
  Next
End Sub
```

17.
```vb
Private Sub btnDisplay_Click(...) Handles btnDisplay.Click
  'Display the course and campus enrollments
  'Define and fill the enrollment array
  Dim er(,) As Integer = {{5, 15, 22, 21, 12, 25, 16, 11, 17, 23}, _
                          {11, 23, 51, 25, 32, 35, 32, 52, 25, 21}, _
                          {2, 12, 32, 32, 25, 26, 29, 12, 15, 11}}
  'Define the arrays to accumulate the information
  Dim campusTotal(2), courseTotal(9) As Integer
  For campus As Integer = 0 To 2
    For course As Integer = 0 To 9
      campusTotal(campus) += er(campus, course)
      courseTotal(course) += er(campus, course)
    Next
  Next
  'Display the campus enrollment
  lstOutput.Items.Add("CAMPUS ENROLLMENT")
  For campus As Integer = 0 To 2
    lstOutput.Items.Add(CStr(campus + 1) & ": " & campusTotal(campus))
  Next
  'Display the course enrollment
  lstOutput.Items.Add("COURSE ENROLLMENT")
  For course As Integer = 0 To 9
    lstOutput.Items.Add(CStr(course + 1) & ": " & courseTotal(course))
  Next
End Sub
```

19.
```vb
Private Sub btnDisplay_Click(...) Handles btnDisplay.Click
  'Load golf data, cumulate totals, and display results
  Dim scores(,) As Integer = {{69, 63, 72, 68}, _
                              {68, 67, 67, 73}, {69, 69, 67, 72}}
  Dim golfers() As String = {"Tiger Woods", "Luke Donald", _
                             "Bernhard Langer"}
  'Compute the total score for each golfer
  Dim total(2), rounds(3) As Integer
  'Aggregate the figures
  For golfer As Integer = 0 To 2
    For round As Integer = 0 To 3
      total(golfer) += scores(golfer, round)
      rounds(round) += scores(golfer, round)
    Next
  Next
  'Display golfer's totals
  lstOutput.Items.Add("GOLFER TOTALS")
  For golfer As Integer = 0 To 2
    lstOutput.Items.Add(golfers(golfer) & ": " & total(golfer))
  Next
  'Display average per round
  lstOutput.Items.Add("ROUND AVERAGE")
  For round As Integer = 0 To 3
    lstOutput.Items.Add(round + 1) & ": " & _
                        FormatNumber(rounds(round) / 3))
  Next
End Sub
```

21.
```vb
Private Sub btnDisplay_Click(...) Handles btnDisplay.Click
  'Display the categories of a university
```

```vb
        Dim ranking(,) As String = _
            {{"U of PA", "U of IN", "U of MI", "UC Berk", "U of VA"}, _
             {"MIT", "Cng-Mellon", "UC Berk", "Cornell", "U of IL"}, _
             {"U of IL", "U of OK", "U of MD", "Cng-Mellon", _
              "CO Sch. of Mines"}}
        Dim categories() As String = {"Business", "Comp Sci.", "Engr/Gen."}
        'Look up the specified university in the rankings
        Dim result As String = ""
        For category As Integer = 0 To 2
          For rank As Integer = 0 To 4
            If txtName.Text.ToUpper = ranking(category, rank).ToUpper Then
              'Append category name to result
              result = result & categories(category) & "    "
            End If
          Next
        Next
        'Display result
        If result = "" Then
          txtOutput.Text = "None."
        Else
          txtOutput.Text = result
        End If
      End Sub
```

23.
```vb
  Dim scores(14, 4) As Integer    'Stores students' exam scores
  Dim count As Integer            'Current number of students stored
  Dim names(14) As String         'Stores students' names

  Private Sub btnAdd_Click(...) Handles btnAdd.Click
    'Add student to array.
    If count = 15 Then
      MsgBox("Fifteen students already stored", 0, "Warning")
    Else
      count += 1
      names(count - 1) = txtName.Text
      scores(count - 1, 0) = CInt(txtExam1.Text)
      scores(count - 1, 1) = CInt(txtExam2.Text)
      scores(count - 1, 2) = CInt(txtExam3.Text)
      scores(count - 1, 3) = CInt(txtExam4.Text)
      scores(count - 1, 4) = CInt(txtExam5.Text)
      'Reset input
      txtName.Clear()
      txtExam1.Clear()
      txtExam2.Clear()
      txtExam3.Clear()
      txtExam4.Clear()
      txtExam5.Clear()
      txtName.Focus()
    End If
  End Sub

  Private Sub btnDisplay_Click(...) Handles btnDisplay.Click
    'Aggregate totals and display report.
    Dim n, temp As Integer
    Dim sum, median As Double
    Dim even As Boolean
    'Display student's semester grades.
    lstOutput.Items.Clear()
```

```vb
lstOutput.Items.Add("Students' Semester Average")
For i As Integer = 0 To count - 1
  'Accumulate sum of scores for each student.
  sum = 0
  For exam As Integer = 0 To 4
    sum += scores(i, exam)
  Next
  'Display the student's name and semester average.
  lstOutput.Items.Add(names(i) & ": " & FormatNumber(sum / 5))
Next
'Display median on the exams.
lstOutput.Items.Add("Exam Medians")
'Determine whether the count is even or odd.
even = (Int(count / 2) = count / 2)
For exam As Integer = 0 To 4
  'Bubble sort the scores array based upon the exam score.
  For i As Integer = 1 To count - 1
    For j As Integer = 1 To count - i
      If scores(j - 1, exam) > scores(j, exam) Then
        'Swap scores.
        temp = scores(j - 1, exam)
        scores(j - 1, exam) = scores(j, exam)
        scores(j, exam) = temp
      End If
    Next
  Next
  'Calculate median depending upon even or odd.
  n = CInt(Int(count / 2))
  If even Then
    'Median is average of two middle scores.
    median = (scores(n - 1, exam) + scores(n, exam)) / 2
  Else
    'Median is middle score.
    median = scores(n, exam)
  End If
  'Display median score for exam.
  lstOutput.Items.Add(exam + 1) & ": " & FormatNumber(median))
Next
End Sub
```

25.
```vb
Private Sub btnDisplay_Click(...) Handles btnDisplay.Click
  'Load data into an array, cumulate totals, and display a report
  Dim totalSales As Double
  Dim sales(,) As Integer = {{25, 64, 23, 45, 14}, _
                             {12, 82, 19, 34, 63}, _
                             {54, 22, 17, 43, 35}}
  Dim price() As Double = {12, 17.95, 95, 86.5, 78}
  'Cumulate totals
  Dim totals(2) As Double
  For store As Integer = 0 To 2
    For item As Integer = 0 To 4
      totals(store) += sales(store, item) * price(item)
    Next
  Next
  'Display report, storing grand total in totalSales
  lstOutput.Items.Add("Sales per store")
```

```
  For store As Integer = 0 To 2
    lstOutput.Items.Add(store + 1 & ": " & FormatCurrency(totals(store)))
    totalSales += totals(store)
  Next
  lstOutput.Items.Add("Total sales: " & FormatCurrency(totalSales))
End Sub
```

CHAPTER 8

EXERCISES 8.1

1. `Hello`

3. `Bon Jour`

5. `You must enter a number.`

7. `Error occurred.`

9. `File AGES.TXT contains an invalid age.`

11. The file WELCOME.TXT is created and has the following lines:
```
Hello
Bon Jour
```

13. The filespec YOB.TXT needs to be delimited with quotation marks.

15. There should be no quotations around the variable *name* as the parameter to the CreateText method.

17. The variable *age* is declared within the Try-Catch-Finally block and therefore is not available below the line End Try.

19.
```
Private Sub btnCreate_Click(...) Handles btnCreate.Click
    'Create a sequential file, and populate it.
    Dim sw As IO.StreamWriter = IO.File.CreateText("COWBOY.TXT")
    sw.WriteLine("Colt Peacemaker")
    sw.WriteLine(12.2)
    sw.WriteLine("Holster")
    sw.WriteLine(2)
    sw.WriteLine("Levi Strauss Jeans")
    sw.WriteLine(1.35)
    sw.WriteLine("Saddle")
    sw.WriteLine(40)
    sw.WriteLine("Stetson")
    sw.WriteLine(10)
    sw.Close()          'Always close the writer when finished.
    MsgBox("The file has been created.", 0, "DONE")
End Sub
```

21.
```
Private Sub btnAdd_Click(...) Handles btnAdd.Click
    'Append to a sequential file.
    Dim sw As IO.StreamWriter = IO.File.AppendText("COWBOY.TXT")
    sw.WriteLine("Winchester rifle")
    sw.WriteLine(20.5)
    sw.Close()
    MsgBox("The item has been added to the file.", 0, "DONE")
End Sub
```

23.
```vb
Private Sub btnAdd_Click(...) Handles btnAdd.Click
  'Add new item to list from COWBOY.TXT,
  'and save in alphabetical order into COWBOY2.TXT.
  Dim flag As Boolean
  Dim item, price As String
  'Open COWBOY for input and COWBOY2 for output.
  Dim sr As IO.StreamReader = IO.File.OpenText("COWBOY.TXT")
  Dim sw As IO.StreamWriter = IO.File.CreateText("COWBOY2.TXT")
  flag = False
  item = ""
  'Loop until we reach the new item to add or run out of room.
  Do While (item < txtItem.Text) And (sr.Peek <> -1)
    'Read the current item from the file.
    item = sr.ReadLine
    price = sr.ReadLine
    'If we have reached the new item, add the new item.
    If item > txtItem.Text Then
      'Add the new item and the new item's price.
      sw.WriteLine(txtItem.Text)
      sw.WriteLine(txtPrice.Text)
      'Set flag true so we don't add it again at the end.
      flag = True
    End If
    'Add the current item and price.
    sw.WriteLine(item)
    sw.WriteLine(price)
  Loop
  'If there are any more items to read, write them to the output.
  Do While (sr.Peek <> -1)
    item = sr.ReadLine
    price = sr.ReadLine
    sw.WriteLine(item)
    sw.WriteLine(price)
  Loop
  'If the new item hasn't been written yet, write it.
  If Not flag Then
    sw.WriteLine(txtItem.Text)
    sw.WriteLine(txtPrice.Text)
  End If
  sr.Close()    'Always close the reader when finished.
  sw.Close()    'Always close the writer when finished.
  'Display a message, and clear the input text boxes.
  MsgBox("Item added to COWBOY2.TXT", 0, "Note")
End Sub
```

25.
```vb
Private Sub btnLookup_Click(...) Handles btnLookup.Click
  'Lookup person in data file to get age.
  Dim found As Boolean = False
  Dim name As String, yob As Integer
  Dim sr As IO.StreamReader = IO.File.OpenText("YOB.TXT")
  'Loop through file until end or name found.
  Do While (sr.Peek <> -1) And (Not found)
    name = sr.ReadLine
    yob = CInt(sr.ReadLine)
```

```
        If name.ToUpper >= txtName.Text.ToUpper Then
          If name.ToUpper > txtName.Text.ToUpper Then
            Exit Do
          Else
            'If name matches, display the age
            txtOutput.Text = CStr(2006 - yob)
            found = True
          End If
        End If
      Loop
      sr.Close()
      'If name not found, then display message.
      If Not found Then
        txtOutput.Text = "Not found."
      End If
    End Sub
```

27.
```
    Private Sub btnLookup_Click(...) Handles btnLookup.Click
      'Lookup book title in sequential file.
      Dim fileName As String
      Dim title As String, quantity As Integer
      'Determine file to open, and then open it for input.
      If mtxtType.Text.ToUpper = "P" Then
        fileName = "PAPERBACK.TXT"
      Else
        fileName = "HARDBACK.TXT"
      End If
      Dim sr As IO.StreamReader = IO.File.OpenText(fileName)
      'Loop until title is found or end of file.
      title = ""
      Do While (title.ToUpper <> txtTitle.Text.ToUpper) And _
               (sr.Peek <> -1)
        title = sr.ReadLine
        quantity = CInt(sr.ReadLine)
      Loop
      sr.Close()
      'Display result.
      If title.ToUpper = txtTitle.Text.ToUpper Then
        txtQuantity.Text = CStr(quantity)
      Else
        txtQuantity.Text = "n/a"
        MsgBox("Book not found in file.", 0, "NOTE")
      End If
    End Sub
```

EXERCISES 8.2

1. facetious

3. A,B,C,D,E,F,G

5.
```
Dim sw As IO.StreamWriter

Private Sub frmBaseball_Load(...) Handles MyBase.Load
  sw = IO.File.CreateText("AVERAGE.TXT")    'Open for output
End Sub
```

```
  Private Sub btnAdd_Click(...) Handles btnAdd.Click
    'Add a name with 0 times and 0 hits to the file.
    sw.WriteLine(txtName.Text)
    sw.WriteLine(0)
    sw.WriteLine(0)
    'Reset input text boxes.
    txtName.Clear()
    txtName.Focus()
  End Sub

  Private Sub btnQuit_Click(...) Handles btnQuit.Click
    sw.Close()
    End              'Terminate the program.
  End Sub
```

7.
```
Dim sw As IO.StreamWriter

  Private Sub frmBaseball_Load(...) Handles MyBase.Load
    sw = IO.File.AppendText("AVERAGE.TXT")
  End Sub

  Private Sub btnAdd_Click(...) Handles btnAdd.Click
    'Add a name with 0 times and 0 hits to the file.
    sw.WriteLine(txtName.Text)
    sw.WriteLine(0)
    sw.WriteLine(0)
    'Reset input text box.
    txtName.Clear()
    txtName.Focus()
  End Sub

  Private Sub btnQuit_Click(...) Handles btnQuit.Click
    sw.Close()
    End              'Terminate the program.
  End Sub
```

9.
```
Private Sub btnConvert_Click(...) Handles btnConvert.Click
    'Convert a sequential file in LSV format to a sequential file
    'in "Comma Separated Values" (CSV) format.
    Dim numFields As Integer     'Number of fields per record
    numFields = CInt(txtFields.Text)
    Dim field(numFields - 1) As String  'String array to hold fields
    Dim sr As IO.StreamReader = IO.File.OpenText(txtLSV.Text)
    Dim sw As IO.StreamWriter = IO.File.CreateText(txtCSV.Text)
    'Loop over all lines in the LSV file.
    Do While (sr.Peek <> -1)
      'Set each field to a line from the LSV file.
      For i As Integer = 0 To numFields - 1
        field(i) = sr.ReadLine
      Next
      'Join the fields with a comma, and write to the CSV file.
      sw.WriteLine(Join(field, ","))
    Loop
    sw.Close()
    sr.Close()
    MsgBox("Conversion completed.", 0, "DONE")
  End Sub
```

11.
```
Structure State
    Dim name As String       'State name
    Dim abbr As String       'Abbreviation
```

```vb
    Dim entered As String      'Date entered union
    Dim area As Double         'Area in square miles
    Dim pop As Double          'Population in 2000
  End Structure

  Private Sub btnDisplay_Click(...) Handles btnDisplay.Click
    'Load data from CSV file, sort on abbreviation, write to new file,
    'and display records in list box.
    Dim temp As State
    Dim state(4) As String     'Current state data, five fields total
    Dim states(49) As State    'Holds all states
    Dim fmtStr As String = "{0,-4} {1,-17} {2,-10} {3,10:N0} {4,13:N0}"
    'Read the data into the states array.
    Dim sr As IO.StreamReader = IO.File.OpenText("csvUSSTATES.TXT")
    For i As Integer = 0 To 49
      state = sr.ReadLine.Split(","c)
      'The field order is name, abbr, entered, area, pop.
      states(i).name = state(0)
      states(i).abbr = state(1)
      states(i).entered = state(2)
      states(i).area = CDbl(state(3))
      states(i).pop = CDbl(state(4))
    Next
    sr.Close()
    'Bubble sort the array based upon abbreviation name.
    For i As Integer = 1 To 49
      For j As Integer = 1 To 50 - i
        If states(j - 1).abbr > states(j).abbr Then
          'Swap elements.
          temp = states(j - 1)
          states(j - 1) = states(j)
          states(j) = temp
        End If
      Next
    Next
    'Write the data to the output file and to the list box.
    Dim sw As IO.StreamWriter = IO.File.CreateText("csvSORTED.TXT")
    lstOutput.Items.Add(String.Format(fmtStr, "ABBR", "STATE", _
                                      "ENTERED", "AREA", "POPULATION"))
    For i As Integer = 0 To 49
      'Copy data into string array.
      state(0) = states(i).name
      state(1) = states(i).abbr
      state(2) = states(i).entered
      state(3) = CStr(states(i).area)
      state(4) = CStr(states(i).pop)
      'Join string array using commas, and write to file.
      sw.WriteLine(Join(state, ","))
      'Write data to list box.
      lstOutput.Items.Add(String.Format(fmtStr, states(i).abbr, _
                                        states(i).name, states(i).entered, _
                                        states(i).area, states(i).pop))
    Next
    sw.Close()
  End Sub
```

13.
```
Private Sub btnCreate_Click(...) Handles btnCreate.Click
    'Write matching records from two input files into a third file.
    Dim name, subscriber As String
    'Open files for reading.
    Dim srBlock As IO.StreamReader = IO.File.OpenText("BLOCK.TXT")
    Dim srTimes As IO.StreamReader = IO.File.OpenText("TIMES.TXT")
    Dim sw As IO.StreamWriter = IO.File.CreateText("NAMES.TXT")
    'Loop over all records in the BLOCK reader.
    subscriber = ""
    Do While srBlock.Peek <> -1
      'Read in the name from BLOCK.
      name = srBlock.ReadLine
      'Loop until the subscriber has been reached.
      Do While (subscriber < name) And (srTimes.Peek <> -1)
        'Read the next subscriber.
        subscriber = srTimes.ReadLine
      Loop
      'If we have a match, then write it to output file.
      If subscriber = name Then
        sw.WriteLine(name)
      End If
    Loop
    srBlock.Close()
    srTimes.Close()
    sw.Close()
    MsgBox("The file has been created.", 0, "DONE")
End Sub
```

15.
```
Private Sub btnCount_Click(...) Handles btnCount.Click
    'Count the maximum number of repeated integers.
    Dim max, lastNum, numRepeats, number As Integer
    'Open data file.
    Dim sr As IO.StreamReader = IO.File.OpenText("NUMBERS.TXT")
    max = 0
    lastNum = 0
    numRepeats = 0
    'Loop over all input.
    Do While sr.Peek <> -1
      number = CInt(sr.ReadLine)
      'If number has changed, then compare its count.
      If number <> lastNum Then
        'If its count is more than the max, update the max.
        If numRepeats > max Then
          max = numRepeats
        End If
        'Store this number as the last number.
        lastNum = number
        numRepeats = 1
      Else
        numRepeats += 1     'Increment the count
      End If
    Loop
    sr.Close()
    txtOutput.Text = CStr(max)     'Display the result
End Sub
```

17.
```vb
Private Sub btnDisplay_Click(...) Handles btnDisplay.Click
    'Display a report on count of raffle tickets by grade.
    Dim grade, gradeTotal, total As Integer
    Dim currentGrade, tickets As Integer
    Dim name As String
    Dim fmtStr As String = "{0,5} {1,7:NO}"
    'Open data file for input.
    Dim sr As IO.StreamReader = IO.File.OpenText("RAFFLE.TXT")
    'Reset cumulative totals.
    grade = 0
    gradeTotal = 0
    total = 0
    'Loop over all records in the file.
    lstOutput.Items.Add(String.Format(fmtStr, "GRADE", "TICKETS"))
    Do While sr.Peek <> -1
      'Read in student's data.
      currentGrade = CInt(sr.ReadLine)
      name = sr.ReadLine
      tickets = CInt(sr.ReadLine)
      'If grade changes, then display current grade's totals.
      If grade <> currentGrade Then
        'If not first pass, display totals.
        If grade <> 0 Then
          lstOutput.Items.Add(String.Format(fmtStr, grade, gradeTotal))
          'Update cumulative total.
          total += gradeTotal
        End If
        'Reset grade.
        grade = currentGrade
        gradeTotal = 0
      End If
      'Add student's tickets to grade's total.
      gradeTotal += tickets
    Loop
    sr.Close()
    'Display last grade's totals.
    lstOutput.Items.Add(String.Format(fmtStr, grade, gradeTotal))
    total += gradeTotal
    'Display grand total.
    lstOutput.Items.Add(String.Format(fmtStr, "TOTAL", total))
End Sub
```

19.
```vb
Private Sub btnUpdate_Click(...) Handles btnUpdate.Click
    'Update phone number master file with file of those who have moved.
    Dim masterName, masterNumber As String   'Master info
    Dim movedName, movedNumber As String      'Moved info
    'Open input files for reading.
    Dim srMaster As IO.StreamReader = IO.File.OpenText("MASTER.TXT")
    Dim srMoved As IO.StreamReader = IO.File.OpenText("MOVED.TXT")
    'Open temporary file to hold output.
    Dim sw As IO.StreamWriter = IO.File.CreateText("TEMP.TXT")
    'Loop over all records in the move input file.
    Do While srMoved.Peek <> -1
      'Read in name that has moved.
      movedName = srMoved.ReadLine
      movedNumber = srMoved.ReadLine
```

```
        'Loop until find a matching record in master file.
        Do
          'Read a name from the master file.
          masterName = srMaster.ReadLine
          masterNumber = srMaster.ReadLine
          If movedName = masterName Then
            'If found a match, then write the new number.
            sw.WriteLine(masterName)
            sw.WriteLine(movedNumber)
          Else
            'Otherwise, write the master number.
            sw.WriteLine(masterName)
            sw.WriteLine(masterNumber)
          End If
        Loop Until masterName = movedName
      Loop
      'Write the rest of the master file.
      Do While srMaster.Peek <> -1
        masterName = srMaster.ReadLine
        masterNumber = srMaster.ReadLine
        sw.WriteLine(masterName)
        sw.WriteLine(masterNumber)
      Loop
      srMaster.Close()
      srMoved.Close()
      sw.Close()
      'Delete the old master, and rename the temporary file.
      IO.File.Delete("MASTER.TXT")
      IO.File.Move("TEMP.TXT", "MASTER.TXT")
      MsgBox("The file has been updated.", 0, "DONE")
    End Sub
```

CHAPTER 9

EXERCISES 9.1

1. The currently selected item in lstBox, Mozart, is displayed in txtOutput.

3. The last item, Tchaikovsky, from lstBox is displayed in txtOutput.

5. The number 3 is displayed in txtOutput.

7. The item Haydn is inserted into lstBox between Chopin and Mozart.

9. The first item, Bach, is removed from lstBox.

11. The last item, Tchaikovsky, is removed from lstBox.

13. The number 2 is displayed in the text box.

15. The list box will be empty.

17. `cboBox.Text = CStr(cboBox.Items(0))`

19. `cboBox.Items.Remove("Shakespeare")`

21. ```
cboBox.Items.RemoveAt(cboBox.Items.Count - 1)
```

23. ```
For i As Integer = 0 To cboBox.Items.Count - 1 Step 2
    lstOutput.Items.Add(cboBox.Items(i))
Next
```

25. ```
Dim found As Boolean = False
For i As Integer = 0 To cboBox.Items.Count - 1
  If CStr(cboBox.Items(i)) = "Cervantes" Then
    found = True
  End If
Next
If found Then
  txtOutput.Text = "Cervantes is in the list."
Else
  txtOutput.Text = "Cervantes not found."
End If
```

27. ```
Private Sub btnDisplay_Click(...) Handles btnDisplay.Click
    Dim total As Double = 0
    For i As Integer = 0 To lstNumbers.Items.Count - 1
      total += CDbl(lstNumbers.Items(i))
    Next
    txtOutput.Text = "The average of the numbers is " & _
                     total / lstNumbers.Items.Count & "."
End Sub
```

29. ```
Private Sub btnDisplay_Click(...) Handles btnDisplay.Click
    For i As Integer = 0 To lstNumbers.Items.Count - 1 Step 2
      lstOutput.Items.Add(lstNumbers.Items(i))
    Next
End Sub
```

31. ```
Private Sub btnDisplay_Click(...) Handles btnDisplay.Click
    Dim smallest, largest As Double
    lstNumbers.Sorted = True
    smallest = CDbl(lstNumbers.Items(0))
    largest = CDbl(lstNumbers.Items(lstNumbers.Items.Count - 1))
    txtOutput.Text = "The spread is " & (largest - smallest) & "."
End Sub
```

33. ```
Private Sub btnSort_Click(...) Handles btnSort.Click
    'Load names from a file into a sorted List Box
    'and write them to another file.
    Dim sr As IO.StreamReader = IO.File.OpenText("POPULAR_NAMES.TXT")
    Do While sr.Peek <> -1
      lstOutput.Items.Add(sr.ReadLine)
    Loop
    sr.Close()
    'Open the output file.
    Dim sw As IO.StreamWriter = IO.File.CreateText("SORTED_NAMES.TXT")
    For i As Integer = 0 To lstOutput.Items.Count - 1
      sw.WriteLine(lstOutput.Items(i))
    Next
    sw.Close()
    MsgBox("The ordered file has been created.", 0, "DONE")
End Sub
```
```

35.
```
Private Sub btnDisplay_Click(...) Handles btnDisplay.Click
    'Convert a length from one unit to the other.
    'The inches array stores the number of inches in each unit.
    Dim inches() As Double = {1, 12, 3 * 12, 100 / 2.54, 12 * 5280}
    Dim result As Double        'Result
    'If input is not specified, display message.
    If (lstFrom.SelectedIndex < 0) Or _
        (lstTo.SelectedIndex < 0) Or _
        (txtAmount.Text = "") Then
      MsgBox("Please select both units and enter a length.",0,"Incomplete")
    Else
      'Convert the first units to inches, then convert to second units.
      result = CDbl(txtAmount.Text) * inches(lstFrom.SelectedIndex) _
              / inches(lstTo.SelectedIndex)
      'Display the decimal places in the result depending upon the size.
      If result < 1 Then
        txtOutput.Text = FormatNumber(result, 6)
      Else
        txtOutput.Text = FormatNumber(result, 2)
      End If
    End If
End Sub
```

37.
```
'Note: This event procedure handles events from all three combo boxes.

Private Sub SelectedIndexChanged(...) Handles _
                    cboBrand.SelectedIndexChanged, _
                    cboMemory.SelectedIndexChanged, _
                    cboMonitor.SelectedIndexChanged
    'Update output if all choices have been made.
    If (cboBrand.SelectedIndex >= 0) And _
      (cboMemory.SelectedIndex >= 0) And _
      (cboMonitor.SelectedIndex >= 0) Then
      txtOutput.Text = "You have a " & cboBrand.Text & _
                      " computer with " & cboMemory.Text & _
                      " of memory and a " & cboMonitor.Text & _
                      " monitor."
    End If
End Sub
```

EXERCISES 9.2

1. The word "Income" becomes the caption embedded in the top of GroupBox1.

3. The check box becomes (or remains) unchecked.

5. The radio button becomes (or remains) unselected.

7. The scroll box moves to its rightmost position.

9. Clicking on the arrow on either end of the scroll bar will move the button the same ("large") distance as clicking on the bar between the scroll box and an arrow.

11. The Tick event will be triggered every *intVar* seconds

13. Any picture placed into the picture box will be automatically enlarged or contracted to fit the picture box.

15. A green rectangle of width 200 pixels and height 100 pixels will be drawn in the picture box. Its upper-left corner will be 25 pixels from the left side of the picture box and 50 units from the top side.

17. `RadioButton1.Text = "Yes"`

19. `RadioButton2.Checked = False`

21. ```
HScrollBar2.Value = CInt(HScrollBar2.Minimum + _
                 (HScrollBar2.Maximum - HScrollBar2.Minimum) / 3)
```

23. ```
PictureBox1.CreateGraphics.DrawEllipse(Pens.Yellow, _
                             10, 10, 100, 100)
```

25. `RadioButton2` is selected and `RadioButton1` is unselected.

27. Check boxes, combo boxes, horizontal scroll bars, list boxes, radio buttons, and vertical scroll bars can receive the focus.

29. Yes

31. ```
Dim box(2) As CheckBox

Private Sub frmCount_Load(...) Handles MyBase.Load
  box(0) = CheckBox1
  box(1) = CheckBox2
  box(2) = CheckBox3
End Sub

Private Sub btnDisplay_Click(...) Handles btnDisplay.Click
  Dim numChecked As Integer = 0
  For i As Integer = 0 To 2
    If box(i).Checked Then
      numChecked += 1
    End If
  Next
  txtOutput.Text = CStr(numChecked)
End Sub
```

33. ```
'This event procedure is called when any of the checkboxes
'or radio buttons change.

Private Sub CheckedChanged(...) Handles _
      radDeluxe.CheckedChanged, _
      radSuper.CheckedChanged, _
      chkMultimedia.CheckedChanged, _
      chkModem.CheckedChanged, _
      chkMemory.CheckedChanged
  'Update the cost of the system.
  Dim cost As Double
  cost = 0
  'Add amounts to the cost based upon selections.
  If radDeluxe.Checked Then
    cost += 1500
  Else
    'Super model
    cost += 1700
  End If
  If chkMultimedia.Checked Then
    cost += 300
  End If
```

```
      If chkModem.Checked Then
        cost += 100
      End If
      If chkMemory.Checked Then
        cost += 50
      End If
      txtOutput.Text = FormatCurrency(cost)
    End Sub
```

35.
```
  Dim phase As Integer          'Current phase of the moon
    Private Sub tmrMoon_Tick(...) Handles tmrMoon.Tick
      'Update the phase, and display the image.
      'Timer Interval setting is 2000.
      'Timer Enabled setting is True.
      phase += 1
      If phase = 9 Then
        phase = 1
      End If
      picBox.Image = Image.FromFile("Moon" & phase & ".BMP")
    End Sub
```

37.
```
  Public Sub vsbFahren_ValueChanged(...) Handles vsbFahren.ValueChanged
      'When Fahrenheit value changes, update the Celsius value.
      Dim celsius As Integer
      txtFahren.Text = CStr(vsbFahren.Value)
      celsius = CInt((5 / 9) * (vsbFahren.Value - 32))
      'Update Celsius value if necessary. If this IF statement
      'is not included, the program would be in an infinite loop.
      If vsbCelsius.Value <> celsius Then
        'This line will cause the other event procedure to execute.
        vsbCelsius.Value = celsius
      End If
    End Sub

    Public Sub vsbCelsius_ValueChanged(...) _
              Handles vsbCelsius.ValueChanged
      'When Celsius value changes, update the Fahrenheit value.
      Dim fahrenheit As Integer
      txtCelsius.Text = CStr(vsbCelsius.Value)
      fahrenheit = CInt((9 / 5) * vsbCelsius.Value + 32)
      'Update Fahrenheit value if necessary. If this If statement
      'is not included, the program would be in an infinite loop.
      If vsbFahren.Value <> fahrenheit Then
        'This line will cause the other event procedure to execute.
        vsbFahren.Value = fahrenheit
      End If
    End Sub
```

39.
```
  Dim count As Integer = 10
    Private Sub tmrBall_Tick(...) Handles tmrBall.Tick
      'Update the value of the scroll bar and label.
      'Timer Interval setting is 1000.
      count = count - 1
      vsbBall.Value = 10 - count
      lblBall.Text = CStr(count)
```

```
   'If at zero, display the message and end program.
   If count = 0 Then
     tmrBall.Enabled = False
     MsgBox("HAPPY NEW YEAR!!!!", 0, "NYE")
     End
   End If
End Sub
```

EXERCISES 9.3

1. The contents of the clipboard are deleted.

3. The text currently selected in txtBox, if any, is copied into the clipboard.

5. The contents of the clipboard are displayed in txtBox.

7. The contents of the clipboard are assigned to the variable *strVar*.

9. The name of one of the 43 U.S. Presidents is selected at random and displayed in txtBox.

11. Two states are selected at random and displayed in the list box.

13. A check mark appears in front of the mnuOrderAsc menu item.

15. The text appearing on the mnuOrderAsc item will be changed to Increasing Order.

17. The String variable *address* will be available to all forms in the program.

19. `txtBox.SelectedText = Clipboard.GetText`

21. `Clipboard.SetText("Rosebud")`

23. `txtBox.SelectedText = ""`

25.
```
Dim randomNum As New Random()
txtBox.Text = CStr(randomNum.Next(1, 101))
```

27.
```
Dim randomNum As New Random()
'A and Z have ANSI values 65 and 90.
txtBox.Text = Chr(randomNum.Next(65, 91))
```

29.
```
Dim randomNum As New Random()
   txtBox.Text = CStr(randomNum(1, 7) + randomNum(1, 7))
```

31. `mnuOrderDesc.Checked = False`

33. `Me.Close()`

35. `The menu item mnuOrderAsc is greyed out and cannot be selected.`

37.
```
Private Sub mnuCopy_Click(...) Handles mnuCopy.Click
    'Copy selected text into clipboard.
    Clipboard.SetText(txtBox.SelectedText)
End Sub

Private Sub mnuPaste_Click(...) Handles mnuPaste.Click
   'Paste clipboard into text box.
   txtBox.SelectedText = Clipboard.GetText
End Sub
```

```vb
Private Sub mnuCut_Click(...) Handles mnuCut.Click
  'Copy selected text into clipboard, and delete selected text.
  Clipboard.SetText(txtBox.SelectedText)
  txtBox.SelectedText = ""
End Sub

Private Sub mnuExit_Click(...) Handles mnuExit.Click
  End        'Terminate the program.
End Sub
```

39.
```vb
Private Sub btnDeal_Click(...) Handles btnDeal.Click
  'Deal five cards at random.
  Dim deckOfCards(51) As String
  Dim suits() As String = {"Hearts", "Diamonds", "Clubs", _
                           "Spades"}
  Dim n As Integer
  Dim randomNum As New Random()
  Dim temp As String
  'Populate each suit of the deck.
  For i As Integer = 0 To 3
    'Populate numbers 2 through 10.
    For j As Integer = 2 To 10
      deckOfCards(i * 13 + j) = CStr(j) & " of " & suits(i)
    Next
    'Populate the honors cards.
    deckOfCards(i * 13 + 0) = "King of " & suits(i)
    deckOfCards(i * 13 + 1) = "Ace of " & suits(i)
    deckOfCards(i * 13 + 11) = "Jack of " & suits(i)
    deckOfCards(i * 13 + 12) = "Queen of " & suits(i)
  Next
  'Choose five cards at random.
  For i As Integer = 1 To 5
    'Choose a card at random.
    n = randomNum.Next(1, 53 - i)
    lstOutput.Items.Add(deckOfCards(n))
    'Swap the chosen card with the one at the end.
    temp = deckOfCards(n)
    deckOfCards(n) = deckOfCards(52 - i)
    deckOfCards(52 - i) = temp
  Next
End Sub
```

41.
```vb
Dim randomNum As New Random()    'Random number generator

Private Sub btnToss_Click(...) Handles btnToss.Click
  'Toss a coin, and keep track of results.
  If randomNum.Next(0, 2) = 0 Then
    txtOutcome.Text = "Heads"
    txtHeads.Text = CStr(CInt(txtHeads.Text) + 1)
  Else
    txtOutcome.Text = "Tails"
    txtTails.Text = CStr(CInt(txtTails.Text) + 1)
  End If
  'Display total tosses and percentage.
  txtTosses.Text = CStr(CInt(txtTosses.Text) + 1)
  txtPercentHeads.Text = FormatPercent(CDbl(txtHeads.Text) / _
                                       CDbl(txtTosses.Text))
End Sub
```

EXERCISES 9.4

```
1. Private Sub btnDraw_Click(...) Handles btnDraw.Click
     Dim gr As Graphics = picBox.CreateGraphics
     Dim x, y, r As Double
     x = picBox.Width / 2
     y = picBox.Height / 2
     r = x / 2
     If r > y / 2 Then
       r = y / 2
     End If
     gr.FillEllipse(Brushes.Black, CSng(x - r), CSng(y - r), _
                               CSng(2 * r), CSng(2 * r))
   End Sub
```

```
3. Private Sub btnDraw_Click(...) Handles btnDraw.Click
     Dim gr As Graphics = picBox.CreateGraphics
     Dim x, y, r As Double
     x = picBox.Width / 2
     y = picBox.Height / 2
     r = 20
     gr.FillEllipse(Brushes.Red, CSng(x - r), CSng(y - 4), _
                               CSng(2 * r), CSng(2 * r))
     r = 19
     gr.FillEllipse(Brushes.Red, CSng(x - r), CSng(y - r), _
                               CSng(2 * r), CSng(2 * r))
   End Sub
```

```
5. Private Sub btnCreate_Click(...) Handles btnCreate.Click
     Dim gr As Graphics = picFlag.CreateGraphics
     Dim br() As Brush = {Brushes.Green, Brushes.White, Brushes.Red}
     'picFlag.Width = 99
     'picFlag.Height = 149
     For i As Integer = 0 To 2
       gr.FillRectangle(br(i), 0 + i * 50, 0, 50, 99)
     Next
     gr.DrawLine(Pens.Black, 0, 0, 148, 0)      'top border
     gr.DrawLine(Pens.Black, 0, 0, 0, 98)       'left border
     gr.DrawLine(Pens.Black, 0, 98, 148, 98)    'bottom border
     gr.DrawLine(Pens.Black, 148, 0, 148, 98)   'right border
   End Sub
```

```
7. Private Sub btnCreate_Click(...) Handles btnCreate.Click
     Dim gr As Graphics = picFlag.CreateGraphics
     Dim br() As Brush = {Brushes.Orange, Brushes.White, Brushes.Green}
     Dim r As Integer = 12     'radius of circle
     'picFlag.Width = 99
     'picFlag.Height = 149
     For i As Integer = 0 To 2
       gr.FillRectangle(br(i), 0, 0 + i * 33, 149, 33)
     Next
     gr.FillPie(Brushes.Orange, 75 - r, 49 - r, 2 * r, 2 * r, 0, 360)
     gr.DrawLine(Pens.Black, 0, 0, 148, 0)      'top border
     gr.DrawLine(Pens.Black, 0, 0, 0, 98)       'left border
     gr.DrawLine(Pens.Black, 0, 98, 148, 98)    'bottom border
     gr.DrawLine(Pens.Black, 148, 0, 148, 98)   'right border
   End Sub
```

9.
```
Private Sub btnDraw_Click(...) Handles btnDraw.Click
    Dim n As Integer
    Dim numbers As String = ""
    Dim gr As Graphics = picBox.CreateGraphics
    n = CInt(txtNumber.Text)
    'Font is Microsoft Sans Serif
    For i As Integer = 0 To n
      If i < 9 Then
        numbers &= CStr(i) & "        "
      Else
        numbers &= CStr(i) & "      "
      End If
      gr.DrawLine(Pens.Blue, 12 + (24 * i), 5, 12 + (24 * i), 15)
    Next
    gr.DrawLine(Pens.Blue, 0, 10, 24 * (n + 1), 10)
    gr.DrawString(numbers, Me.Font, Brushes.Blue, 8, 20)
End Sub
```

CHAPTER 10

EXERCISES 10.1

1. Combined population of the 10 most populous cities in 2015: **209.2 million**

3. China
   India
   Japan

5.
```
Private Sub btnDisplay_Click(...) Handles btnDisplay.Click
    'Display the country names in the order they are stored.
    'Open a connection to the database.
    Dim connStr As String = "Provider=Microsoft.Jet.OLEDB.4.0;" & _
                            "Data Source=MEGACITIES.MDB"
    Dim sqlStr As String = "SELECT * FROM Countries"
    Dim dataAdapter As New OleDb.OleDbDataAdapter(sqlStr, connStr)
    'Fill the data table with data from the database.
    Dim dt As New DataTable()
    dataAdapter.Fill(dt)
    dataAdapter.Dispose()
    'Display the country names (field/column 0) in the list box.
    For i As Integer = 0 To dt.Rows.Count - 1
      lstOutput.Items.Add(dt.Rows(i)(0))
    Next
End Sub
```

7.
```
Private Sub btnDisplay_Click(...) Handles btnDisplay.Click
    'Displays the cities whose populations in 2015 will exceed 20 mil
    'Open a connection to the database.
    Dim connStr As String = "Provider=Microsoft.Jet.OLEDB.4.0;" & _
                            "Data Source=MEGACITIES.MDB"
    Dim sqlStr As String = "SELECT * FROM Cities"
    Dim dataAdapter As New OleDb.OleDbDataAdapter(sqlStr, connStr)
```

```
    'Fill the data table with data from the database.
    Dim dt As New DataTable()
    dataAdapter.Fill(dt)
    dataAdapter.Dispose()
    'Display the city name (column 0) where the 2015 pop exceeds 20.
    For i As Integer = 0 To dt.Rows.Count - 1
      If CDbl(dt.Rows(i)("pop2015")) > 20 Then
        lstOutput.Items.Add(dt.Rows(i)(0))
      End If
    Next
  End Sub
```

9.
```
Private Sub btnDisplay_Click(...) Handles btnDisplay.Click
    'Displays countries and monetary units
    'Open a connection to the database.
    Dim connStr As String = "Provider=Microsoft.Jet.OLEDB.4.0;" & _
                      "Data Source=MEGACITIES.MDB"
    Dim sqlStr As String = "SELECT * FROM Countries"
    Dim dataAdapter As New OleDb.OleDbDataAdapter(sqlStr, connStr)
    'Fill the data table with data from the database.
    Dim dt As New DataTable()
    dataAdapter.Fill(dt)
    dataAdapter.Dispose()
    'Display the country (column 0) and its monetary unit (column 2).
    For i As Integer = 0 To dt.Rows.Count - 1
      lstOutput.Items.Add(CStr(dt.Rows(i)(0)) & " - " & _
                      CStr(dt.Rows(i)(2)))
    Next
  End Sub
```

11.
```
Structure Country
    Dim name As String
    Dim pop2005 As Double
    Dim monetaryUnit As String
  End Structure

  Private Sub btnDisplay_Click(...) Handles btnDisplay.Click
    'Displays countries in descending order of their population
    'Open a connection to the database.
    Dim connStr As String = "Provider=Microsoft.Jet.OLEDB.4.0;" & _
                      "Data Source=MEGACITIES.MDB"
    Dim sqlStr As String = "SELECT * FROM Countries"
    Dim dataAdapter As New OleDb.OleDbDataAdapter(sqlStr, connStr)
    'Fill the data table with data from the database.
    Dim dt As New DataTable()
    dataAdapter.Fill(dt)
    dataAdapter.Dispose()
    'Declare an array of structures to hold the data.
    Dim temp, countries(dt.Rows.Count - 1) As Country
    'Load the data into the array.
    For i As Integer = 0 To dt.Rows.Count - 1
      countries(i).name = CStr(dt.Rows(i)(0))
      countries(i).pop2005 = CDbl(dt.Rows(i)(1))
      countries(i).monetaryUnit = CStr(dt.Rows(i)(2))
    Next
```

```
     'Bubble sort on population.
     For i As Integer = 1 To dt.Rows.Count - 1
       For j As Integer = 0 To dt.Rows.Count - i
         If countries(j - 1).pop2005 < countries(j).pop2005 Then
           temp = countries(j - 1)
           countries(j - 1) = countries(j)
           countries(j) = temp
         End If
       Next
     Next
     'Display the country names.
     For i As Integer = 0 To dt.Rows.Count - 1
       lstOutput.Items.Add(countries(i).name)
     Next
   End Sub
```

13.
```
   Private Sub btnDisplay_Click(...) Handles btnDisplay.Click
     'Displays cities and monetary units
     Dim j As Integer
     'Open a connection to the database.
     Dim connStr As String = "Provider=Microsoft.Jet.OLEDB.4.0;" & _
                             "Data Source=MEGACITIES.MDB"
     Dim sqlStr As String = "SELECT * FROM Cities"
     Dim dataAdapter As New OleDb.OleDbDataAdapter(sqlStr, connStr)
     'Fill the data table with data from the database.
     Dim dt As New DataTable()
     dataAdapter.Fill(dt)
     dataAdapter.Dispose()
     'Load data from Countries table into second data table.
     sqlStr = "SELECT * FROM Countries"
     dataAdapter = New OleDb.OleDbDataAdapter(sqlStr, connStr)
     Dim dt2 As New DataTable()
     dataAdapter.Fill(dt2)
     dataAdapter.Dispose()
     'Loop for each city.
     For i As Integer = 0 To dt.Rows.Count - 1
       j = 0
       'When the city's country is found, then quit the loop.
       Do While CStr(dt2.Rows(j)(0)) <> CStr(dt.Rows(i)(1))
         j += 1
       Loop
       'Display the city and monetary unit.
       lstOutput.Items.Add(CStr(dt.Rows(i)(0)) & " - " & _
                           CStr(dt2.Rows(j)(2)))
     Next
   End Sub
```

15. The two sequential files have a combined size of 498 bytes, while the database file has size 196 KB.

17. Two tables: Publishers and Titles

19. 10

21.
```
Dim dt As New DataTable()    'Data table holds the data.

Private Sub frmStates_Load(...) Handles MyBase.Load
  'Loads the information into the data table
  'Open a connection to the database.
  Dim connStr As String = "Provider=Microsoft.Jet.OLEDB.4.0;" & _
                          "Data Source = STATE_ABBR.MDB"
  Dim sqlStr As String = "SELECT * FROM States"
  Dim dataAdapter As New OleDb.OleDbDataAdapter(sqlStr, connStr)
  'Fill the data table with data from the database.
  dataAdapter.Fill(dt)
  dataAdapter.Dispose()
End Sub

Private Sub btnDisplay_Click(...) Handles btnDisplay.Click
  'Display the state that matches the abbreviation.
  'Convert the abbreviation to uppercase.
  mtxtAbbr.Text = mtxtAbbr.Text.ToUpper
  If mtxtAbbr.Text = "" Then
    'Display error message.
    txtOutput.Text = "Enter a state."
  Else
    txtOutput.Clear()
    'Loop over all states.
    For i As Integer = 0 To 49
      'If the abbreviation matches, then display the name.
      If mtxtAbbr.Text = CStr(dt.Rows(i)(0)) Then
        txtOutput.Text = CStr(dt.Rows(i)(1))
      End If
    Next
    If txtOutput.Text = "" Then
      'Display error message.
      txtOutput.Text = "Not found."
    End If
  End If
  'Set focus back on abbreviation.
  txtAbbr.Focus()
End Sub
```

EXERCISES 10.2

1. Could cause a problem if the country added is not one of the countries in the Countries table

3. No problem

5. (B)

7. (A)

9. (D)

11. (C)

13. `SELECT country, monetaryUnit FROM Countries WHERE pop2005>130 AND pop2005<200 ORDER BY pop2005 ASC`

15. `SELECT * FROM Cities WHERE country='India' ORDER BY pop2015 DESC`

17. ```
SELECT * FROM Cities WHERE pop2005>18 AND pop2005<19 ORDER BY pop2005 ASC,
pop2015 ASC
```

19. ```
SELECT city, pop2015, monetaryUnit FROM Cities INNER JOIN Countries
    ON Countries.country=Cities.country
    WHERE Countries.country='India' ORDER BY pop2015 DESC
```

21. ```
Dim dt As New DataTable()   'Holds the data

Private Sub frmCurrency_Load(...) Handles MyBase.Load
  'Get all fields from the Rates table sorted by country.
  Dim connStr As String = "Provider = Microsoft.Jet.OLEDB.4.0;" & _
                          "Data Source = EXCHRATE.MDB"
  Dim sqlStr As String = "SELECT * FROM Rates ORDER BY Country"
  Dim dataAdapter As New _
          OleDb.OleDbDataAdapter(sqlStr, connStr)
  'Fill the data table, and close the data adapter.
  dataAdapter.Fill(dt)
  dataAdapter.Dispose()
  'Set the list box's data source to the countries field.
  lstCountries.DataSource = dt
  lstCountries.DisplayMember = "Country"
End Sub

Private Sub lstCountries_SelectedIndexChanged(...) _
          Handles lstCountries.SelectedIndexChanged
  'Display the country's monetary unit and exchange rate.
  txtCurrency.Text = CStr(dt.Rows(lstCountries.SelectedIndex)(1))
  txtRate.Text = FormatNumber(dt.Rows(lstCountries.SelectedIndex)(2))
End Sub
```

23. ```
Structure Rate
    Dim country As String
    Dim monetaryUnit As String
    Dim dollarRate As Double
End Structure

Dim rateTable As New DataTable()
Dim rateTable2 As New DataTable()

Private Sub frmCurrency_Load(...) Handles MyBase.Load
  'Get all fields from the Rates table sorted by country.
  Dim connStr As String = "Provider = Microsoft.Jet.OLEDB.4.0;" & _
                          "Data Source = EXCHRATE.MDB"
  Dim sqlStr As String = "SELECT * FROM Rates ORDER BY Country"
  Dim dataAdapter As New OleDb.OleDbDataAdapter(sqlStr, connStr)
  'Fill the from and to table and close the data adapter
  dataAdapter.Fill(rateTable)
  dataAdapter.Fill(rateTable2)
  dataAdapter.Dispose()
  'Set the list boxes' data sources to the respective data tables.
  lstFrom.DataSource = rateTable
  lstFrom.DisplayMember = "Country"
  lstTo.DataSource = rateTable2
  lstTo.DisplayMember = "Country"
End Sub

Private Sub btnConvert_Click(...) Handles btnConvert.Click
  'Convert the monetary unit, and display the result.
  Dim result, amount As Double
```

```vb
    Dim fromRate, toRate As Rate
    Dim fromIndex As Integer = lstFrom.SelectedIndex
    Dim toIndex As Integer = lstTo.SelectedIndex
    'Display an error message if input is insufficient.
    If (fromIndex < 0) Or (toIndex < 0) Or _
        (txtAmount.Text.Trim = "") Then
      MsgBox("Both countries and an amount must be provided.", 0, _
            "Insufficient Input")
    Else
      'Get each row from the data table, and store into a structure.
      fromRate = GetRate(fromIndex)
      toRate = GetRate(toIndex)
      'Convert the amount
      amount = CDbl(txtAmount.Text)
      result = Convert(fromRate.dollarRate, toRate.dollarRate, amount)
      'Display the result formatted with the rates.
      txtResult.Text = FormatNumber(amount) & " " & _
              fromRate.monetaryUnit & "s from " & fromRate.country & _
              " equals " & FormatNumber(result) & " " & _
              toRate.monetaryUnit & "s from " & toRate.country
    End If
    txtAmount.Focus()
  End Sub

  Function GetRate(ByVal rowNum As Integer) As Rate
    'Store the fields from a row into a structure.
    Dim rateInfo As Rate
    rateInfo.Country = CStr(rateTable.rows(rowNum)("Country"))
    rateInfo.monetaryUnit = CStr(rateTable.Rows(rowNum)("monetaryUnit"))
    rateInfo.dollarRate = CDbl(rateTable.Rows(rowNum)("dollarRate"))
    Return rateInfo
  End Function

  Function Convert(ByVal fromRate As Double, _
                  ByVal toRate As Double, _
                  ByVal amount As Double) As Double
    'Convert the amount from the from Currency to the to Currency.
    Return amount * toRate / fromRate
  End Function
```

27.
```vb
  Private Sub btnDisplay_Click(...) Handles btnDisplay.Click
    'Display the data from the data table in the data grid
    Dim sqlStr As String
    sqlStr = "Select player From Players INNER JOIN Teams ON " & _
            "Players.team=Teams.team WHERE location='New York'"
    UpdateGrid(sqlStr)
  End Sub

  Sub UpdateGrid(ByVal sqlStr As String)
    Dim dt As New DataTable()
    Dim connStr As String = "Provider=Microsoft.Jet.OLEDB.4.0;" & _
                        "Data Source=BASEBALL.MDB"
    Dim dataAdapter As New OleDb.OleDbDataAdapter(sqlStr, connStr)
    dataAdapter.Fill(dt)
    dataAdapter.Dispose()
    dgvDisplay.DataSource = dt
  End Sub
```

35.
```
Private Sub btnDisplay_Click(...) Handles btnDisplay.Click
    'Display a telephone directory.
    Dim lastName, str As String
    Dim fmtStr As String = "{0,-30} {1,7}"
    Dim connStr As String = "Provider = Microsoft.Jet.OLEDB.4.0;" & _
                            "Data Source = PHONEBOOK.MDB"
    Dim sqlStr As String = "SELECT * FROM Entries ORDER BY " & _
                           "lastName, firstName, middleInitial ASC"
    Dim dataAdapter As New OleDb.OleDbDataAdapter(sqlStr, connStr)
    Dim dt As New DataTable()
    dataAdapter.Fill(dt)
    dataAdapter.Dispose()
    'Loop over all rows, remembering the current lastname.
    lastName = ""
    lstOutput.Items.Add(String.Format(fmtStr, "NAME, ADDRESS", _
                                      "PHONE #"))
    For i As Integer = 0 To dt.Rows.Count - 1
      If lastName <> CStr(dt.Rows(i)(0)) Then
        'If the last name has changed, then remember it.
        lastName = CStr(dt.Rows(i)(0))
        'LASTNAME firstName middleInitial streetNumber street
        str = lastName.ToUpper & " " & CStr(dt.Rows(i)(1)) & " " & _
              CStr(dt.Rows(i)(2)) & "   " & _
              CStr(dt.Rows(i)(3)) & " " & CStr(dt.Rows(i)(4))
      Else
        'firstName middleInitial streetNumber street
        str = "    " & CStr(dt.Rows(i)(1)) & " " & _
              CStr(dt.Rows(i)(2)) & "   " & _
              CStr(dt.Rows(i)(3)) & " " & CStr(dt.Rows(i)(4))
      End If
      lstOutput.Items.Add(String.Format(fmtStr, str, _
                                        dt.Rows(i)(5)))
    Next
End Sub
```

CHAPTER 11

EXERCISES 11.1

1. Any negative grade will be recorded as 0, and any grade greater than 100 will be recorded as 100.

3. Remove the keyword WriteOnly from the Final property block, and add the following *Get* property procedure to it:

```
Get
  Return m_midterm
End Get
```

5. The properties MidGrade and Final are write only.

7. The property SocSecNum is initialized to the value **999-99-9999**.

9. The keyword New is missing from the third line of the event procedure.

11. The statement **nom = m_name** is not valid.

13. The property MidGrade is write only; it can be set, but cannot return a value.

15.
```
Country: Canada
Capital: Ottawa
Pop: 31 million
```

17. Create a **formLoad** event procedure with the following lines, and change 20 to −20 in the **btnMove_Click** event procedure:

```
round.Xcoord = picCircle.Width - 40
round.Ycoord = picCircle.Height - 40
```

21.
```
Class PairOfDice

    Private m_die1, m_die2 As Integer
    Dim randomNum As New Random()

    Public ReadOnly Property Die1() As Integer
      Get
        Return m_die1
      End Get
    End Property

    Public ReadOnly Property Die2() As Integer
      Get
        Return m_die2
      End Get
    End Property

    Public ReadOnly Property SumOfFaces() As Integer
      Get
        Return m_die1 + m_die2
      End Get
    End Property

    Sub Roll()
      m_die1 = randomNum.Next(1, 7)
      m_die2 = randomNum.Next(1, 7)
    End Sub
End Class
```

25.
```
Dim register As New CashRegister()
Private Sub btnAdd_Click(...) Handles btnAdd.Click
  'Add an amount to the balance.
  register.Add(CDbl(txtAmount.Text))
  'Display the new result.
  txtBalance.Text = FormatCurrency(register.Balance)
  txtAmount.Clear()
  txtAmount.Focus()
End Sub

Private Sub btnSubtract_Click(...) Handles btnSubtract.Click
  'Subtract an amount from the balance.
  register.Subtract(CDbl(txtAmount.Text))
```

```
                  'Display the new result.
                  txtBalance.Text = FormatCurrency(register.Balance)
                  txtAmount.Clear()
                  txtAmount.Focus()
                End Sub

              Class CashRegister
                Private m_balance As Double

                Public ReadOnly Property Balance() As Double
                  Get
                    Return m_balance
                  End Get
                End Property

                Sub Add(ByVal amount As Double)
                  'Make sure balance does not go negative for negative amounts.
                  If m_balance + amount >= 0 Then
                    m_balance += amount
                  End If
                End Sub

                Sub Subtract(ByVal amount As Double)
                  'Make sure balance does not go negative.
                  If m_balance - amount >= 0 Then
                    m_balance = m_balance - amount
                  End If
                End Sub

              End Class
```

EXERCISES **11.2**

```
1. Sub btnDisplay_Click(...) Handles btnDisplay.Click
     Dim fmtStr As String = "{0,-20}{1,-15}{2,-1}"
     lstGrades.Items.Clear()
     lstGrades.Items.Add(String.Format(fmtStr, "Student Name", _
                                       "SSN", "Grade"))
     For i As Integer = 0 To lastStudentAdded
       If students(i).CalcSemGrade = "A" Then
         lstGrades.Items.Add(String.Format(fmtStr, students(i).Name, _
                             students(i).SocSecNum, _
                             students(i).CalcSemGrade))
       End If
     Next
   End Sub

7. Class CashRegister
     Private m_balance As Double
     Event AttemptToOverdraw(ByVal amt As Double)

     Public ReadOnly Property Balance() As Double
       Get
         Return m_balance
       End Get
     End Property
```

```
Sub Add(ByVal amount As Double)
  'Make sure balance does not go negative for negative amounts.
  If m_balance + amount >= 0 Then
    m_balance += amount
  Else
    RaiseEvent AttemptToOverdraw(m_balance - amount)
  End If
End Sub

Sub Subtract(ByVal amount As Double)
  'Make sure balance does not go negative.
  If m_balance - amount >= 0 Then
    m_balance = m_balance - amount
  Else
    RaiseEvent AttemptToOverdraw(m_balance - amount)
  End If
End Sub
End Class
```

Exercises 11.3

1. 4

3. 64

5. `Can move Has jointed limbs and no backbone`

7. The keyword Overrides should be Inherits.

9. The Hi function should be declared with the Overridable keyword in class Hello and with the keyword Overrides keyword in class Aussie.

11. The Hi function should be declared with the Overrides keyword in class Cowboy.

13. The Hello class should be declared with the MustInherit keyword, and the function Hi should be declared with the MustOverride keyword.

15. The Hello class should be declared with the MustInherit keyword, not MustOverride.

19.
```
Public Class frmRregister
  Dim tollBooth As New FastTrackRegister()

  Private Sub btnProcess_Click(...) Handles btnProcess.Click
    'Process the vehicle
    If radCar.Checked Then
      tollBooth.ProcessCar()
    Else
      tollBooth.ProcessTruck()
    End If
    'Display the revenue and number of vehicles
    txtRevenue.Text = FormatCurrency(tollBooth.Balance)
    txtNumVehicles.Text = CStr(tollBooth.Count)
  End Sub
End Class
```

```
Class CashRegister
  Private m_balance As Double

  Sub Deposit(ByVal amount As Double)
    m_balance += amount                'Add the amount to the balance.
  End Sub

  Sub WithDrawal(ByVal amount As Double)
    m_balance = m_balance - amount   'Subtract the amount from balance.
  End Sub

  Public ReadOnly Property Balance() As Double
    Get
      Return m_balance
    End Get
  End Property
End Class

Class FastTrackRegister
  Inherits CashRegister
  Private m_count As Integer

  Public ReadOnly Property Count() As Integer
    Get
      Return m_count
    End Get
  End Property

  Sub ProcessCar()
    m_count += 1      'Process a car: $1.00.
    Deposit(1)
  End Sub

  Sub ProcessTruck()
    m_count += 1       'Process a truck: $2.00.
    Deposit(2)
  End Sub
End Class
```

INDEX

A

Abstract property, method, and class, 591
Access key, 9, 51, 473, 474, 486, 616
Accumulator variable, 261, 265, 301
Active window, 6
Add
    data to a file, 414
    method, 73, 89, 462
    New Item dialog box, 489
Addition operation, 73
ADO.NET, 520
Aiken, Howard, 22
Algorithm, 4, 31
    binary search, 365–67
    bubble sort, 357
    merge, 329
    Shell sort, 361
Aligning controls, 54–56
Allen, Paul, 24
Alphabetic view of Properties window, 46
Alt key, 8, 9
Ampersand character, 51, 91, 115
Analyze a Loan case study, 291–301
And logical operator, 196
Andreessen, Marc, 27
Animation, 502
ANSI
    displaying characters, 613
    table, 611
    values, 194, 605–6
Apostrophe character, 96
AppendText method, 414
Application, 30, 42
Argument, 137, 633
Arithmetic operation, 73
    level of precedence, 80
Array, 308, 309, 401
    control, 341, 401
    declaring an, 309
    higher-dimensional, 383
    initial values, 312, 379
    of objects, 569
    of structures, 345
    ordered, 326
    passing an, 331
    search of ordered, 327
    searching an, 327, 365, 402
    size, 309
    sorting an, 356–63, 402
    two-dimensional, 377–78, 402
    upper bound, 309
    variable, 308, 309
Arrow, 5
Asc function, 194, 243
Ascending order, 326
ASCII. See ANSI
Assignment statement, 60, 76, 78, 89, 127, 316
Asterisk character, 67, 73
Atanasoff, John V., 22
Attaching controls to a group box, 472
Auto hide, 54
AutoSize property, 477, 616

B

Babbage, Charles, 21
BackColor property, 56
Backslash character, 10, 12
Backus, John, 23
Bar charts, 501
Bardeen, John, 22
Base class, 582
BASIC, 4
Berners-Lee, Tim, 26
Binary search, 365–67
    flowchart, 366
Body of a For . . . Next loop, 277
Bohm, Corrado, 23
Boole, George, 21
Boolean data type, 197–98, 266
Brattain, Walter, 22
Break, 437
    mode, 627
Breakpoint, 628, 629
    removing a, 629, 631
    setting a, 628, 631
Bricklin, Dan, 24–25
Brushes object, 497
Bubble sort, 357, 370
Bug, 31, 418, 627
Button control, 45, 50
Button, Tom, 26
ByRef keyword, 155
    overriding, 157
Byron, Augusta Ada, 21
ByVal keyword, 134, 154, 157

C

Calculated columns (SQL), 540
Call statement, 132
Called procedure, 133
Calling procedure, 133
CancelButton property, 617
Caret character, 73
Case
    clause, 220
    keyword, 218
Case study
    Analyze a Loan, 291–301
    Recording Checks and Deposits, 442–53
    Sophisticated Cash Register, 392–401
    Weekly Payroll, 235–43
Catch block, 419
Categorized view of Properties window, 46
CDbl function, 90, 97, 128
Ceil function, 182
Chamberlain, Don, 25
Character map, 54, 613
Check box control, 473–74, 509
CheckChanged event, 473–74, 475
Checked property, 473, 474
Child class, 582
Chr function, 194, 243
CInt function, 90, 97, 128
Class, 552, 553, 601
    abstract, 591
    base, 582
    block, 553
    child, 582
    creating a, 558–59
    derived, 582
    hierarchy, 582
    interface, 586
    level scope, 159
    level variable, 159, 188, 310
    Name box, 62, 63, 65
    parent, 582
Clean-up code, 421
Clear method, 74, 95
Clearing
    a list box, 74
    a text box, 95
Click
    event, 64
    with a mouse, 5
Client area, 502, 504
ClientSize property, 502, 504
Clipboard object, 484–85, 509, 610, 613
Close
    a file, 109
    button, 7

method, 109, 412
    Project command, 56
Codd, Ted, 24
Code window, 62, 67
Coding, 31
Color, 47
    palette, 616
    property, 497
Colorization, 98
Combo box control, 464–65, 509
Comment statement, 96, 141
Compound interest, 172
Computed column, 548
Concatenation operation, 91
Condition, 194, 201, 243, 248, 268
Confusing If block, 207
Connection string, 521
Constructor, 560
Containment, 574, 582
Context-sensitive help, 64
Continue keyword, 284
Control, 19, 42, 127
    aligning, 54–56
    array, 341, 401
    break processing, 437
    Button, 45, 50
    Check box, 473–74
    Combo box, 464–65
    DataGridView, 535
    delete a, 615
    Group box, 472
    Horizontal scroll bar, 478–79
    Label, 44, 51, 616
    List box, 45, 52, 73, 462–64
    Masked text box, 114
    MenuStrip, 486–87
    move a, 615
    OpenFileDialog, 466
    Picture box, 477–78
    place on a form, 614
    positioning, 54–56
    Radio button, 474–75
    related group of, 614
    resize a, 615
    setting properties of, 45–48, 127, 615
    Text box, 44, 45–50, 90
    Timer, 476
    variable, 277, 278, 279, 282, 284, 301, 437
    Vertical scroll bar, 478–79
Converting from VB 6.0 to Visual Basic 2005,
    621–26
Cooper, Alan, 26
Coordinates of a point, 497
Copying text, 484, 610
Count property, 462, 522
Counter variable, 261, 265, 301, 328

Courier New font, 53
CreateGraphics method, 496
CreateText method, 412
Criteria clause, 533
CStr function, 90, 128
CSV format, 432
Ctrl key, 8
Ctrl+Alt+Break key combination, 629
Ctrl+Del key combination, 8
Ctrl+End key combination, 10
Ctrl+F8 key combination, 628
Ctrl+Home key combination, 10
Ctrl+Shift+F8 key combination, 628
Ctrl+Y key combination, 610
Ctrl+Z key combination, 56, 610
Cursor, 7

D

Data
    conversion, 90, 98
    hiding, 552
    table, 520
    type
        Boolean, 197–98, 266
        Double, 76–77
        Integer, 80
        String, 89
    validation, 419
Data adapter, 521, 548
Database, 422, 518, 519, 548
    altering, 538
    Explorer, 519–20, 548
    management software, 519
Data-bound control, 526
DataGridView control, 535, 548
DataSource property, 526, 536
DataTable object, 520, 548
    Columns, 522
    Rows, 522
Debug folder, 110
Debugging, 22, 31, 160, 268, 619–20, 627–36
Decision structure, 36, 185
Declaration statement, 76
Declarations section of Code window, 159, 188
Declaring
    an object, 553
    variables, 76, 80, 81, 89, 95
Default value, 77, 95
Del key, 8, 45
Delete
    a breakpoint, 619, 620
    method, 415
    text, 609
Delimiter, 433

Depreciation, 305
Derived class, 582
Descending order, 326
Description pane, 46
Design
    mode, 627
    modular, 183
    top-down, 140, 183
Desk-checking, 38, 627
Details view, 13
Dialog box
    Add New Item, 489
    canceling a, 612
    Error, 67
    Find, 10
    Font, 48
    Input, 112–13
    message, 114
    New Project, 43
    Open, 15–16
    Open Project, 50
    Save As, 10, 15–16
    using a, 612
Dijkstra, Edsger W., 23
Dim statement, 76, 89, 95, 309, 377, 401
Directory, 13
Disk, 12
    drive, 2
DisplayMember property, 526
Divide and conquer method, 36
Division operation, 73
Do loop, 248, 251, 301
    flowchart, 248
    pass through a, 248
    stepping through a, 635–36
Documentation, 32, 96–97
Double data type, 76–77
Double-click, with a mouse, 5
Double-subscripted variable, 377
Dragging, with a mouse, 6
DrawEllipse method, 477
DrawLine method, 497
DrawRectangle method, 477
DrawString method, 497
Driver, 186
DropDown combo box, 464–65
DropDownList combo box, 464–65
DropDownStyle property, 464–65

E

e parameter, 66
Eckert, J. Presper, 22
Editor
    smart, 133, 226

Editor (*Continued*)
    text, 8
    using the, 609–11
Efficiency of sorts, 363
Element of an array, 309
Else keyword, 201
ElseIf clause, 205
Empty string, 95
Enabled property, 56, 476
End
    Class, 552
    Function, 170
    If, 201
    key, 8, 49
    Select, 220
    statement, 66
    Structure, 343
    Sub, 61, 132, 133
Engelbart, Douglas, 24
Enter
    event, 66
    key, 9, 617
Erase keyword, 316
Error
    detection, 67
    dialog box, 67
    file not found, 414, 420
    For must be paired with Next, 284
    index out of range, 316
    logical, 81
    run-time, 81
    syntax, 80
Esc key, 9, 617
Estridge, Phillip, 25–26
Event, 60–66, 601
    procedure, 61, 62, 127, 618
    user-defined, 571, 602
Exception, 418
    ArgumentOutOfRange, 420
    Catch block, 419
    Finally block, 419
    IndexOutOfRange, 420
    InvalidCast, 418–19, 420
    IO.DirectoryNotFound, 420
    IO.EndOfStream, 420
    IO.FileNotFound, 420
    IO.IO, 420
    NullReference, 420
    Overflow, 420
    Try block, 419
Exists method, 414
Exit keyword, 284
Exiting Visual Basic, 607
Exponent, 82
Exponentiation operation, 73

Expression
    numeric, 77
    string, 91
Extension of a file name, 12, 13, 614

F

F1 key, 64, 611, 612
F4 key, 45, 615
F5 key, 48, 607, 629
F8 key, 628
F9 key, 628
Faggin, Federico, 24
FICA tax, 206, 236
Field
    of a database table, 518, 548
    of a record, 422
File, 12–16
    add data to, 414
    close a, 412
    copy a, 15
    create with Notepad, 10
    CSV format, 432
    delete a, 15
    Delete method, 415
    delimiter, 433
    displaying extensions, 13
    Exists method, 414
    LSV format, 433
    merging, 435
    modes, 414
    move a, 15
    Move method, 415
    name, 10, 12, 412
    opening for append, 414
    opening for input, 108, 412
    opening for output, 412
    opening in Notepad, 10
    processing data from, 261–62
    reading from a, 108–12, 128
    read-only attribute, 519
    rename a, 15
    saving a, 10
    sequential, 412
    sorting a, 430, 454
    text, 12, 412
    writing to, 412
Filename, 12
FileName property, 467
Filespec, 12
FillEllipse method, 498
FillPie method, 498–99
FillRectangle method, 498
Filter property, 466

Finally block, 419
Find
    dialog box, 10
    editor command, 610
Flag variable, 261, 266, 301
Flagged bubble sort, 370
Flowchart, 33, 40
    binary search, 366
    Do loop tested at bottom, 251
    Do While loop, 248
    For . . . Next loop, 278
    If block, 201
    processing data from a file, 263
    search of an ordered array, 327
    Select Case block, 221
Flowline, 33
Focus, 49
    method, 66
Folder, 12–16
    bin, 110
    copy a, 15
    create a, 13
    Debug, 110
    delete a, 15
    move a, 15
    rename a, 15
Font, 48, 53, 127
    dialog box, 48
    setting properties of a, 67
Fonts object, 504
For . . . Next loop, 277–84, 301
    body, 277
    control variable, 277, 301
    flowchart, 278
    initial value, 277
    nested, 282–83
    terminating value, 277
ForeColor property, 47
Foreign key, 531
Form, 42, 43, 65
    center a, 617
    design a, 614–15
    Designer, 42
    modal, 490
    multiple, 489–90
    rename a, 617
Format menu, 54, 55–56
Format string, 105, 128
FormatCurrency function, 105, 128
FormatNumber function, 105, 128
FormatPercent function, 105, 128
Formatting output, 105–7
FormBorderStyle property, 490

Frequency table, 315
Function
    Asc, 194, 243
    built-in, 169
    CDbl, 90, 97, 128
    Ceil, 182
    Chr, 194, 243
    CInt, 90, 97, 128
    compared to Sub procedure, 175–76
    CStr, 90, 128
    declaring a, 170
    FormatCurrency, 105, 128
    FormatNumber, 105, 128
    FormatPercent, 105, 128
    InputBox, 128
    Int, 78, 128
    invoking a, 170
    Join, 434
    Math.Round, 78, 82, 128
    Math.Sqrt, 78, 128
    numeric, 78
    parameter, 170
    parameterless, 175
    procedure, 169, 188
    Split, 433
    ToString, 98
    user-defined, 169, 172
Fylstra, Dan, 24–25

G

Game of Life, 406–7
Gap in a Shell sort, 361
Gates, Bill, 24
General procedure, 132
GetUpperBound method, 312, 380, 401
Gosling, James, 27
GoTo statement, 40, 185
Graphical user interface, 18
Graphics, 496–504, 509
Greatest common divisor, 261
Group box control, 472, 509

H

Handles keyword, 61, 65
Hard copy, obtaining, 619
Hardware, 3
Help, 611–12
    context-sensitive, 64
    index, 53, 611
    IntelliSense, 63
    Member Listing, 63
    Parameter Info, 113, 141

Hierarchy
    chart, 33, 35
    of classes, 582
Hoff, Ted, 24
Hollerith, Herman, 21
Home key, 8, 49
Hopper, Grace M., 22
Horizontal scroll bar control, 478–79, 509
Hourglass pointer, 5
Hover, with a mouse, 5

I

I-Beam pointer, 5
Identifier, 81
If block, 201, 243
    confusing, 207
    flowchart, 201
    stepping through an, 633–34
Image property, 477
Immediate window, 629, 631
Imports System.IO, 415
Income tax, 245
Incrementing the value of a variable, 78
Indentation, 66, 611
Index number, 462
Index out of range error, 316
IndexOf method, 93
Inequality, 194
Infinite loop, 252
Infinity, 81–82
Inheritance, 582, 602
Inherits keyword, 583
Initial value of a For . . . Next loop, 277
Initial value of a variable, 77
Inner Join operation (SQL), 533
Input, 3, 30, 44, 90, 108–12, 112, 114
    devices, 2
    dialog box, 112–13
Input/Output class (IO), 108
InputBox function, 112–13, 128
Instance, 490, 554
    variable, 554
Int function, 78, 128
Integer data type, 80
IntelliSense, 63, 113, 610
Interface, 586
Interval property, 476
Invalid cast error, 418–19
Invoking Visual Basic, 607
Is keyword, 220, 226
ISA test, 583
Item of a list box, 462
Iteration, 185

J

Jacopini, Guiseppe, 23
Jobs, Stephen, 24
Johnson, Reynold B., 23
Join
    function, 434
    of two tables, 531–32

K

Kapor, Mitchell D., 26
Kay, Allen, 25
Kemeny, John G., 23
Key
    access, 9
    Alt, 8, 9
    Alt+F4, 49
    Ctrl, 8
    Ctrl+Alt+Break, 629
    Ctrl+Del, 8
    Ctrl+End, 10
    Ctrl+F8, 628
    Ctrl+Home, 10
    Ctrl+Shift+F8, 628
    Ctrl+Y, 610
    Ctrl+Z, 56, 610
    Del, 8, 45
    End, 8
    Enter, 9, 617
    Esc, 9, 617
    F1, 64, 611, 612
    F4, 45, 615
    F5, 48, 607, 628
    F8, 628
    F9, 628
    foreign, 531
    Home, 8
    member, 370
    primary, 531, 548
    Shift+F5, 631
    Shift+F8, 628
    Shift+Tab, 50
    shortcut, 612
    Tab, 50
Keyword, 61, 81
Knuth, Donald E., 24
Kurtz, Thomas E., 23

L

Label control, 44, 51, 616
LargeChange property, 478–79

Leave event, 64, 66
Left-justification, 106
Length property, 92
Level of precedence for arithmetic operations, 80
Like operator, 533, 542
Line-continuation character, 97
List box control, 45, 52, 73, 462–64, 509
    data-bound, 526, 548
    fill at design time, 464
Literal
    numeric, 73
    string, 88
Load event procedure, 311
Loading a program, 67
Local scope, 159
Local variable, 157, 188, 310
Locals window, 630, 633
Logical
    error, 81
    operator, 194, 196, 243
Lookup table, 368
Loop
    Do, 248, 301
    For . . . Next, 277–84, 301
    infinite, 252
    keyword, 248
    nested, 267, 282–83
    structure, 36, 185
LSV format, 433

M

Machine language, 3
Main area, 42, 43
MainMenu control, 509
Managing
    menus, 613
    procedures, 618
    programs, 607–9
    windows, 619
Mask property, 114–15
Masked text box control, 114
Math.Round function, 78, 82, 128
Math.Sqrt function, 78, 128
Mathematical notation, 73
Mauchley, John, 22
Maximize button, 7
Maximum property, 478–79
Mazer, Stan, 24
Me keyword, 65, 497
Mean, 402
Median, 376
Member
    Listing, 63

of a structure, 343
    variable, 554, 559, 594
Memory, 2, 76, 154, 155, 157
Menu
    bar, 7, 8, 42, 43
    managing a, 613
MenuStrip control, 486–87
Merge algorithm, 329
Merging files, 435
Message dialog box, 114
Method, 73, 555, 601
    abstract, 591
    AppendText, 414
    Clear, 74, 95
    Close, 412
    CreateText, 412
    Exists, 414
    IndexOf, 93
    Name box, 62, 63, 65
    OpenText, 108
    Readline, 108–9
    Substring, 93
    ToLower, 92
    ToUpper, 92
    Trim, 92, 98
    WriteLine, 412
Microprocessor, 2
Mills, Harlan B., 23–24
Minimize button, 7
Minimum property, 478–79
Mod operator, 82
Modal form, 490
Modular design, 140, 183
Module, 35, 183
Module-level scope, 159
Mouse
    clicking, 5
    double-clicking, 5, 56
    dragging, 6
    hovering, 5
    pointer, 5
    pointing, 5
    using a, 5–6
Move method, 415
Moving text, 609
MsgBox statement, 114
MultiLine property, 616
Multiple
    declarations, 80
    forms, 489–90, 509
Multiplication operation, 73
MustInherit keyword, 591
MustOverride keyword, 591
MyBase keyword, 587

N

Name property, 52
NaN (Not a Number), 81
Nested
    Do loops, 267
    For . . . Next loops, 282–83
    If blocks, 207
New
    keyword, 553
    procedure, 560
    program, 50, 608
    Project dialog box, 43
    Project icon, 49
Next
    keyword, 277
    method of Random class, 485
Normal code, 421
Not logical operator, 196
Notation
    mathematical, 73
    scientific, 82
    Visual Basic, 73
Notepad, 6–11, 613
Nothing keyword, 95
Noyce, Robert, 24
Numeric
    expression, 77
    function, 78
    literal, 73
    variable, 75–77

O

Object, 552, 601
    box, 46
    code, 552
    constructor, 560
    oriented programming, 187, 552
    setting properties of an, 63
    use, 582
One-to-many relationship, 541
Open
    a program, 608
    dialog box, 15–16
    Project dialog box, 50
OpenFileDialog control, 466, 509
Opening a file for
    append, 414
    input, 108, 412
    output, 412
OpenText method, 108, 111
Operator
    Like, 533, 542
    logical, 243
    relational, 194, 243

Option Strict, 95
Or logical operator, 196
Order By clause, 533
Ordered array, 326–27
    search of, 327
Output, 3, 30, 44, 90, 105–6, 114
Output devices, 2
Overridable keyword, 587
Overrides keyword, 587

P

Page tab, 43, 62
Parameter, 135, 137, 170, 633
    Info, 113, 141
Parameterless function, 175
Parent class, 582
Parentheses, 80
Pass
    of a loop, 248
    of a sort, 357
Passing, 133, 137
    a structure, 346
    an array, 331
    by reference, 155
    by value, 154
Path, 12
Peek method, 261–62
Pens object, 497, 503
Percent character, 533
Personal computer, 2
Picture box control, 477–78, 509
Pie charts, 499
Pixel, 477
Places bar, 16
Point, with a mouse, 5
Pointing device, 5
Polymorphism, 587, 602
Position, 93
Positioning controls, 54–56
Preserve keyword, 313, 380, 401
Primary key, 531, 548
Prime factorization, 260
Printing a program, 619
Private keyword, 61, 558
Problem solving, 4
Procedure, 188
    called, 133
    calling, 133
    event, 61, 62, 127
    Function, 169
    general, 132
    header, 61, 66
    hide a, 611
    level scope, 159
    step, 620, 628
    Sub, 132

Processing, 3, 30
   control break, 437
   data from a file, 261–62
Program, 3, 30, 42
   changing the name of a, 608
   closing a, 56
   development cycle, 31–32
   documentation, 96–97
   modes, 627
   opening a, 50, 608
   printing a, 619
   region, 63
   running a, 3, 48, 607
   saving a, 49, 608
   starting a new, 50
   terminating a, 49
Programmer, 4
Programming
   stub, 186
   style, 141, 207, 253
Project, 30, 42, 50
Prompt, 112, 113, 114
Properties window, 43, 44, 45–48
   how to access, 615–17
   icon, 45, 46
Property
   abstract, 591
   block, 554, 559, 601
   Get, 554, 555, 559, 601
   Length, 92
   read-only, 555
   Set, 554, 555, 559, 601
   setting a, 616
   write-only, 555
Proximity line, 54, 55
Pseudocode, 33, 34–35, 40
Public keyword, 490, 559
Push pin icon, 43, 54

Q

Quotation mark character, 89, 194

R

Radio button control, 474–75, 509
RaiseEvent statement, 571–72
Random class, 485, 509
Range, specifying in Case clause, 220
Reading a file, 108–12, 128
ReadLine method, 108–9
Record, 422
   of a database table, 518, 548
Recording Checks and Deposits case study, 442–53
ReDim statement, 312, 380, 383, 401

Reference, passing by, 155
Referential integrity, 531
Refresh method, 504
Region directive, 176–77, 611
Relational
   database, 519, 531
   operator, 194, 195, 243
Remove method, 463
RemoveAt method, 463
Removing a breakpoint, 620, 629, 631
Replace editor command, 610
Reserved word, 61, 81, 612
Restore button, 7
Return a value, 78
Return keyword, 170, 176
Reusable code, 116, 186
Right-justification, 106
Ritchie, Dennis, 25
Root folder (directory), 12
Roundoff error, 284
Rule
   of entity integrity, 542
   of referential integrity, 531, 548
Run
   a program, 48, 74, 607
   mode, 627
   to cursor, 628
Run-time error, 81

S

Save All icon, 49
Save As dialog box, 15–16
Saving
   a file, 10
   a program, 49, 67, 608
Scientific notation, 82
Scope of a variable, 159
Scroll
   arrow, 7
   bar, 7, 8
   bar controls, 478–79
   box, 7, 8, 478, 479
   event, 479
Search
   binary, 365–67
   sequential, 334, 365
Second-level menu item, 486
Select Case block, 218, 220, 226, 243
   flowchart, 221
   stepping through a, 634–35
Select statement (SQL), 533
Selected control, 45
SelectedIndex property, 462
SelectedIndexChanged event, 462
SelectedText property, 485

Selecting
    multiple controls, 59, 614
    text, 609
Selector, 218, 220, 226, 243
Sender parameter, 66
Sequence structure, 36, 185
Sequential file, 412, 454
    searching a, 334, 365
    sorting a, 430, 454
Server, 3
    Explorer, 519–20
SetText method, 484
Setting a breakpoint, 619, 628, 631
Settings box, 46
Shell sort, 23, 361
Shell, Donald, 23, 361
Shift+F8 key combination, 628
Shockley, William., 22
Shortcut key, 487, 612
ShowDialog method, 467, 490
Simonyi, Charles, 26
Simple
    combo box, 464–65
    variable, 308
Simulation, 485
Single-subscripted variable, 377
Size of an array, 309
SizeMode property, 477, 478
Sizing handles, 45
SmallChange property, 478–79
Smart editor, 133, 226
Snap line, 54, 55
Social Security tax, 206, 236
Software, 3
Solution, 30, 42
    Explorer window, 43, 44, 609
Sophisticated Cash Register case study, 392–401
Sort
    a file, 430, 454
    an array, 356–63
    bubble, 357
    efficiency of, 363
    flagged bubble, 370
    gap in Shell sort, 361
    method, 370
    Shell, 23, 361
Sorted property, 462
Spaghetti code, 185
Split function, 433
SQL, 532–35, 548
SQL string, 521
Stallman, Richard M., 26–27
Start button, 6
Start Debugging icon, 48
Step keyword, 280, 284

Stepping to debug, 620, 628
Stepwise refinement, 183
StreamReader object, 108
StreamWriter object, 412
StretchImage setting, 477
String, 88–95
    data type, 89
    default value, 95
    empty, 95
    expression, 91
    literal, 88
    substring, 93
    variable, 89
    zero-length, 95
Stroustrup, Bjarne, 26
Structure, 343, 401
    complex, 346
    decision, 36, 185
    loop, 36, 185
    passing a, 346
    sequence, 36, 185
    variable, 343
Structured
    exception handling, 418–21, 454
    programming, 23–24, 185–87
    query language, 532–35, 548
Stub programming, 186
Style of a combo box, 464–65
Sub
    keyword, 61, 132
    procedure, 132, 188
        compared to Function procedure, 175–76
Subroutine, 61
Subscript, 309
Subscripted variable, 309
Substring method, 93
Subtraction operation, 73
Syntax error, 80
System Menu button, 7
System.IO, 415

T

Tab
    key, 50
    order, 617
Table
    ANSI, 194, 605–6
    ASCII, 611
    frequency, 315
    lookup, 368
    of a database, 518, 548
Tasks button, 45
Terminating an infinite loop, 252

Terminating value, 277
Testing a program, 31
Text
    box control, 44, 45–50, 90
    copying, 610
    deleting, 609
    editor, 8
    file, 12, 412
    moving, 609
    property, 46, 50, 463, 465, 473, 474, 486
    select a block of, 609
TextAlign property, 51
TextChanged event, 63
Then keyword, 201
Thompson, Ken, 25
Tick event, 476
Timer control, 476, 509
Title bar, 7
To keyword
    in Case clause, 220
    in For loop, 277
ToLower method, 92
Toolbar, 42, 43
Toolbox, 43, 44, 116, 614
Tooltip, 42
Top level menu item, 486
Top-down
    chart, 35
    design, 140, 183
Torvalds, Linus, 27
ToString method, 98
ToUpper method, 92, 370
Trim method, 92, 98
Truth value, 198
Try-Catch-Finally block, 419
Turing, Alan, 21–22
Two-dimensional array, 377–78
Type-casting, 90, 98
TypeOf keyword, 594

U

Unconditional branch, 40
Underscore character, 97, 533
Undo a change, 610
Until keyword, 250, 253
Update method, 538
Upper bound, 309
User, 4
User-defined
    event, 571, 602
    function, 169, 172, 188
    type (UDT), 343

V

Value
    ANSI, 194, 605–6
    ASCII, 611
    default, 77, 95
    initial, 77, 277
    list, 218
    passing by, 154
    property, 478–79
    step, 280
    terminating, 277
    truth, 198
Variable, 127, 308
    accumulator, 261, 265, 301
    array, 308
    class-level, 159, 188, 310
    control, 277, 278, 279, 282, 301, 437
    counter, 261, 265, 301, 328
    declaring a, 89, 95
    determining type of a, 97
    double-subscripted, 377
    flag, 261, 266, 301
    incrementing the value of a, 78
    instance, 554
    local, 157, 188, 310
    member, 554, 559
    naming a, 76
    numeric, 75
    passing a, 154
    simple, 308
    single-subscripted, 377
    String, 89
    subscripted, 309
Vertical scroll bar control, 478–79, 509
Visible property, 56, 61
Visual Basic, 2, 4
    6.0, 621–26
    controls, 42
    creating a program, 19–20, 60
    events, 60
    exiting, 607
    How Tos, 607–20
    introduction to, 18–21
    invoking, 42, 607
    printing programs, 619
    versions, 21
Von Neumann, John, 22

W

Watch window, 620, 629–30, 636
Weekly Payroll case study, 235–43

Where clause (SQL), 533
While keyword, 248, 253
Wildcard characters (SQL), 533, 542
Wilkes, Maurice V., 22
Windows, 6
    Explorer, 13–15
    how to utilize environment, 613
    introduction to, 4–10
    managing, 619
Wingdings font, 53
With block, 75
WithEvents keyword, 572

Word wrap, 8, 611
Work area, 7
Wozniak, Stephen, 24
WriteLine method, 412
Writing to a file, 412

Z

Zero-length string, 95
Zone, 105